JEALOUSY

JEALOUSY
BY
NANCY
FRIDAY

A Perigord Press Book

William Morrow and Company, Inc. New York

For Richard C. Robertiello

I want to thank Pat Golbitz, Lynn Nesbitt, Dan Stern, Hanna Segal, and Rebecca Burcham. To my husband, Bill Manville, my gratitude and love.

Contents

CHAPTER ONE

Memoirs of a Jealous Woman Part One

*O*nce I met a man who wanted to outlaw jealousy. Long ago his mother had made him take down the Hanes stocking ads he'd pinned to his bedroom wall. More recently his wife had reminded him of the conditions women attach to love: He was lying in bed, looking at a nude centerfold, stroking his genitals. He reached for her. "No," she said.

When we met, he had left his wife and three children and was living in his office, a twenty-foot-ceilinged room in a semi-industrial building that stored old Pathé newsreels, in the West Twenties just off Seventh Avenue. He was beginning all over again, rewriting history: his. I was dying of jealousy in an affair of imminent abandonment: mine. Losing, lost, I was open to suggestion. Jack was a born teacher. Excess was his subject.

I'd never met a college-educated man whose cheerful hello promised orgasm and security. He was such a Nice Man. You'd never met a Nicer Girl than Nancy Friday. Always waiting for men to make me sexual, I offered sex only when asked. And gave no more than the man wanted. What remained untapped was my shameful secret. It was lust.

As each man released that part of me that fleshed his fantasies, I became enslaved to his magic, never dreaming it lay within me. Dependent, already frightened of losing him, I treacherously dreamed of his successor, the next man; one who would reveal me further to myself. I was jealousy personified: Men didn't have to betray me to stand indicted. In my mind, wasn't every man pursuing sex as I would, if only women were granted the male's freedom?

That is what Jack offered. Polymorphous Perverse was his credo. I'd never heard of Norman O. Brown. "Toward pleasure and away from pain" sounded right.

All his life Jack had been leading women to desire, to bed, to orgasm. His dream was turnabout—for some outrageously Wicked Woman to lead *him* the next step. "More!" was what he wanted, and when we first met, the woman sharing his bed was famous for never saying "No." How was he to know it would not be she, but a Nice Girl who would open the door? That "Yes" from a woman in white gloves and a single strand of pearls would be Open Sesame to the loss of control he was seeking?

For the chapter of our lives that began when we met, Jack and I were made for each other. But who thinks of chapters when he falls in love? When his student learns all his lessons and then gives him the highest degree of sexual permission a woman can give a man? Thus making herself indispensable, and *him* jealous.

My official and very proper job at the time was as researcher with a smart Eastside public-relations firm. They had subcontracted for Jack to make a film, the entire project underwritten by the Federal Aviation Administration. To speed the work along, my firm had lent Jack my services. I had been given his address that morning and sent by Yellow Cab crosstown—fateful dividing line, I was soon to learn, not only in the geography of status in New York City but in my own life as well.

In time, the creaky freight elevator to Jack's fourth-floor office would become analog to the slow ascension of the roller coasters of my youth. Anxieties would slip away in anticipation of the more immediate and alluring dangers Jack offered. None of the girls I'd grown up with in Charleston had shared my fascination with those twenty-five-cent thrills. Do all little girls feel different, until they abandon their "bad" selves and become like one another? In those days, I thought I was the only one. I used to love danger, walking on high walls, loose bricks crumbling underfoot. Empty houses with No Trespassing signs drew me in. It was frightening, but thrilling too. Something was being gained, something more important than bcoming like the shy, anxious women who lived in my house. I was trying to be brave, like a man.

Adolescence, breathtaking in its immediacy, held no place for bravery in girls. I would have won a race, written a sonnet, swung from the tallest trees—excelled at any of my myriad "masculine" skills—for the love of the boy for whom I wished on every star. Unfortunately, waiting was the only action allowed. I quickly looked for lessons to the other girls, whose leader I once had been. No one obeyed The Rules of feminine adolescence more carefully than I. Fearing that my wicked desire for those mysterious creatures, boys, ran deeper than that of my friends, I competed in Niceness as once I had in daring and courage. My erotic self went underground. I never knew the full range of my fantasies until Jack. My favorites, old faithfuls that had always pushed me past The Rules and into orgasm, were charged with the forbidden. Until Jack, I was as estranged from my sexuality as every other woman I knew, each one showing me the same prudent and law-abiding face I showed her.

Jack made no bones about it. He was the forbidden.

Indeed, when I took him to meet Fanny, my best friend, she immediately knew him to be the enemy. He sat in her white-on-white apartment, long legs stretched halfway across her living room, and I could tell as she curled in her grandmother's wing chair, miniature poodle in her lap, that she hated him. She hated what he did to me. Jack disturbed the status quo between us.

Supposedly, Fanny and I were adventuresses; nothing either of us did with men was too outlandish not to arouse admiration in the other. One night a married man held her prisoner in a telephone booth until three A.M. and threatened her life unless she loved him. The next week a drunken poet broke down my apartment door when I told him it was over. The competition between us fired our friendship. Men were never felt to pose a real threat to us individually or to the bargain between us. They were within the scheme of things: We controlled them.

Jack wasn't like the men we danced with at Le Club; he wasn't looking for a woman like us. He wanted one who'd break The Rules, and Fanny knew, as his lack of interest in her considerable beauty registered, that I wanted to ride with him. Fanny had never had a taste for roller coasters, but she didn't want me on that trip either. The Rules are bearable only so long as every woman obeys them.

It is hard to describe Jack's fascination for me. He was dangerous. But an equal part of his magic was the visible safety net beneath his life: his intellect, the cultured cadence of his voice, his physical grace, skill at his job, the order and discipline of his life. In effect, his past. I saw it all behind him that first day, as he opened the bright yellow door of his office and offered me a Pepsi: At one end of the high-ceilinged room in which he lived and worked was an elegant Herman Miller unipole system, the office equipment on it as neatly organized as the modular system itself. At the opposite end of the room was a king-size bed. On it two men lay reading copies of *Nude Living*.

"Harry says you're the best researcher he's ever worked with," said Jack, spinning the executive chair to meet me, swinging open the under-counter-fridge door to reveal shelves of soda, fruit juices and Carta Blanca beer. He didn't drink liquor.

"We're going to make the United States government a film on civil aviation to be fucking proud of," he said good-naturedly, smiling up from the work to which he'd returned. He was weighing a mixture of tobacco on a postal scale, neatly funneling it into three Ziploc plastic bags. Even I knew it was marijuana. It was 1963, moments before the Beatles and Lee Oswald changed the world. I shook my head at the offered joint, and smiled a polite apology. For what, I wasn't sure and never had been.

I made myself busy. I dialed U.S. Steel and correctly introduced myself to a vice-president as the voice of the Federal Aviation Agency. I told him his country needed him. The daddy voice told me it would be a privilege to supply the desired footage on the history of the use of steel in aeronautics. Where should his Communications Department send it? I gave him the address where three men were inhaling the forbidden smoke, holding it deep in their chests as they continued their talk. I was watching my training film.

If I'd been happy that day when I met Jack, would it have been a take? If some man had loved me; if my identity had been intact, would I have immediately responded to a man so alien to my life? Does it matter? I'd been spiraling down for months in jealousy's unrelenting depression, shedding those parts of myself I admired most as I lay, unable to sleep, beside a man who no longer wanted me.

I should have left him. I knew he would soon leave me. But rejection was new to the woman I'd made of myself. The child I'd been had known it intimately. It's reawakening was fatefully fast. This man had started out wanting me more than I wanted him. He no longer bothered to empty the lipstick-stained cigarettes from the ashtrays. We slept on sheets he'd stained making love to other women. Just before we met, his wife had left him. He was angry. His revenge was not yet complete. I was the first target to come along.

I tried to save myself. When other men asked me out, the healthy part of me accepted, but as the day wore on, resolve would weaken. I'd call back and lie some excuse, needing to be available for my pusher, should he materialize. Easier to wait for his call than to break a fidelity he no longer asked and had long since broken himself. Games of unavailability used to spark his interest, but I no longer had the cunning energy for manipulation. My troth was to some primitive need within myself that demanded I wait for him, and wait.

When he did call, I would lie beside him after sex, praying the ugly frog would awaken to be again the prince who had once spoken of marriage.

But he never did, and it was I who became ugly, leafing through his agenda in the morning while he showered, writing down their names and addresses, those other women, so dismissable when we met but goddesses of beauty now; powerful creatures will all the glamour I'd possessed that first night he saw me.

I'd entered the room and felt it mine. There was no one there I knew except my hostess, but I enjoyed arriving alone, testing the new magic of my looks; they had arrived so unexpectedly, so late. He'd asked to be introduced. I'd felt his desire to please, to win me, not to be rejected. I felt my power. How soon it went.

That first night we made love—which was our first night—I felt the shift. Therein lies a good argument for postponing sex. Had I got to know him better, I'd have found he was just a pretty face. Not my kind at all. A throwback to the handsome heroes of my youth, those football stars who'd passed me by for prettier, smaller girls. And so I'd developed the second-ary powers of intelligence and humor and learned them best from the men I'd loved. It is always humiliating to be rejected. Even more so when you know the beloved infidel is a fool. Do we ever give up on the past? Damn infantile omnipotence.

I was used to seeking my reflection, my value, in men. For months this lover's eyes had shown me a sad woman's strained, tight lips—my own private image of what anxiety does to women's faces. Seeing myself mir-rored in store windows, I turned away with fear. Where had I seen that face before? It was that part of my mother I'd sworn never to become.

Jack gave me back my sense of self. It was the way he saw me.

"No, you see what you want to see," he said later when I told him this. He didn't want the responsibility, not even for a woman's happiness. He didn't want dependency. Equality was all.

Jack himself searched women's eyes for what he needed. Like Narcissus, he drew up a face to mirror his own: exciting, erotic, full lips. A woman as sexual as he. It was a masque most women did not want to wear. Most women looked away. I put it on and discovered it was me.

There was no rush, no dinner dates or telephone calls to pack with meaning or mark our progress. A formal business decision, made by others, decreed we would see one another every afternoon. A film had to be made. Time was on our side. Our long hours together held no personal demands, no expectations and therefore no recriminations. He didn't ask about him and I didn't ask about her. We got to know one another with the eager but patient curiosity pre-lovers bring to a friendship.

Morning hours in my Eastside office were aimed toward that daily crosstown ride. Each block west lifted the dead weight of the frog prince's rejection. Something new and healthy was coming to life, an emotion that dependency had suppressed: anger. Oh, God, how good it felt to be able to hate that beautiful, silly bastard!

Jack told me about his new life, the money he was trying to raise to make a feature film based on a book written by a man he admired enormously. He and the author had just completed the first draft of the script. The FAA documentary he and I were working on would help finance the "real" movie. I read the book. I wanted to be part of it, the story, the movie, Jack's life, all that energy. I wanted to lose my own iron control, the constraint that had always bound me. It never occurred to me that I had no credentials, no experience in freedom or ease. I had never known love without jealousy.

Every afternoon a woman telephoned him. He told me about her. Weekends on Fire Island. They took mescaline. I listened enviously to the descriptions of abandon, loss of time and place. Mere weeks ago, an old friend had told me of his first high on grass. I'd been haughty in judgmental disdain. But Jack made hallucination, the sense of dissolution of the limits of self, seem an important experience. Also, he had read everything there was to know about the drug in the *Encyclopaedia Britannica* and *The Physician's Desk Reference* and the *United States Pharmacopeia*. The mescaline had been taken in a house he had built himself, once again learning how from books at the New York Public Library. "Where they said use two nails, I used three," he said. It was why I wanted to fly with him. Nothing would fall down.

He taught me to edit and splice film and introduced me to huevos rancheros. He was the first man who expected me to pay my share. It disturbed and excited me. I began to understand why the woman who telephoned every afternoon left souvenirs around the office. Her underwear would turn up unexpectedly under a chair; without comment, Jack would tuck it away in a drawer. Did she leave it—or did he—to let me know now, before we went further, that these were the rules: There would be no rules?

The woman who wore the red bikini underwear was real, but I was not jealous of her. My unfaithful lover's sexual partners lived far more powerfully in my suspicious imagination than she. Jack made his admiration of her very clear. I felt none of this to be a warning. This woman was no rival. She was a challenge. I was a competitor, still rational where Jack was concerned. We hadn't had sex. The heat he aroused in me was unspoken. The decision to give or withhold was still in my hands. I had the power.

I knew Jack two weeks before we made love. He would have said, "Before we fucked," determined as he was to know the difference and for me to know it too. That particular day, he was talking to a musician friend when I arrived. The man looked at my well-girdled ass, my coordinated Gucci accessories and pearls as if I'd flown in from another planet. They were sharing a joint. Usually Jack didn't smoke during work.

"But this is very special stuff, Nancy," he said. "Today's the day."

He'd never proselytized since my refusal that first day we'd met. And so I respected his judgment. I canceled my lunch-hour appointment with the dermatologist. That afternoon, instead of having a wart removed from my index finger, I smoked my first grass.

It does nothing for some people. For those of us who live close to our fantasy world, it can be a trip into the preconscious. I've never done anything I didn't want to do when I smoke. I can go years without it. But I have always respected that it takes me faster where I already want to go: behind the polite smile and the string of pearls. Since that first day, or because of it, grass has always been an aphrodisiac.

The musician, Jack and I walked to a Japanese restaurant. It was three P.M. The place was empty. That was reality. In my fantasy it was packed, with raised tiers of tables so that everyone could see the floor show, like in a 1930s nightclub. Except no one was watching the floor show. Were we it? They were all staring, pointing at my exhibitionistic lust for the man beside me. In reality, I was indeed touching Jack. As I'd been longing to touch him for weeks. I buried my nose behind his ear and breathed his sweet smell. I smoothed his khaki-trousered leg. Then, suddenly aware of what I was doing, I'd switch attention back to the abashed, censorious, fantasy crowd. Up and back I went, stroking the dark hairs on his arm one minute, quickly folding my hands in my lap like a good little girl the next. Laughing, blushing with embarrassment, deeply happy, I felt out of control and safe too. Now and then Jack would pat my hand or stroke my hair, like an indulgent father. Am I mixing similes too wildly? I don't think so. There is something of the good father in every good teacher. For those of us who did not have one—a father—leaders are irresistible.

At no time did my stop-and-go behavior become a topic of discussion among the three of us. The two men talked between themselves, pausing only to smile and reassure me when I interrupted to ask about the crowd. I played my tug-of-war game alone, inhibited at times by paranoid fantasies, but in the end, losing to desire.

The musician watched with envy and concern. I didn't belong in Jack's world. I was an uptown outsider. But the heat I radiated was very real. Good sex crosses all barriers, including Fourteenth Street and Fifth Avenue too. It must have been what drew him back with us to Jack's office. He immediately left when I took Jack in my arms. The musician was right to be confused. It's not every day a Nice Girl makes a clean start: That afternoon the other Nancy, the girl who'd climb the highest tree and take any dare was picking up where she'd been so rudely interrupted by The Rules.

We made love, we fucked, on the king-size bed.

My arm curled around him.

"Don't do that," he said.

The words should have signaled he was running away from something I needed desperately at that time: closeness.

No promises were being broken. Love had never been offered. Nor was it what I'd expected of him just a few short hours ago. So far we'd been absolutely straight with one another; knowing his terms full well, I'd made the first move. But the warmth he aroused in me was a promise of life. Having restored me, he now became life itself. To hold him, to be held by him, was assurance that fear of abandonment would not return. Sex had always been the bridge to love. That was exactly what he didn't want.

In the kind of tight, secure togetherness of which I had always dreamed, sex eventually dies. He knew it had killed his marriage. In over-prolonged, mutual embrace, the distance required between two people for the spark to jump and ignite disappears. No air.

I heard his words. I wanted love and he didn't. But I also wanted sex, to know the full expression of my own. Who was to say that with this man I couldn't have both? Does a man race headlong from suffocation unless he's first known the infinite sweetness of intimacy? I removed my arm and slept; I could handle this.

Later he took me home on his Lambretta. We'd never before left his place together. I rode pillion, holding him tight as he headed east, going fast, expertly, and I was beginning to believe he did everything.

"Next time wear a fuller skirt," he hollered in the wind. "It's safer when you straddle."

I warmed to the inference of our future. When we reached my building, he smiled and shook his head.

"I'm going to see my kiddies and have a shower," he said. "Two privileges my wife allows me." He spoke of her without resentment. I liked it that he missed his kids, that he regretted that his marriage hadn't worked.

"I'm due downtown at eight," he said, knowing what I was thinking. I had forgotten about her. "I never said I had time for a drink." He was smiling, his eyes straight on mine. There was to be no misunderstanding.

"See you tomorrow," I said, smiling back. And he was gone.

After that, things with the other man got better. What was between us hadn't changed. I had. That next Saturday I lay beside him while he commiserated on the phone with his ex-wife about her menstrual cramps. While his continued union with this woman didn't feel good, it was no longer an attack on me. His wife was going to remarry. When I discovered it was to a man I'd repeatedly refused even to have dinner with, I won-dered once again what I was doing with a fool who'd been rejected by a woman who was going to marry an even bigger fool.

I had a fragment of my life back now, a space where I was separate from him. That my regained sense of value came not from within but through attachment to yet another man didn't alarm me. I had always been in love; there had always been a man who could give life or take it away.

Obviously there had not always been a man. But if you had tried then to tell me that my repetitious pattern of jealousy had anything to do with nurseries, mothers and the tears of childhood, I'd have dismissed you. As I had dismissed Freud. I looked down on people in analysis. They were "weak." I was "strong." I dealt with today's reality, shaping it to my will. I kept myself ignorant of the powers of the unconscious. My life looked brilliant and successful, therefore I was.

The degree of energy and control required to make that life appear admirable was in direct proportion to what it took to erase memory of nursery pain, a contest with my sister in which I ran alone. A contest she had won long before I was born. "You don't have to worry about Nancy; she can take care of herself," were the first words my mother sang to me. Literally trying to wrest meaning from her every word—as children do—I thought my independence was what she wanted. That trophies won at school would focus her eyes on me. I won them all, but she was preoccu-pied with something/someone else. The left-out feeling never went away.

That is how I would have described jealousy when I was little: feeling left out and deprived, angry, abandoned, out of control and humiliated. (Though I would never have admitted any of these feelings aloud. Public knowledge of defeat would have increased my humiliation.) Nor had my ideas on jealousy changed much by the time I met Jack—or even when I began this book. I had not yet come to understand *envy*. How could I know that so seemingly petty an emotion would turn out to be the most destructive of all the components of jealousy?

When I was a child, I looked for someone to follow, to emulate; some-one who would keep my bad jealous feelings at bay. I found a tough Irish nurse, an admirable aunt. Mostly there was my grandfather. That he was one of my models is an idea I've only recently come to accept.

Raised to find my identity in men, I measured myself against other females, my competitors for these desirable sources of security. To ac-knowledge myself patterned on a man would threaten my femaleness—my chance at happiness—to the core. But I was my grandfather's child. He had all the power in the family. He enjoyed life on a large scale. Of one thing I was sure: He was never jealous.

My grandfather became my hero and my model. Summer evenings, he would take his big walking stick, whistle for me and his two favorite Dalmatians, and together we would strike out to inspect the grounds, leaving the silly women behind. "Well, Nancy, what have you accomplished today?" he would ask.

My grandfather's esteem for accomplishment, my mother's statement of fact that I could take care of myself, combined to decide my course of action. Little Nancy, Class President, became Big Nancy who took care of herself very, very well. I wore my glamorous jobs and revealing clothes as other women wore perfume. The applause might as well have been meant for someone standing behind me. I felt men's arms around me, but even as the world slipped into sweet balance at last, there came the old fear of imminent loss. Jealousy. I was caught between—driven by—two opposing needs: to mesh as tightly as possible with a man, and to achieve on my own.

Today I say, "I *am* my grandfather." That is how sure I am of whose life made mine and saved it too. Without him, given my desperate need of men, I probably would have married on Graduation Day, as did many of the southern girls I grew up with. Instead, I tried to find a formula for love and work. A responsible worker who could not afford to fail, I hit upon a plan that left me ever available for my daily bread, intimacy. I took only short-term jobs, flashy if only for their brevity. When a long-term career with more money and real power was offered, I refused. Flamboyantly, I declared I wanted freedom. What I wanted was something diametrically opposite: freedom to pursue men at a moment's notice, to give myself to a man in a way that allowed me to drop the rigid control by which I'd run my life and the world around me. If it was freedom, it was to make myself dependent on men. Dependent on them, I had to possess them.

Where did I first read the formula that jealous people tend to have feelings of low self-esteem? Some fashion magazine in a dentist's waiting room? I distinctly remember mocking the idea. I was jealous all right, but far from lacking self-esteem, I suspected I had too much. If I had anything to fear, it was arrogance. Why then was I as quick to feel left out at age twenty-two, to see unbeatable rivals in every shadow, as I'd been at age twelve and, I suspect, at age two?

I had it backward. I had not yet learned that real work, work in which I believed, would give me the security I had vainly sought in men, allow me to love rather than merely depend on them.

You may read my story with Jack and say I was an emotional cripple. That is not how I or the rest of the world would have described me. I had put myself together so cleverly I'd fooled everyone, myself included, as far back as I could remember. Or wish to. It is, I think, how many of us survive.

We construct whole lives on avoidance of painful early emotions, jealousy being one of the worst. We begin so young that not even parents know the face we show is a mask. Life itself narrows to block against ever feeling that old hurt again. The subterfuge works until passion comes along. Intimacy is our undoing.

"Are you jealous?" I ask Tennessee Williams. We are standing in his backyard in Key West. It is two A.M., not quite the end of the party.

He smiles. At that moment, neither he nor I know it is two A.M. in his life too.

"No, darling," he says. "I've given it up."

We don't give up jealousy. We give up passion. It interferes with our work. We've been hurt too often. We're too old to get that close to feelings of dying again.

But intimacy is how we began and why most of us keep trying. Either to regain it or, if we have never had it, to find it at last. My marriage was the first time I believed in love, trusted intimacy enough to question the reality of the person I had put together. There were many reasons I married Bill; one of the most compelling was the knowledge that he was not a man to manipulate jealousy.

The riddle of love and work changed when I stood on that first firm ground to do my first honest work. Freedom from jealousy gave me emotional room in which to move around intellectually, to change. I thought more of my husband's love than I did of myself. In truth, I thought I'd tricked him: I valued the person he fell in love with, someone I saw as not quite me. I wanted to be that self-sufficient, gloriously independent woman he described as his wife. Sure of his love, anchored in it up to my knees, I risked a look at the false Nancy.

I had always taken love, sex and dependency as parts of one global and undifferentiated package. It occurred to me now that each word held a difference in meaning. These musings became the research for my first book on women's sexual fantasies. It did not begin as a personal search, but in writing, I bumped into my own guilt and anxiety. I bumped into mother. The day I finished *My Secret Garden*, I wrote the outline for *My Mother/My Self*. It was another year before I became conscious, for the first time in my life, that I was angry at my mother. How much of my life had been shaped by hiding from that knowledge? More than I would like to say.

"You know, sweetheart, you are different," my husband was saying. *My Mother/My Self* was about to be published. We were having tea. I was standing at the casement window of our apartment, staring at the reservoir in Central Park. He was seated behind me, and though the words sounded like a random thought, he was telling me something important. It was uncanny. He had read my thoughts. I was so aware of it those days, what he'd just said, and that things would never be the same. I had changed.

"Tell me what you mean," I said, unsure myself of just how I'd changed.

"When we met," he began, "you had this independent persona you showed the world. I knew the anxiety inside. Now it's as if"—he paused for the right words—"it's like the inner you has caught up with the outer you. You are more integrated."

He had perceived me better than I had myself. There was new room in my world, so much space in which fear had once lived. Learning to write had taught me to deny the censor in my head, to put down on paper the forbidden before my overly strict conscience had cleaned it up beyond recognition, beyond truth. Once said aloud, the "unspeakable" released its iron grip on me. How ironic. Through this new ability to relinquish control in writing, I had backed into the dreaded Freud.

All my writing has been an effort to sort out the paradoxes of my life. When the contract for this book was signed, assuring a measure of economic independence, I sat on Bill's lap.

"This doesn't mean I don't still need you," I said.

We laughed. A family joke. An ancient cry for help. Success was threatening to do me out of what I still most needed: dependency.

So much rage, so much dependency. All those men in the past, all those jobs, pitted one against the other as if I could not have them both on honest terms. Writing has been my education. Work has taught me who I am. Will writing about jealousy allow me to live as I choose and not as a child?

Already my research shows that if there is one thing on which the fashion magazines and the behavioral world do agree it is that freedom from jealousy, from fear of loss, rests on self-esteem. If Bill is right and I am more integrated, why then do I still dream at night of being left? Why do the men in my dreams walk away from me with other women? I stand alone in doorways and watch couples in each other's arms. I had once thought that when I believed in myself I would be able to carry a man's love inside me. Is my unconscious lagging?

I have answered my own question: I am trying to hang a sense of value acquired as an adult on the skeleton of a child. Something has been left out, something that comes earlier than present-day conviction of worth and power. Doesn't there have to be a *self* before there can be self-esteem?

I began this research intuitively convinced that jealousy was rooted in incomplete *separation,* one of the unfortunate words in psychological jargon. In everyday speech, separation sounds awful, connoting loneliness and desertion. To the psychiatrist—and as I shall use the word—separation has little to do with financial or geographical position. It means something very close to emotional independence. The child or adult who is unseparated is psychologically still tied; has not yet achieved true identity.

How we achieve the autonomous self had long been a field of my research. It was knowledge intellectually and emotionally earned. People who were separate and individuated, thus ran my initial thinking, would not have to fearfully guard and possess. Yes, I thought as I began this book, that *feels* right. People who have separation problems are the ones who suffer that sapping, sinking sense of isolation, humiliation, defeat. We are the ones who suspect betrayal where none exists. We are the jealous ones.

In his famous paper "Certain Neurotic Mechanisms in Jealousy, Paranoia and Homosexuality," written in 1922, Freud says:

> Jealousy is one of those affective states, like grief, that may be described as normal. If anyone appears to be without it, the inference is justified that it has undergone severe repression and consequently plays all the greater part in his unconscious mental life. The instances of abnormally intense jealousy met with in analytic work reveal themselves as contructed of three layers . . . [which] may be described as 1. *competitive* or normal; 2. *projected* and 3. *delusional* jealousy.[1]

What puzzled me was the line Freud drew between "normal" jealousy and pathological. Almost everyone I interviewed who did not deny jealousy—the "severe repression" of which Freud speaks—immediately seemed to go far beyond the normal. They spoke with firsthand knowledge about feelings, ideas and symptoms that Freud called "delusional." Knowing all too well the malign influence jealousy had on their lives, convinced it was always evil and with no remedial value, they would ask me if I had found "a cure."

What exacerbated the puzzle was talks with an array of the most brilliant minds I know in the behavioral world. Again and again, these people who take great pride in claiming that no human emotion is alien to them told me they hadn't thought much about jealousy. "Patients rarely bring it up." When I described some of my most recent interviews, the usual response was, "Ah, that's pathological jealousy. I almost never see that."

I am left with a question: Why do I hear more about jealousy on the street than therapists do in their offices? It may be true that patients do not often present themselves as suffering from jealousy, but one of the great truisms of psychoanalysis is that patients do not know what is making them unhappy. To uncover and name their unconscious defenses is precisely the therapist's job.

Jealousy drives people to murder. It has inspired some of the world's greatest plays, novels and operas. Consciously or not, it infects all our lives. And yet, a bibliography on jealousy compiled from both the New York Public and Yale University libraries filled less than a page when I first consulted the card catalogs. In professional journals, the word *jealousy* rarely appears in titles. Is there some kind of avoidance going on here, and on whose part? The patient's? The analyst's?

My expectation that jealousy could be explained along lines of incomplete separation was short-lived. It had foundered on a question that early impressed itself upon me: In a jealous situation, against whom is the aggression directed—the intruder, the beloved, the self? If we need someone, if we see the beloved as the prime tie to life, we might want to shoot the rival. Never our mate. But a commonplace of police crime sheets is that it is indeed the beloved who is often the victim in a crime of passion. That the emotionally dependent person would want to destroy his source of life was an idea far beyond explanation by any separation theory, no matter how radical.

Another unthought-out conclusion held early on was that men were less jealous than women. This was an extension of the notion that jealousy was a function of lack of identity. Weren't women raised to find their identity only in men? Though I later read that Freud and Aristotle had this same bias—that women were more jealous—my own beguiling intuition rested on two legs. One: Observation told me men were more separate; hence more independent; hence less jealous. Two: My subjective experience was that since men had always made me jealous, they had to be less so. Would the good men I have loved put me in such hell if they had been there themselves? Knowing its agony, didn't I go out of my way to protect my men from jealousy? I know a man can fall in love as deeply as a woman, and be hurt as much. But when he falls in love, a man loses his heart, not his identity. When he is jealous, he does something about it. He moves. He hits his rival, walks out the door; quickly enough, certainly more quickly than I, he is in another pair of arms. Even if he does nothing, he *could.*

In women's eyes, men have alternatives, options, mobility. Women are the sex that waits. Men are women's legs. Without a man, a woman is passive and paralyzed. In my assumption that men were the less jealous sex, it was men's alternatives, their ability to leave without a safe destination, which more than anything else seemed so remedial.

Being less desperate, more able to replace a woman, men were less likely to see rivals where none existed.

Oh?

"Are you jealous?"

I am talking to a thirty-four-year-old physicist, my first interview.

"Yes," he says promptly. "It was a boys' school and I was fourteen. Suddenly one term my best friend became involved with another boy, some homosexual thing between them. The pain I felt was so terrible, I decided then and there I must never feel it again. And I haven't. Before I let myself fall in love, all my life, I had to know she needed me more than I needed her. That she would never leave me."

One interview proves nothing. But if my first bit of research showed men as violently jealous as any woman, I had to wonder what the subjective gain was for me in seeing the psychology of the sexes in such asymmetrical terms.

As therapist Leah Schaefer put it, "Women may seem more jealous because historically women have been more focused on relationships for their identity; men more focused on their jobs, their money, impersonal things. So the seeming failure of a love relationship—jealousy—is more talked about by women. Their core of identity is under attack. A man in love can feel as jealous as any woman but it is not manly to talk about it. He shuts up, and while you may think he is blue about losing his girl, it does not occur to you he is dying of jealousy."

For reasons of my own, I had invented a notion that men were "above" jealousy. My friend Leah hadn't told me anything I didn't already know; merely what I did not want to face. What woman doesn't know that men often deny their deepest feelings? Consciously deciding what to feel or not to feel is a defense, not a sign that the frightening emotion is absent. I had taken the male cutoff stance as indication of male invulnerability. Just as men have to keep women on pedestals or in the gutter to diminish their power, I had to keep men in some immune, dominant position. If men were drowning in incontrollable currents of emotion, who would take care of me?

Not until I read psychoanalyst Melanie Klein, did I come to understand why I was deliberately keeping myself ignorant and naïve. Klein explained the profit in perceiving myself as a powerless little rag doll tossed about by jealousy, while endowing men with cool control. In her great book *Envy and Gratitude*, she explores the central role envy plays in jealousy.

I *envied* men their independence, their mobility, their power over me, and wanted those qualities for myself. Needing men—more than loving them—I could not express anger that they had what I coveted. The unconscious is a hall of mirrors in which the mind plays the game of Opposites. I buried my resentment behind the formidable defense that Klein calls *idealization*. To save myself, I had to idealize men, to see them as "stronger" than I.

I will explore Klein's seminal but enigmatic thinking as we go along. But note: Klein would not say I was jealous of men's mobile qualities. *Envy* is the correct word.

Let me finish the story of the physicist, the man in my first interview. When we spoke, he had just returned to his wife. They had been married twelve years. A year before he had left her for another woman.

"The night I returned to my wife," he said, "I went into the bathroom and sat on the edge of the tub. I wept uncontrollably for hours at what I had done to her. I wept because I could not believe she had taken me back."

He had left her. She had taken him back. In this story, who has the power? Whose self-esteem has been reinforced?

Ten years ago I probably wouldn't have gotten so emotional an interview. Men are becoming more introspective. Male defenses aren't working as well as they once did. Women have changed. In answer, so must men. The barriers to that change are well described by the noted psychoanalyst Leslie Farber. While generally believing that jealousy "is experienced in essentially similar fashion by men and women alike," Farber describes the more enviable position accorded men in traditional society:

"Throughout history," he writes, "the sexual infidelity of women has been punished far more harshly than that of men, ranging from social ostracism to banishment to death, and including the occasional American Indian practice of amputating the nose of an unfaithful wife.

"Traditional assumptions about jealousy are also interesting," he continues. "A man is cuckolded; a woman is [merely] unfortunate. The wife's infidelity strikes at her husband's honor and pride, it humiliates him. The husband's infidelity, however much it hurts his wife, need not humiliate or dishonor her; it reflects upon him rather than her, whereas hers also reflects upon him.

"In short, history would seem to be telling us that a man has much more to lose from his mate's infidelity than a woman has, and that his vulnerability must be well protected by law and custom."[2]

Women's lives have been dramatically expanded. Their mass entry into men's work world will be recorded in history as one of the most important events in this century. Much of what is being asked of men today looks, sounds and feels like abdication. They are being asked to give up the superior, and at the same time protected, position Dr. Farber writes about; to surrender definitions of masculinity and social usage by which their fathers and grandfathers lived and ruled. In exchange, they are promised such uncertain joys as the right to do housework and weep in public.

Men have always given themselves sexual latitude while demanding absolute fidelity from women. The famous double standard. To be jealous was a sign a man did not have his woman under control. A "real man" never had to worry about rivals. His wife's every sinew was bent toward letting him know there never could be any rival. This denial of women's humanity forced men to live with an illusion of invulnerability. The price was high for both sexes.

In a conversation with psychologist Martin Hoffman, I tell him about the man who wanted to outlaw jealousy, my old friend Jack. "If someone else moved in on me, this man would come across the room with a big smile and put his arm around me. 'Isn't she glorious?' he would say. By that, he staked his claim, made me love him more for being so publicly adoring. The other man would be cut off in mid-flight."

"You thought he was without jealousy?"

"I only knew that jealousy paralyzed me. If he was flirting with another woman, I could never have walked across the room and put my arm around *him*. The contrast between us convinced me he was without jealousy."

"If he hadn't felt at least the beginnings of jealousy, he probably would not have come across the room to make the gesture," Hoffman says. "What he may have done was nip the emotion in the bud. It didn't mean he was in fact 'jealousy free.' "

Ignored, repressed emotion does not magically go away. Often it becomes the hidden engine driving mind against body; ulcers, asthma, high blood pressure—some think cancer itself—all may be manifestations of unacceptable and unconscious feelings, eating away at their host.

At times, the mind grows too anxious, too weary, to contain the ugly fear. Devious expression is found, the repressed is pushed "out there." What was the chastity belt of the Middle Ages but a material defense against what used to be called "the gnawing worm, Suspicion?" Once his wife was locked up, the husband could go off to the Crusades for years.

"Jealous?" he could then say. "Never think of it."

He would not be lying. The steel trap in which his wife's body was being held, held his jealousy safely locked up too. In Freud's early cases, forbidden ideas often came back in what used to be called "hysteria" or "hysterical conversion symptoms." The woman who was terrified at how much she hated her mother would find her knee paralyzed. No organic, mechanical or medical reason could be found. The foot that wanted to kick mother had been stiffened by the conflicted mind, and was unable to move.

Forbidden wishes or ideas of which we are afraid or ashamed also find expression in distorted social forms. Before the women's movement gave women a degree of sexual freedom approaching the male's, the term *machismo* was virtually unknown in English. That both ideas came to public consciousness at about the same time is, I believe, no coincidence; action and re-action. The exaggerated, cartoonlike posture of the macho says, among other things, that he is so "strong" that no mere female—liberated or not—is going to make him jealous. When, in Shakespeare's phrase, we "protest too much" to others, we are lying to repress fear. When we protest too much to ourselves, we are fighting recognition of the repressed within.

In the days when father was sole breadwinner, all else was subordinated to keeping him on the job. There was little room for jealousy in his life. It would reduce his efficiency in the "real world"—office, field or factory. Chastity was insisted upon for women. The man had to know the children were his. "Woman's place is in the home" was an absolute tenet believed by men and women alike; it kept woman from roving behind his back and behind the other women's too. Virginity and monogamy stilled anxiety about possible comparisons with a lustier and unknown rival. Did suspicion nevertheless lurk that beneath women's enforced sexual passivity was an unsatisfied sexual voraciousness? As late as the turn of the century, renowned surgeons in this country performed clitorectomies.

Emotions like jealousy were unpaid work, the enemies of production. They were turned over to women. The double standard was reinforced and kept going by women. They forgave the man his occasional lapse (you do not ask the morals of someone who throws you a lifeline) but judged themselves and every other woman with unrelenting harshness. Men were to be left free—emotionally and practically—to build the country. More than anything, it was work that defined manhood.

Women bought the golden cage. They paraded an ironclad fidelity, taught it to their daughters as woman's finest virtue. If ever they felt the urge for sexual adventure, it was quickly stifled. As long as the husband held the purse strings, he held her life. Something else, I believe, also lay behind many women's fidelity, a kind of magical blackmail: "If I am true, he will be too. If I reject the advances of these other wonderful men, won't the enormity of my sacrifices bind him to me?" The symbiotic mind foolishly at work.

What self-delusion we weave; how grimly this kind of story often ends. As the man walks out, the woman's rage can be heard down the hall; it echoes across suburban lawns. "How can you do this to me?" ("After all I've given up for you!" is the unsaid half of the sentence.)

"I didn't ask it!" might be his reply.

She knows he did. Whether they say it aloud or not, most men expect their wives to be faithful. It is a mark of how much men still live in the past. Today the woman is as likely to walk out as the man. Dumbfounded, he turns up at the therapist's office. To whatever question is asked, he numbly repeats, "But I brought home my paycheck every Friday!"

Contraception and their own paychecks have given women room to consider adultery and infidelity as easily as any man. Figures in the studies on women's increased sexual activity are staggering. Fifty-four percent of married women have committed adultery, says a recent study.[3] According to another report, the rate of increase in adultery among young people is higher in women than in men.[4] The statistics may not be exact. The trend is clear. A conflict in underlying assumptions about women's fidelity is going to breed more jealousy than ever in the liberated 1980s and beyond. What my own studies show is that the adulterous act more often than not leaves women confused and guilty. Their attitudes and behavior may be up front; their deepest gut feelings about right and wrong lag behind. What studies do not and cannot report is the effect of women's increased sexuality/adultery/unfaithfulness on men.

Any discussion of jealousy today evokes two highly publicized crimes of passion. The first was the murder of a twenty-year-old girl, the daughter of a wealthy family. She was killed by her rejected twenty-three-year-old lover, a poor Mexican-American scholarship student, graduated from Yale. Bonnie Garland died when she told Richard Herrin she was taking up one of women's new options. She was going to break their monogamous relationship. He split her head open with a hammer. On the charge of murder, Richard Herrin was found not guilty.

The second crime, oddly enough, occurred in the same small suburban town—Scarsdale, New York. It was committed by Jean Harris, the fifty-six-year-old headmistress of the prestigious Madeira School for Girls. When Herman Tarnower, the famous Diet Doctor, told her he would not marry her, Jean Harris broke her own strict moral code and continued the affair. When it became clear he was leaving her for another woman, she too availed herself of a new option. Rejected women usually turn their rage against themselves. Jean Harris picked up a gun and Tarnower died. Jean Harris was found guilty.

What is significant is that each case had at its heart the question of jealousy as motive. I want to discuss Richard Herrin and Jean Harris in greater detail later. I mention them now because I believe both verdicts turn on an inability to define, let alone understand jealousy.

In various versions and translations, the Bible has played a formative role greater than any other in the history of language, and therefore in the history of ideas. "For thou shalt worship no other god: for the Lord, whose name is Jealous, is a jealous God." Thus the King James version, in a verse memorized by innumerable generations of Jews and Christians alike; used century after century in law, worship, catechism and schools; one of the great "givens" that linger somewhere in the recesses of the mind (as it did in mine) long after the exact words are forgotten.

This verse tells us that the emotions under discussion go back to the dawn of monotheism. God still finds it necessary to warn the Hebrews against the worship of idols or rival gods. Perhaps it tells us something even more relevant to this study: From the earliest eras of recorded history, it was recognized that unfaithfulness was so unbearable it made God himself angry. He forbade the ancient Hebrews to make him jealous. If you believe that the Scriptures are literally the Word of God, then "Jealous" is one of the names God gives himself.

"When I'm in a position of power," says a senior partner in a Washington, D.C., law firm, "I think of vengeance rather than redemption and mercy. I've always known I get that from the jealous God of the Old Testament."

No woman, myself included, tells of identification with a vengeful God. I may be retaliatory. It never occurs to me to cite God as justification.

Is He a role model for men?

To my mind, the great latitude and forgiveness usually accorded crimes of passion throughout history may have its roots in Scripture. "Thou shalt not kill" may be one of the Ten Commandments, but if God names Himself "Jealous," how can we not understand that the emotion is so grievous that it can drive a mortal to murder? Biblical scholars may object to this reading. They would say that as used in the Bible, *jealousy* has special meaning. It refers specifically, and only, to the injunction "Thou shalt worship no other god."

All good dictionaries take special note of what might be called this "Godly jealousy." *The Oxford English Dictionary* (OED): "having a love which will tolerate no unfaithfulness or defection . . ." "Demanding exclusive worship and love," says *Funk & Wagnall's New Standard Dictionary. The American Heritage Dictionary of the English Language* goes so far as to give us a somewhat discourteous description of the Old Testament's "jealous God": "intolerant of disloyalty or infidelity; autocratic . . ."

Yes, biblical scholars are not without justification in warning us that *jealous* can have special meaning. A reply might be that like everything else, including the universe itself, language evolves. Is it difficult to see how almost the exact emotion demanded by a jealous God millennia ago can now be demanded by an anxious lover?

Here are two entries in *The Oxford English Dictionary:*

Jealous . . . in love or affection, esp. in sexual love: Apprehensive of being displaced in the love or good-will of some one; distrustful of wife, husband, or lover . . .
Jealousy The state of mind arising from the suspicion, apprehension, or knowledge of rivalry:
a. in love, etc.: Fear of being supplanted in the affection, or distrust of the fidelity, of a beloved person, esp. a wife, husband, or lover.

"Are you jealous?" I ask a twenty-eight-year-old man.

"No," he says. "I don't want very many things. My needs are simple."

"I think you're talking about envy," I say. "A kind of secret bitterness that you don't have a Cadillac the way someone else has. I mean jealousy in the sense of fear someone will steal away your girlfriend's love."

"I've never felt that."

"Ever been in love?"

"No."

If I fear you are casting seductive smiles upon my husband, you make me jealous. But aren't you jealous of me? Meanwhile, anytime you are around, I keep a jealous eye on him. What kind of state is this that cuts two ways, maybe three? There is something important in this young man's confusion of envy and jealousy. I hear it everywhere.

"I envy your life," says a teacher at the local community college. "Being a writer, you work or not as you like." Our neighbor puts it this way: "You make me jealous. If we stay up late tonight, you writers can sleep as long as you like tomorrow."

I will not dwell on these highly romantic notions of a writer's life. What is important is that here is a demonstration, plucked from just one night's conversation, of the way in which envy and jealousy are forever being confounded.

I have come to believe there is some "psychosemantic" signal here. Clarification might start with this: Jealousy is used far more than envy. "Oh, jealousy is the real killer!" interviewees are quick to assure me. "I have no trouble with envy. It's jealousy that drives me crazy." In fact, while we all use *jealous* for *envious,* almost no one uses *envious* for *jealous.*

When did you last hear a lover, threatened by loss to a rival, say that he or she was envious? Is there something admirable and large-scale about being jealous? Why do we run away from the use of *envy,* a word like any other? *Psychosemantic* is a pun on *The Psychopathology of Everyday Life,* in which Freud taught that verbal slips, puns and mistakes are not "mere" semantics. They are avenues seized upon by the unconscious in an effort to speak to us *en clair* at last.[5]

Doesn't the Bible, which has lasted over the millennia, speak at least as powerfully of and to the unconscious as any source we know? It is therefore hardly surprising that an ambivalent relationship as central to human experience as *envy* and *jealousy* should be mirrored in Scripture.

"You will not find a neat description of envy and jealousy in the Bible, complete with suitable illustrations from Bible stories," warns church historian Mary Frances Albert. "Joseph had a dream he would one day rule over his brothers. The King James Version used *envy* to describe what the brothers felt. The Revised Standard edition, the New English Bible and Jerusalem Bible all used *jealousy*."

"And Cain and Abel?" I ask.

"The Bible does not speak of Cain and Abel, Esau and Jacob, or the elder brother of the prodigal son in terms of jealousy or envy. In order to use Scripture to illustrate these terms, one must first decide what the terms mean and then go to the Bible for stories which one *subjectively* determines to be appropriate."

"And the sermons we grew up with, were these stories used to warn against envy and jealousy . . . ?"

"I'm not saying Bible stories are not right in those sermons. The Bible does give lots of good human characterizations. It is not on its own, however, a lesson in clear word usage. Some of the confusion in English usage of *envy* and *jealousy* may find its origin in the Hebrew of Scripture. The pun on *Bible, Babel, babble* is apt."

In the original Hebrew of the Old Testament, the words *Qana* and *Qinah* can mean "jealousy," "envy," or "zeal," depending on the context. The same holds true for the words *zelos* and *zeloo* which were used to translate the Hebrew into Greek. Our word *jealousy* has its origins in that Greek word *zelos* even though there was a real difference in the meaning of the two words.

Dr. Marion Severynse, etymology editor of *The American Heritage Dictionary*, explains, "A lot of words in English came to mean what they do because they were used in particular ways to translate a particular word in the Bible; and the translators didn't always understand what the word they were trying to interpret meant. Sometimes that led to ambiguous definitions. Maybe people got used to hearing the word *jealousy* in a particular biblical passage or with reference to a particular biblical event and they got it associated in their minds with something that wasn't positive. You really can't predict what a word will do.

"*Jealousy* has a checkerboard history. In Greek, *zelos* meant 'emulation' and 'rivalry.' But the word could be either positive or negative. In fact, it was more often positive than negative, according to the dictionary. It implied a friendly rivalry. Competing with someone indicated strong ambition and desire to achieve. But then *jealousy* got used as a technical word in Christian circles and it probably took on more ambivalent meanings because of the words it was translating. Once it became an English word, it started to be used in negative context and thus became a negative word."

Envy, on the other hand, is derived from the Latin *invidia*, related to the verb *invidere* (from *in*, "upon," and *videre*, "to see"), meaning "to look maliciously upon" or "to envy" (OED); or "to look askance at," "to look maliciously or spitefully into," "to cast an evil eye upon." *Invidia* is one of the seven deadly sins, as is avarice or greed.

As language has evolved, the original close link between envy and such "spoiling" words as resentment, malice, spite, and begrudging has weakened. The sequence of ideas in *Webster's New Dictionary of Synonyms* points to the transition: "Envious," says *WNDS*, "may imply either a gnawing, often malicious, desire to deprive one of what gives him gratification, or a spiteful delight in his dispossession or loss of it. Frequently, however, the stress is on coveting."

The way we speak today, *envy* more often than not embodies the last part of the *WNDS* definition—not so much a desire to spoil another's possession as a desire (secret or not) to have that possession oneself. Envy can even lead us to work hard and emulate someone, to become as good or skilled as he.

After the King James Version of the Bible, Shakespeare is the most powerful influence on the English language. It is usually said that *Othello* is a play about jealousy. But there is disagreement on the specifics: Who is jealous of whom or what? Whose jealousy is more intensely felt?

Depending on the critic, Iago can be interpreted as a latent homosexual who is fond of Othello and jealous of Desdemona. He can be a misanthrope, misogynist or masochist. Othello's own problems can be traced back to a deeply rooted oedipal complex. What is rarely understood by the popular audience is that *Othello* is a classic demonstration of the power of envy.

Once again, we must begin by wondering what jealousy and envy meant to the Elizabethan audience.

In *Shakespeare's Tragic Heroes: Slaves of Passion*, Lily B. Campbell surveys books on moral philosophy published in English before 1605 and looks for usages that might have been available to Shakespeare:

Jealousy was, in the thinking of the Renaissance, not one of the simple or elementary passions but a derivative or compounded passion. It is a species of envy, which is in turn a species of hatred. Hatred finds its opposite in love and is opposed to love, it rises often from love. And like envy it has something of grief or fear that comes from seeing another in possession of that which we would possess solely for ourselves, or from fearing that another may possess it. It is this curious mingling of love and hatred with grief or fear that we see in jealousy.[6]

Or this, in which I feel Campbell misses altogether the spitefulness and meanness, the nihilistic destructiveness of envy:

And of envy there are four kinds, according to *The French Academie* (1594 edition) again: 1) the envy that we feel because the profit of others is so great as to hurt our own; 2) the envy that we feel because the welfare or profit of another has not happened to us (being in reality a type of covetousness); 3) the envy that makes us unwilling any other should have a good which we desire or which we have wished for and could not get; and 4) the envy which makes us feel ourselves hurt when others receive any good.[7]

The confusion between jealousy and envy is as evident in Shakespeare as it was in biblical times and still is today. It is important to grasp the basic tenet of modern etymology. Words do not have fixed, absolute or eternal meaning. This goes against our natural desires for certainty. We want to believe there are usages that are "right" and "wrong" and that all "authorities" agree on them. Dr. Tamara Green, chairman of Classical and Oriental Studies at Hunter College, stresses that words derive their meaning only by how they are used at any one time or place. "Speech and language are dependent upon class and social structure," she says. "They are influenced by those who are forming the language."

If the English use the word *lift* where Americans say *elevator*, neither can be faulted. Individuals may be wrong—an American using the word *lift*, for instance, when he is not in the United Kingdom may well be described as pompous or affected. However, all that can be said about the use of words by different cultures is that they often use words differently.

Dictionaries do not define or coin words. What they do is report usage. When Swann and Odette agree upon the name of an orchid as their private synonym for making love, they have every right to do so. The communication in their community (of two) is perfectly clear. If, on the other hand, Proust himself, in writing about them, had gone on to use the same word as *his* synonym for making love, the word might well have passed into the language, to be used by all of us, and so have found its way into the dictionaries. He did not, so it did not.

At the same time that *envy* is softening in connotation, scholars agree that *jealousy* is taking over more and more of *envy*'s territory. The way American-English is going, *jealousy* will soon come to mean what we once called *envy;* and *envy* is coming to mean what we once called *covet.*

I asked an etymologist what this change in language means.

"Means?"

"What gain is there for people to say they are jealous rather than envious?"

"Psychology is not my frame of reference."

But he said my question was very interesting. "When you have determined what this change means, I would be grateful to hear your opinion."

Indeed. At this point it would be difficult to persuade me that the nasty thicket of words is not man's devilish defense against knowing what he does not want to know.

Despairing of the semantic problem, I turn to the behavioral world to describe the emotional *feel* of envy and jealousy. "What do the others say?" asks one analyst after another.

Do you know how unusual it is for anyone in this field to express interest in another's opinion? Usually they are so envious of one another, they will rarely quote anyone not safely dead.

Whenever you begin an original piece of research, you can be sure half a dozen other people are feverishly caught up by the same idea. Several weeks ago I came across mention in the morning paper of work on jealousy being done by Dr. Gregory White.[8] As if in response to all the unanswered questions chasing themselves around in my mind, the article said that Dr. White was a social psychologist. This meant he came at the problems of jealousy from an empiric direction.

Unlike the psychoanalyst's, the social psychologist's principal interest is not necessarily individual therapy. His aim is to put psychology on as firm a quantitive basis as physics or chemistry. The vague and conjectural are eschewed; only what people overtly hear, say, see and do is noted. The methodology of social psychology includes questionnaires, statistics, biofeedback, self-report. Above all, results must be capable of being replicated:

When asked if they were jealous, X percent of respondents said this, Y percent said that . . .

The replies could be broken down by age, sex, married, divorced—any category you cared to name. *Data*—not anecdotes or case histories. I telephone Dr. White and ask if he feels men or women are more jealous.

"Neither," he promptly says. "My study says that once you have accounted for who has the power in a relationship, the sex differences almost completely drop out."

Were there personal reasons for his interest in the subject? I ask.

"I began thinking about jealousy when something happened to me in graduate school. I was at UCLA."

"You never felt it before your twenties?"

"Ordinarily, I am not jealous in my relationships. It was so surprising I eventually decided to study it."

"What was different this time?"

"For a year I dated a woman who was a research assistant. Then it ended. Four months later, she started dating one of the professors. Ironically enough, he had once been jealous of me, merely for being friendly with his then girlfriend. Suddenly, I was the jealous one."

"Was it territoriality? You felt he had taken your possession?"

"No," he quickly corrects me. "It connected with my feeling that I was in the less powerful position. In a relationship, the low-power person is likely to be the jealous one. This new man she had taken up with was a powerful professor, with whom I identified. He was well known in the field. He had been preferred to me. My identity as a social psychologist, at a time when it was very important to me, was called down."

"Your jealousy wasn't that you still felt passion for her," I ask, "but that he was the bigger man and he had taken her?"

"I felt powerless to influence my former girlfriend."

"Why should you be able to? Your relation to her was over before this professor came along."

"But I had a relation to him! He was more powerful than me."

"What did you feel toward him? Competitive?"

"I felt depressed. That gave me insight into one of the sex differences people clinically report in jealousy. Any person in a lower power position, if they can't affect the other person, the only area of power they have left is to affect themselves. That explains why women who are jealous tend to get depressed and guilty, while men tend to get angry."

"You're not saying that women are biologically given to depression when jealous?"

"No. In our society, women are usually raised to see themselves in the low-power position in a relationship. In economic fact, they are indeed mostly in the low-power position."

"Did it bother you that you found yourself in what your studies indicate is usually the feminine position—a state of depression?"

"A more accurate way to describe my depression was not that I was in the feminine position vis-à-vis this professor. I was in the less powerful position."

I like it that White is not threatened by questions of gender: "All men do this, all women do that. . . ." He is thirty-two years old, a member of the generation to whom the job of redefining sexual roles has been passed, to be worked out in their own lives. His flexibility raises hopes in me.

We talk about the effort of the hippies to conquer jealousy. "You can't just talk it away with slogans," White says. "I once lived in a commune myself. The chant was 'We will not be jealous. . . .' Everybody talked a lot of ideology about freedom, nonpossession and so on, but when there was a real attraction, there would be a move to bond in pairs and exclude other people. Oh, a special revolutionary language would be used to explain why this pair or that were exceptions. 'We happen to share this same, mutual cosmic consciousness. . . .' Et cetera. But what they were *doing* was just what their parents had done."

"Let's go back to your studies on power and jealousy. My feeling is that when you talk about power in a relationship, it is close to what I have heard others call self-esteem. Either way, the more power you have, the more self-esteem, the lower you are supposed to score on being jealous, right?"

"For me," he says, "jealousy flows from threats to self-esteem or threats to the equality of my relationship. Being in a low-power position is one of several ways that either or both of these threats becomes magnified. Low-power position, so to speak, sets one up for eventually feeling threatened by a real or imagined rival."

"By anything you can measure," I say, "I should not be in the low-power position with my husband. My jealousy has nothing to do with earning ability, intellect, status among our friends, success in the world. We are equal in every way."

"How does your feeling of being in a low-power position come out?" White asks.

"Once I was in a rage at Bill. Suddenly I felt like I wanted to kill the man I had loved five minutes earlier. An analyst colleague pointed out that my fury was out of all proportion to what had just happened. The roots of all that fury didn't lie in my relationship to Bill. It belonged to a time prior to my even knowing him, to when I was little, perhaps an infant. Knowing this lessened the rage and preserved our union. I felt more in control, able to function again."

"What if there were no psychotherapists?" White asks. "What if a social psychologist explained to you that from time to time in any relationship, it is common for people to have these murderous feelings. Then you could understand from a different point of view. Wouldn't that help?"

I know the relief that comes from realizing that what you feel is not unique and monstrous; that you are not isolated in your guilt and self-horror from the rest of the human race. "Yes, it is reassuring to find you are not the only one," I say to White. "But in the end, I also want to know the *why* of what I feel."

"As a social psychologist," White says, "I look at the interactions between people, at the unspoken rules and codes that define our feelings and actions. To me it sounds like you want to blame the unconscious for jealousy. But as a social scientist, I think there is much more to jealousy than the workings of some hard-to-define unconscious."

It is a polite good-bye, a gentleman's agreement to disagree.

Not that I have dismissed White's notion of power. As soon as he used the word in connection with jealousy, I knew he was naming something central to the problem. My puzzlement is in the emotional meaning of power itself.

In human relationships, what constitutes power? Where do we get it, how do we lose it? Take the two-hundred-pound truck driver who is the brawling bully of the road-stop bar and grill, but is henpecked by his ninety-nine-pound wife. He may be the stuff of TV jokes. He is not rare in real life or we would not laugh in recognition at the jokes.

My own feeling is that interpretation, intuition, denial, empathy, projection—and above all the ambivalence between what the mind may think, the tongue say and the body do—cannot be avoided if we are to understand the power relationships of human beings. It is baffling to deal with the unconscious. The psychoanalytic view of life may be closer to art than science, but I believe that social psychologists buy their rigorous certainty too dear.

This is my bias. Therefore let me quote Dr. Gordon Clanton, himself a sociologist and colleague of Gregory White. He explains why the self-report system may not be reliable. He cites the case of a young man, Glenn:

"When another man asked Glenn's date to dance . . . Glenn punched the guy out. When a bystander suggested that he was a very jealous fellow, Glenn growled, 'I wasn't jealous. I was pissed!' By relabeling his jealousy as simple anger," Clanton writes, "Glenn was able to deny it. And if he responded to White's six-item jealousy scale, he would score very unjealous. Semantical difficulties and the apparent complexity of jealousy require that we devise more sophisticated and subtle measures of it."[9]

My objection is more fundamental. The indeterminancy of emotion, the irrationality of our conduct—in a word, the unconscious—may forever put a full explanation of human behavior outside any science that depends upon measurement.

This is where the social psychologists and I go separate ways, they to invent ever more sophisticated calculations to explain conscious experience of jealousy; I, drawn back in time to the epitaph Bill says he will have chiseled on my tombstone: "What does it all mean?" Gregory White says he felt jealousy for the first time when in graduate school. A "new experience." How can a man as sensitive as White have had twenty-odd jealousy-free years, while jealousy runs as far back in my remembered life as love itself?

Ah, for the old certainty that women were the jealous sex, that jealousy was rooted in nonseparation and as such was infantile and did no one any good. Today I listen, all defenses down, as the noted anthropologist Lionel Tiger tells me that men are at least as jealous as women. In fact, because women do not recognize the volatility of this, he says, the future of both sexes will remain "strenuous."

"One of the great factors in evolution and natural selection," he says, "is male competition for the female. Now that women control contraception, it is a whole new ball game, a whole new biological scheme. People don't want to recognize we are playing with powerful, vital and highly significant existential forces that have been bred into us for millions of years. I see jealousy as a positive force. If a relationship is good, it is worth fighting for. Put it this oversimplified way: There will never be a gene for sexual generosity.

"If jealousy had not served an important purpose, it would have evolved out of the species. I think men are *absolutely* more jealous than women. They have to know who their children are—knowledge it is difficult to be sure about."

In sharp contrast to Dr. Tiger, psychoanalyst Robert Gould believes, "Jealousy has its roots in unhealthy patterns of development. It is tied up with possessiveness and ownership. As such, it is always pathological."

Gould, who is an M.D., has long specialized in the problems of adolescence and has done authoritative work on the hippie movement of the sixties. I have always been intrigued by the role jealousy played among the hippies.

"One of the most powerful tenets," I say to Dr. Gould, "was that 'freedom' meant sexual exclusivity had to go. What led them to the intuition that jealousy was one of the cornerstones of their parents' lives and that as such it must be rebelled against?"

"The affluence of the sixties was unprecedented in world history," says Gould. "The total focus of life as an economic struggle softened. Young people began to see there was something missing at home, even after there was a second or third car. Not much love between the parents, not much love shown the child. The parents had everything, but their children felt impoverished. From the start, kids felt programmed to want possessions. How do you argue with the American Dream? But they could see that this kind of ownership brought their parents not much happiness. They also saw that the fallacy of owning things carried over all too easily to the idea of owning people. 'My' wife. 'My' husband. Keep off the grass.

"The hippies banned private ownership in the name of love and community. The communes fell apart, in my opinion, not because jealousy is a 'given' in human nature but because hippies were the children of our culture. By the time they were old enough to leave home, they had incorporated their parents' values. They took jealousy with them on the road to San Francisco."

Is all jealousy pathological as Robert Gould believes? Is it the positive force that Lionel Tiger says is bred into us? The two ideas are mutually exclusive, but I admire both men.

Two things occur to me: Either I've been getting ready for this work all my professional life and learning about jealousy will be the sanest thing I've ever done; or it is a backbreaking effort to reassert infantile omnipotence over a subject too vast for my powers.

I do not use the term "backbreaking" lightly.

My back is my emotional barometer. Five pain-free years ago, I corrected the galleys of *My Mother/My Self* lying on the floor, my back in severe spasm. If I finish this book on the floor again, or seated in the steel-ribbed orthopedic corset that I wear at my desk, will the integration my husband said he saw in me be complete?

What I know now is how little I know; that in so loaded an emotional field, where almost nothing has been studied or written, other people's prejudices and biases will teem as abundantly as my own. I must be ready to change my mind about anything before this book is over.

Will my old friend, Robertiello?

He has been telling me for years that he is not jealous, ever. However, when I told him the subject of this book, his response was electric. "When can we start talking about it?" he asked. His eagerness belied his supposed noninvolvement in the emotion. A question: Can he be so different from the rest of the human race? More to the point, can he be so different from me?

The date for our first formal meeting is penciled in my calendar. The day after Labor Day, traditional return of the psychoanalysts to Manhattan. I look forward to our talk.

Richard Robertiello is an M.D. and a psychoanalyst who has been in private practice for thirty years. He has served as director of psychiatric services at various hospitals and has published nine books on psychological subjects. He has been my mentor and friend for eight years.

Ours is an odd relationship. We talk. Not as patient and analyst—he has never been my analyst—but as provocateurs, battlers against one another's defenses. In our innumerable harangues over the years, he has revealed himself to me as fully as I to him. There has never been a time in his life when he has not been in love and/or in despair. His last marriage ended a year ago. He is deeply in love again today.

Denial of jealousy from so open and passionate a man, one who has built his entire life and career on unrelenting self-examination, is dismaying. I know he would not lie or stoop to self-serving deception. I see his denial as a red flag. He taunts me to charge, *wants* me to charge.

Robertiello has taught me that "Know thyself!" is not just a pious platitude, not even merely the beginning of wisdom. For people like Robertiello and me, it is the necessary prelude to any life free of pain.

He began as the most orthodox of Freudians, but has slowly hewn out his own eclectic paths during years as a teacher, a training supervisor of other analysts, and in his own private practice. Unlike more conventional analysts, he uses his own life to shed light on the nastiest bits of denial. I assume this enthusiasm for discussing jealousy means he is ready not only to add to the meager research available but to question at last his own claim to be jealousy free.

We met when I first went to interview him on the subject of the mother/daughter relationship. I never left. I had been doing research for almost a year, postponing putting a sheet of paper in the machine, typing Chapter One, Page 1. As luck would have it, Robertiello had just finished his own book on the subject of separation and individuation. It was he who encouraged me to make this the theme around which to organize my own book. I sat down to write, knowing he was only ten blocks away.

During the three years of writing *My Mother/My Self*, when anxiety choked thought, when repression settled like a black cloud, he pushed me past defenses. Learning, denying, fighting him all the way, I accepted at last the truth about women's attachments to, and rages at, their mothers. It was material learned from other people too, but always best learned in discussion with him.

What he liked about our talks, oddly enough, was my persistent and often angry demand that he be ever more clear, more lucid, more imaginative. "You make me doubt," he would say. He put his life on the line alongside mine; the terrible realization that my intimate relationships were patterned on what I had had with my mother became acceptable when he explained that his were too. One day, speaking with the full weight of his fifty-six years, he said, "Nancy, separation is an ideal. No one ever fully achieves it."

I remember sitting in his office, watching him read the last manuscript pages of *My Mother/My Self.* He was crying.

In turn, he taught me to see the male position, that my angers and disappointments were not caused by the malice and perfidy of men, but derived from the same cultural stereotypes that leave men outraged and disappointed in what they perceive to be the malice and perfidy of women. It was with him that I came to accept the similarities between the sexes, to recognize how much we are alike; not enemies. These realizations led me to write *Men in Love.* You see how much I owe him.

I have always thought people who said they were not jealous were lying or emotionally opaque. Robertiello is neither. After reading the galleys of his last book, a highly autobiographical work based on men's relationships with their fathers, I suggested that perhaps he had revealed too much intimate detail.

"In your position as a well-known psychoanalyst," I said, "maybe you show yourself subject to too many demeaning weaknesses."

"Nancy, the prime rule of psychoanalysis is . . ."

". . . to freely associate with as little self-protection as possible."

"I ask it of every one of my patients."

He would ask no less of himself.

This is where I thought I would catch him up. He is too much like me not to be jealous. Oh, we know each other, he and I. Not all our talks were on lofty, abstract plains of theory. We've called each other names, quarreled like children, letting the regression rip because we both knew it was a path *in;* not entirely different from dreams. As friends, we had one rule: We were not to be afraid to hurt each other's feelings. Anything said in the interest of getting at the truth was useful. In the unique push-pull of our endless questioning, we will come at last to some understanding of my vulnerability to jealousy, of his denial and defenses.

"Don't think you can retreat into some superior Freudian silence and hide in that Barcalounger of yours!" I yelled at him one day after shooting home some particularly ugly accusation. "I'm not one of your patients! Say something!"

Silence.

A beating heart. Had I gone too far?

"Nancy, I'm wondering what anxiety is working to hurry me past what you just said, without really taking it in. . . ."

Later, when I said good-bye, I apologized.

He shook his shaggy head. "No," he said. "I have my best talks with you."

Robertiello's beginnings were as lean as my own. He was raised in a house where he felt hated by his highly competitive father—an unloving man who totally dominated Richard's mother, and forbade her to pay the boy any attention. An already unmaternal woman, she obeyed. Richard grew up feeling as left out as I did. His separation anxieties are even more intense.

A year ago, before leaving for his summer vacation, he said something to me so mean, so needlessly cruel, I was depressed and wounded the whole time he was gone.

"Why so blue?" he asked cheerfully upon his return.

Word for word, I quoted back his harsh farewell.

"But I was going away," he said.

"You were the one leaving for sunnier shores, Richard, not me!"

"Nancy," he reminded me, "when you fear abandonment as much as I, it doesn't matter who's doing the leaving. Separation is in the air."

Oh, no—there is no way Robertiello can help but be jealous.

As September approached, I reread Melanie Klein's *Envy and Gratitude*, which he'd been the first to recommend. I found her powerful and magnetic, but strangely repellent too. More than anything, I had to talk to Robertiello about Klein. I cannot take in the importance she gives envy in engendering jealousy.

I see Robertiello and me as the Lewis and Clark of jealousy. My dear, brave and bearded professor and I (his pith helmet barely grazing my shoulder), journeying together to where no man has been, to the headwaters of an emotion that has soured so much of life. If I am jealous, he has to be too. Once he has accepted that truth, he will explain my jealousy to me.

Our first discussion is a disaster. It's not going to be Lewis and Clark.

His maid is cleaning the inner office; we sit in his waiting room, the tape recorder on the table between us. It's an old battered Sony that has seen me through all my books. The handle is broken. How many years ago did I decide that it would be simpler to leave it here permanently? Other interviewees get another machine. This one is ours.

An African witch doctor's rattle rests beside the Sony; Robertiello loves all things primitive and spooky, the powers of the irrational. Once he went on a tour to Africa that was supposed to include powwows with real witch doctors; he was very excited. But he never met a single witch doctor and the accommodations were terrible. On his return, he sued the psychoanalyst who had organized the tour. How many Italian psychoanalysts do you know? He is proud of his ancestry, to which he smilingly attributes his "operatic" taste for sex and revenge.

I open the discussion with a tentative outline for this book. I tell him I plan to proceed developmentally. First, early vulnerability to jealousy due to incomplete separation and lack of strong identity formation . . .

"Don't get confused," he interrupts. "When you're jealous, it's not just an issue of separation. Lack of separation makes it worse, yes, but . . . I'll give you an example. With all your success, you're still very symbiotic. . . ."

"It's maddening," I admit. "I'm very independent in my work. But when it comes to love, I still get fierce separation anxieties."

"That's Step One in the confusion," he says. "When jealousy enters, it's not just separation anxiety; envy is there too. You, Nancy, don't want to face that. Have you read Klein?"

"I'm working on it. I can't take but a page at a time. Her language is so difficult . . ."

He cuts through that. "Something frightening too?"

"Yes."

"*What is frightening is the perception that envy works to drive away the symbiotic love object.* Klein explains why you are envious of Bill's power. Which feeds your jealousy."

" 'Bill's power'? That's exactly why Klein drives me nuts. Bill and I are equal in every way!"

"No," he says. What makes Klein such an original thinker is that she does not see power in the conventional way. It has nothing to do with money or success. Bill has the power to make you happy or take it away. You suspect the reverse is not true."

"You, Richard, are as symbiotic in your attachments to women as anyone I know," I say angrily, not exactly sure why I feel such heat. "Your mother ignored you. Your father hated you. You're totally dependent on women today for the psychic nourishment you did not get as a kid. You are no less jealous than I."

His look is level:

"No."

The word is shocking.

Robertiello deals in nuance, the continuum of the emotional spectrum. Isn't he always warning me off too-large generalizations? "Richard, you may be the rare exception, but are you saying all men are like you? That men are less jealous than women?"

"*Absolutely.*"

Again, a one word reply, an obiter dictum that stuns me into silence.

"In over thirty years of practice," he continues magisterially, "I have seen maybe three men with pathological jealousy, meaning obsessed with it. I can't tell you how many, many women I've seen like that. There is absolutely no comparison in the amount of jealousy in men and women."

"Richard," I plead, "can't you consider that maybe jealousy is so painful that you've built a life avoiding it, that jealousy is the one emotion you are totally defended against?"

"If you're saying that men express their jealousy through defenses . . ."

"I'm not saying 'men' do it. I'm saying you do it!"

He begins again as if I had not spoken. "If you're saying that men express their jealousy through defenses, then they are not expressing it. Jealousy is based on being afraid that you'll be out in the cold. The more you feel that you can either defeat your opponent or replace the love object, the less jealous you are. That is why I repeat that women are infinitely, more consciously, overtly, phenomenologically jealous than men. It would be ridiculous not to say that."

"Look at you," I shout. "You never leave this office. You control your life so that you never see people or a world that would arouse your jealousy. . . ."

"You mean *envy,*" he says imperturbably. "That may be. But I am not jealous. You are talking about defenses against something. You can't equate that with the thing itself. There is no doubt women are the jealous sex."

"Are you a broken record? Every analyst, every psychologist, anyone who has thought about the subject tells me there is absolutely no data showing women are more jealous. No one agrees with you."

"They are wrong."

For several moments, only the vacuum cleaner in the next room can be heard. I pray for him to fill the void with his customary patient, thorough explanation that has always before taken me past misunderstandings of his meaning, my own stubborn defenses.

Nothing.

He sits in silence. I could swear he is sullen. Mopey Dick, that was the nickname they gave him in school. "Won't you consider," I implore, "that maybe it is not that men are less jealous, just that they have learned to protect themselves against it better? Don't they literally 'jealously possess' their wives, stowing them out of temptation's way in the suburbs, where each wife can watch the other . . . ?"

"That is different. That's a real semantic error. If they have defenses *which work,* they don't feel the emotion. You can say, 'Everybody is a killer at heart.' But some people go around slashing people on the street and others . . . well, they read mysteries. The two ideas aren't the same. People have their own unique defenses against unconscious impulses and consequent behavior. These other people you've been talking to, if they think there are as many jealous men around as women, it just isn't true.

Men have successfully employed certain kinds of stances to prevent jealousy, like marrying virgins. . . ."

"Eight years ago I would have told you I wasn't angry at my mother, but I was!"

"But you weren't," he corrects me. "You may be now, but you weren't then. That's the point."

"I loved her but I was angry too. I'd led a whole life of elaborate defenses to make sure I never felt or expressed it. Defending against that anger distorted my life."

"I understand what you're saying," he says calmly. "And it's a very important semantic issue. Don't get trapped by it. The fact is, you didn't hate your mother then. Consciously, you really didn't. In your unconscious, you and everybody else hates their mother. The difference is between people who hate their mothers and *know* it, and people who don't know it. You can't say they are the same."

"The semantic problem is important. What concerns me is how jealousy, consciously or unconsciously, dictates the pattern of our lives. For instance, I interviewed a man who is so conscious of how jealousy has ruined every relationship in his life, he can trace it back to when he was age two and his little sister was born. They caught him going upstairs with a knife. Another man I've interviewed told me he used to be insanely jealous. 'Now,' he says 'I'm not into it anymore.' When I asked him what he did now, he said, 'I just hang out with whores.' "

"Well, then, he's *not* jealous," says Robertiello. "His defenses are working."

His voice lacks sympathy, empathy, resonance. Why does he sound so uninterested? His answers are flat, imperious; uninviting of any rejoinder, any tentative question, the continued discussion from which he ordinarily derives so much pleasure. Take it or leave it.

Is all this technical discussion of male defenses a form of stonewalling, contrived to keep me at arm's length? Why can't he see he is protecting himself against recognition of his own jealousy? I feel as if I've shown him the first draft of a book and all he wants to talk about is the quality of the paper on which it is typed.

My alarm is total. I've been counting on him. In the most formal and profound sense, he is my mentor. If he is resisting me, his all-too-willing student, who is sitting in the doctor's chair? If he isn't going to accompany me through the contradictory mazes of jealousy, I am lost.

"Maybe you don't hear your male patients talk about jealousy," I say bitterly, "because, in Sullivan's phrase, you are 'selectively inattentive.' "
If a patient reports a dream about his mother and father, and the analyst makes a brilliant connection between the patient's dream mother and a

problem he is having with his wife, the hour's conversation has effectively been steered away from the patient's connection to and conflict with his father.

"Nancy," he says, "if a patient came in here obsessed by something, especially jealousy, there is no way I could steer him off the subject. Nor would I want to. The fact is that my male patients are not aware of being jealous. The subject doesn't bother them, so they don't come in here and talk about it."

To someone who did not know him as well as I, his flat denial of male jealousy could be termed chauvinism. Robertiello is proud that a female patient once dubbed him "an honorary woman" for his ease in expressing his own so-called weak and feminine emotions. This adamant separation of the sexes pertains to only one idea: jealousy.

Am I slighting him by accusing him of selective hearing? I don't think so. I do it myself. It is why I have learned to use a tape recorder in all my interviews. Practice has taught me that I'm an unreliable reporter of conversations that are emotionally painful. How many times have I left an interview thinking, What a waste of time, what a dullard that guy was. Only when I listened to the tape at home did I begin to hear the brilliance, the cascade of ideas and explanations that had gone right past me the first time around. So self-protective is my hearing that even after listening to the tape, it is often only when the interview is typed and I've read it that yet another layer of meaning is made available.

At a loss as to where to turn, I try to restore a common ground between Robertiello and me. I tell him about my talks with etymologists and we discuss the importance of distinguishing between envy and jealousy. It is baffling, we agree. (How heartwarming to have him with me again, if only in this.) Each of the two words is like an umbrella covering a host of meanings. Even professionals in the behavioral world confuse the two.

"They say things like 'I am jealous that George has gotten into print before me. . . . ' "

"The correct word would be *envy,*" says Robertiello.

"Right. George's wife might be *jealous* of his work, meaning she sees it as her rival for his attention . . ."

"But a colleague, feeling a touch of resentment that George's work might outshine his own, is not jealous. He is envious."

"We tend to think of jealousy in exclusively sexual terms," I say. "It's too limiting. For instance, Bill told me that while he was poor at math as a kid, the study of Euclid's geometry was the opening of a magic door. 'Classroom work became almost a private conversation between the teacher and me,' he said, 'with everyone else in the class just listening, mouths agape.' Then some new kid moved into the school district. He was even better at geometry than Bill. The two-way dialogue turned into a three-way conversation. How Bill hated that new kid!"

Robertiello and I agree that envy is a two-party transaction, and that jealousy entails three. We envy a good another person has. We are jealous of a rival who threatens to take away someone we love. More sophisticated definitions no doubt will arise as I proceed. At the moment this formulation is very satisfying. I had come upon it first in the pages of Melanie Klein. It was interesting that in our conversation, Gregory White had also used the schematic that envy is two and jealousy is three.

When I'd asked him if he agreed with Klein that envious people have an inborn tendency toward jealousy, his answer was that he did not find her concepts useful in understanding "the normal course of jealousy."

When I repeat this to Robertiello, he is uncharacteristically angry.

"Who are these assholes you are interviewing?" he growls. "Envy feeds right up the ladder into sibling rivalry—you want what your brother or sister has. It goes into reinforcing and embittering the oedipal conflict— you want what your mother or father has with the parent of your own sex. How can all this *not* lead into, *not* intensify any jealous disposition you had to begin with?"

"I find envy hard to understand as a factor in jealousy. . . ."

"They are very different," says Robertiello, "but connected. You, Nancy, are having such a hard time accepting envy because it is a much more despicable emotion than jealousy."

"I don't deny I'm envious!" I say, angry myself and near tears as well. "I don't deny I feel the whole catalog of nasty emotions. But you, you're envious of anyone else I interview. You call them 'assholes.' You hate every word I repeat to you other than your own."

He pauses, his own uncustomary burst of emotion forgotten. Nor does my pain affect him. He's used to tears. A couch, two chairs and a box of Kleenex, that's all an analyst needs. My accusation of envy has posed him a professional problem. He brings all his introspective powers to bear.

"No," he replies carefully, going through his emotional closet with almost audible exactness. "I've always had high self-esteem. That is why I'm not jealous."

"That's a slogan I read in *Vogue* magazine," I say angrily. "Can't you do better?"

"I don't care where you read it. It is a classic formulation. If you feel you are the best thing for someone, you are not going to be afraid that your lover is going to replace you with someone better. If you believe you are irreplaceable, the idea that she might make it with someone else is less threatening. You really should reread Klein. You will never understand your own jealousy until you understand envy. You, Nancy, are far more envious than jealous."

I look at the mean African masks on the wall and feel a total absence of the camaraderie I associate with this room. What is this distance he keeps putting between us? He is Simon Pure and I am . . . what? The fact is that I haven't denied that I am either envious or jealous. Robertiello knows me so well, knows my dependence on him. His holding back, his labeling me in a way that separates us, feels crippling.

"Has it ever occurred to you," I say evenly, "that you are envious that my books are more successful than yours?"

Though he has taught me over the years that there is nothing I cannot say to him, accuse him of, until this moment I'd never have suggested this.

"No," he repeats with his unflappable honesty, "I don't think I'm envious of your success. Nor have I ever been jealous of any of my wives or girlfriends."

"That's because you pick women who won't make you jealous! They are too dependent!"

"One of my wives was outrageously flirtatious," he says matter-of-factly, "and I never felt jealous. Even when a handsomer, richer, more charismatic man than I came on with her. And those were my insecure years. She would practically be screwing guys on the dance floor in front of me, telling me the next day that my friends had called and tried to make it with her. But it didn't upset me. You, Nancy, would have gone bananas in that situation. That is the clear difference between us."

What is he up to? There is something besides my own emotions being expressed in this room. There isn't an atom of warmth or friendship in his look. I sit, visibly beaten. I don't want Lewis and Clark. I want to be led. I want my old professor. And I have lost him. What is more, I can intuitively feel that he wouldn't care if I never called again. I could kill him.

He unplugs the tape recorder and we head for the door. His next patient is due and he is always prompt, no matter whose life is teetering on the brink. The maid is leaving too and we smile. Without thinking, I'm reminded it is Wednesday. That is how well I know these rooms. The maid comes on Wednesday.

I don't want to leave on these terms. He loved the subject when I brought it up. He was eager for our talks to begin. Now he is acting like a stranger. If I were an analyst and he a patient, I would have no hesitation in saying he is resisting. But if he is, it is unconscious. It is beneath him, unthinkable, to lie or use his brilliance to gain some intellectual advantage over me. Before he can close the door, I make one last stab at connection.

"What about that time your girlfriend was five minutes late telephon-

ing you? In your own words, you were 'almost out on the window ledge,'
you were so suicidal."

"That was fear of abandonment," he says, deadpan as ever. "Fear of
abandonment and jealousy are very close, but not the same. I have tremendous fear of abandonment, but no jealousy. I'm scared to death I am
going to be left but I never fear I'm going to be left for another man."

"Good-bye," I say.

I am out on the street before I realize I haven't made another appointment. He hadn't asked. I feel suddenly dizzy, unattached to the world
around me. Abandoned.

In my wallet is a frayed cocktail napkin from George's Bar in Rome,
where Bill and I used to drink around the time we were married. On it is
drawn an Italian flag, circled by Bill's lettering: THE ITALIAN SEAL. Above
this, in very large letters, he has printed: IO TE ABANDONARE MAI. Generously translated, this means, "I will never abandon you."

My marriage may have given me freedom from fear of loss. But that
strength depends on Bill, on how constant he is; on his character, not
mine.

Robertiello is right about the difference between us: Unlike him, I
would be insanely jealous if Bill left me for another woman. I would also
feel humiliation, rage, betrayal and a painful host of other emotions. But
mostly, I think, I would feel abandoned. Fearing abandonment—as
Robertiello says—may be different from fearing the loss of the beloved to
a rival; but are they not connected in the early complex, emotional growth
that leads to jealousy?

"Talk to me about abandonment," I say to Dan Stern. "Was that a sigh
I just heard, Doctor?"

We laugh. He had indeed sighed at my request. No one likes abandonment.

Dan Stern knows about beginnings. He is an M.D., a psychoanalyst in
private practice, but most important to me right now, chief of research
and developmental processes in the Department of Psychiatry at New
York Hospital. It is a baby/infant laboratory.

I've come to him because I'm fed up with sophisticated psychoanalysts
who live in the defensive adult world—no names mentioned. Stern treats
adults but he also studies and observes the behavior of babies. If I am to
get at the roots of jealousy, I must know more about the first years, the
first months—Klein says the first days—of life.

"I would say," says Stern, "that the feeling—the fear of being abandoned—and the biologic response to it change very little from nine
months until we die."

CHAPTER TWO

Remembrance of Things Lost

*I*f his mother's sister hadn't taken the photo, he probably wouldn't have remembered.

He is two years old and his big brown eyes stare bewildered and frightened into the lens, into the woman's face, waiting for her directions: "Run, Tommy! Poppa is at the front door! No, no, he's at the back door!" Unsure of which way to turn, unable to move because one foot is caught inside his diaper, he hesitates, near tears at the thought of missing his beloved Poppa. "Hurry, hurry! He's leaving . . ." He clutches his diaper with one hand but it is too late. He is falling. His aunt and cousin laugh merrily. His tears spill. The camera clicks.

He laughs too as he tells me the story now. He is twenty-seven, a successful young executive in a large advertising company. He loves his aunt. She wouldn't do anything cruel. The photo is kid stuff, something that just happened to surface during our interview, like the time his aunt's daughters wouldn't change his diapers.

"I didn't want to be dirty. I was a very aware kid. And very coordinated. I'd try to work those safety pins myself. I was angry as hell, but they'd just laugh."

"Oh, God, how mean," I sigh.

"Aw, it was just a joke," he says, and as if to excuse his cousins' behavior, explains, "I was the first boy born into my generation. I was raised by women. All my aunt's children were girls, not that much younger than my mom. She was the baby of her generation and the beauty."

He has her looks, and he is very charming too, with a powerful sense of self-confidence. One imagines that women come to him easily; it is unlikely that they will have that kind of power over him again.

"I didn't see much of my parents the first couple of years of my life. They were nightclub entertainers, on the road a lot. I was raised by my mother's oldest sister. I still call her Mama Lynn. We have a big close family. One day my mom and dad came back to collect me for a visit. My aunt said, 'Go to your daddy.' I went to my uncle.

"After that my parents took me with them. We were always together. I'd sleep in their dressing room. If they were having drinks with friends after the show, my mom would put my blanket on the table or on the banquette, and I'd curl up and go to sleep. It was terrific. My dad built me into the act. At the end, I'd come out in my top hat, with my cane, just like his, and take a bow with them.

"My mom was a singer, and she really was gorgeous. The men were always after her, and she didn't exactly hide it from my dad. Him, he had a real eye for the ladies. Boy, did they fight! They were both so jealous, real killers. I was little, so they didn't think I understood, but I knew what was going on. They did terrible numbers on one another . . . always accusing, always fighting . . . but they really did love one another. It was like a sickness with them."

"Were you jealous when your sister was born?" I ask. "You'd had your parents all to yourself up till then. . . ."

"Oh, no, never," he interrupts. "Know what I'd do when my dad picked her up? I'd run and get my top hat and my cane and I'd start singing and doing his routine and right away he'd drop her. He'd give her to someone else to hold and come to me and say, 'No, no, son, this is how you do it.' No, I was never jealous."

"When did your parents divorce?" I ask.

"When I was six. My mom couldn't take it any longer. He really was involved with this other woman. She was humiliated. After that, I felt very responsible for my mother. By the time I was fourteen, I had a job, assistant manager in a men's clothing store. I always looked older than my age. And I had my own band. We played for school dances in the small towns around where we lived."

"How about girls?"

"I was into sex early. Women have always been important to me. Even when I was a kid, back there in Nevada, I always had to have the hottest girl in town. I was really kind of screwed up, drugs, cars, all that stuff that means status when you're a kid. I really was immature. If I'd not got that scholarship and come East . . ."

The woman he lives with has just come in the door. Her name is Mary. She is pretty enough, quiet, low-key. When she hears we are talking about jealousy, she rolls her eyes.

"Have you told her about Alice?" Mary asks. She fixes us fresh drinks and discreetly excuses herself, allowing us to finish the interview.

I know about Alice. He had shown me the scar on his chin where she'd hit him with a bottle for talking to another woman at a party. They were college sweethearts. She was the most beautiful girl on campus, an obvious choice for the man who was used to "the hottest woman in town." Except there is a big difference between being big man in a dusty little Nevada town and achieving the same rank on a fancy eastern college campus. The transition for Tommy had been painfully reminiscent of other losses in his life, other times when he had felt left out. His clothes were wrong, his family was wrong, everything about him was wrong except the prize-winning intelligence and charm he'd long practiced to survive in the face of childhood abandonment. In time, the good things came to him, including Alice. But Alice too was a new kind of woman. Like her family's wealth and prestige, Alice's beauty was a gift at birth. She hadn't had to struggle for anything. Power, for Alice, was a given. She was a prize; one he was never sure of.

"I had to work damn hard," said Tommy. "I had to keep my scholarship. But Alice didn't want to study. She'd ask for the keys to my car. She'd go to the bars. She'd get drunk and come on with my friends. But if I so much as looked at another woman . . ." He pointed to his chin.

"What happened to your father?" I ask.

"He used to come and see us. But my mom was real down on him. She used to make me go out to his car and do this whole guilt trip on him: 'How can you love that other woman more than Mom?' And she'd tell me not to be nice to him until he gave us some money."

"That must have been hard for you," I say.

"I missed my dad. But my loyalty was to my mom."

"Do you still see him?"

"We talk on the phone. The last time I saw him, two years ago, it was really ironic. I'd met this actress. She was beautiful. Older than me, but I like older women. My dad happened to be in town and we three went out to dinner. I was so proud of myself, walking in with this knockout woman. Can you believe it? She'd known him; they'd been lovers. It was also clear she was still attracted to him. God, what an awful night."

We smile ruefully and sip our drinks. Suddenly he stands, shakes off the past—mothers, fathers, Alices—and says comfortably, "I've got it under control now."

The power balance has changed. No longer a child dependent on his parents, or a scholarship student on a campus where status can be gained or lost by the beautiful woman on your arm, he now moves in the real world. His job is his power, the look of respect in other people's eyes adjusts to a known and established standard he is mastering: The more money he makes, the greater his self-esteem. He moves with assurance; can pursue success and have the comforting love of a woman too, with no energy-draining jealousy. The woman he lives with today is not another Alice.

Mary's entrance into a bar would not arouse immediate passion. Nor would she go to one without him. She is studying for her Ph.D. He is paying her tuition. She used to dress in jeans, but he has walked her into smart Madison Avenue designer boutiques, and paid for her Charles Jourdan shoes. She is Galatea to his Pygmalion, dependent on him. Above all, she adores him. She will not interrupt his concentration on his career by arousing jealous anxieties. He is wide open to pursue the real security he has missed all his life.

Mary walks me to the corner when I leave. She is on her way to buy groceries. She asks what started me writing about jealousy.

"Just the usual nightmares of being left," I smile.

"Like Tommy," she says. "He looks so big and cocksure, but you know, when he's curled in bed, and I kiss him in his sleep, he makes these little baby noises. I think that's when I love him most. He is so vulnerable. He spends his life changing that. I don't give him any reason to be jealous, but I watch him dealing with it all the time. I admire that, his conscious effort not to say something when a man just talks to me. I'd never leave him. I know he'll be the one who goes."

On a standard jealousy questionnaire, where power is measured in terms of who makes the decisions and has the money, Tommy would rank as the less jealous person in this relationship. And yet jealousy—the determination never to feel it again—has structured his life. So has ambition. A pendulum of loss versus power he must keep ever tilted in his favor. Never again to feel abandoned, impoverished, terrified of being left; small and meaningless in a world of giants. Would Robertiello say that because this man's defenses are working, he is not jealous?

I agree he no longer feels it. He's got life "under control" now. But at what expense? The woman who loves him sees the energy he spends preserving his self-esteem. She loves him for this lack of total power, what he would call his weakness. I interview people like Mary and envy their ability to love without the need to possess. She knows Tommy will leave her one day, but there is no rage in her. Sorrow yes, but not the kind of intolerable fear and anger Tommy would have in her position. Why are some of us able to love in this way, to be grateful for present happiness, even accepting our beloved infidel's expanding universe—one that will eventually leave us out? Mary lives in the moment, feeling love whole, its edges not eaten away by anticipatory anxiety. Tommy, Robertiello, me— people like us respond to the hint of loss as if it were a wound reopened; revealed as not only unhealed but suppurating worse than ever. Present love is immediately forgotten. The wound is all.

Two thoughts, voiced by different people in interviews a year apart, converge: "I see abandonment," psychiatrist Dan Stern once said to me, "as a very close cousin to depression." Willard Gaylin, also a psychiatrist, said, "I feel the word *despair* has something to do with loss of the love object. Despair is a sense of helplessness, a diminished sense of self. When you lose someone, and become depressed, it means that with that loss, you also lost respect for yourself and your capacity to cope, either by earning love or by survival. It is a bankruptcy of the self . . . depression."

The loss of a parent, the death of a sibling, these losses knock the ground out from under us. When we are little, such loss is almost apocalyptic. We build defenses to protect against ever feeling such pain again. We control, ourselves and others. But loss cannot be avoided. We cannot control anxiety or suspicion. Further loss—real or imagined—always has attached to it the original feeling of being devastated.

"Who are the people," I ask Stern, "who deal best with loss?"

"I guess people who haven't had any."

Any study of jealousy must begin with this: the vulnerability, the susceptibility to loss. Perhaps the word *loss* carries special poignance for me. Let me try to clarify: jealous loss is not loss of a possession. What has been taken away is not a thing we own, but something we are. When we are jealous, there is the sense of being diminished, reduced, lessened as a person. If the loss is public, jealousy is all the more intense. Humiliation.

This sense of loss begins in a developmental era so archaic, not even Robertiello's therapeutic wizardry can touch it. His work reveals him to himself and protects him too. Psychoanalysis leaves out the years before speech. Freud took a verbal route. The only way *in* was what the patient *said* was his experience. Technique became almost synonymous with speech, with imagery and symbolization. Psychoanalysis has been called "the talking cure." The word *infant* comes from the Latin *infans*, which means "unable to speak."

It is often speculated that one reason Freud paid little attention to the preverbal years was that when he was ten months old, a brother was born.

A rival who usurped his special place and whose early death left Freud with lifelong guilt. Did Freud begin his examination of life at the oedipal period—age three or four—because he could not bear examination of his own earlier years?

Robertiello was two years old when his sister was born. No one explained where his mother was going when she left for the hospital, or why he was being sent to unknown relatives in the country. When he returned, his bed in the parental bedroom had been usurped. The experience was all the more powerful for what it reawakened: the feeling of abandonment when he was six months old and his mother had to go to the hospital for minor surgery. He had been abruptly weaned.

Tommy was less than a year old when his mother left him with her sister. When his parents reclaimed him, it was the sheerest bliss, but it was abruptly cut short by the arrival of a baby sister. Did this make him feel jealous? Absolutely not! he insists. Only four years old, but he already had strategies to protect himself. Feeling left out, abandoned, threatened because father was holding the baby, Tommy knew how to recapture attention. He was clever in the dangerous world of imminent deprivation. How early had he learned these defenses? How many of Tommy's choices today in work and love are in reaction to this vulnerability, this memory of loss, which I hesitate to call unconscious? Let's say he half remembers.

As he becomes more powerful, more successful, his mastery over early, painful emotions may well be reflected in his choice of ever more beautiful women. Mary knows this more consciously than he. Will recently won power keep this exciting new woman—the kind of woman his father admired—faithful to him? And if she is faithful, will his early history of loss reawaken suspicion whenever she spends an extra minute talking to another man? The neat formulation that the person with less power will be the more jealous rings true, but does not sound complete. The world sees us as rich, successful, powerful. It is how we may even see ourselves. But how do we *feel?*

Edward VIII was King of England. Wallis Simpson was a twice-divorced American of no enormous wealth, youth or beauty. He gave up his throne for her. The calculus of power is never simple. She touched a vulnerability, a fear of loss—not covered by his crown.

I leave Tommy's interview with a haunting picture: the baby straddling his diaper, as women send him tottering from front door to back, desperate not to miss his Poppa. Only two years old and already struggling not to feel abandoned, again. For those few years, the women's power over him is complete. They love him, yes, but the women tease him, finding something irresistible in a little boy out of control. Click goes the camera. And then the boy, only a few years older—even more in need of his father who has come to visit—sent out to the car, not for an embrace, the feel and reflection of the man he loves. Sent as carrier of women's revenge. "Don't be nice to him until he gives your mother some money."

How many fathers are lost to us, and so soon? How to live with such loss, and with the anger that they would abandon us? How not to?

From the time we are born, we suffer loss until we lose life itself and die. Some loss is inevitable, part of growing, changing, aging. Loss would be unbearable if it were not countered by love. The infant must depend on others to right the balance. Our ability to redress loss ourselves when older, not to suspect treachery where none exists, is determined by our earliest history.

Robertiello says he is not jealous. The rivals he fears are as intangible and abstract as Death, who took away his sister. That is why he fears abandonment. He says it is different from jealousy. Semantically, he is correct. Emotionally, I feel that abandonment is part of jealousy's web.

In delineating fear of abandonment as different from jealousy, I am beginning to think Robertiello is strengthening his defenses. Abandonment is not quite the same as loss to a rival. But the roots of jealousy are what interest me, all the different beginnings of all the different emotions that feed into that one overused and misunderstood word. Freud says that experiences in later life may be healing to the psyche. They can never establish the granitelike foundations of security known to those who had good enough early mothering. As an infant, Robertiello experienced every kind of loss. For sheer survival, for self-mastery in the face of insurmountable odds, he deserves the highest praise. But the very success of his defenses makes him unreliable to me in this work.

More than anyone, he has taught me the best defenses are not straw men, easily knocked down, but strong points, set up to draw attackers to waste their strength on the wrong targets. In the psychoanalytic wars, these false strong points take on many guises. Screen memories. Reichian armor. Simple denial and even "forgetting." Defenses can be so cunningly built into character formation, they seem part of the structure, not one of its flaws. "We don't want to admit we are fundamentally dishonest about reality," says Ernest Becker, "that we really do not control our own lives. . . . All of us are driven to be supported in a self-forgetful way, ignorant of what energies we really draw on, of the kind of lie we have fashioned in order to live securely and serenely."[1] What Becker seems to be saying is that full comprehension of our condition might drive us mad. Conversely, deliberate incomprehension can also drive us mad.

Perhaps it is my overly mystical belief in the infinite possibilities of life that draws me away from orthodox psychoanalytic intellectualizations and pulls me toward the work of people like Dan Stern, the Baby Watchers. For fifteen years Stern has been observing and writing about infant behavior.

I believe it is the most fascinating work being done today: the study of preverbal infants. The first months are not empty. On a level too primitive for speech, *we feel*, and with enormous intensity. If you believe the Baby Watchers—as I do—the capacity for memory is there too.

Jealousy is a triangle, involving the feeling of loss to another. Does it occur developmentally later than those first months so fascinating to the Baby Watchers? By the time we are old enough to take in a world containing more than the mother/child dyad, don't we already have an emotional backlog of loss, a sensitivity to it, depending on what we had with mother? Later jealousy—loss to a sibling, oedipal loss—gets its first fuel from the time when there were just two of us. When love was everything and mother's absence was death.

Stern and I are in a small room adjoining his office at New York Hospital. The Baby Theater is in action. An assistant focuses a TV camera on a "stage," a tabletop on which a mother is holding her eight-month-old child. The baby actor is happily pulling apart a stuffed frog.

"Where does the sense of abandonment come from?" I ask Stern.

"I think it's a bottom-line thing," he says. "It has a more universal, psychobiological core than does something like envy or jealousy. They are more complicated. The basic response to abandonment is almost automatic, it is so deeply biological."

"You mean it's constitutional? Some people can take abandonment better than others?"

"I don't know about that. What it does to your body, how it feels, is probably the same for all people. It's built into the species. That's the constitutional issue. What determines how high or low a threshold you've got for this response, or exactly what kind of situation will elicit it, depends on your life history. As we get older, we elaborate more into our response to abandonment. But whatever your threshold, once you feel abandoned, I think the basic response is fairly universal—and in that sense wired in by nature and evolution."

I watch the loving interaction between mother and child and wonder out loud, "Do we have to first experience love, and then be left, to know abandonment? I mean, if we didn't have love at all, didn't have loving parents, could we fear abandonment anyway?"

Stern opens the door and calls down the hall before answering my question: "Any more babies coming in today?" He sounds like the director in *A Chorus Line*.

"Before you can experience psychic abandonment," he says to me, "most agree that you first have to get attached, form a special relationship. Once you have an adequate memory to realize somebody isn't there, *then* the psychological and physiological responses aren't very different no matter what age you are."

"You said earlier that abandonment feels the same whether you're nine months or ninety. What's so special about nine months?"

"Most theorists say that the baby spends the first nine months *becoming* attached. Only at that age has the infant formed a notion that there is this special creature out there, of whom there is only one on earth, and whom he can then experience the loss of. Before that, presumably, the baby's mind is not sufficiently organized to come to this complicated conclusion. I partially disagree. My own view, and that of others too, is that the baby is sufficiently attached to experience some forms of loss much earlier."

"Earlier than nine months?" I ask excitedly.

Why am I encouraged by the opinion that the memory of pain begins sooner than most people believe? Because no one I have studied so far— not Freud, not Margaret Mahler and her brilliant separation theory—has even begun to explain the burning rage of jealousy in otherwise intelligent adults.

To a baby, emotions are matters of life and death. That's why they are so titanic. When mother—food, warmth, life—is absent too long, the infant's rage reaches killing proportions. In time, love and care—the socializing, civilizing forces—blunt the murderous edge. The infant learns alternatives. But when we accept the frustrations of reality because we are forced to, rather than through a growing and agreeable sense of self-mastery, the resentful, killing component of rage is merely masked. We have learned defenses. And they work. Until someone is late or spends too much time talking to a stranger. When the rage erupts, we are bewildered. It is so out of proportion to what has happened. We are humiliated.

Our reaction to jealousy has much to do with what is reawakened—our history of loss. For instance, two psychiatrists from the famed Massachusetts General Hospital recently reported on a group of children who were mysteriously taken ill. During an elementary-school graduation ceremony, a wave of dizziness, chills and faintness spread from one child to another. A form of mass hysteria no microscope could probe. Doctors Gary W. Small and Armand M. Nicholi, Jr., found evidence that a probable key ingredient was early childhood experience of loss.

The graduation assembly contained several such elements: The principal was being transferred, the sixth grade was graduating, and a camping trip had been scheduled during which many children would be away from home for the first time. "The researchers found that a significantly larger share of the hospitalized children came from divorced families . . . a significantly higher percentage had experienced a death in the immediate or extended family. . . . These findings suggest that in children at least, *episodes of early loss intensify vulnerability to new situations of loss* [emphasis added]."[2]

How to come to terms with loss in a world where, as the philosopher Heraclitus says, "Everything flows and nothing abides; everything gives way and nothing stays fixed."

Dan Stern talks about research that shows that the capacity for memory begins earlier than we ever thought, and some of his work indicates that an infant very early has a pretty good memory of emotional events. "At nine months," says Stern, "when mother leaves the room, the baby's got the capacity to *do* something about her loss. He can anticipate an immediate future without mother. The memory has been there all along, but now he can follow her, yell and cry. He is good at throwing tantrums. He has effective measures to counter feelings of loss. What happens initially at nine months is that he gets pissed off when he can't control her and the immediate future. . . . Distress and sadness often enter immediately."

"He hasn't just lost mother. . . ."

"Right. He's lost his omnipotence. It ain't working. He is also having a reaction to his own failure of mastery as well as to the loss."

While most Baby Watchers generally agree on when certain reactions, like the separation reaction, begin, Stern is under attack these days for questioning some of the accepted psychoanalytic explanations for these reactions, and for challenging the chronology of Mahler's work on symbiosis and separation/individuation. He has just in fact finished writing a book on the development of the infant's sense of self. Stern is filled with praise for pioneer work already done, even though studies in his own lab often lead him not to agree. When he can, he uses their ideas. He is not one to throw the baby out with the bath water. Stern is a low-envy person.

Stern and his colleagues don't take a psychoanalytic or even a psychodynamic perspective. They watch. I think they know. In a baby's first months, the earliest patterns of intimacy or distrust are forever grooved into his soul. When we were most dependent, when the world was small —like us—the people who mattered, who meant life and death, hardly ever changed. How could this pattern of dependency and intimacy not leave a mark, not *be* the mark against which we try to right the world later on? We do mesmerizingly convoluted things with this memory, trying to recapture it, change it, deny it, "forget" it, but we cannot say the emotional feel of the person who met our earliest needs—or did not—doesn't matter today.

Conscious or unconscious, our anticipation of love, expectancy of loss, our need to lose/find ourselves at any risk, is in reaction to a time we cannot remember. It is embarrassing, humiliating, to accept that our mature, intimate lives are determined by baby stuff. But it is inescapable.

The Stoics believed that life was inherently painful, and that the main cause of pain was desire. The wise man wanted as little as possible so that if he did not get it, he would not miss it. An existence in which the absence of pain is seen as the major good might be said to be a formula for a life of little envy and jealousy; if you think about it, one adopted by a lot of people who have never read a page of Greek philosophy. To my mind, it means opting for a small life. It is a betrayal of the self, lest others do it to you first.

If part of jealousy is loss, diminishment of the self, failure of omnipotence, Day One is the appropriate time to begin investigation.

Or earlier?

The Baby Theater: The Dr. Seuss Experiment

Pregnant mothers were each given a story written by Dr. Seuss to read to their tummies five times a day. Soon after the babies were born, a tape recorder played sounds of the story that was read aloud by the mother, and sounds of a story the mother had never read. A nipple in the baby's mouth had been hooked to a metering machine.

By monitoring the infant's sucking pattern, the Baby Watcher can tell when the baby is hearing sounds of the Dr. Seuss story that had been read aloud to him before birth by his mother. The response is stronger than to the story his mother had never read aloud.

The baby has remembered across the birth chasm.

Experiment by Dr. Anthony J.
DeCasper, University of
North Carolina at Greensboro

The fetus lives in perfect balance; the ceaseless thud, thud, thud of mother's heart, the steady temperature, food swishing in through the blood stream. Hunger, cold, loneliness—all are unknown. Constancy. The first change a living creature knows is consciousness itself. One psychological system tries to base all neurosis on the "birth trauma": the shock of coming into the world. *That* is the fundamental illness that we never get over. The slap on the ass. Life is change and pain.

Be that as it may, once born, we have a longing for the old unchanging rhythms. It is wired into our very structure, perhaps into the biological preconscious.

Infantile omnipotence, the belief that we control the world, that we *are* the world and the universe too, begins at birth. Frustration is magically met. When the infant expects food, when he is cold, mother is there. In symbiotic oneness with her child, she anticipates his needs: The breast, the blanket are offered almost before hunger or cold is felt. The baby's thoughts are answered before they become conscious even to himself. What power!

But frustration cannot be postponed. The period of time it takes for reality to enter is debatable. Alas, it is not very long. No mother, no matter how good or loving, can keep her infant in his omnipotent heaven. Nor should she.

What she can do is soothe the loss entailed in surrendering this grandiose state; appease his fury at losing the power to demand automatic, instant satisfaction. A good enough mother kisses away his tears and offers her love as a substitute. Slowly, sadly, the infuriating realization comes home to the baby that not every wish will immediately come true.

What makes the gradual letting go of infantile omnipotence bearable is her sweet mothering. It diminishes the pain of learning limits: where he ends, where she begins. The reward is this: If mother is *not* him, but someone else, she can have opinion of him. The beam in her eye, her constant assurance of praise and love are reward for his surrender of magical power. "That's a good boy," she says when he does not immediately set up a howl at learning that if he knocks over a glass of water it has the impertinence to wet him. "What a brave boy!" She is rewarding him for learning to put up with frustration/reality. In time the baby becomes resigned to losing his place as King of the World. In mother's admiration for the abdication he finds recompense, but the surrender of glory is never done without regret.

Witness people who acquire vast powers. How often they maniacally regress to states of infantile omnipotence. When they are most able to control their lives—and the lives of others—they make Canute-like demands on reality. The happiness and success that once seemed the unattainable end of the rainbow no longer are enough. Alexander wept because there were no worlds left to conquer.

Our culture raises us to seek success but we are not taught how to live with it. Infantile omnipotence, as the name suggests, should end in infancy. In an adult, it is a regressive step toward madness. Colossal pride that heralds self-destruction. The Greeks called it *hubris.*

The formative work of weaning us from omnipotence, teaching us to live with loss and to anticipate love, is still done almost exclusively by women. No one has more control over another than a mother over her child. The fact is that even the most loving mother in the world is inevitably going to be seen by the child as an inhibiting force. If every time he runs into the street to play among the speeding cars, a child's mother runs out after him, and at the risk of her own life and body, pulls him back to safety, the child is not necessarily going to thank her. All he knows is that whenever he is having fun she stops him.

"Thirty years ago," writes Sylvia Brody in *The Psychoanalytic Quarterly*, "the advice to avoid a facile leap from a mother's faulty infant care to infantile neurosis was necessary. The issue long since is not one of blaming mother or of expecting or desiring freedom from later conflict. It is to recognize how early, how much, and how subtly an infant's experience in his particular environment and with his particular parents . . . can advance or impede his ego and character formation."[3]

That the necessary, difficult and often thankless job of child rearing is left to one sex is a major loss to us all. It is my own opinion that the unhappinesses described in this book would best be ameliorated if a child were raised from the day he was born with two sources of love, two sources of discipline, two models to imitate, and last but not least, two outlets to divide his inevitable rage.

Nevertheless, the job in our society is left to women. When I refer to the person responsible for child rearing as "she" it is merely recognition of reality.

Nothing has the glue, the sweet stick-with-it-ness of love carried to the point of adoration in the first years of life. The Adoration Banquet. The celebration of our life that we remember as if in our blood, always. It is expressed as a sense of trust in others and in ourselves. In such early symbiosis, says Mahler, lies our strength to separate and find our own identity. According to psychoanalyst Heinz Kohut, pioneer in the new thinking on narcissism, herein lies the groundwork for healthy self-esteem. Even constitutional envy, which Melanie Klein says we bring into life in our genes, is lessened by good mothering.

Things can go wrong later. But we do not anticipate loss. We do not build a life as a defense against it. Should someone leave us, we ache, we feel our hearts will break, but if our earliest experience was love as a given, the reaction to loss is not "That is how life is"—but to find love again.

For this belief in love to happen, the Adoration Banquet is not enough. It has to end. And the ending must be as loving as the beginning. You could say that the leavetaking was what the banquet was all about; nourishment for the journey. The richer and more satisfying the banquet, the stronger and more eager and ready the child is to be off into the world.

Some mothers cannot love. Others cannot let go. Either way the child loses. Within the sweet symbiosis with her baby, a mother often finds the only love she's ever believed in. Here is a creature who cannot leave her, who needs her. "As close to heaven as I have ever been" is how one mother describes her first months with her infant. There is no sacrifice in meeting her child's needs. Filling them is like filling herself, with warmth, with food, with love. In the first months, both mother and child bask and benefit from the oneness.

Then one day baby has had enough closeness. Perhaps no one ever told mother she had to let go so soon. Society still eulogizes the mother who gives up everything for her child, though it is a gift a child may guiltily feel he can never repay. Perhaps her own mother did not easily let go. She went from mother's arms, to Alma Mater, to husband. Now she has a baby. He is *hers*, the only person who ever belonged to her, to whom she feels she belongs.

"But she is my best friend!" a twenty-year-old mother cries to me from the audience. I am lecturing at a small midwestern university, emphasizing how important it is for mothers to encourage their children to seek love from others as well as from themselves. Her "best friend" is eighteen months old.

When the child is ready for his own life, this kind of mother sees his separation as a threat to her happiness. When a pediatrician says to a mother, "You only have to be 'good enough,' " it cuts two ways. It can be reassurance to a mother anxious because she must work outside the home. It is also a warning to the overprotective mother that she should not try to be too good, to do too much for the child too long. This inhibits independence and keeps the child tied.

The English child psychologist D. W. Winnicott defines it this way: "The good enough mother . . . starts off with an almost complete adaptation to her infant's needs, and as time proceeds she adapts less and less completely . . . according to the infant's growing ability to deal with her failure."[4] As the child surrenders his unrealistic need to have mother act as his agent, the good enough mother gives herself a bit of time for her own life, for her own private pursuits. In this she is the reality principle at work, teaching the child the satisfactions of self-reliance. The child decides he'd better learn to handle the environment himself.

If she has been a good enough mother, he does this out of satiation, even boredom. The world is safe and happy, but so small! If his need for symbiosis has not been sated, separation will be reluctant. He will resent it and look for someone else to take mother's place, someone who will satisfy the feelings of dependency appropriate to age one or two, but crippling in a grown man or woman.

The life force that propels so many of us so far in life, even though we didn't get that early adoration, is awesome. Even more so is the motivation that makes a child, who has all the love in the world, want to leave.

And he does, he will, if he is allowed. The first year of life is not yet over, the infant is in Eden, but he crawls away. We are drawn to life, to find ourselves, separate and unique from everyone else. Why else would an infant leave paradise? Real security is not in someone's arms, but in the discovered self.

People often say, "Oh, I left home when I was eighteen. I've been separate for twenty years." Separation is not defined geographically. Though we begin with the physical act of crawling into the next room, whether we indeed become separate will depend on an *emotional* process. The self we show the world can be handmade, an external persona, put on for protection, even bravado. Intimacy unmasks us either as the truly separate people we are who can be generous with love, or as the frail needy ones, who never learned to believe in love, and so must possess and control the beloved against loss. Somewhere within the infant's faith in love begins an understanding of our own lack.

Separation. The beginning of life on our own. It is the spirit in which mother aids the process that will ever after move us. The fuel is her faith in us, ours in her love—which we carry inside, and which is not diminished by the distance we go. Our reach and our courage, our intellectual and emotional curiosity, will be rooted in her generosity. Did she make us feel guilty for wanting to go? Did she project her own fear onto us, making us unsure we would find the way?

The baby's needs are selfishly two-headed; he wants his own life, but he wants hers too. And he wants them simultaneously. Much as adolescents do, repeating this hold-me-let-me-be-myself separation process ten and twelve years later. When the baby, not yet a year old, crawls into the next room on his own for the first time, he experiences an excitement, a place, a moment all his own. Self-discovery. A new, bigger reality.

It is swiftly followed by realization that he is alone. Frightened, he rushes back to where he left her. If mother picks him up, consoles him, assures him that neither she nor her love have gone away, he is restored. "Re-fueled" is what Mahler calls it. Sure now that he can have both the excitement of the next room *and* her love, he will try an even farther room the next time. Again he will feel the thrill of discovery, followed by the panic that he's lost her. Again he will hurry back to home base. She is there. She loves him. "Everything is all right."

In time, with enough journeys and enough re-fuelings—enough of what Mahler calls *practicing*—he learns that new things he wants to do for himself won't lose him what he still needs most: her love. It becomes a given; he knows that she will always be there for him. Now when he runs back to her, it is not out of fear that she might have abandoned him, or that she will love him less for moving away. When he returns—in what

Mahler calls the *rapprochement* stage of separation—it is to share with her his extended life.

Practicing *his* separation with *her* love has taught him that he need lose nothing. Life becomes all about growing, changing, having an even bigger life. Our choice of partners later will be made not out of a need for safety but out of desire for the even richer life she has taught us to seek. The final stage in Mahler's separation theory is called *object constancy.* It means the good enough mother is internalized. We carry her love inside like the memory of home on a cold winter's journey.

If, however, the child's panic at discovering he is alone in the next room is met by mother's anxiety or reproof when he hurries back, he will not be re-fueled. "See, didn't Mommy tell you? Stay close. Be good." The child will not try to go as far the next time. His explorations have made her angry. He thinks of leaving as dangerous, a threat to love. Abandonment. He becomes guilty, timid, emotionally burdened. Growing up, moving away from her, engenders reprisals. Love feels most constant and unambivalent when *she* is in control. This becomes his model: He can count on love only when he makes the rules for himself and the beloved too. From this it is just a step to ideas of possession. You are mine; even one of your smiles, given to someone else, is stolen from me.

"Are you jealous?"

"Oh, no," he says. He is a retired bank executive from San Diego who now owns a house in Key West. "There's lots of wonderful women out there but you don't have to own one."

"What kind of verb is that—'to own'?"

"I've been married four times."

"You mean you're tired of women?"

"Not tired, but when you're involved with a woman, you either own or you're owned. You're jealous. The two go together."

According to Mahler, the process of separation and individuation begins in the second half of the first year of life and should be complete by age three. In fact, separation is something we work on most of our lives, giving it names like fear of being alone, fear of being left, fear of losing our piece of the pie.

The Baby Theater: The Visual Cliff Experiment

A twelve-month-old infant sits on a glass table. His mother stands at the opposite end, about ten feet away. Beside her is a beautiful toy ferris wheel. Directly beneath the glass is a red-and-white checkered cloth. The lighting is controlled so that the glass is invisible, thus giving the baby the feeling that the cloth is solid ground. Halfway between the mother's end of the table and the baby's end, the checkered cloth *beneath* the glass drops precipitously, giving the impression of a cliff. (The glass surface on which the baby sits remains as it was.)

As the baby crawls closer to the halfway point, enroute to mother and the ferris wheel, he comes to the edge of the cliff. He looks down. He is uncertain. On the one hand, he is scared, a natural fear of heights. On the other hand, he wants to get to mother and the pretty toy.

Unable to resolve his ambivalence and uncertainty, the baby looks at mother's face to see her emotional feeling about the situation. The Baby Watchers who did this experiment call this "social referencing": When the baby doesn't know what to do, he references mother and picks up her affect state and takes it into himself.

If mother has been instructed to show fear on her face, the baby will not cross the cliff and, in fact, will often retreat and become upset. But if the mother gives a nice smile, conveying the message "You're doing fine, honey," the baby will crawl toward her, over the "cliff."

> Experiment by Dr. Mary Klinnert, Dr. Joseph Campos, and Dr. Robert Emde
> University of Colorado at Denver

Stern tells me that the Visual Cliff experiment was not originally set up to research separation. I ask him, however, if it doesn't show how mothers can encourage it.

"Absolutely," says Stern. "When a mother lets her child know that the world is a dangerous place, he is going to stay close to home."

"On the other hand, her smile, if he becomes frightened, can show him that his fears are imaginary?"

"It is up to her to help him practice bravery and curiosity."

Practicing. Such a simple word. One of Mahler's stages of separation for a two-year-old, and something we continue all our lives when confronted with the new. Without practice over and over again, the untried remains fearful forever. Overcoming fear of the unknown is not best done theoretically or through explanation. It must be gone through existentially. It must be physically done. It must be practiced.

When we are jealous, what are we afraid of? If we live with fear, if we haven't entered into the dark corners and faced the serpents, we will never learn that we have resources to fight the good fight if indeed the rival is there; at worst, to replace the person who has left us, should the rival win.

Without practice in separation, we may appear to function well in the world but the *self* is not rooted in our center. Our sense of security lies not in who we are but in the connection made to another. Driving home after a party, a husband and wife are angry at each other. She because he danced too much with a pretty woman. He because he feels locked up. There are many emotions loose in the car: fear of abandonment, of betrayal, of being left out in the cold; chagrin at defeat by a superior rival. Resentment at being owned, possessed, suffocated. Loss of warmth, trust, power, self-esteem, sex. The permutations and combinations are endless. If the two people in the car could give precise names to what they are feeling, it would enhance their chances of resolving their differences. They use a shorthand instead, calling everything *jealousy*. No wonder the argument comes up again and again.

Some of the most beguiling and successful people had unhappy beginnings. The most lovable man I know stood in hushed expectation at the top of the stairs in his little blue blazer on his third Christmas, secure in the knowledge that he'd been a good boy. He watched his mother disappear forever in the arms of the family chauffeur.

One afternoon in Los Angeles, Robert Morley, the portly British actor, tells me a story while we are waiting in the green-room to go on the *Merv Griffin* show. Having been a fat little boy, he says, had its advantages; he was forced to find other ways to win love and admiration. He learned to speak; he became articulate and amusing. Beauty fades, but the brilliant conversationalist gets better and better. In time, even the man's size becomes part of why we love him.

At times I think it's a rule of thumb, this business about bad beginnings and later triumphs (though I wouldn't wish a wretched childhood on anyone). It's a gamble that doesn't always work: some people who don't get loved or taken care of on a consistent basis die. Or they go quietly under; they never really try. They don't have the genes to fight, or the luck to find alternatives to mother. They go through life never quite feeling it, never being wholly alive.

But when it does work, when home base runs dry, when that "good enough" mothering just isn't there, and a tiny child has a capacity to find love, it is a tribute to human nature. Survival working at its most creative. For me, the restorative process is *the* life force. We cannot overestimate the importance of mother love. But there is something more miraculous. And that is the tiny child's ability to go looking for the love he needs to stay alive.

Just in case Number One fails to ignite, we've an auxiliary motor. If there is not that spark in her eye for us, the reserve engine will try for someone "out there." If there is an emotionally receptive father, an aunt, a grandmother, someone who picks up on the attractive needy quality we've developed, and whom we see as worthwhile so that their love is meaningful, restorative magic begins to happen. It can save our life. Now, in addition to feeling lovable, we've this talent, these qualities we've worked on since maybe the first year of life: We know how to get people to see us, to pick us up and hold us.

And yet, as marvelous as our ability to find love may be, if we have to work for it—if it is not lavishly given at the right time, unasked for and without strings—we never quite believe in it. Not as wholeheartedly as those lucky ones who began life getting love as their accepted due. Literally drinking it in so that they never question whether people will love them or leave them. The Adoration Banquet, a short time in life when the infant gets everything he needs. Did you sit at it, or lie at it, as it were?

Few of us can remember infancy, but I believe we know on some unspoken level whether we received this bountiful beginning. We know it if only from comparison with others who seem to have an ease with love, giving it, getting it, believing in it, unafraid it will be taken away. When we get it later, from a nurse, a sister, a mother surrogate, we never believe in it as positively as those who get it at the appropriate time.

Stories of gloriously successful people who made it on their own, without early constant love, are an inspiration. But what if they'd had the Banquet too? If my wonderful friend's mother hadn't run off with the chauffeur, would he be as dear today? Would he radiate that irresistible energy for all of us that never seems to go out, that he never dares let go out? If Robert Morley had been a beautiful, thin little boy, would he be just another nice overweight guy today? Does he ever stop talking, being amusing; dare he? (That night on the *Merv Griffin* show, it was hard to get a word in; it was as if he would disappear if his lips weren't moving.) Would Proust have struggled with his genius if his remembrance of things past had been a happy stroll down memory lane, instead of terrifying loss every time his mother did not kiss him good-night? Would I be writing this if I hadn't feared loss ever since I can remember?

We would like to relax with love, but do not know how. Giving neither ourselves nor our partners enough room to breathe, we complain of boredom. They complain of suffocation. One of us wanders. Jealousy erupts. The relationship breaks up. We have contrived to get what we feared most: We are alone. And if new love is offered, once more the feeling is that it will be withdrawn unless we *keep* them loving us. It all becomes a trick, a skill, an endurance test, because essentially we do not feel lovable. Failure looms. We are the kind of people who jokingly say, "I'm going to leave you before you leave me."

Still in control, if only of our own loss.

The least jealous people must be those who don't have a need to control. Where do they get the courage? They have such an ease with love (how I envy them!). They do not confuse it with suffocation, nor see the beloved's independence as prelude to treachery. They are capable of letting go, allowing the beloved to lead the fullest possible life, never fearing that a momentary happiness elsewhere means he will not come back. But who would leave them?

Those are the people who repeat with others the gift of being at home with love that mother gave them. They are also the ones who return to her when grown, not out of guilt or dependency but with gratitude.

Here is a running argument with Robertiello: Would you rather be someone who got loved and loved and never let go—or someone left on your own emotionally, forced to develop talents for winning love that you then never quite believe in?

The answer, of course, is not to have to choose; to be loved *and* let go at the right time.

Proust was insanely jealous. So is my thoroughly lovable friend. So am I. And so, I am beginning to believe, is anyone who did not get the Adoration Banquet, followed by practice in separation. There is a developmental chronology to life, optimum times for getting what we need to grow up strong and healthy. Later love may save our lives. We seek it, drink it in thirstily, being so parched. We may even feel loved. Until something happens. Suspicion enters:

"I didn't think I was jealous," says a twenty-eight-year-old woman. "But the phone rang the other day. A woman's voice said, 'Is Jimmy there?' It was the intimacy of her voice. Suddenly I felt everything drain out of me. It was an ache, a pain deep in my gut. I went into the park. I sat quietly and began to breathe deeply, regularly, trying to diffuse the *thing.* I know that woman means nothing to Jim. I *know* that! But when she asked for 'Jimmy' in that way . . . As I sat in the park, I could feel energy well up. By being quiet, something changed and it altered direction. That incredible energy that was the jealous feeling, it became mine. My reason returned."

The woman speaking is my Tai Ji teacher. Twice a week we practice the ancient Chinese exercise that I hope will keep my body aligned during the years I work on this book. The man she loves is gentle, less dynamic than she. The loss of control brought on by the intimate note in the other woman's voice cannot be explained by today's reality. It touched a pool of vulnerability damned up within her long before she met Jim.

"Consumed by jealousy" we say because jealousy is an energy that takes us over. A tornado sweeps up all feeling throughout our body, bearing down on our brain, our gut, the central nervous system. Jealous suspicion spoils everything. Before we felt it, we were in love, beautiful, and had the power that comes from both. How can a woman's faith in love be eroded by a voice on the telephone? How can that voice be stronger than what she feels for the man she is going to marry?

Even the decision to marry someone who will not betray us is no protection. The seed of suspicion lies within. Jim has to do nothing. He is accused and convicted without a word. Though jealousy requires three people, the third person in the cast may be in our heads alone. My Tai Ji teacher's story might well come under Freud's heading of pathological. Among the people I interview, her story is resonant. They have been there. It is normal.

"Are you jealous?"

"No more sleigh rides," he answers. He is driving my taxi in Chicago, an actor filling in between roles.

"What does that mean?"

"I just met a new woman. I'm not going to make her into the moon and stars, like I did with all the others. She's a lovely woman. That's enough."

"Meaning no more sleigh rides?"

"No more jealousy."

I have my own view in the argument with Robertiello on the question of whether it's preferable to be safely cut off emotionally or to be tossed about on the sea of passion and jealousy. I opt for the highs and lows because the heights are the best moments in my life. The promise they hold carries me through the lows. That is how I am, a decision I have made. Having your own biography, you may work out a different equation between love and control.

I find the example of the tiny child to be so brave. Totally dependent, the infant looks for scraps of love on which to build a life. Twenty-five years later, older and stronger, able to feed and clothe ourselves, we give up when love is threatened. Why is someone paralyzed by jealousy? Someone else, with the same emotional start, is not. Jealousy breeds a lack of courage which, ironically, is often born out of fear of our own desire to do murder. When we don't fight for someone we love, when we abase ourselves before a rival, it reflects our vision of life not as a feast but as a pie with just so many slices—and ours has been taken.

When adult love is offered to the unseparated person, the response is regression, a rush back in time as if to find what we never received, or never relinquished. The masquerade is intense. It has all the components of life and death. So does our jealousy.

To the dependent, unseparated person, when loss is in the air, it is intolerable. The disappearing beloved robs us not only of himself but of the identity and security found through him. This is not to say that people who are healthy and separate are impervious to the pain of losing someone they love. That school of thinking which looks to a dawn where there will be no jealousy ignores the irradicable and unavoidable fact that feeling loss is neither weak nor strong, neither good nor bad, but human.

In any love relationship there are good and even pleasurable dependencies. Meeting these mutual needs is part of the magical exchange. But love that is based on the need to survive means you must structure it in such a way that your partner can never leave. The irony of control has mad, Proustian logic: You make the other person your prisoner; you run, control and dominate their lives because you fear they are stronger, can live without you.

Who is weak? Who is strong? The words are absurd.

Even as the beloved promises eternal love, if there is no clearly defined "I" separate from the sweet "We," we cannot be held or hold on tight enough. All the sacrifice and fidelity on our part cannot guarantee that some rival will not take away the beloved, ending the "We" and thus life itself.

And so I began this book feeling that women are the jealous sex. Men get more practice in separation than their sisters. A mother will be more courageous for her son. Even if she wants to hold onto him, society forbids it. If he stays tied to her, she will be "a bad mother," the worst criticism that can be leveled at a woman. When the baby boy tries for the stairs and falls, her inclination may be to pick him up and hold him to her breast. Training, her intellect, her husband's voice behind her, all say, "Don't baby him."

That is how the boy learns. First the next room, then the neighbor's yard, the next block, another town. Getting on an airplane, starting a new job, *being alone* are not filled with terror but with a growing sense of mastery. He has a small scar on his chin from where he fell from a tree when he was five. It hurt then. He wears it with a kind of pride today.

The first time he takes the initiative and calls a girl, he is terrified, but he already has a backlog of experience in trying and failing and trying again, until he succeeds. The first time he touches a girl, kisses her, leads her to bed, the new risks fill him with anxiety. He is reinforced by remembrance of having dealt with anxiety in the past, often with a degree of success. With each kiss, each touch, sex becomes less anxious.

The boy develops a strong sense of self-reliance. He knows where he begins and others leave off, an emotional differentiation that began with mother and now extends to others. "I love you," a woman says to him. He doesn't say in a little voice, "Do you really?" and ask for documentation. He believes her. Not because he thinks he's the best man in the world but because he knows whom she's talking about: him. He has a self in which to deposit her love. That self grows as she speaks. Love strengthens a man. It is an additive. For women love is often subtractive. Even if the man is walking out the door to go to work, she has a sense of being diminished. She is smaller without him. Losing the woman he loves can be the worst pain a man has ever felt. Even in pain a man knows who he is.

"I've always had a sort of rule for myself," a forty-year-old man says. "I remember it from the time I was a kid. I always said, 'I have to make myself do anything I'm scared of.' I don't know where I learned it, but it's been my code: If I'm scared of it, I've got to do it. It simplified everything. I could never allow myself to avoid something because I'm afraid of it."

This man is no tiger. He is somewhat shy. His feelings are easily hurt. But he takes risks. Finding out that he eventually masters things that once scared him has taught him something: When a woman leaves, when loss is in the air and you think your heart will break, life doesn't end.

My editor warns me against generalizations. "Nancy, the only person I know who totally fits your description of women's dependency in these pages is a man." Her warning carries weight. Women are changing. They are trying in their private lives to exercise the same kind of courage they show in their professional lives. However, until women have been raised from the beginning to value autonomy in themselves, until they have practiced accepting rejection as every teenaged boy must, when a crisis of intimacy occurs, they will respond as their mothers taught them.

"I get turned down in business all the time," says a twenty-seven-year-old real-estate broker. "I pick up the phone and make another deal. But it takes all my courage to call a guy for a date. If he says no, I die. If we wind up in bed and then he does not call, I die even more. It's not a business contract being rejected. It's me."

Social or sexual rejection is personal pain. It hurts more than being turned down professionally. A man may "die" over rejection too. He has learned, however, that you are always reborn to try again. He picks up the phone and dials a second woman, a third . . . Sooner or later, life has taught him, he will be lucky. For a woman, rejection by a man reinforces mother's implanted message: "It's more womanly to let the man make the first move."

Nevertheless, women grow increasingly tired of being the sex that waits. They are learning what men have always known. The privilege of taking the initiative carries a price. My own studies show that for many women the price is too high. As the real-estate broker above put it, "I'm crazy about my job. I'm going to cool it with men for a while."

When you are the one who takes the initiative, there is a psychic gain whether you are rejected or accepted. Each time you try, you are accustoming yourself to the idea of risk. Practicing separation. Small wonder that a woman who has waited to begin the practice of risk taking until she is twenty-five or thirty feels acutely vulnerable. Rejection not only makes her feel unlovable, unwanted; it also undermines whatever good feelings of self-reliance she has gained through work.

One of the difficulties of not learning autonomy at the appropriate childhood age is that we have to first *un*learn a lifetime of reinforced dependent responses. Sadly enough, it is easier for a woman to forge her identity in the "man's world" of business; the emotional temperature is cooler than when she is dealing with a specific man on a personal basis. He reawakens the old symbiotic desire to find someone to lean on. The very desire she has striven so hard to overcome. And so women feel they must choose between men and independence.

One night I sit under our avocado tree in Key West talking with a pretty fifty-year-old woman whom a friend had brought for drinks.

"Is that your manuscript in there?" she asks. We are on the deck just outside the studio where I work.

"You know," she confides, "my husband made me so jealous that since our divorce, anytime I feel the slightest twinge of that emotion, I back away from the man."

I ask her if that means avoiding passion.

She smiles sadly, reflectively. "I just don't want to feel that much anymore."

This woman runs her own business in Washington, D.C. In her mother's time, people didn't get divorced over jealousy. She had enough courage to leave a philanderer whose wealth protected her. Her enterprise in business is unending, but she cannot afford emotional risk. If she's even in the vicinity of jealousy, she tells me, she doesn't work well. She sees only men who allow her to stay in control. On this trip, she is traveling with a man, a friend, but he is safely homosexual. How can a woman be so brave in everything but love?

Women's lives today are both different than they used to be, and the same. The economic need to work, as much as desire, is teaching women the practical and unavoidable truth: They can take care of themselves. Discovering through a paycheck that you can support yourself and run your life—mastery—echoes the thrill the baby feels when he makes it into the next room on his own.

If men were ever-encouraging, all-accepting, totally loving and omnipresent, it might be said that women could practice separation with their help. *But those adjectives describe a mother.* It is not a man's role, nor what women really want from men.

Many mothers today want to teach their daughters some of the courage they've won themselves. Intellectually, they know a daughter must be prepared for the egalitarian world they themselves helped win. But motherhood has a way of regressing a woman. She sees herself in her daughter. How many narrow escapes she herself has had, trying to be different from her own mother. She fears the girl may not come through the dangers, the risks, as successfully as she.

The idealism, the high professional expectations of today's college women is amazing. Studies show they expect to shoot right to the top in their chosen careers; they anticipate totally egalitarian marriages. At the same time, their attitudes about mothers and men illustrate that the deep conflict—need for symbiosis versus need for separation—has not yet been resolved.

In a recent survey, college women were asked, What message do you think you give to men? Three choices were given. Women want to: 1) Be treated as equals. 2) Be taken care of. 3) Both. Sixty-nine percent of respondents checked *Both*. [5] (In the margin of the page, several acknowledged the impossibility of what they were asking. "Sorry," they apologized.)

No wonder men are baffled. No wonder women are.

Young women today talk of their mothers' lives like so much baggage they must carry in addition to new expectations. "If only my mother weren't so self-sacrificing; if only she'd stick up for herself!" they say. Many seem more adamant, more anxious about changing their mothers' lives than their own: They already see themselves becoming like her. Not the admirable mothers they love, but the very parts of her character they hate. The desperation to see their mothers change, to *make* their mothers change, now, in front of them, while they are both still alive, says to the daughter that the legacy might then be broken. "If only my mother were her own person" really means "I cannot be my own person because she is me and I am her. If she does it first, I will be able to do it too."

That is not independence talking. That is symbiosis.

"Are you jealous?"

"I was," she says. She is thirty years old, an industrial engineer for a major airline.

I laugh. "Did you take a pill to get rid of it?"

"What I mean is that I'd never felt it before, until recently. It was a very new emotion to me."

"What brought it on?"

"I think I was feeling insecure," she says.

"You were in love."

"Yes. I was really in love with this man in a way I'd never been before. I wanted to become the kind of woman I thought he wanted. A woman who would let him appear to be on top, in charge. When we met, I thought he was very sure of himself."

"You discovered he wasn't."

"But by then I had already tried to make myself into something I wasn't. Playing a role makes you very insecure."

"So you became jealous?"

"Of every woman he looked at. It was humiliating. He ended up telling me *I* was insecure."

"It must have been frightening," I say, "to have experienced jealousy for the first time at thirty."

"It would have been easier if I'd begun to learn about it when I was sixteen."

"Hadn't you been in love before?"

"I'd always gone out with a lot of men, but nothing had ever been this serious."

I ask her if she thinks she will marry some day.

"Oh, maybe."

She is a beautiful woman, warm, empathic. Fifteen years ago, she would have waited, with men vying for her as a prize. Today, she will choose. She doesn't seem all that passionate about marriage. Not as eager and confident as she is about the job ahead of her in South America. There, this woman who tried to make herself look dependent and small in love will be instructing a group of industrial engineers, all men. Will her recent brush with the pain and humiliation of jealousy steer her away from another passionate involvement? Will she decide to leave men out of her life?

"Living alone is a thoroughly bizarre circumstance," says anthropologist Lionel Tiger. "An unnatural state and an unspeakable nonpractice."

Strong words. But something in me responds to Tiger. We live in a world without constancy. Half the marriages today end in divorce. Once children grew up with fears of bogeymen; these were symbolic fears. Today the symbols have become real. Studies show that what children fear most, what their nightmares are about, are the real anxieties of losing a parent—to drug abuse, to cancer, to divorce. The only given is insecurity itself.

"Are you jealous?"

"Only when I'm not in control," he says, not missing a beat. He is thirty-two. He says it so unapologetically I can't help smiling. Most people bury those feelings in verbal acrobatics. It is certainly possible to live within a loving relationship free of jealousy, but to structure a marriage or an affair, to pick a mate in order to avoid jealousy, seems emotionally limiting. Perhaps not. No one said all of us had to live life to the hilt.

"Does that mean you like passive women?" I ask him.

"Absolutely not. I like independent, strong-minded women. But if I feel things are getting out of control, out of my control, it makes me jealous."

"When does the effort to control begin?" I ask Dan Stern.

"Three months," he says. Just like that.

Obviously, the baby does not control his world. What Stern is talking about is the three-month-old's manipulation, the effort to get his way through the use of other people. It is not dissimilar from methods of the unseparated adult. Especially in love. He wants to lose himself in the beloved. But he wants to keep the upper hand too.

Power. Control. Manipulation. Not nice ways to look at love.

When I married, I suffered the first insomnia I had ever known. Overnight I had merged so totally with my husband that some part of me was frightened of losing my self. If I let go of reality and slipped into unconscious dream sleep, I might never return. Just as I refused to learn to braid my own hair as a child—to keep my beloved nurse Anna from ever leaving me—today I postpone learning how to change the outgoing message on our telephone-answering machine. Bill does it. When it is I who want a message changed, and he is reading a book, I have to get him to do it for me in a way that doesn't irritate him. You could say I am exercising power. I get my way. It is manipulation. And manipulation, no matter how successful, leaves you vaguely dissatisfied and angry. It is a reminder you lack real power. The manipulated person is angry too. Something within feels tricked; it was not his idea.

Dependency is a part of love, not its role. As a way of love, it kills. One person has too much power, the power of life and death. The feeling that you cannot live without the other person is the essence of romantic love. It is also how an infant feels about its mother. Perhaps we should ask ourselves if the life-and-death relationship between a mother and her baby is the appropriate pitch at which to live our adult lives.

How many of my angers, my sudden, inappropriate rages, my jealousies, stem from my own self-imposed dependency, which up to now I have inappropriately called "love"?

"You ever wonder if you're capable of genuine love?"

"We discussing me, or wondering about you?"

He makes me smile. He knows me so well. "Oh, hell—about me, of course."

I am talking to Robertiello. He phoned me last night. He wanted me to read an article by psychologist Bruno Bettelheim in the current *New Yorker*.

"He's really pinned down the bastards who translated Freud into English! What a disservice they did him by using artificial words like *id* and *superego*. They took the heart and soul out of him. They gave Freud this phony hard-edged scientific sound. Essentially his language was an expression of his genius. He was always clinically correct, but he put things in words that were fluid, emotional . . . spiritual."

I told him I'd get the magazine as soon as we hung up. The call was uncharacteristic—it's always me who picks up the phone. I wanted him to continue. It had been a long time since I'd heard so much enthusiasm in his voice. Was something more than the Bettelheim bulletin involved?

"Maybe Freud's translators were afraid of what Bettelheim calls 'the dark side of their souls,' " Robertiello hurried on. "Maybe that's why they took the primitive, mystic stuff out. I mean, for Freud, *soul* was practically synonymous with *psyche*. What those translators did by using distancing, technical words was make it sound as if Freud were talking about other people, 'sick' people. God damn it, Freud was talking about every single one of us!"

After we hung up, I walked around the apartment, strangely excited myself. Like Robertiello, I'd always admired Bettelheim. His Pulitzer Prize–winning book, *The Uses of Enchantment*, had told me so much about the meaning of symbol and language in children's fairy tales. Ideas so important they were kept alive through oral tradition for centuries until people like the Brothers Grimm finally wrote them down.

It made sense that Bettelheim would be the one to point out how much more effective the simple word *I* would be instead of the formalism *ego*. Also, what in hell is the *id* anyway? How much more recognizable *it* would be. When a child wakes up in the grip of a nightmare, he yells, "Mommy, mommy, it almost got me! It frightened me!"

The child cannot describe what *it* is. He doesn't have to. The good enough mother knows the dragon-who-eats-children isn't out there. The fear is in the child. "There, there, honey," she says and the child sleeps again. That is all that is needed in childhood.

General, nondefined reassurance is not sufficient in psychotherapy, which is concerned with making the unspeakable anxiety understandable by naming it in words. But what does the doctor say to the patient? "The ego suffered narcissistic injury." The artificial, third-person language invented by Freud's translators, and now used by the analyst, has alienated the patient from his own emotion.

I have always hated the words *id* and *ego*. I like the word *it*. Whatever it is, *it* still scares me.

Freud never intended psychoanalysis to fall into the hands of the M.D.'s. "Have you ever thought of the kind of personality it takes to get through the tough grind of medical school?" Robertiello once said.

"Rigid, obsessive, very success-driven. That's why Freud thought the question of lay analysis was so important. He once wrote Jung a letter. He said that in essence, psychoanalysis was a 'cure through love.' Tell that to a smooth young graduate of Columbia's College of Physicians and Surgeons today without attributing it to Freud. He'll smile at you for talking a lot of nonscientific nonsense and go back to figuring out who should be his tax lawyer. The drive of medicine today—including psychological therapy—is to reduce the doctor's involvement with patients. To *process* as many per hour as possible. An exchange of love between doctor and patient? That would scare the shit out of most doctors today, including therapists."

Bruno Bettelheim puts Robertiello's thought more formally; to my mind, very beautifully:

"The purpose of Freud's lifelong struggle," Bettelheim writes, "was to help us understand ourselves, so that we would no longer be propelled, by forces unknown to us, to live lives of discontent, or perhaps outright misery, and to make others miserable, very much to our own detriment. In examining the content of the unconscious, Freud called into question some deeply cherished beliefs, such as the unlimited perfectability of man and his inherent goodness; he made us aware of our ambivalences and of our ingrained narcissism, with its origins in infantile self-centeredness, and he showed us its destructive nature. In his life and work, Freud truly heeded the admonition inscribed on the temple of Apollo at Delphi— 'Know thyself'—and he wanted us to do the same. But to know oneself profoundly can be extremely upsetting. It implies the obligation to change oneself—an arduous and painful task. Many of the current misconceptions about Freud and psychoanalysis have arisen from the fear of self-knowledge—from the comforting view, abetted by the emotionally distancing language of the translations, that psychoanalysis is a method of analyzing selected aspects of the behavior of *other* [emphasis added] people. Freud's insights threaten our narcissistic image of ourselves. . . . By selectively accepting only some of Freud's ideas about the role of the sexual drives in man's makeup, and by misunderstanding his tragic belief that man's destructive tendencies spring from a dark side of the soul, and perverting this belief into a facile theory that the negative aspects of man's behavior are merely the consequences of his living in a bad society, many of Freud's followers have transformed psychoanalysis from a profound view of man's condition into something shallow."[6]

I was halfway through the Bettelheim article when it occurred to me that if Freud's interpretation of dreams, and Bettelheim's of fairy tales, both deal with terrors within ourselves—and not out there—isn't that what Melanie Klein is trying to do, too?

She writes that the infant in his rage wants to cannibalize the mother, to smear her breast with excrement and tear her apart. When I first read her, my feeling was that she had been badly translated. I now know she wasn't translated at all. She wrote in English. She means what she says; she wants us to feel the full horror of the destructive side of our nature. She didn't use terrible words *in place of* other words. It is I who have been looking for translation, wanting someone (Robertiello) to soften her for me. Wanting to distance myself from her. I cannot bear to take in her nightmare language because her words mirror my own impulses.

The insight gave me courage to get her book out and try again: "One of the consequences of excessive envy is an early onset of guilt. . . ."7 And then one grim paragraph that filled me with the deepest sadness. Jealousy, Klein says, my kind of jealousy, which stems from symbiotic need to attach myself to someone, is often expressed in this greedy desire to totally possess the people I love.

She is telling me that my love is not love at all. And she is signaling with a word that captures so much of my life: guilt. It is my secret name. Is Robertiello's phone call a signal too? Does he also want to get past technical semantic discussions that have been distancing the two of us? Does he want to enter into an emotional exploration of what Klein has to say about him and about me? I hope so. I call him. We meet.

"All my life, whenever I fell in love, I had to control everything. I almost had to lock him up in order to be sure of him. How can that be love?"

We are in Robertiello's office. It is the next day.

"Is that what Klein means by the child's greed?" I continue. "This drive to suck all the juice and goodness out of the mother, to devour the beloved like a cannibal?"

The strength of the images frightens me. I am trying to retain the connection with Klein I made last night. I can only do it by using her language.

"Good God, Richard, I can accept that a dependent, terrified, infant has these feelings, but if I, an adult, if I am so selfish and greedy—"

"You are beginning to understand Klein. What you are feeling isn't jealousy. It's your envy of the other person's power over you—to give you love or withhold it. In envy, the very person you love is the person you want to do in. That's why you feel so guilty."

The old buzzing starts in my head. I feel as if I'm trying to hold too many thoughts, juggle too many ideas.

"Richard, you're losing me. Maybe it's because you're a man. Women are so guilty. Why are we so much more guilty than men?"

"Because you're angry. And you're not supposed to feel it. In our soci-

ety, men get points for being angry. In fact, anger makes them feel good;
they can get genitally hard on anger. Women lose points for showing
anger. They're supposed to keep the relationship together. Biologically,
they welcome the man in."

"So when we feel anger, we bury the emotion and feel guilty instead?"

"Exactly."

When Robertiello is undefended like this, seeing both the man's position and the woman's with evenhanded clarity, the sun comes out for me.
I sit up and tell him about the young woman who was washing my hair at
the beauty salon yesterday. " 'I'm so guilty about my jealousy,' she said.
'I've ruined every relationship with my possessiveness. Maybe I should
give up on love and stick to friendship. I'm good at that.' "

"When a man threatens to withdraw," says Robertiello, "well, hell hath
no fury like a dependent woman scorned. She wants to kill the son of a
bitch."

"*Men* make weapons, *men* make war, *men* get angry and destroy . . .
but nice girls are raised, well, to make nice."

"Their smile hides their rage," he says. "But behind the smile women
still feel it. That's why they're guilty."

I remember my first realization of the enormity of women's guilt. I was
collecting women's sexual fantasies for *My Secret Garden.* In fantasy after
fantasy, the great barrier to sexuality was guilt. The emotion that dictated
the scenario was shame at even wanting to feel sexual. Nice girls did not
lust in 1970, not even in the privacy and safety of their own minds. The
fantasies were mostly about anonymous brutes who "forced" women into
wildly sexual scenes for which they were not responsible. . . . "He made
me do it, Mommy!" The orgasm was thrilling. Nice Girl status preserved.
So well preserved that the fantasy itself was "forgotten," suppressed.

Women's fantasies are changing. While the guilt factor remains the
major barrier to push past, to reach full sexual heat, more contemporary
emotions now dictate scenarios. Ideas of triangles, notions of sharing the
man with another woman. Ten years ago, ideas such as these were too
frightening for women to play with. They were filled with jealous poison.

This kind of reverie is still almost exclusive to young women. The new
generation feels more equal to men. They own their sexuality more than
their mothers did. There is less of that terrible dichotomy between male
power and female neediness. Being more separate, more in control of their
real lives, the terrifying fear of loss of the man doesn't inhibit these
younger women from playing with multiple partners—at least in the
safety of their own minds.

It occurs to me now that I've never discussed these new fantasies with
Robertiello. He and I have been talking about the meaning of men's and

women's fantasies for years. More than anyone, he has taught me ease
with forbidden material. I tell him about one fantasy that represents this
new departure, and which may tell us something about a change in wom-
en's traditional form of jealousy *in reality.*

In the fantasy, a twenty-two-year-old imagines her wedding night. She
goes into her bedroom. Her husband is there. Plus his best friend and two
other men who'd been in the wedding. She has wild sex with the others
while her husband watches, smiling with total approval. Then her husband and one of the men have sex together.

"Ten years ago," I say, "I never heard a whisper of a fantasy where a
woman got aroused thinking about her husband watching her with other
men. Not to mention her watching him with other men. Every kind of
jealousy-provoking situation is being played out but they don't make her
angry or frightened. They excite her."

He is frowning. "My emotional and intellectual reactions are that it
sounds sad. The woman is getting into the same place where men used to
be: circuses and acrobatics rather than an intimate, loving relationship."

"But it's a fantasy! Don't you think it's interesting that women can
allow themselves to imagine such ideas? Doesn't that say to you that in
reality they must feel less guilty about sex, that maybe they won't be so
dependent and jealous?"

"I hear anger. A desire to do what men used to do. A kind of wanting to
be on top, and use men as sex objects. It's like she's doing it as a vengeance. . . ."

"There's not a trace of vengeance. . . ."

"These kinds of women are very cut off—just the way they have always
accused men of being."

"You used to say that when men had this kind of fantasy—of wanting
to share their woman with another man—that it was about wanting to see
the woman aroused. Wanting the woman's permission. You said they were
loving. . . ."

"Some of them."

"Most of them were loving!"

"Some times."

"Most of the time!"

There is anger in his voice.

When we met, Robertiello repeatedly told me men were dying to meet
sexually aggressive women. He most of all. Men's fantasies do indeed
frequently star women on the edge of sexual explosion. My own experience and that of other women is that in reality it turns men off. Can
Robertiello be frightened of women's new sexual assertiveness? Envious?

He is holding back. . . . I don't know how to work with him when he is angry, closing doors in my face when I know he wants me to enter.

I reach for cooler ground between us. "In the jealous situation," I ask, "do you think it's important which person's jugular you go for—the rival or the beloved?"

"Now that's important!" he says, loving the question. He knows exactly what I mean. It is he who taught me that our hottest rages are reserved for the people we love most. "If you want to 'kill' your lover," he says, "that sounds closer to envy than jealousy. According to Klein, if you're jealous, you want to kill the intruder."

"Who'd you go for?"

"When one of my ex-wives walked in on me, that time I was literally making it on that couch in the waiting room, she went for the woman. She tried to kill the other woman."

Why is he leaving himself out? I ask about him and he gives me a story about his ex-wife. I try again, talking about myself to encourage him to open up. A technique I learned from him. I tell a story about when I was fifteen. The Citadel cadet I was in love with left the Christmas hop with a girl from Atlanta. "She was my house guest," I say, "but I didn't give a damn about her. He was the one I was mad at."

"Of course you didn't give a damn about the other girl. More than jealousy, it was envy of his power. He could have loved you but chose not to. You wanted to tear him to pieces, right?"

Am I the only awful person in this room?

"Let me read it to you," he says, reaching for Klein and miraculously opening to her diagnosis of *my* envy, *my* jealousy. I don't want to be read to. I've read that book three times. Richard, I need your full, emotional identification with the problem and with me. I want a talk in which the pronouns are *I* and *Thou, Us!*

By now, he's pushed the button on his Barcalounger and his feet are up in the air, putting him in his favorite cradled position. He reads:

" 'When jealousy is experienced, hostile feelings are directed not so much against the primal object but rather against the rivals.'[8] That is important for you to understand, Nancy. Your anger at men, when you suspect loss, is not jealousy but Kleinian envy, which you hate me to talk about."

"I don't hate you to talk about it. I need you to change information into knowledge, so that I feel it comes from inside you . . . not something you're preaching down to me."

"Envy is not one of my big issues. For you it is. Calling your envy jealousy is your way of hiding something from yourself. That you resent the power men have over your life. You've got to get these Kleinian under-pinnings right. Otherwise, you'll get into a lot of semantic snarls."

"What about your sister?" I say. "The one who died. You hated her. How can you say you never hated a rival?"

A cruel thing to say, but nothing said in this room is either kind or cruel. In fact, he is suddenly more animated.

"I hated her guts," he says matter-of-factly. "She was five when she died. My fantasy was that some bad man had come into the room and killed her. I was seven. Of course, the bad man was me. So you're right. I certainly wanted her dead. A part of me did."

"You never told me that fantasy before."

"I didn't? It wasn't deliberate. I never got in touch with my feelings about my sister until the end of my analysis. No one ever brought her up. Not until my last analyst. Didn't I tell you how he went with me to her grave, and how all that hate came out?"

He did tell me, maybe five or six years ago. I didn't know enough about psychoanalysis then to realize the significance of this omission. Twenty years in analysis. Six different analysts. How could his sister never have come up? If Robertiello's many doctors had left out one of the most important people in his life, no wonder he kept changing therapists and going back for more.

Robertiello's analysts, I have begun to suspect, are not unusual in this omission. Sibling relationships are just beginning to come into their own as an important issue in psychoanalytic theory. I tell him about some new work that shows men consistently have more difficulty than women re-membering and talking about early sibling relationships.

"Can you remember," I ask him, "what happened at your sister's grave?"

"I expected to experience a tremendous sense of loss. Instead, what spontaneously came out at the grave was all this rage at her for stealing my act, for acing me out. No love came out, just hate. How glad I was she was dead . . ."

"Because she got all your parents' attention?"

"They loved her more even after death than when she was alive. She became their angel. The one they were always talking about."

"Richard—you were jealous of your sister!"

"But I also loved her. For who she was, and the bond between us. We were clinging to one another against all these other terrible people in the house. We played a lot together; we had fantasies in common. I was idealized by her; she was crazy about me. She was the only one who made me laugh."

"So it was the familiar business of a love/hate relationship."

"Yes, my sibling rivalry is enormous. To this day, I can't stand it if I go home and Susan is talking on the phone to her sister. I want her to hang up and pay attention to me. My father was that way too. If he came upstairs and my mother was talking to her sister on the phone, he began to yell. I couldn't care less if Susan talks to a former lover on the phone all night. You see, I'm not talking about sexual jealousy. This is all sibling stuff—a replay of what happened with my sister."

"Sibling stuff?"

He looks at me. "Yes, sibling stuff."

"Not jealousy."

"Not sexual jealousy."

The stubbornness is back. Safe as a baby, Robertiello lies in his chair while I search for a neutral question, an attempt to regain camaraderie. I know he is pleading guilty to lesser crimes—first to fear of abandonment; now to sibling rivalry. To avoid . . . what?

How can I describe how big I see this man? It is not my purpose to show him as petulant. I am not out to win an argument. It is only when Robertiello has broken himself down to his most ignoble parts that he and I recognize each other. *That's when we cook.*

"When someone is jealous," I begin again, "where does this killing component come from? Some people walk out the door; others pick up a knife."

"I keep repeating this and you keep resisting hearing it: People who want to kill the beloved in a jealous situation are run by envy. Envy has gone up the ladder and intensified jealousy to the point of murder."

"And you've never felt that."

"Don't set up a kind of magical symbiosis between us. If you feel something, that doesn't mean I feel it too. The only way we're going to clear this up is to personalize it. Just because I say I don't worry about it day and night, that doesn't mean it hasn't happened to me. I've lost women to other men. But I've never wanted to kill either one of them. You would."

"Then help me grasp it. Once a man I was in love with actually made it with another person, with two people, when I was in the next room. Yes, I could have killed all of them. I was losing the person I loved; therefore I was jealous. How could that be envy?"

"I think you have a larger component of envy in your genes than most people. You are both envious and jealous."

He says it just like that. Talk, talk, talk. *Bullets.*

"Are you telling me that when a man kills a woman in a fit of passion, he does that from envy? Not out of some oedipal jealousy?"

"Categorically right," Robertiello says. "Oedipal jealousy is a later stage in life, when the superego is well on its way to full development. Shit, I sound like one of Freud's translators. Murder is *infant* stuff. The conscience is not yet fully developed."

He sees the blank incomprehension on my face. He tries another tack.

"Remember the time they made you and Bill move out of a good seat at a movie preview so that some famous critic could have it? Bill thought nothing of it. That was the nature of show biz, he said. But you had a very specific reaction. You were still upset four days later, which was when I saw you, and I don't think that reaction of deep humiliation had anything to do with separation or with your father not being around when you were a kid, and so on. What caused such bitter resentment was envy. The envious feeling that your favored position—the good seat you had—the good Kleinian breast—could be taken from you at the whim of another. Envious people have terrible problems with humiliation."

He has named me.

"And that is different from what *you* felt when your sister took your place?"

"Sibling rivalry, oedipal rivalry . . . as you get older, other things come along and intensify the early envy. But, at bottom, what we're talking about, where the virulence comes from is envy. In your case, constitutional envy."

"I was born that way?" The tape recorder catches the horror and dismay in my voice. "The bad seed? Oh, no . . ."

"Yes," says Robertiello. "That's it. Absolutely."

I am cut off from him. Alone. He used to love my refusals to accept his intellectualizations, my dogged angry insistence that he find emotional language that could allow me to feel what he knew. Whatever I was learning, in getting me there, he was learning it more profoundly himself. He came along with me on the journey. It was as if we were mountain climbers together. Only as he helped me come to the top of belief, a height from which I could see the unconscious laid clear, could he get up there himself. It is different with envy and jealousy. He is not sure of Klein *from the inside*. The emotion of envy is not "in his genes."

The mountain-climber metaphor I have just used gives me away. Mountain climbers are tied together with a life-and-death umbilical cord. Despite my vaunted separation, it is not totally achieved. Is his? In our work together, I suppose I have always thought of us as symbiotically tied; I had hoped in a mutually nourishing way. But he is cutting me loose, cutting me off.

He sees me as someone against whom he must protect himself.

I have lost more than just an interview.

CHAPTER THREE

Envy:
The Bad Seed

"My mother always said, 'If anything good happens to you watch out, because the next thing will be bad.'"

The man talking is a fifty-one-year-old historian. His publishers called this morning to tell him his latest work has been selected by a major book club. He has previously written four scholarly books on the American Revolution. This is his first popular work. You may not have heard of him. There is a very good chance you will in the future. Never a guarantee, being named a Main Selection is nonetheless a writer's dream.

"How did you feel when you got the news?" I ask.

"I felt ill," he says. "Immediately."

"How do you define that?"

"My stomach seemed to fall out and my mind went blank. There were four editors on the conference call. So I knew it had to be good news. They expected me to shout, 'Wow, yahoo!' But that's not my style. I couldn't say anything. I merely said, 'Oh, that's great.' I am my mother's son."

"In what way?"

"Something terrible is going to follow anything good. My mother is a jealous person. She is angry with men. Especially me. I was her Prince, but she would also undermine me. If I was going to the movies or wanted to buy a house, she'd say, 'Why look for trouble? Don't do that.' "

"Why is she angry with men?"

"My mother is the kind of woman who wanted to work. She'd been a bookkeeper for a large insurance agency before she married. My father wouldn't let his wife have a job. After we were grown, she went to one of those meetings and signed up to be an Avon lady. When she came home, my father said, 'Where were you?' and she said, 'I'm going to be an Avon lady.' And my father said, 'Oh, no, you're not.' She said, 'It will only be in our apartment building,' and he said, 'Oh, no, I don't want you to do that.' He was very insistent. The Avon lady felt bad for her and let her keep the badge. She wanted that job very much. She didn't really want to be a housewife."

"Did she raise you? Was she the one who nursed and fed and bathed you?"

"I think so. But I remember a lot of baby-sitters. There was a Polish one with great legs."

"For instance, were you breast-fed?"

"I'd always thought so. But two years ago when our son was born, I turned to my mother and said, 'You breast-fed me, didn't you?' and she said, 'No.' That made me very angry." He laughs.

"Why were there so many baby-sitters if your father wouldn't let her work?"

"He let her work for him. At his office. She could keep his books, but he wouldn't let her have her own career."

"Are you the only child?"

"Virtually. My sister is six years older."

"What is the relationship between you?"

"Awful. My sister's very jealous of me. And with reason. She's very angry at my mother. They're frightened of each other. I once tried to explain to my mother why she and Jocelyn, my sister, have such a terrible relationship. I said, 'You know, Mom, when I came along, I was the Prince. You dropped Jocelyn like a hot potato.' She said, 'You weren't the Prince; you were the King. Nicholas the King.' "

"Is she still unaware of how that made your sister feel?"

"My mother never quite got it. They did everything for me. They cut my lamb chops. No wonder my sister hated me. She married at seventeen."

"She must have been desperate to get away."

"My family promoted the jealousy between us. When I got out of the army, my father bought me a Cadillac convertible. He said, 'Look what I bought Nick.' My sister said, 'What are you going to buy me?' He said, 'You're such a jealous bitch.' "

"What about today? Are you jealous?"

"Before I was married, I was extremely jealous. There was a time when I wanted to know exactly what the woman did and where she did it and exactly how she did it. That kind of overwhelming jealousy."

"How did you deal with it?"

"I always ended it. I was the one who was the bad guy and left."

"Your wife is very pretty," I say.

"But she doesn't do the jealous numbers. That isn't her trick. She has made me jealous, twice. Both times it was when she was in an extremely insecure situation. She felt like she had no credentials. It was before she got her terrific new job. Before that, she felt she was there only as my appendage. Twice she came on with men and it was as if to say, 'Look, I have some value too.' That was before we were married. But she's not the flirtatious type."

"If you had walked in on one of your former lovers and found her with another man, who would you want to attack?"

"I would feel great anger at *her*. Rage. In the Freudian sense, of my mother betraying me again."

" 'Again?' "

"All through my youth she betrayed me. Someone would say, 'Your son's so good-looking. So smart.' She'd say, 'He's not so smart. He's not so great.' She never felt good about herself, so she couldn't be proud of me. She identified with me. In her mind, I was just like her."

"On the one hand you were the Prince. On the other . . ."

"On the other, she was angry at me. At all men. My mother never praised anything I did. She would say, 'It's not so good. We'll see what happens. I wish you were happy. Don't put your money on it.' "

"How do you think you would handle enormous success?" I ask. "Because of your new book, there's a good chance it could happen."

"It would be very difficult for me. I would never feel I deserved it. There would be that gnawing thing; fear it would be taken away from me in the next minute."

Six months later, Nick and I talk again. Bewilderingly, his book has come and gone—virtually vanished with less than a half-page advertisement from his publishers. He has left them for another company and is well into his next book. He is bitter about the lack of support from his former publishers, but in a way, he seems more relaxed. He looks better. Optimistic about the future. He likes the new book he is working on. He's also finished a screenplay, a new area for him.

"Lucky I had my father's influence," he says. "My father was a great risk taker. Everything I do, I take a risk."

"In spite of your mother's warning not to take them?"

"My father was very different. My mother saw me as my father's son. She'd say, 'You're just like your father.' Which means I was selfish and didn't care about her and only thought about myself. She really wanted me to be a failure, as she perceives herself. And my father in some ways did too. He said he'd support me if I was a schoolteacher."

"He didn't want you to succeed as a writer?"

"He was very dichotomous. Half of him wanted me to succeed and half of him didn't. Whatever drive I do have for success I got from my father."

"Was he affectionate; could he express it physically?"

"That was one of the problems: He didn't know how. He had a purely public presence. It took him two years to die. He had this terrible stroke. He became like a child. Whenever I came in the room, he'd say, 'Nick, kiss me.' He never kissed me when I was a kid. When I was thirteen, he held out his hand and said, 'Shake hands. From now on, no more kissing.' I said, 'You never kissed me. What are you talking about?' "

"About what happened to the book," I say. "Or didn't happen. Do you ever think, Well, it's good you didn't count on any overwhelming acclaim? That in some way your mother's warnings about not counting on success came true?"

"No." He pauses. "But maybe yes. 'Don't sing in the morning or you'll cry at night.' That's what she'd say. Part of me never believed there would be a big success. I have that built in. When something doesn't pan out, I say 'Ha, my mother was right.' And I keep going."

"Are you on good terms with her these days?"

"Absolutely. My mother thinks I can do no wrong. She has our wedding picture magnetized on the refrigerator. She's coming to stay with us for a month."

"Any mixed feelings about that long a visit?"

"It'll be great. She loves the baby. She and my wife get along beautifully. My mother won't make a move these days without getting our approval. My mother's always been there for me when I needed her."

Is it possible there is something deranging and dangerous in fame, riches, power? During our first interview, Nick felt threatened by imminent success. What other word would describe his certainty that "something terrible is going to follow anything good"? The phone call that tells him how his new book has been chosen by a major book club causes him to feel "ill, immediately." What strange comfort does he take in his mother's slogan "Don't sing in the morning or you'll cry at night"? Why has he taken it as a leitmotiv for his life?

I play the two tapes over, two interviews done six months apart, and can hear the change in Nick's voice. Why was he most anxious when it seemed his new book was going to take him to heights he had not known before? When it did not happen, he was audibly relieved. His attitude about his mother changed; no longer the jealous person who undercuts him, she is now the beloved mother who needs his protection. He is like two people: as hardworking, competitive and risk-taking as his father when he is struggling for the success he envies in others. When the prize is within reach, he becomes his mother's son, fearfully waiting for fate to deal him a nasty blow.

The noted American anthropologist George Foster points out that in cultures all over the world, any person who stands out above others is regarded with ambivalence. He cites a study of a Philippine village by fellow anthropologist George Guthrie. A certain ritual phrase is used when someone's success makes his neighbors envious: "He will be brought down."

"In the face of this outlook," Guthrie says, "individuals feel obliged to deny their own effort, insisting that their achievements were a matter of luck and that their successes were undeserved."[1]

In his own fascinating study on envy among a primitive Spanish-speaking tribe of Indians in Mexico, Foster writes about the "Image of Limited Good." These Indians seem to feel that there are only so many rewards in the world. If you get something good, I must lose something good. Therefore, I am constantly playing down anything fortunate that happens to me; I fear arousing your anger at being left out or diminished. Flattering someone is a terrible social mistake. For instance, if I compliment you, that means you have something the rest of us do not have, and therefore you become a target for our hatred. Foster says, "If good exists in limited amounts which cannot be expanded, *logically an individual or family can improve its position with respect to any good only at the expense of others.*"[2] Hence, if you do or get something much admired, you are a threat to the entire community, despoiling the rest of us. Economists, sociologists, anthropologists, psychologists—practically every social science has made note of this all-too-human phenomenon, calling it "The Zero-Sum Game."

A man tells me a story. In his teens, a friend took him for a summer afternoon sail off fashionable Newport, Rhode Island. "There they were," he says, "dancing on the afterdecks of hundred-foot yachts, eating lobsters on country-club lawns, servants opening more champagne." His friend turned to him and said, "You know, they *all* can't be unhappy."

Is the near universal belief in the unhappiness of the rich and famous merely a secret revenge on our part, a palliative bit of folklore to ease our envy? Unlike Guthrie's Philippine village, our society *says* that the American dream is to rise from a log cabin to the White House, that your fellow Americans will admire your yacht, your limo, your penthouse, taking it as an example of what might happen to them if they too work hard enough. Ah! The unlimited American dream! But why does the morning paper carry still one more story of the divorce-drink-and-drug problem of this famous actress, the suicide of the Pulitzer Prize–winning playwright, the strange and lonely death of one more billionaire who has begun to fear everyone in the world wants to kill him? "Be careful what you wish for," goes the old adage; "you might get it."

"It is remarkable how seldom the vernacular forms of different languages permit one to say directly to another person: 'Don't do that. It will make me envious!' " writes the German sociologist Helmut Schoeck. "Instead we tend to talk in abstract terms of justice, saying that something or other is intolerable or unfair, or we relapse into sour and bitter silence."[3]

Instead of fearing envy because it is so terrible, Schoeck thinks that Americans deny its nastiness by using the word loosely. "Americans," he writes, "prefer 'envy' to the obsolete use of 'emulation,' but are quite unaware of the shift of meaning. They have forgotten envy's spiteful, destructive aspect."[4]

We knock on wood against misfortune waiting up ahead to pounce upon the naively optimistic. "How kind of someone of your magnificence to enter my lowly hut," goes the politely self-demeaning formula of an old-fashioned Chinese mandarin, ushering a visitor into his palace. Who hasn't heard of "the evil eye"—the curse of the lucky?

Are abstruse psychological explanations necessary? I think they are. Manners, verbal usages and superstitions don't endure over centuries by mere chance. They have a sound psychological basis: Ritualistic social usages are demonstrations of the unconscious at work, giving us formulas and ceremonies to guard against fears not fully understood. What then is so frightening about acquiring success, fame, wealth?

Why are some of us afraid of being loved? Melanie Klein says that fear of our own ascendance is directly linked to a time in life when someone else had power over us. As much as we loved and needed mother, we also resented and hated her for being the stronger . . . the supplier of all our needs. In Klein's words, we were *envious*.

How does a book about the jealous fear of loss of love to a rival become a discussion of envy and power? Because Klein has convinced me that the triangle of jealousy cannot be deciphered without first examining the earlier base—and basic—emotion:

"Envy is the angry feeling that another person possesses and enjoys something desirable—the envious impulse being to take it away or to spoil it. Moreover, envy implies the subject's relation to one person only and goes back to the earliest exclusive relation with the mother. *Jealousy is based on envy* [emphasis added], but involves a relation to at least two [other] people; it is mainly concerned with love that the subject feels is his due and has been taken away, or is in danger of being taken away, from him by his rival. In the everyday conception of jealousy, a man and a woman feels deprived of the loved person by somebody else."[5]

Envy, says Klein, is a developmental step that comes earlier—and leads into—jealousy.

Historically, three great minds dominate the beginnings of psychoanalysis. Freud led the way, the first to systematically explore the unconscious. Jung's contribution was the "collective unconscious," a semireligious line of thought Freud eventually found inimical. Adler completed the triumvirate. He coined the term "inferiority complex." His disagreement with Freud was this: It was not sex, Adler felt, but the drive for power that was the supreme satisfaction sought in life.

"Every neurosis," Adler said, "can be understood as an attempt to free oneself from a feeling of inferiority in order to gain a feeling of superiority."[6] (Isn't this a description of every devious move a jealous lover makes? How often people I interview simply shrug and say, "I guess I'm jealous because I have an inferiority complex.")

In time Jung and Adler fell—or were pushed—out of the Freudian movement. My feeling is that Adler's loss was especially unfortunate. Recognition of the role of power in human relations was relatively neglected until Melanie Klein came along. She too began as a fervent believer in Freud. In time, she too came to differ, though some say she tried in the beginning to twist her theories to fit within the Freudian framework. But her thinking was too seminal to be a footnote to anyone else's. There are Freudians, and there are Kleinians.

Melanie Klein, born in 1882, was "petite, beautiful, feminine, proud—even vain, fearlessly honest, intuitive and a dedicated product of *fin de siècle* Vienna," writes James S. Grotstein in *The Psychoanalytic Quarterly.*[7] She was the youngest of four children in a professional family. She had never heard of Freud until she read his popular book *On Dreams.* She was psychoanalyzed by Karl Abraham and Sandor Ferenczi, two of Freud's foremost adherents. Abraham was impressed by her work in child analysis, and in 1921 she moved to Berlin where she established a psychoanalytic practice with adults as well as children. In the same year, she published her first papers.

The notion of using games and toys for access to the child's unconscious is almost universal today. But in 1927 when Klein arrived in London with her technique of child analysis—which she called play analysis—fully worked out, it was an unheralded idea.

"Klein's stroke of genius," writes Hanna Segal, "lay in noticing that the child's natural mode of expressing himself was play, and that play could therefore be used as a means of communication with the child. Play for the child is not 'just play.' It is also work. It is not only a way of exploring and mastering the external world but also, through expressing and working through phantasies, a means of exploring and mastering anxieties. In his play the child dramatizes his phantasies, and in doing so, elaborates and works through his conflicts."[8]

In observing children playing with tiny figures labeled by them as mother, father, sister, brother, Klein could see with utmost clarity that the ideas that frighten and horrify us as adults (defecation on the mother, murder of a sibling) were the ordinary stuff of children's reveries. The use of very small toys lent "themselves particularly to play analysis," writes Segal, "possibly because the smallness makes them specially appropriate to represent the inner world. Donald Winnicott [the famed British child psychologist] said that he considered her introduction of these tiny toys as the most significant advance in child analysis."[9]

In England, Klein became one of the most important, and in time controversial, members of English psychoanalytic circles. "To her dying day," writes Grotstein, "Klein was puzzled by the rejection of her work by her colleagues and was disappointed that Freud did not more positively espouse her views, which she believed to be so congruent with and an extension of his work."[10] A loyal daughter to the end, she didn't like her theories labeled Kleinian. It separated her from Freud. "She helped to expand the locus of developmental importance from the penis to the breast [that is, from father to mother],"[11] writes Grotstein.

No wonder the paternalistic Freudians disagreed with Klein, calling her unorthodox and labeling her work inconsistent with Freud's. As if that by itself—Q.E.D.—made it wrong. One of the basic assumptions of psychoanalysis is that the earlier the anxiety, the more fundamental to all further organization of psychological systems. To have moved the focus of conflict to a time earlier than did Freud himself was Melanie Klein's great achievement.

Klein's most important work is called *Envy and Gratitude*. In a short, densely packed essay, she gives us an enormously powerful theory of human development. Freud focused on instinct gratification and the oedipal years, roughly ages three through seven. Klein placed more importance on the struggle between parent and child in the first months, the first days of life. Many American analysts feel that her timetables are off, that she endows the newborn infant with more complicated emotions than evidence can support. But I have yet to meet a professional whom I admire who does not acknowledge her genius. The work of the Baby Watchers has already established that complex mental life begins far earlier than clinicians imagined. Time will tell if indeed Klein's timetables are off. Whether they are or not, I feel her basic theory cannot be shaken.

No one is more dependent than an infant. Life immediately begins to teach him there is something/someone out there who controls his destiny and who can neglect or hurt him. To his not-yet-fully organized central nervous system, mother is too vast a continent to take in as a whole. His first knowledge of her is the breast; this wonderful, warm mystery, which feeds him when he is hungry but at times, maliciously, selfishly, withholds itself. It disappears, leaving him cold, lonely, frightened; raging with hunger and hatred both. *Someone else has all the power.* That is Klein's serpent of rage in the dependent infant's paradise.

"For the urge even in the earliest stages to get constant evidence of the mother's love is fundamentally rooted in anxiety," says Klein. "The struggle between life and death instincts and the ensuing threat of annihilation of the self and of the object [breast/mother] by destructive impulses are fundamental factors in the infant's initial relation to his mother. For his desires imply that the breast, and soon the mother, should do away with these destructive impulses and the pain of persecutory anxiety."[12] Klein's last sentence is especially important but especially obscure. Feeling both love and hate toward mother, the child assumes it is up to her to do away with the pain and anxiety he feels at containing these conflicting emotions. It is up to her to rid him of his fury and anger. Doesn't she have all the power?

One of the things that makes Klein difficult to understand is that the above paragraph would be summed up by her saying that the infant *envies* the mother, *envies* her power. It is of the utmost importance to remember at all times this special meaning Klein gives the word. It is not how most of us use envy. However, Klein's use is not so much opposed to popular understanding as a very special extension. Here is *The Oxford English Dictionary:*

to envy: To feel displeasure and ill-will at the superiority of (another person) in happiness, success, reputation, or the possession of anything desireable; to regard with discontent another's possession of (some superior advantage which one would like to have for oneself). Also in less unfavorable sense: To wish oneself on a level with (another) in happiness or in the possession of something desireable; to wish oneself possessed of (something which another has).

envy: The feeling of mortification and ill-will occasioned by the contemplation of superior advantages possessed by another. Mortification: The feeling of humiliation caused by a disappointment, a rebuff or slight, or an untoward accident; the sense of disappointment or vexation.

envious: . . . vexed or discontented at the good fortune or qualities of another.

Klein is saying that the infant begrudges the breast its power and covetously wants it for himself.

Philosopher Max Scheler elaborates in a manner very close to Klein: " 'Envy,' as the term is understood in everyday usage, is due to a feeling of impotence which we experience when another person owns a good we covet. But this tension between desire and nonfulfillment does not lead to envy until it flares up in hatred against the owner, until the latter is falsely considered to be the *cause* of our privation. Our factual inability to acquire a good is wrongly interpreted as a positive action *against* our desire —a delusion which diminishes the original tension. Both the experience of impotence and the causal delusion are essential preconditions of true envy."[13]

How fatally easy it is for the very young infant to fall into the "delusion" Scheler talks about. By not always appearing the instant we want it, the breast is seen as taking "positive action *against* our desire." The breast is not merely passive; there are times when the infant feels as if it is actively, malevolently working against him. Klein's theories begin with the baby's relation not to the mother-as-a-whole but to the breast-seen-as-mother. It is the very anatomy of power.

In a visceral rage too primitive for words, the infant feels that if the all-powerful breast wanted to, it could take away all his fears and discomforts, and thus rid him of his anxiety and fear of death. The selfish breast is keeping all the good things, all the milk, warmth and companionship, for itself. The child loves the breast; the child resents the breast. To sum up in Kleinian terms, the child *envies* the breast. And what he envies is its power . . . envies it even at the moment when that very power is being used to satisfy his wants!

Mother is wonderful and she is my life, but it is in her gift alone. I resent being dependent on her, and I am in a rage at feeling impotent and helpless without her. I love her breast but I hate her too. No matter that she loves me and does all she can for my happiness. It all depends on her decision, not mine. I do not care that she makes me happy. I resent her. I deny her power. I will show her:

The infant bites the breast!

Here is Klein talking about how infants express their resentment:

"Envy . . . seeks to . . . put badness, primarily bad excrements and bad parts of the self, into the mother, and first of all into her breast, in order to spoil and destroy her."[14]

The baby has no words for his rage, his resentment that mother can either offer him the breast or take it away. He does not know about knives or guns. When he is mad at mother, Klein says, he has preverbal fantasies of eating her up, tearing her flesh apart, smearing her with feces—imagery born of the only experience he has: that of his own body, its pain and functions.

I didn't just close Melanie Klein the first time I read her. I took the book out of the room in which I sleep and put it in a closet upstairs. As I keep going back to her, I see that she makes sense out of why we spoil so much of the love we seek. Intuitive acceptance of a theory may not be the firmest beginning. But when you read Klein, when I read her, a certain instinctual faith takes over. Something absolutely right keeps bringing me back to her, to what I once found to be her confusing, terribly upsetting sentences and images. Her ideas resonate with my dreams at night.

I must assume that you will have at least some of the difficulty I did with Klein. How often I have wished that she had coined a different word than *envy* to express what she is talking about; some verbalization that did not come to us already freighted with associations and meanings. Let me give you my own formula; whenever Klein uses the word *envy*, I read it to mean the rage and resentment that the dependent person feels at the power someone else has to make him happy or sad, to give life or take it away. In one of Klein's most significant phrases, "We bite the hand that feeds us."

Here is a story from a thirty-year-old bank officer. It illustrates the destruction caused by infantile envy when it is carried over into adult life:

"I had been looking forward to the weekend with my wife all Friday at the office. That night when I got home, I knew if I went over and put my arms around her, it would be a wonderful weekend. But some nasty voice inside me said, 'No, I'm not going to give her that satisfaction.' And so I didn't. And so we had a crappy weekend."

Like an infant, this man resents the power his wife has to make him happy. Even though he too would have had a lovely weekend if he'd caressed her, that would only have made it all the clearer that his emotional well-being lay in her hands. His contentment would have been the sign of her power. He did not want to give her that dominance. *He envied her.*

He would rather be unhappy, preferring a lousy weekend—spoiling the relationship if necessary—rather than acknowledge his wife's ability to give or withhold happiness at her will. How can we come to terms with Klein's image of the infant wanting to smear the loving breast with feces? In his own words this man gave himself a "crappy" weekend. Didn't he make shit of it? The parallel to Klein is clear.

The children she treated were so young, so close in time to their earliest, most primitive ambivalences about the breast/mother, that Klein could reconstruct from their dreams, games and seemingly random verbalization what went on in the first year of life.

The grotesque language, the cruel and often disgusting imagery with which she presents us are not figments of *her* imagination. They come from close observation of how very little children repeatedly act out their most violent, most hidden feelings through play with the tiny figures who represent the most powerful people in their real lives.

Klein didn't write about envy in a political or sociological sense. But I find her horrific descriptions of the envious rage of the baby who bites the proffered breast parallel much of what we see today. The fished-out lakes that used to feed us, the polluted streams and seas around the world, are examples that come immediately to mind. Better than any economist, Klein explains the destructiveness of greed.

"Virtually a third of the psychoanalytic world today," writes Grotstein, "is either 'Kleinian' or has been significantly affected by her work. The rest . . . [have] chosen to shun her and her work, at times with an absolutism which even today seems puzzling."[15]

That Klein remains relatively unknown in this country is one of the puzzles psychoanalysis itself has yet to solve. It is my belief that her detractors may be impelled by more than professional refusal to accept a theory outside learned orthodoxies. Resistance goes back to the emotions she asks us to face, which include primitive, even cannibalistic, urges against the mother. Most people, including analysts, do not wish to recognize such ideas in themselves.

In her recent best-selling novel *August*, Judith Rossner makes a dramatic issue of her analyst heroine's determination to go against accepted Freudian theory and examine her patient's preverbal, pre-Oedipal experiences—the time Klein studied so carefully. "This was the most difficult and frightening period of life," Rossner writes, "for the obvious reason that words did not exist that were adequate to describe the overpowering feelings engendered in an infant who did not yet have words to describe and sort out those [cataclysmic] feelings."[16]

I have already commented on the semantic confusion between *jealousy* and *envy*, noting that most people use them interchangeably, the great majority preferring to describe themselves as jealous. Yes, there is a certain grandeur about jealousy, a sexual implication and passion. Look at how easily people admit to oedipal conflict. Isn't that nothing less than a declaration of desire for incest? Why is admission of envy so much more painful?

"How remarkable it is," says George Foster, "that one can admit to feelings of guilt, shame, pride, greed and even anger without loss of self-esteem, but that it is almost impossible, at least in American society, to admit to feelings of envy. I think the explanation of this difference, or at least a very important part of the explanation, lies in the fact that in feeling guilt (etc.) a person is not necessarily comparing himself to another . . . with respect to some quality or characteristic. But in recognizing envy in himself, a person is acknowledging inferiority *with respect to another;* he measures himself against someone else and finds himself wanting. It is, I think, this implied admission of inferiority, rather than the admission of envy, that is so difficult for us to accept."[17]

"Some of us were discussing the topic of your book," says poet John Malcolm Brinnin one night in Key West, where we have our share of poets—James Merrill, John Ciardi, Richard Wilbur and Brinnin to name but a few. "We just could not agree on what envy means, what jealousy means."

I ask John what I ask everyone these days: Does he find much envy, jealousy among the people he knows?

"Poets tend to ignore the world other writers have to compete in," he answers. "They forget money and celebrity and recognize fame only on their own terms. On those terms, the stakes are immortality—who's going to be remembered when the prizes and best-seller lists are forgotten? Who's going to figure in the schoolbooks and anthologies fifty years from now? When they suspect that one among them is a good candidate—for immortality, that is—they may take the lead in publicly idolizing him or her . . . or retreat into a private fury about their own neglect that can end in the asylum or suicide. The instances of madness and self-inflicted death in my generation have made the lives of the poets a study in morbid psychology.

"Envy is a kind of giving, I think, a recognition of superiority made by someone capable of understanding its nature. . . . Jealousy does nothing but consume the jealous and rob them of the very objects they were jealous about. But what a thrilling and terrible emotion it is! I've felt the kink of it in my personal life, God knows. But, professionally speaking, not at all . . . unless envy is a form of self-deception that disguises it. Knock wood."

If poets, whose life is the precise use of words, cannot agree, how can the rest of us?

The Pulitzer Prize–winning play *Amadeus* has been on Broadway for five years. It dramatizes envy so poignantly that when a friend took me to see it, the small hairs rose on the back of my neck throughout the performance. Around me, people smiled, nodded and applauded, drinking at the bar between acts as if we were not all witnessing the most ruinous emotion. I reminded myself I would have behaved as coolly two years ago, before Klein entered my life.

In the play, Salieri, the official court composer for the Austrian emperor, conceives an enormous hatred of the young Mozart. This boy, he moans in fury, can compose and transcribe entire symphonies in his head! With the hunger for infantile omnipotence of the truly envious, the composer enters into rivalry, not with Mozart, but with God. *(Amadeus* means "love of God.")

"Of what use is man," the composer cries, "if not to teach God a lesson!"[18] He invents fantastic manipulations to keep Mozart poor, unrecognized and suffering throughout his short life. Salieri himself loves Mozart's music. But envy of Mozart's genius—the "good breast" which an all-powerful but capricious God chose to give to the prancing fool Mozart instead of to his hardworking self—leads him to want to destroy God's favored child.

As we left the theater, my friend said, "You know, I sympathized with Salieri." His voice was matter of fact. I stared at him in amazement. Hadn't I just witnessed murder? "There was a guy in school," he went on, "who never had to study and always got top grades. I worked like a demon. God, how I hated him! I had to admit to myself a long time ago I'm no genius. I got where I am today by sheer hard work. Oh, yes, I know how jealous Salieri felt! Or do I mean envy?"

"Envy."

Who among us doesn't indeed remember some "genius" who skated through school effortlessly getting A's while the rest of us slaved? Who among us didn't envy him? What makes Salieri so fascinating a character is that he speaks to each of us, giving such unashamed and unguarded voice to our own sneaky envy that, like my friend, we leave the theater purged and able to speak the unspeakable.

The usual understanding of envy is that it is a rankling emotion felt by someone looking *up*. I envy what you have . . . your fine character, your fine car, your fine tennis game. Since they are better than mine, I secretly hope your character is a lie, your car gets dented and that next time you step onto a tennis court, you trip over the net and break your leg. I want your good things spoiled, since they give you pleasure and me pain.

Quoting from *Crabb's English Synonyms*, Klein writes, "Jealousy fears to lose what it has; envy is pained at seeing another have that which it wants for itself. . . . The envious man sickens at the sight of enjoyment. He is easy only in the misery of others. All endeavors therefore to satisfy an envious man are fruitless."[19]

Envy is like an illness. It takes the joy out of life. If I envy you enough, I will eliminate you; that is, if you come here, I will go there. If you are in the room with me, I will not look in your direction, and if you speak, I will close my ears. I have removed you from the face of the earth. Psychologically, isn't this murder? Envy kills what it most admires and cannot have for itself.

Nick's story, with which this chapter began, is a clear example of how difficult it is to recognize envy. With his considerable scholarly and literary accomplishments, financial success, a happy marriage and a wonderful new son, if there is envy around, Nick would seem to be its natural target —not one who feels it himself. And yet Nick has named himself to me as an envious person. His entire interview is freighted with the curious sense of nemesis that haunts the successful person in Guthrie's Philippine village: "He will be brought down."

Just as liars suspect that all other people are liars too, the envious person fears you hate him for his success just as much as he would hate you if the positions were reversed. This characteristic of playing down good fortune, which is so evident in Nick's story, of becoming anxious and/or depressed, of spoiling the good things that do happen, is central to Klein's expanded description of envy. The envious person resents your achievements and power *but doesn't enjoy his own either.*

An analyst talks to me about a woman patient:

"Basically, she feels pretty good about herself. Until something good happens to her. Then she has one of these attacks of putting herself down, of feeling she is awful, horrible. Usually accompanied by alcoholic binges. We have traced the last several of them. What it is about is that she feels badly about outdistancing a friend, her sister, whoever. Last time she got a promotion, her sister said, 'Boy, are you ever lucky!' Maybe it was an expression of genuine goodwill; maybe it was indeed envy. The patient *always* reads it as envy. To protect herself from what she perceives as rivalrous hatred coming at her from others, she makes herself small and ignoble. That's what the drinking's all about. Who envies a sloppy drunk? 'Don't hate me for my success. Pity me for my weakness.' "

Envy cannot be understood, Klein says—and this is one of her important formulations—until we see that it runs both ways. You may be envious of other people, but if you are, that envy is predictive that you will equally fear their envy of you. In this understanding, Klein posits a different idea of power than does social psychologist Gregory White.

You may remember that Dr. White's studies showed that in a jealous triangle, the low-power person, realizing he cannot affect the other, turns the anger upon himself. He becomes depressed. More exactly, he depresses himself. "I'm not surprised she picked him. He's the better man. Smarter. Richer. I'm not much. No woman will ever want me." The process makes good common sense and needs no complicated psychological theory for underpinning. As Dr. White said to me, in formulations such as these, the concept of the unconscious is not necessary because one's feelings of self-esteem are being attacked on an everyday level.

In our competitive society, the notion of self-esteem is comparative. "It does not matter that someone's doing better than you is not at your expense," writes philosopher Jerome Neu discussing the work of fellow philosopher Robert Nozick. "Even though your absolute position on a scale is unchanged, the scale is extended by their performance and your relative position on the scale looks worse, so you must think less well of yourself." Neu quotes Nozick directly: "Self-esteem is based on *differentiating characteristics;* that's why it's *self*-esteem."[20]

The form of power of which Klein speaks lies in the unconscious. It is the power of hatred, the underdog's resentful wish to bring his superior down, even if it means his own destruction. Taking a completely opposite tack from White's, Klein says that in envy, it is often the *high-power* person who depresses himself.

"When I was little," a man tells me, "we lived in a big penthouse apartment. I was always aware that my mother would never tell a new elevator man our floor if anyone else could hear. She would wait until we reached their floor and they got out. If she had to say the word *penthouse,* she worried that other people would dislike her."

"You have no idea of the taxes, the government regulations, alimony, lawyers, I have to deal with every day," cries the millionaire. "Don't envy me. I never have time to enjoy it." The laments of the very rich are usually marked down as laughable hypocrisy. Perhaps we ought to pay a bit more attention to the strange music underlying the words.

The higher we go, the more convinced many of us are that everyone out there is wishing for our fall. Much safer to attack ourselves before their hatred is fully aroused. The prize we've worked so hard to win doesn't feel as satisfying as we had thought it would. "I only won it as a fluke," we say. "It couldn't happen again." The cheers ringing in our ears are disquieting because if those people knew how little we deserved their praise, they would have contempt for us. All is vanity. Life is empty. "Don't envy me," Woody Allen seems to be saying as he ducks adoring crowds and makes yet another film that says he too fears impotence: "I'm the only man I know who suffers from penis envy."

Who could hate such a nebbish—even if he is a millionaire movie star?

Says psychoanalyst Leslie Farber: "Envy, which tends toward diffusion, hiding and effacing itself behind all things, escapes identification and confounds experience. I suspect that envy, because of its talent for disguise, may promote greater mischief [than jealousy], and I am convinced that the envious man is miserable, even though what he knowingly feels is not envy but perplexing pain."[21]

In my life as in my work, I have come to see how right Farber is. Few of us ever see envy bare. What you will more often recognize are three defenses, which Klein names *denial, devaluation, idealization.*

Let me illustrate all three in a little story. A young woman has worked long into the night to sew a dress for a party. In her fantasies, she sees herself entering the room, proud and shining, wearing a gown lovelier than any in the local stores. Arriving at the party, she sees her friends admiring someone in a St. Laurent just brought over from Paris. *Denial* is almost invariably the first defense.

Is she envious? Absolutely not. "Me? Envy? You're crazy!" The denial is flat and immediate; an almost childlike refusal to face reality. Sometimes denial is not enough. Another emotion may be expressed: *devaluation of the other.*

"A St. Laurent in our small town? Why, its pretentious! She couldn't possibly have afforded it on her salary. Some man must have paid for it."

Envy has spoiled the party for her. Unable to smile over her anger and tears, she pleads boredom and goes home. Later, her mother finds her weeping in her room, the dress thrown into a corner. She has now switched defenses. She *devalues herself:*

"What a fool I was to make this dress," the daughter says. "I can't sew; I can't design. I hate this dress. It was the ugliest dress at the party."

The dress in which she saw herself as Queen of the Night has been devalued too.

"It may not be a St. Laurent," her mother says, "but it was a very pretty dress."

"It's the worst dress in the world!"

Can you hear the tiny bit of victory that devaluation brings? Humiliation is avoided, even if only in retrospect. She never had much hope for the dress. There is even a bit of left-handed pride here: That dress may seem good enough for you; it is not nearly good enough for me.

To make the Kleinian parallel clear, we could say that before the evening began, the young woman felt the dress had the power of the breast/mother: to make her happy. Instead, the breast/dress has made her miserable. The entire evening has been a disaster, but at least the final destruction has been at her own hands: She threw the dress onto the floor. The infant has emerged, ruling the world by destroying it.

Let's remember that envy runs two ways, not only from the bottom up but from the top down. What about the young woman who wore the St. Laurent, who was the center of attention?

"You really like it? Look, it's got a spot on it. That's why I got it on sale so cheap." *Devaluation* again but in another form. It is not a new dress; it's damaged goods. I do not feel beautiful in it—and therefore enviable. I am constantly aware of the spot. Please don't envy me, don't hate me because I have outshined you.

Once again, the object that aroused anxiety in the Envy Sweepstakes has been destroyed, if only verbally.

To illustrate Klein's third defense, let's take a third woman who has just entered the party, looking terrific, feeling so too. Her husband is also buoyed up by his wife's good feelings about herself. Suddenly she too sees the woman in the St. Laurent. Her husband naïvely comments on the lovely stranger's appearance.

"Oh, she's gorgeous," the wife says. "She's better than a movie star."

The other woman is, in fact, merely pretty. However, to quickly distance herself from what she really feels—that she would like to scratch the other woman's eyes out—the wife *idealizes* the rival. She decides the other woman is the most glorious creature she's ever seen, beautiful beyond comparison, *out of her league*. Distancing the rival to this degree protects her from envy. Had she truly *admired* the other woman, she would have praised her realistically: a pretty woman, a pretty dress. The exaggerations of idealization give envy away.

Just to be sure she is safe, the wife could employ devaluation as well, belittling her own good looks. She is not in the race at all. She suddenly feels drab, unattractive. When she hurries into the bathroom to look into the mirror, *her face has changed*. It is as if someone has turned on harsh, unflattering lights. Her fire goes out. She has indeed become less attractive.

Her husband is baffled. He arrived with a woman who shone with vitality and radiance. The party is ruined for him too. His wife has "spoiled the good breast," Klein would say; in our terms, she has spoiled the good evening, the good dress, the good husband, everything. But she has protected herself from something more important: the hateful, gnawing tooth of her own envy.

The idea operating within her is to elevate the St. Laurent woman into an inhumanly exalted class of being. For good measure, the self is covered with shit. Between two such totally different people, how can any notion of competition enter? The self is defended against conscience's accusation that she wants to destroy the other woman. "Destroy her? You're crazy. I found her the most wonderful woman on earth. We're having lunch tomorrow."

On the phone the next day with a best friend, it might be confided, "Oh, I did feel a twinge of jealousy last night." But unless the other woman (or the husband) set up a triangle, in which the wife felt she was going to lose a relationship she loved—what happened at that party was not jealousy, but pure envy.

But we don't like to use that word.

Let's go back to Nick. The principle defenses he uses are varieties of devaluation. He does not shout, "Wow, yahoo!" when his editors put through a conference call. Sniffing that something wonderful is about to happen, he goes into a decline, a depression. "Oh, well," he shrugs, devaluing the success he's spent ten years working to achieve. A friend meeting him on the street might say that his reserve regarding success is more akin to gentlemanly good manners than to a nasty psychological process like envy. But Nick knows better. An intelligent man and well aware of the subject of my book, he unhesitatingly zeroes in on his real reason for avoiding enjoyment of being chosen as a Main Selection. "I am my mother's son," he says. "Don't sing in the morning or you'll cry at night."

Nick has not read Klein. But he does know that when he is in this frame of mind—close to happiness but unable to enjoy it—it has to do with what he calls his mother's "jealousy" of him and other men too. The risk-taking courage he gets from his father is such a secondary characteristic—having entered Nick's life so late—he can only emulate his father when success and power are far away. To understand Nick, we have to understand his mother. He tells us as much.

Perhaps his mother is "jealous." What Nick goes on to describe is her envy. A kind of envy silently borne by women of Nick's mother's generation. She is seventy-four. When she was young, a woman with a prosperous, loving husband, who would not "allow" his wife to go out to work, was considered fortunate. But Nick's mother wanted to work, wanted a career. To someone like this—male or female—the dependent position is especially intolerable.

Too much rests on the other person. The bigger the husband, the more powerful, the wider the gap between the dependent one and the powerful one. It is a wonderful feeling to be taken care of. Its pleasure resonates on the earliest level of life. But behind the dependency lurks fear; fear the other might withdraw, fear of the power of the other to make us happy or sad, to give life or take it away. Klein.

The powerlessness of dependency made Nick's mother angry. What more natural target for her anger than the people who had the freedom and independence she wanted: Men. That her husband gave her a fine house, a car and furs made her happy but filled her heart with rancor too. Love by definition means an exchange of dependencies; but when one person's dependence far outweighs the other's, leaving the first with a feeling of powerlessness, it is breeding ground for envy.

The old bargain used to be that the man would provide and the woman would nurture; a traditional picture I need not further dwell on. In retrospect, the old bargain seems to have worked; at least the defenses held. Rages were buried; families stayed together. I am not saying the old days were better or healthier, merely that the angers between the sexes were not as free-floating as they are today.

Nick's mother's lonely efforts to free herself from the dependent role, I find to be heroic. This was long before the feminist movement, long before she had an accepted framework in which to see herself or the comfort of numbers to back her up. Her husband refused to let her work, except for him. Which is not the same as working on your own and knowing you can make it by yourself.

A dependent wife cannot control her husband. She can control her tiny son. We must begin by understanding that Nick's mother both loves her son and is angry at him. He is her Prince. Simultaneously, she envies him the opportunities he will have to become big and powerful—as it would have suited her to become. One day the boy she loves will leave, taking with him the only real power she has ever known. Unless she clips his wings. Are you thinking these paradoxical ideas cannot coexist in a loving mother's head?

Nick knows better. He is especially aware that his mother's ambivalence intensifies when he is closest to becoming powerful and successful. She not only gave him life; she "cut his lamb chops" too, blatantly favoring him over his sister—thus creating an even more fertile family ground for envy and jealousy. She called him The King. (God only knows what she called her husband.)

Here is the heart of the problem: Women's envy of men's power must be understood to exist alongside and simultaneously with women's love of men. In the right circumstances, the right coupling, a woman can still find a satisfying sense of identity and security as the extension of a loving and powerful man. But how can the flip side of such dependency not be fear/ envy? "What would happen if he meets another woman, if he died, if he didn't come home tonight?" At the heart of the sweetest dependency lurks a bitterness: The other person holds all the power, holds life and happiness in his hands. I am happy only at his sufferance.

This is duality, an all-too-human ability to feel conflicting, equal and opposite emotions, both at the same time, one as true as another. It is a difficult fact of life to understand. In writing about love and hate in the mother/daughter relationship, for instance, I found this the hardest reality for women to face: Most of us feel our rage will destroy the people we love. If acknowledged, it will bring about our own destruction at their hands. This is primitive thinking, the reasoning of a dependent child who cannot see its mother as a whole, both "good" and "bad." Accepting elements of rage in our love frees us to love more honestly and deeply.

What makes envy difficult to grasp stems from this conflict: Envy is a nasty, negative emotion. How can we feel such a shitty thing against someone we love? We are consumed by guilt.

When I ask Nick about his childhood, the quality of his early mothering, he remembers a parade of baby-sitters. But in his fantasy he had a perfect mother, an idealization that is abruptly shattered when in our second interview he tells me that he recently learned he wasn't breast-fed. "That made me angry," he says.

Why? Why would a fifty-one-year-old man, a recent father himself, become angry that his mother didn't breast-feed him almost five decades ago? Nick wavers between idealizing the relationship to his mother and devaluing it. One day he talks about her as perfect; the next he describes her as always out to get him, undermine him.

What Nick is doing is technically called *splitting*—one of the central concepts in Klein's work. It is a defense mechanism that goes back to earliest childhood, when it is a matter of life and death for the tiny child to retain the image of the all-good breast/mother. He does not have the sophistication to understand that the same breast/mother who feeds him and comforts him, and whom he loves, might also be the origin of his misery when he is hungry and she is not there. Unable to contain his own destructive feelings, he splits them off from himself and puts them into the "bad" mother; what he is left with is the connection between the good child and the good mother. Unfortunately, splitting does not end with childhood.

"I'm aware of something very strange going on within me since my mother's doctor told me she has cancer," a fifty-seven-year-old architect tells me. "When I was little, I was angry at her. She preferred my brother and does to this day. I never understood the popular veneration of mothers. I never liked mine. Now that she is dying, I can no longer see her as all bad. I don't know why exactly, probably because I want to keep something of her alive, some good feeling about her. All of a sudden, I don't hate her anymore and I catch myself almost thinking of her as a saint. The curve on all this is that whatever anger I used to feel about my mother now seems to get dumped on my girlfriend, or on my ex-wife. I'm crazy about my girlfriend. Why do I suddenly feel that she's letting me down, that she's not as wonderful as she used to be? I'm sure it has to do with my mother dying. Strange, isn't it? A woman who I thought for all my fifty-seven years was all bad, I now see as all good." Splitting.

Integration is another word for maturity. As we grow up, the good mother and the bad should fuse into one person; someone we can see whole. As the saying goes, someone in whom we can take the rough with the smooth. Listening to Nick, I can't help but remember how many years I idealized first my relationship to my mother, later my marriage.

Each had to be presented to the world as perfect. It was a bleak day indeed when I finally *heard* Robertiello: "Nancy, listen to me. You're feeling guilty for not loving your mother or your husband in the way you believe you should. Also because you have a lot of need for symbiosis and the need to possess. What you're doing is splitting, idealizing Bill, idealizing your mother, saying the relationship with both of them is perfect. You do this not only to maintain the connection to the love object, but also in some kind of envious competition with the idealized picture you have of other people's marriages, other people's relationships to their mothers. Envious people always want to look good. You present this perfect picture to the world because there is a tremendous amount of humiliation that goes along with envy."

How could Nick not experience, literally take in, his mother's envy, along with the envy/jealousy generated between him and his sister? His sister had had six years of being the only child. When Nick was born, the first male child in the family in fifty years, Jocelyn clearly felt a tremendous drop in her value within the family. Within the jealous triangle, she must have also envied Nick for having this special quality she lacked: He was male. Nick didn't become envious because his sister envied him, but he certainly became more afraid of other people's envy because of her. She was older, stronger. To a two-year-old boy, an eight-year-old sister is big enough to kill him.

I have mentioned how often people who have been in therapy tell me that the relationship to their brother/sister was rarely an issue. We are just beginning to learn how important these relationships are, how unfortunate it is that their relevance has been so long neglected. Within a family, the sibling relationship is often the one that carries the most open hostility/jealousy/envy. In Nick's case, these poisoned competitive emotions were openly promoted by his father. In such families, the favorite often learns to cool anything good that happens because he is surrounded—not only in his own mind—by enemies. Nick got a Cadillac. His sister got nothing. When she complained, the father called her a jealous bitch.

Nick was very open in our second interview about his envy of other people. Once he was spared the overwhelming success a best-selling book would have brought, he felt free of the envious hatred of others. One simple example is the easy way he admits his envy of his wife's favored position with their son. Being a writer, he works at home, and has been involved with raising the boy from birth. When the two-year-old in his arms reaches for mother, Nick is devastated. When a friend gets a terrific review for his book, he admits he is envious. Recently he bought a house. When his mother saw his friend's house next door, she said "Now *that's* a real house!" Nick tells the story and laughs. It is only when he himself becomes enviable that the screens, the defenses, go up. When success threatens to come to him, he feels he would not "deserve" it. "There would be that gnawing thing that it would be taken away from me in the next minute." Just as he wanted to take away his friend's house, his friend's good review.

Here is the heart of my allegiance to Klein: She explains the paradoxical price we pay for protecting ourselves against envy: So much of what we love and want, we spoil.

Take a husband and wife out for a Sunday drive in the country. It's a lovely day; they know a nice restaurant near a lake. Only pleasure lies ahead. But the moment they get into the car, the wife begins: "Don't drive so fast. Don't go so far over to the side. You're braking too hard. Did you get the oil changed?" Et cetera, et cetera. By the time they get home, they've had a quarrel, eaten their meal in the nice restaurant beside the lake in complete stony silence. *The day is spoiled.*

What is there so awful, so universal about the idea of the *backseat driver?* Why is the name usually accorded women?

Your grandmother, perhaps your mother, can remember the time when you seldom saw a woman behind the wheel. It was always the man "in the driver's seat." In control. He is running the car, a pretty good image of the way he runs/controls her life. Where is she? Beside him, working the invisible brake pedal, totally powerless, dependent upon him to keep her safe and sound. Women's backseat driving is a perfect example of Kleinian resentment/envy of the man's power.

Have you noticed how many recent novels by women—especially from California—deal with the image of a woman behind the wheel of a car? Driving is an exercise in power. Being driven is a state of dependency. My worst arguments with my husband have been in automobiles. And yet, it has just occurred to me how many women I know who have refused to learn how to drive in order to suit their dependent symbiotic needs. Even as it keeps the man tied to her as chauffeur, simultaneously any pleasure of possessing him is undermined by his mastery of the car, his power over her.

We are familiar enough with the housebound wife who envies what she imagines to be her husband's freedom to go out into the world every day. A lot of her feelings are justified. A lot of it is pure envy. She lashes out at him: "You aren't watering the plants right," "Why don't you rinse the dishes better?" "Look at these peaches you bought; they've got blemishes on them." On a printed page, these sentences almost automatically are put in a woman's mouth.

If there is one characteristic of mother that women recognize in them-selves—*and swore they would never imitate when they grew up*—it is her constant nagging and criticism. To nag someone is to pull him down, to undermine. Why do women repeat the behavior they hated most as chil-dren? A woman dependent on a man cannot afford open anger. Nagging is what slips out from under the lid she has put on her envy of his power over her. She wants to spoil his imagined happiness. She spoils her own happi-ness too.

The worst thing you can tell a woman is that she is castrating. Women hate the accusation that they are controlling. One tells her analyst of a dream where she is sitting at a table with her husband's penis on a plate, carving it up and eating it. The analyst shrugs. He has heard the dream before. Generations of women have been in a rage at their powerlessness/dependency. The Freudian interpretation of these dreams, simply put, is that the woman envies the man's penis, wants one for herself and is angry that he has what she desires.

Klein sees penis envy differently. It is not that women want an actual penis. They are envious of its power, not only to confer sexual pleasure but in a broad symbolic sense. The penis stands for the power once held by mother, now held by men. Women don't want male anatomy. They want their share of power.

How often have I heard grown children agonize over what will happen to mother when father dies. They've never seen their mother leave the backyard without her husband. Suddenly she is a widow. Instead of col-lapse, there is metamorphosis. Mother goes to Europe alone, gets a driv-er's license, joins the Fred Astaire Dance Studio. The ability to take care of herself, to be in charge, was always there. It was the direct effort of keeping it in check in order to fit the required mold of good wife that resulted in the nasty hisses of nagging and criticism.

What is less familiar is the husband's side of the picture. Perhaps he is dissatisfied with his job, has come to a point in life where he realizes his boyhood dreams of overwhelming success are never going to come true. But the mortgage, the need to pay for the children's schooling, the daily bills, all seem to leave him no other course but to plod on. And there's his wife using her "ignorance" of money to blithely redecorate the living room! To take expensive classes so that she can be a real-estate agent. When she makes her first sale, he refuses to praise her. In our male-valued society, how could the husband admit he envies a woman?

"A man with a woman is always in a condition of fascination, and fear," says Italian filmmaker Federico Fellini regarding his film *City of Women*. "He senses that she is stronger. So now I make a picture about a man who to the ancient fear has added a new fear—that of feminist rage."[22]

Men deny they envy women's power. Not Robertiello. After his last divorce he said to me, "I've always been much more afraid of what a woman will do to me than a man." Oddly enough, I feel women share this fear: We too are far more anxious about reprisals and revenge from other women than from men.

Perhaps the oldest way men protect themselves against the demeaning awareness of envy of women is to combine two of Klein's defenses, idealization and devaluation. The famous Madonna/Whore split. By refusing to see women whole, they halve women's power. They put them on a pedestal as perfect wives and mothers, and fuck them as sex objects. In neither event is the entire woman confronted. Divided she falls. Men love women. They also want to "keep them in their place." The man on top, the woman below. Not only a sexual metaphor, but one of power too.

One of Klein's ideas, which orthodox analysts find most difficult to come to terms with, ironically grows out of an agreement she had with Freud. Late in life, Freud formulated an instinctual opposition between Eros and Thanatos, love against death. He said the battle goes on in all of us. Many analysts, no matter how they admire Freud in everything else, cannot accept this. A "death instinct"? It was just too literary, too abstract; too mystic and Jungian. Freud was growing old, said his admirers, morbidly influenced by his cancer of the mouth. Too bad . . .

Klein too sees this tragic element in life, an inborn, constitutional instinct for aggression and destruction. In some of us the murderous heat was softened by good enough mothering. But all of us have it in our genes. Something in us smiles when a waiter drops a tray of fine china and it goes *smash*.

Most psychiatrists look at a cooing, gurgling baby smiling at mother and see only an epitome of Freud's life instinct. While any human being is capable of anger and fury, they say that is entirely reactive, not inborn. Treat a baby kindly, and you'll find no hate or destruction in him at all. A child's hostility is merely reaction to an enmity the child first perceives directed against him by the environment (parents being a major part of the environment).

The idea is immensely appealing. It gives us a hopeful, meliorative view of human nature. So distinguished a psychoanalyst as Heinz Kohut adheres to this belief. "We are born," Dr. Kohut writes, "as an assertive whole, as an affectionate whole, not as a bundle of isolated biological drives—pure aggression or pure sexual lust—that have to be gradually tamed."[23] At worst, goes this school of thought, the baby is born with a clean psychological slate, neither happy nor sad; constitutionally given neither to love nor to hate. Environment is all.

And yet, doesn't the evidence contradict this rosy notion? Anyone who has read a single history book (or this morning's newspaper), and still believes that human nature is not in perilous tension between war and peace, love and hate, life and death, is lulling himself to sleep. Given this ominous polarity, which writ small is the story of our lives, writ large is the history of mankind, the task Klein set herself was, How do we put ourselves in the service of life and love? What psychological paths must be followed to help Eros prevail over Thanatos?

Klein will not settle for cosmetic or merely pretty slogans. Unblinkingly, she centers on a terrible image, one reported by mother after mother, clinically observed by pediatricians and developmental psychologists so often as to become a commonplace in the literature: Offered a full, loving breast, many a hungry baby will choose not to suck, but—as noted earlier —will bite instead!

Why does the baby ignore the fact that this may drive away the breast, which is about to appease his hunger? Classical Freudians would call this "oral rage"—the hungry baby's anger at the breast. Logical enough at first glance. It fails in this: The orally fixated infant would be appeased when the breast at last is offered. He would stop crying and use his mouth for a greater satisfaction: to take in and suck the breast.

Another child pushes the breast away, bites it. Why? Here we see the importance of Klein's insistence on Thanatos, the destructive/aggressive instinct. The urge to rebellion, to the denial of the other's power and the assertion of one's own at any price, is in us all. We will gain primacy even if it brings the world down about our ears.

What emotion in a tiny infant could be greater than hunger? *Rage,* says Klein—the terrible rage of powerlessness and dependency triggered by the absence of the breast the very second the child wants it. Endowing the breast/mother with a will, which he obscurely decides is opposed to his own—certainly not under his control—the infant is driven to murderous fury. How dare the breast not be there when he wants it? The bite tells mother he is not appeased now that she has deigned to offer him what he wants in her own good time. His teeth tell mother he resents, he *envies*, her power.

Teeth are a primary organ of aggression. A bite is the first way we can hurt anyone. Aggression may become inhibited when we are grown; even as we lash out at the people upon whom we are angrily dependent, we don't strike as hard as we might. We are afraid we might lose them, destroy them, or even bring about our own destruction at their hands. Turning our anger against ourselves, we grind our teeth. Even as we sleep, we gnash in rage. Ask any dentist how many adults come to him, teeth ground down to the gums. How many others must he fit with protective plastic retainers?

Klein says the infant who bites has greater *constitutional* capacity for anger and envy. That is, he is born with more of the devil in his genes.

In this country we don't like to think of being born with something we cannot fix. If envy is constitutional, what is left to psychoanalyze? How can we pull ourselves up by our bootstraps and be good Americans?

Melanie Klein goes right against the grain of this Yankee optimism: "I consider that envy is an oral-sadistic and anal-sadistic expression of destructive impulses, operative from the beginning of life, and that it has a constitutional basis. . . ."[24]

Note the word *constitutional*. There is much disagreement about what it means, and as in so much of psychiatric theory, a certain ultimate vagueness cannot be overcome. One cannot set up controlled laboratory experiments to test ideas of heredity using human beings as subjects. Therefore, let me tell you how I understand Klein's idea of constitutional envy.

It means something we bring with us out of the womb. It is not something we develop in reaction to experience. Two newborn infants reach for the breast. Both find it is not there. One will react with more fury than the other. That fury, that demand not to be frustrated by someone more powerful, *that envy*, is innate. Constitutional.

Freud too started out with belief in the constitutional. For instance, he believed there was a constitutional difference in people's sex drives. In time, the genetic got less and less emphasis in psychoanalytic theory. Today, if a man with a low sex drive enters therapy, his analyst will probably focus on oedipal difficulties, on a punitive, puritanic superego. The analyst feels this will help him toward easier sexual expression. Perhaps it will. But even after years of psychoanalysis, someone with a low biological component of sexuality will never be as erotic as a man who may have had a terrible upbringing but came constitutionally equipped with a high supply of the male sex hormone, testosterone.

I believe in Klein's constitutional theory. I've always felt other people

handle envious/jealous situations more easily than I do. The way I was
raised enters into it. Basically, I am beginning to agree with Robertiello's
bad seed theory: I was born that way. Nor am I surprised. I think my
grandfather—the model in my life perhaps more than anyone else—was
an envious man. (Though in his day the desire to have everything bigger
and better than everyone else's was thought ambitious and admirable.) I
also come from a long line of women who did not sit comfortably when all
the power rested in men's hands. My grandmother defied her authoritarian husband and left him (temporarily), taking the children with her. In
her day, an action of unheard-of, scandalous will and rebellion. Recently I
discovered that her sister (my great-aunt) was also what Jessica Mitford
calls a "bounder"—a woman always bounding over the fences of domes-
ticity. My mother eloped against her iron-willed father's wishes.

Robertiello and I may agree that Klein is right in stressing the death
instinct and the constitutional element of envy. You may feel differently.
You know your mother and father. Are they envious people? Were your
accomplishments denigrated, constantly compared to cousins'? Was there
a sense of resentment that neighbors had bigger cars, houses, better times?
A feeling in the house that enough was never enough?

A handsome man I interview remembers with an almost tactile sense
his mother's envy of him as a baby. Like his father, he was beautiful. She
was quite plain; he always had the feeling she was "ready to kill me
whenever I was admired by people." He also remembers her as the kind of
woman who was never satisfied with what they had, though his family was
wealthy. She constantly compared her life to her sister's, which was less
conventionally successful, but contained a contentment and ease that in-
furiated his mother.

"Why did you choose the woman you married?" I ask him.

"Because she never arouses my jealousy," he replies instantly.

Did this man "catch" envy/jealousy from his mother's behavior, or did
she pass it to him in his genes?

While Klein's emphasis is on the mother/breast, father cannot be left
out, especially if you believe in the genetic inheritance of the capacity for
envy. We are all familiar with the father who is competitive with his son.
What about an earlier emotion? Fathers are often ambivalent in their
feelings toward their newborn children. The baby threatens the special
relationship a man has with his wife. "I felt terribly left out when my wife
became pregnant," a man tells me. "I wanted the baby desperately, but
she didn't include me in the experience. Did I envy her ability to carry
'our' baby? Yes, I did. But how does a man say that? I remained silent. You
could say I kind of withdrew."

If the father was a very envious kind of man before his child's birth, then constitutional elements will be added to environmental. We wonder why fathers, "left out" by the finality of divorce, often refuse to support their children. It may well be that the rage/envy of the mother/child relationship, suppressed by the man while he was part of the family, now finds expression in withholding money.

Here is a thirty-five-year-old woman reflecting on the reasons her former husband refuses to help support their four-year-old child: "Before our son was born, we had an idyllic marriage. It was the happiest time I've ever known in my life. After the baby, I think he felt he came third. Our son, Barry, was first, my work was next, and he was third. My being the major breadwinner never bothered either of us until there was the added complication of the kid. Suddenly there was divided energy and divided attention, and the fact that we were both in love with the kid. We both found another baby.

"One of the ways you make a marriage work, where there is unequal earning power, is that you baby each other a lot. You can't really do it to the same extent when you have a baby. Our son was taken care of by three of us, my husband, the nurse and me. My husband did a lot of child care. He was wonderful with the baby. He did as much caring for the child as I did, but I think . . . it overwhelmed him. Maybe men feel humiliated by the giving up of the self, giving up time from their work, that child rearing implies. I can be a very selfish person, but I felt no humiliation. I think I finally accepted it as my lot because I was the biological mother.

"I was working very hard at my job, which was going very well, and I was nursing the baby. Meanwhile, my husband's career was not taking off in the way he wanted it to. It was a coming together of a lot of different kinds of envies. Womb envy. Money envy. Work envy. And maybe not getting enough attention . . . feeling jealous. Who will ever know?"

This woman wants another child. She is thinking this time of artificial insemination. She will simply leave the male out.

When I read of the growing number of women drawing sperm from banks, my blood runs cold. When a woman sets out to have a child without a man, withdrawing his sperm as if it were a fluid she was entitled to, she is denying the man his right to paternity. Even more important is what she is denying the child. If we exclude men from the very act of creation, conception, what envious rage can we then expect? If we continue to raise generations of children without fathers, envy of women's power, resentment of women, will grow.

"To some extent, envy in the parents will provide the conditions for envy in the child . . . ," says psychoanalyst Leslie Farber, in an essay, *Faces of Envy*. "Where envy is habitual to the parents, it is more than likely to direct itself sooner or later toward the child, and, strangely enough, to fasten on those qualities and capacities of his that the parents most admire. The child will probably at first find the invidious comparisons to which his parents' envy subjects him bewildering, arbitrary, and jolting to his own wavering experience of himself. In a house where envy is in the air, however, the child need but look, listen, and breathe to be instructed in consolation and counterattack. . . . *If* he accepts the conditions offered him and agrees to be instructed by the example of his elders, thus will their envy breed his own."[25]

Sibling rivalry is more intense in the constitutionally envious child. While competition between children for parental attention is unavoidable, if one child has a stronger capacity for envy, every gift or favor shown the other will be all the more bitterly resented. "I always felt my brother kept a constant, watchful guard over what I got in life," a twenty-five-year-old man tells me. "If I got a fire engine, and he got a sailboat, he wasn't interested in his present. He wanted mine. He's still that way. I was my mother's favorite. That promoted a lot of tension. But I swear he came out of the womb resenting the hell out of me."

According to Klein, envy feeds right up the developmental ladder:

> There is a direct link between the envy experienced towards the mother's breast and the development of jealousy. Jealousy is based on the suspicion of and rivalry with the father, who is accused of having taken away the mother's breast and the mother.[26]

> In both male and female, envy plays a part in the desire to take away the attributes of the other sex, as well as to possess or spoil those of the parent of the same sex. It follows that paranoid jealousy and rivalry . . . are in both sexes, however divergent their development, based on excessive envy towards the primal object, the mother, or rather, her breast.[27]

What Klein is saying is that jealousy begins in the cradle, before father is thought of as either sexual rival (by boys) or sexual desire (by girls). *The seed of jealousy precedes the oedipal conflict.* Father is seen by both boy and girl infants as a rival who has the ability to take the beloved breast away and keep it for himself. To Klein, before sexuality arises as an issue in jealousy, the infant resents father because he is taking away the attention of the person who holds all the power in the infant's world.

Freud's oedipal battle for sexual confirmation—happiness, if you will—can thus be seen as being fired by the earlier Kleinian struggle for more primitive joys: power. The child's inchoate fury is that no matter how much mother loves him, the choice is hers, not his. She can always say *no.* She can decide to give life or take it away. To the dependent infant who lives on in the unconscious, no matter what the calender says, the Kleinian mother has two faces. One is smiling and warm. The other is death. The power to decide which to show is hers alone. Who wouldn't envy such power and want it for himself?

Bizarre? Think of the adult, jealous lover. Doesn't his beloved show him two faces? With just a smile and a touch, she can lift him to heaven. When she turns away, perhaps to smile at someone else, he is left in a despair unto death. "I was her Prince," Nick says of his mother, "but she would also undermine me."

"Unlike classical analysts," writes James S. Grotstein, "the Kleinians speak from the point of view of very primitive phenomenology. . . . They relate to a stage . . . even more buried and forgotten than does the classical infantile neurosis. If they are right, however, it is a stage which we ignore at our peril."[28]

Klein's images and metaphors of cannibalism, of biting and chewing the breast, tearing apart the mother, spreading feces on her, are difficult to take. Not just for me—they perplex clinicians who claim that she observed small children, not infants. How did she know, her detractors ask, that these surrealistic nightmares go on in the mind of the baby at the breast?

I remember taking this plaint to Robertiello.

"The horrible images that Klein talks about," he told me "are recurrent; they are always turning up in dreams reported every day on every analyst's couch. To what other period of life could we trace these anarchic and murderous ideas than to infancy? That's before conscience is born."

I catch a taxi over to the East River to see Dan Stern. At a red light on Third Avenue I notice that three horror films are running. One of them is *Alien*, in which a man's belly explodes in giving birth to a monster that destroys him. When I saw the film, adults cringed and closed their eyes. The children in the audience loved the gore. Still close enough in time to the origin of these emotions, they joyously yelled, "Go, Alien, go!" Klein may scare me and the doctors. She doesn't scare them.

Wearing his clinical white coat, Stern sits in his small office adjoining the room where the Baby Theater is housed. Robertiello doesn't wear a white coat. That is not what makes them different. Stern is more at peace than either Robertiello or myself. I realize that is why I came here today. I need a cool nonenvious, nonaccusatory voice. I'm sure he didn't have a father who hated his guts and a mother who abandoned him, like Robertiello. A kind, concerned man, who spends his life looking at and being fascinated by the behavior of little babies, Stern strikes me as the epitome of "Doctor." I ask what he thinks of Klein's developmental timetable.

"I think she begins too early, at least with what she puts into the infant's mind," he says. "I think aggression has a constitutional element. *That* feeds into envy, yes. But I don't think envy is 'primary.' By primary I mean innate."

"Did you see in *The New York Times* the other day that they're finding more and more supposedly psychological traits have a constitutional basis? Depression, alcoholism—"

"—even shyness too; yes, I saw that. And I agree. I feel shyness is more innate and earlier than envy."

"That's because you're shy," I say fondly.

At the door of Robertiello's consulting room a six-foot carved wooden figure greets his patients. It is half a woman: one leg, one breast, headless. "A perfect Kleinian image," he once said, "split and spoiled, not much use to anyone." His favorite bookshelf is lined with grotesque tiny gargoyles from every country he has visited.

Over his desk, Stern has a nice photo of a sailboat. The rest of his office is taken over by stacks of manuscript for his new book and the odd stuffed frog. I spoke to him after a recent psychoanalytic conference where the members rose against him in a body. He was neither angry nor pejorative. If anything, he enjoyed it as a good clarifying fight. I remember the furies Robertiello went through when he resigned as head of the Psychiatry Department of the Long Island Institute for Mental Health. "Unless they give me complete authority, I'll never serve on one of those boards again!" When it comes to dissenters, Robertiello is no less imperious than Freud.

"I don't mean that envy isn't important in our lives," Stern is saying. "It's dynamite."

"Dan, if you were in a jealous situation—someone took your woman away—you would feel . . . ?"

"Abandoned. Angry, humiliated, devalued, my self-esteem lost. Furious, murderous and all of these in some amalgam, depending on the situation."

"Then where do you disagree with Klein?"

"I think an infant can get frustrated at not getting what it wants, but frustration is not envy. I think in order to be envious, to feel the kind of rage that Klein talks about, the baby would have to have far more ideas of the intentions, motives, notions of possession and other things out there in the world that he can yet have. Envy is cognitively way beyond frustration, and the infant hasn't yet the cognitive equipment to elaborate envy."

"You don't think the infant has a sense of his own dependency?"

"Envy implies you could get what you want but aren't getting it. Until you have an expectation of what you should have, what's rightfully yours, what's to be anticipated as yours, I don't think you can really be envious."

"Klein doesn't use envy that way. . . ."

"Yes, she does. She says the baby is envious because of the inequality of power. That implies an alternative, that things could be different."

"When would you say the Kleinian process begins?"

"She says at birth. I believe maybe eighteen months."

"You disagree with Mahler too. My, my, you certainly do dissent."

"Mahler doesn't think the infant makes a distinction between himself and mother. I think the child is developing a concept of self and a concept of other from the very beginning. Mahler's notions are reasonable, but once again I can't go along with her timetable."

"Then it sounds to me like you're not all that far from Klein . . . to her concept of the newborn infant's realization of his impotence versus mother's power. . . ."

"Look, Nancy, don't let disagreement about timetables get in the way of your work. Klein was a genius. I may not go along with her that envy is constitutional, but I do think that the constitutional givens of rage and aggressiveness will determine how we react to envy and jealousy."

If Stern agrees with Klein's theory but says the whole machinery begins to work perhaps eighteen months later than she, I am not going to quibble. No one knows better than Stern, whose career is baby watching, that the results are not yet in. Let the theologians, philosophers and psychoanalysts—and as Freud himself encouraged, yes, the poets too—decide the time and tide of envy. For what it may be worth, I stick with my feeling that Klein is right. Envy is inescapable.

Correctly understood, however, it can lead to love.

While we are all born with some degree of envy and some of us are born with a greater capacity to feel and express it, *Klein says this predisposition will be heightened by bad mothering and ameliorated by good mothering.* If our parents act out their envy and jealousy, our genetic tendency will be reinforced. If they are loving and generous in their actions, it will be diminished.

No one human being can meet all an infant's inexhaustible demands. As Freud writes in *Civilization and Its Discontents*, it is the parents' painful duty to socialize the child. What child will thank you for teaching him the discipline of controlling his sphincter even as he sleeps? Some children's demands are often contradictory. "You want to go out?" mother says to her two-year-old. "No." "Do you want to stay in?" "No." Mother can't win.

The child is furious because he wants something, and even though he doesn't know what it is, mother is not furnishing it. Mother cannot be God, nor should she try. Even if she were perfect, even if she and her love were available day and night, the child would still resent needing her.

We don't like to think of the mother/child relationship in terms of power. We prefer words like responsibility and sacrifice, but these apply only to one person in the partnership. It is only when we get past the idea of "blaming mother" that we can usefully analyze the infant's point of view: The breast is either given or withheld. The baby is warmed or left cold, cuddled and caressed or left wanting. Mother may be late, overworked, ill, forgetful, tired. These are good and human reasons. We have taken into account only one person's emotions: mother's. The inner life of the infant is unwittingly assumed to be as small as his size.

How can his emotions be comparable to what we feel when someone stands us up, for instance, leaving us wretched, abandoned? When we are big and powerful, we deflect our rage onto others. If we are neurotically sophisticated, we know how to suppress our rage and turn it against ourselves. The infant experiences helplessness in a pure state. He feels rage/destructiveness flat out.

Since this all-consuming and insatiable dependency of the infant is one of life's givens, is Klein telling us we are all doomed to a life of envy and rage? We must remember the full title of her book, *Envy and Gratitude.* Envy is a developmental step, the first in an ironic process that Klein teaches can lead to gratitude and love.

The newborn infant does not so much love his mother as need her. While he may be furious that he cannot get what he wants the instant he wants it, if mother is "good enough," she will mitigate his envy of her power. Eventually he sees that mother tries to give him what he needs as best she can. Even if the breast doesn't appear the moment he wants it, it soon will. A bit of reality is taken in: The world is not set up solely to make him happy, but if he learns to wait a bit, it will do its best. The appearance of the breast, again and again, despite his anger for having been kept waiting, teaches him that his powerful but frightening fantasies of revenge, of destroying mother, have not succeeded. He is learning the thought is not the deed. His hatred is not omnipotent. He wanted to kill her because he was so wretched and hungry, but look—here she comes again. She is not dead. She does not hate him back for hating her. In fact, she is smiling, giving him the breast. Mother is so nice. Why does he have these mean feelings about her? The child begins to feel guilty.

Guilt, says Klein, is the paradoxical beginning of the turn away from envy/hatred and toward gratitude and love. How could he want to destroy the good breast/mother?

Reparation is the next step. Atonement for the malice he once felt toward someone who has done so many nice things for him. The baby "makes nice" with mother. He smiles, strokes, touches her, wanting to share some kind of tender emotion with her. Rather than feeling, I hate you because you made me wait thirty seconds before you put the breast in my mouth, he understands that mother is basically a good person.

Gratitude has entered his life. He is grateful for the milk and the cuddling and the aura she provides of being loved.

Envy. Guilt. Reparation. Gratitude.

And gratitude, says Klein, opens the door to love. Let me quote her at some length:

> One major derivative of the capacity for love is the feeling of gratitude. Gratitude is essential in building up the relation to the good object and underlies also the appreciation of goodness in others and in oneself. Gratitude is rooted in the emotions and attitudes that arise in the earliest stage of infancy, when for the baby the mother is the one and only object. . . . This early bond [is] the basis for all later relations with one loved person. While the exclusive relation to the mother varies individually in duration and intensity, I believe that, up to a point, it exists in most people. How far it remains undisturbed depends partly on external circumstances. But the internal factors underlying it —*above all the capacity for love—appear to be innate* [emphasis added]. Destructive impulses, especially strong envy, may at an early stage disturb this particular bond with the mother. If envy of the feeding breast is strong, the full gratification is interfered with because . . . it is characteristic of envy that it implies robbing the object of what it possesses, and spoiling it.
>
> The infant can only experience complete enjoyment if the capacity for love is sufficiently developed; and it is enjoyment that forms the basis for gratitude. Freud described the infant's bliss in being suckled as the prototype of sexual gratification. In my view these experiences constitute not only the basis of sexual gratification but of all later happiness, and make possible the feeling of unity with another person; such unity means being fully understood, which is essential for every happy love relation or friendship. At best, such an understanding needs no words to express it, which demonstrates its derivation from the earliest closeness with the mother in the preverbal stage. The capacity to enjoy fully the first relation to the breast forms the foundation for experiencing pleasure from various sources.[29]

Klein's continuum from envy through gratitude to love is very persuasive. The question is, Why does so much of the world we see around us find it impossible to complete the process? Why is there so much envy and greed? Why so little gratitude and love?

My answer would begin with denial of envy. Hiding it from ourselves keeps us from recognizing the need to change. We are left with a kind of sullen, free-floating guilt. A current, popular assumption is that guilt is old-fashioned, a hang-up, a waste of emotional energy. We'd be better off without it. Wouldn't it be wonderful if some pharmaceutical manufacturer discovered a Freedom-From-Guilt pill?

No.

"Guilt," says psychoanalyst Willard Gaylin, "the sense of anguish that we have fallen short of our own standards, is the guardian of our goodness. It is necessary to the development of conscience in children. . . . The failure to feel guilt is the basic flaw in the psychopath, who is capable of committing crimes of the vilest sort without remorse or contrition. Guilt results when we betray an internalized model of behavior.

"In early childhood, good behavior is enforced mainly through parental induction of guilty fear, the fear of punishment for violating a code of behavior," *The New York Times* sums up Gaylin's ideas. "But as the child grows up, an 'ego ideal'—a form of father figure—becomes internalized as a model of correct behavior. . . . By adulthood, people seek to punish themselves when they betray that model. . . . The lack of appropriate role models or father figures [is] one cause of the growing rash of guiltless antisocial behavior among young people today."[30]

If we fully understand Klein, we come to see that guilt is not meaningless "neurotic" suffering. A pain in the body is a warning of physical sickness. Guilt is an ache in the soul. We are doing something we don't want to do, something we dislike in ourselves, but find terrible joy in doing anyway! Once we recognize that the guilt felt is not vague and nameless, but resentment of the power someone we love or admire has over us, guilt can serve a purpose. It says, *Envy is here.*

If we can admit to envy, we can say we are sorry. We can allow ourselves to get past the false pride of "never apologize, never explain." We can make amends; in Klein's phrase, make reparation. Every love relationship is a balance of power. The rate of exchange today is unstable. To the traditional envy each sex has of the other's power, we have now added the new dynamic of women in men's world. The defenses against envy that protected our parents no longer hold. In any relationship, the beloved is bound to frustrate, sooner or later, wittingly or unwittingly. If we do not understand that we are envious of their power to begin with, our anger will take a destructive turn.

"Steve and I worked in the same office for over a year before we became lovers," a thirty-year-old woman tells me. "I'm sure part of why I fell in love with him was how much I admired him. He seemed to have all the answers. Now that we're living together, whenever he tells me about something good that's happening to him professionally, I don't want to hear it. I don't know where my anger comes from. His raise means more good times for both of us, but I'm always angry at him. It comes out in little things, like forgetting to pick up the dry cleaning. He's talking about leaving me. I can't blame him."

She loves his power. She hates his power. She envies anything that makes him bigger than she, and therefore more capable of withholding love.

As women do become as powerful in the marketplace as their mates, studies show the relationships darken, sour. The man's identity has been threatened. Also, his defenses against envy of women's power have been destroyed. She already had too much power and now she has his too:

"New marriages where the wife is ambitious are less stable. It is not that an ambitious wife necessarily grows dissatisfied with her marriage or seeks greener pastures. Rather, it is her husband who does not want to live with such an ambitious or successful woman. Among married couples who have broken up, we find that the more ambitious the wife, the more likely that the husband wanted the relationship to end."[31]

Guilty about relationships we've botched through possessiveness, resentment, envy and jealousy, more and more people seem to be giving up on love. "I'll just whore around," the man says. "I'll live alone," the woman says. Do I often hear self-pity in the admission of inability to love? There is also fury, a kind of sullen resentment in the cry. Like angry children who punish their parents with fantasies of running away—"and then you'll be sorry"—we nurture our anger at the opposite sex who *could* make us happy, but is withholding instead.

Since most of us do not have Kleinian analysts sitting at our elbows, let me give you an example of how envy is treated professionally. An analyst tells me this case history:

"The patient came in the other day, disgruntled and angry. He considered some interpretation I had made in the last session incorrect. He also began bitching at my lack of caring. I pointed out the unreality of his allegations, that I hadn't been negligent. What he was doing, in fact, was destroying and spoiling some very good work we had done together in that particular session. By the end of the hour, he'd made the connection. He remorsefully began to realize that he'd ruined his relationship with his wife in the same way. Every time she gave him something good, he made shit out of it. Eventually they divorced.

"Over the past year," the analyst continues, "this had been the consistent pattern the man had established with me. He would attack the previous session, then become remorseful and apologize. Only recently has he begun to feel grateful for how patient, understanding and responsive I've been with him."

"How did his envy come out in relation to his wife?" I ask.

"She would make him a nice dinner. He would complain there wasn't enough seasoning. This made her furious. Sex with his wife had started off by being magnificent. In this too he would start complaining, telling her what was wrong with her sexually. He stopped pursuing her. Of course she would then get enraged and withhold sex for months because she was so angry at him for spoiling everything."

"Was he afraid of needing somebody and then not having them available to him?" I ask.

"Exactly. He was afraid that if he ever let himself love and appreciate his wife, then if he lost her—by death, sickness or to another man—it would be devastating."

"That sounds to me like fear of abandonment."

"In part it is. But you have to know the man's history. When he was six months old, his mother went off on an extended trip, leaving him with a nurse. He was abruptly weaned. There was suddenly no mama there. The whole world had been cut out from under him. So he'd had some relatively good mothering and then it had been taken away. For a six-month-old child, that is the worst thing that can happen."

"Does the constitutional element of envy enter in here?"

"I do know the mother was envious, envious of her relatives, her brothers and sisters. What's more, the man calls himself envious. All through his childhood he'd been the poor relation and he had an aunt who was a millionaire. Her son was his age. Not only was this cousin rich, but also handsome, sexually attractive, highly intelligent. The cousin outdid him in everything. Everyone in the family always compared him to the superstar cousin, and he does himself, still. So even though this man is now successful and makes seventy-five thousand a year, he continues to compare himself to his cousin, who makes one hundred forty thousand. The comparison makes his own real accomplishments seem worthless—the true mark of envy. Here he is in the top earning percentile, and he feels like a failure."

"Devaluation."

"Yes. Now he feels tremendous guilt at having spoiled so much of his life. He spends sessions just crying and crying."

"It strikes me that in envious people there is a perverse kick out of knowing you have ruined something."

"Destruction, tearing the house down, is a manifestation of your power. The envious person is terrified that if he loves someone, they will use their power against him."

In the kind of irony that drives people mad (or to the divorce court), the envious person will hem the beloved in, guard her, watch her; will erect ever-higher barriers against her ever being exposed to real or imaginary joys without him. "Your possessiveness is suffocating me," cries the beloved. "No, I love you more than anything on earth," cries the other. But if it is love, why does the beloved feel she is being eaten alive? Her freedom and right to experience, her individuality and self being swallowed in some insatiably suspicious maw?

The beloved warns, If you don't give me room to breathe, I will leave you. The envious person cannot stop. This is envy's other face, the desire —the need—to possess all the goodness that can be extracted from the beloved, sharing it with no one, demanding it all to some insane degree in which the supposedly supreme love relationship is destroyed. Greed demands more and more and more. Even if it is to the beloved's detriment.

Why is there always something unfinished, restless, unsure—something more that must be done—hovering at the corners of my good fortune? Klein has made me acutely aware of how little gratitude I see about me, my own included. One morning last week I sat in a beautiful garden (my own), eating papaya with fresh lime juice (from my tree), complaining about something so inconsequential I can't even remember it, that was already ruining a heavenly Key West day. I clipped the following from the Miami Herald:

"In a realistic sense, enough is always enough," wrote columnist Sydney J. Harris. "Or, as Mother used to say, 'Enough is as good as a feast.' But . . . almost nobody thinks he or she has 'enough' in one department of life or another. . . . Fame is not enough. Talent is not enough. Honor is not enough. Power is not enough. Wealth is not enough. . . . Gompers said that the aim of organized labor was 'More', but this seems to be the aim of nearly everyone. . . . 'Gratefulness' is the quality most wanting here. Gratitude for the gift of life, for being given what we have and being what we are. Enough, as my mother never knew, is better than a feast—it is a blessing."[32]

Once we've accomplished what we set out to do, once we've achieved and accumulated all we can use, why do we continue to overacquire and overaccumulate? When is enough enough? In envy's eyes, enough never is. Somebody else always has something we want.

Men who are already billionaires plot and scheme and stay up nights to corner the silver market, almost bringing down the world banking system in the process. In the end they lose millions, perhaps billions—for what? Unless they collect nuclear aircraft carriers, neither they nor their heirs can ever spend all they already have. But money is power. The envious person can never be powerful enough.

Envy, jealousy, *greed*. The three are related, but Klein says that distinction should be drawn between them.

"Greed," Klein says, "is an impetuous and insatiable craving, exceeding what the subject needs and what the object is able and willing to give. At the unconscious level, greed aims primarily at completely scooping out, sucking dry and devouring the breast: that is to say, its aim is destructive introjection. . . ."[33]

You may not recognize yourself in these mean words. Many people *are* satisfied with their lot and take genuine pleasure in the success of their friends. My bet is that they had a good enough mother, a good enough father; they have developed what Eric Ericson calls "basic trust," a deep down feeling that on the whole other people are going to wish them well, and not resent any success that comes their way. When they fall in love, it reawakens remembrance of something sweet. The people I know who've had this kind of mothering give me the feeling that they are rejuvenated by human connection. They do not want to hungrily, greedily devour the other. They admire, as well as love.

Envy begins with admiration. We like what another has. Why doesn't the emotion stop right there? Why isn't the world filled with people awash in admiration of the fine qualities or possessions of others? John Kennedy may have been the last public figure who aroused a global feeling of admiration. As I remember, there was little envy of his high office, quick intelligence, good looks, lovely wife, family. We called his brief period in history Camelot. A last gasp of good feeling about him and ourselves before our present age of envy.

It is interesting to speculate on why an important quality like admiration is almost as absent from everyday language as is envy itself. Most compliments you hear are *pro forma*, ritual formulas that carry little emotion. You seldom hear someone praised to his face. Why is it so difficult to give praise? Because in some crazy way, to compliment someone else makes us feel as if we are enhancing their power. "My friends tell me that my husband raves to them about my success," a woman says. "But he never says anything encouraging or flattering to me."

Admiration is the generous heart's way of coming to terms with the fact of someone else's greater virtue or virtuosity. For a moment, we have a chance to enrich our world through emulation of whoever/whatever it is we admire. But for the envious person, admiration is too competitive; it passes through the mind before it can become conscious. It is denied with the speed of light.

"Envy," says British journalist Henry Fairlie, "will not let into its heart the notion that those of us who are only mediocre are not therefore necessarily to be counted as failures; and so it equally will not let into its heart the notion that those who excel can ungrudgingly be given our admiration and respect with no diminishing of ourselves."[34]

Instead of the expanded sense of life that admiration could bring, the envious person feels deprived and rancorous. Instead of making the day shine, the admirable one has suddenly spoiled everything. We are nothing.

"Now envy and antipathy, passions irreconcilable in reason, nevertheless in fact may spring conjoined like Chang and Eng in one birth. Is envy then such a monster?" writes Herman Melville of Claggart's envy (not jealousy) of the heroic, handsome Billy Budd. He continues: "Well, though many an arraigned mortal has in hopes of mitigated penalty pleaded guilty to horrible actions, did ever anybody seriously confess to envy? Something there is in it universally felt to be more shameful than even felonious crime. And not only does everybody disown it, but the better sort are inclined to incredulity when it is in earnest imputed to an intelligent man. But since its lodgment is in the heart, not the brain, no degree of intellect supplies a guarantee against it."[35]

Can we begin to see why envy is so often automatically denied? Not only does it label us as feeling inferior, but the emotion itself is too confusing to recognize easily, carrying as it does a compound of such seemingly diverse emotions as anger, admiration, hostility, competition and desire to both emulate and destroy. Since the cost to ourselves of denying what we feel is so great (if only through never knowing what it is that is disturbing our peace of mind), it would be helpful to try to take envy's measure.

Here is my own yardstick: The more removed from me, the less known personally, the cooler is my envy; the easier it is for me to admire. On the other hand, the more intimate and loved someone is, the more heated the envy.

For example, I may envy Mary McFaddin's famous ability to design beautiful clothes, especially since I have sometimes thought I might have some talent in that direction. But I do not know McFaddin; my desire to design clothes is closer to a whim than something by which I measure my self-esteem. Therefore, while there may be a touch of envy mixed into my feelings about McFaddin, my rivalrous feelings carry little heat. There is no *GRRR* in my envy. What is more, since I am not in any way dependent upon McFaddin for friendship or love, I feel no urge to undercut her, to make her less powerful so that she cannot arouse such nasty emotions in me. Instead, a feeling begun in admiration will remain just that.

Admiration is a positive gain. The world feels a more cheerful place for having talented people like McFaddin in it. The next time I see one of her dinner parties photographed in *Vogue*, I will take her as a model. I will emulate her style. And since I genuinely feel this, my vague feelings of competition and envy are far outweighed by admiration. Meeting her, I would wholeheartedly express my admiration and feel better for doing so.

I have just described in miniature the process which is Klein's resolution for the problem of envy: I feel gratitude. Buying a McFaddin dress, feeling good when I wear it, has enhanced my life.

Now, take someone a step closer to me than McFaddin. Say I read a glowing review of a book by someone in my field. The feeling in my gut would be different from what I felt toward McFaddin. Even if I didn't know the author, my envy would be warmer. I am a writer myself and here is praise that I would like to have gotten for a book of my own. But since the author is not a friend, not central to my life, my envy might move into healthy competition.

I would use the idea of this other writer as a rivalrous spur, going to my typewriter and working harder to emulate or outdo the other person's success. Whatever complexity of admiration, envy and competition I would feel, it would be very different, in terms of heat, from what I would feel if the terrific reviews had been lauded upon a novel written by a good friend.

I would like to say that I would feel only happiness for my friend. That would be a lie. My admiration for McFaddin never developed into envy because my relationship to her is marginal. The relationship to a friend is another matter. It "derives" as Klein would say, from structures and un-conscious memories of the earliest familial experiences. If it did not, we would not recognize enough mutual emotions and resonances in each other to have become such good friends. Now that her book is nationally praised, Kleinian emotions come to the fore. I would feel many things toward her, good wishes among them. But I would feel anger too, and fear. Her success has taken her out of my league. She will meet new people, more successful people, people she will like better than me. Jeal-ousy has also entered, the fear of being abandoned, left out, passed over in favor of others. My envy would be hot, hot. Envy of my friend, envy of the new people who have entered her life—these envies feed and inflame the jealous situation. The only minor, saving feature is that my work is nonfiction and hers is a novel.

I remember getting such news, an early morning call saying that a mutual friend had received rave reviews. "Oh, I'm so happy for her, it's made my day," said the caller, so genuinely that I felt like a worm.

"I'm envious," I announced to my husband whose typewriter never hesitated at the news. Confessing my sin out loud, I felt like a doctor ineptly trying to treat his own ulcer.

I telephoned the writer whose book had been so well received and told her I was envious. I congratulated her. By afternoon my fever was down considerably. The fact that she was not a particularly close friend contrib-uted. By evening, I had become almost an objective observer of my own discomfort. I was having dinner with the woman who'd telephoned the news that morning. I told her of the envy her call had aroused.

"You, envious?" she said, putting down her fork and staring in amazement.

"Why are you surprised?"

"Because . . ." She hesitated, embarrassed.

"Because . . . ?"

"Because I have always held you in such high esteem," she said carefully, eyes lowered.

I put my arms around her and decided never again to mention envy at dinner.

As for what I would feel if an even closer friend should win a top award in our mutual field, I can only imagine that I would turn the aggression against myself. I would deny envy, devalue myself and my work. I have done it before and I have seen others do it with me.

"You mean you could envy another author?" says a famous writer. She is a good friend who has limited her sphere, her entire world to people she has so outstripped that envy never arises. Protected by denial of envy, she doesn't seem to hear what she is saying. Who would she or I envy more than another writer? My own envy, guilt at feeling so mean toward someone I love, who loves me . . . it would all be so overwhelming the emotions would distort and block inside my head. "Sicklied o'er with the pale cast of thought,"[36] is the way Hamlet's inability to act against a rival is described by Shakespeare. Nor do I think it irrelevant to the discussion that the emotion Hamlet is unable to act upon is the desire to do murder.

The more power someone has over us—*the more we love them*—the more heated the envy. Unconscious eddies of murder begin to roil at the back of the mind. Inhibition sets in. The Kleinian infant does not know the difference between beating out someone and killing them. In simpler and sadder terms, it is easier to admire a stranger than your best friend.

Until I began this research, I had no name for emotions that soured my life. Now I do. One word to describe everything from coveting your pretty hat to the desire to murder you for outstripping me. I had thought of calling my feelings about your hat "admiring envy," the other "competitive envy." The etymologists I talk with agree that this is the way the word is evolving. I find it confusing. Everyone is entitled to use words as they wish, of course. But isn't trying to fit positive value into *envy* a trap? A word already freighted with the most deadly connotations used in conversation as a compliment?

How do I know if you say you "envy" me whether you (a) admire me, or (b) secretly wish me to fail? Can the study of semantics be the study of a society's defenses? Are we hiding behind words, hoping that some of the soft connotation of hat-envy will rub off on, and so mitigate, the desire to do murder?

"Some people are less envious than others," says psychoanalyst Louise Kaplan. "They don't walk around with a consuming sense of deprivation. They don't have that feeling of 'Everybody else has and I have not.' The more a person has this diminished sense of self, and the more they feel humiliated, the greater part envy will play within the jealous situation."

Oscar Wilde never heard of Klein, but did not need her theoretical framework to help him explain the rage of envy we feel toward the beloved's power over us. "Yet each man kills the thing he loves" is the way he put it, a sentence I'd read a hundred times but thought only a cliché until Klein put her lens to my eye.

During the writing of this chapter, two other writers came to hand. I thought neither had anything to do with my research. I took up their books to read before going to sleep. Both spoke eloquently to my subject, in voices I once never would have heard.

Here is John Fowles's apprehension of how envy works within the jealous triangle. The book is *The Magus:*

> December came, and we were still writing letters. I knew she was hiding things from me. Her life, as she described it, was too simple and manless to be true. What I hadn't expected was how bitter I should feel, and how betrayed. It was less a sexual jealousy of the man, than an envy of Alison; moments of tenderness and togetherness, moments when the otherness of the other disappeared, flooded back through my mind. . . . I wrote a letter in reply to say that I had been expecting her letter, that she was perfectly free. But I tore it up. If anything might hurt her, silence would; and I wanted to hurt her.[37]

The second quote is from the bound galleys of Nora Johnson's autobiography. Describing the failures of various marriages and remarriages—her mother's, her father's, her own—Johnson says:

> All of us married to be taken care of. All of us, on some profound level, felt ourselves to be helpless, useless, almost nothing as long as we were alone. At the same time we resented the power that came with protection. *We bit the hand that fed us* [emphasis added], we resented our own dependency. At worst we hated the person who dared to love us, rotten kids that we were.[38]

These are remarkable paragraphs. Both deal with the symbiotic need I once thought explained all jealousy. Both begin with the earlier seed, envy. Fowles's hero recalls that transcendental love when we lose ourselves in one another. To love is to risk. Fowles's hero lost. Is he grateful for the love he was given? No. He wants to hurt. He tears up the letter.

Johnson too writes of infantile fears of being alone, infantile resentment of the love that is offered. Klein couldn't have said it better: "We bit the hand that fed us."

"Some people just never can be grateful for what is given to them," says Louise Kaplan. "They don't even know when somebody is giving to them, so they are always disappointed. Somebody may even be trying to love them but they cannot take it in. So when they become jealous, one of the angry things they feel is 'You never gave *me* anything. You're giving to *that* person what you withheld from me.' When less envious people are jealous, they can remember that they were given something. They can remember something good about the beloved and be grateful."

Once I took Robertiello a gift, a show of my gratitude. It was a hand-carved, early-American butter mold, a mysterious wooden form on squat legs with a plunger, on which were engraved two *R*s. It was as primitive and handsome (I thought) as pieces of his African sculpture. He could hardly look at it, nor examine it in my presence. He put it down quickly with a mumbled "thanks." Weeks later he confessed he had trouble with gratitude. "I can't express it," he said.

I'd been hopeful that Robertiello would help me cover the ground between envy and gratitude; find language I could accept and relate to my own life. He did not succeed. Did he fail—or did I? There is no one I admire more. He and I are going through an atypical period right now, one in which he seemingly refuses to be my wise and patient professor. To do so he would have to admit to his envy. It is my belief that my brilliant mentor has problems in this area. These problems are his defenses and they support his life.

I remember a Lamaze instructor telling me of an expectant father. "He hated being intimately involved in the birth of his child. He called it 'woman's work.' His defenses held back so much emotion that when they finally did come down, he was the best student." I feel the same could be true of Robertiello. When he read Klein twenty years ago, he told me he dismissed her as so much gobbledegook. His citadel was intact. He would have nothing to do with her because she had nothing to do with him. Now she does.

Perhaps it is the destructive, greedy times in which we live. Perhaps his patients have brought envy's dead cats into his safe room with its grass-covered walls. Why does he insist again and again that I read and reread

Klein? Is he hoping that if he and I talk long enough his defenses will crumble? I can no longer wait for Robertiello.

"Of one thing I am quite sure: The infant is not born pure. If the infant was born pure, where would all the nasty adults come from?"

Hanna Segal is speaking into the mike I have pinned to her woolly sweater. She is perhaps Melanie Klein's foremost living disciple. She was psychoanalyzed by Klein and later worked with her, becoming an eminent psychoanalyst and author herself. They were friends. Last night I flew three thousand miles to see her. I am in London, sitting in the high-ceilinged Victorian house in which she lives and works.

"Everyone I interview denies feeling envious," I say. "It's jealousy they recognize."

"To admit envy, to admit that the object you love, admire, desire—the person who is good to you—to admit *that* is the person you envy and hate and want to destroy . . . nobody can really admit to that."

"No one wants to think that their hottest hates are the people they love most," I say.

"You can admit hatred if the person you love frustrates you. That's admissible. You can hate the person you love if they are unfaithful. That's admissible. But to admit that *because* they are good and you love and admire them—and that is why you want to destroy them—that is not admissible."

I stare at the photograph of Melanie Klein on the bookshelf behind Mrs. Segal. They are both such smiling, warm, almost twinkly women. How can they be so jolly in this jungle of semantic snakes? "Melanie Klein has such a wonderful face," I say.

"I have photos of her when she was young. She was very beautiful. A lovely sense of humor, enormous *joie de vivre.*"

"How did she get into all this horrific material?"

"Genius." She laughs.

I ask Mrs. Segal why people use envy and jealousy interchangeably.

"Semantic confusion often covers psychological confusion. Using the right words for the right thing is important. For instance, a man feels 'jealous' when other men have success with women, quite irrespective of the value any single woman has for him. That could be part of oedipal jealousy, that every woman is mother. But what I think is mostly behind that kind of jealousy is envy. He's not really jealous because A, whom he loves, loves B. He is envious of the qualities B has—potency, charisma or whatever."

"He could also be envious of A because she has the power to withhold love when she could love him instead."

"What you see in the genuine jealousy situation is 'I love her; therefore I am jealous of *him* and hate *him.*' When you are jealous—as opposed to being envious—the object of love is generally protected from your hostility. When the predominant emotion you feel is hostility toward the beloved, though you may call it jealousy, it is envy."

"We think of jealousy as noble and envy as ignoble. . . ."

"And for a good reason. Jealousy at least implies loving, the capacity for passion. Real jealousy . . . it feels less destructive than envy."

"Just the opposite from what most people think," I say. "Why do so many child psychologists have the opinion that envy is too complicated for the infant to feel, too elaborate?"

"The fact is," says Mrs. Segal, "that envy is much simpler than jealousy: 'This is marvelous—you have it—I *smash* it if I can't have it.' It's a terribly simple feeling. Primitive envy is one of the simplest feelings. Let me tell you a story. Henry Moore was doing a big sculpture and making these big holes in it. When a friend came into the room he said, 'I am making a mother and a baby. That's what babies do, don't they? They make big holes in mothers.' " She chuckles.

"Klein."

"Yes. And you remember Klein's cycle: envy, guilt, reparation, and then gratitude. Well, years later I read an interview with Moore. When he was young he massaged his mother's back because she suffered from arthritis. So here is where the reparations come—as though he were a child who made all those holes in his mother's body and now he has to use his hands to put her back together again."

"People say, 'I envy your hat.' Does Melanie Klein really mean us to understand that *all* envy goes back to the infant's desire to destroy what it loves?"

"*Conscious* envy is not necessarily destructive. When your pretty hat makes me feel envious, I am aware of the feeling. There may be a touch of hostility and competition in my feeling toward you. But your hat is not an issue of life and death to me, the way a breast is to an infant—or one lover is to another. The heart of the matter is whether the other person is someone we depend upon for our existence, for glory, for the deepest feelings of security and value. When another person is that close, that important, then terrible rages inevitably arise. That is what Mrs. Klein described as primitive envy."

"Tell me how primitive envy works in the jealous situation."

"If the unconscious, underlying envy is very strong it will mobilize the original primitive destructiveness. You will want to destroy the rival; you will want to destroy your love object. If you feel deficient in love yourself, you will be envious of their relationship, of their capacity for having such a relationship."

"You mean, that if I doubt the quality of my love . . . doubt that I can really love—"

"Then it is not so much that you are jealous of A or B but envious of their capacity to have a relationship that you are not capable of. The jealous situation depends on the intensity of the underlying envy. For instance, if there is real love and low envy, one can imagine the injured partner forgiving both parties. Feeling abandoned, feeling the pain, feeling the loss, but saying, 'That person I love is happier with the new one.' If the love is strong enough, eventually you forgive, you mourn, you stop wanting to possess. You yourself are then free to fall in love with someone else."

"Loving someone, wouldn't you want to regain him?"

"If you can. You would look to your own failure. You would want to compete with the rival, to be better than you were. But say you lost the competition. Then maybe for his sake, because you loved him, you would let the object go. You would have to go through a mourning. That is important. It is all very well to say, 'He will be happier with her; I'll let him go.' But you must go through your own mourning."

"You have just described a jealous situation where there is more love than envy. What about people who are obsessed with hatred and revenge?"

"If your jealous pain is mostly wounded vanity—vanity being a derivative of envy—then you are more preoccupied with hatred and revenge."

"On both of them?"

"More against your love object."

"Because of the envy . . ."

"Envy. Not jealousy."

"Against the beloved . . ."

". . . *not* the rival."

I sigh. Relief. After months of dealing with my own fears of the material—intensified by Robertiello's defenses—Segal has confirmed my growing comprehension of Klein. At the same time, her clarity and completeness of thought tell me how much more I need to understand, beginning with Klein's use of *envy* itself. I say how much I wish Klein had invented a different word or phrase.

"It isn't how we think of *envy* in the English language."

"I think it is the right word."

"Can we backtrack?" I ask. "Are you saying that envy of someone's hat is related to the destructive, primitive envy the infant feels toward the powerful breast?"

"These feelings are not identical," she says, "but they both derive from the same early root."

"And jealousy . . ."

"Intensely jealous people, when you scratch the surface, they are in fact envious people."

This then is how I will use the word *envy*. Polite usage be damned. When I write *envy* it will in no sense be a compliment. It will carry the weight of Scripture and Klein: the mean intent to possess, hurt and destroy even, and especially, those we love.

CHAPTER FOUR

Self-Esteem, Self-Centeredness and Grandiosity

"Jealousy has so many masquerades. Last night my boyfriend was talking bitterly about his ex-wife. Then his tone became sympathetic. 'Well, maybe now I can understand why she did that.' It made me uneasy. I like it better when he's angry with her. There'll be no reconciliation. I think my jealousy is based on fear of abandonment."

The woman I am interviewing is an attractive thirty-one-year-old. Hair, clothes, makeup, everything has been carefully thought out to present an optimal picture: poised young woman, one who speaks with wit, insight and self-assurance. Not likely to strike you as one who fears being left out in the cold.

I smile in recognition of the familiar gap between appearance and reality. "Did you get angry with him last night when he turned sympathetic toward his ex-wife?"

"That's jealousy wearing its disguises. At the time last night, I didn't want to face it. Today, I can see he was making me feel extremely jealous. Instead, I tried to live up to my ideal of myself. I'd be ashamed to admit feeling jealous. You're not supposed to feel insecure. So I just sat there and said, 'Oh, what a shame she did that. Tell me all about it.' My role was to be there for him, as a friend. But I didn't feel friendly. Inside I was scared.

What if he fell back in love with her? I'm jealous that he and she may reconcile, that I will lose him, that I will be alone. I'm jealous they have children together, that they share things I never will. I'm even jealous that his children love her more than they love me. That shows how irrational jealousy is."

"In your jealous moments," I ask, "do you ever think, 'I, Janice, am not easily replaceable'?"

"It's not rational. I cannot sit and tell myself I'm prettier, more success-ful than she. . . ."

"Are you?"

"Yes. But that doesn't make any difference when I get one of these attacks."

"Of jealousy?"

"It's like a sudden pain in the heart. The reality is, he does love me more than he ever loved her. Nevertheless, I was furious last night, but as I said, you aren't supposed to be jealous. It only came out this morning. All this disguised rage, directed at him."

"Give me an example."

Janice laughs. "For instance, I found myself yelling at him. Like, 'Oh, shit, why did you drop that crumb on the floor?' Last night, I wasn't aware that I was jealous. But now I realize that is what the angry morning scene was all about."

"How about jealousy in the past?"

"The other half of jealousy is being the target of someone else's jeal-ousy. I've experienced a lot of that. Not with my real sister, who is five years older than me, but with my stepsister. My mother married her father when Lucy and I—we were both eight, born only twelve days apart. There we were, practically twins, except we had nothing in common, not even the same name. For my stepfather's five kids, it was all brand-new. So my stepsister, Lucy, she was very jealous of me. It was *my* town, *my* maid, *my* mother. Lucy always perceived me as the favorite. I got more than she did, my mother loved me more, I had more girlfriends, more boyfriends. Con-sequently, I had to play down everything good that ever happened to me. If I got an A on a test, I would never mention it. If she found out, she'd scream at me. It was easier to let her think she was on top. I didn't want a confrontation."

"You call what went on between you and your stepsister 'jealousy.' You and Lucy were rivals for your mother's attention. But most of what you say went on between you and Lucy sounds more like envy."

She looks puzzled. "That sounds right, but you know, I've never really made a distinction between them."

"One of the characteristics of envy is that the closer the person is to you, the hotter the resentment of the other person's success. And here were the two of you, 'practically twins.' Comparisons had to be made on both sides."

"Exactly!" she says, her face alight at this recognition of her emotion. "In college, I ranked in the top ten of my class and made Phi Beta Kappa. But I didn't tell anyone at home. I didn't want Lucy to hear about it. If she did, that awful face would come over her and she'd want . . ."

Janice's face twists into a terrible grimace. She can't find words to complete her sentence. My feeling is that she *can* complete it, but the words are too frightening. I try a bit of neutral prompting:

"And she'd want . . . ?"

". . . and she'd want to kill me!"

She said it—words right off one of Klein's pages. Preverbal infants cannot express their rage, but when the words come out thirty years later they are as absolute and murderous as a child's. "I'm so angry I could kill you!" we say most ardently to the people we love.

"A woman I know wanted to do a TV series on envy," I tell Janice. "The network insisted she change the world *envy* to *jealousy.* No explanation was given. But people seem intuitively to know that envy involves something they're ashamed of. It comes from an earlier, more savage stage of development than jealousy. Maybe that's why you found it hard to complete the sentence about your stepsister. Envy is all about spoiling things. At the bottom, it's a desire to destroy."

"I've had women jealous of me over a man. That doesn't bother me too much. Maybe a part of me even enjoyed it. But what I felt from my stepsister, being the object of someone's envy, you carry the memory of that around with you forever. I once headed a department of eight women. I'd come in and say, 'I'm going to the Bahamas on a short vacation.' People started to move away from me! I'd see the terrible looks on their faces. My old cover-up mechanism would go into gear, just as it used to with Lucy. I'd say, 'Really, it's not going to be such a great vacation. It will probably rain all the time.' Or if I get a new car, and mention it to someone, and I see that black look, I say, 'Listen, it was a used car; it didn't cost much.' "

"Did you ever wonder why you were so sensitive to your stepsister's envy?"

Janice's father had been terminally ill when she was born. She'd been "brought into the world" to be a companion to her full sister. Her parents knew her mother would be absent a great deal. First at the hospital with her husband, and then after he died, she'd be going to work outside the home.

"Is it possible," I continue, "that maybe you could sense envy so keenly because you yourself envied your full sister? She had those five years with your mother and father before you were born. Your father was healthy, your mother wasn't always anxious, and they were a happy family."

"But my sister never really knew him either," Janice interrupts. "She didn't have that happy little family nucleus you're thinking of. Oh, maybe a couple of years before he became ill. But I think she was very confused because he took all of Momma's attention. She saw Momma as someone who took care of *him*, and nursed *him*, and there was no time for her to be a little girl. She wasn't played with. She wasn't, you know, paid attention to."

"Do you think she resented your arrival?"

"I think she was grateful. It was such a gloomy house. My being there, I think, was a pleasure to her. She's always been a mother to me because my mother was always working. My older sister literally took care of me. So there was never any competition between us."

"You strike me as very adventurous and self-confident," I say. "Do you have a strong sense of self-esteem?"

"Well, yes. When I try something, I'm surprised if I can't make it work. Most people assume they will fail, so they don't bother. But I have this . . . it's almost a conceit. My feeling is, if I think it's a good idea, it probably is no matter what other people say."

"Do you think you got this self-esteem from your mother? Was she a good model?"

"I didn't want to be like her. She was anxious about everything. You know, 'It's raining, don't go out, you might slip.' The elements, things you can't control, worry her a lot."

"Is she a maternal woman?

"Very. Very. Even now. Even more now. But she was more so with my sister, she says, because she was the first one."

"Then you feel you got a lot of loving and holding from her when you were a baby?"

"Absolutely. I was raised by my mother. But she was always worried that we'd go off on our own and do something."

"You certainly did," I laugh. "Did you get an idea of how to be from your stepfather?"

"No, he was an ill man too. He was sort of . . . vague."

"How about negative models, ways you didn't want to be?"

"I didn't want to repeat my mother's life. I couldn't imagine standing in that kitchen—there was a big counter—with all her seven kids, her own and the stepkids, crowding around and each shouting a different breakfast order and my mother would stand there and go, 'Pancakes? Eggs? Toast? Anything?' And I thought, She's crazy. I'll never do that, no matter how much I want someone to like me. She wanted to please everybody so much."

"But isn't that a powerful force in your life?"

"*Oh, yes!* When people envy you, they don't like you. If they feel sorry for you, they can be nicer to you. I remember when my boyfriend was made president of the company. My old friends stopped being my friends. They left me because I was elevated to a new position. That's not paranoid. It happened. People tend to be more sweet and sympathetic when they feel on top."

"So you keep yourself little, even though, in reality, you're very successful."

"Yes. If I'm down there and they're up there, it's easy. But if I'm the one who's up there—I have to look out."

"We don't like to recognize our envious feelings. We pretend they're too petty to discuss, but—"

"—but you hate them!" she interrupts. "For instance, I've been out apartment shopping. I made offers to buy several and was convinced each time *that* was the one for me. But I kept reading the classified section. I was never satisfied with what I had. Even now that I've taken an apartment, I still open the paper every Sunday to see what else is around. Maybe someone else has something better, maybe . . ."

"Maybe you'll end up dissatisfied again?"

"You're right about not letting yourself admit that you have these nasty feelings. When I was a department head, I was criticized for not delegating, for not hiring good people to work for me. My people kept making mistakes and I had to do everything myself. Management's idea was 'Maybe she's threatened by a good person working under her.' And if I was really honest, I would say that's true."

"Have you ever been afraid that if things got too terrific—too much success, too many lovers, too good an apartment—that you might get so high, go too far . . ."

"The Achievers' Disease!" she cries triumphantly. "That's what a successful woman friend and I call it."

"Describe it."

"Fear of flying," she immediately replies. "In an airplane. I have that phobia a lot, usually when I'm flying someplace pleasurable. When you think about it, when there isn't a lot of turbulence and you look out the window, it's a beautiful experience—feeling up, feeling high. If I allowed myself to feel it, I'd probably get to like it. But I'm convinced that if I let myself feel the slightest bit relaxed on an airplane, God will come down and strike me dead and crash that plane. It all gets back to not letting yourself feel that good because somebody will kill you."

"I know what you're talking about," I say. Ah, yes . . .

"If you're feeling good and experiencing success, either someone will kill you, or you will be a killer. See, that's another thing I've thought about a lot. That if I'm too good, too successful, I will kill somebody else."

Murder again, envy seen as pure emotion, stripped of rationalizations and/or disguise. I am stunned. I had asked Janice for an interview because of her eager interest in this book, and her engaging candor. Five years ago we had worked together briefly on a short-term project, but I do not know her well.

I ask Janice to state in her own words how she thinks the idea of envy relates to murder. Remembering that Klein says envy stems from a time before the conscience is formed, thus allowing the destructive impulse full play, I feel like a chemist in a lab, watching a litmus paper turn—as predicted—a revealing color.

"It's a feeling I have," Janice says, "that everything trails off onto someone else. We don't live in a vacuum. If I'm good, get a good job, apartment, someone else will get a worse job, a worse apartment. Someone else will have to suffer consequences for my goodness."

"So they'll want to . . . ?"

"To kill you. That's how they'll feel."

"What do you mean by 'goodness'?"

"Successful, attractive to men, whatever achieving and success is all about. I win something; someone else loses something. It's as if God doles out seven million success drops and seven million failure drops, and each of us takes away from somebody else, addition and subtraction. You can't just be happy and successful without somebody falling over the side."

There it is again, envy's Zero Sum Game. The guilt of the "haves" makes them magnify the danger they are in. If Janice were a "have-not" wouldn't her intensely envious nature want to murder the "haves"? Projection.

"Not everyone thinks this way," I say. "Some people are pretty envy free. But power, fear of our own and other people's, is a primitive issue. Once someone had complete power over us and we never want that to happen again."

"What scares me is when I feel I have too much power. Last week I was telling my best friend how terrible I 'made' my boyfriend feel. She said, 'You didn't *make* him feel anything. No one is that powerful. He's feeling that all by himself.' But I always did have the idea I had this power . . . that I could be—what's the word?—voracious, too demanding, too strong. That I could make someone feel small, make someone shrivel. So what my friend said made me feel better. She took a great burden off my shoulders."

"Aside from last night, does your boyfriend make you feel secure, relatively free of jealousy?"

"Absolutely. That's part of why I picked him. I want to be free of this stuff. Not like the last man I was involved with."

"What was he like?"

"A looker. I mean, a real looker. We'd walk down the street and his neck would turn. I thought, If he is satisfied with me, why should he look over there? In this city, there are a lot of great-looking women. And if you try to compete with all of them, you'll be very tired."

"Did you tell him how you felt?"

"He said, 'I think beautiful women are wonderful, they're works of art.' Bullshit, I said to myself. It was especially bad in restaurants. So I used to say, 'Why don't we have dinner in my neighborhood?' Where he lived, on the Upper Eastside, the women are more attractive. I live downtown. In the restaurants there, I'm usually the star because I have long red hair and great clothes. Downtown, mostly they don't. Uptown, all those women are decked out like they want to meet Richard Gere that night and it's really all competitive. I figured I'd have his full attention if I was the big fish in the small pond. I tried to manipulate the whole thing and I was tired all the time because it took a lot of energy to make sure that he didn't see anyone but me. I couldn't stand those sudden losses of self-esteem. It was humiliating, infuriating."

"How do you think you will handle the loss of beauty and youth?"

"I don't think about that. I'm happier each year of my life. I've been on a climb. When I was little, I really was not a happy kid. Now it gets better all the time. Nowadays, when I feel the old jealousy coming on, or what you call envy, I try talking myself out of it by saying: I have *this*. And the *this* could be the fact that I just won a new free-lance account or somebody just sent me a check. I've always loved getting paid. Ever since the first check that had my name on it. It wasn't something my mother gave me. I had earned it. I never forgot the feeling. I still look at a check and hold it up to the light. When I see someone who is prettier, or has a fancier apartment, I tell myself that *this* is something that is mine, that I earned."

"If you were to walk in on the man you love, and he was with somebody else, what would you feel?"

"The first thing I would feel, and I've felt it a lot, is physical pain. As if I were going to have a heart attack. My heart begins to pound and then, and then . . . I'm always worried I could murder someone."

"Who would you go for, your rival or your lover?"

"I remember in college finding my boyfriend in his dorm room with this female. They weren't doing anything, just talking. But he told me he would be somewhere else. And one of the things I hate most in the world is being lied to. I have trouble trusting people anyhow. So lies drive me nuts. On top of that, this woman with him was very beautiful. She was my friend and I kind of knew she had designs on him. I didn't hesitate. I walked in and slapped him really hard across the face. It was very dramatic! Then I turned and walked out. I didn't say anything. They looked at each other like I was crazy."

"Did that end the relationship?"

"He pleaded. He called and said, It's not what you think. But I would not even talk to him. And I didn't, not for a long time. He begged. I mean, I got him down so low."

"Was that your revenge?"

"I never trusted him after that. From then on, I constantly tested him."

"How?"

"I made *him* jealous. That was always my tactic. When I feel vulnerable, jealous, I quickly turn the tables and make it look like *I* am up to something."

"I understand that tactic all too well."

"But I go too far. You know, I never really end any of my relationships. I've had several affairs, lasting maybe six months, maybe a year or two. I'm the one who always leaves. But I never throw out their pictures. I keep them as friends. I have them all in this stable," she laughs now, "just waiting."

"In case Numero Uno doesn't watch his step?"

"I let the current one know that I am in great demand and 'You'd better watch your step, buddy, because if this doesn't work out, I have my stable just waiting.' Also, if he does start looking elsewhere, I can always phone one of these others. Then I let Number One know I'm doing just that."

"Has this always been your pattern?"

"It's always a nice foundation to have these 'in abeyance' romances. But I'm going to stop. I've decided what it really does is make the guy you're with angry. Why should he trust *me?* I've decided I finally have to take a chance and put all my eggs in this one basket."

"Have you told the stable, Listen, guys, this time it's for real, goodbye?"

"It's a new me. I'm not sure how convincing I am," she laughs.

"Then you haven't released the whole stable?"

"Even when I was engaged, I didn't wear my diamond ring. I didn't want to scare off anybody else. I never admitted I was engaged."

"I didn't know you'd been married."

"When I was twenty-two, for five years, but we lived together for only two years. I married a package. I really liked his parents. Particularly his father. I'm not clear exactly how much I liked his father and in what way. But they were this terrific *family*. His mother was young-acting, and the four of us played tennis together a lot. His father was a great guy, very handsome and had great clothes, and everybody liked him. As far as I was concerned, they were just neat people. They especially didn't have any weird step-things and parents dying. They all had the same last name. Two parents and two children. They were so regular. I'd always felt like a weird kid in school. In fact, I was identified as, 'Oh, that's the poor kid that doesn't have a daddy.' 'That's the kid whose father died.' "

"I know what you mean," I say. "I felt the same thing."

"The night before my wedding I almost called it off. Walking down the aisle, I knew it was a big mistake . . . there weren't going to be any children. One of the hardest things for me in splitting up was losing my in-laws."

"Was your mother-in-law more your kind of woman than your own mother?"

"Yes. She had a great job. Her friends were Jackson Pollack and Larry Rivers. She was very aggressive, cool. She did all the things that I really like to do."

"So now you're going to try to trust a man?"

"I made myself a real princess for a lot of years. What was right for me wasn't right for him. By which I mean, I never wanted him to have women friends, while I kept all my male friends."

"You know all about wanting to possess, that greedy kind of love," I say, recognizing a sister.

"It's time for me to grow up. We're going to live together and have the same address and phone number . . . although I'm keeping a private line for myself and I'll still play tennis with Jeff on Thursdays. . . ."

She laughs ruefully, guiltily, triumphantly.

I wonder what Janice would make of the bit of wisdom I read in *Vogue* magazine so long ago: The best defense against jealousy is healthy self-esteem? When we have a good opinion of ourselves, runs this idea, we live with reassuring knowledge: If the beloved should ever leave, in time someone else would find us lovable. Loss isn't something we look forward to—and it may never happen—but if our history shows that giving and receiving love are not once-in-a-lifetime events, not flukes or wildly lucky accidents, fear is diminished. As surely as we count on our ability to find a new job if the current one does not pan out, sooner or later we'll find someone new to love us. We *know* this.

The problem with a neat, logical-sounding formation like this is: Why doesn't it describe Janice? She looks, talks and acts as if she has everything. Feelings of value? Her fear is that if anything, her opinion of herself may be too high; she may be too strong, too powerful.

And yet her interview shows she lives with constant jealousy and envy. Janice churns with fears of abandonment, loss, betrayal and humiliation. Why does her self-esteem not support her when her lover merely turns to look at another woman passing in the street? Janice cannot be understood until we differentiate between true self-esteem and those meretricious counterfeits of the real thing.

Self-esteem is a basic, deeply rooted good opinion of ourself; self-confidence based not so much on a constant stream of reassurance or flattery from the outside world as on the feeling of value given us first by mother and then later by others important in childhood. Healthy self-esteem should not be confused with:

Self-centeredness. The self-centered person did not get the attention he needed as an infant and so must manufacture it for himself. He is unable or reluctant to take a realistic view of himself as just another person in the world, sometimes playing a star role, sometimes not; most often, neither star nor audience, but a human being getting on with life like any other.

Self-centered people forever need to wrest attention from everyone else. They are preoccupied with their importance or lack of it, always looking in mirrors, talking about their friends and never interested in yours. Ironically, the hypochondriac, always telling us about his ulcers, his weight problem, the pimple on his nose, is self-centered too. The clue to the self-centered personality is whether he is telling you how big and marvelous he is, or how small and near death, he must always keep himself the focus of conversation, the center of attention. People often say he has a "big ego." The fact is he has very little "ego" at all.

Jealous? The self-centered person, afraid he isn't worth anything, always suspects that if his lover even looks at someone else, he'll lose. In the jealous triangle, how can he win? In his heart he knows he's inferior.

Grandiosity. This person goes an exaggerated step beyond self-centeredness. His car must be the biggest, his house the most expensive, his parties the most lavish. He is a name dropper, a place dropper. It is not enough for the grandiose person that his wife loves him. She must treat him like a god. He doesn't just want her constant attention; he needs to be the one and only focus of her unfailing admiration.

While he may live with fear of being carried away by his own inflated importance, he is often unconscious of his arrogance. As Hanna Segal put it to me, "He has a secret conviction that 'nobody has what I have or is as good as I am. Therefore I have no reason to feel envious of anyone.'

Unconscious envy manifests itself very often as this kind of arrogance."
Or to turn it around, arrogance is a defense against envy.

The grandiose person never got his infantile omnipotence satisfied at an
age-appropriate time; behind his boasting he hungers for it still. Conversely, mother may have encouraged this state in him too long. *Archaic
grandiosity* is the technical name, meaning it goes back to an era so infantile and forgotten—so ancient in development—that "archaic" exactly
describes it. Jealous? The grandiose person knows in his heart that his
exaggerated claims are not true. His archaic grandiosity was not successfully modulated into healthy self-esteem. When a potential rival appears
his hot-air balloon is punctured.

On any objective test of self-esteem devised by social psychologists,
Janice would undoubtedly rate in the top percentile. "Who makes the
major decisions within the relationship?" "Who is more likely to quickly
establish a new relationship?" "Who is perceived to be more attractive?"
Etcetera. We can easily imagine the self-confident answers Janice would
give. Nor would she be lying.

Janice does have a certain amount of self-esteem. But it is handmade.
She has worked hard to earn it: Phi Beta Kappa at school, ownership of an
apartment, checks arriving weekly in the mail, an attractive, pulled-to-
gether image, the many men in love with her. The problem is all these
accoutrements are an attempt to make up for what she missed in her early
formative years.

Janice is right to question her self-confidence and to wonder if it may
not be "conceit" instead. Conceit is another way of saying she suspects
she may be self-centered and grandiose.

Why else wouldn't her high marks in self-expressed self-esteem give her
peace of mind? "I get so tired!" she says of her maneuvering and manipulations, keeping whole stables of men on the string, having to do all the
work at the office herself because she cannot hire people as competent as
she. Even when she wins—keeping the upper hand—she loses. Her men,
sensing there are rivals around, grow angry, don't trust her. Even if they
do trust her, she is anxious. She can never totally believe they have not
seen through her efforts to control. Of course, they will leave her! She
would never stay with a person like herself.

Hanna Segal: "If you've invested all your self-esteem not inside your
own feeling of identity but in possessing the other person, if you lose
them, you lose all control. People who are insecure feel they have to
control everybody. If you can't control your rage, your jealousy, your envy,
then in order not to stir up these feelings, not to explode, you must control
everybody and everything else around you."

Janice works for love but sets up unrealistic conditions in which it must end by being spoiled. Imperiously reserving the right for herself to have as many admirers as she chooses, each man must "see" only her. Her self-esteem is intact only as long as their eyes are fixed on her.

Take her notion that by changing the locale of the restaurant where she and her lover meet, she can control the kind of woman he might see. Janice is not there for the food. She is the heroine in a secret little drama. "Mirror, mirror, on the wall, who is the fairest of them all?" The chef, the waitress, the other customers—in her eyes, they all have an opinion of her.

Isn't this a demand to control the randomness of life itself? Janice cannot be satisfied thinking of herself as an attractive woman. She must be the most beautiful woman in the room, in the world. She is on stage all the time. "Tiring," indeed. The self-centered have little energy for anyone else. The beautiful clothes, the long red hair, the glamorous apartment, vacations in the Bahamas—all are used as attention-getting devices for a self that feels it is not worth much. Sooner or later, of course, another pretty woman will come along, catching her lover's eye. Janice calls her ensuing rage "jealousy." It is rage and humiliation at not being the focus of all eyes. "If he is satisfied with me, why should he look over there?"

To someone like Janice, playing with notions of omnipotence, her college sweetheart's actions were an unwelcome dose of reality. She asks something unfair and one-sided, the kind of double standard justified only by her secret self-image of being a "princess," to whom ordinary rules do not apply. When she found him talking to another woman, this showed he did not agree with her inflated opinion. She says she slapped his face because she was jealous. Perhaps a better explanation would be that she punished him not because she feared the loss of his love but because he had punctured her grandiosity. He had humiliated the Princess. And the Princess took her revenge: "I got him down so low!"

This abasement of a man she supposedly loves puts in question a popular misconception of jealousy. As philosopher Jerome Neu points out, jealousy is not necessarily a sign of love. In fact, it can betray an obvious lack of trust, reveal a superficiality in depth of affection. It is only in romances, in fiction, in TV serials that jealousy is taken as a sign of true love.[1]

For most of us, sometimes we have self-esteem; sometimes it comes mixed with self-centeredness and grandiosity. Sometimes we merely play or bluff at having it, sometimes we fool ourselves into thinking we have it, sometimes it deserts us just when we need it most. One thing is clear: Self-esteem is not like an electric light, either on or off.

People with healthy self-esteem may feel some diminishment if their lover is charmed by another face. They live with these little fluctuations, but on the whole their sense of self-worth has a certain constancy. The benchmark of the grandiose person is the violent swing of emotion. He is either Rockefeller or on welfare.

"I'd be ashamed to admit feeling jealous," Janice says. It is a nasty, inferior position. But she feels it anyway when her lover's tone of voice runs momentarily sympathetic about his ex-wife. Janice feels "jealous" but is ashamed of herself for feeling it . . . all the more jealous for feeling ashamed. Indignity has been added to injury. Self-esteem sinks lower than ever.

In simple but eloquent terms Dr. Leslie Farber describes this process: "Issues of the [jealous] conflict—loss and gain—are external to character and even to self-esteem *(what causes humiliation and the fall of self-esteem in the jealous person is not the wound of his loss, but his jealousy itself)* [emphasis added]. . . ."[2] This formulation turns *Vogue* magazine on its ear. Janice is not jealous because she has low self-esteem. *She feels low self-esteem because she is jealous.*

"Suspicion" used to be another name for the kind of jealousy that is based not on fact, but on state of mind. It is a useful concept to remember in connection with Janice. Why shouldn't her lover have an occasional moment of sympathy for his ex-wife? It is only Janice's suspicion that reads it as betrayal. In the regressive grip of one of her sudden "attacks," how can any of Janice's esteem-building achievements in the grown-up world help? They are not built deeply enough into her central feeling of self to help at moments when anxiety inflates real and/or imagined rivals into figures of total superiority.

Jealous suspicion is not so often born of the real world outside; it is the enemy already within the gate. It carries a hundred spears. One of the cruelest is self-humiliation: a terrible acknowledgment, a sickness in the heart. You know that your lover is right to leave you for the other. You *are* the inferior.

While I am concerned with how we develop genuine self-esteem, and how we are tricked or trick ourselves by substituting feelings of self-centeredness and grandiosity that do not support us, I believe moral issues enter as well as psychological. As adults, are we responsible for our feelings? "I'd be ashamed to admit feeling jealous," Janice says. Is it indeed "shame" Janice feels or is it "guilt"? Once again we have two words that are constantly misused.

Shame has to do with how other people will view us, the image we present to the outer world. It is connected to humiliation. When Janice says she'd be ashamed to admit to jealousy, she means it would present her boyfriend with a petty and ignoble picture. She doesn't want to have it herself.

Guilt is something we feel because we have failed to live up to some expectation of ourself—*even if no one else knows it.* It has to do with the ego ideal. We feel guilt, for instance, when we are supposed to love a parent and know we do not. Janice is guilty about her jealousy because it makes her feel murderous thoughts toward someone she loves.

Janice's jealous feelings make her feel both *ashamed and guilty.* How can self-esteem not drop?

A distinction should be made between sudden "attacks" of low self-esteem and chronic low self-esteem. People like Janice have nose dives of confidence because their self-esteem comes mixed with grandiosity. Usually they bounce back because they do have a reserve of genuine self-worth; it is only their grandiosity that has been flattened. People who suffer from *chronic* low self-esteem begin by having a low opinion of themselves. Reversals and rejections are simply confirmation of what they thought all along.

Having introduced the important notion of self-esteem (and its relation to jealousy), let's now see how it meshes with Klein's theories.

A tutelary example might be a married couple going to the theater with a new friend, a bachelor. Between the acts, the husband goes off for a smoke. He returns to find his wife and friend whispering together. When they see him, they quickly pull their heads apart. If the husband has a strong sense of self-esteem, suspicion does not immediately begin to gnaw at his heart. His sense of worth tells him where he rests in his wife's affections. Even if she's indulging in a little flirtation of the moment, where is the harm in that? It adds a bit of sparkle to her evening without in any way diminishing the fact that he is the most important man in her life.

Many other husbands, shakier in their self-esteem, would say they felt a stab of jealousy.

"Of whom?"

"I felt jealous . . . of him. I mean, of her. Of both of them! I don't know, just jealous."

Language seems to be failing again.

You will remember Klein's shorthand notion that jealousy is a three-party situation. This naturally brings the oedipal triangle to mind. Envy, Klein says, derives from an earlier age. It is a transaction between two people, modeled upon what went on between mother and baby before any third person (usually, of course, father) enters.

Therefore, while the little scene in the theater involves three people, and thus undoubtedly contains elements of jealousy derived from oedipal conflict, isn't something else going on too? Specifically, doesn't the husband have an individual relation—one at a time—with each of the other two people?

He *envies* the rival's seeming ability to win the wife's love. He *envies* the wife's undoubted power to take her love away from him. He *envies* them both their suspected happiness because in envy's Zero Sum Game, every "good luck drop" (as Janice calls them) that goes to you is one less for me. Endowing the other two with power and glamour, which envy assures him he does not possess, the husband is belittled in his own eyes. He is disturbed, anxious, humiliated, frightened. Suspicion has killed his self-esteem; the death of self-esteem has raised suspicion to greater heights. *Within the jealous situation, both are going on at the same time.*

"Despair," writes Kierkegaard, "is never ultimately over the external object but always over ourselves. A girl loses her sweetheart and she despairs. It is not over the lost sweetheart, but over herself-without-the-sweetheart. And so it is with all cases of loss. . . . The unbearable loss is not really in itself unbearable. What we cannot bear is in being stripped of the external object, we stand denuded and see the intolerable abyss of ourselves."[3]

"The intolerable abyss of ourselves" in the less eloquent but perhaps more pedantically exact language of the behavioral world is *deficient self-esteem.*

I lie in bed in the morning trying to visualize jealousy, to sort out the layers and contradictions. Its roots and tangled growth are like giant wisteria, those ancient Methuselahs in the gardens of the South where I grew up. Almost impossible to follow one individual vine with the eye, to keep it separate from the dozens of others that twist and turn back in upon themselves.

It's a mental picture of jealousy I'm looking for, a clarification in my mind's eye that I can't work out on paper. I couldn't learn to ski, couldn't understand the dangerous absurdity that was being asked of me, until I worked through the picture of the precipitous mountain turn in my head. I trusted it. And then I did it out on the slopes.

I trace the various individual developmental lines in the first year of life that lead into jealousy: envy, abandonment, separation, and now problems of self-esteem. Before the first year is over, these issues—and others I suspect but have not yet explored—become intertwined, feeding one another, adding anger to fear. Some envious god doesn't want us to understand this tangle of contradictions. The ambivalence of love is brought to its acme in jealousy. Why do we kill, or want to kill, those we most love? Does the jealous person love too much?

I have carried one answer in my wallet for five years:

"In jealousy there is more self-love than love."

The message came in a Chinese fortune cookie. In psychoanalytic language, it tells us that when jealousy arises, narcissistic issues are more powerful than those of object relations. In English, this means that jealousy is self-centered, self-preoccupied. We are more concerned with our own insult, injury, hurt pride and loss of face than with the needs of the beloved. As Kierkegaard says, the real beloved is the empty self. Today's political climate in China may not leave much room for romantic love, for Danish existentialists or for psychoanalysis. But the wisdom of the fortune cookie is ancient. It is time to take a closer look at the empty self; time to see how narcissistic issues fit into jealousy.

Not so coincidentally, this week's "Science" section of *The New York Times* carried a lead article titled "New Focus on Narcissism Offers Analysts Insight into Grandiosity and Emptiness."[4] Narcissism is one of the hottest subjects under discussion in the behavioral world.

"American psychoanalysts believe they are finding new ways to treat a large and possibly growing group of patients," the article begins, "whose problems used to seem nearly insoluble to traditional analysis: the joyless men and women who cannot love anyone, but spend their lives desperately seeking admiration to counteract their feelings of inner emptiness."

The article went on: "These people suffer from what is now being called 'a narcissistic personality disorder,' which paradoxically involves self-hatred as well as self-love. They have a grandiose sense of self-importance or uniqueness, and react with rage or deep humiliation when their superiority is not recognized."

In the upper right-hand corner of the article was a small box listing five danger signals: SIGNS OF NARCISSISTIC PERSONALITY DISORDER. With the clutched heart one feels on checking for the telltale signs of cancer, I read:

- A grandiose sense of self-importance or uniqueness.
- Recurrent fantasies of unlimited success, power, brilliance, beauty or ideal love.
- A craving for constant attention and admiration.
- Feelings of rage, humiliation, inferiority, shame, emptiness or haughty indifference in response to criticism or defeat.
- At least two of the following:
  a) Entitlement—the expectation of special favors.
  b) Exploitiveness—taking advantage of others and disregarding their rights.

c) Oscillation between extreme over-idealization and devaluation of others.

d) Lack of empathy—inability to recognize how others feel.

I make enough check marks to render me certifiable. I call an analyst friend and read her what was in the box. "Sounds like a disturbed personality to me," she says.

Last night in a taxi with several friends, I recited the check list. "Oh, my God," was the amused consensus, "that's me!"

"Me too!" echoed the cab driver. "I checked the whole damn list and threw the goddamn paper out the window."

This morning I called Robertiello and asked him how he'd rated on the test. He too had checked most of the boxes. "But I hate this idea of diagnostic categories being taken as absolutes," he says. "All this talk of 'borderline schizos,' 'narcissistic personality disorders'—they make people sound like specimens in the zoo. Neither you nor I are classically in those diagnostic categories, but we have an awful lot of those features. So we put checks in every box and decide there's something terribly wrong with us."

"Our self-esteem plummets," I say.

"But the people who have strong defenses against facing their problems are sitting around right now saying, 'Well, I only checked one or two boxes, so I'm fine.' The truth is, they pay a high price for not being as openly narcissistic as you or I. Look at me—I'm beginning to work through my defenses. I'm so depressed. . . ."

"Your defenses against envy?" I can't believe what he's just said.

"I've been reading, doing some writing and working a lot of this out with my patients. . . . Why don't you come see me anymore? It must be six months. . . ."

Traditionally, psychoanalytic thinking labeled all narcissism as pathological, regression to a more infantile stage of development. The word itself comes from an ancient Greek legend in which a beautiful youth, Narcissus, falls in love with his own reflection in a mirroring pool. Fascinated by himself, he does not move. He dies.

The narcissist is so in love with himself that he has no energy or emotion left to invest in other people. In psychoanalytic terms, narcissism did not necessarily mean someone merely vain about his or her own beauty. To Freud, the narcissist was like a baby so enrapt in discoveries of his body and self that he does not notice a stranger entering the room. The narcissist maintains this self-obsession when grown.

"There is universal agreement that narcissism crystalizes in the first three or four years of life," says Dr. Aaron Esman in the article quoted above. "And if a disorder has its origin in very early development, it is always difficult and time-consuming to treat."

In the same article, Dr. James F. Masterson describes one of the new ways psychiatrists are beginning to look at the disorder. Dr. Masterson tells of a "brilliant researcher who was astounded to find he had been passed over for a promotion and even more surprised to find that he lost out because of his poor relations with the staff.

"When this man turned to his colleagues and family for sympathy," recalled Dr. Masterson, "he was shocked to hear them say that they agreed with the boss. For such narcissists, other people exist only the way a hamburger exists for them—to make them feel good. . . . They may charm you and manipulate you to make you see how wonderful they are, but as soon as they get your admiration, they'll drop you."

Don Juans of the mirror. Once they've seen the admiring glint in your eye, they are off for new worlds to conquer.

Several names are preeminent among those who have done new work on reexamining the roots and functions of narcissism. If I choose to be guided by psychoanalyst Heinz Kohut, I must confess that my first reasons were not objective. From the day I met Robertiello, almost ten years ago, he spoke glowingly of Kohut's work. In fact, he is the only man I have ever heard Robertiello idealize.

"To Dr. Heinz Kohut, the world's greatest living psychoanalyst . . ." reads the dedication in Robertiello's own book on narcissism. But if I merely followed my mentor in the beginning, I have my own reasons now. Like Mahler, Klein and, yes, Freud himself, Kohut makes sense out of my life. It is Kohut who coined the diagnostic phrase in the article quoted above: Narcissistic Personality Disorder. Unlike earlier thinkers on this subject, Kohut and his followers believe there is—to use the shorthand that pops up even in the professional literature—both "good" narcissism and "bad."

In this view, at a certain stage in early development narcissism is as natural as breathing, *a necessary step for building self-esteem*—a firm buttress against jealousy. What matters is that we get our narcissistic needs satisfied at that early stage of life. Basically, Kohut says there are two major steps toward developing "good" narcissism. The first requires having a mother who adores you, in whose eyes you see a reflection of yourself as a veritable Christ Child; a mother who gives you the feeling you have the best seat—the only seat—at the Adoration Banquet.

Nothing represents this more pictorially than Renaissance paintings of Madonna and Child. Earlier Christian art includes an even more literal touch to the exchange going on: The artists paint a gold beam or ray passing from the eye of the Madonna to the Child, connecting them so that her adoring eye seems to replenish Him, raising Him above all other mortals. According to Kohut, at that time of life, that is exactly how the infant needs to see himself reflected.

If this first step of Kohutian development is nourished and satisfied by mother for a long enough period of time, we grow increasingly able to relinquish the unrealistic demand to be the most important person on earth. The baby can almost be said to grow sated with the tiny world he rules in the first, adoration stage. We reach out to explore a further, bigger reality. We are ready—eager—to proceed to Kohut's second step: *the idealization and introjection of the fine qualities we admire in other people who love us.*

Part of our ability to turn away from mother and find ourselves lovable in other people's eyes as well depends on our having taken in those qualities of mother we love most. *We will have taken in the good mother.* But to be effective, for self-esteem to grow, the process of idealization and introjection must extend out beyond her (after all, she can't be everything). It should encompass father, grandparents and others to whom we can get close. Think of self-esteem in terms of ongoing layers, accretions: The greater number of admirable people we take in, the better. It is a process that can and should go on as long as we live.

If this process sounds familiar, it is because once again we are talking about good mothering and, yes, once again about the first year of life. An awful lot going on between the same two people—mother and child—but each of these developmental lines makes its own contribution. While they all influence jealousy, each has its own logic.

For instance, one of the processes going on is symbiosis, a phase in which mother and child are merged. If the need is met, the child should have begun to separate by the second half of the first year of life. The mother who has a more defined sense of self can, however, continue to beam on her infant without merging with him . . . without using her love as an excuse to "own" him. In contrast, the intrusive mother retards separation. The child continues to feel tied to her.

The more separate we are, the greater our autonomy, the higher our self-esteem. It is important to keep these ideas distinct. *Separation* and *self-esteem* coexist and influence one another—a child with healthy self-esteem is obviously going to be able to believe he can make it on his own. He will be more independent than the child who never had his need for attention and importance satisfied. In the same way, and at the same time that symbiosis/separation is going on, we must understand that Kohut's idea of the mother beaming adoringly at the baby, and thus laying the cornerstone for self-esteem, is going on too.

I am not positing either Klein's nor Kohut's ideas as absolutes but as provocative possibilities for better understanding of envy and jealousy. There is the usual dissension in the rivalrous behavioral world as to just how correct Kohut is. Some analysts feel he puts too much emphasis on the infant's need to feel he is paramount on earth. Another criticism is leveled against his notion that mother's adoration cannot go on too long. Kohut says it is self-correcting: The child will willingly surrender his omnipotent fantasy of himself when ready to take in the greater excitements of reality.

I myself am sure of only one thing: Certain developmental needs are age-specific. If they are not met at the right time, attempts to satisfy them later will help but will not be as firmly built into character. A plant that does not get enough sun or water early on will never grow to full height no matter how much fertilizer we give it later.

A child needs as much of his parents' (both mother's and father's) love and attention as it is possible to give. It is more important for him in the first year than in the second. It is more important in the second year than in the third. And so on. By the time we are old enough to summon forth memories of how things were for us as a child, the major events in our development—both good and bad—have already occurred. But there are clues. The way we speak, the way we think of ourself and others, our ease and/or anxiety in the world, our capacity for envy and jealousy—all are evidence, if we could but fully understand them.

I have come to think of the kind of narcissistic need Kohut talks about —the infant's demand for attention—as almost an evolutionary requirement. At some early period of the human race, doesn't it make sense that children who did not make these demands on their mothers, whose natures did not clamor for attention—which means *safety*—didn't these children tend to die more frequently than the others, their low-narcissism genes thus selected out of evolutionary survival?

Nowadays, of course, physical survival is more assured, if only because there are so few saber-toothed tigers around, but the infant's need for attention has not lessened. It now serves a psychic function: If the child's narcissistic needs are met in the first years of life, he changes and develops, grows outward, matures into healthy self-esteem. When the child does not get enough attention and admiration from mother at the right time and is also thwarted from idealizing and taking in other admirable people, such as father, poor self-esteem results. If he does get it, it is like a lifelong annuity. A psychological feeling of worth and security he does not have to wring from other people.

As the baby signals to mother that he is willing to accept more frustration, mother's focus must change. "In this, the baby teaches the mother;

the mother doesn't teach the baby," says pediatrician Berry Brazelton, who has come to be regarded as the Dr. Spock of our time. "The goal of attachment is detachment."

With mother's loving help the baby is ready to face the fact that the cat will not obey him. If he bumps into a chair, he learns it will not comfort him (as mother once did). Slowly he takes in the news that everything out there does not exist solely for his pleasure. This is the reality principle at work, and all of mother's skill and patience must be used now to show him it is not she who is thwarting him, but things-as-they-are.

As Klein would say, the infant can now tolerate the breast/mother not being there the instant he yells. As Kohut would say, he's felt his magnificence reflected long enough in his mother's beaming eyes and is satisfied. He is growing, developing. The message is that reality—which includes other people—is more interesting and more exciting than the world the two of them up till now inhabited.

Because the child has a good feeling about himself, Kohut says, an inner core of self-esteem has developed. He can abide inevitable little defeats. The growing process is exciting; reality has its own rewards. The way the world works, separate from his ego, is a marvelous puzzle. The surrender of infantile omnipotence is made up for by pride in himself. Extending his area of control and power, he can suffer to find out he is, after all, a small fish in a big pond. His self-centered preoccupation with his own needs shifts outward. He focuses on the wonders of the pond, and the people out there.

All around him there are fascinating beings—father, grandparents, aunts and uncles. The healthy baby experiences these giants as new sources of love. Mother is wonderful, but when father holds him in his powerful arms, the baby senses an ease with the world, a lack of anxiety that mother perhaps didn't have. The child wants that ease. Older brother has a talent to make him laugh; his aunt has an infinite patience in teaching him little games. Admiring these qualities, wanting them for himself, he doesn't just imitate them but proceeds on a level higher than mere mimicry. In Kohut's words, he *idealizes* the people he admires. Having identified with them, he introjects their qualities. They become part of his growing self-esteem.

Here is yet another semantic snarl for the unwary. Both Klein and Kohut use the same word—*idealization*—but mean almost contradictory ideas.

To Klein, we idealize people *to keep them out.* Idealization, she says, is a defense against envy, a process by which we elevate people to a stratum so far above us they have no connection to our lives. To Kohut, we idealize people *to take them in*. We see them as shining figures upon whom to model our lives.

Why does Kohut feel we need to idealize people before we can use them as models to grow on? Perhaps the best explanation begins with hero worship. Children know the need for heroes. They go looking for them.

"Do you like me?" asks a three-year-old. "Why?"

The child is doing exactly what Kohut suggests we do throughout life. Knowing why people we like like us back speeds the process of introjection. The child needs to hear the admirable person say out loud those words he is hungry to hear: that he is brave, talented, attractive. Having these traits confirmed by a hero strengthens the child's self-image.

For most of us it is fortunate that Kohut's steps do not have to build one upon the other. That is most desirable, but we have met admirable people who did not go through that first step. Perhaps their mothers were ill, absent, nonmaternal, or just too busy; whatever the reason, mother just did not beam adoringly upon her baby. In a family like this, Kohut's second step—idealizing and taking in an empathic and loving father (for instance), can be a lifesaver. Idealizing and internalizing a beloved nurse, an older sister or brother—or even years later, when we are six or eight, a wonderful teacher at school—all these people too can give us a model, admirable images of a way to be. Kohut's second step represents a second chance. As Freud said, life itself is often the best therapist.

"I was always afraid of growing up like my father," says the forty-two-year-old mayor of a small town. "I remember thinking as a kid that neither of my parents behaved like the parents of my friends. They went out every night. And there'd be terrible fights when they came home. My father had what I used to think of as an Errol Flynn syndrome. He was a play-boy, an addictive kind of man. He loved drinking and gambling. Loved them too much. I remember the night of my tenth birthday. There was a knock at the door. It was the sheriff. They were repossessing our house."

"That must have been terrible," I say.

"It was humiliating, an emotion I can't take. I try to stay in control of myself at all times. Even if I fall, slip in the snow, and someone tries to help me, I push them away. I watch my liquor, never let myself get too high on good times. I'm terrified that I may have my father's genes, an addictive personality. If I got a little out of control, people would perceive me . . . well, as I perceived him. So it takes me a long time to drop my guard and get close to people. And I really enjoy closeness."

"That comes through," I say. "Did you get that from someone in your family?"

"My grandmother. She really loved me. My parents, especially my mother, were very possession oriented. 'When's enough?' my father used to say. With my grandmother there was always joy in the simplest things. She is a fabulous woman who relishes my happiness as if it were her own. No one else ever gave me that.

"My mother recently told me the reason I felt so neglected as a child was that she loved me more than all my brothers and sisters combined. She was afraid to show it because they would be jealous. Those were her exact words. She said, 'You must never tell them.' "

"Do you believe her?"

"I have peace about my mother and father today. But when I have a holiday, it's my grandmother I go to see. She's the one I admire; she's the one I try to be like. Not just because she loved me . . . but her values. Even as a kid, I knew she was a better person than my parents."

Should our heroes return our affection, the process of idealization/ introjection is speeded. For this kind of mutual admiration to be set up, *mother must first surrender her possessive and exclusive demand for the child's love.* It is an idea I choose to put emphasis on. I've said before that we prefer to see mother's role in terms of responsibility and sacrifice. We neglect to see that it is also a role of power. In a time when many roles describe many women, a woman may be reluctant to give up the role that most absolutely defines her.

The unselfish mother who encourages her baby to love people other than herself is one of the finest examples of human generosity. It is born of the most human caring. Sadly, parents are not always overjoyed by their children's attachments to others.

"I remember my first summer job," a thirty-eight-year-old man tells me. He is an industrial designer in his father's firm. "One night I came home and told my father about my new boss. It's not as if I praised the guy. Just said how hardworking he was. My father became angry. It's such a clear memory. He didn't say anything specific, but I knew never to talk to him again about other admirable men."

It is a basic psychological proposition that children need to believe their parents are perfect, an idea parents mistakenly abet. Where do we as parents get the idea that we have to have all the answers? That if a child goes looking for them elsewhere, we have failed? Emotional gifts and skills learned outside the immediate family are felt to be an implied criticism. If a child is to surrender his grandiosity, so must his mother and father.

Where are children going to find these admirable uncles and aunts and grandparents I talked about earlier? That is no longer how we live. More and more children don't even have two parents. And in many single-parent families, that parent is working outside the home. If Kohut is right —and I believe he is—then children must be given more than passive permission to look for heroes outside the home. They must get spoken, heartfelt encouragement to get out there and find all the sources of love and emulation they can. Children need to believe in their bones that if they come home with tales of glory about the giants "out there"—the athletic coaches and drama teachers, parents of other children—their discoveries will be hailed with enthusiasm and generosity.

If the child feels that his loving others, becoming like them, is felt by parents as betrayal, the accrual of self-esteem slows. The child needs to feel love at his back as he goes, warming him on the journey. He doesn't want to hear the accusation "Where did you learn to do *that?*" Praise for learning it keeps him looking for more.

"I don't know why she's so crazy about her Uncle Larry," a mother says of her daughter's attachment to her brother. In the mother's eyes, Larry has settled for too small a piece of the pie. He is not ambitious. But her daughter has seen something glamorous and wonderful in Larry's love of music, a way she would like to be herself. If the girl is lucky, Uncle Larry will love her back, her mother will be generous enough to smile upon the friendship, and in time the child may internalize Larry's ear for Mozart, the way he could navigate a boat. The way Uncle Larry "was" becomes a part of the daughter's good feeling about herself, her self-esteem. She borrowed Uncle Larry's love of music, his patience in teaching her to sail, the manual dexterity and independence that went with the skill—qualities her parents never had—and made them her own. Having a larger life, a larger self, she will be less vulnerable to loss, less envious that others may steal her piece of the pie. She may never make a million dollars, but she can sail a boat to Florida.

When I ask a fifty-five-year-old film director, whose parents were farmers in a tiny Iowa town, where he got the idea of leaving, the courage to think that he *could,* he pauses thoughtfully and says, "I don't know." We talk about his Fulbright Fellowship and the grant from the French government that allowed him to leave home. We talk and talk. Maybe two hours later, he "remembers" his mother's sister, the opera singer, with whom he'd spent his childhood summers. And her husband, the handsome European impresario. Then the man talks about a lifelong sense of guilt about his parents. Because he didn't repeat their lives? Because he "betrayed" them, by taking admirable others as his models? "I don't know," he says sadly. "I don't know."

When we do not remember the people who helped give us our lives, we are cut off from the joyful sense of gratitude. I used to think that the reason we "forgot" the surrogates and models who helped us grow was a kind of Yankee determination to "be our own person."

Forgetting our surrogates and models speaks of a bit of unresolved, leftover infantile omnipotence. "No one helped me. I did it all by myself." Wouldn't a true sense of pride and accomplishment leave room for gratitude to those who gave us so much? Wouldn't it be better training in reality?

Kohut says it is never too late to jack up self-esteem. Two psychological systems keep most of us from doing it. Some people who hold back, he says, are too self-effacing, afraid to shine. Popular usage calls these people "modest" or "shy." Perhaps they tried to win admiration and approval long ago but were painfully slapped down. Their efforts won humiliation instead.

"Stop showing off!" mother says one day when we sit down at the piano to play her favorite song. When we were smaller she would insist we entertain her guests. At what point did she stop enjoying the attention her child received, taking it almost as praise for herself? Why did she start teaching "modesty" instead?

Culturally, we have a powerful taboo against boasting, seeking praise. Just about the most stinging accusation one kid can make of another is "You're conceited!" Where do children learn this sophisticated, killing criticism if not from their elders? At what awkward point in development did becoming bigger/smarter/prettier suddenly turn from being a "good" accomplishment into a "bad" attention-getting device?

Robertiello has always said he belongs to this first psychological group Kohut talks about—those who are afraid to shine. As a result he leads a retiring life, never spends money on himself. Even his voice is a dull monotone, as if to hide the luminous clarity of what he is saying. Is the reason he refuses to write more than a single draft of his books fear that if he polished them, if they shone, then he too would be thrust into the limelight? I must ask him.

Robertiello puts me in Kohut's second psychological group, those who are the opposite of shy: the extroverts, the exhibitionists; we who tap-dance our way through life. Alas, it garners us little self-esteem. When the applause begins, we are not warmed. It is as though it were meant for someone standing behind us. Nonetheless, we keep on dancing. As Janice says, the need for constant attention is "very tiring."

This narcissistic uneasiness is also traced back to childhood. As Kohut says, if as infants we aren't adored, if our grandiosity isn't acknowledged by the smile in our mother's eyes, for the rest of our lives we try to get it satisfied on a giant scale. Conversely, if we have an overindulgent mother who never weans us from the early sense of being the Light of the World, we grow up expecting everyone to see us as mother did.

Adults with this kind of archaic grandiosity are haunted by fear that if we believe the praise and applause, we will rocket right past satisfaction into loss of control. Fear of humiliation keeps us from taking in the recognition for which we worked so hard. We will not gain self-esteem but soar off into megalomania instead.

For instance, we know from Janice's interview that her mother was often distracted and absent. Her older sister stepped in to fill the breach, but one little girl trying to mother another little girl cannot make up for what Janice missed in Kohut's first, adoration phase of development. Nor did Janice get a second chance through idealization of a father. Her real father was dying; her stepfather was not healthy either. Neither man was someone to get close to and take in. Death and abandonment were in the air.

An absent father, a wounded mother—a role in the family needed filling: that of competent, healthy, successful breadwinner. Janice took on the social role of husband/father, not only because she didn't want to be like her mother, not because she was unfeminine, but because, as small children will, she sensed a vacuum.

One of Janice's difficulties is that she has been so successful, her grandiosity almost seems to have a basis in reality. This frightens her. "Feeling up, feeling high," as in an airplane, says Janice, "is a beautiful experience . . . but I am convinced that if I let myself feel the slightest bit relaxed . . . God will come down and strike me dead and crash that plane." In Kohut's terms, she suspects the irrationality of her highflown view of herself. If she got too high, she might plummet to earth. There is a certain confident steadiness in the lives of people who have good self-esteem, but the inflated personality is marked by tremendous swings of mood. Life is lived at the top or at the bottom.

Before we can understand the full complexity of what Janice calls her "jealousy," Klein's theories should be seen working hand in hand with Kohut's. The same distracted, often absent mother who did not nourish Janice's self-esteem (Kohut) was also too distracted and absent to have mitigated Janice's envy (Klein).

How she must have envied the fine healthy people around her. But her anger at others for having so much, being so big when she had so little, inhibited Janice from going through Klein's healing steps. Her own envy is always denied. It is others who are envious, who "move away" and want to "kill" because *she* is so big and successful. Never having acknowledged the guilt that accompanies envy, Janice has not been able to make reparations to whoever it was—uncles, aunts, teachers—who must have given her the models she needed to survive. Denying envy, denying guilt, she robs herself of the sense of gratitude, which, Klein says, opens the door to love.

There is a wonderful description of the process of gratitude and introjection at the end of Judith Rossner's novel *August*. A patient has just finished a long and troubled psychoanalysis. Her name is Dawn. She is a painter, young and blond. During the analysis, she had always thought herself to be smaller than Dr. Shinefeld, though in fact she was taller by inches. She was also especially fond of a certain red dress that the doctor occasionally wore. About to get married and move to Washington, D.C., Dawn gratefully leaves Dr. Shinefeld a present before she goes:

"[Dr. Shinefeld] turned on her desk light to look at the framed oil painting that Dawn had left with her. Done in a more primitive style than the one Dawn usually employed, it showed a young woman emerging from what might have been a subway kiosk in a city whose buildings resembled Washington's. The woman had blond hair and wore a dress in a brilliant print of purple, red and blue. Painted inside that large woman, so that she contituted a good portion of but not the entire body's interior, was another considerably smaller woman whose small head reached the place where the large one's heart might have been, whose tiny arms fitted into the other's large ones, and so on. The small woman wore a brilliant red dress and had dark hair close to the color of Dr. Shinefeld's."[5]

Five years ago I didn't know why I refused to throw away my fortune-cookie paper—"In jealousy there is more self-love than love"—whenever its tattered remains turned up in my wallet. Five years ago I thought I was envious and jealous because I was a Bad Person. While I had a certain high regard for myself, enjoyed a certain degree of self-esteem, behind it always lurked the Bad Nancy. Whenever a compliment came my way— and God knows I worked for them—they were a momentary glow, not money in the bank. The praise flew past me because Bad Nancy didn't deserve it.

It has taken all my talks with psychiatric colleagues, my readings of people like Leslie Farber, Kierkegaard, Willard Gaylin, and the unknown sage of the Chinese fortune cookie; above all, my effort to come to terms with Melanie Klein and Heinz Kohut have helped me understand how I am like Janice: 1) I keep myself dependent as a way of defending myself against the envy of others (Klein) and, 2) I limit the enjoyment of my life out of fear that if I really believed in my success, really got high on it, I would become totally grandiose (Kohut). I would be an object not of admiration but of ridicule.

If others saw me as big and powerful, the way I did in some omnipotent part of my soul, they would hate me. And since another, more realistic part suspected my power was self-willed and fraudulent—"conceited"— their hate would be successful. They would kill me.

Here are the last images, all I can remember of my dream last night.

As usual, the place is a hotel or a large house where many people live. Everyone is paired off, hand in hand, couples; except for me. I wander alone, left out; I stand in doorways, a spectator at other people's happiness.

The action shifts. To my surprise I am in a room where I see one of my mother's sisters. I almost don't recognize her. She has cut her hair very short, and dyed it blond (as I did myself only a month ago). She seems to be my age. In fact, for a moment I almost think it is me. She is very happy. Then another woman with dark hair walks into the room. She is weeping, tragic. Suddenly she takes out her breast which is very large, swollen. She points to terrible scars on it, especially the nipple. It is unclear what caused the awful mutilation. And then I think, Are those teeth marks? I feel so frightened I wake up.

This morning at the breakfast table, my back betrays me. A red-hot pain shoots down my right leg as I try to walk, sending me screaming to the telephone. My orthopedist is on vacation. The physiotherapist who always got me through previous back miseries does not answer his telephone. I don't usually weep. I do all the way to the acupuncturist.

I am home now, lying in bed, waiting for the pain-killers to work. The Kleinian symbolism, the scarred mutilated breast connects the dream to my work. Is the happy, cheerful blond young woman in the dream the *me* I would like to be today? Is the terrifying dark woman both an earlier me and my mother compressed into one? Is my back punishing me for not understanding—or for understanding only too well—the crimes she and I committed and suffered?

Robertiello loves dreams. He used to teach a course in dream interpretation at The American Institute for Psychotherapy and Psychoanalysis. I phone and tell him mine.

"That's a meaningful dream. It ties your book into your life," he says, confirming my thought.

"I'm giving up the book. I'm in pain; it's crippling my back. Nothing's worth it."

"You felt like this when you were writing *My Mother/My Self*. You don't remember, but I do. Nancy, this is your work. You can't give it up. Come see me."

"No. Talking to you about envy and jealousy is like talking to a wall. You deny your feelings. I don't trust you."

"Remember I told you I was depressed? One of the reasons is that I've come to understand my WASP Princess idea."

"Ah, you're envious of their power."

"They're WASPs and Princesses and beautiful. They come from good families, good schools. So there's tremendous envy."

I lie in bed, the telephone cradled in the pillow. *He's admitted to envy.* Can admission to jealousy be far behind? I feel myself smiling. There is a pause. I can almost hear his machinery working, trying to find what else he must say to get me to trust him again.

"One way I even up the score is to bag the WASP Princess and do her in. That's the way it's been, Christ . . . since childhood. And I never realized it until we began our talks."

Robertiello doesn't care about my back. He isn't someone you go to for sympathy. But he can cure your soul. Ten days later, when the burning nerve in my leg has relented enough to allow me to walk, I take a cab through Central Park to the familiar brownstone. Ring three times, up the stairs, through the padded door, and here I am again, lying on his shabby carpet, the tape recorder between us.

"Maybe you should keep this anonymous," he says from the depths of his huge Barcalounger. "I have these fantasies of the woman I'm involved with, Susan. She's making it with a lot of other men."

Robertiello and I have been discussing sexual fantasies since the day we met. Never before has he mentioned a fantasy of his so resonant with jealousy. But does he see it that way? Something in me knows that if I mention the word *jealousy* too soon, it will shut him up. This is the first time he has asked me to keep anything private. Up till now, there has been nothing in Robertiello's world too humiliating, too shameful to talk about, to write about, and, yes, to publish.

Please understand that in my talks with him, I am not playing analyst. Something is going on here that depends on his saying the words out loud, and my—specifically—hearing them. "Nancy," he once said to me, "I can't talk to anyone else like I talk to you." I am the goad; I am the mirror; the job of seeing himself more clearly is Richard's alone.

The idea of being "left out" of my book has upset him. More important, was some therapeutic process within himself aborted when I stopped coming here six months ago? He is depressed. For the first time in our years of friendship, I feel he needs me.

"Keep talking," I tell him.

"I'm not sure what this fantasy means," he says.

"Are you in the fantasy? Are you watching?" I hope my voice is not too curious.

"No, no, I'm not in it," he continues enthusiastically. "The scene I imagine is that the delivery boy comes to Susan's apartment and she's so hot she makes it with him. And she makes it with the super and the guy who comes to collect the rent. That is one of my biggest turn-ons."

"These fantasies don't make you jealous?"

"Just the opposite. I like to think of her as very sexual, orgasmic, ready to take on any man who comes along. I used to analyze it as a way of dealing with my residual, little-boy guilt that women didn't like sex, and that I was awful to make any woman do it."

"But if she herself is so red hot . . . ?"

"Exactly! Since we've begun our talks, I've begun to see another element. Some kind of Kleinian resentment of the woman. A desire not to let her feel she's all-powerful. A desire to get my own back."

"A lot of anger too."

"Anger isn't something I would hesitate to admit. For a lot of men, anger is easily associated with sex. It makes them hard. I also realize there's a lot of humiliation in this fantasy."

He returns Susan's love for him with a fantasy of seeing her fucked by the delivery boy, groveling for sex. "You resent her power to make you happy or make you miserable," I say. "So you devalue her."

He smiles. "Pure Klein," he says. "You know, Nancy, I've missed our talks."

The house in which Robertiello grew up can only be described as Early Dickensian Italian. His mother was totally dominated by her husband, who was so rivalrous that Richard's mother took no interest in the boy. In the end, the tyrannical father handled his envy by turning the boy over to his own father to raise. Richard is the only man I know who was reared by his grandfather, a man so intrusive that he used to examine little Richard's stools during toilet training.

The old man saw in the child entrusted to his care the opportunity to create the genius he had always wanted to be. The rigorous standards of toilet training were extended to every aspect of Robertiello's early life, especially schooling. When the grades weren't good enough, he was literally beaten. "My grandfather was all over me, twenty-four hours a day. My father was around but he never looked at me. He hated my guts." That's how Robertiello remembers his childhood. "My father wanted to kill me."

Little wonder Robertiello had such mixed feelings about the "little blond angel" sister, who was born into this cold and competitive family when he was two and a half. It was only when he scored perfect grades that a rare acknowledgment of his right to exist was grudgingly given by the "drill sergeant" grandfather. His sister had only to be, to exist, to be loved by all. As I mentioned earlier, he loved her, but not so surprisingly, he hated her as well.

"They sent me to a fancy private school. I felt like this little immigrant Italian. I didn't belong. All those beautiful little WASP Princesses, they aroused all my envy and rage. I wanted to kill them, but I also wanted to love them and have them love me. They were like my sister who had all this beautiful stuff that everybody loved while I was cast aside. They got so many good things just for being beautiful and privileged . . ." He pauses.

"Ever since I've realized how many defenses I've erected against my envy, I've been able to see this as one of the reasons I've wanted to snare WASP Princesses."

"Even though we moved to Charleston when I was little," I say, "I always felt different. No father and a Yankee to boot. I didn't belong. I've come to believe the feeling of being left out leads to terrific vulnerability to jealousy."

"Or terrific defenses against feeling it," Robertiello quickly adds. "Take my last girlfriend. I set her up like some golden princess who was out of my league, whom I could only adore. I can see now that the way I handled my envy was to idealize her."

"Doesn't it go back to those little blond princesses in that fancy private school?"

"From the very first grade, I made them into queens. Like my sister."

"Aha, I always knew you were jealous—"

"Not of WASP Princesses!" he interrupts. "I was envious; that's not jealousy. I envied their beauty, their warmth, the fact that all they had to do was exist. They didn't have to produce, *just be.* Just like the women I get involved with today. I make them so wonderful, in a different league from me, beyond envy. *Idealization.* Classic Kleinian stuff."

"You're protecting them, and yourself, against your enormous . . ."

"Rage," says Robertiello, who's been married four times.

"You'd rather idealize them out of your orbit . . ."

"Than kill them."

"Like she's a Madonna . . ."

"And I'm a mortal. But it works! How can you be in rage at a goddess?"

"In some unconscious way, didn't you also want to do them in? In the fantasy of Susan and the delivery boy, in the end what is expressed is anger at her."

Characteristically, he proceeds to lift the discussion to a more interesting, more complex level. "But I am angry at women starting out! Right along with all the idealization, there are a lot of other fantasies about me being an African chief. She's the missionary's daughter and I capture her. I make her into my sexual slave. By devaluing her, I keep the power."

"You never told me you had these fantasies. . . ."

"The hidden agenda with all my WASP Princesses is to reduce them to my size. To humiliate them. Like those dirty movies where you put a quarter in the slot . . ."

"Boy, you give them a double whammy. You idealize *and* devalue . . ."

"I *know*, I *know*, there's nothing rational about this. Only a certain crazy internal logic."

"Let's go back to your sister," I say. "It seems to me you always avoid connecting your jealousy with your sister."

"My *defenses* against jealousy," he corrects me once more. "Take a sultan in the Ottoman Empire. If one of his wives betrayed him, he would feel jealous. What he does instead is put all his women into a walled harem. The only men they ever see except him are eunuchs. So he never feels jealous. The harem was an institutional defense against jealousy."

"So the sultan was protected by the structure of the society in which he lived."

"Yes."

"Six months ago you said you almost never had patients with problems of jealousy or envy, especially men. Do you think you practiced a kind of selective inattention? When free association brought one of your patients to the edge of these feelings, you steered him away because you didn't want to hear about jealousy and envy in your own life."

"I think you're right," he says in that matter-of-fact way in which he will admit anything, if it is conscious. "I used to deflect the subject. Now I deal with it every day, with more and more patients."

"Are they aware of their envy?"

"A man comes in, he doesn't say, 'I'm envious.' He says he's depressed, anxious. In getting into what's wrong with him—I'm thinking of someone I saw today—I'm very aware that his basic issue is envy. I wouldn't have seen that ten years ago. Or five years ago."

"Six months ago?"

"I didn't recognize it as a core issue then. But I still see a lot more envy than jealousy."

"Are you deflecting again?"

"I'm not saying that envy and jealousy are not related. For instance, I have a patient who says he's jealous about his wife. In his case, this means he's afraid she will abandon him. He has problems of separation; also low self-esteem. What I have to do is help him build up healthier self-esteem. Then I can encourage his independence. When he's more self-reliant, has a greater feeling of self-worth, he'll be less jealous."

"Abandonment, separation, narcissism—so many of these issues jell in the first months of life . . . it gets you down."

"Let me tell you what happens, à la Kohut. The analyst is the empathic maternal figure the patient never had. A lot of us are beginning to think now that maybe the most important thing that happens, no matter what analytic school you follow, is that you, the patient, get the feeling you've finally found somebody who really understands you. And really cares. So that his correct interpretations of your feelings and behavior is evidence of his supreme concentration on you . . . highly focused attention you did not get from your mother. What is important may not even be the correctness of the interpretation as much as the fact that someone cares about you, cares enough to think about what knotted you up."

"That's close to what Hanna Segal said to me when I was in London. That in Kleinian analysis, the psychoanalyst's role corresponds to that of mother. If mother is good enough, she can take the destructive projections of the infant, contain them, and in a way detoxify them. What the infant gets back from mother is a response that makes him feel his envy is not overwhelming. His malevolent feelings don't seem so omnipotent. . . ."

"In the same way," Robertiello says, "the patient sees that the doctor contains his fury and returns understanding in its place. When mother isn't around, the infant can eventually contain his bad feelings without being afraid they will destroy everything. When the patient introjects the good analyst, the same thing happens."

"Not everyone believes in therapy," I say, "or can afford it or has the time. How does someone build enough self-esteem, on his own, so that jealousy doesn't make every telephone ring the signal of impending doom?"

"It's difficult for an adult but there is a way. It may sound simple-minded if I put it into words."

"Try."

"My belief is that an adult can move toward greater self-esteem if he or she is courageous enough, lucky enough, to set up a two-person transaction that replays the intensity of the mother/child dyad. A relationship in which you let go of your control, and your resentful envy of the other person's power, long enough to submit yourself to his judgment."

"When somebody says, 'I love you,' that's not enough?"

He laughs. "Has it ever been?"

Rue takes the form of laughter in me too. "No."

"You see, 'I love you,' while very nice, is not specific enough. To really grow, you have to pick somebody—or somebodies—whose opinion really matters to you, whom you yourself admire very much. You also have to do it in an atmosphere where you both realize the seriousness of what you're doing. The other person has to let you know he takes it so seriously he's not going to lie to you to be nice. In other words, the other person has to be someone who responds to the real things you have, knows the things you don't have, and is willing to take the risk of your anger or disappointment at giving it to you straight. They must 'see' you. It's not just a matter of your asking them, 'Don't you think I'm great?' That doesn't do it. Once you've set up this extremely emotional situation, with all your defenses down or melted, then you have to specifically ask them for what you want to hear. And you have to do it directly, risking the fact that they may choose to tell you that you're wrong about yourself . . . that you're not as generous with others as you imagine, more possessive than you thought, not as loving, or whatever. *You have to risk the fact that you may not get what you want.* In other words, if you have manipulated the answer you want to hear up front, it's no good. Anything you get gratuitously, or from a setup, anything you haven't earned . . ."

"I got here through hard work! Doesn't that count?"

"You tell me."

So simple an answer. So profoundly right. Any success I've achieved, any work I've done—nothing has yet reached down to still anxiety that it will all end tomorrow, everybody will find out that I'm basically selfish and unlovable, my work really wasn't good enough . . .

"If your archaic grandiosity wasn't satisfied when you were an infant, you have to say to this important other person, 'Tell me in what ways I'm admirable.' And then you have to believe what this person tells you, to take it in. That, I think, is how an adult gets a new chance to build self-esteem. It rarely happens. As you say, Nancy, you have a better opinion of yourself now than before you became a writer. But you're still highly vulnerable to narcissistic wounds. Your self-esteem can plummet at just a word. It is very tenuous. . . ."

"It's always had a great deal to do with the men in my life. If I feel the faintest whisper that I'm losing him, I'm wiped out. Any success I have in any other direction—none of that matters."

"Your men aren't narcissistic extensions so much as positive reflectors."

"Positive reflectors? Sounds like something on the back of a bicycle."

"In other words, you don't pick a guy who is a superstar so that you'll feel adequate. That's the narcissistic extension business, where the woman feels the more powerful the man, the better off she is because she gets her power through sharing his. What you, Nancy, look for is somebody who reflects you positively. The way a photographer backlights a star to make her glamorous."

"In Kohut's terms, you mean a 'self-object,' " I say.

" 'Object relations' is analytic jargon for what goes on between two people. A self-object is this other person, but one who has little meaning to you other than his relation to your *self*. And that relation is that he is a fan. Somebody who always flatters you. A self-object is not seen as some-one who has a life of his own outside his job of reflecting back marvelous things to you. An equal, a peer, someone you love or even hate, that would be a 'real object.' In Kohut's terms, *who* the self-object is doesn't matter, just as long as his applause for you continues."

"I was writing about that . . . but I didn't know it was me. . . ."

Calmly, implacably, Robertiello's voice goes on speaking, as if I were not drowning in appalling self-accusation: "Your need," he said, "is for a man who thinks you're the greatest thing around. That way, you get your self-esteem artificially boosted. The fairest of them all. Not necessarily literally, or only in terms of beauty, but all around. But the guy whom you've chosen to be this positive reflector, if you suspect he's withdrawing his attention—either in fact or fantasy—it's a tremendous blow. Not because you're losing your narcissistic extension, but because he is your self-object. Your beauty is in *his* eye. Losing his good opinion, you realize you've only borrowed that good opinion. You haven't made it part of yourself. Without his flattering positive mirror to see yourself in, you don't see anything. *You've lost everything.* The difference between being a narcissistic extension and needing a positive reflector is very important. The narcissistic extension involves attaching yourself to someone who is very powerful. The positive reflector—it doesn't matter who he is, rich or poor, powerful or not. He gives you the illusion that *you* are the beautiful or powerful one."

"You make me sound so mean. That's a terrible reason to pick a man . . . because of how he reflects you. So when I'm losing him, I'm jealous because . . ."

"Well, not exactly jealous, but very, very anxious. Your self-esteem is based not in yourself but on his specific response. You don't have any money in the bank from momma loving you or from having a father around to idealize. . . ."

"When I'm 'jealous,' part of my anxiety is that he's with another woman. I immediately think that. And I immediately think of finding another man first."

"Someone to replace him. Because he's really there more as a reflector than he is as a person whom you love, esteem or care about. Right? That's a hard thing to acknowledge."

"I knew we'd end up here: Nancy's incapacity to love. I wish I'd never got out of bed this morning. I don't think I can take any more brilliant insights. Besides, you're wrong: I feel very close, very caring of the people I've loved. In the beginning, what you say may be true, that they are more reflectors than people who have value in themselves. But in time, I do love, I do care. . . ."

"Nevertheless, he's replaceable by another self-object."

"I'm not like you, Richard. Let's not get confused. I'm not the one who's been married four times. I don't replace people."

"You think about doing it."

"When I feel betrayed."

"When there's a disruption in the flattering positive reflection."

"That has always been my quick Band-Aid."

"And it makes sense that you should grab for that Band-Aid just as it makes sense for me. It's a desperate situation and you're going for a life raft."

"When Susan's late coming home, you never think she's with another man?"

"That's the difference between men and women. As we talk, it's clearer and clearer that men are much less jealous than women. They are light years away. I've always said that."

"You're crazy! And no one agrees with you! Society gives men more defenses against jealousy. . . ."

"Even putting it your way, even calling it defended jealousy, I think there is much less jealousy among men than women."

For reasons I don't yet know, jealousy is something he still can't acknowledge. I want to rescue the rapport we had going. "If I'm kept waiting, if the phone doesn't ring, I feel abandoned, my self-esteem plummets."

"You're always getting your feelings hurt—and feeling jealous—because you have to maintain this exalted idea of yourself."

"I knew this was coming."

"Being afraid of humiliation," he says, "is connected with grandiosity."

"Tell me, as a patient rather than as a doctor, how is self-esteem connected with envy and jealousy?"

"Am I the patient or the doctor? Who's the patient?"

"You've got your share of grandiosity."

"Let's start with you," he says. "You've told me that when you go on television you have these fantasies, even while you're on camera, of saying the wrong thing, having the strap that holds up your dress break; being humiliated. You do have a certain degree of self-esteem. But you also feel you have to knock them dead so much you'll be elected Queen of Television. That's grandiosity."

"When I do well, I do get high. If I walk into a restaurant after a show and they give me a lousy table, I'm furious. I'm shot down."

"You're more aware of your defenses than of your grandiosity. You go for the applause but you don't take it in very much. Then you belittle your performance. I've heard you, 'Oh, I wasn't so great.'"

"I've just been writing about this woman, Janice. While I didn't fully identify with her, I did to some degree. She acted the way you describe me, but I'd never go so far as to slap my boyfriend just because he talked to another woman. I can apply your ideas to her. Why don't I feel them about me?"

"That's what I mean by your defenses. If you could admit to your grandiosity, acknowledge it, laugh at it, you'd suffer less from it. But it would mean the final surrender of the secret hope that maybe you *are* Queen of the World."

"Because I didn't get that Kohut stuff as a baby—a mother who adored me, a father to idealize and take in . . . ?"

"It isn't enough for you to have everyday, normal self-esteem. You have to be the greatest. Always. This is where I feel your resistance."

"You do? Now?"

"Remember when you talked to me about my resistance to some of the envy stuff? I can feel that blankness in you now."

"How?"

"You set yourself up like royalty. You dress like a queen. You have a Versailles of an apartment. . . ."

"Come on, Richard! What's wrong with enjoying a beautiful apartment? It's not like I want twelve of them."

"I mean, that's like a king's coat you're wearing, right?"

"Do you envy my coat?" I'm laughing.

"Listen, I think we're onto something now," he says. "I mean, if people have tremendous grandiosity, like you, they have a lot more to lose; if somebody takes my girl away, okay, I'll be wounded . . ."

"You'd jump out the window."

"Because I feel abandoned. But it's different with you. If you lose your man, what you lose is not just him but your whole grandiose structure."

"Listen, you're crazy for admiration yourself. You're too shy to go after it the way I do, but you want it. You stay in this one place, this office, where you are The Greatest. You even bought yourself that African king's throne in the other room. You're doing just what you did with envy: making *me* killer envious, making me outrageously grandiose. I won't be your scapegoat, carrying all your sins!"

I hesitate, out of breath. Have I gone too far? I reach for a question. "These back problems that keep me from the typewriter—do you think I'm afraid to finish the book?"

"As long as you tie your books in with fantasies of having them prove you are The Greatest of Them All, that's possible." The deliberation and careful choice of words tell me that as usual, he's taken no offense at my attack. "You are not perfect, Nancy. That is the fantasy you will not give up."

"Boo hoo."

"When you're not perfect, you feel like the Bad Nancy. Your self-esteem goes to zero. After you finish your book, you'll know what the bad part is and you'll be able to say, 'I have it, but it's not so bad.' Because everybody else has it too."

"What is this *it* that's so bad?"

"That primitive part of you that is envious, greedy, destructive. . . ."

"Aw, come on, Richard," I guffaw.

"When I told you that five years ago you got very upset. Just now you laughed like it was almost a relief to you. You should think about this because it's really what makes you crazy," he says, reaching to unplug the tape recorder. "It's time for my group."

"Hey, don't pull the plug! I want to talk to you about what Christopher Lasch wrote. He says that writing is one way to take exhibitionism and archaic grandiosity and convert it into something socially acceptable."

"Right! Even though your back is in pain, you should finish your book. In the long run, it will result in less pain, physically and emotionally."

"Because I'll understand my life better and also get some of my narcissistic needs satisfied?"

"But in an appropriate way," he says. "Oh, this ties right in with something Hanna Segal wrote." He is excited. "She says the difference between art and pretty pictures is that real art contains the essence of the destructive, the Thanatonic element . . ."

". . . the old death instinct again."

"Yes. That's what your writing is about—all those horrible monsters. Your job is to put your book together in a way that helps people face their envy and destructiveness in order to become better people. People who can love."

"Segal's ideas on art really parallel Klein's cycle of envy/guilt/reparation/gratitude."

"Creative work sets free the destructive part of the artist. He disintegrates old ideas, old habits of seeing and thinking, old forms . . ."

"Old neurotic defenses . . ."

"Yes. Then the creative part of the artist enters and makes reparation. Which is the work of art."

"I have to die before my book is finished?"

"You have to kill the narcissistic, greedy infant in you. But that's the part you don't want to live with anyway. That's what drove you to write."

"Death and resurrection?"

"Want to make another date?"

"Forward and up," I say, rolling onto my side and rising in the correct Alexander Method.

Twice a week my physiotherapist, Tom Lemens, puts me through the rigorous exercises designed by the Australian F. M. Alexander to teach body musculature to function correctly. Unlike the grandiose orthopedic specialists I've spent a fortune consulting, Alexander has got me back on my feet.

I can see Robertiello watching me with concern. It is not my pain that furrows his brow. It is my indecision about going on with the book.

"I'm meeting my accountant on Thursday," I say. "I've got to know what will happen financially if I stop writing."

"But this material is fascinating. You can make a contribution . . ."

"My life used to be a lot happier."

"I love the way we've been talking. I'm practically having a whole analysis."

"Can I charge you?"

". . . so many issues I've denied or ignored . . ."

"If I go on, you won't withdraw again? You won't start denying again?"

"You know me—I want to get in touch with all this."

"You should hear my early tapes: denial, denial, denial. You're one of my most interesting cases, Doctor."

"Look, I'll write the book."

"No!"

"See you on Monday?" he says. He's holding open the soundproof door. In the waiting room, his group is quietly milling about.

"You've been saying some pretty self-incriminating things. But don't worry, I won't use your name."

"Oh, use it!" he says. "Say it's me."

"I do use it when you're the brilliant Robertiello, the wise analyst. But when Richard, the angry little boy, starts talking . . ."

"They're both me," he says. "Use my name."

I laugh and kiss him above the beard. It's only when I'm out on the street that I realize I'm still holding the note I'd written to myself: Make him talk about his sister, the one who made him jealous, the one who died.

CHAPTER FIVE

Memoirs of a Jealous Woman Part Two: Projection

*R*emember Jack? The man who wanted to outlaw jealousy?

How he and I crested and fell looks different today than it did then. I'd like to finish the story. That time with him is my qualification to write this book.

I never did mention the name of the man with whom I was involved when I met Jack. I'm not surprised. I'm embarrassed to have loved such a fool. His name, would you believe, comes from the English peerage. Let's just call him Noble. He was a truly dumb man.

Why is there so much going back in growing up? Why don't we let them go, those people we wanted when we were twelve who didn't want us? How much time is wasted winning them at twenty-two, only to find we don't want them. Small wonder there are so few grown-ups.

Noble did serve one good purpose. Having him in my life, a secret of my own, allowed me to get to know Jack. Allowed Jack to fall in love with the self-reliant Nancy I wanted to show him. So long as I had Noble, I could handle Jack's other woman. One weekend, Noble and I ended, badly.

We were at his Long Island house. He had his four children for the weekend. The mother/ex-wife had removed all the furnishings after the divorce, except for the beds on which we slept and Noble's wing chair in the library. The children loved the mausoleum, probably seeing in their mind's eye paintings and carpets where I saw only ghostly blocks of light. Usually after Noble and I had made love in his old married bed, he would drive me to the guest room of one of his married friends, to sleep what remained of the night. In the morning, he would come to retrieve his Maiden. In front of my host and hostess, we would go through the charade of Chaste Reunion. That last night he stopped protecting my reputation; no longer needing my Madonna image, he allowed the whore to spend the entire night in his bed.

Noble had taken an apartment in town. Having never been a bachelor before, he didn't know what to do with the city or his "freedom." He was happiest among old married buddies in wealthy suburbia. A way of life I thought I'd rejected. But I went along with the weekends, trying to mesh, to undo the woman I'd made up since leaving home. In some crazy convoluted way, the adolescent me had to prove she could win the man my mother had always dreamed I'd bring home one day to the country club.

I was the only single woman in his crowd of friends, and the youngest. A titillating novelty for the boys; a threat to the women. His wife's abandonment had humiliated Noble. I gave him back his balls, and a very attractive pair they must have seemed too. His best friend's wife set out to seduce him: "I want you," she wrote on a piece of paper that last night. Noble would never violate a male friendship; he was King of the Locker Room Boys. But he was angry at women for what they'd done to him; he left the note for me to see on the bedside table. I listened to him sleep the deepest, most satisfying sleep and wondered if his revenge was complete.

By morning, my terrors of abandonment had raced down all those eerie, empty corridors, awakening every separation anxiety in the house. The place was alive with Someone Going Away. Poor children. Had I touched off their memories of a lost father, a home divided—still too fresh to be unconscious? The youngest child sat spreadeagled on the kitchen floor, weeping, he knew not why, into a jar of Skippy peanut butter, which he was slowly licking clean with his finger. Only the daughter responded to her father's jolly efforts to rally us to the scheduled daily events.

"Am I your Juliet?" she teased, hanging on his neck. I was leaving; she had him to herself. Don't think I read too much into the children. Their reactions were honest compared to ours. Still close to life's primary emotions, they had none of our corrupt, adult defenses. Their antennae picked up pure feeling and played it back to us.

Noble had a terrific son whom I loved. He was nine, the oldest. While the others let me hold and hug them, he'd yell and run away whenever I reached for him. But he knew I loved him best. We'd compete in sports and wrestle in the snow, and sometimes we'd walk in the woods and I'd tell him the kind of stories my favorite aunt used to tell me. Real stories about real bravery, like Brigham Young's march to Utah. But even when he'd lean against me, caught in the story, should a kiss be imminent, he'd whoop and tear away. "No kisses!" he'd laugh.

I hadn't seen the boy all morning. There was a ten A.M. train to the city. I was determined to be on it. While I washed scrambled eggs from the breakfast dishes, Noble prattled on about how he couldn't see why I wanted to waste this beautiful day in town. "You'll miss the racquetball at the club," he scolded, choosing to read my departure as a sudden change of weekend plans rather than the final good-bye we both knew it was.

But the boy, the dear one who looked like him, whose strong young body was toughening itself against women's caresses, knew exactly what was happening. He suddenly appeared beside me and found my hand. Then he led me into the garden. "I'm saving my allowance," he said. "And when I get enough, we'll have dinner." Then he put his arms tightly around me and I bent down and held him too.

I've always wondered what touched him: sympathy for the pain of someone he knew cared for him? Competition with his father, and the stepfather-to-be? Still child enough to need his mother, he was old enough to know being a boy meant unlearning all the soft things about her he loved most. And that the path away from women was won in part by competing for them with other men. I'll never forget that little boy. In elevators, I still smile at nine-year-old toughies; they lower their lids, shy and sweet at having been seen.

I never felt the slightest desire for revenge on Noble. The drama had little to do with him. He'd been sent by Central Casting to play out something I had to go through. When it was over, I realized the worst pain hadn't been losing him. It was losing that admirable self I had so painfully constructed. So many weeks, months, of the worst despair; wondering whom he was with, what he was doing. Acts of spying and suspicion, at a pitch of panic that could have been healed and put to sleep in an instant by another man. The seed of jealous pain was in me. Yes, Noble had other women, but they were nowhere near as plentiful, as beautiful and powerful as they were in my imagination. Yes, he was unfaithful. But not as often or as passionately as I'd have been were I in his place.

Another man had indeed stepped into my life. But so far Jack had played second lead. Now he was the star. I continued to see him every day in our work, but his nights were reserved for The Other Woman. I knew I had to be patient and clever. He must never see my neediness, the way I responded to songs about *forever*. The man who was going to outlaw jealousy must never suspect he was dallying with its Queen.

That Monday afternoon he congratulated me for ending the affair with Noble.

"What kind of motherfucker gives you something like that?" he said and removed the gold circle Noble had pinned on my breast last Christmas. I never wore one again. Nor much underwear either. "You have great nipples," Jack had observed, which took care of bras. As for the panty girdles my mother/my self wore, "They give you a mono-ass."

Jack telephoned his service and said he'd return in an hour. Then he grabbed my arm. "Come on."

Outside, the hard December sun didn't make a dent in the chill, but he wore no coat. Striding along that depressed Seventh Avenue of lost souls, talking out loud to themselves as they delivered invaluable documents for Rapid Messenger, I could feel my pulse return; a wish to attach myself to him, this man, source of new life. People turned to watch us pass, the tall lanky fellow in khakis, his chin tipped up, and the girl in the purple fox coat, also tall but double-timing to keep up with him.

At the Chase Manhattan Bank he barely broke stride as the guard swung wide the door. Jack walked in front of me (he also didn't pull back ladies' chairs).

"Good afternoon, Mr. Hanson," the man in uniform said, touching his hat.

"Good afternoon, Officer," Jack said in his resonant radio voice. At the foot of the marble stairs, another officer jumped to his feet in recognition, unbolting the gate from inside.

"Good afternoon, sir."

"Good afternoon, Officer," smiled Jack, and followed him through a ritual they'd obviously often performed. Each inserted his key in the safety-deposit box. Handing Jack the drawer, the officer asked if he'd like his usual room.

"Please."

A mahogany door was unlocked, bows exchanged. Jack locked the door from the inside. There were no windows in the small room. Just a conference table and some horse paintings on the walls. Jack motioned me to a chair, set the drawer on the table and began to unpack it.

"I know a guy, works at IBM, brings his secretary here every Friday and fucks her."

"On the table?"

"Wonderful service these banks provide."

He took a Ziploc plastic bag out of the briefcase he'd been carrying. There was only about a half ounce of grass.

"If we're going to finish that fucking film by next Monday, I've got to keep this shit out of my office. Doesn't pay to have it around when you're feeling neurotic."

For the first time, I realized his buoyancy wasn't from the heart. Money problems. Pressures from his estranged wife. Jack was of the positive thinking school of self-therapy. He never laid his problems on you. Using a cosmetician's tin funnel, he transferred the grass to one of the glass jars in the drawer, while cheerfully acquainting me with its other contents.

"I keep the usual odds and ends at my friendly Chase Manhattan," he said, holding up each item in turn. "My will, army discharge, and, ah, yes, the separation papers from my wife. I loved her breasts. They were too saggy, she said. Wouldn't let me touch them. Like to see some photos of my kiddies?"

Three little boys. All with his blond curls. "They're beautiful," I said.

"Yes," he sighed deeply, and gave each photo a loud smack with his full lips. "Jesus, but I miss them. However, no gloom. Toward pleasure and away from pain!" He lined up a variety of little brown glass bottles, each neatly labeled, in front of me. "A little Jamaican ganja? Ah, no, not today," he said, taking away a different bottle I'd selected. "You show unerring good taste, but that's for when we have more time, like three days." He decided on the ganja, rolled a joint and leaned back in the leather executive chair, his olive sneakers on the table.

"Why do you keep this stuff here?" I asked.

"My kiddies' pictures because they'd bug the shit out of me if I had them in the office. The psilocybin, mescaline and LSD because it's safer. The grass I only keep here when I've got a deadline."

"I think you do it for the kick. Putting on the Chase Manhattan. If I smoke this," I said, "you realize I won't be able to work this afternoon?"

Soon I was between his legs, his cock in my mouth. He made so much noise when he came I had fantasies of men with guns breaking down the mahogany door. "Look," I said, "the horses in the paintings, their eyes are moving."

He licked the saliva and semen from my face. "You're beautiful; come back to the office immediately."

We sprayed the room with Caswell-Massey's English Gardens, also in the drawer. Outside, the guard jumped to his feet. Once again they went through the formality with the keys.

"Thank you, Mr. Hanson."

"Thank you, Officer," we chorused.

That afternoon, when The Other Woman telephoned, we were half conscious, each too aware of how far we'd gone this time to sleep. Unable to use the cool words that had so far marked our affair, we'd been lying in silence for maybe half an hour. Usually, Jack took the aggressive lead in sex. Today I'd matched his talent for abandon, taking him with me. I'm sure there was gratitude in the way he'd loved my body as no other man had, as he never had before. Though when I told him later, he used familiar words:

"It's all in your head, Nancy."

Where else? My head or his, he awakened parts of me that should have died from neglect. Nerves, muscles and an erotic aggression that scared and excited me. Does desire ever die? Long ago, we were promised love if we didn't love our bodies. We took our little hands away and turned our minds against our sex. We got kisses for the bargain.

But the kiss we dream of is the one that gives us back the erotic self. Desire waits in all of us, as eternally young and powerful as the day we first denied it. Isn't that what Sleeping Beauty is all about? The kiss of life. Children, still close in time to having made the bargain, love to hear it told; fears and anxieties about their bad secret selves are put to sleep by dear parental voices telling a fairy tale of unconditional love: a kiss that awakens a princess and seals a union. Once upon a time, the same mouth that warned "Don't" kissed our mouth for being good. I've always believed that is why a kiss, a mouth, on that unlovable part of us, gives our bodies back to us. Who wouldn't love such a Prince?

Once a woman pitted her love against Jack's feelings for his body and won. Thirty years later, his wife tried to make the same bargain. He'd refused. What incredible glamour did sex hold for him? Like other men, he was ambitious in his work. There the similarity stopped. The sexual revolution was just beginning; not yet fully defined. Jack was already dedicated to the credo that the key to his identity lay in the erotic. As he would say, in his cock. Having once divided him from his body, women must put him back together again. That afternoon, he recognized my desire and ability to help.

I watched him walk naked around the room, carrying the phone that connected him to her, and knew I had become important to him. The role of seductress-without-strings would be a new one. Already rewarding, it nonetheless demanded qualifications that were in opposition to my possessive, overly needy way of being in love. But he was involved too and I could see that this triangle that had been created between him and two women wasn't what he'd counted on. Or was it? In a world without jealousy, he should be able to have the two of us.

If I was to win, I had to play it his way. Knowing about The Other Woman—his knowing that I knew—gave me the opportunity to become his dream woman.

"Don't bug me," he said to her.

Did she know we were together? Was she jealous? *I would not be.*

With Noble, the rules had never been clear; he hadn't known what he wanted. And so my imagination, my suspicions, had run wild. Jack knew, and the kind of woman he wanted was how I wanted to be: open, sexual, accepting. Not jealous. Doing it often enough, I would become that way. And he would love me.

That next weekend we never left the office. We worked nonstop on the FAA film. He taught me how to run the Movieola. He would mark the miles of footage I'd assembled, and while he slept, I would splice it together. Then I'd take his place in bed and he'd return to the cutting room, which was at the opposite end of the hall from the office where he slept. The building was empty and overheated. We wore no clothes. Trotting naked along the corridors was exhilarating. The public washroom was filthy but Porthault linens had brought me little happiness that year. The woman in the cracked mirror over the basin had never looked better. We had our meals at the greasy spoon on the corner. Sunday night, when we'd finished, he took me a block farther for a celebratory meal at his favorite Mexican restaurant. Jack was broke. I liked that about him too. I'd been around too much inherited money lately. It makes men soft.

We had been together, in bed and at work, for almost sixty hours. The job that had brought us together daily for two months was finished. The intimacy, I assumed, would continue, but on what terms? Dinner dates formally made by telephone? His evenings, so far, had belonged to The Other Woman. Fresh out of an affair in which my waking and sleeping hours had been filled with fantasies of betrayal, I was in a unique position: I could try to love in a way diametrically opposed to what I'd just been through. There would be no love, no sex, if Jack suspected the kind of jealous hold I wanted on him.

I didn't want to be that kind of woman either. Exciting as sex had been with Noble, it was a means to an end: to ensnare him, yes, but also to put myself in that weightless, out-of-control state of rhapsodic high which I called love; but which was dependency. Until Noble, I'd prided myself on the men I'd loved—writers, architects, musicians—men who brought to my life not just sex but a vitality born of their work, which enlarged my own life. I'd grown dependent on them too, but when it was over, when we parted, I was more formed.

Looking back now, I would say I chose Noble not just to prove that I too could win a gridiron hero but because I was afraid of how independent I was becoming. If I got too big, how would I find a man to mother me? We are never totally unconscious of how ungiving these bloodless types are when we choose them; I may have been looking for someone to take care of me, but I chose exactly what I'd had in the first year of life. I was going to squeeze the love out of this dry herring that I'd never been able to wrest from my mother. Infantile omnipotence revisited. Of course, I failed.

One night I'd had a terrible dream about Noble. I saw him sitting on the toilet in his bathroom, the bedroom door open between us. There beside him on the floor were his genitals, looking like so much ugly meat, butcher-shop trimmings. I am ashamed of this dream because I don't want you to think badly of me. I include it because I've only understood its grotesqueness since reading Melanie Klein.

While I was responsible for creating my state of dependency with Noble, I had not anticipated his not wanting me; nor the rage my helplessness would arouse. I was furious at the power this man had: to give me happiness with a phone call, peace with a caress, utter bliss with his body and words of permanence. I had never had a dream of a man's butchered genitals. It terrified me.

I was very much ready for a new set of dreams. Jack loved my independence. That I got out of bed and went my way, and didn't "bug him" with questions like "When will I see you again?" It had been easy when work brought us together daily and I'd had a man to balance his woman. Now I was alone. If I could learn to be easier, take the sex and love Jack gave, and not possess, perhaps I could help him outlaw jealousy. I was certainly back on the track of "my kind of man," ready to learn.

What Jack saw in me at this crucial time in his life has always puzzled me. While he liked attractive, intelligent women, there were others around. And though he may have guessed at my sexual potential, his companion of the moment was light years ahead of me in sexual abandon. I did prove to be a quick learner. I think all my life I'd been looking for a man who would knock down those Nice Girl rules. Herein lies the answer to my question. I think my attraction for Jack was a combination of all these things. If he could get me out of my white gloves, if I was willing to lower those formidable drawing-room controls I'd been raised to think of as the very essence of being a woman, if I would follow him into all the sexual forbidden corners he'd dreamed of—no matter how taboo—and not judge or abandon him, then he would have pulled it off, experienced his sexual limits with a woman's love and approval. And no jealousy.

What value is the approval of a woman like my predecessor, who'd follow any guy anywhere? The real test was to take on a pillar of society. Like me.

I don't think any of this was conscious on his part. I knew he had lots of misgivings about taking me on for the serious experiment. It didn't take glasses to see I was possessive. But I was a student. I had the necessary heat, and I was a peer, at least starting out. In the beginning, there was no rage because there was no dependency; he might be the leader, but I brought my own dowry to the experiment.

For several months we coexisted, me and The Other Woman. It became an endurance test. I bit my jealous tongue. I did have advantages over her. I could make things happen with my contacts. I had money of my own, a paycheck that allowed me to pick up my half of the bill—or all of it, which excited him. I explored my sexual fantasies for ever wilder ideas to beguile Jack. But the time came when I could no longer tolerate finding her hairpins in "our" bed.

I got myself a magazine assignment to do a travel story on a California island. I convinced the editors that Jack was a professional photographer. Our departure brought on a jealousy attack of unprecedented proportions from The Other Woman. That morning when I picked up Jack in the limo that would take us to the airport, his glazed expression told me she'd signed her own fate.

"Drink this," I said, pouring him more champagne as the jet roared up from the February slush into the sun. First Class, all expenses paid for two weeks. Jack was awash in admiration for what I'd pulled off. In complete control of his happiness, I exuded so cool an aura of independence he pinned me in my seat. "You are the most creative, outrageous woman in the world and I can't wait to get my cock inside you."

During the months that followed, I worked to become the woman of his dreams. I was too successful. The experiment began to get out of hand. Out of my hands. Jack wanted "more." The crowd we saw in the Village were his friends. Their sex had already gone into multiples. New and wilder hallucinatory drugs appeared. When I wanted to leave the party to return to our magic dyad, I knew Jack wanted to stay and enlarge it.

He had never asked for monogamy. But I was the faithful type. Until our trip to Guadeloupe, that second winter. I'd been getting more and more anxious, frightened of what he did those evenings we weren't together. I had suspicions, fantasies. Looking back now, I don't think he wanted to leave me out. Quite the opposite. He wanted me to join him; better still, to be the one who invited others to join us. That is what the woman of his fantasies would do. I could not. I loved him in the only way I knew: one-on-one. He had brought vitality into my life. I had grown into myself, a person who never would have emerged without him. It was due to the profound sexual energies he released in me.

What I did in Guadeloupe was act like a man. Having written that sentence, let me tell you what I mean: having mobility, being straightforward, aggressive, especially sexually. As a woman, raised to wait, these are words, actions, emotions that had always *belonged* to men. But they described how I was, deep down inside.

People didn't use to talk about gender identity. Not that my emotional conflict was in the correct sense one of a confusion as to whether I was a man or a woman. What had troubled me on and off all my life wasn't fear that I was born in the wrong anatomical skin. It was that so many of my spontaneous reactions were those I had been brought up to label masculine. Temperamentally, genetically, I am not passive. It was only training in love that rendered me dependent. A basic contradiction I could live with until jealousy. Fear of loss of the beloved meant I had to "act like a man." "If you are going to fuck around with someone else, then I will too, double." I had to restore myself.

Since we'd begun, I'd felt desire for no man but Jack. I had tried, feeling his permission at my back. But when a new man responded to my cue, I retreated. Many people fear that if they are unfaithful, they will be found out and abandoned. To my symbiotic thinking, my fidelity ensured his. Projection.

Why then the young Frenchman in Guadeloupe, the soldier I picked up on the beach?" *"Bon jour,"* he said and sat at the foot of my beach towel. I knew immediately I would play it out with him. We left the beach and showered together, making love as we soaped our bodies. On the ferryboat back to the mainland, we made the most complicated plans to meet again the next day, miles away, where he would be practicing regimental maneuvers on a different beach. He had no car.

I try to avoid driving because I have no sight in one eye. It's congenital. I see flying objects where they don't exist. But I found that godforsaken beach the next day, where my soldier was playing war games. We went into the woods and fucked until his sergeant's whistle recalled the troops.

When I got back to the hotel where Jack was working on the final version of the film script he'd been rewriting since we met, he asked no questions. I offered no explanations as to where I'd been or why I'd taken up driving. The next day my soldier paid a prostitute for the use of her filthy bed. *"Pauvre Jules,"* he gasped when our hour was up and his cock lay spent in my hand. He was smiling. He led me to a restaurant in Pointe-à-Pitre which Jack and I'd never seen. It was very simple and very French. He never took his eyes off me. I paid. Then I drove him back to his barracks.

I'll never know how I found my way back across the island to the hotel. There were no lights on the dusty road, no other cars, and the night was filled with flying objects. When I discovered that Jack was not in our hotel room, I was suddenly frightened at what I had done, but I did not wish it undone. I was on a survival course. The next morning he was in the bed. We made love and drove into town. It was Mardi Gras. The streets were filled with music, drunks, and men dancing in women's clothes. The parade pushed into the bars, which emptied the drunks and dancers back into the streets. In between, my soldier and I would meet, press our bodies together in an alley, disentangle, vowing to meet again at the little restaurant. Somehow Jack and I also found and lost one another in those streets, and while my heart clutched at the various women in his arms, I left him again to share the whore's bed one last time with my soldier.

I had never risked so much. Never been so daring, let go of so many of the Nice Girl rules by which I'd lived. I was far from free of Jack, his hypnotic hold on me. It would be years before I could lie in another man's arms and not be returned to Jack, back to the man who had taught me to let go. Guadeloupe was what he'd always wanted. And not wanted. For the woman he loved to wander, to be the one who broke privacy, thus giving him loving permission to do the same. Complete expression of the nonjealous bargain.

My fantasies have always been of sex in near-public places. Not very original, I've discovered in my research. But special to women, to whom sex is so forbidden. Did it pain Jack when I lived those fantasies with my soldier, the two of us just barely out of sight, my pink Brooks Brothers shirt flagging our fucking on beaches, in woods, making bargains with whores for their beds?

Jack never asked anything. Except what did I think about getting married? He said it on the plane going home. I didn't want marriage. I didn't want to lose him. Mostly, I didn't want to lose. Whatever happened, I would leave him before he left me.

How clearly thought out I make it sound. As if I knew what I was doing. As if I had a plan. I had none. No clear understanding of my own motivations, no real evidence that Jack was up to anything. I had been living for some time with free-floating suspicions of Jack; fear of losing him. If I had been forced to give it a name, I would have said I was jealous. I was totally unconscious of how I fed it, of how much *my jealousy was projection onto him of my own desire for infidelity.*

All my life I feared men would betray me once out of my sight, out of my arms—out of my control. How could I trust them? They were free to do all the things women were forbidden. How could they *not* betray? No amount of love on their part could convince me otherwise. Fidelity had nothing to do with love. It had to do with sex, lust. Not theirs. Mine.

Which I'd never owned. I knew I was a sexual person only when men aroused me, and to the degree they did. The need to give myself in symbiotic union to one man ruled out any conscious feelings of lust for another. Certainty of the man at hand allowed me to relax; only then could I release some of my still-buried musk, drawing other men to me.

But the thrill of the forbidden was short-lived. Quickly I turned my back on the exciting stranger, fearful of gambling with the loss of Number One. There was nothing moral, ethical or even intelligent about this. I both knew and didn't know my pattern: that I had to have the tight closeness I'd never had as a child. That I was terrified of any desire to break that monogamous relationship.

I'd been raised, trained and rewarded for fidelity—to mother, to family, to Sunday School, Church, the Girl Scouts, and to those binding Rules laid down by The Other Girls. It was not guilt that kept me from infidelity. A far more honest explanation would be terror. Terror of being abandoned should I be found out. We learn lust later than symbiosis.

Had Jack been seeing other women in New York? I'll never know. But if I were a man who wanted to outlaw jealousy, I wouldn't stop the experiment with a possessive woman, no matter how good a fuck she was. By the time we reached Guadeloupe, I'd had a year of my own intense fidelity, fired by suspicions that every night he was not with me, he was having even wilder sex with an even wilder woman. From my own experience, I assumed that once a man had great sex with a woman, he would never want to leave her. He would be in love. By the time we got to Guadeloupe, I had to do what, in my mind, he was doing.

Jealousy gives the mechanism of projection full play. When the suspicious person projects his errant lust onto his partner, he wipes clean his own slate. A perfect defense. When it works, successful projection means that we who suffer from jealousy are kept safely unconscious that it is *we* who are the ones desirous of infidelity. (However, it should be remembered that calling projection "successful" does not mean it is without pathology. The process is always a distortion of reality.)

Projection explains many of life's thickets. Yet most people I interview aren't familiar with how it works. And so are deprived of knowledge that could heal their lives. For instance, let's say there is discord in the air between us. The cause may be that I hate you, but am ashamed to own up to such ugly emotion. One way I can deal with my shame and anger is to say, I don't hate you. *You hate me!*

By projecting my hatred onto you, I disown it in myself. This frees me of accusations brought from within by my superego or ego ideal. (Superego is largely the collection of rules and values we have taken in from our parents; it tells us what they want us to be. The shorthand name for it is *conscience*. The ego ideal is what we think we ought to be.)

"What are you talking about?" cries the innocent partner, who was indeed merely having a conversation with an attractive stranger at the party. But the jealous person reads in, suspects—*projects*—that something more is going on. Isn't that exactly what he would do if . . . if what? If his religious, moral, ethical code allowed, if his guilt wasn't so enormous, if his fear of abandonment (should he be found out)—and a dozen other things—didn't prohibit him from acknowledging his own sexual desires.

Our partner would not necessarily leave should we dally in casual flirtation, but in our own minds, some of us are afraid to even look at an attractive stranger. We expect our partner would be as jealously enraged as we would be. Projection again.

It is important to remember that what Hanna Segal calls "real jealousy" is not all bad. "Real jealousy," she says, "is when the love object stops loving you or is actually unfaithful. Pathological jealousy is based on something like a smile he gives someone else. What is enraging is feeling he has taken something away from you, stolen what belongs to you and given it to someone else. It is pathological to believe you should own all of the love object's smiles. People like this think possessiveness is love."

Popular magazines are beginning to write more and more about jealousy. Unable to differentiate between normal and pathological, they only add to the confusion: "Jealousy is a freak of nature. . . . It serves no purpose except perhaps to inspire some great literature. . . . Jealousy does not protect love. . . . It blinds, it warps, it distorts."[1]

No. Let me quote a more informed voice, psychoanalyst Willard Gaylin: "In normal jealousy, where you find your mate is having an affair, or is playing footsie with someone, what you are feeling is a signal. Jealousy is telling you to watch out. Something may be going wrong. That feeling of 'Hey, what's going on here, I'm being neglected,' et cetera may be alerting you to the fact that you are not examining the real world."

There is such a thing as normal jealousy. It is so important, I'd like to repeat the opening lines of Freud's 1922 paper:

Jealousy is one of those affective states, like grief, that may be described as normal. If anyone appears to be without it, the inference is justified that it has undergone severe repression and consequently plays all the greater part in his unconscious mental life. . . . There is not much to be said from the analytic point of view about normal jealousy. It is easy to see that essentially it is compounded of grief, the pain caused by the thought of losing the loved object, and of the narcissistic wound, in so far as this is distinguishable from the other wound; further, of feelings of enmity against the successful rival, and of a greater or lesser amount of self-criticism which tries to hold the person himself accountable for his loss. Although we may call it normal, this jealousy is by no means completely rational, that is, derived from the actual situation, proportionate to the real circumstances and under the complete control of the conscious ego; for it is rooted deep in the unconscious, it is a continuation of the earliest stirrings of the child's affective life, and it originates in the Oedipus or family complex of the first sexual period. . . ."[2]

Normal jealousy is what Freud called the first layer or stage of jealousy. Here is his description of *projection*, the second layer of jealousy:

> The jealousy of the second layer [after normal], the *projected*, is derived in both men and women either from their own actual unfaithfulness in real life or from impulses towards it which have succumbed to repression. It is a matter of everyday experience that fidelity, especially that degree of it required in marriage, is only maintained in the face of continual temptation. Anyone who denies this in himself will nevertheless be impelled so strongly in the direction of infidelity that he will be glad enough to make use of an unconscious mechanism as an alleviation. This relief—more, absolution by his conscience—he achieves *when he projects his own impulses to infidelity on to the partner to whom he owes faith* [emphasis added]."[3]

Freud's third layer of jealousy, the *delusional* type, "also has its origin in repressed impulses towards unfaithfulness—the object, however, in these cases is of the same sex as the subject."[4] The homosexual component of jealousy, as described by Freud, I choose to leave for a later chapter. While this third, irrational layer always arouses strong argument, Freud's lucid description of everyday jealousy and projection are rarely discussed. For this reason, perhaps, the vast majority of people I interview are unaware that some jealousy is inevitable; that the painful emotion, like a high temperature, is not "bad" but a normal reaction to a real threat. Since projection explains so much of jealousy, let me explore it more fully.

For instance, finding ourselves in a jealous situation, we have the opportunity to ask important questions: Have I been neglectful of my mate, taking him/her for granted? Have I been blind to obvious, real signs, seeing only what I want to see? If so, this jealousy is telling me that I'd better pay attention, make repairs, or I might lose what I love most. On the opposite tack, we might ask, Am I projecting my own feelings onto my beloved? My suspicion may be ruining a perfectly fine relationship because of inability to own up to desires that are inside *me*, not in my mate. Two radically different diagnoses.

It is not always jealousy that "blinds . . . warps . . . distorts," as popular magazines accuse. Projection does that. We draw the desire for infidelity up out of ourselves like so much venom and inject it into our mates.

When we are "in love," both of us love Beethoven, Chinese food, open fires . . . anything that makes us feel good, we assume makes the beloved feel good. This too is projection. Is it such a giant step to see this kind of symbiotic thinking at work when the motivation is not pleasure but fear? For instance, when a handsome stranger begins to flirt, as flattered as we may feel, our stirrings frighten us. We move away. When, ten minutes later, we see our beloved in a similarly tempting situation, we are not so sure of his fidelity. We "forget," deny our recent desire. We project what the handsome stranger stirred in us onto our mate and decide he must be planning a rendezvous. How could he, the traitor! We are good. He is bad. Jealousy.

There is another important idea in my interview with Gaylin: "The person who lives with chronic jealousy, like the coward, always lives in a life-threatening situation, even when none is there. He sees himself as vulnerable; life is a place where he's walking through minefields."

Gaylin was describing the pathologically jealous person. I told him that when I was in love, his description pretty well fit me. Unless I was totally sure of my man—in control—I was "walking through minefields."

"The pattern runs so consistently through my life," I said to him, "you would probably classify me as pathological."

"That's probably right," he said. "The fact that you choose to write about jealousy suggests to an analyst that it isn't merely pie in the sky to you. We tend to be attracted to the things that hit home. But when I say behavior is 'pathological,' I don't mean *you* are sick. Some of us have dominant emotions. I, for instance, have a lot of guilt and can be up all night for something trivial—I didn't write that letter, I didn't call my parents. But I feel very little anxiety. I feel compassion for my friends who are anxious people."

"*Paranoia*'s another word people throw around," I said. "Again, it scares people, makes them deny jealousy, diminish themselves. A lot of the Freud paper on jealousy is about paranoia."

"I think jealousy and the paranoid go hand in hand, but they are quite different. There is a sense of vulnerability in paranoia, where we are not sure of our ability to survive, nor of our integrity. That is the link between the jealous person and the paranoid. I'm using paranoid in a very delicate light. I don't mean the person who thinks everyone is out to screw him. I'm talking of a person who has a heightened sense of social humiliation, who is very sensitive to slights, ready to be hurt. It's not just a fear of being taken advantage of . . . it's a fear that you aren't going to be valued enough or properly respected. It stems from your own insecurity about the worth you have. Have you watched people in restaurants? They are always worrying that they are being given the wrong table. You'll find a very high percentage of paranoids in our society." Gaylin paused. "There are also a lot of people who experience plain old jealousy."

"My kind . . . ?"

"I never said it was a rare pathology."

Jealousy may not be a rare pathology but I am aware that most analysts —according to their own accounts—see very few patients suffering from "pathological" jealousy. Is the self-report system at fault?

For instance, when I mention my work to a thirty-five-year-old woman I have just met, she denies knowing how jealousy feels. She says it in a pleasant voice and is surprised when the man she is with raises a skeptical eyebrow. Several months go by before I see her again. It is during intermission at a concert in Carnegie Hall. "Remember what I said at dinner that night?" she says eagerly. "Well, I've been interviewing for a new job. When the application said to list my major characteristics, I wanted to put down 'Jealous, jealous, jealous.'"

She later tells me in a private interview that when she travels on business she alerts the doorman to keep track of any women who visit her live-in lover. When they go out with friends, she "goes crazy" when he stays too long at the bar, dances with other women. Therefore, they stay home a lot.

"Why did you say when we first met that you were never jealous?" I ask.

"I simply never gave my feelings that name. I am used to being in charge in my work. It carries over into my personal life. I never saw it as jealousy because as soon as I felt it, I rearranged things to eliminate it."

Professionally, economically, socially, this woman would seem to have far more power than her young lover. His power lies in the love relationship. She envies/resents his ability to make her unhappy, make her lose social poise just by talking to another woman. She constantly manipulates, constantly controls him. Consequently, she lives with a pervasive sense of guilt. Loving him, but also aware of her destructive feelings, she is forever making reparations. She introduces him to people who can help him professionally; she helps support him financially, spends hours talking to him about his career. She gives him everything but independence.

"Mrs. Klein placed a great deal of emphasis on the fact that part of love is making reparations," says Hanna Segal. "The capacity to recognize when you damage what you love, followed by the wish to repair it. But there is something I call 'manic reparation,' in which you are quite willing to repair love objects and go on repairing them forever, provided they are never completely repaired and therefore never able to leave you."

"I think parents as well as lovers constantly make these reparations," I say. "Guilty at wanting to possess their children or lovers, to control them —knowing they are limiting their lives—they throw them little gifts. But never enough so that they can make it on their own."

"And they don't know what they are guilty about," says Hanna Segal.

If the thirty-five-year-old woman in the interview above went to an analyst, most likely her complaint would be not jealousy but that she cannot find a good man. She vacillates between men twice her age and men younger than she. Inevitably the relationship ends when the older man goes back to his wife, when the younger man finds a young woman. If she didn't use the word *jealousy,* would the analyst?

In Shakespeare's time, *suspicion* was a commonly used synonym for jealousy. How many Shakespearean plots would lose all dramatic tension without the suspicious fantasy of the beloved's betrayal? Without projection? Just as shyness with strangers may be taken to the point of pathological blushing or stammering, so does jealousy for many people invisibly come to pervade all their thinking.

"I had a little paste-up job to do the other afternoon in the office," an art director of a well-known fashion magazine tells me. "Just two photos and a headline to be arranged on a piece of paper. It should have taken me three or four minutes. When I looked up at the clock—one of the two photos still in my hand, the work hardly begun—I found that a half hour had disappeared. It worried me. When I thought about it, it all came back. That half hour had been spent as if I were in a movie, a passive spectator of all kinds of pornographic cartoons about my wife and an old friend of hers she had run into lately at the supermarket. Just to remember those thoughts makes me shudder."

"Do you think any of this 'cartoon' is justified by fact?"

"I got so upset, I took a piece of paper and divided it into two halves. One half was facts; what I knew was true. The other half was made up of conclusions I drew from those facts. When it was all done, the only 'fact' I had was that she had spoken of him in what I could only think of as a special voice."

"So there is no hard evidence of infidelity?"

"No. But if you'd heard that special voice—this sounds crazy, I know—but if you'd heard the way she talked about him, you'd think something was up too."

If we should see our mate holding hands under the table with somebody else, the world would say we are well justified to be jealous. But the pathologically jealous person is suspicious when there is no "game of footsie" going on—except in his/her own fantasy. That is the mischief of projection.

Many women feel guilty if, while walking down the street, they just think of having an affair with a passing man. Instead, they project. It is not they who have these desires. It is their husbands. They construct a fantasy about the husband and his secretary. Not very Shakespearean, not very epic. But very ordinary and universal. These women are so guilty about their fantasies—which are not even conscious—that it is more comfortable to be jealous of the husband who hasn't done anything.

I have just described a traditional woman. Someone whose sense of identity comes through and from her man. As does her sexuality. *He* makes *her* sexual. The idea that her sexuality is her own is frightening. It separates her from him.

To protect themselves even further, many women bury their sexuality altogether. The Doris Day wife is born. The more important—if nonsexual—union to the husband is maintained. Neither husband nor wife understands what has happened to the sexual woman she used to be. No one can say she isn't perfectly faithful. No one can convince her that he isn't enjoying all the sex she has denied herself.

Even a woman who thinks of herself—and acts—in a highly sexual manner often finds herself suspiciously wondering what the man is up to. How could she be jealous, you might ask. She has three different lovers. "If she doesn't acknowledge that it is her initiative, her desire," Robertiello once said, "that is taking her to the bedroom so often, she doesn't own her sexuality. Women like this often think of sex as something they do to hold onto the man; so he won't go looking for it elsewhere." By projecting that sex is the man's idea, not hers, she endows him with enormous and unsatisfied desires. She is jealous.

Let us take a woman more in touch with her sexuality. She tells about her inability to choose between two men. She is a bright, attractive young social worker. One of her lovers is a social worker too. He is self-effacing, not very assertive. Sexually, he often suffers from premature ejaculation. The woman used to be his supervisor. Her other lover is an eminent surgeon. He is handsome, intelligent, very amusing and extremely rich. Part of her wants to choose the powerful, sexual man: He is everything she wants—fantastic in bed, nurturing and fun to be with. Twenty years ago, women dreamed of marrying such a man. This young woman will probably choose the man who is less powerful than she. She is more comfortable with him. She will feel free to grow in her career, develop her full potential, unencumbered by an ambivalent wish to sink back into the department role of the surgeon's wife. She may have been raised for this role, but it carries the threat of abandonment by the more powerful person.

"I love every minute with him," she says of the surgeon, "but when I am not with him, I'm always wondering what he's up to. I'm sure he loves me, but you know how women love their doctors . . ." her voice trails off. In Kleinian terms, she envies/hates the power he has over her, the withdrawal of his love that could topple her budding sense of security. The surgeon has never betrayed her, never given her the slightest indication that he would. The betrayal is in *her* mind: If she were in his place, if *she* were free to respond to beautiful adoring patients, would she resist? No.

Better to choose the other man, the one who is dependent on her. It would free her from ever being jealous again. Perhaps she will be faithful to him forever. But the unspoken addendum to her choice says that if anyone is going to stray, it will be she.

"Possessiveness is certainly a defense against jealousy," says Hanna Segal, "but it's also a defense against envy. I can allow you to be beautiful and clever and good provided you are a part of me. If you show signs of independent life, then I not only feel abandoned, but I immediately become envious of your qualities because I no longer own them."

"Is possessiveness also a control against desire to destroy the envied love object?"

"There is a link between possessiveness and projection," she says. "What you want is to own the other person's mind. You want to be inside, controlling their thoughts. This is very much a defense against envy."

"You don't want the beloved giving the goodies to anyone else. . . ."

"You don't want the object to be separate enough to be enviable."

If you own and control the good breast, your fury at its power is eased. Why would you want to destroy it?

It is hard for men to lose touch with their sexuality. Popular culture, advertising, mass media—all spend millions to reinforce male sexual fantasies. Even President Jimmy Carter admitted to lusting "in my heart" for women other than his wife. Can anyone imagine Rosalynn Carter making a similar confession in *Playgirl?* The pressure to alleviate guilt through the mechanism of projection is not the same for men and women.

While Freud used the word *projection* to describe both men's and women's efforts to protect themselves from unacceptable desires for infidelity through transference onto their mates, the key word is *unconscious.* In successful projection, we do not merely deny that we have the impulse, we are not aware there is anything to deny! We get rid of the feeling *completely.*

Melanie Klein enlarged on Freud's idea of projection by distinguishing between conscious and unconscious desires for infidelity. For instance, a man talks to me for three hours of his wife's adultery. They have been married fifteen years. He is convinced she is having an affair with the man for whom she works. Though she denies his accusation, he has evidence. Overheard telephone conversations; matchbooks from "the kinds of restaurants in which you don't do business"! Finally, with genuine self-righteousness, he says, "I guess I should know how to spot this kind of thing. Hell, I've had my share of whoring."

Is this man "safely" unconscious of his own desires for sex outside marriage? No. By accusing his wife of betraying him, he has not purged himself of knowledge of his own desires for infidelity. He makes himself sound a wronged man, but he is no innocent. A cuckold perhaps. An upholder of the double standard, certainly. The only thing he is *unconscious* of is his use of projection. He has laid his own lustful feelings on his wife, but retained them in himself as well. *It could be said the projection has failed.*

Melanie Klein calls this Projective Identification. The man does not hide his illicit desires from himself but projects them onto his wife. He does not present himself as Simon Pure. He is just as "bad" as she. In fact, even as he feels his jealousy going out toward her, it boomerangs:

"She has always been jealous of me," he says, convinced she is checking up on him. He "knows" she is as suspicious of him as he is of her.

This kind of half-successful projection is often found in fathers of young girls. They dislike every young man their daughter goes out with. Nothing will convince father that the young man is not planning his daughter's seduction at the earliest possible moment. What must be remembered here is that the father may be right, he may be wrong. The only evidence he has is projection: memory of the time when he was the young man's age and seduction of every maiden was indeed his heartfelt goal. Even more unconscious is the inevitable oedipal component, the father's own desire for his lovely young daughter. What projection does for him is to split off that part of himself that he disapproves of or is afraid to know. He puts it into the young man. And hates him for it. "I know what these young bastards are like."

Robertiello and I have endlessly discussed the difference between projection and projective identification. It is baffling. What a relief when in one of our conversations, Hanna Segal advises me to just leave Klein's term out.

"Projective identification is a broad concept," she tells me. "It still needs a lot of elucidation. In fact, it's something of a misnomer. Mrs. Klein couldn't use the word projection for what she wanted to say. Freud had used the word in a different way. So she was short a term. If I were you, I would call all of it *projection.*"

Robertiello objects, the only time he disagrees with anything in my London talks with Segal. "You can't just say 'Don't use Klein's phrase!' " he says. "Orthodox phrasing may sound like jargon but it's the shorthand by which people immersed in the field can understand each other quickly and without ambiguity." That might be the ideal. The reality is that no one agrees how much of Klein's projection mechanism is conscious, how much is unconscious. Therefore, using *projective identification* does not promote clarity. I will go against my professor's advice and follow Segal

With this important understanding: Call it what you will, the fact of projection exists. It can be best understood if we distinguish between *successful* and *failed* projection.

Successful projection: I do not wish to have an affair. You do! You treacherous rat. I am good. You are evil. My conscience is clear. This is classic Freudian projection. I have so completely split off any bad desire from myself and put it into you that I remain unconscious that I ever had the desire to begin with.

Failed projection: I know you are betraying me. While it is true that I have thought of betraying you—and may indeed have done so—right now, you are the villain. If I am bad, you are worse. In this formulation, the projection has only half succeeded. The conscience is not entirely clear, but is somehow angrily soothed by "knowing" you are guilty too. *You* carry all the guilt for what both of us have done.

There is a state between conscious and unconscious that Freud called the preconscious. This gray area, I believe, is where many women's sexuality resides. Not quite buried, not repressed, it lies there, available for projection onto the main if/when the woman refuses to own up to her own desires. But also waiting to be acted upon by the woman. Which is what happened in the women's movement. Overnight, it seemed, women became sexual.

It used to be that the double standard—the great stress on female virginity, female fidelity—protected men from uncomfortable notions that their women might have sexual appetites similar to their own. Didn't women have to be talked into sex? If they enjoyed it before marriage, "something happened" when a woman became a wife and even more so when she became a mother. Women were different from men; they didn't want, didn't need sex the way a man did. Those who did were great for a one-night stand, but not the kind of girl you took home to mother. Men's sexual fantasies have always starred the seductive woman, a queen of lust who is as hot a sexual animal as he, or hotter. These fantasies worked because they were just that: private images tucked away safely in the man's mind, under his total control. The dream, the fantasy, was so far from reality, how could a man know how frightening such a woman could be? How jealous she could make him if she should appear in real life?

Today women are no longer confined to the manless world of diapers and kitchens and the mutually inhibiting world of other women. Women move around the world—and the bedroom—with new assertiveness. Men's own favorite magazine, *Playboy*, announces a staggering finding: "The more partners a man has, the more likely he is to say that he gets enough intercourse. The more partners a woman has, the more likely she is to say that she wants *more* intercourse."[5] Industries now exist to feed women's sexual appetites. Even if a woman doesn't want it—for moral, religious, personal, ethical, whatever reasons—she now has sexual options, just like a man.

This means the death of the double standard. A forty-five-year-old man who has lived through this historic role reversal tells me that jealousy has entered his life for the first time.

Lou is also in love for the first time. Cheryl is twenty-one. A wide age gap, but hardly uncommon. What is terribly unsettling for this sexually attractive man is that when his beloved is not in his bed, he imagines her in another man's.

"I've been trying to figure out why I'm so jealous all of a sudden," he says. "I can't get her out of my mind. . . . I see her holding me, loving me, fucking me, touching me, but doing it with someone else too. If she says, 'I can't see you tonight, I'm going out,' then I automatically see her with another man. I know it shouldn't be a threat. I'm very comfortable with myself, but I just can't tolerate what I see in my mind's eye . . . even though I know it wouldn't be the same as it is between us."

"She's as much in love as you?"

"So much so that she's afraid."

"Has she been with other men since you two fell in love?"

"No, no," he quickly answers. "Not yet. But she could be. As I could be. I've gotten very involved with her on a level that I haven't experienced before in my life. It's not just sex, it's everything. She's incredibly intuitive, very bright, very sensitive about herself, about me, us. She's afraid it's going to end and she's going to be hurt, and that she'll never fall in love again."

"You're faithful to her?"

"For the first time in my life. I was married when I was twenty-two. Really dumb. I knew three years later it wasn't going to last. What happened was I got invitations from women. They'd come up to me, and I started taking advantage of it."

I believe him. He is a man who sends out sex like an invitation.

"Did your wife know?"

"She was seeing other men. I didn't know about it until we were married ten years."

"Would you call it an open marriage?"

He laughs ruefully. "The way I found out about it was she moaned this guy's name in bed one night while we were making love. When I say it wasn't an open marriage, I mean nothing was talked about out loud. I was suspicious. I think she wanted me to approve."

"Of her affairs?"

"They weren't affairs. It was just fucking. I knew one of the guys. His wife and my wife were friends. But I didn't think he was the one betraying me. I blamed it more on my wife."

"So you didn't give your approval?"

"I gave her a divorce. But don't get the wrong idea. . . . I had maybe seventeen, twenty-seven relationships during that marriage."

Every time Lou mentions what might look like an advantage a woman has over him, he quickly equalizes it, turns it around, and makes it his. During his marriage he'd had—seventeen, twenty-seven?—other women sexually. When he found out his wife had been playing the same game, and with a man he knew, he turns that into an advantage too: The man becomes his best friend. The betrayer was his wife. To protect herself from being hurt by him, by his leaving, Cheryl is seeing other men. Even as he talks about this independent move of Cheryl's, he corrects himself. He lets me know it is *his* idea. "I'm planning a retreat on her behalf." He must have all the power. All the time.

In love for the first time, he seems genuinely afraid of the power this twenty-one-year-old woman has over him. He is a strong and healthy forty-five, but not as young, as powerful, as once he was. "I have this idea," he says, "that I could die suddenly, this afternoon. My father died a few years ago, just like that. From being a very vital, alive person who was in tiptop shape, he just suddenly had a stroke. No sickness, nothing—just all of a sudden . . ." He snaps his fingers.

"Putting off mortality . . . Is that part of the attraction of a much younger woman?"

"Sure. The tight ass. All those old fantasies."

"When people get successful, they often start up with someone much younger. It's a way of going back and rewriting those earlier years. . . ."

"Exactly. It is a return to the past in a sense. Cheryl is twenty-one. When I was that age, I didn't know anything. When I'm with her now, it's like I knew then what I know now. And with her, I do know it. It's incredible."

"Were you shy when you were young?"

"Very. I didn't know where to put it. I didn't know what I was touching . . . and the fear of pregnancy! I didn't have intercourse until I was nineteen. I'd get involved with girls, and I'd always be like their best confidant, the nicest guy they met."

"Maybe that's why you're 'in love' for the first time," I say. "Maybe it's the idea of losing her that makes it so special."

"This is the first time in my life it's been this way. It was always that women fell in love with me and I was nowhere near in love with them. 'You shouldn't be falling in love with me because it isn't what I'm looking for,' I'd say. Now I'm feeling what the women must have felt. There's a part of me that's guilty for the amount of pain I've caused women. I can understand why Cheryl feels she should see other men . . . why," he corrects himself, "why I tell her she should see other men."

It occurs to me that Lou would rather lose the woman than fall more deeply in love—let it take him over, allow himself to lose control, *lose the power.* I ask him how jealousy feels:

"Threatening. A threat. Loss. Anger and pain, neck and neck. Angry at myself, angry at her. If I say to her, 'What's going on Wednesday night?' and she says, 'I'm going out,' my mind clicks onto a videotape of what I *assume* is going to happen, in the sexual sense. Our sex has been incredible, phenomenal. The loss of that, it's terrible. It underscores what I know about myself, the incapacity to stick with it. Even though I want to this time. The incapacity to commit myself. Even though I'm in love."

What does Lou mean by love? He tells me that when he was little, "I was my mother's best human being, best child, could do no wrong. I was the oldest. She was a great woman, a great athlete. My very existence was enough in her eyes. The fact that I was there and alive was all I had to do. It really fucked up my later relationships."

He knows he's a difficult man to be in love with. He has to be Number One, the Totally Adored One. The woman must reflect him positively at all times, as his mother did.

"If the infant is very narcissistic, and the mother encourages it," says Hanna Segal, "then jealousy is not merely jealousy. It is a dethronement."

Even as Lou regrets his former incapacity to love, there is braggadocio in his lament. "Poor me, I can't help it if I break women's hearts." He is so defended against loss of his position as King that he has constructed a life in which he will never again lose. There was a younger sister. Did she usurp his place in his mother's heart? All I know is that he momentarily forgets her name during the interview. The person he did lose was his mother. She died when he was fifteen.

How many other emotional sources feed what Lou calls his first and unique experience of jealousy? As in most of our lives, his jealous situation is overdetermined. What keeps him awake at night is projection: the "videotapes" that flash through his mind. He fears Cheryl is doing what he would do in her place, what he has done to other women he's betrayed in the past. He feels her jealousy coming back at him, a terrible round robin of jealous fears . . . *though neither has yet really betrayed the other.*

And there are other projections. Lou has a daughter who is exactly Cheryl's age. He knows full well how sexually aware twenty-one-year-old women are today, how much they own their sexuality. Is he projecting his daughter's sexuality onto Cheryl? As well as his own oedipal desires for a lover the exact age of his daughter? A possibility he himself brings up.

And what of the wife who betrayed him? How can he not imagine that this new woman will repeat her infidelity? Projection again. Finally, he knows that the mother he adored had been unfaithful to his father. That tells a little boy a lot about how women are. Will Cheryl do to him what his mother did to his father?

Since his divorce, Lou has enjoyed years of leaving women before they left him. Ten jealousy-free years. But his defenses no longer work. In love with a woman half his age, "so tiny she could pass for a teenager," he feels the rejuvenating shot of sexual adrenaline middle-aged men have always enjoyed in the company of younger women. But very young women used to be faithful to the "daddies" whose power protected them. Even if Cheryl is faithful, how can a man with Lou's experience not project his feelings onto her and be jealous?

I agree with Freud that fidelity, "especially that degree of it required in marriage, is only maintained in the face of continual temptation." Without putting any value judgment on monogamy, could it not be said that the more *conscious* we are of our desire for fidelity *and the temptations away from it*, the more responsible we can be for our decisions?

Let me tell you what I have come to think about my jealousy. As I become more aware of what I really want and feel, jealousy has less power over me. Understanding reality better, I have less need to control others. The more I own up to my own ambition, ability, desire, and drop those Nice Little Girl Rules that are false for me, the less I have to deny, suppress and thus project onto others what I want but cannot allow myself to admit. I do not so much feel these days that I am "walking through minefields." That is, on good days. There are bad days too.

When we are little and experience the jealous situation, we learn how to avoid being blown away. We must. We devise defenses against any further jealous situations. Walking through minefields demands a lot of control. Who wants to admit he is in such jeopardy? Small wonder so many jealous people deny they are.

The woman I am going to tell you about almost didn't appear in this book. She told me she was not jealous. I believed her. She was so self-contained, sure of herself in a way that lent her great mystery.

"Jealous?" the man beside her said. "Beth is paranoid on the subject!" Puzzled, I looked from him to her. Was he calling her bluff?

"No, no, I didn't say she was jealous," he quickly corrected the misunderstanding. "What I meant was that if I just say 'What did you do last night?' she tells me not to be a fucking concierge. She's very jealous of her privacy."

His name is Frank. He was clearly in love with her. Her calm, her "privacy," made it hard to know exactly what she felt for him. "If I even sniff it in the air, jealousy, I never see that person again," she said. She did not look at Frank. He understood the rules. That was when we first met. It is different now, six months later.

I was wrong about all that calm control. And Beth was wrong about herself: She is jealous. But even now when she cannot sleep, when her suspicion is about to destroy the relationship, she will not use the word. To be jealous is to admit that someone has power over you, that you are not in control. Beth is in love.

Now it is she who telephones Frank: Where was he last night? When his hoarse voice tells her he was up late, she dies inside. There are fights, tears, accusations. Frank loves her but he isn't sure how much of her vigilance he can take.

She doesn't want to lose him. Today she wants to talk about this thing called jealousy, which she prefers to call "a sense of insecurity."

"It's not jealousy per se," she says. "What causes this bad feeling in me —this is real hard; I've never said it out loud before—is not knowing where I stand in relation to him and his view of other women. If that's jealousy . . . but isn't a better word *insecurity?*"

"It feels like a blow to your self-esteem?"

"No, I think I'm a pretty nice person. Worthy, important, to myself . . . but I don't know if other people realize it. . . ."

"Has Frank actually done anything to make you feel . . . insecure?"

"In my mind's eye, he did. Frank's an affectionate, *physically* affectionate person. Women are always coming up to him, putting their arms around him, and these people are just casual friends. . . . I mean bar women!"

Frank is a local bartender. "If this is how he is with *them,*" I say to her, "you must wonder how that makes *you* look."

"Exactly! I think to myself, If I did that, that would not be casual. There would be a helluva lot more going on there than meets the eye. He's so different from the way I act with people that I guess I put my own motivations on him—if that makes sense."

Beth is thirty-four. She owns her own small real-estate firm. She deals with people all day, in her cool, distancing way. It is easy to see the attraction for her of a warm, easygoing man like Frank. He is fifty and has been through two marriages. Frank wants life to be simple now, and thought he'd made it that way by choosing this younger woman, who seemed so undemanding and nonpossessive. "Say you see Frank driving in a car, with another woman," I say. "In your mind . . ."

"Where is he going? Why didn't he tell me he was doing that? Who is

that woman? How does he know her? I've never seen that woman before.
. . ."

"Are you thinking, I know what he's up to because if I was in that car, I
know what I'd do next?"

"Oh, yeah. I've said that to him and he tells me I've got to stop infusing
my interpretations on his behavior."

"In your jealous fantasy, he's doing what you would do if you were he.
That's projection."

"Rejection?"

"*Pro*jection."

She nods, accepting, understanding. I'm taken aback by her candor. I
can see she is telling me these things because she wants to understand. It
is indeed very hard for her to admit to such humiliating feelings. I ask her
if she believes Frank when he tells her he is totally faithful to her. I believe
him. He's as open as she is closed.

"I don't think anyone is the faithful type. Yes, I've known women
who've been faithful, not men. Men never are. And I am not, as a rule.
I'm faithful, monogamous, until the relationship doesn't feel good. It gets
boring or I'm not getting the feedback that I need from the other person.
The excitement is not there. There's no communication. Whatever happens to a relationship after three or four years."

"Then you're no longer faithful."

"When I was young and not a wise woman, I was not jealous. I began
showing strong feelings of jealousy, maybe five years ago. In the last serious relationship. It was being so trusting of him and finding out in the end
that I had no reason to be trusting. I lost all security. I learned not to trust.
Not feeling jealousy—not being concerned about what the other person
was doing—was a foolish way to be."

"Becoming wise meant . . . ?"

"Knowing the nature of the beast. That fidelity is not to be counted
on."

Beth was married at nineteen to a man who was "smotheringly jealous."
I ask her if that was part of the attraction, being prized so much.

"I think I was too dumb at nineteen to know I had options," she says.
"He was the boy I'd dated in high school and when you date someone for
two years and you sleep with them, then you get married. My parents
were moving and he said, rather than do that, let's get married."

"Some alternative to moving house!" I say.

We both laughed.

"I don't think I was that thinking a person then, Nancy. I don't think I
had reasons for doing things. I just drifted into marriage."

"Was his jealousy a problem in the marriage?"

"It was burdensome. But I didn't know that people weren't supposed to be that way."

"Did you do things to arouse his jealousy?"

"I was true blue."

The marriage lasted three years. Before Beth allowed herself to get into another serious relationship, she made the man promise the fidelity she told him she needed.

"He agreed," she says. "He gave his word. But he lied about it. He worked at home and I knew there were things going on with this woman next door, but he would never admit it. I really loved him. I couldn't stand the pain of knowing I wasn't enough for him."

"Would you say what you felt was a feeling of betrayal?"

"For me it is the fact that the other person doesn't value me as much or in the same way as I value him," Beth says, switching to the present tense, which obviously includes Frank. "They do not find exclusivity necessary, vital to a relationship, as I do. That causes me extreme jealousy. Does that make sense?"

"Is it, If I'm going to be faithful, then you must be too?"

"No. It's more. It's, I don't think you can really love me unless you want to be monogamous. Jealousy means . . . if you make me feel this way, that means I'm not as important to you as you say I am. You don't need me enough. You're enough for me. If you make me jealous, then you don't think I'm enough for you and we're out of kilter."

"In that last relationship, when you learned 'the nature of the beast' . . . what did you do?"

"I told him that I'd met another man. That I was going to start seeing him. He became so jealous, he locked himself in the bedroom with a gun. He swore he'd never see another woman. But I never trusted him, or anyone else again."

"How about your own sexuality? Are you conscious of what you really want sexually?"

"I was always very aware of my sexuality. I began masturbating very young, maybe six, seven. My mother caught me doing it one day, swinging on one of those low kitchen-cabinet doors. I'd put a towel over the door and straddled it. I didn't hear her come into the house. . . . It was bad!" Beth half sighs, laughs. "She yelled at me and told me she was going to tell my sister."

"Your sister!"

"She was the beautiful daughter. She was the cheerleader. The golden girl. She's eight years older. We've never gotten along well. There was always rivalry. I thought she was the perfect daughter. She always thought

I was allowed to do whatever I wanted with my life. She was the one who got married, had three children . . ."

"Followed the script. The good daughter. You're the one who got away."

"She was so good she got knocked up at sixteen!" says Beth. "She thinks she gave her life away. She looks at me and she's still jealous."

"Were you pretty as a young girl?"

"No. Oh, no. I had a jawbone—a malformed jawbone that made my face—it was a malocclusion. I took it for granted from the time I was very young that I was not pretty."

"Having a very beautiful sister can be hard. Even little girls know they've missed out on something. . . ."

"No, it was never a consideration for me because all the pretty girls I knew, I thought they were silly. They didn't have . . . they weren't as smart as me. Perhaps I have a poorly defined realization of the importance of beauty."

"Unattractive kids . . . we develop other talents, more lasting ones, to make up for the lack of beauty. . . ."

"I look at pictures of myself back then and I don't think I was that bad-looking. It's strange. I think they, my mother, did me a disservice. It was she who made me feel I was not attractive. She was beautiful, like my sister. And sexy. Though she didn't acknowledge it. She showed no sexuality. She was not a role model for me."

"Were your parents happy?"

"No. I know now that my father, well, he traveled a lot, and there were other women. I'd always thought my father was a man of steel morals. Until he told his 'war stories' to my ex-husband."

"There must have been a lot of jealousy flying around that house."

"All unacknowledged. But sure, I must have been very aware of my mother's jealousy."

"Recently I interviewed a woman," I say, "and the first thing she said was, 'I learned my jealousy from my mother. My father always made her jealous and it was from her that I learned not to trust men.'" Beth nods her head. I ask her how old she was when she had intercourse for the first time.

"Thirteen. With a twenty-two-year-old man. No, it was not a good experience because I was so young and didn't know enough not to let it happen. We were on a date, necking, and it just progressed. I was frightened. No, he didn't coerce me. I got right into it. I felt like I was in over my head, drowning. Not because he was bigger and older, stronger. It was my own sexuality that frightened me."

"You got 'swept away.' You really wanted to do it?"

"Yes, I did. But I was so anxious afterward, about pregnancy, that I'd put myself in such jeopardy. My sexual feelings frightened me. I never got close to anyone again, until my husband. I learned to trust myself sexually in time, but men . . . take Frank . . . the more seriously I become involved with him, the less easy it is to have a relationship. The more I love him, the less I can trust him."

"How about if he didn't work in a bar, wasn't always around women?"

"You mean if he was a banker? It wouldn't make any difference because he could still . . . It might even be worse because I couldn't see him in his business. I couldn't see how he acted with people. And wondering how he was acting could be worse than being there and watching him do it."

For months now, Beth has spent her evenings sitting at the bar where Frank works. He works nights, she days; but she's there—sitting at the bar —often until closing. When she doesn't see him, when she can't monitor and control everything because she has to stay home and work, the sort of thing happens that almost ended their relationship two weeks ago.

It was Frank's night off and when she said she couldn't join him, he said he'd probably go and have some drinks with friends. The next morning his whiskey voice told her it had been a long night. He told her he'd gone to one bar and then another, where he'd run into a mutual woman friend and her girlfriend and they'd all finished the night on brandy. "End of story," says Beth. "And I say to him, 'Did the two women go into the other bars with you?' And he said, 'No, the one went home.' I said, 'What about the other one?' He said, 'Yeah, she came with me to the other bar.' And I said, 'How did she get there?' 'I drove her,' he said. I said, 'Oh, how'd she get home?' 'Well, I drove her home.' And I went up in a blue light. I was furious, couldn't work. I had to close the office and go to his place. We had a terrible fight. . . ."

"What did you accuse him of?"

"He hadn't told me everything! I had to pry it out of him! If he had told me, it would have been different. He said he hadn't told me about driving her home because he knew I'd get upset. I said, 'Frank, I only get upset when you don't tell me everything and I have to ask questions. What if I ask the wrong questions? What if I had not said, How did she get to the other bar, how did she get home?"

"Does it ever occur to you that he's just driving her and not fucking her?"

"It's beginning to. I don't think he did fuck her. But when he doesn't tell me, it's like he's lying to me. It suggests there is something he's trying to hide. . . ."

When Frank doesn't tell Beth everything, when she can't watch his every move, when she can't control him, the things he leaves out—which she calls lies—encourage her to "infuse my interpretations on his behavior." To project. Is he doing what she would do? What she has done to other men? What other men have done to her? What her father did to her mother? Beth says her history of not trusting people/men began five years ago. But her life is filled with half-buried memories of loss and betrayal, of feeling left out of the special relationship between her "beautiful, sexual" mother and sister, a relationship that she was born into, of rivalries with the sister and her two brothers, memories of parents who betrayed one another, and her too.

Like many children, Beth learned that her control would avoid the pain that ran like an artery through her life. When she fell in love for the first time, Beth lost her control. And learned "the nature of the beast." "The more seriously I become involved with Frank," she says, "the less easy it is to have a relationship." All the promises of fidelity in the world aren't going to put her fears to sleep. It seems there is no way she can fall in love and not be jealous.

She says what she wants is honesty. Even if Frank had sex with another woman she could live with it—*if he told her.* Perhaps. "How can I be a jealous person," she pleads with me, "how can jealousy be my problem if I can handle that?" It is as if I can exonerate her from an admission she hates. The admission that love gives someone else so much power over her.

"It's not knowing, it's the unknown that's frightening," she says. What is known can be controlled. Left with the unknown, her fantasies are worse than reality. How can she count on his fidelity when she cannot count on her own?

Beth splits the man she loves into the Good Frank—who doesn't arouse her envy and jealousy—and the Bad Frank, who does. In this she is like the infant who cannot long maintain the notion that he hates the mother he loves. "Splitting comes to infants very naturally," says Hanna Segal. "Especially since they have little integration. The baby has the problem of needing the breast, wanting its love but at the same time feeling that the breast maliciously wants to withhold, which means death to the child. So the baby creates the fantasy of what Mrs. Klein calls the good breast and the bad breast. In this way he tries to keep his good feelings in relation to a good object. He maintains the good mother."

"And the integrated person, the grown-up . . . ?"

". . . allows the good beloved to have some bad characteristics, and the bad beloved to have some good ones."

"In other words, the object is allowed to be integrated too."

"Otherwise, the relationship does not last."

"It's filled with too much unreality."

"Yes."

"So you can allow your beloved to talk to an attractive person without
. . ."

". . . without wanting to kill. You can suffer jealousy, you can be angry, but your world doesn't come to an end. If you have sufficient internal
integration, you don't have to possess the other person."

I tell Mrs. Segal how many of the people I interview admit they cannot
bear the beloved to have too much happiness with someone else.
"Wouldn't you find that more in adolescents?" she says.

"There are an awful lot of adolescents who are forty years old," I say.

"Yes," she laughs. "A lot of forty-year-old adolescents."

Projection. You learn a word and wonder how you got along without it.
What did I use to call the mechanism that word describes? Ah, but that is
the beauty, the mischief of projection. We don't know what we're doing if
the defense is working perfectly. How could I understand so much of my
jealousy when projection was not only successfully defending me from my
own desires for infidelity but laying them on my mate instead?

There was no mention of projection in the fifty-page outline for this
book. Once understood, I never questioned it. I remember the talk several
years ago with Robertiello when I "discovered" it all by myself. "That's
called projection," he said. The name gave me an intellectual grasp on an
emotional mechanism I both knew and didn't want to know. With just a
word, he had given me an increase in power over my life.

The symbiotic person does a lot of projecting. Which is more or less
what I was saying to Robertiello that day: "When you lose your identity in
the person you love, it's frightening to accept the idea you are sexually
attracted to someone new. So when he walks out onto the terrace with the
beautiful other woman, you're convinced he's having it off with her behind the bushes because that's what you would like to do!"

"Nancy, with all your problems about not being separate, you're a helluva lot more in touch with your sexuality than a lot of women. Maybe you
don't know that. There are a lot of women who just want the symbiotic
relationship."

It occurs to me that if I made the mistake at the beginning of this book
of thinking that Robertiello was like me—jealous—because of our intellectual symbiosis, could it be that he has been projecting his envy onto me?
After all these years, I think we are mixed up in one another's heads. All
that vehemence about *my* nasty, killing, envious nature, while he remained Simon Pure.

He is in session when I telephone to ask about this but he gets back to
me between patients. We make an appointment to meet.

"I've been reading back over years of interviews," I say, "and it's suddenly struck me that there's a certain projection on your part regarding Nancy and her envy!"

"Yeah, well, I'll buy that." Just like that, he says it.

I am relieved, and as always, struck by his flat-out honesty. But I am miffed too. I took a lot of abuse.

"I don't mean your envy of me," I explain. "I'm talking about how in the beginning you denied you were envious and were extraordinarily vehement about *my* envy. Yes, I am envious, but you were, well, almost accusatory in your pronouncements against me. You unloaded all your stuff onto me."

"Yes. I understand. I was saying that you, Nancy, are the envious one, not me."

"So! How about grandiosity? There were several days, you were just out of control about *my* grandiosity. While you owned none!"

"Yeah, well, that's a good example of projection. I don't doubt I did it. It's perfectly reasonable."

"Even my editor remarked on it when she read the last draft. In the margin she wrote that the way you put down my apartment—like I had a lot of nerve living in a 'palace.' It made her wonder where *you* were coming from. 'What's wrong with wanting to live in a beautiful place?' she said. 'He's the one who sounds envious. . . .' "

"Sure. Fine. I might have been envious of you and so I put you down for being that way."

"You didn't just project your envy onto me, you also denied your grandiosity. By projecting *that* onto me too!"

"You and I both have our share of archaic grandiosity. . . ."

"You admit there could be some of that in you too?"

"Well, of course!"

"Oh, Richard, how far you've come!" I laugh. He smiles.

"Look, we both try to do that, to re-create what we missed out on when we were little," he explains. He is his old lucid self, no longer competitively putting me down. In control of this material as though it had never been repressed for almost sixty years.

"Take my anger at women," he says.

"—and your fear of them too," I cut in. "Don't you fear angry women?"

"And how I do!" he agrees. "A lot of that is—if you will allow the term —projective identification. I put my rage onto them, and then I'm afraid it'll come back and they'll kill me. I'm petrified of that. It's mostly connected with primitive rage."

"There's a certain reality in it. You act so awful; you're so cruel to the woman once you leave her."

"That's projective identification again. I just cut off from the woman completely. I'm so scared to death of her rage that I am almost phobic about her. I have to put as much distance between us as possible."

"Have you ever felt like that about a man?"

"Yes. These projective mechanisms aren't always about jealousy, nor do they work only across the sexes. I remember one night a guy double-parked and kept me from a concert I was going to. When he came out, I found myself rolling up the window and locking my door."

"He wasn't a rival? Was a woman involved?"

"No, no. Just a guy who double-parked and stymied me. Even as I was locking my car door, I was wondering, What the hell am I doing? I mean, I could go out there and beat the shit out of him. Why am I going into this cowardly position? Then I realized that I was cowering because I was afraid that if I ever got out of my car, I would have killed the son-of-a-bitch. I was afraid of my own aggression—and therefore, saw it in him."

"Do you think that explains your cruelty to a former wife or lover . . . that you see your own cruelty in her?"

"She becomes the primitive witch. She's going to destroy me. I have to get away from her. I don't think it is because I am innately cruel. It is because I fear her. To the woman, I may seem cruel. She feels destroyed because she's not only losing me as a lover, but also losing a friend, a confidant. . . ."

"Come on! She's losing the whole magic thing you promised her. Just when she came to depend on it, when she needed it most, you took it back!"

"When you put it like that, I can understand her fury. I've felt like that about people who did it to me. You're talking about breaking promises. Like momma. That's what she did to me."

"Well, if we're talking about how you deal with women, we have to start with the first one."

"I'm still enraged at my mother," he says. "When I'm in a room with her, people tell me the hate is so strong they want to run out the door. And I don't even know about it!"

I tell him about a woman I recently interviewed who had just ended a passionate love affair. "She and the man had been equally possessive. In fact, they relished the intensity that their jealous demands gave the relationship. As long as they were together, they protected each other and never did numbers to arouse the other's anxiety. When she ended it, she was convinced he was going to kill her.

"She called all their friends and alerted them not to answer any questions of his about her movements. She told the doorman she did not want him allowed in the building. When she heard his voice on her answering machine, terror gripped her. She left town for several months. In fact, he never threatened her, never made an attempt to hurt her in any way. It was all in her mind that he would do her physical harm if he found her. What is interesting is that at the same time, she told me she felt his pain so deeply, she wept for him and wanted to hold him in her arms like a baby."

"Two projections," says Robertiello. "I understand her emotions very well. When I break up with someone, I'm scared of what she'll do to me. Like, my momma destroyed me by cutting me dead—especially after she promised in one way or another that she would always be there for me. That's the promise she made before my sister and brother were born. Then she acted as if she had never made it. It's the broken promise, no matter how trivial, that drives me crazy."

"Hanna Segal says that we all take mother's early care as a promise. She quoted a great line from a book by Romain Gary. It went something like 'At the dawn of our lives, mother gives us a promise that is never fulfilled. . . .' "

He sighs. "You know, Romain Gary committed suicide. Look, you and I are not so different from each other in this. We were never responded to sufficiently, as if we were the adored Christ Child, when we were little and needed to be. So we're always looking for that fantasy to be fulfilled . . . for people who will put us in that category."

"The admiration and adoration you didn't get as a child . . . you have to feel that you are one of the best analysts in town. . . ."

"Who can say who's the best? There's no reality yardstick."

"You have a whole gang of people who think you are."

"Yes."

"Like me."

"I'm glad to hear that."

Friends.

We make a date to meet again in two days. When we do, I ask him to elaborate on the link between symbiosis and projection.

"I have a couple whom I see separately. The woman is always imagining the guy being unfaithful, and the guy never even brings it up. From time to time, the woman thinks of having an affair with a colleague. In fact, the guy is faithful and doesn't think of other women. He is never concerned about her being unfaithful and she is always concerned about his being unfaithful."

"The woman doesn't know it's *she* who wants the sex. . . ."

"If I push her hard enough, she admits it. It's a very important idea.

Biologically, any individual woman can have as much sexual desire as any individual man. Social forces and how she's raised make a woman put these sexual feelings away someplace."

"Often, onto the man. It makes you wonder about the effect on men's behavior. If a woman begins by expecting him to be unfaithful—'That's how men are'—and then accuses him of having the sex she can't allow herself to have . . .'"

"I used to feel that a lot. One of my wives was extremely jealous. She thought I was fucking everyone who came into this office. And I was totally faithful to her! I resented that. If I'm going to be accused of it anyway, I might as well do it. To be accused of something unjustly makes you want to do it. It's that self-fulfilling prophecy thing. A guy might not even think of screwing another woman, but he comes home and if his wife keeps saying, Who have you been screwing?, it puts the idea in his head. And, besides, he's mad at her for the unjust accusation."

"Bill once wrote a story about a man who keeps telling his woman he loves her and she keeps saying, 'No, you don't,' until finally he says, 'You're right. I don't love you.'"

"If your feelings aren't acknowledged, whether it's love or fidelity, it gets you angry. Finally you say, Fuck her, I won't be faithful to her. If she doesn't give me points for being faithful when I am faithful, then I might as well do it. I'd say most of the women I've been with—affairs, marriages, casual relationships—there's always an expectation that I'm going to cheat on them."

"I don't think most men really get what's behind the form of women's jealousy expressed through projection. How can a man understand the degree of hands-off sexual training a woman goes through? It's hard enough for her to admit she wants one man. To want two is unthinkable."

"Even today most women haven't got past all that stuff that puts polygamy in a negative light. But underneath, who doesn't want variety? So they make their men polygamous in their fantasy. Projection."

"Off the top of your head, Doctor, are you worried Susan is screwing somebody else?"

"Never. She's worrying that I'm screwing you during this interview."

"My goodness."

"And it's not like it's just her. Almost any woman I've been with would think like that. And I never think that, even when they are screwing somebody else. A man doesn't have to project his desires, his lust. He feels it and acts on it."

"You don't mean men act on every impulse towards infidelity. . . ."

"No. But the impulse isn't taboo. He's acted on enough of his sexual desires not to feel he has to anxiously suppress his sex and project it onto her to protect himself. There are very different dynamics for male and female sexual jealousy. Male jealousy is *not* based on projection and female is. . . ."

"Hold it!" I say. "We're talking about a matter of degree here. Also, you're forgetting Freud. You're leaving out men's projection of their forbidden homosexual desires, where the man has jealous fantasies of his woman with another man: 'It's not *me* who wants him,' the jealous husband defends himself. '*She* does.' "

"Nobody believes that Freud stuff anymore. . . ."

"For God's sake, Richard, you're not going to desert me again. . . ."

"But that 1922 paper—I mean, it's bullshit. I know it's bullshit for me. I've had fantasies of other men . . ."

"You have? You never told me . . ."

"And I *know* they're not about homosexual desires."

CHAPTER SIX

Competition

I knew a woman who slept easily at night and moved gracefully through the world by day, happy in the reflection of her husband. The protective umbrella he offered was enormously satisfying: dark good looks, professional stature that grew steadily through the years together. Eighteen of them. His suits were tailored by Huntsman of London, Turnbuller and Asser made his shirts, and though her clothes were pretty, they were demure, quiet. The way she looked complemented him.

The arrangement seemed to work, a mutual bargain; over the years he fulfilled his potential in the spotlight which her deliberate soft-focus presence afforded him. He became more articulate and sure of himself. A certain shyness he'd had as a boy was overcome as the resonance of his voice and his fine sense of humor drew respect from people around him. He had chosen his partner wisely: a woman content to let him grow and shine. She was content. They were content. Things had never been better. Until that eighteenth summer, when another woman sidetracked him off the serene course of their marriage.

It happened one weekend. The wife was absent. It should have been mended by the next. But so meager was her vision of herself, so accustomed to gaining strength, her very existence through him, that she didn't know how to fight for herself. Without him she had no center. Oh, I'm sure she'd won her share of arguments when they were alone, in the kitchen, in bed; more than anyone she knew the uncertain boy at his core. But the entrance of a rival turned her back into the little girl; one who'd been taught to acquiesce when there was a third party. A triangle. She had no talent for competition, no practice. Faced with the possibility of loss, she saw no chance of winning.

I'm sure that was in part why he had chosen her. He was easily made jealous, couldn't afford a woman who provoked it. To look to him, one would have thought he could stand a peer. He was so physically and intellectually brilliant. But he knew his limits and the emotional room he required to become and remain the man he seemed. There wasn't time in his life for the consuming distractions of jealousy's fires. The fat little boy he'd once been still didn't quite believe in the handsome skin he'd grown into. For his maturation, he needed a gentle woman's presence, not beauty's power.

Then suddenly, the way things happen, the status quo of eighteen years changed dramatically. Their second child followed the first to boarding school. The son's leaving hadn't affected him, but he loved his daughter dearly and missed her presence. Now for the first time in their marriage, they were alone. Her role as mother ended, she looked wistfully to him for direction. He encouraged her first tentative moves to become a photographer's representative, working out of their apartment.

With his full support and assistance (there is nothing rational about this story), she mailed out the brochures he had written for her. Magic of all magics, agencies asked to see her client's work. She was suddenly in business, moving around the world, making and meeting appointments. She began joining the conversation at dinner parties, voicing opinions different from his. When men spoke to her now, she smiled back, interested, interesting. He hadn't foreseen how these changes would affect him in his fortieth year; who does? In that timeless moment when his image of himself wavered in his own eyes, a glamorous woman appeared. Quickly, the twinge of uncertainty he'd felt was forgotten in the blaze of her vision of him as male, dominant and sexually desirable.

The newcomer was formidable. Whatever the husband may have thought entering this dalliance, she had her own immediate plans for them both. She abandoned her husband literally overnight, and announced to her lover she intended to follow him when he left their idyllic Vermont retreat.

He was a gentle man, responsible, guilty. He was at a loss, half looking back over his shoulder for the partner he'd loved and relied on for eighteen years to come and get him; perhaps more than half overwhelmed and flattered that such a woman could be so aggressive in her desire for him.

Did this clever newcomer recognize a man in flux, nest empty, role as father/provider in question? What she did was make herself totally dependent on him: "My husband says I will never see my children again," she said. Upon such notions of operatic despair and life-wrecking guilt are these stories made. Her self-wrought dependence on him was her strength. He was no match for her determination.

Nor was his wife. Her emergence as someone in her own right was too recent, had been too brief to stick. It was as if it had never happened. She came apart, torn so violently by pain and rage that she could take no action. "How can I get him back?" she cried, but all ideas, all suggestions were futile. How could she compete? She felt herself defeated from the start.

Had she confronted the problem head on, had she fought, shown the kind of self-confidence and determination the rival displayed, demanding the rights the other woman did not yet possess, I believe she would have him still. For instance, had she "forgiven" him and, in the name of their eighteen years together, asked him to give their marriage another try, I think he would have done it. Had she taken a lover (as a friend suggested), or led him to believe she had, he might have returned. Jealousy would have been the excuse, the catalyst he needed to reclaim the life he knew fit him best. This other woman was too aggressive, too handsome, too outspoken; too much his equal. In guts she outstripped him. She hung in there. He surrendered.

Something that should never have happened—I say in my Olympian detachment as storyteller—was over before any real struggle took place. The only time the wife flew into action was at one of those MGM coincidences, when all players ended up at the same restaurant one evening. The betrayed wife's companions tried to avoid the confrontation. "No!" she cried, breaking away and dashing back into the restaurant. "I want to *see* her!"

("Every woman I've known who has a problem of jealousy," says an analyst, "always wants to see the rival. She has to know what she looks like. It is the most important thing, to *see* the other woman.")

The wife made some last tearful, desultory swipes at his guilt, which was enormous. She abandoned her small business to resume her old accustomed, dependent position. In the end, her fury and revenge focused—at the suggestion of her lawyer—on his wallet. He set up house with the new woman, put on weight, lost much of his ebullient charm and a business promotion. Today, he scrambles for blood money to pay a woman he'd never intended to abandon while he lives with a future that was meant to be only a sexual dalliance.

Faced with a rival in love, threatened with loss, why do some of us fight, others fade?

Where does the competitive spirit come from? Why is it so highly developed in some, not at all in others? Equally important, why do some of us have it in certain situations—sports or work—but lose it so often when faced with a rival for the person who means life itself?

"Competition is one of the actions you might reasonably take following jealousy," said psychologist Martin Hoffman. "You could compete with the rival for the person you love." I'd gone to see Hoffman, a colleague of Dan Stern's, several years ago. I didn't yet have a form for this book, didn't know what to leave out, what to put in. The subject of competition, and its relation to jealousy, was one of the darkest enigmas. I'm beginning to see now why Hoffman's seemingly unexceptional statement has stayed to puzzle me for so long. "You could compete with the rival for the person you love," he had said. I could not.

I can compete in everything but love. Intimacy is my bread. Faced with a rival, why then don't I challenge her? Or him? It is how I've always been: a winner on the baseball diamond, in a game of cards. In a jealous situation, a loser a priori.

Nothing has yet happened. There may be only a whiff, the merest scent of suspicion. My heart freezes over, a subjective feeling of defeat. Defeated by whom? The rival, the beloved? In a way it has nothing to do with either of them. A memory has been aroused, a pain earlier than the one facing me. A pain so primitive that people like me try to construct life so as never to feel it again. The "it" is often called jealousy. For people who cannot compete in love, what we are avoiding isn't so much jealousy as losing again.

It would be misleading to say that the woman in the story above was not competitive. She and her husband often played tennis together. At first, he had always won. Perhaps she wanted him to. In time her game improved. She was more sure of him, of his love. She enjoyed beating him, safely releasing some of the anger that accrues in the happiest dependencies, in a ferociously fought singles match. Afterward, she would lovingly tease him. He could never lose gracefully. But the day always ended well. After all, in their life together, he held all the aces. Since her identity came through his, that is how they both wanted it. His power was hers.

It is important to remember that while he had chosen her for her sweet passivity, she wasn't just a cookie on a plate. She had chosen him too. While she may have envied the power he had over her life—it was total—

she had been raised to be taken care of. Eighteen years ago she had responded to him because she recognized his need/love of a woman like herself. In his own way, he was dependent on her, jealous of other men who admired her quiet prettiness. This pleased her, made her want to be even more that way. Because he was the kind of man who would never leave her, she wanted to be ever more his kind of woman.

Having invested her life in this man, knowing him far better than her opponent, why didn't she plant herself between them in that restaurant, look the other woman in the eye and declare, "He is my husband. The father of our children. Just try to get him away from me!" And then lead him home. He would have followed her. She *knew* that. Something earlier than symbiotic need of him destroyed her courage; something earlier than a sense of her importance to him wiped out her self-esteem.

The point I would like to stress is that she had a *right* to be jealous. "The social function of jealousy," writes sociologist Helmut Schoeck, "[is] mainly to stimulate defensive behavior whenever an interpersonal relationship . . . is threatened or disrupted by a trespasser not admitted by the culture as a legitimate rival."[1]

Exactly what psychological force rendered the wife unable to act?

Freud tells us that sexual rivalry gets its fire from the oedipal years when the child finds himself at one corner of a triangle, mother and father at the other two. How adults respond to the jealous situation, to the possibility of losing someone we love, is patterned in this competitive struggle. It begins in the third or fourth year of life and ends about age seven. Freud applied this to both sexes. General psychoanalytic opinion today is that the theory is more satisfying and complete when applied to males.

The little boy is strongly attracted to mother. He wishes to defeat father and have her for himself. This arouses fear of retaliation from the bigger man, which Freud called "castration anxiety." But it is not that simple. While the boy wants to beat out father, he also loves the older man. He needs him as an ally and model in his battle to separate from mother, for formation of a sense of self, to reenforce gender identity as a counterweight to his aggressive, libidinal drives. Mixed feelings. The boy is guilty.

Optimally, the oedipal complex is not resolved out of fear and guilt alone. When things are right within the family, mother should be able to convey to her son, in words or attitude, "I like you very much, darling, and you are an attractive boy. Even though I know you want me—and paranthetically, it is all right to want me—I want your father more. You should have no trouble going out and finding a girl your own age."

From his corner of the triangle, father must also acknowledge what is going on. Ideally, he is not too competitive with the boy, neither silent nor withdrawn. He lets the son know he is aware that there is a rival in the house. However, contrary to the boy's fears, father doesn't resent the competition. While reinforcing mother's message that his son will have to find a girl of his own, father proudly lets the boy know that his sexual emergence shows he is "a chip off the old block."

If father and mother both do their parts in recognizing the boy's competitive sexual desires, they ease his anxiety. The terrible fear that only one man can win and the other must suffer is tempered. While he has lost this contest with father, he may well win the next one. Mother still loves him. Father admires his competitive spirit. A general live-and-let-live spirit reigns in the family. "I'll let Daddy have Mommy," the boy feels. "I'd rather have her, but if I can't, I'll get my own girl."

One psychiatrist I know, aware of his six-year-old daughter's seductive behavior with him, and of his wife's unspoken competition with the girl, actually had such a talk with his daughter. "The next week, she fell in love with the little boy who sits next to her in the first grade."

But aren't there rivalries earlier than the sexual? Contemporary theory has come to recognize that by age three or four a child has already won and lost countless competitions. To the baby, anything that takes mother's eye away from him is an intrusion. Margaret Mead went so far as to suggest, "The true oedipal situation might not be the primal scene but parents talking to each other in words the child does not understand."[2]

The child's problem is how to win mother's attention back, away from daddy, siblings, grandmother, TV, her work. These early competitions are inevitable. How we fare in them sets the mood for how we enter the oedipal years.

"You might say that competition is learned in two stages," says Dan Stern. "Stage One is pre-oedipal. It is when we learn *how* to compete. We fight for what we want. The oedipal period would be Stage Two. A dangerous and new element has been added—sex—bringing with it guilt and fear of retaliation. This is when we learn how to inhibit competition. The goal is integration: to compete but do it within safe limits."

For the girl, oedipal competition (something called the Electra Complex) is more complicated than for her brother. She begins with a more symbiotic relationship with mother. How can she recognize mother—her prime connection—as a rival? No matter how angry the boy's rival, father, may become, he still has mother. The tie to her is never in jeopardy. But if the girl arouses antagonism in *her* oedipal rival, she loses the person upon whom she most depends for love and identification.

What is the likelihood of mother's congratulating her daughter on becoming sexual, of fondly acclaiming her "a chip off the old block"? The question answers itself. The daughter's emergence as an uninhibited coquette turns the mother's attention back onto her own sexuality. An un-resolved or ambivalent issue.

Inherent to the oedipal struggle is that competition exists, not only in the daughter but in the mother too. Even as she openly contends with her daughter over dress, behavior, discipline—the very stuff of sexuality—my research shows that the first thing a mother will admit is that she is sexually competitive. *Her* mother didn't admit to competitive emotions. She won't either. It is unwomanly/unmotherly/unnatural. The little girl is introduced to sex in the same way her mother handled every competition between them: denial. The symbiotic tie is as important to mother as to daughter. Competition threatens it. The subject is too awful, too danger-ous even to mention.

The little girl is dancing for her father. A four-year-old can be outra-geously flirtatious. How does he respond? Fathers take cues from wives where daughters are concerned. It's women's business. "Stop crawling all over your daddy," says the mother. Recognizing her tone of voice, the man walks away. That is unfortunate. "When a father stands up for his daughter against the mother," says psychoanalyst Erika Freeman, "those daughters can never fail."

Most women I interview remember adolescence as the time when they literally felt dropped by their fathers. When the girl is four, father can easily remain unconscious of his incestuous feelings; mother can more easily deny her competition. When the girl is thirteen, the unconscious pressures grow an edge. "I had always been my father's girl," a grown woman remembers. "We had always done things together. But when ado-lescence came, he turned away from me as though something terrible had happened. It was awful."

If the first and most important man in our lives not only fails to applaud our sexuality but rejects us because of it, how can we believe we will be good at attracting other men? If the first woman in our life betrayed us by instigating that rejection, how can women ever be trusted? Like mother, they will deny competition even as we sense they are sharpening their knives behind our backs.

"Unfortunately, the mother's competition is usually unconscious," says Erika Freeman. "If it were conscious she would perhaps stop herself. Most mothers aren't evil. Someone should tell them that the psychosexual reac-tions are going to happen so they can be on the lookout and not be afraid and not always have to deny them."

This thought of mother as enemy is literally unbearable. The idea that mother doesn't wish her well is repressed by the daughter. "Sensing that things are amiss," Freeman continues, "the little girl knows it has some-thing to do with father. In her confusion, the girl heads for mother because mother is safety. The girl has learned that it is very dangerous for men to love you and for you to respond to them because then you may lose mommy."

Life and love are not an infinitely expanding universe but a pie with just so many slices.

The girl loses the first oedipal battle in the saddest kind of way. She has lost the first man—as she must—but with no compensation. Her sexuality has not been accepted and encouraged. Mother's denial of competition haunts the girl with the unknown nature of women's reprisals. By never displaying her own rivalrous feelings opposite the one person who should be her safest opponent and best teacher, the girl's own competition grows ever more destructive, more killing for being so long buried. Simple projection leaves her feeling that other women are the same. Fear of becoming sexually involved isn't so much fear of the man (or sex), as fear of other women's condemnation and retaliation.

"It's not that women aren't competitors," says Martin Hoffman, "but women feel stronger restrictions than men. I don't think there is a need to teach girls to be competitive so much as there is a need to stop discouraging them."

Obviously these remarks are general. There are so many ways to negotiate early sexual competition as there are daughters. For instance, an analyst tells me of a young woman patient who has periodic eruptions of sexual interest in triangles involving another woman and a man. "But in this case," he says, "the other woman was not the mother but the sister. The father was a powerful and charismatic figure for whose attention the patient and her sister were always in competition. The central theme of the patient's fantasy is ultimate victory over this other woman who symbolizes the sister. Just winning the man doesn't mean anything. The rival has to be there and to be defeated or the system doesn't work."

He goes on: "Contrary to popular opinion, there are women who not only can compete but cannot perform sexually unless there is a competition with another woman."

Some women's competition takes the form of being attracted only to unavailable men. A familiar example is the woman who chooses married men, repeating again and again the early oedipal contest of trying to win another woman's man away. Despite their reputation as home-breakers, they rarely win. Nor, frequently, is that what they want. Loss is a signal sent back through time, a reparation to the unconscious mother of childhood: "See, Mommy, I'm not a bad girl. I didn't take Daddy away from you. I love you best of all."

"Contemporary Freudians think most people resolve the oedipal complex weakly at best," says psychoanalyst Willard Gaylin, speaking of both

men and women. "That forever after, there is an excitement in the unavailable man because that is what father was. When we are adults, the
threat of losing our partner returns us to the oedipal situation. The other
two people are the grown-ups, the powerful ones in the triangle. The loser
feels not only partnerless, but impotent, pushed back again into the role of
a child. You can call it 'castration,' but I don't like those fancy words.
Something has been taken away from you, not something you own, but
something you *are.* You are diminished, lessened as a person, *reduced.*"

Like Gaylin, I don't like the "fancy" word *castration* either. It never
spoke to me. "Reduced" is something everyone can understand. One moment we have a life, a family, a position in society—we are a competent
adult in every way. And then something is said, a covert smile exchanged.
It is as if someone has pulled a plug and all the stuffing has drained out,
leaving us impotent, small and powerless as a four-year-old. Jealousy has
reduced us to a child opposite giants.

We are paralyzed from one direction, Freud tells us, because of the fear
of our own oedipal rage. The destruction it can wreak stops us from
competing. Murder is in our hearts and we are afraid to act on it. On the
other hand, there is this feeling of being reduced and impotent, which
Gaylin mentions. This is also inhibiting because it says, even if we wanted
to compete, we would lose and be further humiliated.

Some people, luckier in their genes, in their early development, carry
the conviction that should a rival come along, they could probably beat
him out, at least put up a good fight. Some even relish competition. They
feel they are winners; they *know* they are not easily replaceable. To them,
competition is like a healthy flexing of the muscles. Should the worst
happen, and the beloved be lost, they are fortified by inner certainty: They
will soon find someone else to love them.

The more deeply these ideas are knitted into the grain of existence, the
less jealous we are going to be.

The role of competition within the jealous situation is often misunderstood. Once again we use one word to describe two different forms of
expression. First there is *open and behavioral competition.* The emotion is
acted upon, visible for all the world to see. The second form is *internal
and subjective.* While this process is hidden within the self, it is no less
competitive.

It is a common mistake to label only people who are openly rivalrous as
the competitors, while taking silence and inactivity to be withdrawal,
noninvolvement and lack of rivalry. The fact is that if I'm competing with
you, I don't have to do anything visible. I can be deadly competitive while
keeping it all inside. I say to myself, "You're pretty attractive, but I'm a

much finer person." I've silently declared myself the winner. In a more vulnerable moment, I can once again decide the contest in my mind. "You are my superior and I don't stand a chance." Nothing overt has happened but I have competed and lost, internally.

Because men's competition tends to be open and behavioral, I had always thought it the male province. Yes, I knew something powerful—even dangerous—went on between women. But it was covert, disguised, called by other names. For men, the game was all-important. As boys they learned that disputes were part of the give-and-take of the overall process.

During the course of a study on which psychologist Carol Gilligan reports, boys were seen to quarrel often during a game, "but not once was a game terminated because of a quarrel. . . . In the gravest debates, the final word was always, to 'repeat the play.' . . . In fact, it seemed that the boys enjoyed the legal debates as much as they did the game itself, and even marginal players of lesser size or skill participated equally in these recurrent squabbles. In contrast, the eruption of disputes among girls tended to end the game. . . . Rather than elaborating a system of rules for resolving disputes, girls subordinated the continuation of the game to the continuation of relationships."³ For girls, who won and who lost is not as important as avoiding the heat that is at the core of competition.

Without putting a value judgment on playing the game to the end versus maintaining the relationship, it is important to realize that games teach children to see themselves through one another's eyes. Sometimes you're the batter; sometimes you're the fielder. Sometimes you win; sometimes you lose. Respect for the rules is another lesson. They are not arbitrary. They are the structure of the game, established to keep both the game and the players from getting out of hand. By coming to see that disputes must be resolved, the value of compromise is learned. The fiery heat of competition is cooled and socialized in order to keep the game going. Further, losing one day doesn't mean you won't win the next.

If the game is called off because of a dispute, these existential lessons are not learned. The competitive rage remains, untamed, unexpressed, more frightening than before. After a hard-fought game, men walk off a playing field in great camaraderie. Women's hidden competition often breaks up friendships. When the women's movement vehemently labeled competition as nasty and unsisterly, many women felt more confused than ever, alienated from their own emotion. When competition exists, *it exists*.

Something more is learned in games. Courage. When you stand toe to toe with your rival, when you look your opponent in the eye, and do not allow yourself to be faced down, a lesson has been learned. If emotions are not allowed to run hot, there is no reality testing, no exploration of those possibilities of courage that I think men and women share. In the haste to maintain the relationship, women are deprived of learning what they are capable of in an antagonistic situation. They remain frightened.

Fear of being left out in the cold, fear that we cannot beat our opponent, fear that we will be humiliated, fear that we will not be able to replace our love object . . . again and again, in definitions of jealousy there is the concept of fear of loss.

In another study by Carol Gilligan, men and women were shown pictures of people in various degrees of closeness and asked to create stories about what they saw. As people in the pictures were brought closer together, there was an increase in violence in the men's stories. In the women's stories, violence increased as the people in the pictures were moved farther apart.

"Each sex perceives a danger," concludes Gilligan, "which the other does not see—men in connection, women in separation."[4] Gilligan, whose principal interest is in moral development, traces these different reactions back to the way boys and girls are raised by their mothers. She feels the women's concern and sensitivity to the needs of others and to maintaining relationships has *incorrectly* been seen through history as a failure to mature morally. That may be so. My own feeling is that until women can choose to compete or not, they may be fostering relationships not through conscious choice but out of fear.

With these ideas in mind, let's go back to the wife in the story that opened this chapter. In addition to whatever unresolved oedipal conflicts she may have had, and her learned feminine inhibitions against competition, what else kept her from acting in her own behalf with in the jealous situation? "Oh, there's nothing I can do!" Like many people she blamed her immediate acceptance of defeat on "insecurity." Yes, her marriage was threatened. But what made her "insecure" was her *subjective perception* of the other two people and of herself opposite them. She saw them as holding the power of life and death over her. When we feel others have this power, Klein says, we are *envious*.

Envy wipes out any possibility of competition. To see how this happens, let's examine the crisscrossed trajectories of emotion among the three players. First of all, the husband took an almost passive position between the two impassioned women. When you are the prize and the game could be fatal, it is often safest to do nothing at all.

In the contest with the wife, the newcomer saw merely a rival. Yes, she may have resented the wife's entrenched position, the children and the past she shared with the husband. But it was not so much envy she felt as competition. She knew her power over the man. Her desire was still new enough to be unambivalent; it was closer to passion than love. So far, she had everything to gain and nothing to lose. In time, love shows its other face and we resent/envy the power it gives the beloved over us. This envy of the power he would have over her in time had not yet slowed her down. She had all her considerable resources available. Seeing how her determination dazzled the husband, she subjectively rated herself a winner.

She entered combat without envy, without inhibition. "I will have him!" she was heard to say.

From her side, the wife certainly did envy the newcomer's sirenlike hold on the husband, the aphrodisiac lure of the stranger. But was the rival so irresistible? So beautiful that the husband would forget the wife's loyalty, his high opinion and love of her, their years and children together? Absolutely not. She was pretty, but nothing more. *It was the wife's envy* that escalated the rival's beauty onto some unearthly level. How could she even dream of competing? If she did compete with such an (idealized) goddess, the pain of losing would be even worse and she would be humiliated. The very idea of envy tells us we are overmatched.

To the wife, the husband was not merely a prize. She was dependent on him, her identity invested in him. But something even more paralyzing than the threatened loss of her symbiotic connection kept her from fighting the good fight. Integral to the wife's inability to compete was envy of the husband's total power over her. It was far stronger than envy of the other woman.

For eighteen years she had quieted and buried envy of her husband's power. They had a bargain, an agreement. Marriage and children sealed it. Now he had betrayed her. He had broken the promise. Betrayal blew the lid off the socialized control of her envy, as it does in most divorces and separations.

Overwhelmed by an awakened sense of his advantage over her, when she looked at him something in her must have said, "How dare you hold this kind of sway over me, this ability to take away my life or restore it, to abandon me in hell or come back, *either one by your will alone?*" The jealous situation had reduced her to the impotent position of an infant. Symbolically the husband had become the breast/mother, who could give life or take it away. She wanted him back. She also wanted to kill him. Whatever were the factors in the wife's psychology that kept her from murder, we don't know. Fortunately, her rage frightened her. Unfortunately, it frightened her so much she could not act in her own behalf. Unable to move, unable to compete, the wife took her rage to her lawyer.

I find the phrase *the jealous situation* more useful than merely saying someone is jealous. It allows us to step back and examine the whole picture, the interaction among all three people instead of focusing on a single emotion, which may not even be the most important. According to Klein, if the most powerful dynamic in the story above had indeed been jealousy, the wife would have gone for the rival. Did she threaten her, spy on her, send her poison-pen letters? No. The wife was jealous of the other woman, but that was not the crucial emotion. All her obsessive thoughts, her threats and fantasies, were centered on the husband. He was all she could talk about, think about. "How can I get him back?" she wept to everyone who would listen. The drama was between her and him. The major emotion within this jealous situation was envy.

This goes against the popular notion that jealousy comes from low self-esteem. Most of us think that is why we cannot compete. Klein teaches us that we have it backward. *We are envious first; low self-esteem follows.* As a defense against envy, we devalue ourselves. We idealize the rival. Of course we can't compete—not only would we inevitably lose, but we would be further humiliated in the process. Putting the rival out of our league, making ourselves feel tiny and worthless, the dynamics of envy say we are outstripped before we begin.

More than oedipal jealousy, it is envy that brings murder to the heart. This is the core of Klein's message and is reflected in contemporary psychoanalytic thinking. The little boy does not want to kill father as much as he wishes father would disappear, go away for an indefinite vacation, leaving the son alone with mother. Even if the boy wishes father dead, such a thought is far different from wanting to kill him. A highly symbolic illustration of oedipal conflict is the game of chess. The king is never killed, just "checked." It is a healthy resolution to competition. Once the king is defeated, we don't have to kill him.

If the urge to kill does not arise from the furies of the oedipal years, where then does it come from? Freud did not do extensive research into the passions of the first years of life. Klein did.

While she theorized that there is oedipal conflict in the first year, behaviorists today mostly agree with Freud that sexual competition, per se, doesn't begin until three or four. In the first year, erotic feelings are still polymorphous perverse, autoerotic, diffuse. The sexual drive isn't organized and directed into specifically heterosexual channels, nor toward a heterosexual object, until age three or four. But while sexual competition may not begin in the first year, other violent battles do go on. These early struggles, Klein tells us—and she has no peer at explaining the killing aspects of jealousy—are what feed developmentally right up the ladder into later sexual competition. It is the envious, preoedipal infant in us who wants to do murder.

"If you walked in on your lover with someone else, who would you want to kill?" I asked a young man.

It is only now, after years of studying Klein, that I can understand the profound shorthand of his reply. He doesn't hesitate.

"I'd go for the source."

The question has become basic to my research. Even before I had read Klein, I knew from my own experience that jealousy did not center on the rival. In this, I had always been at odds with oedipal theory, which says that in the jealous situation, the one who gets shot is the rival. What made the oedipal explanation incomplete and unsatisfactory to me was that in my own triangles, the other woman didn't really engage my strongest emotions. Yes, I would be jealous of her, but like the young man above, I too would go for the "source."

So did Proust. *Remembrance of Things Past*, one of the world's supreme works of art, turns upon the seemingly trivial fact of whether or not a bad-tempered husband will allow a boy's mother to kiss her son good-night. If the father forbids it, the boy is in despair, choked with asthma. When he does get mother's kiss, he can literally breathe again.

With the omnipotent power of an author, Proust not only kills his mother in the novel but kills her twice over, decreeing that his grandmother—whom the narrator loves with practically the same intensity as he does the mother—must die too. ". . . it is because they thus contain all the hours of days gone by that human bodies can do such injury to those who love them," Proust writes, "because they contain so many past memories, joys and desires, already effaced for them, but so cruel for one who contemplates and carries back in the domain of Time the cherished body of which he is jealous, jealous even to the point of desiring its destruction."[5]

With Marcel's total and envious awareness of the beloved's power to raise him to heaven with a kiss, or force him to spend a night choking in hell by her absence, it is not coincidental that Proust's novel is the most profound study of jealousy and envy we know in fiction. He deals not in behavioral competition with the father—who, after all, is the one who decides whether the boy will be kissed good-night or not—but with the more deeply rooted, hidden Kleinian envy of his mother. That is the novel's power. Competition with the father is never expressed openly, or even made conscious. That is the narrator's tragedy.

A comment on my choice of words: "In the jealous situation, who would you want to kill?" I learned quickly that many interviewees did not immediately know what I was talking about. It was only when I cooled the question several degrees—"At whom is your major emotion directed, the beloved or the rival?"—that they understood. Three years ago I would have told you my question was rhetorically exaggerated. I realize now that using "kill" conveyed honest feeling. While I am not a killer, I am apparently closer to it than some people I interview. Most of us have socialized our killer furies into more acceptable channels, such as guilt, anxiety, hypochondria, ulcers, compulsive criticism/nagging of the beloved. Perhaps most often we turn it against ourselves and become depressed.

Sometimes the socialization breaks down. The self is threatened. Defenses that so carefully constructed an image of poise, politeness and control can no longer contain the fury within.

Twenty-three-year-old Richard Herrin had been high-school valedictorian and a Yale scholarship student. He was also a Mexican-American, an illegitimate child from the barrios of Los Angeles. Twenty-year-old Bonnie Garland was the daughter of a wealthy and prestigious lawyer from Scarsdale, New York. They were lovers. After Richard's graduation, Bonnie announced that while she still loved him, she was going to see other men too. Richard Herrin picked up a hammer and in his own words, hit her until "her head split open like a watermelon."

When I read about the murder, I was confused. I did not yet know the difference between jealousy and envy. If it was a crime of passion, a jealous crime, why hadn't Richard gone for the rival?

"Richard Herrin had severe attachment problems," says psychoanalyst Willard Gaylin. While Gaylin did not testify in court, he conducted extensive interviews with Herrin and wrote a book about the case. "He had no true identifications except with his mother and those were very powerful. All that intense, possessive feeling he had with his mother, he moved it all onto Bonnie."

Richard had three years invested in the relationship with Bonnie, and she still loved him, still wanted to see him. Why didn't he think he could beat out his rival? It was to answer this question that I had come to see Gaylin. "Richard had successfully competed for scholarships to several of the best colleges in the East," I say. "Why didn't he compete for the woman he loved?"

"Richard could not compete. He had no father, no close boyhood friends, no man to identify with. Because of his strong identification with his mother, his hold on manhood was shaky. The idea of being compared to another man automatically meant to Richard he would lose. If Bonnie started up with another guy, Richard was afraid his sexual inadequacy would be exposed."

Winning Bonnie was more than a romantic triumph for Richard. It promised an end to his feeling of isolation, of not belonging, of feeling left out. In Bonnie he found an emblem of success and acceptance, an identity he had missed all his life. He and Bonnie became inseparable. Holding hands with her—*being seen* holding hands—was a symbol to the world and himself that he existed; that he had triumphed.

"In the trial," I say, "they tried to make it sound like a case of macho revenge, a Hispanic man being humiliated by his girl's rejection. But in your book you bring up more central issues. It wasn't enough for Richard to hold Bonnie's hand; the whole world had to see it. . . ."

"Richard always felt the world was watching him. That is what made the public hand holding important, because then the whole world knew he not only existed, but existed as a man who had won the heart of a beautiful and desirable woman. The world has more important things to do than watch Richard and Bonnie holding hands. But Richard had paranoid ideas of reference, that all eyes were on him. When Bonnie left him, he was wide open to public humiliation."

"Are you saying his public role with her meant more than his private feeling about her?"

"With people like Richard, two things matter," says Gaylin. "The first is private knowledge that the beloved prefers someone else. Even more important, more wounding, is the public announcement of defeat. Competition was very important to Richard, as it is to all jealous people. He had to win."

"I had the feeling reading your book that if the world had only seen him with another woman, if he'd slept with that stewardess he met on his last flight back to Bonnie . . ."

"There might have never been a killing of Bonnie Garland," Gaylin finishes my thought. "She was as replaceable as the queen of diamonds by the queen of hearts."

Reduced, rejected, diminished, the self on the verge of falling apart, Richard did not attack his rival. It was Bonnie who bore the full burden of rage as well as love. If she didn't love him, that meant nobody did. Gaylin has answered my question: Richard went for what he felt to be the "source" of his anguish: Bonnie/mother.

"When Richard Herrin lifted that hammer," says Gaylin, "there was more than one woman being killed."

The violent act as an attempt at restoration of the self.

An act of envy.

An instructive comparison of how two fascinating women handled competition—the one behaviorally, the other subjectively and internally—turns up in Wilfrid Sheed's biography of Clare Boothe Luce. The second woman in question is Luce's old friend, colleague and rival, writer Helen Lawrenson. I think it no accident that the three major reviews I read are all preoccupied with the role of envy in Luce's life. All three were by women.

"Clare caught a lot of hell from the envious for being beautiful, outspoken, and a raging success,"[6] writes one critic. According to Sheed it was the cause of many disappointments, among them rejection by the witty and savage Algonquin Roundtable, which "was out to get her even more than they were out to get most people. There seemed to be that inevitable feeling that she had bought her way in with her looks, that she didn't belong, which has followed her everywhere and shaped her view of life. . . ."[7]

If Luce had been more envious herself, would she have been able to compete as well? She did recognize envy enough to defend herself: "No doubt a serious woman," writes Sheed, "had to be very no-nonsense indeed (or else very plain-looking), to get a fair hearing in those days. When Clare's sex appeal was turned off, it was like a new ice age. . . . Her ardent desire to be taken seriously could have made her unintentionally funny, except for a strange note of self-mockery, which suggested it was meant to be funny. . . ."[8]

Helen Lawrenson had the same self-mocking humor as Luce, and perhaps for the same reasons: She too was a beauty, a woman ahead of her time. I didn't meet Helen until she was in her sixties. She had come to live in Rome where Bill and I had an apartment. She settled into the Rome Hilton with an enormous trunk filled with blank yellow legal pads (she was afraid you couldn't buy them in Italy) and layers of memorabilia. "I'm finally going to write that book about my life," she said.

Her wonderful dark good looks and wit made me dizzy to think what she must have been like in the thirties when she and Luce were the two stars at *Vanity Fair,* competing both editorially and for the affections of publisher Condé Nast. They must have been quite a pair, Rose Red and Rose White, enjoying professional success, sexual freedom and the mobility few women then had, or even dared to want. That was the quality in herself Helen valued most, I think—her daring. At least it was the only aspect of her character she never denigrated with her customary half smile.

Imagine a woman in 1936 writing an article for a national magazine entitled "Latins Are Lousy Lovers!" By her own account, Helen had been the hottest girl on the block. No one ever contested *that.* "Helen was the most outrageous woman I knew," photographer Eve Arnold said to me. "We were together once on an assignment in Havana. Helen had had a romance on the boat going over, another lover awaited her in the Hotel Nacional, and on the way there, she was making love to yet a third man in the taxi."

Her looks and professional success made Helen, like Luce, a target for the envious. Like Luce, she constructed an ironic defense. Even if she did have two lead articles published that month, and was the most beautiful woman at the Cotton Club opening night, she had a stain on her dress. I loved those stories, and that her eclectic range of lovers never interfered with her work.

Until she met and married Jack Lawrenson, the legendary, tough, handsome organizer of the New York waterfront. Jack was a folk hero in the Greenwich Village bars, often reputed to be the character played by Marlon Brando in *On the Waterfront.* He was also a famous womanizer. Helen stayed home with the children. Valid enough decision. But what did the woman who once had a man in every port do with her jealousy and envy? Not only was the man she loved unfaithful to her, but the woman against whom she measured herself more than any other, Luce, was vaulting professionally/economically/socially out of her league.

Helen was in love with Lawrenson but he had all the power. She turned her anger against herself. The brilliant articles appeared only now and then. The reclusiveness that would later take over her life began to set in. She became depressed. Her competitive spirit was no longer actively played out; it turned inward, became hidden and sour.

From her left-wing political stance, Helen would comment ironically to me on Clare's Catholic conservatism, the "boring, snobbish" parties at the Luce's estate. From her position as wife and mother, she mocked Clare's ambassadorship to Rome. These stories about Luce's life and career were told with verve and élan, but not even Helen's wit could mask what I always felt to be jealousy of Luce. (Now, of course, I know it was envy.)

Shortly after we met, Helen described a novel she'd begun. It opened with a certain beautiful, blond journalist giving head to a certain millionaire in the private car of a train headed to the Democratic convention of 1936. Even as I laughed at Helen's brilliant narration, I couldn't help thinking, Is that the way you write about your best friend? Luce was godmother to Helen and Jack's daughter, while the famed financier Bernard Baruch was a friend of both women and godfather to Helen's son. In fact, while Helen's best stories were about "Bernie" and "Condie" and Clare, the friendship between the two women didn't sound like anything you would want for yourself.

Helen had once been famous for going after and getting the men everyone else wanted. When we met she was still a beautiful woman. Jack Lawrenson had been dead for years. Her interest in men, her sexuality, was almost palpable. You don't just turn off all that heat. But when a famous film star (one whose aging, rough good looks reminded me of photos of Jack Lawrenson), responded to her cue, Helen drew back. She denied her flirtation, his interest, her ability to beat out other women. In classic fashion, after denial came devaluation: "Who, me?" she said incredulously, when Bill and I asked if she would see him again. "Compete with Miss X?" She named a famous film star. Does it matter that I think she could have beat that other woman? I'd seen the way that man looked at her.

Somehow Helen never convinced me of the satisfactions of her life's choices. The thinly disguised novel never went beyond that first chapter. It was laughingly dismissed as not being worth her time. Helen's profiles in *Esquire* were famed as among the best that magazine had ever published. "Oh, they're not much," she would dismiss compliments. If journalism was so unsatisfying to her, why didn't she write "The Big Book," the one about her own life, the one that would have brought her the respect and eminence she so deeply craved?

I think Helen felt the world had outstripped her, which is why she had taken herself out of the literary sweepstakes. To compete would mean certain defeat. It would be humiliating. Looking back now, it seems her whole life had become a fortress against envy. I can say this because I was present when the lid blew.

It was now the early 1970s. Bill and I had moved to London, and by coincidence, Helen had too. One night a writer friend from New York came to dinner bringing stories of the impassioned books being published about the women's movement. Helen flew into a tirade. "Women's equality goes against nature!" she cried. We were all bowled over. We couldn't believe that the sexual rebel of the 1930s, when "bad girls" died in movie after movie, would denounce her sisters in sin. Which was exactly why she hated them: The new sexually liberated woman was stealing the title Helen cherished most, "the fastest girl on the block."

A whole generation of younger women was about to make the best years of her life look ordinary. On top of that, two of her own contemporaries and competitors, Marya Mannes and Lillian Hellman, had just published their memoirs to great acclaim. Helen's own memoirs might never have been written if honest anger hadn't blasted through her defenses. Self-protective humor gone, the white-hot envy inside was exposed: "God damn it, my life was far more interesting than theirs!"

Out came the trunks filled with material for the famous Big Book. Out came the Stork Club napkins, the matchbooks from dives in Havana on which were scrawled what Irwin Shaw whispered to her in 1937. Helen's memory was amazing. She knew what people wore to parties in 1939 and the scandal they swapped in elevators in 1942. *Stranger at the Party* was published in 1975.

"Do you think they'll shoot me for bad manners?" Helen asked Bill when the book came out. Though said as a joke, was the reference to murder entirely accidental? In envy's insidious circle, we don't just resent the brilliance of others. We assume that if we are brilliant, their envy would make them want to shoot us too.

Projection.

There was plenty about Clare Luce in *Stranger at the Party.* You can be sure it was all very amusing. Helen's "funny" revenge.

Sheed sums it up: "At some point Lawrenson chose the acceptable female role of sniping . . . instead of competing, and of immersing herself in her husband's life, while Clare went careening along as herself. It must have been tempting indeed for Lawrenson to shoot her old patroness on the wing."9 ("Patroness" indeed! How Helen would have resented that.)

At the end of Sheed's book, Luce summons him back to discuss a new emotion she has just discovered in herself. She thinks it belongs in the book, and she is right. Sondra Day O'Connor had just been appointed first woman on the Supreme Court bench. Luce tells Sheed she doesn't know whether she is envious or jealous. They decide on envy, the more despicable of the two.

"I don't want to *be* her," says Luce. "I would just like to have had that kind of chance."10

Luce may call this envy. What I hear is more nearly a response to rivalry and challenge. A behavioral competitor to her fingertips, how could Luce not have wanted a crack at so eminent a position, one closed to women in her day? It is fascinating to speculate what effect a young Luce would have on the feminist movement today. And how would *they* deal with *her?* All that power, all that beauty.

Luce once wrote an article for *Life* magazine in which she attributed Marilyn Monroe's death to the loss of beauty. Perhaps an intimation of Luce's own vulnerability, an admission that she felt, in her heart of hearts, that her biggest strength was not her talent, wit or formidable intelligence. It was her drop-dead beauty.

She says as much to Sheed: "What I do miss [most today] is my looks."11 A telling confession, all the more so because Luce gives honest priority to an asset that many women today feel necessary to denigrate—often in the name of sisterhood. The sentiment is noble. Is it in accord with reality?

I can understand Sheed's surprise at Luce's confession. But I was surprised myself when it was echoed by the women reviewers. One even went so far as to comment, "Good-bye to power without responsibility!" I couldn't help but think she had labeled herself either hypocritical or envious. The Mount Rushmores of the Movement may have rejected Raquel

Welsh's offer to lend her voice to the cause (now *that* is envy!) but I don't think Luce would have been so easily dismissed.

While I admire Luce's asking Sheed to reopen his finished manuscript to include her envy of Sondra Day O'Connor, it raises a question. Luce has more success, fame and riches than most. When she reads the newspaper every morning in her beautiful estate in Hawaii, do the achievements of others awaken a nostalgia in an old competitor's heart, or do they sour her life?

What of the younger women Luce envies? Are they indeed enjoying the competitive opportunities Luce yearns for? Or does the harsh psychology of envy remain the same, changing times or not? Recently an article appeared in *The New York Times* by a woman who seemed endowed with much of Clare's old fire and spirit—even while thinking it a "monstrous" aspect of her own character.

"I glimpsed her on the street some months ago," the writer begins. "For a moment, I was surprised to see her looking so well, walking around. Part of me still thinks that I nearly killed her. We had been friends, and competitors, years ago. At the time, as I recall, I felt she had some kind of leg up on me—she seemed to get waylaid less than I, had a firmer sense of purpose, a bouncier step, a more cheerful disposition. I must have possessed some qualities that she envied as well, for the rivalry worked both ways: We competed—daintily, tiptoeing around the subject—in our work, our friendships. At one point we quarreled, over something silly, and afterward she informed me that I had looked . . . as if I had wanted to kill her. It still unhinges me, that remark."

Not enough to stem her competitive reflex: "When I meet up with a rival, I am—despite a kind of keyed-up friendliness that covers for it—calculating all the while: . . . which of us has scored the most points?"

In amusing but dead serious tones, she rankles over the disclaimers of competition made by women friends, *even as they push to get ahead.* This denial, the discrepancy between what her friends say and what they do, is her despair. Is she the only one filled with competitive "poisons," the only sinner in a world of cooperative and womanly saints? Didn't mother say envy and competition were bad? " 'If another girl admires something you're wearing, you should give it to her.' . . . It was an act of generosity I only rarely rose to," she writes.

The real poison is that she is half in agreement: "Girls should have more grace than to compete, to envy or be envied. Better to ward off rivalry with a gift. Let me be that girl, I sometimes think, the one who gives away her sweaters and cares nothing for competition. Not the one who is forever looking over her shoulder, or ahead, keeping a gimlet eye out for the other runners."

Sapped by conflict, at the end of what is only a short newspaper article, she subsides, denies her nature. Of competition—clearly the very stuff of life to her—she finishes: "Ideally [it] should be beside the point." She has again become her mother's daughter.[12]

I am so saddened by her resignation, but so taken by her honesty and courage, I telephone around to find her age. She is twenty-seven.

"The greater aggressiveness of the male is one of the best established, and most pervasive, of all psychological sex differences," write psychologists Eleanor Maccoby and Carol Nagy Jackson. The evidence is less decisive as to "whether males as a group are more competitive or assertive."[13] Unfortunately, in our society, competition and aggression are often taken to be synonymous. When a woman is labeled competitive, she hears it to mean she is aggressive, i.e., unwomanly.

In a world where success is determined by competition, how can women not envy men their socially granted, socially encouraged ease with competition? On the other hand, I do not wish to set up as ideal the mindless, unending competition that notoriously drives men into early graves. Isn't there a median, a healthy measure for what is after all one of life's emotions? I'd like to give competition a good name.

"So many of the women I know are driven people," writes Anne Taylor Flemming, "more afraid of failure than of success, more afraid of complacency than of competition, more afraid of one another's successes than of the successes of the men in their lives."[14]

Competing at the job is different from competing in love. Professional competition is behavior learned late. If we are to understand the form of jealousy to which women are particularly susceptible—passivity, acceptance of defeat before the contest even starts—we must look back to the woman who very early taught her daughter *not* to compete. Since this is so important, let me repeat: If we are afraid to enter the race, if we are certain a rival will beat us out, we are wide open to jealousy.

No man goes through boyhood without repeated competitive experiences of winning and losing. Unlike his sister, he must be *seen* to compete. That is how boys are. That does not mean anyone enters the fray without his own individual and internal mind-set, largely determined by how he fared in early family battles for position and place. No less than his sister, he carries a subjective scoreboard of what his chances are.

"Are you jealous?"

"To me that means comparison," says a thirty-seven-year-old art director. "If I imagine my girl with another man, what upsets me is that she will compare me to him. I get, you know, tense and excited, anxious in competitive situations. I've developed strategies against being compared.

At a party I separate my girl over in a corner. I promote a 'you and me against the world' psychology between us. We are a pair. To keep her focus on me I try to be very entertaining. If we are allies, she won't compare me and I won't be jealous."

"But you can't control the world," I reply. "Say you're at dinner, and she pays too much attention to another guy. . . ."

"I've worked out other strategies. I've got this way of broadcasting displeasure by going into a sort of aggressive moodiness. It's an emotional version of suddenly coming up with a broken arm, a way of silently getting her attention back to me.

"Another way I compete without showing it is a kind of manipulation I've practiced all my life. When I'm around competitive people, I make competition seem less desirable than remaining cool and noncompetitive. That way, competition itself is a form of losing. What I do is change the rules of the game and make the game players feel foolish. I win.

"Underneath it all, I think, is a desire to be the best in the world—to be fabulous—to be a star. The result is I've got an almost pathological fear about standing up in front of an audience. Or even having everybody's attention at the dinner table. What if the joke doesn't go over? I'd be humiliated. For me the discomfort outweighs the potential rewards. I hate competition because underneath it all I'm intensely competitive."

He is an extremely attractive man, reasonably successful, and despite his fears, very articulate. He has no trouble finishing sentences and, in fact, often interrupts to finish mine. I ask him where he thinks his problems with competition began.

"I think my dislike of it was worked into me through my family. I was not only the first child, I was the first grandchild, the center of my adult world. Because my parents included me in everything I began to talk very early. My sister was born when I was about one and a half. Suddenly all attention shifted to the baby. She was a girl and I guess my mother wanted a daughter. They had something special between them that left me out. Or I experienced it that way.

"My parents gave us all a lot of praise for achievement. Comparisons were always being made not only between me and my brother and sister but with our cousins too. I wanted my parents' approval for being the best. In fact, I was told I was the best and felt I had to live up to that. I liked to read those boys' books about heroic people. Winning or losing big became too important. So I rejected the whole idea. When I used to play baseball, I'd hope the ball wouldn't come to me. I remember being very relieved if the game would end before it was my turn to come to bat. It wasn't great to be up at bat. Trying and failing, or even failing to win big, the whole picture arouses too much anxiety in me."

I ask him if "the whole picture" today includes comparison with other men sexually, or in terms of power, money. . . .

"Sure, sure," he interrupts. "If I'm impotent and my lover gets involved with somebody else who's the opposite of impotent, then I feel sexual jealousy. But jealousy doesn't have to start with that big a deal. It could be that he's a better conversationalist than me. He never lets those long silences develop during dinner."

I can't resist asking if he is aware of never letting me finish a sentence, as if speaking over my last words gave him an advantage.

He smiles. He knows exactly what I'm talking about. "When we were kids at the dinner table, we all talked simultaneously. We learned to talk and listen at the same time. No one dared stop for breath. If you did you lost our parents' attention. That's what we were fighting for. My brothers and sister and I laugh about it now. We are friends. Back then, from the time they were born, I cut them out of my life, pretending they didn't exist. I never spoke to them."

The area in which this man chooses to compete is the one that posed the first threat. When he thinks a woman might leave him, anxiety does not focus on his bank account or penis size. He is afraid that another man will outtalk him. The root of his jealous competition for women's love is not so much oedipal as sibling.

If our self-esteem rests not within but in the eyes of others, of course we fear comparison. "How can another's activities or characteristics affect one's own self-esteem?" writes philosopher Robert Nozick. "Shouldn't my self-esteem, feeling of worth . . . depend only on facts about me? If it is me that I'm evaluating in some way, how can facts about [someone else] play a role? The answer, of course, is that we evaluate how well we do something by comparing our performance to others, to what others can do."[15] And the first "others" we compare ourselves to are members of our family.

This man's sister was born before he was two years old. As he experienced it, his mother turned away from him because the baby had something he did not. A comparison had been made, and it was to his detriment. The feeling was exacerbated by the parents. First, they set extraordinarily high goals for him to reach. Second, they constantly compared one child's achievements with the other's. The obvious inference was that love would be withdrawn unless one not only won, but "won big."

"A lot of competition grows out of jockeying for a more favored position in the family," says Dan Stern. "But there is often a lie at the heart of the contest. A child gets the feeling that if he were better looking, like his brother, got better marks in school, like his sister, or excelled in sports, he would win favor. That is, improve his status in the family pecking order. This makes for a lot of competition of a very vicious, unsatisfying kind because the lie is that your parents already know how much they do or do not favor you. Nothing is going to change that."

It reminds me, I tell Stern, of Tennessee Williams's *Cat on a Hot Tin Roof.* It doesn't matter what the prodigal, alcoholic son does—he may be homosexual—Big Daddy loves him.

"A parent gets an idea in his head," says Stern, "about how a certain child is. He may be wrong. He may be just seeing an illusion of how he wants the child to be or who the child 'takes after.' That doesn't matter. Functionally speaking, who you are is in part what the parent perceives you to be. If you are the favorite, it is so often irrational, like 'chemical reactions' between people. It is very, very hard to change.

"In a family like this, siblings enter the race for what the family claims it values, but they never win. How can they? Someone has secretly won before the race started. The competition goes on and on. The belief is that the next prize is going to still the gnawing inside, but since the true prize is love of a parent who always favored your brother or sister more— *and who always will*—you never win but never stop running. . . ."

"And there's no nourishment in what you do win."

"Exactly," says Stern. "Another form of competition within the family is cross-generational. Sisters and brothers who never resolved problems of sibling rivalry often pass them on. Their children become pawns, stand-ins for their parents' competitions. You see it all the time at family reunions. Grades earned at school, pictures painted, medals won in races, all are brought out and compared by the parents in front of the children, the aunts, uncles and grandparents. Nothing the child does is valuable in itself. Its value is in the eyes of the aunts and grandmothers. How does it stack up in comparison with the feats of the cousins? That is what matters. It's a kind of generational lay-down of what constitutes positions of favor. Kids pick it up in a snap."

Jealousy, envy, competition, sibling rivalry, oedipal conflict—we give the strands of human nature discrete names, as if they can be picked apart and examined one by one. It is a perfectly valid scientific method, in which large systems are broken down—reduced—to their component parts for clarity of analysis. But in human existence, isn't the whole greater than the sum of its parts? In the interview that follows, all strands intertwine, affecting and changing each other, resulting in the complexity of life, seen not under a microscope but as a whole.

Until Sally was eighteen, she never felt pretty or desirable or had a boyfriend. Then she fell in love. She came from a conservative Catholic family. Sex before marriage went against her whole background. "But he was just smitten with me," she says. One night, alone at his parents' house, they had sex.

A month later, she learned he was having an affair with another girl. "I thought I was going to die. I really wished I would."

As she tells the story, my heart sinks for Sally. We have been close friends for ten years. We were both raised in the South. We know a great deal about one another, much of it told in terms of fear of abandonment, and of the separation anxieties we share. I have never heard this story.

"What did you do?" I ask.

"I was too much in shock to do anything. I went to bed and stayed there for three weeks. I couldn't talk to anyone about it. I had no close girlfriends and I certainly couldn't tell my mother or father. I was stunned that I could make this decision to have such an intimate relationship with someone and be so wrong. I suppose I had told myself that he was the person I would marry . . . maybe to justify the act. That he could have another girl friend . . ."

"Would you say what you felt was jealousy?"

"Mortification. I felt he had broken a promise."

"Ah, betrayal . . ."

"Not that he'd made any promise of fidelity. But I'd assumed. It was so humiliating, a terrible blow to my self-esteem."

"Didn't you feel abandoned too?"

"You know my separation anxieties, but it wasn't so much that . . ."

"Rage?"

"I wasn't aware of feeling any anger until years later. It came out in my therapy. These other emotions were what I felt—this terrible shock, humiliation. Before this boy I'd had no social life, didn't go with a crowd of girls. I felt like a misfit."

"You've said that so often before. I've always found it hard to believe." Sally has more loyal friends today, more people who love her, than anyone I know.

"It seemed to me in high school that no one was interested in me. Love and romance, they were the most important things in the world when I was an adolescent. I *lived* at the movies. What's odd is that since then I've found out that a lot of people did notice me. They even had crushes on me. But I wasn't aware of it."

"You've always told me how much praise your family gave you. . . ."

"I got a lot of acceptance at home. I had a lot of intellectual confidence and I thought I was a good person. In childhood I'd been very oriented toward my family. That changed in my teens. My mother didn't understand why I wanted pretty clothes. She and my father didn't value things that are important to adolescents."

"Did you ever see that man again, the one who betrayed you?"

"After a few weeks he stopped being interested in the other girl and came back to me. That established a pattern. It went on for three years."

"He repeatedly went off with other women?"

"Don Juan. He had this compulsion to pursue and win other women. Once he had, after three or four weeks, then he always came back to me."

"And you took him back?"

"I had two reasons. First, because he did come back and that was what I wanted. The second one is an odd sort of thing: He came back of his own volition. This ended up giving me the feeling that I was the most attractive person to him after all."

"Power."

"The other women he would get interested in, they were always completely different from me. I could go to a party and pick out exactly who was going to be the next one."

"How did you feel when you spotted your next rival?"

"Very jealous. They were always what seemed to me to be very good-looking. Blond and good figures and tall, modely looking."

"In time you knew your power. He always came back. Why didn't you ever stand up to one of those tall blonds?"

"I didn't know how to compete. I always suffered the jealousy within. I was jealous of their wonderful qualities, being so blond and sexy. Jealous was the word I used for myself then. I know now what I really felt was envy."

"And you felt no anger toward him?"

"At the time, no. I felt a lot of pain. Today, of course, I believe that behind the pain there had to be a lot of anger. That's what put me to bed the first time, literally knocked me out."

"Instead of killing him you turned the murder against yourself."

"Later on I did get a certain malicious satisfaction turning him down when he wanted me to marry him. He begged me to break my engagement to a new man I'd met."

"Revenge."

"I felt like, You finally got your comeuppance! He was devastated that I would marry someone else. He kept calling me for years, even after he got married."

"Why do you think he kept coming back to you?"

"He would say that I was like no one he'd ever known, that sex with me was terrific. I didn't know what he was talking about. I had no way to make comparisons. I had always been interested in sex, from the time I was four years old. But I knew nothing about it. Maybe it was the intensity of my interest . . ."

"Did he know what pulled him back to you?"

"Years later I asked him, but he's not a person who knows how to answer those questions. I think that's what he liked about me, that I was always thinking about the psychological aspects of relationships. He liked to ask me about how women felt, and I was always ready to talk about myself."

"You sure are!" We laugh. I've had more conversations with Sally about the what-does-it-all-mean of sex/love/romance than with any other woman.

"You probably also asked him about himself and listened in a way no other girl did. It must also have fascinated him that you weren't looking for someone to give you an identity."

"I've never done that."

"And you loved him in that very special way. How many women would keep taking him back? Where was he going to find someone like you?"

"But after him I determined I would never again be in a relationship with anyone who would become interested in another woman while he was with me."

"How do you do that?" I ask. "A woman in love with love—how do you protect yourself against jealousy? It's so unpredictable."

"In my adult life, no woman has ever taken a man away from me. After that first one, I decided never to expose myself to jealousy again, and I never did."

Control.

The uncharacteristic absolutism in her voice catches me up. Sally has had an extraordinary and varied love life. In all her many relationships, no man ever got away? No woman ever presented a threat? But I know in myself how it is: When your life depends upon a subjective interpretation of events, you shade reality. What does that one man, the one night in Seattle, matter?

"Once I'd had that first boyfriend," Sally says, "I was never without one. If I felt drawn to a man, I was always able to win his interest."

"Wouldn't it be truer to turn that around, that you were only drawn to men if they showed interest in you first?"

"Obviously, yes. I can't get any man in the world. But once I felt attractive, I felt very powerful. That first man shattered my self-esteem, but in the end he built it up even higher by coming back to me all the time. That was a very powerful and formative three-year period I spent with him."

"You're not saying that all your power came through sex? I know you better than that."

"I began by thinking women's power was beauty and glamour. I grew up in the movies of the forties. But my parents had always taught me the value of work, of earning your own way."

Sally combined the two ideas. Her parents' charitable work in the community was tireless. Much to her mother's chagrin, Sally chose to be an actress. By the time she was twenty she was part of a well-known repertory company in Boston. I've seen her photos in old theatrical programs. My, she was pretty!

"I had this feeling that if you were in show business, you were automatically glamorous. I began earning money, having boyfriends, feeling glamorous—it was all simultaneous. But show business was too undependable. I liked working and I realized I was going to be a working person all my life. Before I was thirty, I went back to college and got my degree in anthropology."

Sally may not depend on men for her identity, but she has never been without one. How to control your life in such a way that you can have work you enjoy and intimacy too? She knew that the kind of man she wanted was the kind who would never leave her. She needed to find a form of work that would reinforce those traits of character that were her real power, power that would last until the end of her life. When she chose to become an anthropologist, she was acting on something she had known since that first man. He didn't repeatedly return to her because she was beautiful. He came back because she has a unique empathy no one can resist. She wears her heart on her sleeve.

"Tell me about the man you married," I say. "Was he a grand passion?"

"No. I liked him. I won him away from a girlfriend who was crazy about him."

"You stole your friend's man?" My voice shows my surprise. The Sally I know would never openly compete with another woman. A few women we know in common might have been professional competitors. Sally has turned them into close friends.

"But he wasn't hers. She would like to have had him. . . ."

"Was that part of his allure, that you could get him when she couldn't?"

"I guess so. He was very attractive, but we were too young. We were divorced in less than a year."

In less than another year, Sally was married again. In all she's been married four times. I'd always believed that the pattern of Sally's life with men echoed her attachment to her mother, a woman so identified with her only daughter that when she sent Sally clothes they were in *her* size, not Sally's. I still believe that the need for a symbiotic closeness, the fear of separation—topics that have laced our conversations over the years—continue to dominate Sally's intimacies. But now for the first time in our friendship, she has sounded a new emotional theme: competition. The importance of the other woman as well as the man.

Immediately after Sally's second marriage, war broke out. While her husband was in boot camp a thousand miles away, Sally was becoming successful as an actress. Successful with men. She began to have affairs.

"I shared an apartment with two other girls," Sally says. "They were actresses too. We took acting classes together, dancing classes; we often worked together. I was the only married one, but wherever we were, men ignored them and became interested in me. They were very jealous . . . or is it envious?"

"Envious of what you had, but jealous that they lost the men to you."

How much of her decision to begin having affairs was based on passion? How much on beating out the other girls?

"The tables had turned," says Sally. "In my adolescence, I was jealous of the girls who had boyfriends. Now these two girls were jealous of me. Night after night they would watch me going out, and they couldn't stand it. Oh, they went out, but not nearly as much as I did. You have to understand, all this time I was so thrilled to be having so much attention. It was still very close to the time when I'd had none. When I'd been the one staying home."

Sally had intended to tell her husband she wanted a divorce when he was discharged from the Marines. There would have been no mention of other men. "I would never intentionally hurt him by arousing jealousy. Never, never, not after what I'd been through!" But one of the women who shared the apartment told him.

Sally laughingly says of the next period of her life, "Married men became my hobby."

"Against whom do you think you were playing out these affairs?"

"Against my mother. Becoming involved with married men was my unconscious way of competing with her for my father. It was a jerky sort of compulsion but it was a way of symbolically winning him, proving I was the person he loved most. That I was better than she. More romantic, more desirable. I always wanted to be my father's favorite person in the world, for him to acknowledge me above her. My father was very clear about how he felt. He had this legal clarity. After all, he was a state supreme court judge. He adored my mother; he absolutely adored her. I think I was his favorite child, but she was his beloved."

"He did exactly the right thing. He let you know where you stood. That he loved you, but she was his mate, the one he wanted to sleep with."

"He was perfect! He was clear, but I wasn't. I resolved it with those married men."

"Most women involved with married men live with a kind of defeated feeling. They can't get him away from his wife."

"That's not how I felt," says Sally. "I never felt, 'Poor me, he won't leave his wife for me.' I always felt I was more desirable, that he loved me more than her. Wasn't he here with me tonight?"

"Was your mother competitive with you?"

"I never realized it till much later. Since my father was so crazy about her . . . in my eyes she had everything. How could she be jealous of me?"

"What do you think you had that she wanted?"

"She never had my opportunities. She was a very talented woman, strong and brilliant. Like her own mother. Her parents were immigrants and had nine children. They were very poor. My mother had to work hard. She had to raise all her brothers and sisters. She watched them all go off to college. She was resentful of that. . . ."

"Envious . . ."

"Yes. She went to work so early she never even finished high school. She knew she was brighter than all the rest. I think her envy, her bitterness, it all got channeled into work. She devoted her whole life to charity. She always bought me secondhand clothes so she'd have more money to give to the missionaries."

"But she wanted you to go to college. . . ."

"In the literature, there is an idea called the Spartan Complex. Parents who had a hard upbringing often get angry at their children for having it easier—even if the children's ease is due to the parents' own efforts. My mother was like that. . . ."

"There was always that resentment?"

"She begrudged me going to college. She was an envious woman."

"Envious that you had what she didn't."

"The last time I saw my mother she was in a nursing home in Atlanta. She told me my father had always wanted me to be a lawyer. He thought I was a gifted child. This was long, long before the law schools became swamped with women. It was unheard of in the thirties for a father to want his daughter to have a legal career! But she never told me. Not until that last visit. Now I think it was because *she* would have loved to have some kind of learned career."

"Since your mother was so identified with you, wouldn't it have been enough for her to live through your achievements?"

"That didn't mean she wanted me to outstrip her."

"When a daughter is symbiotic with her mother and in love with her father, competition becomes difficult. . . ."

"My competition with her was always secretive. For instance, her side of the family had bad teeth, something genetic. When I had my teeth capped, I didn't tell her, but once it was done, I felt absolutely glamorous, free of her. But I was afraid for her to find out."

"You *had* outstripped her."

"When I was a child, I loved her. But when adolescence came, it was hard for her to understand her daughter might value things she did not. My mother always thought she was right about everything and for everybody. She was a wonderful woman, very imperious, but she needed me in a unique way. I was the only girl in the family."

"So while she was envious and competitive with you, you were her favorite?"

"Oh, no! I was two years old when my brother was born. I didn't realize until much later how threatened I felt. His birth was my first trauma. It all got forgotten, buried, until I tried hypnotherapy. I felt like I was in Dante's Inferno. I saw myself running through these corridors, the corridors of Hell. When my brother was born, I felt I was going to be lost, abandoned. Everybody would care about this new baby more than me. That hopeless feeling stayed with me for many years."

"Did you resent him for being her favorite?"

"*She* was the one I resented. I felt he knew how to get things from her, her attention. But *she* gave in to him."

"How did competition with him express itself?"

"I was never competitive with my brother. We had a wonderful relationship. I never blamed him for getting what he wanted from her."

"Come on, Sally . . ."

"No! I blamed her. I blamed her for being that way."

For being withholding. Not only when the baby came. From the beginning.

Like most of us, Sally traces her sexual pattern to her first experience. Who wants to think that childhood, infancy, has anything to do with sex? And yet, was Sally's decision never to lose to another woman really born of that betrayal when she was nineteen?

She and I go back down the ladder of her defeats. We reconstruct the envies and competitions that added up to her iron determination never to lose again, nevermore to be outstripped by tall beautiful blondes. First there had been "the loss of my whole adolescence," as she calls it. I never understood my friend's fixed memory of herself as a friendless, ugly teenager. It had no consonance with the reality of the woman I know today. But when she sensed that her sexuality threatened the love of her prime connection to life, she capitulated. No, she wasn't sexual; no, she wasn't attractive; no, she wasn't popular. To be a rival to the other, bigger woman in the house was frightening.

People she knew in school tell her today they had crushes on her. She couldn't afford to see herself as desirable. What is usually not recognized about the popularly named "inferiority complex" is that it is devaluation —a defense against envy.

Sally's pattern wasn't set by her first boyfriend. It wasn't even set by her adolescence. Oedipal conflicts? While Sally's father was clear about the roles of the two women in the house, this solved only half of his daughter's Electra problem. Sally and her mother were not clear at all. Sexual competition between mother and daughter was repressed, hidden. The mother held all the cards. She deflected the rivalry. Her secrecy deprived Sally of her father's ambitious plans for his brilliant, beloved daughter.

Sally's denial of competition with her brother sounds unbelievable. Could she be reaching for a more honest, more basic emotion? Sally was only two when she lost supremacy in the family. The real figure who sent her "racing through the corridors of Hell" was her beloved mother: By turning from Sally to shower attention on the favored boy, Sally's mother displayed her other face: the withholding, death-dealing mother of Klein's nightmares.

"The older I get," says Sally, "the less I have to idealize my mother. She was envious. And if envy is constitutional, I've probably got it in my blood too. That's why I always feel I must have control. I can't bear a relationship in which a man has power over me. From the time I was little, I couldn't wait to grow up and make money. I wanted to be an adult, to go to work and be able to buy myself all the things my mother wouldn't give me. To have pretty clothes, cosmetics—it seemed to me, you know, that it was making money and your mother making it possible. . . ."

"Mother making it possible?"

Sally laughs. "Did I say that? My mother didn't make it possible. Earning my own *money* made it possible."

"What a slip! You unconsciously substituted money for the good mother. Talk about power. You have your mother locked up in your bank account."

"She gave me the most important thing in my life. Dedication to my work comes from her."

Robertiello has been out of town for a month. Another August. This year he's gone to Italy, back to the small town where his father and grandfather were born. After years of preoccupation with the mother/ child relationship, he's turned to seek out his male heritage; all those highly sexed Italian men to whom he attributes his survival as a man. His intense competitive spirit.

We'd had a quick visit the day before he left. It was Saturday. He was on his way to play tennis. I was depressed, not just over his going away but because I was about to begin the latest draft of this chapter. I watched him trot around his office, grabbing tennis balls and sweatbands. With the padded door to the waiting room open and Robertiello in his white shorts, the place revealed itself as what it was: the apartment where he'd intermittently lived over the past twenty years, whenever one of his marriages broke down. His mismatched furniture, now old and shabby, was the residue of various wives' tastes. He liked it that way, he'd told me. He said it reminded him of Freud's consulting room in a famous photograph. I asked him why this chapter held such special despair for me.

"I've done three drafts. But each time I try to make sense out of the relation of competition to jealousy, I choke."

"The intense bond between your mother and sister was set up before you were born. How could you compete? Jealousy for you always carried this a priori defeat."

"I feel like I'm swimming underwater, that I'm not going to make it. . . ."

"That's great," he said, never breaking stride as he closed up the apartment and turned off the air conditioner. "The more pain you go through in writing, the better the book will be. That's what makes it good, right?"

The thought of taking his beloved ancient spear from some other August's trip to Guatemala and thrusting it into his heart entered my mind. I had learned from him that part of what I was feeling was displaced separation anxieties; it is less painful to feel anger than admit how abandoned I would feel without him.

"You any good at tennis?" I asked

"A killer at the net," he grinned. "I've always been a competitor."

I told him of a woman I was interviewing. "She calls herself 'a terrible person' for wanting to compete."

"At least she can admit it. That's better than defending yourself by going under because you're envious of your opponent's power."

He told me about a beautiful actress in one of his therapy groups. "All the women want to do her in, but aren't up front about it. When I talk to them about their envy, ultimately they admit it."

"How do you get them to do that?"

"We talk about their fantasies. That onstage, they'd really like her to fall flat on her face. Or have somebody scar her with acid."

"Oh, my God . . ."

"I know it sounds horrendous, but it's important to know how you feel.

If you don't acknowledge how you really feel, you won't be able to compete."

We left his office and walked out onto sunny Madison Avenue. Robertiello swung his racket at an imaginary lob shot, clearly destroying his opponent.

"Look," he said, "don't get the idea that women are the only ones troubled by competition. I once had a lawyer patient who would urge his wife to pick up other men. Then he'd watch them in bed. There was a homosexual element in it. But he was also putting himself down and making the other man better than he. There was a lot of competition, but with him losing. He really wanted to experience himself as setting up the triangle and then losing . . ."

". . . because the other man was better than he?"

". . . *only as he perceived him to be in his own mind.* That was his defense against castration anxiety. He did the same thing professionally, as a lawyer. He was always submitting to his partners or opponents. He needed to lose across the board to appease his very powerful father. Unconsciously he needed to say to Poppa, 'I won't compete with you. If you won't cut my balls off, I'll even let you have my woman.' "

"You see many patients like that?"

"Twenty years ago that was the main thing men came into analysis for. Oedipal conflict. The goal was to get to be able to beat father rather than having to submit to him . . . with the consequent raising of self-esteem."

"Has this change in your male patients got anything to do with the sexual emergence of women?"

"Yes, in that women are more available nowadays. It used to be harder to find a woman to make it with unless you married her. So there was more sexual competition with other men."

"Now the envy and competition is between the sexes."

He nodded. "Envy is a dirty word," he said. "Even sophisticated patients who are therapists themselves, when I first point out their envy, they deny it. They tell me I'm crazy. All kinds of resistance. Envy is very difficult to accept in yourself."

Crowds of shoppers, happily defended against envy, were buying up every luxury in sight. More than they needed. More than they wanted. When is enough enough? I was still loath to say good-bye to Robertiello, and determined to do it on an up note. How many Augusts had we parted on arguments, angry, even hostile to one another?

I especially hate him when he goes away in the middle of one of my books. One year he had lent me a "transference object," a security blanket to remember him by—one of the little monster figurines he'd collected from his travels around the world. They sit on a shelf behind his Barcalounger. "Those monsters," he had told me, "carry a lot of projections of my earliest, nastiest feelings. That's how I disown the monsters inside of me." He'd smiled at my choice, a gargoyle. "All primitive art is endowed with a kind of magic, both creative and destructive."

We were in front of an art gallery, a lovely soft Impressionist painting in the window. Two lovers in a garden. If I turned the painting over, would I see their other faces?

". . . see, if envy makes you afraid you'll kill"—Robertiello hadn't stopped talking—"then you'll put a damper on how aggressive, how assertive you can be. You won't put up your best effort to win whatever—the job, the man. But if you've openly admitted you'd like to see your rival killed or tortured or destroyed—acid thrown in her face—because you're envious, then simply trying to ace him or her out of a job or a lover isn't such a big deal."

I'd been looking at Robertiello's legs. "You know, you're much better looking with fewer clothes on."

"So I've heard."

"How would you rate yourself on a Bo Derek scale of ten?"

"Eight." He spoke without hesitation.

I laughed out loud. But I envied him his sureness, his ease with competition. To paraphrase Luce, "I don't want to *be* Robertiello, I would just like to have had that kind of chance." The chance to have grown up with more practice in handling my competition. To have learned the civilizing rules of the game at the appropriate time, as a child. Rules that tell competitors how to win and lose. To have rehearsed again and again the dumb, existential experience of learning opponents don't die just because you want "to ram the ball down their throats," and that they don't want to kill you back for feeling that way.

Instead, here I am—and clearly I'm not alone—stuck with this archaic response whenever the jealous situation threatens. I go straight from envy into immediate self-devaluation, denial, and idealization of my rival. Anything to eliminate the possibility of open competition. And what is left? A sense of peace? No. Only the conviction, as Robertiello put it, of a priori defeat. Behind it, the old roiling, primitive feeling of repressed murder.

"Want a lift home?" Robertiello offered, gingerly opening the door of his ancient Chevy. The roof was rotting through.

"No chance of anyone envying you that heap."

"I'm not worried about losing my girl to a guy with a Jaguar," he smiled. "Only a fool would own an expensive car in this city."

"Who would you be jealous of?"

He started the engine. The car backfired. "A smarter analyst," he said, waving, impatient to kill his opponent. Good-bye to August.

I stood there on the sidewalk for a few minutes after he left. He is almost sixty years old and lives with a woman half his age. Like Picasso, Casals, Supreme Court Justice Douglas and all those wrinkled movie moguls in Hollywood, I'm sure he'll die with a lovely young woman beside his bed, or in it.

"Women are like streetcars; there's always another one coming along." His terrible joke. For him, women are interchangeable. But while each one is with him, she holds his life in her hands. That is why he has his streetcar philosophy. You don't hear women joking about men being streetcars. Experience hasn't taught women to see black humor in disaster.

I've seen Robertiello's bereavement when the phone didn't ring or a letter didn't arrive. No woman suffers more over the possibility of loss. But he can live with his fear that women may abandon him, knowledge of his vulnerability, rage that they have power over him. Reality has taught him that in time he does recover, another "streetcar" comes along. Losing the tennis match today doesn't mean he won't win next Saturday. He does his work and enjoys his women too, without constant fear that some bigger man will come along and take away his one-and-only forever.

It wasn't always that way.

His father was a deadly competitor who refused to recognize his son's existence. There could only be one "man" in the house. Robertiello positioned himself as weak and noncompetitive opposite his father. He found ways to win points outside the house. By competing at school for the top grades that his tyrannical grandfather demanded, he strove to win attention from his loveless family. Thanks to his grandfather's grueling academic regimen, he entered Harvard at sixteen. Harvard had too many geniuses. Robertiello had to find himself a new arena in which to prove he mattered: sex.

He'd always fervently attributed much of his early survival to qualities he'd taken in from the other men in his family, Italian uncles and cousins, who, to listen to Robertiello, were cocksmen all. I used to laugh at what I thought to be this macho overemphasis. But now I understand why he repeatedly stresses how much he owes to their maleness.

While the nice Harvard boys were too inhibited to touch a Wellesley girl, Robertiello was clearly a rabbit, programmed and primed to do what Italian men do best. "It was a combination of genetics and role models," he'd told me. "A lot of it is ethnic, I think. I had a lot of better male sexual introjects than the WASPs and Jews at Harvard. I was obsessed with sex. I put so much time into it, I was so insistent on it with girls, that I succeeded. My early sexual experiences were very reinforcing of my adequacy as a man. I knew I could beat out all those other guys for a woman because I knew what I was doing. I had the guts to go after women. It's all subjective. Men like me, who have these kinds of early successes, are sure we'll win in a sexual competition, right?"

It was World War II and men were scarce. If the nice Wellesley girls were afraid of sex, Robertiello found townies in Cambridge who would "do it" in doorways and behind bushes. Chubby Mopey Dick won himself another nickname. In his dorm, he became known as The Dong.

"Because of my father and my grandfather—in that house it was life-and-death competition—I had to beat my father or die. I had to be a winner or die. In sex I found a field in which I was the best. Or anyway, women told me I was. Whether it was objectively true or not, I felt it was. Once I was convinced I could beat out any man for a woman, I was much less threatened. Prior to sex, I thought I was a loser. But from then on, I felt women loved me."

Does it matter that he confused women's postcoital symbiotic attachment to him with his sexual prowess? All he knew was that once he got a woman into bed, she was his. In his mind, sex became his power over women. It also gave him status among less sexually daring men. It was a competitive status he couldn't afford to lose. When his girlfriend threatened to see other men unless he married her, he proposed the next day. He was nineteen.

"I was suicidal at the idea of her seeing other men," says Robertiello. We are back in his office. I have lived through thirty days. September is here. August is over. We pick up the conversation. "My supremacy was based on not being compared. If she was with anyone else, she would leave me for the other man because he would be better. Whatever better meant and not just necessarily better in bed. I mean, better all around as a man.

"Sex was that central to my existence. A year after I got married, I had my first extramarital affair. I was top of my class, an intern, had this beautiful wife, and I didn't give a damn about this new woman really. I was impotent. I took sleeping pills and was in a coma for ten days. My life experiences had somehow made me feel okay as a man, but it was based too much on my penis, on sexual performance. Impotent, I felt destroyed all over again."

"What made you so sure you could beat out any man when Wife Number Two came along?"

"I think it was my analysis when I was twenty-three. I worked through my oedipal problems. Instead of feeling I had to lose to my father, because I was afraid of castration—all the old chestnuts—I got so I wanted to beat my father. And in the end, believed I could. That analysis was the turning point. My second wife was the very sexy one who used to come on with all my friends. I was never in the least jealous. My internal view of myself had become that of a winner and that is what made me one. In competition the subjective idea makes all the difference; it's whether you believe you're going to win, or believe you're going to lose. In reality, my second wife could have left me. But I believed I had everyone beat hands down, and so I wasn't jealous."

"Come on, Richard, not because you had this magic cock. That isn't what women want. Not for the long haul. A great lover is wonderful but the real reason that women don't leave you is that you have something more powerful than sex. You know how to get inside their heads. You find out what their needs are, and zero in, convincing them that you are the answer. They can't survive without you. That's your magic."

"My father was treated as a god because of his magic as a doctor. I'd always been aware of the amount of power he had throughout our extended family."

In the medical hierarchy a psychoanalyst outranks a general practitioner. Becoming an analyst didn't just give Robertiello power over women. It gave him stature among men.

"My father got an enormous amount of points from everybody," he says, "even people who were richer, more successful, whatever. So imagine the points a psychoanalyst gets. He's the magician, the guru. I wanted to beat my father at his own game. Becoming a psychoanalyst made it a sure thing, like being the head of the family."

"Your father never acknowledged it."

"He never acknowledged anything," says Robertiello and we both know what he means.

In one of his books Robertiello describes how as adults, we can get a second chance at improving self-esteem. We must go to the significant person in our lives, he writes, and ask for what we need to hear. I remember the summer the old man died. That August Robertiello stayed in town to be the good son. He practiced what he preached. He went to his father's deathbed, said he loved him and asked for his approval for thirty years of dedication to healing.

What the old man said was, "If only you had made professor at Harvard."

Robertiello is pursuing his own line of associations. "What's the name of that analyst you've been talking to—Stern?"

"Dan Stern."

"Once in a while, during my travels in Italy, I'd get a whiff of terrific anger at this guy. I want to talk about it now. Whenever you tell me about him, I growl. I don't want you to think he's a better analyst than me.

Remember I used to tell you I was never jealous? Well, *I'm jealous of him.*"

I say nothing. I don't want to break his train of thought. It is the first time Robertiello has ever admitted to jealousy.

"Are you sure it isn't envy?" I ask at last.

"No, it isn't envy because I don't think he's smarter than me. It's jealousy because it's a three-party transaction. You're in the middle of it, and I'm vying with him for your respect. That's one of the things that came to me while I was away. That jealousy need not have a sexual component. It's invading some territory that's singled out as being a special bond. For a macho, if she makes it with somebody else, anybody else, that is invading his special, privileged zone of connection. Sex. But while the competition I feel with Stern is purely intellectual, it's still jealousy because you're in it. I don't want you to like him better than me. I need you to think I'm the best analyst in the business."

"Here's an idea of my own," I say in turn. "It's a way to further distinguish between envy and jealousy. Envy is additive. You want something someone else has. Jealousy is subtractive. You are facing loss. Stern could win me away if he were smarter than you. I'd stop coming here. I'd talk only to him."

"And I'd be devastated!"

"When I come in here quoting something fascinating some other analyst has told me, you don't become envious and sulk. You go into your killer competitive stance. Either you put him down and destroy his reputation—'what kind of a schmuck would have a dumb idea like that?'—or else you really turn it on to dazzle me. Competition really wakes up your adrenaline. That's when I learn the most from you."

"That's when I educate myself," he says. "That's why I like our talks so much."

"That's the 'something special' between us that you don't want to lose."

"I can fuck a hundred different women but what I have with you is unique. If you go out with some other guy who's a better lay than me . . . I mean, even if I were sleeping with you . . . I couldn't care less. Because that's not what's special. But if someone else muscles in on what's really special and unique that we have together, then I'm very jealous."

"Tell me exactly how you feel when you imagine me listening enthralled to some other brilliant man."

"They're cutting into my territory! That's the feeling. This stuff you and I do together is private. So when Stern invades that territory—and we're now getting into territoriality, which I think is important—that pains me. I either have to feel pain or I have to destroy him by denigrating what he's said."

"What if your hero Kohut were still alive and I was interviewing him?"

"I would have felt there was no way I could beat this guy. He's got the same kind of magic going with you that I do, but his is better."

"You couldn't compete?"

"I would have gone into depression. We're getting at something important here. . . . For some people, sex is not all that important. I would genuinely not be jealous if Susan had sex with another guy. Because I know that is not the special thing that binds her to me. What you and I have, I can't have with a lot of people. I don't have it with anyone but you." He laughs. "I feel as if I should break into song."

I laugh, but I'm blushing, pleased. He'll never leave me. He's right about jealousy. It is that terrible feeling of loss of something special you share with someone. As children, we all knew it when our best friend found another best friend.

I tell Robertiello something Arthur Koestler wrote about the end of his friendship with Jean-Paul Sartre and Simone de Beauvoir. He called it "intellectual jealousy" on de Beauvoir's part: "She resented Sartre's repeated offers of 'unconditional friendship'" were Koestler's exact words, "and such influence as . . . [I] might have on him. . . . Simone's own influence on Sartre aimed in the opposite direction."[16]

In other words, de Beauvoir felt that Koestler was intruding on and ruining *the something special* she had with Sartre.

"Come to think of it," Robertiello says, "I've always been very jealous of the therapists my girlfriends see. I've resented their looking to a third person for help. Empathy, insight, that's my magic. That's my territory."

"And all this came to you in Italy? That was quite a trip."

"What I want to talk about next are my defenses. There's a useful question in the business: When the patient is afraid, how does he act? You see, our behavior betrays our defenses. They must be analyzed right along with what is defended against."

"You drive me crazy! When we started these talks, I told you this book was going to be as much about people's defenses as about jealousy itself. You dismissed the idea totally. All you cared about was protecting yourself: 'If their defenses work,' you said, 'then they're not jealous.'"

"It's hard for me to remember, but I don't mind your showing me defensive. I put Klein away for twenty years after reading her. That was a defense against recognizing my own envy. My resistance to you, Nancy, always took the form of not wanting to analyze my defenses."

"Now we're talking!" My enthusiasm is genuine. It is a moment of admiration for his ease, his eagerness to have a look at his newly discovered jealousy. He's forgotten to push the recline button on his Bar-calounger. He's uptight.

"My first defense is to limit my spheres of interest to what I'm best at. I manipulate my environment in such a way that I practically never . . ."

"Yes?"

". . . feel jealous. For instance, I wouldn't be jealous of losing my woman to a more attractive man because I don't value looks. Nor do the women I choose. I define what is important, limiting it to intelligence and empathy. Since I feel I'm best in those areas, I know my woman will never leave me."

"On the smart, empathic charts, you're right up there."

"Also I make the woman very dependent on me."

"She's dependent starting out. You only choose wounded pigeons. Unless you can set up the power relation in your favor, you don't get involved with a woman ever."

"That's why I was never jealous! I felt I had this special magic, to give her something irreplaceable. So what if a better-looking man comes along? Or a richer one? She's not going to leave."

"You must have once felt jealousy, very powerfully, to put up such rock-hard defenses. Look at the expense. Doesn't it boomerang in the end? How many of your relationships have I seen end as you become increasingly bored and angry? You're doing all the nourishing, all the giving. It's your strength, but nobody's feeding poor little impoverished Richard."

"But they get angry at me too! The need me, they want me, they can't live without me, and that's exactly what infuriates them. I have all the power."

"It's the same with your male friendships. You're always saying how you miss having a close tie to another man."

"It's true. I have a yearning for a closeness with men."

"Did you belong to a boy gang when you were young?"

"I had friends . . . but no. I didn't feel I was into the male world in the way you are talking about. I graduated from high school when I was fifteen. Most of the people in my class were two or three years older than me. There was such a disparity in ages and experience. I had gone out with one girl on a date when I was fifteen."

"Not belonging to a gang of boys, it must have intensified all the earlier feelings of being left out. That fancy private school you went to, where you were the only non-WASP . . ."

"I really felt like I was not allowed in that club at all. I felt very left out and rejected. . . ."

"And the pretty WASP princesses . . ."

"I remember the first grade, where everybody was showing each other their thing, and I suppose I could have joined in that. . . . I wanted to! It wasn't that they kept me out, but I felt as if I couldn't make it with them. Like they were unattainables . . . princes and princesses and I was just a peasant."

"Feeling left out . . . it's such a terrible pain."

"A lot of my anger at women and my wanting to do them in comes from my not having been acceptable to the little girls in that first grade. I felt very left out . . . a feeling that began in the family where my sister was acceptable, was 'let in,' and I wasn't."

"Even your grandfather . . . he only let you feel 'in' if you brought home straight As."

"Later on, I practically never went out with Radcliffe girls. I just assumed they wouldn't have anything to do with me . . . all those Seven Sister ladies. Actually, I was wrong. But at the time I didn't feel I had a chance. I felt very left out by them. And also by the WASP Harvard men. I was furious at their being privileged."

"Some people I interview, when I ask them to describe jealousy, they say, 'I feel left out.' "

"Even in groups that happens a lot. When a new member comes in for therapy—into an established group—they almost invariably have the feeling that they're going to be excluded. There's no way they're going to get in. They defend themselves in a variety of ways. By saying the group is no good anyway, or whatever. Or else they just feel very left out for a very long time. It's a common preoccupation."

"One of the early threads that feed into jealousy."

"Oh, yes. The early family thing has so much to do with it. If you really had a good sense of belonging to a family unit, that decreases your vulnerability to feeling left out later on. But there are fewer good strong family systems now."

"To get back to your desire for good male friendship with a peer. The one or two male friends you introduced me to are yo-yos."

"I only meet people professionally. That's where limiting my world comes in. . . ."

"Your women are either in the field or you get them into it. Either way, you're on top."

"I'm always the boss. The people I know are always patients, supervisees, people in the clinic. In the end, I always have to be the big fish in the little pond. That kills any chance at friendship."

"The disparity of power. Tell me how women get angry at you."

"There was a woman I was living with. We once went to a dirty movie. There was a scene where a guy had six women. She became absolutely outraged at *me*. It brought up all her rage that I had opportunities like this before I knew her. Even more important, it brought up rage at me for having so much power over women, specifically her."

"That wasn't jealousy; it was envy."

"Not just envy of my masculine power, 'penis envy.' The biggest envy with her and with a lot of other women is that they feel that if I break with them, they can be replaced in three days. And there is no way, they feel, they can do that. That's why so many women are afraid of getting involved with a guy. They say, 'I'm losing myself; I'm losing my autonomy because you're so big and I'm so small.' It makes women very angry."

"How about you and Susan . . . Does she get angry at you?"

"We had a terrible fight last night. I was absolutely furious. She was crying and moaning and groaning. I'd really laid her out. She was suffering. She was doing all the things that would ordinarily make the man feel guilty. I didn't feel a drop."

"What were you arguing about?"

"She wanted me to pay a higher share of the expenses and I felt she was trying to rip me off."

"My, my, what a 1980s argument."

"And I really laid into her. I said no way."

"This new preoccupation of yours with money," I say, "it just doesn't sound like you. You becoming greedy in your old age?"

"That argument with Susan was about my not wanting to have all the power in the relationship. If I did, then she would go under like all the other women I've known. I wanted her to feel she was pulling her weight."

"Balls. That isn't at all what you were saying."

"Really?"

"You weren't going to give up any of your bloody power!"

"That's funny you heard it that way. I'm surprised. . . . But I am very conscious of my money giving me power. Much more than I was two years ago, five years ago."

"When I met you, I don't think money was anything you thought about."

"It really wasn't. And it is now. Tremendously."

"The world's more expensive. You'd be a fool not to be more aware of it."

"I used to think I had enough money to get whatever I wanted for the rest of my life. I don't feel that now. Maybe now that I'm older . . . No, no, I'm not that old. Money is not my only power. But I do think the idea of money being the major source of power is different. I would have felt power in being a very competent professional five years ago, ten years ago, certainly thirty years ago. But that doesn't seem to have much value anymore."

"Five years ago you were proud of the fact that you hadn't raised your fee in maybe fifteen years. You used to tell me that was the most important thing your father had given you: the image of a caring, total professional. He was a lousy father but a wonderful doctor."

"That idea still has value but I'm much more concerned about money as my power base. I know that. It's so clear to me now."

It used to be that Robertiello had to marry every woman he fell in love with. It was the only way he knew to "lock them up." He says he doesn't feel this compulsion with Susan. He feels he has her locked up anyway. I wonder. My friend has changed and it's more than his age. It is the time in which we live.

When I listen to him talk about women, there are all sorts of threats in the air. He told me he has sworn Susan to fidelity. He fights with her over who pays the electric bill, though he earns maybe five times more than she does. Yes, I can imagine him almost smiling as he wins the money battle, reducing her to tears.

As he deals with his newfound envy of women, as he allows himself to see them as full, powerful people less in need of his "magic," is his center of balance shifting? His need for male camaraderie has new emphasis. Money has become a frequent subject. Is he feeling a reluctance to stand alone in the world, unbuttressed by some form of male solidarity and the security of a nice bank account?

Stripping himself of the archaic form of power over women he once gloried in, is he finding an ironic new freedom—the freedom to show women he doesn't have to be the kindest, wisest and most loving man in the world? It's almost as if Robertiello's growing awareness of his envy of women has escalated into greed. Not that he is alone. Money remains the major source of marital arguments; more so since women are earning their share.

"It's like another view of the battle between the sexes," I say. "The envy between men and women today."

"Remember I used to tell you I saw very few men in here with problems of jealousy? That's because their old-fashioned defenses worked. They'd get a woman in their control and she would have to put up with whatever they dished out. She had to pretend to like it. That way he didn't have to feel guilty. Since he felt no pain, why should he look for an analyst?"

"Haven't you ever wished for a woman who's an equal?"

"I've known some who had a lot on the ball. Who did have nourishing qualities and could really have given me something. But I always had to keep an edge on them. The power. Sometimes they loved me. I suppose that meant they needed me least, and therefore probably had the most to give back. . . ."

A moment's silence, the sad contemplation of what might have been.

"How does it feel to lose a good woman to another man?"

"I remember one. . . . I lost her to another analyst. I had the strangest fantasy. That I was going down on him, the guy she'd left me for. Isn't that crazy?"

"In Freud's paper he writes that the man's fantasy of sharing his woman with another man suggests the major emotion is between the two men."

"That's bullshit," says Robertiello. "Freud's interpretation has nothing to do with me. I see my thing as a kind of sick masochistic fantasy. A glorifying humiliation. Either I had to kill him or submit to him in some way."

"You're making it into a game of tennis, like it's competition, not jealousy. Look, I never liked that Freud paper either. Until I talked to this guy who's psychiatrist-in-chief at New York Hospital. His reading of that paper was so exciting . . ."

"Where do you find these idiots? That's the old 1920, 1940 point of view. . . ."

"You don't even let me finish telling you what he said! *You're jealous.* Remember you once told me your fantasy about Susan making it with the delivery boy and other 'lowlifes'? Didn't you identify with those men? Didn't you imagine yourself one of them?"

"That's different. I see plenty of that in my practice; it's a whole different story. That's wanting to introject a male model so men can know how to be men."

"Doesn't that include a sense of wanting to be close to the other man, at least in fantasy? In a way that the world forbids in reality?"

"Sure. That's fine. But that isn't queer or gay. It's more like the Greek idea of us men together, learning how to be men and reinforcing our masculinity. But we're all men."

I've never heard Robertiello use the words gay or queer that way. Isn't he always encouraging male patients to be physically close to one another, to touch, hug, confide in each other? Here he is defending his fantasy as if it were tainted. I remind him how often we've discussed the way young boys have heroes whom they worship.

"And they do have very close relationships," he adds.

"Even sexual closeness," I say.

"Mutual masturbation . . ."

"Peeing games . . . innocent stuff," I say.

"Innocent," he says, "in the sense that they aren't going to become gay. It's all in the service of reinforcing their heterosexuality, ultimately. That's not what Freud said. My fantasy, that's not homosexual."

"I never used the word homosexual."

CHAPTER SEVEN

Be a Man!

*T*hese are Phil's earliest memories.

He is being bathed by his mother. She is crying. He asks why.

"Because your father isn't here," she says.

He stands up in the bathtub and puts his arms around her. He is two years old.

"I am here," he says.

"That isn't enough," she sobs.

And then a year later. Father, back from the war, taking mother out to dinner. Aside from father's few brief furloughs home, the little boy has had his beautiful mother to himself for almost three years. Now he stands in the yard, weeping, calling her back.

"No, no, Mommy, don't go!"

The man turns to his son and orders him to be quiet. When Phil doesn't obey, father takes a newspaper, rolls it up and comes after him. Round and round the garden they go until the boy is caught. Held screaming by a man he hardly knows, the child looks to his mother. She stands watching, says nothing. Doesn't she have all the power in the world? Why has she betrayed him?

A sister is born in the same year. Before mother left for the hospital she said she would bring back his favorite candy bar. Instead, this other person, another child, *another rival*, is brought home. To the little boy it is a broken promise.

"Call *her* Isaac!" he cries, hating the name he will later change. They are the only Jewish family in a small southern town. An early feeling of being left out; later rekindled in the East Coast school in which he is enrolled.

Another memory: He is four, too young to enter kindergarten. But his mother is eager for him to begin. "If he can reach the urinal," the teacher says, "we will take him." He and his mother, accompanied by the teacher, descend to the basement. He is very eager to please his mother. The teacher stands him in front of the urinal.

"Too little," the teacher says.

Once again he has failed to measure up.

His grandmother loves him. He is the first male grandchild. "But you will never be as fine a man as your father," she says.

"Try," says his mother.

Indeed, his father is the most successful man in town. Their house is the biggest, their cars the newest. In the morning, the little boy sits on the toilet seat watching father shave. The thing between father's legs must also be the biggest in town. It will be almost forty years before a loving woman convinces the man that his own firm genitals are more beautiful than the sagging testicles of his father. Until then, he has been sure that every woman judged his balls inferior. The only women with whom he felt comfortable were whores; their judgment didn't matter.

The little boy begins to imitate the bigger man who has usurped his place with mother. He puts Vitalis on his curls and parts his hair in the middle. Saturday afternoon he sits in his father's office; when allowed, in his father's chair. Has it always been understood that he will join his father's medical practice when he grows up? It seems so. His mother takes it for granted. Not, of course, that he can ever be "as fine a man." Actually, he sees very little of his father, who works into the night, giving so tirelessly to community affairs that he seldom comes home until long after the boy is asleep.

The lonely wife turns to her "little man," the person with whom she has shared constant warmth since he was born. The person who will never leave her. Oh, he will grow up, marry and have children of his own. But he will be nearby, on call, her husband's future partner and her boy, always. She is a powerful woman within her extended family. A day does not go by that she doesn't speak to her mother and younger brothers. As for her husband's family, over the years she has found reasons to distance if not ostracize them.

She tucks her little son in bed and lies beside him, massaging his back, talking to him softly. He is six, eight, eleven years old. He lies and waits for the sound of her slippers on the carpet. He knows her smell, the feel of her soft, white nightgown. Though he dare not touch it or her for reasons he is not quite sure of. He curls away from her in bed, facing the wall so that she will not know his body is betraying him.

There is nothing overtly sexual in her behavior. She never touches his genitals. No one would call her a bad mother. But how characterize the desires she arouses in him? He is sure they are bad. But she is all good. What then is he?

"Come lie with me, Mama," he calls out on those nights when he fears she might forget.

Phil tells me that when he was little she called his genitals his "sissy box." He repeats the terrible phrase now with an easy laugh. He has no doubts about his manliness. No doubts he could rationally flesh out. Not only is he powerful professionally, his body is hard, muscular. He played football in college, was president of his fraternity, ran the campus radio station. But he is still shy with women. The sureness he felt in front of the microphone didn't carry over to girls, whom he desperately desired.

"I don't think my mother was eager for me to get real involved with girls. She was possessive. Calling my genitals my 'sissy box' was a way of keeping me close to home. This was not conscious, mind you, but she wasn't the kind of woman who sat easy with my father having all the power. She was a traditional woman, so she had to seem to conform. But she was very competitive and I think she worked a lot of that out through me. She wanted me to get ahead, but on her terms."

Phil's sexual drive went underground. Saturdays he worked in his father's office. Upstairs among the inactive files, he would read *Playboy* and masturbate. His favorite Playmate was a woman walking up a flight of stairs, the soft folds of her peignoir pulled away from her breast as she smilingly turned to extend a hand to the man she was leading to bed. It was easy to imagine oneself being that man.

Two things happened when Phil was nineteen. He got his first summer job at the local TV station and knew that this—not a medical practice—was what he wanted. Second, the county fair came to town. He discovered there were women who would let you lick their cunts for a dollar.

How tell his mother that he wasn't going to become his father's partner? How find a girl you could take home to mother, one who would let you lick her cunt?

In the next twenty years he proved himself to be even more successful than the man his mother had lionized. He worked longer and harder than anyone else. "But I've always hated overt competition," he said. "I'm a tough competitor, but my secret strategy is to keep everyone from regarding me as a rival until after I've blown them out of the water."

As for women, "I only approach those I am sure will accept me. I never let them see the side of me I can show a whore, a woman in a massage parlor. The idea of falling in love with a woman and then being left for another man . . . I just couldn't stand it. The rewards I get from my work give me a great deal, a good feeling about myself among men. But women . . . I am so afraid of rejection that I wait until Thursday to call for a Saturday date. That way, if she rejects me, I can always say it was because I called so late."

Women would find it difficult to believe he is frightened of them. Professionally, he makes a practice of promoting women on his staff. To the irritation of many men, if it's a toss-up for a top position, he gives it to the woman. "I have a great deal of respect for women in the work force," he says, and the women I speak to about him return the favor. Professionally, he has certainly "measured up." The television ratings give him daily proof.

"What about the other half of your life?" I ask.

"I take most of the blame for the failure of my marriage. Maybe my wife lost her sense of herself in my world. She was successful but she never thought I was behind her. She felt I tried to overwhelm her. When we met, she was sexually assertive; it's what I loved. That disappeared overnight. She didn't like the way I kissed, didn't like the way I 'thrust my cock' at her. We've been divorced almost a year."

"How about the women you see now?"

"There were two women I saw on a pretty regular basis. But what I learned from my wife held for them too: They didn't want to hear about any of my glories in the work world. They got angry. It disturbed me how compartmentalized my life had become."

"What does that mean?"

"Work, separate from the women I dated, separate from whores. Love and sex kept getting divided. In the kind of role women expect me to play, there was no way I could reach the loss of control I find with a whore. These women I dated and slept with, I couldn't show them what I showed a whore! They'd laugh, reject me.

"I don't know what would have happened if I hadn't met Julie. In typical fashion, I waited to call her when there were only three days left before I was to leave town on an extended business trip. I suggested drinks. She said come to dinner. She's the kind of woman I'd never dare to call until recently. She's beautiful. She's as successful in her field as I am. Our first night together was one of the most exciting in my life. After dinner, I was sitting on the sofa, holding my drink, and when she came back from putting on some music, she just leaned over and kissed me. The kiss went on forever. Then she held out her hand to me—Yes, yes, my Playmate fantasy!—and led me to bed. We made love until four in the morning. I've never had orgasms like that. Never showed a woman that. And the more I showed, the more she loved it.

"When I left, I stood on the street and looked up at her lighted window. 'What happened up there?' I thought. I couldn't believe it. But I didn't call her the next day. Wonderful as it had been, I was a little frightened. She called me. She was so happy, so open, she left herself so vulnerable . . . well, we had one last night together before I left. There was nothing she would not do sexually. Nothing about me she didn't want to hear or see. There was so much . . . mutuality between us. And when I'd start to withdraw into myself after we'd had sex, she'd call me on it. 'Hey, where are you? Come back!'

"Two months apart, the geographical distance between us gave me the space I needed. It made me aware how much I missed her, how she filled the emptiness in my life, brought my two worlds together. I don't think my confidence has ever been higher. Still, it's crazy. The last time I flew back to see her, it was so wonderful, so exciting, that I really became terrified. A few days after I'd left her, I was lying in bed masturbating one morning, remembering what we'd done together. After I came, after the joy of this extraordinary orgasm produced just by the memory of her, I felt cold terror. Is she going to expect that kind of performance from me every time?"

"Did you tell her of your fear?" I ask.

"I said to her, 'I think I'm too old for you.' She laughed. She loved it. She is actually two years older than me. I wasn't kidding. She has so much lust . . . which is what I love . . . but I'm anxious she might meet another, really young guy while I'm away. When I telephone her late at night and the phone rings more than three or four times, I imagine that she's going into another room to be able to talk to me."

"Are you jealous?"

"All the time. But it's in my head. I believe her when she says there's no one else. All my life I've chosen women who wouldn't arouse jealousy, women I wouldn't care about losing. But then I'd go looking for someone else, something more. I want to make it with one woman. . ."

"You want to end the compartmentalization?"

"To have sex and love in one person. If I don't take the risk with Julie, I may never get another chance. The last time we spoke she said, 'You know, I really am your fantasy woman. Tell me what you want; I'll do anything. I love being that woman of your nineteenth summer, the dollar-a-lick woman.' My heart turned to jelly. I'm terrified that my fantasy woman has come true."

Fantasies gain their energy by separating out exactly what we want so as to exaggerate its satisfaction. In reality, a man who lived on chocolate cake alone would soon get sick of it. There is in all of us a drive for the satisfaction of a fully integrated life. Phil wants a woman who would allow him, as he puts it, to stop "compartmentalizing" himself, one who would encourage him to bring into view the half-ashamed, half-proud, fully sexual person he had assumed no woman would ever want to see.

Having found such a woman, the heroine of male fantasy—She Who Never Says No—he is anxious. Her assertion and eroticism ease his burdensome iron control but lose him the safely dominant position. The terror is: Will he measure up?

Phil grew up thinking that women expect you not only to provide for their material well-being but to make them sexual as well, give them orgasm. *That is what a man does.* The night Julie asked him to dinner, she solved the problem for them both. She gave him the orgasm and took her own. What does that make him?

I choose to print this man's interview because he is taking a risk at a time when the old blueprints—the way our parents were—no longer work. He is a man who has given a lot of thought and time to sex, trying to integrate his fantasies with reality. He feels he hasn't got much more time. "Most men my age are burned out," he says. "The work does it." Firmly established at the top of his profession, no one—no man—could weaken his hard-earned sense of himself as a man. A woman could.

"I'm forty years old," Phil says. "How can I still have three orgasms a night? Sometimes I think life would be easier back in the massage parlors."

But he wants the big sexual woman, the dream his mother awoke in him as she "innocently" lay beside him when he was a boy. If Julie should reject him for another man, a younger man, he would not only have to face his jealousy—loss to a rival—but would also be put back in touch with his envy of women. Of their power to give or withhold the breast at their will alone. Envy of their power to come to your bed or not, to arouse emotions they can choose not to accept.

"Am I too old for you?" Phil half joked the first night with his lover. Do I hear a knell in those few words? Do they signal an end to the era in which men were confident that their bank accounts, their large houses and worldly wisdom would safeguard them in possession of women against the depredations of younger men who had nothing to offer but virility? D. H. Lawrence realized the poignant significance of this idea. He located male power within male physicality. Lady Chatterley left her rich, titled but crippled English lord for a physically magnificent servant. If a titan of industry takes a woman to bed and finds himself impotent, all other dominions are suddenly revealed as superficial. He begins to envy the lifeguard at the pool.

Are men, like women, beginning to feel that they too are endangered by age? It is well known that the curve of women's sexual desire goes up with age; men peak in their teens and inexorably ride down. If more and more women can find economic security on their own, will biology vanquish economics and tell us this is a more natural way to live? The older woman, the younger man; Mother and Son as avatars of the race's innate and reciprocating cycles of sexuality.

Popular thinking says that male sexual development is easier than the female's because his moves in a straight line. Beginning with mother, it is always the female sex he will love. Less obvious in this lifelong love affair is that in his journey from mother to girls to women to wife, he carries an unconscious resentment: women's power to accept or reject. He needs/loves them, but also feels the old rage/envy.

A woman's efforts to make him love her reawaken the ambivalence. Women are wonderful but they are also possessive, nagging, guilt-inducing, and disapproving of his sexuality. What he loves in each woman may be new, as she herself is new. What he hates is the old, familiar emotional baggage he has carried since life began.

Speaking of men for whom the image of mother inhibits the erotic life, Freud said, "Where they love, they do not desire, and where they desire they cannot love."[1] The man in the interview above calls this "compartmentalization."

How to have a woman of his own and not be seduced back into passivity by those warm, all-powerful arms? Intimacy with a woman is redolent of the symbiosis he loved, but from which he so painfully extricated himself to begin life as a man. If he surrenders now, how can he be sure he will reemerge as powerful as he was? In his swooning immersion in Cleopatra's spell, Mark Antony grew befuddled, lost his hard, ambitious self; lost Rome. Samson fell asleep in Delilah's arms. He was shorn of his strength. Women have always played this, their most powerful card; wooing men back into the primitive weightlessness of the ocean bed where they, the emotional sex, live.

After sex, men fear too much intimacy; they want to separate again. Women want to talk, to continue the merging, melting fusion into one. Postcoital conversations keep the woman's power alive. Through unconscious severance, by falling asleep, the man regains his self. Writes Leonard Michaels, "Sex wakes women—think of Sleeping Beauty—and puts men to sleep."[2]

"In an adult, dependence on a loved person revives the helplessness of the infant and is felt to be humiliating . . . ," writes Klein. "There is also fear that love will lead to too much responsibility and that the object will make too many demands. The unconscious knowledge that hate and destructive impulses are operative may [cause someone to] feel more sincere in not admitting love either to himself or others."[3]

Women assume that a man believes in his power. It doesn't occur to a woman that his sense of himself as a man is something he must maintain on an almost daily basis; something that he feels is always at risk. The word *machismo* was necessary and so, if not invented, successfully taken over from another language because it fills an immense need. It quiets worries about masculinity in just three syllables. The feminine equivalent has not been incorporated into English.

Who thought of dividing women into Bad Girls and Good Girls? While women are one another's cruelest jailers, quick to ostracize the tainted sister from the sorority—lest her experience of sexual pleasure arouse envy among the virgins—until recently history has been interpreted by men. What purpose did it serve them to divide the female sex into good and bad?

The power of female sexuality disturbed the gods themselves. In the famous argument between Zeus and Hera as to which sex experienced the greater pleasure, the question was referred to the seer Tiresias, who had been in turn both male and female. From this impartial position, says historian Peter Gay, Tiresias "awarded the palm of pleasure to woman, nine to one."[4]

"Nature has given women so much power, that the law wisely gives her little," said Samuel Johnson. Behind Greek mythology, hidden in fairy tale and legend, lurks male suspicion that if left unbridled, women's sexuality would be all-consuming. Dividing woman into Good/Bad, Madonna/Whore, Witch/Mother, cuts her down to size, literally in half.

The mechanism tips the balance. The man is defended against the jealous situation. He will not lose his source of love. He will not be detrimentally compared to another man. He is also protected against finding himself unable to slake woman's insatiable appetite. Guaranteed paternity is perhaps the most important benefit of all. Men's fear and awe of women is often dated from the earliest prehistoric connection made between sex and reproduction.

Young women have long been married to older men for social, economic or political ends. These powerful husbands, says Joseph Campbell (in George Leonard's *The End of Sex*), "invariably took their property rights in the women they had married very seriously. They might be away for years on Crusade; the wife was to remain inviolate, and if for any reason the worm Suspicion happened to have entered to gnaw the husband's brain, his blacksmith might be summoned up to fit an iron girdle of chastity to the mortified young wife's pelvic basin. The Church sanctified these sordid property rights . . . with all the weight of Hell, Heaven, eternity, and the coming of Christ in glory on the day of judgment. . . . So that, against all this, the wakening of a woman's heart to love was . . . a grave and really terrible disaster, not only for herself, for whom torture and fire were in prospect, but also—and more horribly—in the world to come, forever. Hence, in a phrase coined by the early Church Father Tertullian, which long remained a favorite of the pulpits, woman— earthly, actual woman, that is—awakened to her nature, was *janua diaboli,* 'the devil's door.' "[5]

In many societies clitorectomy was a mark of female "respectability." In our country, as late as the turn of the century, clitorectomies were still regularly performed. How could a man tame a continent if half his mind was anxiously at home, jealously imagining his wife in the arms of another man?

Better to think of women hating sex, better to sleep with a frigid wife than allow the furnaces of industry to go half stoked. If women were capable of feeling and even searching for sexual fulfillment, "The whole world would be a bordello," says Krafft-Ebing, in his famous *Psychopathia Sexualis,* "and marriage and the family unthinkable."[6] The desexualization of women contributed greatly to the Industrial Revolution. "The bourgeois," goes the withering accusation by Karl Marx, "sees in his wife a mere instrument of production."[7]

In time it was no longer necessary to remove a woman's clitoris. Emotional training did a better job than the surgeon's knife. Automatically repeating their mothers' lives, women buried and denied the lust that made them guilty. It left men with good companions, fine mothers for their children, partners for life. Safe, sexually boring women. A society had been built that was a good if not perfect defense against jealousy. Lust? Bad Girls took care of that. It is notorious that the sexual expression found in the brothel is the kind a man feels he cannot show his wife. Prostitution gives men a formal, institutional outlet for their rage/envy of women.

Does this mean that men go to whores to play out essentially sadistic fantasies? No. What men pay for is a nonjudgmental but erotic woman who dispenses freedom from guilt. What men seek in fantasy is *permission* and the great male secret is passivity. If there is to be any sadomasochism, fifteen years of research tells me the majority of men choose masochism. Punishment, humiliation, any form of passivity at the hands of a woman puts a man back in touch with a time when a woman totally ruled his world. However, this time the little boy's sexuality will not be denied. The price is—he must first acknowledge her power.

"Be a man," father instructs his four-year-old son. The boy is crying but something familiar is being asked of him. To rise above, to go beyond whatever he may be feeling. There is an urgency to prove something; a higher order of importance than "mere" feelings. Something is at stake that might be lost, that he has not yet even won. The command is frightening but not unwelcome. Lovely as life may be in mother's arms, the boy knows that woman's place cannot be his. Her world is what he knows most intimately. Her flesh is life itself. Her warmth comforts him. But a woman's body is not his. He must find his own power.

Proving his manliness, maintaining it, fearing its loss, regaining it: emotions anxiously tangled in the boy's psyche as far back as he can remember.

"Take that beachhead," the sergeant yells twenty years later. Once again the man must face the test, live up to what society expects of him as a man. The sergeant's command is no less frightening than his father's. And no less welcome. Why else would men wage wars and remember battles as their finest moments? These were times when they were closest to death but most complete as men.

If a man puts himself at risk of death, even if he loses an arm or a leg, he is a hero, more of a man. Being male is dangerous stuff. Perhaps the reverse is more apt: Dangerous stuff is being male.

"When I was a freshman in college," a man says to me, "my roommate and I were both on the wrestling team. Because we were the same weight, we always worked out together. He was far better than I. And a really good-looking guy. There was this big match, and he got pinned. You know, he lost. Afterward, the coach said to him, 'Know why you lost? Because you've got no guts.' The next day he walked down to the railroad tracks and lay down. He put his head on the track and watched a train run over his face." (I could not believe the words when I heard them and wrote them down then and there. I've checked my notes. I remembered them perfectly.)

I will say it again: A man can love as deeply as a woman and be pained as deeply by loss. The emotional history, the developmental strains he brings to jealousy in many ways mirror his sister's, feeding into what will become *someone* who is more or less vulnerable to jealousy's threat.

That having been said, *someone* who is male will anticipate and guard against jealousy differently than someone who is female. Our losses are different. Our defenses too.

Just as "good enough mothering" eases the dependent infant's envy of the power mother has over him, adult love puts to rest the envy between the sexes. We momentarily "forget" all the rages suffered since when we were born. We lay down our arms—our shield—and find the peace and ecstasy we have always craved. In *Parallel Lives,* Phyllis Rose describes love as "the momentary or prolonged refusal to think of another person in terms of power."[8] Marriages, she writes, often do not work because the partners' love is no longer young enough or strong enough to inhibit the struggle for power.

To the boy, power begins as a totally female province belonging to the one who feeds and holds him, who maintains his life. For her love, he even learns to control his bladder as he sleeps. To a two-year-old, her power is invincible. When he cries in the night, when bad dreams attack, what kind of magic is it that this person has? She picks him up and with a kiss saves him from the dragons. Who wouldn't want to own this kind of power? Who would not want to use it on others, making them love and fear you?

"From the very beginning, most people are raised by women," says psychoanalyst Robert Michels. "This means the recognition of her own femaleness is probably easier for the young girl than is the recognition of his masculinity for the young boy. As a result, males have more conflict about their gender identity. Conversely, girls have more conflict about their separateness and independence from mother. Boys know they are clearly different from mother. They may be less sure just *what* they are."

Male and female infant lie against mother's body, physically and psychologically taking in her warmth and strength, taking in *her.* But for the boy, imitation of the person to whom he is closest is exactly what must be avoided. The boy wins himself through negation; the first male identification is a no-compass journey into a vacuum. *A male is someone who is not female.*

This is so abstract, so difficult and reactive a concept, the boy is ever haunted by fear he has not fully succeeded. "When I was a little kid," says a thirty-year-old man, "I had this dream in which I had breasts. It was so scary I have never forgotten it." It is not enough to establish oneself as separate. That self must be established as male. Those arms that hold him, that body that comforts him must not be his model. His voice must not imitate hers, which he loves, and remembers from the womb.

If the phrase *gender identity* has passed into the language, it is largely due to the work of Dr. John Money, professor of medical psychology and pediatrics at Johns Hopkins University. Gender identity refers to an inner conviction that we are either boy or girl. It is a statement about where we fit in the vast dichotomy of the world in which we find ourselves. Money doesn't agree with the general consensus that boys have a more difficult time establishing gender identity than do girls. "Even if you're a little boy," he says, "and you don't have a father at home, you can compliment yourself because of the approval you get from your mother or sister. A mother acts differently to you if you're a boy or a girl."

"But all the little boy has that is different from his sister or mother," I say, "is his penis. At that age, how can it feel more important than his need of mother, his need to identify with her power? Identifying with mother reinforces the girl's sense of herself as female. It puts the boy's masculinity at risk."

"It's just different for the two sexes," says Money, "not harder, not easier, just different. You've been hanging out with psychoanalysts too long. They promulgated these ideas first."

"That gender identity is easier for girls?"

"Yes. It's a matter of professional prejudice whether you follow the party line of the sociologists, the bird biologists, the cultural anthropologists, or whoever. The psychoanalysts have their own ax to grind. Just choose the camp you like."

This disagreement among the authorities illustrates how little we know about how and when we form that inner psychic certainness of ourselves as male or female.

"Very early on the infant knows there is a difference between the sexes and that he is inescapably one or the other," says Dan Stern. We are sitting in the Baby Lab next to his office, about to watch an experiment done by one of his colleagues.

"And it has nothing to do with whether you have a penis or a vagina?"

"Gender identity is a cognitive and emotional thing. We don't think it's inborn. We're beginning to believe infants may recognize the differences between the sexes much earlier than two years, when gender identity seems to be well formed. But that does not mean they acquire a gender identity for themselves as soon as they can tell the sexes apart. Telling the sexes apart is one thing. Being able to place one's self into a sex category is another."

Stern switches off the lights. A TV screen comes to life. "This is going to blow your mind," he says. "Under certain conditions, babies have a better percentage of knowing which sex they're looking at than adults do."

The Baby Theater: The Moving Lights Experiment

Reflective tape is put on the hips, ankles, knees, shoulders, elbows and wrists of infants who can walk. They are photographed so that what appears on the film is patterns of reflected light as the infants move. These films are shown to other infants. Tests show that babies in the audience can tell by the movement of the lights which is the infant boy.and which is the infant girl: Baby boys consistently look longer at boys and girls at girls.

This suggests that they not only can discriminate between the two movement patterns but that they can also identify their own sex's particular pattern of movement. Furthermore, experiments show that an infant is better able than an adult to determine the gender of another infant merely by watching the movements of lights.

Dr. Tom Bower, Department of Psychology, University of Edinburgh, who performed this experiment, believes the fact that a baby spends a longer time looking at his own sex implies identification, the result of a "like-me" judgment. This could be an important mechanism by which infants and children learn sex-appropriate behavior from each other; a method possibly even more important than accepted notions of adult modeling.

Experiment by Dr. Tom Bower,
University of Edinburgh

"Unless he's practically starving, any baby worth his salt would rather look than eat," says Stern. "That is what babies spend most of their lives doing, looking and listening. They have an avid push to explore what's going on outside."

Stern tells me of another experiment, which shows how good babies are at seeing that a female face and head are different from a male. "The slope of the head in relation to the slope of the nose is different," he says. "The position of the other features in the face differ too. Since most scientists and psychologists know little of this, Joe Fagan, who did the experiment, went to police artist. The artist said, 'Oh sure, a female face is different from a male face. Everybody knows that.' But everybody does not know that. Babies do."

"At what age," I ask Stern, "does the little boy think, 'I am a boy'? When does he begin to try to act unlike mother so he can be more *boy?*"

"I don't think boys are too worried about that until they get around a lot of other kids. This gets us into gender or sex roles, which is different from gender identity. Gender role is more an externally socialized idea. It takes in all the things you are or are not supposed to do because you are this sex or that. Such as boys play with trucks and girls play with dolls."

Sex role is sometimes called *sex role behavior* or *gender role.* Professionals often prefer to coin their own phrase rather than use a competitor's. Call it what you will, *sex role* (my choice) is learned later than gender identity. The masculine or feminine role is made up of our construct of what society/family deems appropriate feelings and behavior for people of our sex.

The distinction between gender identity and sex role is profound. For instance, a transsexual's anatomy tells him he is unmistakably male. Nevertheless, ever since he was born he has felt trapped in a grotesque, terrible mistake. Inside, he knows he is female. In terms of gender identity, these people are as fixed as concrete, volunteering for castration surgery as eagerly as going to a victory celebration. *They are women.* The more quickly they are restored to what nature intended them to be, the better.

I have met many homosexuals with equally unshakable masculine gender identity. They have no question about their maleness. It is rebellion against cultural dicta of what is a masculine sex role that makes their behavior different from that of more traditional males.

"People's lives have the potential for lots of different fantasies or psychological structures," says Michels. "But only a few of them are used by any given person. For instance, you may have lots of books in your head. You've only written four or five. Everybody has the potential for a hundred plots, but generally they are preoccupied with *their* four or five. Which ones you pick will depend on early life experiences, on social factors— things that are different for men and women. But the potential keyboard is pretty much the same."

Women's new position of power and dominance may unsettle them. "Do you think I am acting too much like a man?" They ask a therapist. What they are questioning is not their gender identity but their sex role, which is in transition. I do not mean to minimize this anxiety and fear of loss of femininity as women move ever deeper into territory traditionally defined as male. However, sex roles are culturally defined, and in time what women are "allowed" will catch up with what women are in fact doing. The point I want to make is this: No one ever says to a woman: "Prove you're a woman." From the day she is born, it is a given; not something she has to attain or win, that she is always at risk of losing.

It is not that easy for men. When a man is jealous he protects his self-esteem. When a woman is jealous she protects the relationship. Old-fashioned as this may sound, psychologists and sociologists agree: For most women, even today, their self-esteem *is* the relationship. Not enough time has elapsed for this to have changed.

Says sociologist Gordon Clanton: "Recent social scientific research does not show a consistent pattern as to which gender is more jealous, but the research does reveal differences in the way men and women react when they *are* jealous. Men are more likely to blame the woman (or the third party or the universe) and to retreat from the relationship. Their reaction is self-protective. They may go out and drink with friends. 'Who needs the bitch?' they say. On the other hand, women are more likely to blame themselves and are more willing to adapt to men's demands for the sake of the relationship."

Whatever power a woman accrues on her own, when she falls in love there is an emotional shift. Even today, according to a national study in a leading women's magazine, though readers recognized that they were "as strong, confident, intelligent and capable" as men and would never stand for being made to feel less equal, they simultaneously announced that they ranked "love . . . the most rewarding thing in life." They wanted more romance, a more passionate man. What else? One third stated their preference: "the old-fashioned, chivalrous type."9

Men grow ever more confused by this double message. More envious. They do not have women's options. Their own are no longer exclusively theirs.

"Are you jealous?"

"Three years ago, when I was passionately in love," he says. He is twenty-five, a postgraduate student in comparative religion at a midwestern university. "One spring we went to Haiti. I was going to research primitive religions. She was extremely beautiful and I don't think had ever been in love before. She was used to being a little princess; that was part of the problem. She didn't like not being in control. She was always figuring out ways to keep the upper hand."

"She induced jealousy?" I ask.

"She was making sure that I loved her. Making me jealous proved that I did. Then she'd cool out. To fight her fear that I'd look at another woman, she was always flirting with other guys. My problem is if I really love someone, I'm not interested in anyone else. We were very physical with each other. Not only sexually. We fought all the time, usually over stupid things because we couldn't admit we were jealous. I guess we were both too used to being in control.

"I was very serious about my work and my studies. She was just going to school to get her degree and meet some guy. When we went to Haiti, all I wanted to do when I wasn't working was lie in bed and fuck all the time. That's not true—I just wanted to be with her. When we would close the doors, be in bed together, we were at our best. It wasn't enough for her. She wanted to socialize. One night she gets out of bed and says she is going down to the hotel bar where we'd met some people. I told her, Go ahead. But I couldn't sleep. I was afraid she'd go off with someone else. I don't think she ever did, but that was always my greatest fear. Maybe I was afraid because what was between us was so overpowering. There was just too much there. I'd never felt that kind of passion before. I'm not really sure you could call it love.

"She didn't come back to bed that night. I went downstairs. She was in the bar with some man's arm around her. I said a stupid thing: Either she came back to the room with me or it was over. She laughed. I went upstairs alone. I wanted to leave her, but the idea made me suicidally depressed. I said, This has got to stop, it's no good, I'm too tired of this physical thing. It's not what it should be. Then I prayed, really prayed to the Haitian gods to save me from this woman. To get her out of my life and my gut.

"The next thing I knew I was in this Haitian priest's house, the man I'd been studying with, and I'm sitting there with her clothes on. One of her flowing dresses and her bra and panties. And when I look in the mirror, I have on her makeup. I was terrified.

"Then the priest explained. She was very feminine, had all those very strong earthy female qualities. He said I was very tied to that and that I was trying to exorcise her. He said I had a very strong maleness and we both fed on each other. But our hearts were different. Part of exorcising her was to take on her attributes. Take her powers, neutralize and integrate them into myself so that I could be free of her. The priest said it was also a breaking of the male ego, breaking away from wanting to possess her. Putting on her clothes, I put on her magic. And I lost that macho male thing she used to play on.

"The priest gave me a herbal bath and I went back to the hotel. She saw in my eyes something had changed. Over the months, sex slowed and then stopped. I was free of her . . . didn't need to possess her anymore. It ended badly. I was free and she wasn't. She got insanely jealous and there was a terrible fight. She came to my door one morning with a knife. The police came."

"What do you think the experience taught you?" I ask.

"I got free of that male ego thing, always needing to prove, always having to be macho."

Knowing how much Robertiello loves dreams, trances and all things mystical, I ask him to listen to the tape of the interview. This is what he says:

"In Kleinian terms, this man was the needy child. The woman was the powerful mother who could leave him. When he went into the 'fugue state'—the dissociation in which he didn't know how he got from the hotel to the priest's house—it allowed him to express something his conscious mind would never allow, to split off from his total self. He became her. To him this meant he neutralized her and took on her female powers. It had nothing to do with his wanting to become a woman. He was always worried that she was going to fuck around with somebody else. So, while they were both jealous, she had the edge on the relationship. Power over him—which she used. By becoming her, the mother, the woman, the powerful one, he acquired that power and reversed the situation. He became the one who left her rather than being the infant who was constantly afraid of being left by mama. He dealt with his envy of her power by entering the fugue state and becoming her. By constantly making him jealous, she was reassuring herself that he would have to put up with her power. She too may have been scared to death he would leave her. She had to underline that she held the edge and keep him in this vulnerable child position. When he dressed up like her, it was all reversed. He was the powerful mama. He could and did do the leaving."

Much of men's supposed disdain of women is born of fear, and yet the idea that men *fear* women runs so counter to everyday perceptions it is likely to strike the reader as contrary to experience. Man may be irritated at women, angry at their bossiness—but afraid? A lucid exposition of the fact behind the facade comes from Isaac Asimov:

"Men are tyrannized by women from birth (or feel themselves to be— which comes to the same thing, of course). The young boy is hounded unmercifully and continually by his mother, who is perpetually at him to do what he does not want to do, and *not* to do what he *does* want to do. (The father is inevitably a more distant creature and, unless he is a monster, is more easily handled.) . . . Naturally, then, the male gathering is the one place (it seems to the man) where he can escape from this unending, lifelong feminine domination, and where he can retaliate, in safety, by telling jokes in which women get what they deserve."[10]

Jokes get their kick from the release of aggression. If men weren't so afraid of women, they would not tell their dirty jokes behind women's backs, and the jokes themselves would lose their retaliatory punch. If some anxiety in the male unconscious did not recognize how much they need women, men would not have to erect these jokey, flimsy defenses. The statistical fact is that men die without women: "Men [are] much more likely to die within several years after the death of a spouse than are people of the same age group who are married." On the other hand, "a husband's death [has] almost no effect on the mortality rate of women."[11]

Hanna Segal remarks that as a defense against envy of women, men devalue the empathic side of themselves, the womanly side; and devalue women too. Women are weak, women are silly, they never write great symphonies, great novels—so who would want to be a woman? Denial has turned anxiety into triumphant gender-aggrandizement. Forget the magical power the boy once found in mother's touch and smile, his childish belief that her love conquered all. That's all it was—childish, babyish, *woman* stuff.

I have long wondered why an infant would want to leave the paradise of symbiosis with mother. As cogent as I find Mahler's description of separation/individuation, she never describes the earliest motive for the baby to begin the long, painful (if ultimately rewarding) process. Surprisingly enough, the answer may well be envy. This is the only good thing Robertiello and I have found to say about the emotion.

"Kleinians don't use Mahler's word *separation,*" he says, "but the earliest envy involves this feeling of rage, which can make you want to get away from mother. You realize you can't totally depend on this person. You begin to think, 'God damn it, I'd better start depending on myself, or find other people. . . .'"

There are other angers against mother that help the boy push away. For instance, when father comes home, why does her voice change, why does she abdicate the house she ran so competently in his absence? Here she is, serving him meals, taking his word as law, watching him with a respect and concern the boy lavishes on her and so badly wants from her in return. Worst of all, why does she turn him over to this bigger man for punishment? Hadn't they been settling everything between the two of them? Now she lets this interloper—who has not been involved in the most important aspects of his life so far—hurt and humiliate him. She doesn't stand up for him! This memory, of women's treachery, is one that I have heard from man after man. The boy thought mother was the Giantess of the Nursery, who could move heaven and earth, but here she is, passively surrendering him to father. She is weak, unreliable—who would want to grow up to be like that? Masculinity again begins with negation.

Abandoned by her to the harsh treatment of men, how could the boy not think: Very well, these are the people upon whom I will pattern myself. The process is called "identification with the aggressor." Twenty years later, when a woman betrays him, she quickly learns the lesson he was taught: Men are brutes and they hurt you.

". . . what is apt to be salient" for the boy, writes Dorothy Dinnerstein, "is that resentment of the father's claims upon the mother threatens to interfere with a crucial opportunity that is now opening before him." He wants to develop his attachment to this newly interesting and powerful male figure in his life. Father "represents solidarity with his own sex, a solidarity upon which much of [the boy's] thrust toward worldly competence is starting to depend. His main task is to find a balance between two contrasting varieties of love, one that provides primitive emotional sustenance, and another that promises—if rivalry over the first can be handled —to offer membership in the wider community [of men]." The old attachments to mother have now become an obstacle to the ties he wants with people of his own sex. These competing loyalties "help form the basis for the eventual adult feeling that love for women must be kept in its place, not allowed to interfere with the vital ties between men."

Dinnerstein adds, "What is reflected in man's unilateral possessiveness, then, is not only the original, monolithic infant wish for ownership of a woman but also a second, more equivocal feeling, rooted in early boyhood: that attachment to a woman is emotionally bearable, consistent with the solidarity among men which is part of maleness, only if she, and one's feelings toward her, remain under safe control."[12]

The sad fact is that most fathers don't find children interesting until around age four. In the developmental timetable, four is very late. Important stages of emotional growth have been negotiated; character formation is well under way. The little boy wants desperately to identify with something big, important, *male*, but father is remote, almost abstract. What does "going to the office" mean? When he is around, the attention he gives his son isn't the kind of emotional, in-depth, *brooding* watchfulness and concern the boy gets from mother. Father is hard to get a fix on, a hold on, a feel of.

Freud wrote that little girls feel damaged because they do not have a penis and thus envy little boys. This narcissistic blow convinces women of their inferiority and seems to give a certain logic to the masochistic position Freud posited as feminine. In 1942, Clara Thompson wrote a famous paper that summed up the objections many people had long felt. Penis envy, she said, was a neurotic mechanism and not inevitable in female development. It grew out of a culture, she said, where all power rested in the hands of men. For women, the penis was symbol of male power. They didn't envy the man his literal penis; they didn't want to exchange their genitals for his. What they did envy was the male's dominant position.[13]

"Such states as penis-envy or breast-envy," writes Leslie Farber, "which have occupied much of the psychoanalytic literature . . . are of this literal variety, mistaking possession of the physical attribute for the various prerogatives of adulthood."[14]

A girl's need of her father is enormous, but she doesn't have her brother's even greater need to establish gender identity, to get close to the parent of the same sex. Is it farfetched to suggest that some of the same kind of envy/rage that children first feel toward the power of the breast/mother carries over and in time is felt toward the later, learned power of the penis/father?

The first and most recognizable feature that distinguishes a boy from mother and identifies him with father is the penis. So much of his character has up till now been formed in negation of femaleness. His penis is the positive symbol and fact of maleness. Standing side by side with father for a pee in the woods, the boy steals a glance. What a giant father is! Is this the mysterious power he has over mother? Will the boy's own tiny penis ever measure up? "Leave it alone, son, and it will grow," father laughs, remembering comparison with his own father. Few men ever forget the shock of realization of how enormous a penis can be. It doesn't require a great leap of the imagination to emphathize with the boy's feelings that size is proportionate to maleness. How big? becomes all important. It is an emotional exchange between men, a competition about maleness that has very little to do with women.

Because penis size played such a large part in their development, men make the logical mistake of thinking the importance of size preoccupies women too. Sex counselors and therapists I interview tell me almost unanimously that when women complain about their lovers, it is not about the size of their penises. What women want is more seduction, foreplay, tenderness, kissing, touching. Robertiello once told me that in all his years of practice, he'd only had two women patients comment on the small size of a man's penis. "By coincidence, they were both in love with the same man. But each thought his sexual performance was terrific, each thought the man himself was wonderful and both wanted to marry him. His size didn't matter at all."

My research on sexuality began in the late sixties; in the years since, along with their age, marital status and family background, men have invariably sent me their penis size, flaccid and erect. I didn't ask for it. How could I know its importance? My discovery of men's vulnerability has come out of an effort to understand the strength they showed me. Though women are preoccupied with breast size, no woman has ever included bust measurements in the sexual autobiography she sent me. The power of the large breast is a male ideal in a society where bigger is best. Among themselves, women are ambivalent about breast size. Like beauty and youth, the power of large breasts is time-related. If envy begins with admiration, and the covetous desire to have what another possesses, it is not women but men who suffer from penis envy.

"I used to wonder why all my patients had small penises," says Dr. Willard Gaylin. "As an analyst, I would hear that complaint all the time. This is crazy, I thought, because I knew that there was actually very little difference in the size of men's penises. In time I realized it wasn't just my patients who had this fear. Most men in our culture think their penis is too small."

In a 1976 *Penthouse* magazine survey, "all respondents, with the exception of the most extraordinarily endowed, expressed doubts about their sexuality based on their penile size."[15]

If father's arms held him from the day he was born, father's smell and touch and voice soothed him, the boy would have symbols of strength other than the penis to idealize and introject. He would not have to run away from nurturing, tenderness, emotion itself to prove himself a man. He would be less angry at women for having all the power. If, when he was at his most dependent, a man as well as a woman had been there to make things right and to restore life, the step into identity as a male would be more confidently taken. It would be known and tested ground. But studies show the average father spends mere minutes a week with his son.

I ask Hanna Segal what would be the developmental effect if a child had both parents present from the first day of life. "It would make a tremendous difference," she says. "It would reduce the rage both sexes feel toward women. If father is absent, the child feels totally in possession of mother. He cannot express his anger at her for fear of losing her love. She is the only source. If there are two sources, the child can afford anger at one and feel the consequent guilt toward someone who has been nice to him. He can afford this negative expression because he has the love of the second parent backing him. From this position, he can then go on to make reparations." And reparations open the door to gratitude and love.

The usual reason given for fathers' neglect of their children is the amount of time demanded by the workplace. I would suggest there are others, less obvious. Even the best-intentioned fathers-to-be find themselves filled with uncertainty and fear. What do they know about being a caring, nurturing father? Yes, the magazines make it sound fine and easy, but their own fathers were mysterious, absent. *Today's fathers have no models.*

The ideal of shared parenting suffers from another bit of hard reality: mothers' possessiveness. Says pediatrician Berry Brazelton, "Even as she asks for her husband's involvement, a wife builds a wall around the baby and won't let the husband in. There is rivalry between mother and father for the child. Feeling excluded, incompetent, the father withdraws. He 'concedes' that the mother is instinctively the better parent."

Dr. Brazelton continues: "There is a kind of competition that comes up that is unconscious. I want to state it here to make it conscious. Everybody who cares about a small baby is in competition with everybody else who cares about a small baby. There is a basic drive on an adult's part to have that baby, to possess and contain it. Therefore, the more men are included in parenting, the more the competition is going to be felt between men and women around that baby. However, if the competition is accepted, dealt with, it can be a very positive force toward keeping the family going and raising the kids."

A man needs almost constant reinforcement from his wife not to abandon the parenting role. Whatever the reasons, should he withdraw, to the boy it feels like deliberate withholding.

With unthinking arrogance father wins the competition for mother's attention by simply walking in the door. How easily father could include him in man's world, the boy feels. Instead, he leaves him stranded in a world of women. In Kleinian terms, father takes on the powers and attributes, the ambivalence and malignancy of the primitive breast.

The boy's dilemma is how to have father's love, how to identify with him while in a rage at his cruel withholding. Robertiello sees the struggle as both literal and symbolic. "The more envious the boy is of the father's power/penis," he says, "the more he resents him. And the more he feels this competitive anger, the less the boy is able to have that satisfying gender confirmation of being a chip off the old block."

As a child I was addicted to cowboy movies. Every Saturday at the Gloria I would listen to the heroine beg John Wayne not to fight. Neither the hero nor the man he was about to kill bothered to explain. They just kept strapping on their guns before taking the long, slow, ritual walk toward each other outside in the street. They didn't have to explain. Both of them knew. So did the audience, male and female. They were defying —more important, defining—each other's masculinity.

If father were "good enough," wouldn't envy of his power be assuaged? Much as the boy's fury at the breast/mother eased up when he learned she did her best to meet his needs? He would be able to take in and introject the good father, as he did the good mother. If father gave his son a deep sense of the complexities of all the things a man could feel and be, wouldn't the need for a large penis (and fear of an even larger one) shrink to realistic size? If there were more things male that filled the vacuum for defining himself as different and other than mother, he would believe more in himself as a man and less in his penis as the determining factor of maleness. He would be less jealous.

Years later, when his beloved looked at another man, he would not wonder, *What* is she looking at? *What* is she comparing me to? In the envious male imagination, the other is always bigger because the bigness/power of the first rival in life never became his. He never got close enough to father. It is ironic and sad that a man measures his sexual identity, his sexual life with women in memory of a situation that had little to do with the female sex. Statistical evidence shows that as late as 1981, 26 percent of college men preferred a virgin bride;[16] someone who could not compare him to another man. If so many admit going against what has become the cultural mode, how many more men really feel that way in silence? Intensifying the anxiety is a startling statistic: "Young women today are losing their virginity at an earlier age. *[Playboy]* found that 58% of the women . . . who are currently under 21 lost their virginity before the age of 16. Only 38% of men in the same age group did so."[17]

Psychoanalyst Robert E. Gould believes that "sexual jealousy would probably not result if we all grew up feeling equal love and attention from both parents. This almost never happens. Freud himself was typical of Middle European culture, where the man was away from his family all day. When father came home, mother catered to him. So children did feel that whenever daddy was around he took mommy away. We are now beginning to study families where men take a more equal role in bringing up the child. We will see if this kind of oedipal triangle is inevitable. My own theoretical bias is that it is not. But the proof is not yet in."

When a man is jealous, it is obvious he fears losing the beloved. Less obvious is that jealousy puts him in touch with the fury he feels toward the withholding father. Says Hanna Segal, "Some men choose women to be their emotional links to life. When such a man is jealous, he stands to lose his emotional half; he is pained, in a rage. Her leaving him, or being 'stolen' from him, opens him to *all* the things jealousy means. This includes his envy of women's warm, empathic qualities, but also his envy of the mysterious power of the bigger man."

Some men avoid jealousy by getting angry. "Me, jealous? Hell, no! I just don't like that guy's attitude. I probably shouldn't have hit him." Says psychoanalyst Louise Kaplan, "Depression is another way of denying jealousy. It protects the love object from the rage. In my experience, women are much more ready to say they are jealous. Men are more defended against it. Jealousy hurts their pride, their self-esteem, their sense of manliness. It's a question of appearance and reality. What is manifest in men is sometimes not what the true picture is about." The proportion of men admitted to mental hospitals today goes up steadily and there are three times more male suicides than female.

It is usually said that women are a meliorating influence on male furies; without women, men would be constantly at war. I would suggest another conciliatory influence. It is that period in a man's life that comes after the baby battles with mother and father. He is five or six and has begun to get out of the house. He finds other boys his age and size, eager allies in his search for maleness. Not every man is lucky enough to have had this companionate span of years. Those who did remember it all their lives.

So long as the boy is little and at home, he's too dependent on mother and father to afford conscious envy/resentment of their power. In bands, in groups, in clubs, he now pins down for himself the mystery father would not share with him and deals with envy of the omnipotent mother by devaluing all things female. Harry Stack Sullivan calls this period in a boy's life "chumship." I find the phrase awkward because I have never heard a man use it. Allen Ginsberg puts it this way: "The social organization which is most true of itself . . . is the boy gang."[18] Ginsberg is talking about the artist; I would widen it to include all boys. "Boy gang" has a toughness to it, a universality. It combines the fierce rites and loyalties of comradeship with an even fiercer taboo against women.

Getting a communal fix on masculinity requires a clear focus on what girls are. Most of all they are *clean and good.* Since women have always made him feel just the opposite about the part of his body that is different from theirs, he must assume that what is between a female's legs is like a rose. Why else would she be so offended by what he has? Didn't women teach him to think his penis dirty and untouchable? Very well. Rebelliously, the boy sets out to confound women by proving they are right. In the company of other good fellows, he proudly masturbates, urinates, writes dirty words on the wall, and in time competes to see who will be the first to be able to come, who will shoot his sperm the farthest. Together boys test their maleness. Even if one loses the contest, he still wins. He is showing women how boys are. He is breaking women's rules. How awful. How wicked. How satisfying.

Little wonder that the penis plays such an important role in early boyhood games. The only kinship he has known has been family. Now, his body and those of his friends are common ground; anatomy proclaims them brothers. Mother of course has not lost her power. The boy still needs and loves her. But she is safely somewhere else, at home. She doesn't know the dirty, secret, all-male things her son is doing.

His guilt only heightens the excitement. Comparing bodies, showing each other their penises, boys intensify their sense of community, solidarity; *of maleness.* At this age, the dread word *homosexual* isn't thought of. Nor should it be. "When I was eight," a man tells me, "we had what we called a Fucking Club. I don't think we knew what the word actually meant. What we did was pee and shit together in an abandoned lot."

There is a wonderful scene at the beginning of Italian director Bernardo Bertolucci's film *1900.* The two male protagonists are first seen as little boys masturbating in a meadow. The scene is as innocent as a summer's day. When the three-hour film is over, we have lived through almost eighty years of battle between the two. In the end we see them as two doddering old men, quarreling and wrestling on a dusty road beside the green meadow. Bringing the film full cycle is the return to physical closeness they once knew. Not homosexuality but friendship, founded in intimacy that gave each of them what he needed most when he was six. A feeling of male camaraderie that is in the end more important than all the years, wars, politics and women they have fought over.

In boyhood games and rituals, when a six-year-old sees a seven-year-old has a larger penis, his feelings are close to admiration. The sense of not measuring up to father may also have begun in admiration, but very quickly soured into envy. Father was too big. Father had too much power. How could anybody compete with father? Father could have put the world right. He did not. Father withheld.

The older/bigger boy doesn't have that kind of life-and-death power. He does not evoke the infantile desire to murder. Here is the hero the younger boy always wanted, someone larger than he but not by inches and feet, merely by centimeters. The bigger boy represents the figure Kohut says we all need: To build self-esteem we must get close to someone, find someone to idealize and take in. Whatever anger and competition the young boy feels at the bigger one for besting him, he takes him as model, identifying with him as he will later identify with the male star of a porno film; his gigantic penis stands for *all* men.

Being a man, proving it, is what the boy gang is all about. And it is all the more intense for arriving so late in the boy's life. Five, six years have been lived in a system run on women's ideas, a household of female objects and rules. The gang will have none of that. If they have a club-house, ideally it will be made of rough boards, and if they want, the boys will piss on the floor. Anything goes that is not female. Girls and their pretty yellow hair are left out. The boy is discovering the great satisfaction of being male, equal to women, *superior*.

"Excuse the cigar smoke, the rough language," men say to women. "Sorry I forgot to shave." These are late-learned, adult apologies; not altogether genuine in their professed sorrow, nor entirely free of a male stance of superiority. Here is the ancient male resentment against those rules, first learned from mother, that seem to posit man in his "natural" state as somehow falling below society's standards. The battle James Thurber called "The War Between the Men and the Women" goes on and on; for boys, there is a never-to-be forgotten period of truce, the halcyon years when women are left out of their lives.

Defending his membership in various all-male clubs, William Buckley quotes a lifelong and universal masculine dream. "Someday, damn it, we'll have a treehouse of our own. We'll build it out in the woods where Mother can't find us. And we'll eat when we want, what we want. We'll bring our friends. Have a secret club. And no girls."[19]

His sister doesn't understand the secrecy of brother's intense new life. What is so exciting about being dirty and bad? Girls have clubs and private diaries. These too aid separation. But usually girls are just switching partners, going from mother to other girls for the same old kind of symbiotic closeness. They get more energy out of leaving one another out, passing judgment, ostracizing the miserable other—and thus intensifying the closed union—than challenging one another to discover their sexuality in a larger world. Even today, I cannot imagine little girls sitting in a circle masturbating. Too bad. They could stand a share of the sexual discovery and mutual pride a boy feels in handling his genitals in the company of other boys.

Tight girl groupings are not so much about the emulation of the bravest and the best as about setting up rules and limits beyond which no one is allowed to venture. Girls are not angry at boys; they do not slam the door shut. Why should they? Father may not have been much present in his daughter's life, but he didn't withhold the mirror of gender identity. It is notorious that a boy's sister would love it if he played house, played family. Daddy opposite her mommy.

While boys are not innocent of leaving one another out, the principle of the boy gang is to prove oneself worthy of being "in." The idea of life as an expanding universe, where you take the other fellow's gain as a mark against which to set your own ambition is best learned here. In the boy gang he gets a chance to turn admiration into healthy competition. When a boy cannot do this—when envy turns so rancorous he breaks the rules to his own advantage—he is automatically out of the club. In fact, that is exactly the word the British use. A man other men don't like is called "unclubable."

Instead of allowing desire for what someone else has to end in envious paralysis, the ethos of the boy gang encourages open competition. The object is not to denigrate the best player but to become just as good. It is practice in learning how to handle later sexual jealousies. A man's friend has just won a beautiful woman, one he would have liked for himself. Instead of devaluing himself, idealizing the woman or using any of Klein's other defenses against recognizing envy, the competitive spirit has taught him to go out and find an even better woman for himself. "Men have a kind of unspoken agreement not to go after their buddies' women. Mostly that holds up," a man tells me. "Your friend's wife is off limits. That taboo runs deep."

Not all men were part of a boy gang. Not all men respect the taboo against bedding a friend's woman. I suspect there is a cause-and-effect relation. Here are two stories.

The first from a man who had very intense feelings of having belonged to a boy gang. "One drunken night in Paris, I found myself behind a velvet curtain in the Crazy Horse Saloon, necking with my best friend's wife. She was a very hot number. I got so upset, I left the nightclub and went back to the hotel alone. At dawn I took the first plane to London."

The second story concerns a man who had a three-year affair with a friend's wife. "I didn't see anything wrong with it," he tells me. "He was having an affair himself—with my sister."

He goes on to tell me about another woman, whom he'd met through a mutual friend. At a party at his house one night, he'd asked her to stay. She declined. Driving to work the next morning he saw her car parked in front of the "mutual friend's" house.

"Were you angry with this guy?"

"I was furious with *her*. I never called her again. They began an affair. When it was over she called me. Eventually we got married."

"When you were a kid, did you belong to a boy gang?"

"No," he says. I do not have to define the term. He knows what I mean.

"Did you feel left out?"

"I've always missed those kinds of friendships with men. I did have friends, but we were the loners."

"What you call 'the boy gang' is tremendously important in a man's life," says Willard Gaylin. "Women tend to form good friendships all through life—that is, those women who are capable of friendship—and continue to do it later than men. If men don't have these close friendships early on—boyhood, high school, college—later, they don't have the talent or energy. The workplace drains them. They go through life with a sense of exclusion."

"What do you mean when you say you are jealous?" I ask people in interviews. "How does it feel?"

"Being left out," a man tells me. "I am excluded. It's not the same as abandonment. With abandonment there is no hope. You've been cut adrift forever. But being left out . . . What hurts is that you are present at what is happening. You *could* be included and you are not."

"Losing the oedipal battle," says Dr. Louise Kaplan, "is a narcissistic injury. It says you are small, not important enough to be included. The fear is that something is going on and you have no way of imagining what it is. This stimulates all kinds of fantasies: What is going on behind the closed door? What are they hiding from me? Even when there is some lighthearted fooling going on between the parents in the kitchen, the child has the feeling, 'Something is going on here and I'm not part of it'. This stimulates envy, rage, grief, disappointment. A sense of being shut out of the adult mystery.

"But these feelings do not begin in the oedipal triangle. They have been going on all along. Take the primal scene; there is a misconception about that. Usually the primal scene is not so much about what the child saw as about what he didn't see. This is why childhood clubs are so important. They tame the power of the old infantile fantasies stimulated by feelings of being left out. If you have a sense of belonging to the group, all the earlier fears of being left out now get directed within the group, where you *can* affect what happens. The emotion is replayed with far less of the earlier painful intensity."

"It's all so complex," I sigh at the end of my interview with Kaplan.

"Keep it that way!" she urges. "That is jealousy."

According to Freud, there is a period after oedipal conflict and before adolescence—roughly ages seven to eleven—called latency. It is a time of reaction. Having lost the parent of the opposite sex, children retreat to the company of children of their own sex. Supposedly, sex goes to sleep. It is "latent." Many of the analysts I talk to today suggest that Freud was correct but incomplete, right for girls but not for boys. Boy gangs do not retreat from sex. On the contrary, sex is of great importance. Women are out, but the need to get gender identity reinforced is vital.

Almost imperceptibly the treehouse grows into the clubhouse and the boy gang transforms itself into an athletic team. This is the time of life when one man can love another and learn from him too. Hero worship, especially in sports, is a safe area where a boy, eager to measure up, can take in another man. In love with his speed, his strength, his grace and beauty—in love with him—the younger/smaller boy pines, watches and imitates.

I do not wish to idealize the boy gang. There are dissenting points of view, with much of which I agree. "Masculinity celebrates the exclusive company of men," writes Paul Theroux. "That is why it is so grotesque; and that is also why there is no manliness without inadequacy—because it denies men the natural friendship of women. It is very hard to imagine any concept of manliness that does not belittle women, and it begins very early. . . . Nothing is more unnatural or prisonlike than a boys' camp, but if it were not for them, we would have no Elks' Lodges, no poolrooms, no boxing matches, no marines. . . . Any objective study would find the quest for manliness essentially right wing, puritanical, cowardly, neurotic and fueled largely by a fear of women. . . . I regard high-school sports as a drug far worse than marijuana, and it is the reason that the average tennis champion, say, is a pathetic oaf."[20]

Another writer, Phil Gailey, also sees the sports arena as overly glorified. "The sports world is a snug, untouchable refuge from the standards that society imposes outside a stadium, a sacred bastion of sexism, violence, greed and hypocrisy." Growing up as a nonsporting male made Gailey feel he must prove manhood in other ways. "I started smoking, chewing tobacco, cussing and talking tough with gas-station ruffians, none of which I particularly enjoyed at the time, but which I did to stave off the sissy stigma so easily attached in rural Georgia."[21]

Persuasive as these comments are, they ignore a situation that these fortunate men—Theroux and Gailey—seem to have overcome: Most boys grow up in a world where they do not get enough contact with their fathers. I find the boy gangs and the athletic contest developmentally important because within rules established by generations of men who have gone before, the boy safely tests the limits of his competitive fury. Yes, continuing the boy gang into a state of adult machismo does seem close to arrested development. But in youth, the gang, the club, gives the boy a chance to vent his leftover anger against people he loved but against whom he could not compete, mother and father. Losing is painful, but every boy must learn what the game is about. You shake hands with the winner because the next victory may be yours. Win or lose, you are a man among men, a friend among friends.

Though I have never doubted the happiness I can bring a man—that only a woman can bring—I've always known men shared another joy, which left me out. All my life I've watched that mysterious union that falls over men like a cloak when they are together in a bar, watching football, sailing a boat. Even today my intellectual understanding doesn't eliminate the jealousy I can feel when I lose my man momentarily to other men. A mood, a way of talking together, a form of laughter between them predates my importance in their lives. Its very nature excludes women.

I don't think women fully understand the primary satisfactions men find in one another's company. Or perhaps they do, and that is why they would like to deprive men of their time alone together. In traditional symbiotic attachments to men, women often feel any interest men have outside the house—other than the necessity of going to work—is a form of betrayal. Something that should be hers—his attention, time and emotion—is being stolen. My own feeling is that women would be smart to let men have their times alone together, an idea in which I include the all-male club. While it may be unfair to exclude professional women from these powerful powwows, to my mind equality should be fought for on fronts that are less threatening to men. All-male groupings are not merely a social or business idea. They are a biological necessity. So long as men are raised exclusively by women, they will need fraternities to reinforce masculinity. When we live in a more ideal world, in which father shares the burden of rearing children with mother from day one, then Theroux, Gailey and I can have another discussion.

"It was my twelfth birthday," my husband once told me. "I remember sitting under a tree in the park thinking, each year lately life has been getting better and better. Can it go on this way? And then girls came along."

Adolescence. My husband's timetable was impeccable. The idyll of boyhood ends with the flood of testosterone in the blood, the rush of girls and their beauty to the brain. Beautiful girls who arouse unexplainable new energies and the desire to move mountains. They are also extremely bewildering.

Girls have a special certainty not given to boys; the specific date of their advent into sexual maturity is marked by the beginning of menstruation. Boys have no such biological reinforcement; male puberty rites take place at an arbitrary age, which mysteriously differs from culture to culture. "If cultural emphasis followed the physiological emphasis," says anthropologist Ruth Benedict, "girls' ceremonies would be more marked than boys'; but it is not so. The ceremonies emphasize a social fact: the adult prerogatives of men are more far-reaching in every culture than women's, and consequently . . . it is more common for societies to take note of this period in boys than in girls."[22] While I feel this is true and that it reveals some unfairness to women, I do not believe that is the main thrust. Might there not be a universal recognition of the fragility of male gender identity, which leads almost every culture to put compensatory emphasis on male puberty rites?

In all places and in all times, cultures respond to deeply felt and often unconscious needs and fears through religion and ceremony. Yesterday's premenstrual girl is today's menstrual woman. The fact is plain and needs no further confirmation. But the boy did not grow a beard overnight. His penis is not bigger today than yesterday. Besides, being male involves ideas far beyond the physiological. Indian boys were tested for physical courage and endurance, yes—but they also had to have the correct dreams. Little wonder that the boy needs an important psychological ceremony to tell him he has negotiated what would otherwise feel like an abstract rite of passage. No blood runs from his body, announcing to the world he is now capable of childbirth—surely the greatest and most mysterious power.

The balance between the sexes must be righted, indeed tipped in men's favor. With rituals as mysterious as manhood itself, with fires, dancing, prayers, blood, music and large assemblies of people, the boy's fears of not "measuring up" are stilled. "Today I am a man," the Jewish boy celebrates on his thirteenth birthday. At the heart of the ceremony, solemn thanks are given to the Creator for not making him a woman. In Orthodox synagogues, women are seated separate and unequal. When they bleed, they are untouchable. Because they are inferior? Or because bleeding is a monthly reminder of the power no amount of male ceremony can ever dismiss?

With adolescence comes a profound revolution in values. The goal used to be to win the game as an end in itself. Now you fight to win the game so as to win the girl. She is the greatest prize of all. Yesterday's best friend is today's rival for the girl only one of you can have. What happened to friendship?

Afraid of losing his independence to women, afraid of losing out to another man, the boy enters adolescence at an emotional disadvantage he will never right again with the certainty he had in those days when women were left out. It is ironic that he will never be as sure of himself as a man as when he was a boy.

When the best woman—meaning the most beautiful—chooses the best man (in other men's eyes), the loser can almost be said to understand. "Though my heart is broken, I can accept why you have picked the more powerful man." But women cannot always be trusted to play by men's rules. When they do not, when women's passions interfere with the delicate structure of brotherhood, the defense system crumbles.

I have my own feelings about why so many young men today linger uncertainly at the threshold of heterosexuality. How powerful, how sexually assertive and knowing, even demanding, young girls are! To decide to remain in the company of men may not be so much a sexual preference as a refusal to risk losing the degree of masculine certainty and independence so recently won. It is easier to be a man among men, to be homosexual, than to be a man among women.

Last night on television I watched King Arthur build Camelot. Though Lancelot was the more powerful warrior, he bowed to the King's dreams of brotherhood. Even more than personal glory, Lancelot wanted to be part of a world where envies and jealousies were settled by the rules of a Round Table of men. He wanted it even more than he wanted the beautiful Guinevere.

Consumed by passion, the handsome Lancelot lay on bare ground victoriously wrestling with his lust. It was she, the woman, who could not, would not, control her desire. "Damn you!" I yelled at the TV screen as the hussy galloped toward the poor fellow and fell upon him, flesh on flesh. Lancelot didn't stand a chance. As they burned the ground with their naked bodies, Camelot fell in ashes around them. Begun by Guinevere, the havoc was finished off by a second woman, the evil witch Morgan le Fay.

On my way to the refrigerator, I marveled at how skillfully the director/writer had galvanized hatred against Guinevere. I know too well how few women have the resources to ride out of the castle and pin down the man.

King Arthur is a story, a film told by men. Is this how men perceive women, ruining everything with their uncontrollable lust? Morgan le Fay learned her magic from Merlin, but in the end used it against him. The lesson is clear: Women are evil, and must be kept from power. Where do grown men, who hold the real power in the world, get these fears of scheming and deceitful women who will destroy them?

Fairy tales of childhood abound with witches and evil stepmothers who incorporate all the bad, destructive parts of the mother. It is an example of *splitting*. In the child's effort to preserve contact with the good mother he loves, he splits off aspects he hates, and creates the wicked witch/step-mother. When adolescence arrives, when the beautiful Guinevere enters a boy's life, he is already in love with, and afraid of, her. Girls seem frighten-ingly skilled in seduction, as if they've been practicing love, closeness and intimacy for years. As they have. While the boy was learning autonomy, individuality and independence, girls have been developing their needs for love, sex and symbiosis. These are presented to the boy all wrapped up in the pretty package labeled romantic love. It is confusing.

Women do not tell you what they want, misleading you with their sighs and smiles, their heat and quickness to insult, their *nos* that mean *yes*. The boy's body urges him to respond. "Careful," warns his head. If he gives in to her, will he reemerge whole and his own man? Her magic, her power is enviable.

We meet in adolescence like people from different planets. The girl has never touched herself. Aroused by moonlight, music, films, she cries for "More, more!" She asks the boy for kissing, holding, for romance. The boy assumes that her arousal, like his, wants sexual expression. Perhaps not penetration—which is still a mystery to him—but doesn't she want him to touch the rose between her legs? Doesn't she want to touch his penis? Absolutely not! She has her rules. They are her power.

Almost automatically he repeats the defenses of childhood, this time splitting her along sexual lines. The good girl will give him the nurturing and emotion of which he deprived himself in the name of manhood. The bad girl will satisfy his lust. Either way, she is cut down to size.

In this diminished state she is valueless in helping him define himself as a man. He falls back on the measure he knows best. Men will decide who the real men are. The boy has come to understand at last the power of father's wallet. Being a man isn't about shooting baskets or running the fastest mile. Being a man is being a good provider.

Jealousy would lose the adolescent boy everything he has worked so hard to become. His need to avoid jealousy is constantly juggled against wanting the beautiful woman. "The only advice my father ever gave me," says one man, "is don't pick a woman you can't keep." In its doggedly commonsense way, this bit of paternal wisdom parallels an often-heard female injunction. "It is just as easy to fall in love with a rich man," mother tells daughter, "as a poor one."

Having a beauty for your own may be exciting. It is also risky. She increases your self-esteem but other men would constantly be after her. It would be lovely to provide for the very sexual woman, one who takes half the burden of initiation/responsibility off your hands. But if she showed that much lust last night, what guarantees she will not entice another man tomorrow? Someone richer or more potent than you. Young women rush eagerly into love. The young man is more cautious. Perhaps this is the genesis of the idea I once had that men were less jealous than women. In a triumph of their defenses, they do not allow themselves to fall in love until they are totally sure of the woman. It is notorious that women are more eager to marry than men.

Young girls think boys hold all the power. Mustn't they wait for the boy to take the initiative? Girls overlook the fact that by waiting to be asked, they retain the power to say no. If overt rejection is going to take place, she is going to be the one to do it.

"When I was an adolescent," says a thirty-one-year-old man, "I thought girls held all the aces. When you call for a date, you are sitting there wide open. She can slam the door in your face. Boys become each other's rivals. Girls are allowed to keep close relationships with other girls all through life. I see a lot of grown-up men who miss their high-school pals. They have no friends.

"When I was thirteen, I fell in love with this great, great, beauty. She really broke my heart. I remember taking her home from a dance. My father had driven us and was waiting in the car. I took her to the door. She turned and said, 'I don't want to go steady with you anymore.' Just like that. I asked if I'd done something. 'No,' she said, and gave me back my ring. When I got back to the car, my father saw me weeping. After that, I never let a girl get to me again. I really treated girls like shit." Young men are not less jealous than young women. They learn to be more careful about avoiding the jealous situation to begin with.

"You hold my honor in your hands" was the way Victorian husbands put it to their wives. They meant that if the wife was unfaithful, the husband would be laughed at. What they meant by honor was "face", self-esteem. The man whose wife cheats on him feels as if she has taken his manhood away. What burns is that she has given it as a gift—a scalp—into the hands of a rival. This is the final humiliation; not the loss of the woman, but the contempt in which he is convinced other men now hold him.

"Go after the ugly ones," says another of the defensively derisive male rules. "They'll be grateful." They'll also make you less jealous. I remember a party attended by Raquel Welch, whose escort for the evening was her female secretary. Half a dozen men made a play for the secretary. Raquel Welch went home alone in her chauffeured limousine.

"Those wedding bells are breaking up that old gang of mine"[23] goes an old song. A lament at the power that love gives a woman to dissolve long-standing solidarities. Can you imagine a woman singing such a song?

Masculinity was once such an easy idea: Sheer numbers did it. Hanging out with the guys. One by one now, as each man goes off alone with his chosen woman, he learns that just as each woman is different, so is each couple. Your buddy is learning something he cannot share with you. Locker-room wisdom is eagerly exchanged, but never quite believed in.

"Are you jealous?"

He looks bewildered. He is twenty-eight, comes from a traditional family, and is already a successful lawyer. "I can't imagine my wife making me jealous," he says. "It never happened."

"Think hypothetically," I say. "What if some man was coming on with her and she was really responding . . . ?"

He does not hesitate. "I'd take the guy and I'd throw him against the wall. You mean if I came home and he was there? I'd take off all his clothes—first taking out his wallet so I'd have his name—then I'd throw his clothes down the incinerator and lock him out in the hallway, naked. Then I'd call his wife—"

"Who said he was married?"

He doesn't hear the question. Life is preconceived. The answers are known. "I'd call her and tell her what he'd done. I'd tell her to do with him whatever she wanted. Then I'd talk to my wife and try to find out why this happened. If it was maybe something I'd done or didn't do. Maybe I'd been neglecting her, working too much or too long—"

"What if it was just plain lust?"

"Whose?"

"Your wife's "

"Lust?"

The idea is literally beyond him. The inability to associate his wife with lust for a stranger is one of the principal reasons he married her

Being a man is hard, tiring work. Competition in the workplace uses up all his powers and emotions. Home must be a refuge, a place to refuel. I've always felt one of the lures of business (even more true in the military), is the ladder of hierarchy. Every man knows where he stands and the ladder-symbol itself is an implicit (if illusory) promise that each man may eventually get to the top. Infighting within the corporation may be bitter, but even if you lose the argument, it's all between men.

If a man dies of a heart attack at his desk late at night, or as Gulf & Western empire builder Charles Bluhdorn recently did on the company plane, he dies a man's death. Above all, Bluhdorn was a man's man, notorious for humiliating senior executives by publicly pitting one against the other; yelling at them to kill one another in the fight to get ahead. Being railed at in this way made him a part of the club. As in the famous "roast" dinners men give each other, the more insulting Bluhdorn's jokes, the more his executives were flattered. It proved he knew they could take it. Mutual insult is the coin of affection passed up and back in male pack behavior. As long as the power was being shifted among men, one man could wrestle dominance from another. Being rallied by Bluhdorn was like being fired up by the warrior chief—a tribal indoctrination for braves only.

In what might be called a willed failure of the imagination, men have tried to pretend that competition in business is a continuation of the kind they had once known on the playing field. But boys play for fun. Businessmen notoriously play for keeps. "Hardball" they call it. "We have a lot of fun," men say after a board meeting, where the victory of one faction means that a dozen men will lose their jobs and have to forfeit their mortgages and homes, take children out of private school. It is a mutually consoling lie, so long as men tell it only to each other.

The all-male bar, the club, the golf course remain the only places where men can relax and try to restore the healing illusion that they are still a band of brothers, all good fellows well met. Entry of women as competitors in the marketplace makes men seek out these all-male bastions all the more desperately. One man puts it this way: "That mild risk [of an all-male poker game] is as close as any of us is likely to get in a given week to allowing our eternally immature, pre-acculturation urges to take over, which helps to explain why poker remains essentially a man's game. The presence of a woman at the table would be infallibly inhibiting. . . . The competition in a long-running game must be serious—but without malice. Otherwise, it would explode the group. The two-man confrontation in a dramatic hand enhances the camaraderie; the winner does not gloat, the loser accepts his fate in a manly way. It is a moment of intimacy. Poker represents our perhaps pitiable effort to awaken more intense feelings than our several livelihoods allow. . . . For a woman to enter . . . would do more than discourage bad language; it would rob the game of its deeper appeal."[24]

"The good provider." I remember how shocked I was years ago when I first read that was how the majority of men and women of all ages defined masculinity. How horrible, to have one's sense of self measured by how much bacon you brought home. The role also means providing image and status in the community for wife and family, and of course, providing sexual initiative and gratification too. A burdensome role. But so long as women were compliant and stayed safely out of men's world, men felt they had an OK bargain. Their masculinity was confirmed. Defenses against envy of women's power held.

Barbara Ehrenreich suggests that the male revolt against the breadwinner philosophy in general, and against women in particular, predates the women's movement. In a recent book, she says that the male "flight from commitment" began in the 1950s. "The corporation may have been the enemy of men's initiative," she writes, "but it was men's ally in the struggle against woman . . . and if the corporate work world benumbed men's minds and crushed men's spirits, this too could be blamed on women."

It was the editorial opinion of *Look* magazine, Ehrenreich continues, that indeed female dominance was one of the causes of the much deplored "organization man." " 'What he is doing,' " Ehrenreich quotes *Look*, " 'is just building his own masculine world. His office is *his* castle. . . .' In a dizzying reversal of nineteenth-century domestic sentimentalism, home had become forbidding territory, and the corporation was man's 'haven in a heartless world.' "[25]

The fifties was the era of emergence of the Beats and by no coincidence, of *Playboy* magazine too. Both celebrated a disguised misogyny. As a defense against anxiety, "In every issue, every month, there was a Playmate to prove that a playboy didn't have to be a husband to be a man."[26]

Being the good provider was less draining before television inculcated envy in every heart. That too began in the fifties. In 1960, one American home out of four had no car at all. Today the carless family measures only 12 percent; over half own at least two.[27] In 1960, 300,000 households had color TV; by 1984 that number had risen to 75.8 million.[28] The comparative increase in affluence holds true for everything from electric can openers to trips to Europe. However, as one unsatisfied member of the new rich put it, "It's strange what happens when you begin to have money— you just start spending more. But I don't feel rich, and I don't feel responsible."[29]

"It's a greedy world," says Hanna Segal. "Insatiable greed. And very much based on envy because it's to keep up with the Joneses. You must have this because your neighbor has that."

Psychologically and economically, the biggest change of all is that the marketplace—long the male province—has come to be invaded by women. "Demoralize thy neighbor" is the headline on an ad for an expensive car in this morning's paper. "Investing in The Age of Envy" is advertised in the book section. It may take two paychecks to meet today's ever-rising curve of expectations. That idea totally deflates the male's former pride in being the family's sole support. Never has male resentment of women's power been greater. Never has the definition of masculinity been shakier.

"It's such a weird thing society asks of men," says writer David Rabe, whose play *Hurlyburly* opened in 1984. "It asks them to go into a domestic thing and yet it nurtures this other thing. Most guys are given the double message by the society. 'Be hard, think clear, don't let emotion muddy your thoughts, sleeping around is a good thing.' And at the same time, you're told to have your feelings available, be a good father. So you take the guys in this play who have all been flung out of their marriages. They're all back in this adolescence. They have the bitterness and disappointment of having failed."

Talking of growing up male, Rabe says, "There is that whole process of testing and it necessitates a certain type of control of your feelings—the feelings that you think of as 'weak.'[30] . . . I guess the theme of the play is this guy and his effort to control his life and everybody around him. And his feelings—you have to control them or you can't control everybody else."

Speaking of a close male friend who had recently died of drink, Rabe says, "He was a great, great person, a wonderful actor. He died of an inability to live with masculinity. He just couldn't hold it together. It really is true that he opened my heart in a certain way to whatever this play is about. . . . A lot of people say the play is anti-woman. . . . I don't think that's true. It's about the price some guys pay to be men."[31]

Afraid to acknowledge for the first time the difficulty of manhood, we get angry at men already angered at themselves for failure. "I want to say something about men and their troubles with the thing we call commitment," writes columnist Ellen Goodman. Though this particular piece is almost two years older, she seems to be in dialogue with Rabe. "In each case, the man [comes] up to the threshold of promise. In each case, he [experiences] it less as a doorway than as a line drawn in the sand. A line he [can't] cross. . . . We teach men in a thousand ways that relationships are encumbrances that hold them back, trap them, catch them. It's the men, almost always, who become our lone rangers. . . . Men who equate maturity with independence meet women who equate it with connections. Our fears collide."

Goodman goes on to tell of a man she knows whose inability to make a commitment had ended a relationship. "It was hard, he said, but he would get through it, tough it out. I had the sense that he regarded this breakup as a challenge. Re-enacting some primal scene, he was again a real man, alone. In some odd way the new bad feelings felt right. He will . . . deal with his loneliness. It will be easier for him that way, making no commitments."[32]

Like the Spartan boy who lets the wolf gnaw his vitals rather than make a sound that would betray him, the jealous man must hide his pain. In a 1981 survey of college women, 98 percent said men felt it important to control their emotions; 79 percent of the men agreed.[33]

Murder is in the air and that is frightening. He could challenge the rival. But what if he lost? What if he was beaten in public? Physical humiliation would be added to the psychological. He'd be less of a man than ever. Where does a man find a model to sustain him in the face of these new threats? One fills the horizon. Your own woman has brought him to your attention. He is your rival. His is the indefinable essence of masculinity, of dominance, for which she betrayed you.

"There are two ways in which the obsessive character of jealousy tends to exert itself," writes psychiatrist Leila Tov-Ruach. "One is the *need to know,* the endless tests and investigations and spyings that are so characteristic of jealousy. The other is the *need to visualize. Both obsessions seem to make the jealous person less passive, less helpless because he is actively engaged in investigating or imagining* [emphasis added]."[34]

The curious excitement is that your rival can teach you more about manhood than anyone else. His actions don't lie. The corporeality of him is important. He makes the abstract—*a man*—into flesh. You can learn from him what women really want, what it is he has that you don't, something you always secretly suspected made you less of a man than the other guys. You may hate him. You cannot let him go.

"Men don't ever totally give up their early camaraderie," says Dr. Michels. "This is exactly where jealousy so often comes up. Jealousy is a theme that includes unspoken homosexual links among men while their official relationships are with women. Jealousy encompasses the whole set of competitive, rivalrous, hate-filled-and-yet-fascinated interrelationships —with sexual overtones to them—between men."

On a flight from Key West to New York I watch a movie that is so bad you probably never saw it. The film stars the late John Belushi as a well-known newspaper man. He is on the trail of a famous woman bird watcher. She has sequestered herself alone atop a mountain to study a rare species of eagle. She is angry at Belushi's arrival and openly contemptuous of him. One day Belushi jealously spies her in the arms of a "wild mountain man." She isn't alone after all! The two men are soon at the point of killing one another over the only woman on the mountain.

The script sidesteps a true struggle through dawning camaraderie on the part of both men. The "wild man" turns out to be a former pro-football player. Belushi has long been a fan of his. On his side, the wild man has long been a fan of Belushi's hard-hitting sports coverage. How could they hate each other? They don't. They admire each other. The men become instant friends and the jealous triangle is settled between them. Since they are both good fellows, either one could make the woman happy. By mutual decision, the woman is awarded to Belushi.

We are asked to look at this movie as a love story. Between whom? Whatever sex/love exists between each man and the woman is not as moving or believable as the bonding between the men—camaraderie each man had felt before women entered his life, and to which Belushi and the wild man have now gratefully returned. The woman is not allowed to choose, not allowed to get in the way of the male relationship.

Driving into town from the airport, a loose end bothers me. Why do I feel the resolution of male jealousy has been too neat even for a Grade B movie? Envy has been left out.

The film never acknowledges the power of the woman, the unique role she plays in each man's life. In order to make the plot move, we are asked to believe that both men love her. How can we? The woman herself is devalued. Her love is never given the power that is given to male friendship. "Please don't leave me," goes another of Robertiello's awful one-liners. "It'll take me two or three days to replace you." The message of the joke is the true message of the film. If an infant misses his mother, will any other woman do? No. In the same way, the woman in this movie is supposed to be irreplaceable. But envy of her ability to come between the men is too strong. Her power must be denied. She is an empty character in an empty movie.

"Are you jealous?"

I am talking to Howard Sackler, author of the Pulitzer Prize–winning play *The Great White Hope*. Our conversation has touched on childhood, a lost father, a hated stepfather.

"There were two occasions," Howard says, "in which jealousy seriously interfered with my life. Both times I stayed with a woman—once for years —long after I'd lost all interest in her. I couldn't bear the thought of her falling into the arms of another man."

I am confused by his answer. Though it is spoken in immediate response to my question, Howard's words sound rehearsed and overly literary. Memories of Proust come once again to mind; Swann's jealous tragedy in which he gave up career, social position, everything, in an effort to possess Odette. "To think that I've wasted years of my life," he muses on his deathbed, "that I've longed to die, that I've experienced my greatest

love, for a woman who didn't appeal to me, who wasn't even my type!"[35]
As if life in twos isn't difficult enough, here is Howard, inventing a third
party—a man who exists only in some nebulous future of the woman's—
against whom to compete, of whom to feel jealous.

Last winter in Key West, there was a couple who ritually enacted a
jealous passage at arms as prelude to lovemaking. Wiggling like a Playboy
bunny, Betty would find a new man in a corner and enter into flirtatious
talk. Her husband, Steve—a massive, brooding hulk—would then pick a
fight with the stranger. Embarrassed to tears, Betty would rush out into
the night. Steve would knock the rival down and go searching for her
along the deserted beach (she never ran home).

I once asked Betty why, since her husband was so jealous, she wasn't
more careful about arousing his anger.

"When we make it afterward," she said, "we have our hottest sex."

Says social psychologist Gregory White, "In a society where I define
myself through competition with other men, and another man is getting
my woman, the move is to recapture her, not necessarily out of love for
her but out of face-saving or the competitive urge. Also, of course, when
another person shows interest in your lover, it revives what may be a
flagging desire. The idea that somebody else finds your lover valuable
increases her value. In a materialist culture, this kind of thinking is common. How does one know anything is valuable? Because other people
want it."

Knowing the torments of jealousy, I could not conceive of it as aphrodisiac. But Betty knew her man. Showing Steve another man wanted her
did increase her value. His reaction proved he loved her. Perhaps Betty
herself felt some excitement, the power of being the connecting rod between two male forces, the end result of which was the release of increased sexual energy in her lover.

Dr. Robert Michels: "Classically, the little boy is desirous of his mother
and mad at his father for interfering. But he is also in love with his father,
desirous of father's attention—even though father is his rival in the jealous
triangle in which mother is the pivotal corner. To say that a jealous person
is angry at the third party for interfering is a commonplace. What must be
realized is that the jealous person *at the same time*—consciously or not—
frequently has a special fascination with the third party. This special fascination may be more important than the relationship to the woman."

I have had a hard time accepting Michels's words; the tape I am listening to is almost three years old. When I first read Freud's paper on jealousy, which notoriously deals with the ideas Michels was trying to make
me examine, I didn't like it. Commenting on my resistance, Michels

urged me to reread the paper. Just as I have recently urged Robertiello to reexamine his own homoerotic fantasies. How accessible, reasonable, even eloquent I find Michels's interview on rehearing it today.

"Jealous rage is not just hate," Michels's voice continues, "not just murderously destructive. It includes fascination and intrigue with the nature of the other man's experience. Clinical evidence tells us again and again that jealous men are preoccupied with knowing exactly what happened. They want to find out everything, get as close to it as they can. They will pursue and harass their partner for details. 'What did you do with him, how did you do it, where, how many times, how did it feel, *what went on?*'

"What I'm saying is that embedded in jealousy are also elements of a positive nature toward the third party: identification and vicarious excitement and pleasure. It is not an either/or situation. It is both. The jealous person is angry at his woman being taken by another man. At the same time, he also has opportunity for a rich fantasy *about the other man.* This may be more intense than his relationship with the woman. It may be the only permissible way he can have psychologically exciting, sexually toned fantasies about men."

Hearing Michels's words three years ago was like staring at the sun: One giant word blotted out everything else. How many psychoanalysts have I interviewed since? Not one of them showed Michels's straightforward interest in discussing the homosexual aspects of jealousy. I have little doubt that homophobia is one of the major reasons an analysis of jealousy has never gone much beyond Freud's sixty-year-old paper.

Does unconscious speak to unconscious? As I have become comfortable with Michels's exposition of Freud, my interviewees too have become comfortable telling me stories like this:

"When I have a really deep, long-standing relationship with a woman, I find the two of us becoming extensions of one another." The man talking is thirty-three. His name is Ted. "Naturally, not mystically. Partly because you've learned about sex together, you're kind of in each other's skin. But also, psychologically, you know how the other responds. That means if your partner is with someone else, a rival, to some extent you're in bed with the other person too."

"Which makes you feel . . . ?" I ask.

"Exposed. In a relationship I nurture togetherness. I like being close. The triangle destroys that security. You're exposed to the comparison your lover can make between you and the other guy. In some strange way you're exposed to intimacy with the other man. Competitive intimacy. But also, since you've become part of your partner, and she's part of you, now you're in that bed with that man. It's very disturbing. . . ."

"When someone is unfaithful to you, do you ask about the other guy?"

"When I was married, my wife was having an affair. The way I handled it was I became very depressed, I didn't want to know. I couldn't afford to ask but I must have wondered. I felt they were together, judging me. I also wondered what he had that I didn't. Once you're left out like that, well, it's like in childhood. In childhood you wanted your mother to love you no matter what you did, right or wrong. When you're grown-up and have a woman's commitment, that's what you want again. I think I got that to some extent from my mother, but didn't get it from my father. And so I looked for it in lovers. Somebody who . . ."

". . . would love you right or wrong."

"Yeah. My father always had a short fuse, not much flexibility. It's exactly what a little kid picks up on. My mother had a kind of divided loyalty between us, first to him, but also to protect me from his tensions. I know I do the same thing to my kids and my father got it from his father. I can't help it. I'm not accepting when I wish I were. The emotions I keep showing them is that I disapprove of them, that they aren't enough. . . ."

"Do you have strategies for avoiding jealousy?"

"I try to tie her up emotionally," Ted says, "to compete and perform so well she won't even look at another guy. I hate jealousy. In these triangles you're no longer two people doing something together. Suddenly your lover is the audience and you must perform. Even worse is the fantasy of watching them and *being* them. . . ."

Since jealousy is a problem in emotion, a woman may hate it but does not feel unsexed by having to deal with it. For the man, as Freud said, "normal jealousy" is bad enough. He feels "grief, the pain caused by the thought of losing the loved object, and of the narcissistic wound. . . ." He also suffers "feelings of enmity against the successful rival, and of a greater or lesser amount of self-criticism. . . ."[36] So far, good plain common sense.

But, Freud goes on, in some people jealousy is "experienced bisexually; that is to say, in a man, beside the suffering in regard to the loved woman and the hatred against the male rival, grief in regard to the unconsciously loved man and hatred of the woman as a rival will add to its intensity." Freud went on to describe a case history with striking parallels to Ted's: "I even know of a man who suffered exceedingly during his attacks of jealousy and who, according to his own account, went through unendurable torments by consciously imagining himself in the position of the faithless woman. . . ."[37]

What is highly traumatic, what knocks men for a loop when they find themselves the victims of jealousy, is that they are invaded by foreign emotions—violent, intrusive tensions they have never known before. "This isn't me; I don't act like this." The man is not used to feelings he can't overcome, can't rise above, can't forget or ignore, and yet, here he is, being made to feel intensely about another male. Loss, pain, hatred, anger, grief, goddamn it, yes—but how come to terms with this sickeningly heated mixture of curiosity about the successful rival, desire to get close enough to find out all about him, the need to *see* him? How keep from shuddering at the shameful intimacy, the secret tie between them formed by the woman's body they share? Father was aloof, too competitive or absent. Aside from ritualized locker-room horsing around, men don't touch. Contact with this man is almost physical. It's unbearable, too close . . . in a word, unmanly.

Paranoid ideas of homosexual allure make the subject difficult for men to discuss. That is, a man may find his rival so attractive—in Freud's phrase, so "unconsciously loved"—that the emotion is intolerable. He pushes these threatening ideas outside himself, and projects them onto the woman. It is not *he* who finds the rival so magnetic. *She* is the one. The man can then spill out his fear, disguised as righteous anger. The other man is a disgusting coward. The woman is a treacherous harlot. The whole world is filled with lies. Or "mendacity" as Big Daddy roars out in Tennessee Williams's play about hidden homosexual feelings.

Spectators at these not-so-rare scenes are embarrassingly aware that misdirected, misnamed, and inappropriate emotions are flying about. Supposedly sophisticated people mutter to each other about "latent homosexuality." Does this prove Freud was right? No. Merely that he is often misinterpreted. Nothing described above means that the man who expresses these emotions is necessarily homosexual. Haven't you ever, in excess irritation cried out, "Stop that or I'll kill you!" Does that mean you are a murderer, "latent" or not? Nowhere does Freud say of the man who imagines himself to be the faithless woman that he had committed a homosexual act. The thought is not the deed. Only the psychologically illiterate believe that all fantasies are suppressed wishes.

"One way of thinking about jealousy," says Dr. Michels, "is that it is a frequent residue of homosexual interest, where overt homosexual desires have lessened or evaporated. So rather than ask, Where does a man's sexual fascination with his rival come from?, we might be wiser to begin with a recognition. While people are omnipotential sexually, in the usual course of development, overt homosexual interests are likely to wane or disappear. Jealousy remains as a kind of primary residue. Think of it as an adult version of earlier, explicit homosexual interests that are universal in children."

On the biological level half our genes come from the female parent half from the male. Psychologically, every child is aware of two immense sources of love in the house; again—one male, one female. How can we not find ourselves bombarded with emotions, ideas, fantasies, fears and fleeting desires taken over from both of them? It is easy (safe) to imagine ourselves a child, wondering what it would feel like to be the parent of the same sex. Is it possible we did not have at least unconscious curiosities about how it might feel to have the erotic experiences of the opposite sex? I don't think so. "Heterosexuality is seen classically and currently by most analysts as a developmental achievement, a product of mental differentiation and not only of physiology,"[38] says Dr. Allan Compton. We are not born emotionally male or female.

Gender identity is the result of the child's endless research into the questions of what is male, what is female, which one am I? Freud's patient who fantasized he was the faithless woman being made love to by a successful rival . . . my interviewee Ted; I admire both of them. They consciously will themselves to think deeper into the unthinkable than most of us could bear. Their fantasies are almost psychotic breakthroughs into intolerable knowledge, bringing them to the heart of the existential puzzle: How does it feel to be "a real man"?

What I like about Michels is that he treats Freud's ideas as what they are, everyday facts of life. "Emotions like jealousy," he says, "are embedded in universals that make up all relationships. Some experiences that are labeled as deviant or pathological, I would call normal. They pick up fundamental themes that run through everyone. They are often expressed in unexpected forms and so, once again, get labeled deviant. Jealousy involves triadic relationships, even if the third party is imaginary."

"A stranger?"

"Psychologically, there is no such thing as a stranger," replies Michels. "You wouldn't be jealous of the stranger unless you had already invested him with attributes and characteristics that come from within you. The stranger is from Central Casting, on loan to your fantasy."

As I listen to the tape of Michels's voice, a bit of free association floats up. There is an important question I will never be able to ask Howard Sackler. When we spoke three years ago, he told me jealousy had made him unable to end affairs after he had lost interest, in order to keep the woman from "falling into another man's arms." I did not know enough then to ask Howard about these shadowy rivals. What attributes did he himself invent for them, for him to envy, fear and need to thwart? How describe this contest with the unknown man? What was the gain? Why was merely depriving the rival of a no-longer-loved woman so exciting that Howard put up with boredom with her "for years"?

The role we write for the stranger may be painful. It brings secret

satisfactions too. He expresses something within that wants to be said
. . . furnishes an ambience we find intensely, strangely exciting. He has
been created to fit our needs. The price of such ambivalent joys can be
high. I cannot ask Howard these further questions. Tragically and unexpectedly, he died six months ago. The shortness of life. The years that
jealousy can waste.

When I consider how competitive men are about their masculinity, I
am surprised that not once in the thousands of sexual fantasies I have
collected has one man introduced another for the purpose of edging him
out for the woman, thus proving himself superior. Men do have Walter
Mitty fantasies of beating up the other guy, winning the woman and
carrying her off for a victorious fuck. But they are not invented for erotic
stimulation. On the contrary, what does make many a man hot is watching the woman in the arms of another man. Cooperative triangles and
groups are among the great themes of the erotic male imagination.

An intriguing question is: At what point in a man's life does he begin to
introduce other men into his fantasies to serve sexual ends? I have never
run across this scenario in a fantasy from a male virgin. The erotic dreams
of these young men, still in their teens and early twenties, fall into two
broad categories: wildly sexual red hot women who seduce them, or totally
inexperienced young girls who cannot compare them. Either way, no vir-
tuoso performance is called for. The anxious idea of measuring up never
enters.

It is only after a boy has lost his virginity, after women have entered his
real life, that he begins to resummon old male comrades. He writes them
into his sexual reveries, but not as rivals. Some are even presented as
bigger studs than he. Is he envious? No. The need to have masculinity
reinforced by the comforting presence of a hero makes him ejaculate all
the harder.

Not all men enjoy these fantasies. Some men don't have them at all.
"But those who do," says Robertiello, "and get upset over them, may well
be projecting very forbidden homosexual impulses. Let's remember that
statistically about one third of all men have had some real homosexual
experience. Far higher than for women. These men may have consciously
decided never to try it again. But the presence of another man in their
fantasy signals reemergence of impulses they want to deny. That's why
they are so frightening. If I'm sitting here with a fantasy in my head of my
woman making it with my best friend, and I get a kick out of it—that's
one thing. If I'm eating my heart out over it, then very likely I want to
make it with him myself."

It is not hard to understand why a sexually inexperienced young man would find all the stimulation he needs in dreams of being alone with a woman. He is still close to his days of the boy gang and its attendant homoerotic horseplay. If another man were present in his fantasies, anxieties would arise. It is only after sex becomes a known quantity that his fantasies begin to change and become complex.

He knows now that he is not gay, but there are other problems. Is he satisfying the woman enough? Why doesn't she respond? Is she judging him? Having other men along divides the responsibility. They help him make the woman hotter than he ever could alone and bring her to a greater climax. At the same time, the presence of other men allays his fear that the woman will consume him, take him over. Nor can a woman in bed with more than one man be seen in any way as a maternal figure. Perhaps best of all, the other men become his allies against the power of women. They are all heroes. Gender is reinforced.

"A lot of times a guy who has a fantasy of his wife making it with another man," says Robertiello, "he may not really want his wife to do it, but he likes to play with the idea because it makes *her* seem more sexual. For instance, I have a patient who went to a sexual surrogate. She wasn't particularly great, but he said the one thing it showed him was that for the first time in his life, he met a woman who really liked to fuck. He didn't think there were any such people."

"What I've never understood about these fantasies," I say to Robertiello, "is what do these men do with their competition?"

"That's the whole point," he answers. "These fantasies deny rivalry, jealousy, competition. They take what could be a scary triangle and turn it into a sexy one. A man eliminates the issue of competition by the way he structures the fantasy."

"Are you saying that these fantasies allow him to deal with competition . . . ?"

"He doesn't 'deal' with it, Nancy. You're not getting it. Competition is *left out* as part of the given. The fantasy takes his anxiety about competition and circumvents it."

A moment of recognition. In real life, when women came along, they put him in competition with other men. Jealous men are always hiding their women away. In fantasy, he can take his male allies right into the bed with him. Lo and behold, neither competition nor jealousy enters; it's a lot of fun for him, the woman and his friends too. Fantasies take the very ideas that make us most anxious and turn them upside down. That is their magic.

I tell Robertiello that before coming to see him, I had read through three years of our interviews. The progression of interpretation of his own sexual fantasies is fascinating. For instance, the first time he mentioned ideas of Susan with the delivery boy he said it was in the service of making Susan more sexual, as red hot for sex as he. When the subject came up months later, he had just uncovered the full extent of his envy of women's power. At that point he admitted his fantasy also contained a desire to debase and humiliate Susan. By inventing scenes in which Susan fucked any stranger who came to the door, he was proving she was a hot number, yes, but also that she was "no fucking Princess."

"Do you remember," I ask him now, "that when these fantasies first came up, you asked me to keep them confidential?"

"That's so unlike me. I can't believe it."

"I have it on tape. I'll play it for you."

"I wonder what I was so frightened of? That's fascinating. I asked you to keep it a secret? And now I've forgotten asking you to do so? I'll have to work it out."

This is what he does all the time, and, I think, why he became an analyst. Depressing insights someone else might want to bury even deeper excite him. I recently read something that describes Robertiello perfectly:

"Working through . . . signifies . . . triumph over the clandestine operations of neurotic life," writes Dr. Mark J. Sedler. "Nowhere is this truth expressed more eloquently than in Shakespeare's *Macbeth* [V, iii, 40–46]. Lady Macbeth, counselor and *agent provocateur*, has gone mad. Macbeth summons a physician and asks,

> *Canst thou not minister to a mind diseas'd,*
> *Pluck from the memory a rooted sorrow,*
> *Raze out the written troubles of the brain*
> *And with some sweet oblivious antidote*
> *Cleanse the stuff'd bosom of that perilous stuff*
> *Which weighs upon the heart?*

To which the physician replies:

> *Therein the patient*
> *Must minister to himself."*[39]

"You're the most competitive man I know," I say to Robertiello, "and yet, when you analyzed your fantasy of going down on the guy who'd stolen a woman from you, you said it was a 'glorifying humiliation.' Is that interpretation complete? Maybe it was simply wanting to get close to another man. Look, don't get upset again. I'm not saying you're homosexual. . . ."

"I was just thinking of that yesterday," he says calmly. "That was the only time I'd ever had a homosexual fantasy. She said he was exactly like me. He was a therapist. He had a beard, like me. It was as if she'd found a carbon copy of me—no pun intended—because he was black. Was I making it with myself, some narcissistic . . . ?"

"He was the only sexual rival you'd ever recognized as equal."

"At the bottom of that fantasy was fear of being intruded upon by men. Most men are afraid that if they get too close to a woman, they'll be taken over. Since I was raised by my grandfather, my fears are different. He was extremely intrusive. Checking my stool, monitoring my time to the minute, telling me what to wear. He was the quintessential, intrusive Jewish mother figure."

"You never had a woman who was even interested in you when you were small, so why should you be scared of getting too close to a woman? You're the reverse of most men. To this day, you still complain that women don't give you enough nurturing."

"Since the intruder was a man, I didn't have gender identity problems. What I did have were identity problems. My grandfather was really wiping me out."

"I still don't understand about the black analyst. Let me quote from my notes. On March ninth you said you were *jealous* of him. Referring to your fantasy of going down on him, you said, 'That strikes me as a weird way of mitigating the jealousy. . . .'"

"I said I felt jealous of him? I didn't think that was what I was feeling. . . ."

"Didn't you care about that woman?"

"Yeah. I did."

"Okay, you lost something special. Lost someone special. If you were jealous of him, what other emotions in the jealous situation could you be feeling?"

"All right . . . well, let me . . . don't interrupt me! Let me try to reconstruct it. First of all, it was one of those deals where I wanted her to leave her husband and marry me, right?"

"The old Robertiello number."

"Magic, yeah. So anyway, what happened was, first she said she would, then on her way to getting a lawyer and starting divorce . . . she wouldn't."

"She realized you were not a reliable number."

"No, that wasn't the reason. I was just too good for her."

"Ha ha."

"Anyway, we kind of got back together for a while and she told me while we'd been separated she'd been seeing this other analyst. I didn't feel I hated him, or I wanted to destroy him. I didn't feel jealousy."

"You called it jealousy on March ninth, Richard! You said, quote, 'I was jealous.' "

"There was a triangle and some guy beat me out, yes—but I didn't have the feelings people identify with jealousy. I didn't feel the terrible pain. . . ."

"Because your defenses functioned so well! It's like you took an aspirin before going to bed so that you wouldn't wake up with a hangover. What you do with your life in order to avoid feeling an emotion—the defenses you erect—are just as revealing as if you suffered the emotion itself."

"Agreed. So when I said I was jealous, I meant it in the context of the old defenses I erected. They worked very well. Like, Who needs you. You're no good anyway. . . ."

"You devalued her."

"Yes, so I didn't feel I was losing anything. But what strikes me as strange was the emergence of these homosexual fantasies. . . ."

"Why a homosexual fantasy as a defense against feeling jealous?"

"I don't know. On some level he has to be my brother or my son beating me out for my mother or my wife, right?"

"Or your father."

"OK, father/sibling. But it's strange I didn't feel angry at this other guy for replacing me. . . ."

"Maybe . . ."

"Let me finish! You tell me I shouldn't interrupt you! So, maybe by making him gay I'm cutting his balls off."

"But you said you were going down on him. . . ."

"That doesn't necessarily matter . . . although in a certain sense, of course, it does. Because I was . . ."

"A slave."

". . . being more feminine."

"With your Italian dominance number, why did you go down on him?"

"Basically it's all a defense against competition. It wasn't that I was afraid of his castrating me. I think it's much more that I was afraid of killing *him*. So I went down on him to prevent my killing him. The fantasy says, 'Let's not be enemies, even though we're fighting over the same woman. Now that you've won her, let's be friends. I don't want to kill you; you don't have to kill me. It's as if I'd finally found a parent. . . . It was like I was taking him in . . . sucking . . . a parent from whom I could take something in, in a loving way."

"You had your grandfather shoved down your throat."

"Right—his cock, if you will—but that was no loving exchange. This fantasy was a displacement upward. Like I wanted to take in their brains and that's the same as taking in their cocks. Oh, this is extremely interesting!"

"Let me suggest something else. Doesn't the fantasy say to the woman, 'The hell with you. This guy wants me more than he wants you anyway.' Your anger was really at the woman, not the man."

"That's right. It's what we were talking about the other day. That men are more important to men than women are."

"In real life, you've told me several times about trying to set up some man as an intellectual equal, or even superior . . ."

"Yes, I wanted to think they were stronger, smarter than me, someone I could learn from. He would be my guru, my teacher, my father. But each time I went through that, it was a terrible disappointment."

Is Robertiello telling me he can't find an intellectual peer? "You've always been afraid that if you got too close to a man in real life, he'd be like your father, deadly competitive. . . ."

"This fantasy says that despite these fears, I'm looking for that man . . . still."

"Sometimes when I listen to you talk about how you have to have sex every day, and how you wouldn't put up with a woman who wouldn't provide it, I get the feeling that you're competing with women. You're such a he-man, you can have more orgasms than any old woman."

"Maybe I exaggerate my certainty of gender identity. On some level, my preoccupation with sex could be preoccupation with masculinity. When I first got married, when I was twenty, I remember it was important to be able to say, 'My wife.' That meant, I have a wife, therefore I am a man."

"It's weird. As unusual as your childhood was, you still tend toward the norm. You do have problems of gender identity just like most men. You also have the desire other men have for a good father, the desire to be close to other men. And like a lot of men, you can't let yourself. Did you know statistics show that even today something like twenty-five percent of young men say they share their private feelings with no one?"

"Heterosexual men are a lot more homophobic than you'd like to think. It all ties in with Freud's paper."

My jaw drops. "So Freud's paper isn't 'bullshit' after all?"

Robertiello doesn't pick up on my I-told-you-so. He shrugs; the point of our conversations is to push forward. I look for another quote that I've brought with me. It sheds light on something he's been telling me from the beginning, something I used to think was one of his defenses. He has always said it wasn't sexual jealousy he suffered from, but sibling rivalry.

"In *Fathers and Sons*, Yablonsky says, when children are born, 'many men experience a variety of acute anxieties as a result of unhappy memories over their own unhappy childhood, of rivalry with brothers and sisters, or of a fear of competition with the new child for the wife's affection. . . .'[40] Does this describe what goes on between you and your son?"

"My son is like a sibling. I'm always calling him by my brother's name. In my unconscious, I have my son and my brother totally confused."

"How did you feel when your son was born?"

"Terribly jealous of my wife's attention to him. Just like the passage you read me, it rearoused all my old sibling stuff. Remember that I told you that the first time I saw my mother breastfeeding my brother I ran away from home."

Every once in a while, Robertiello tells me he is going to make a conscious effort to do better by his son than his father did for him. Nothing much ever comes of his efforts. It's tragic to hear a man who knows that his father's love could have saved him say that he is unable to give that same love to his son.

"We used to say how difficult it was for mothers to give good mothering if they hadn't received it. Fathers aren't bastards. They don't set out to do their sons in. Why can't they give their sons the feeling that they're a chip off the old block?"

"That's what I've been talking about," he says. "Sibling rivalry. Expectant fathers have entirely different fantasies than their pregnant wives do. They often see the unborn child as a sibling rather than an infant."

"A pregnant woman isn't going to think of the child she is carrying in terms of a sibling. It's so different for a man!"

"I once had a patient whose wife was pregnant. He dreamed he destroyed the fetus. It was so awful he came to me for help. He and his wife were very close. What was agonizing was juggling the idea of feeling competitive with the unborn child and loving him at the same time. On top of that, breaking up of the exclusive union he had with his wife—even if the intruder was his own child—rearoused memories of rivalries with his brothers and sisters."

"If the father shares parenting with the mother, wouldn't that diminish his rivalry with the child?"

"That's one of the best reasons for shared parenting. It involves him with the child in a parental way rather than seeing the child as a competitor. When a father sees his child as a narcissistic extension of himself, that helps too. The child is a little him, and when the child is loved by the mother, he experiences it as being loved himself—not as love being taken away from him."

"The mystery to me has always been that you never felt jealous when another man came on with your wife. But you were insanely jealous of your son."

"My wife was crazy about him. It left me consciously furious, ready to kill them both."

"Are you saying that sibling rivalry is more wounding than the oedipal stuff?"

"Sexual jealousy is a much later development. The sibling business is early; much deeper, more poignant. It's one thing for someone to take away a piece of ass. It's something else to take away a piece of food. Maternal love, that really is life and death."

"You transferred the hate you had for your siblings to your son. . . ."

"Even more than I transferred the hate I had for my father."

CHAPTER EIGHT

A Real Woman

"We're the sex that has it all. My five-year-old daughter reminds me of it daily. You know what Molly said the other day at some kid's birthday party? 'When I grow up,' she said, 'I want to be famous like Shakespeare.' A little boy her age said, 'What's famous?' "

Erica Jong is speaking. We are sitting in my office in New York. An early day in June. We sprawl on sofas facing one another, bottle of cold wine and tape recorder on a table between us. Freud said poets were close to the secrets of the unconscious. Erica is a poet.

"What do you think is men's fear of women?" I ask.

"Control. Not all men, but many. It reduces them to a feeling of being little boys again. They find themselves doing things they don't want. They know somehow the woman got them to do it, but they don't know how. Control is also behind men's fear of women's sexual voracity."

"You're not boiling down women's power to the old multiple orgasm argument, are you?"

"That isn't so daunting to a lot of men. Some are excited, their egos bolstered by the notion they can make a woman come six times in a row, whether they themselves come once, twice or not at all."

"But it goes beyond that," I say. "I was reading your book about witches. Why were people so terrified they burned them?"

"If you trace the witch back, you find the Mother Goddess, the life giver. She made things grow, plants to seek the sun. She brought men and women together in the desire to re-create. She presented the positive side of womanliness, our connection with the psychic world, with elemental emotions, healing, birthing. Whoever controls life controls death. The witch is the reverse of the power that used to be worshiped in the Mother Goddess."

"So the witch to represent fear of woman's unbridled passion, her youth. . . ."

"And also fear of her old age. Killing the witch, torturing her, was men's—and women's—way of curbing and punishing women for their freedom and passion."

"I used to balk at the notion that people—especially men—feared women's power. What power? I didn't feel any. It contradicted the world as I saw it. Maybe men understood it. . . ."

"They did, and that's why they set up sanctions against it . . . the patriarchal society."

"Young women today still resist recognizing how many new options they have."

"They know they have them but they're afraid to exercise them. Part of it is because they realize it makes men uneasy."

"I interviewed the president of a large ad agency. He said that the minute a woman steps up the corporate ladder, men in middle management get absolutely terrified."

"We are the stronger sex," Erica says, wandering around the room. She grew up just down the block. The window of her childhood bedroom is visible from my office. "At the stage of civilization we have reached, muscle power is not as important as brain power. And there is no doubt our intelligence is as high as men's. What's more, we live longer, we are more durable. And we can have babies."

"This advertising executive said something else," I say. "That men in the workplace are terrified of angry women. Especially when the woman works for the man. Something about the angry woman going out of control . . . that she'll attack him and he won't be able to defend himself. 'I don't know what that's all about,' he said."

Erica nods knowingly. We both know what "that's" all about. Men and women alike are terrified of an angry woman out of control.

"Is this you?" Erica asks. She has picked up a small, silver-framed photo, looking from it to me for recognition.

"It's my mother." I can hear her voice: "Oh, Nancy, you don't have that picture of me out for everyone to see!" It is my favorite. She looks so pretty and sexy, sitting on that South Carolina beach in a two-piece bathing suit, her legs protectively tucked under, as she smiles into the camera. She is about thirty-two years old.

The bathing suit was a beautiful yellow. She gave it to my sister; I had nothing to put in the top. My sister filled it perfectly. Oh, how I envied their bosoms, which my mother quaintly called *ba-zooms*. It's curious. I spent most of my life denying my mother's sexuality. Now I sense I need it.

"She's pretty," says Erica. "You resemble her a lot." I smile appreciatively, though I cannot take the compliment seriously. In my eyes, the only time I look like my mother is when I see her anxiety in my reflection in store windows.

"In some ways I'm glad I resemble her," I say. "Other ways, I'm afraid I do." I sigh. "We all resemble our mothers."

"We're supposed to. Among my own women friends," says Erica, "the ambitious ones do work harder than men. They're more driven, single-minded."

"What frightens these corporate guys is that they relate hard-driving women to their wives at home. They fear that their wives might begin to act the same way . . . demanding, aggressive."

"This is a terrible thing for a feminist to say," says Erica, "but I've come to believe the secret of being attractive to men is to realize they want to be constantly fed, given good wine, stroked on the forehead and have their problems listened to."

"That's what I want! Everybody wants to be taken care of."

"What is confusing is that de facto we increasingly live in a matriarchy. But the rules are those of a patriarchy . . . all this puts women in a terrible bind. We've been brought up—brainwashed—to think we're insufficient, lack a penis, blah blah blah. It's hard for us to realize our power."

"Men find it very confusing. We have power, and yet we act like victims. Do you have any trouble taking the initiative with men?"

"I have a lot of trouble with rejection."

"Men tell me it always hurts. The fear of being rejected never goes away. But men keep trying. Women get angry or devastated the first time a man rejects them, and don't try again."

"I'm not vulnerable to rejection until I'm in love," says Erica. "Then I see rejection where there is none. If I'm not in love with a man, I can call him up and take no for an answer. Once I'm connected to him, and have an expectation, I'd rather die than be turned down."

"Are you jealous?"

"Not until I fall in love. If it's friendship, if I see him only on Tuesdays, I can easily see him go out with another woman. Once I'm attached, I will be tempted to go through this diary and figure out where he's been on Wednesday and Saturday. I'm ferocious, a terror in my fantasies; but I try not to let it show!"

"What's horrible is the compulsive quality of jealousy. You hate what you're doing and thinking. Do you remember Rona Jaffe's book where she goes through his garbage?"

"I've done that."

"Once I went through a man's dirty laundry. God, it was demeaning. Tell me, if you walked in on your lover and he was with another woman, whose jugular would you go for?"

A pause.

"I think hers. I don't know. I can't imagine putting myself in a situation where that would happen."

"Did your ex-husband have affairs?"

"Several."

"Which ex-husband?"

"The shrink."

"Did you know?"

"I suspected."

"Did you ask him?"

"I sort of twitted him. It was part playful, part knowledge I was afraid of. I would say, Are you sleeping with this one or that one? He always denied it, but with a smirk. Then I would feel guilty. *He* would be sleeping with someone, but *I* would feel guilty even for asking."

"And you never imagined walking in on them? Never had a little picture in your mind of what you would do?"

"Now that I think of it, he was the one I was mad at, not her. When I found out, I was enraged at him . . . and at myself."

"Because . . . ?"

"Because I had wanted to fuck around and didn't do it. What was enraging was that he made me feel guilty about my jealous suspicions, and all along he had been seeing other women."

"Just as you suspected."

"I knew a lot of analysts did in fact have affairs, right on the couch in their office. It's so easy for a shrink."

"But you'd never played out any of your fantasies.   ."

"I'm very faithful when I love someone. Monogamous. I thought he was perfect, the daddy figure who knew everything. I was this guilty little person who had disloyal fantasies, and wrote disloyal books."

"Did you tell him about your fantasies?"

"I was too ashamed. Remember, we're talking about the way I was fifteen years ago. I mentioned these ideas to him only once. 'You're really fucked up,' he said. 'You'd better go back to your analyst.' "

"And he'd been doing it all the time!"

"I wrote all those books . . . they made everyone think I was a nymphomaniac. But it was only my fantasy life I wrote about. He did it in reality. I wanted to kill him."

"How do you feel about getting older and losing your looks?"

"Scares the shit out of me."

"Men have money. Women have beauty. But you can save your money up and it will grow."

"In the fifteenth, sixteenth centuries, earlier, women were burned because they were so young and sexually attractive, 'bewitching' to men. Simone de Beauvoir wrote that women were burned as witches simply because they were beautiful."

"The double standard of aging. Craggy old rich men have always had little trouble getting beautiful young women. Will power in craggy old women ever be seen as aphrodisiac?"

"I find old male flesh unappealing," says Erica.

"You don't need an old rich man's power. You've got your own. At the Jockey Club in Washington, I interviewed a young bartender. He said it killed him to see so many gorgeous young women coming in with those fat old guys, limos purring at the curb."

"Remember Leah in Colette's *Chéri?* She was forty-eight; her lover was twenty. She compares herself to a vampire feeding on young flesh. I read it when I was twenty. I didn't know what the hell she was talking about. I read it again recently. It was unbelievably compelling."

" 'Never die wondering,' she wrote."

"Leah was a courtesan, still beautiful. She said she would rather die than give herself to an old man."

"Since I never knew my father," I say, "you'd think I would be a setup for older men. But I've never been attracted to them, no matter how much money they had."

"We have the same disease."

"It has to do with running your own life. . . ."

"I was the middle daughter. I was supposed to be the son. The achiever. I always felt that. My mother says, 'You're just like your father.' She means in terms of a drive to achieve, excel, and make money."

"I always felt that expectation too. And so here we are."

"I think powerful women will seek beautiful young men."

"I can understand that when you're fifty and he's thirty," I say. "Can it happen when you're seventy-five and he's thirty-five?"

"It's very difficult for women to conceptualize what turns men on."

"I think women fear the old woman even more than men," I say. "We're the ones who *become* the witch. The skin begins to sag. . . ."

"The old crone. The witch's sagging flesh was symbol of our fear and detestation of her power."

"Control," I say. "It *is* about control."

"Mother and child. Who's bigger, who's smaller."

"And that runs right through the adult man/woman relationship. I think the only couples who last are the ones who give up control. You have to learn to trust enough to stop controlling him, controlling yourself."

"Nowadays," says Erica, "people don't stick together long enough ever to reach that point. Wouldn't that be nice? To stop controlling. Until I do, I will never marry again."

Erica lay in her powerful husband's arms and guiltily dreamed of other men. Jealously, she suspected him of having affairs. When he denied it, she felt even more guilty. Her suspicions proved correct. But if they hadn't, wouldn't she still have wondered and worried that he was enjoying the forbidden sex of which she dreamed but which she denied herself? He was the big man, daddy, "perfect." She thought of herself as this "little person." That was fifteen years ago, but even then it went so much against the grain of who and what she was that we must ask, What did self-diminishment gain her?

> *There's a somebody I'm longing to see:*
> *I hope that he*
> *Turns out to be*
> *Someone who'll watch over me. . . .[1]*

Erica and I can watch over ourselves. We have found our voice again, the power we abandoned when we were young girls for the behavior expected of us. We manage our own businesses and households and will stand up to anyone. Until we fall in love. Then we cringe from rejection. Jealously, we go through his dirty laundry, secretly read his diary.

> *I'm a little lamb who's lost in the wood;*
> *I know I could*
> *Always be good*
> *To one who'll watch over me. . . .[2]*

This Gershwin song is one of my favorites. Late at night, sitting out under the stars in Key West, mellow on wine, good food and company, I'll slip on Zubin Mehta's soundtrack from *Manhattan*. The string section of the New York Philharmonic stills every voice, lifting each of us into private reverie of past or future surrender.

One night a man and woman drifted inside to dance. High on violins, near tears for everyone we'd ever loved and lost, we sat around the wooden harvest table, humming, strumming, watching from the pitch-black darkness outside as the couple in the spotlight held one another in their arms, dipped, paused, and twirled as one. The people around that table were in their twenties, in their fifties. Wanting to be taken care of is specific to neither age nor sex. Everybody wants it. When we find it, no one wants to lose it. Not a child to a sibling; not a lover to a rival.

"And when you love," I say to Hanna Segal, "what you envy is any life of their own they might have."

"Any life they might have of their own, yes," she repeats. "I can allow you to be beautiful, rich, clever and good, as long as you are part of me. Possessiveness is absolutely a defense against envy."

"But if you show signs of independent life, of being able to exist without me, I not only feel abandoned . . ."

". . . I immediately become envious of your fine qualities because I no longer own them."

"So, if you are possessive, the very things that make you love someone, that's what makes you hate them in the end."

"You have realized their qualities don't belong to you," says Hanna Segal.

"We're the sex that has it all," exults Erica Jong, in love with life and its manifestation in her five-year-old daughter, Molly. If women are so powerful, why is our strength unavailable to us when loss is in the air? I would suggest that we grew into it too late. Perhaps Molly's self-confidence will become hers, be integrated at an earlier age. Says analyst Robert Gould, "The emergence of feminist values means we're going to see a radical change in how jealousy works."

In the old days, the bargain of male as good provider and female as caretaker was rooted in economic necessity. Economics have changed. Nobody knows what the new bargain will be.

"Traditionally women were assigned responsibility for the emotional side of the relationship," says sociologist Gordon Clanton. "Therefore, women are more likely to express jealousy. This doesn't say that if a woman is jealous she is sick or weak or defective. She may be putting up an early warning signal that the relationship is in trouble. Jealousy is no more deeply wired in women than in men. The social changes in sex-role expectations that we are undergoing today inevitably produce a certain amount of confusion. And that confusion is a source of a lot of contemporary pain, including jealousy."

Under the old bargain, some men were bad at providing, some women incompetent caretakers, but the need to survive as a unit gave each partner self-esteem. There were grim jealousies and envies, but families stayed together. Without putting value judgments on it, that is what families did. Even when the man wandered, women lived with their jealousy, their fear of loss, their rage. That is what women did.

How ironic! Women felt powerless in a system based on fear that they had too much power.

Oh, women got their way often enough. They nagged, withheld sex; they cut men off from their children. They manipulated. But manipulation is not power you hold in your hands as of right. You get it slyly, through someone else. *Women felt powerless because they so completely bought the defense against their envious rage at men: female devaluation.* And nowhere did they devalue themselves more than in that place where they exercised the most power: raising children. No job has more influence on the future of the world. No job has less value attached.

There is nothing like divorce to show the compulsive quality of a woman's defenses, the need to devalue herself, to idealize the man. How often divorce lawyers have told me that even after a man has broken his wife's arm on his way out the door, she still believes he will take care of her. It is almost impossible for her to give up the image of him as the White Knight. If she abandoned the idealization, she would be face to face with her furious envy of his power. Years of it. She would kill him. That is what lawyers want and why divorces are so bloody. The war is fought on the no-man's-land between two power bases: his money, her children.

In a woman's eyes, men still have the power. Not enough time has gone by to change old perceptions. She envies the man for taking care of her. It shows he has all the power. She envies him for not taking care of her. He could and has decided not to. She envies him his place in a system that pays her sixty-three cents to his dollar.

She is in open rage at him—all defenses down—because he will not solve the double bind she is in. She has been raised to believe he could. Study after study shows that women have one foot in the old, and one in the new: Take care of me. Treat me as an equal too.

"It is a universal problem," says Dr. Michels. "It is easier to act the way your parents did because it is familiar. You learn by observing them. If you and your contemporaries act in totally new ways, you are in a much more anxiety-provoking situation." Without the generational imprint of having seen initiative and self-reliance in her mother and in her mother's mother, a woman fears her power is illusory. Manufactured by herself in her own lifetime, it is too fragile to depend on.

The media trumpets the glory of the independent woman, but the same mothers who encourage their daughters' independence acquiesce to their husbands. Fathers who preach courage to their daughters but expect their wives to remain "the little woman" also teach a double standard. Who is the real woman? The one father married or the daughter he taught to conquer the world?

Women have always gazed over their shoulders, questioning the distance they have moved away from mother's role. Small wonder college women today gaze back more anxiously than ever for a sign of rebellion on their mothers' part. If mother can be less dependent on father, daughter too may be able to resist the temptation to mesh with a man and succumb in his arms.

Meanwhile, young women postpone marriage. In 1970, 35.8 percent of women twenty to twenty-four were single. In 1984, this had jumped to a full 56.9 percent.[3] A not surprising corollary: In 1960, among women ages twenty to twenty-four, 24 percent did not have children. By 1982, the percentage of that group who did not have children had gone up to 43 percent.[4]

Economics and careers account for much of this postponement. The explanation usually neglected is that as long as a woman remains single she can control her life, can avoid the difficult comparisons between her life and her parents' that become so automatic, first when we marry, even more when we become parents ourselves.

Erica Jong thinks powerful women will seek beautiful young men. Some may. Others will not take the risk. Many a woman holds her newfound self-reliance and freedom in her hands, weighs the temptation of finding someone to watch over her, and decides against the unpredictabilities of love. Never again to feel the weightless, high, heartbreaking balm of being taken care of. Never again to feel out of control.

"All the good men are married," women say. "All the single ones are gay." "There are no good men."

That isn't true. Men haven't changed. Women have. Just as they once idealized men as a defense against envy, so do women today devalue men. With men thus "put in their place"—worthless—the terrible rage of envy is blocked. A woman can get on with her life. I think this is a new idea in human history. Never before have women been able to afford to belittle men in the certainty that they could take care of themselves. That is the new economics.

Leaving men out gives the woman a sense of control. There will be no rejection. No jealousy paralyzes her ability to work. No "other" holds her happiness in his hands. It may be lonely. Never mind. Discovering at age twenty-five what she should have begun to learn in the first years of life is thrilling. For many women, a conbination of exhilaration and peace fills the void where a man's love might have been. Women are finding what men have always feared: Alone, a woman can make it emotionally more easily than can a man.

She can even have a baby by herself, having withdrawn sperm from a bank or a passing lover. Not a generous choice. Surely not a "natural" one —if that word means anything. Not a way we are going to live for long, I hope. A transition perhaps. How to understand the "liberated" woman's anger at men? How to understand the resentment such a woman must feel to deny her unborn child a father?

"The Madonna thing enters here, doesn't it?" says Hanna Segal. "First there is the woman's own infantile desire to have a Madonna mother with no father to take her attention away."

"And then comes the woman's desire to be a Madonna herself?" I ask.

"But a Madonna is also a prima donna, isn't she? There is an envy of the woman's own mother. A statement that she can do it better. She can become a mother all by herself. It's also a form of narcissism, envy of the man, absolutely annihilating his function. To begin with, it's theft."

"It's what?"

"Theft. Stealing semen from the man and then denial of the theft. Pretending she did it all by herself. But she didn't. She had to steal the semen from the man."

A man and woman meet and fall in love. Each experiences transcendence, having at last found "someone to watch over me." In the morning, she is still high. She needs to know, almost as does a child, that she will continue to be taken care of. "When will I hear from you?" The swooning weightlessness hasn't gone away. She *knows* it has for him, *knows* that men have this ability, this talent for falling in love for a night.

Psychoanalyst Bruno Bettelheim: "Many females who consciously or subconsciously experience sex as something 'animal-like' . . . feel quite differently while enjoying themselves with the man they love during the night. But once the man has left them, in bright daylight the old anxieties and resentments, including the jealousy of one sex for the other, reassert themselves. What seemed lovely at night looks different by day, particularly when the world with its critical attitude toward sexual enjoyment . . . reasserts itself."[5]

These popular "animal husband" fairy tales neatly sum up a woman's anxiety that once the man has had his pleasure, he will leave her. This neglects the man's side of reality, that he may very well be just as in love with her this morning as he was last night. But he feels other things too.

The need to work, to regain a sense of self, is a balancing reflex action to intimacy—not its denial. In fact, he will work better having loved her.

What does she know of his ability to separate love and self? She will not work better for having loved him. He now carries part of her with him.

"Please God, let him telephone me now," begins Dorothy Parker's famous monologue. "Dear God, let him call me now. I won't ask anything else of You, truly I won't. It isn't very much to ask. It would be so little to You, God, such a little, little thing."[6]

When a woman succumbs to Gershwin, she cannot be sure she will be able to walk away from the totality of surrender. Sex, love, to her they are bottomless wells and when you sink, you inevitably find they flow together. When she hears certain music, sees certain films, they make her feel "that way." Her body hasn't taught her that romance is something else again, different from both love and sex. In her mind they are confused. Without an erection, an outward indication of sexual arousal, how easy to confound lust and romance.

In a study entitled *The Sexual Adolescent,* 46 percent of males gave appetite or desire as a reason for their first intercourse. Only 16 percent of females agreed. But 42 percent of the females said they had sex for the first time because they were in love. Only 10 percent of male respondents said the same thing.[7]

When a man is rejected, he has options. He has had to learn them. He can walk, telephone, find himself a willing—if not beloved—partner. He may choose to do none of these. But he knows he can. He has had to recover from so many reversals and rejections that life has taught him that while it hurts, the world does not end.

It does for a woman. Or so it feels. This is the opposite of a man's streetcar philosophy. Much of women's jealousy begins with the conviction that each man is the last; if she loses him, there will never be another.

"I haven't grown but my husband has," writes a woman named Carol. I received her letter following a lecture at a small midwestern university. "We are both forty-eight years old. I am envious of his position in life, which I realize I share only by being his wife. I am jealous of his relationships with younger women, and even with younger men. They have taught him new tricks and we do not agree on these new tricks.

"My jealousy is based on nothing but intuition. When you live with a man, you *know* certain things. My husband is constantly thrown together with young people through his work. I can't imagine he is *not* having sex with these pretty young women. He may be too shy to initiate a first move. They are not!

"I see women my age and older starting all over again, even having love affairs. I was a virgin when we married. I left it to him to set our sexual pace and I never dreamed of another man. I left responsibility for my life to him. It may have been a foolish decision but in those days it was thought to be a womanly gift, something that made him feel more manly. I didn't want to 'wear the pants' in the family. I never dreamed I'd ever contemplate being unfaithful. I don't now. He is the one with the opportunities. Men are never too old to philander.

"I can't imagine a man would want me. I look at young women today and they are so sure of themselves. Could I walk right up to a man, as they do, with a smile on my face that is a sexual invitation? Maybe I could have, when I was twenty and pretty. But, in my day, girls did not.

"I don't know how to change, or if I should even try."

There is a form of jealousy in Carol's letter that cries for attention: She *knows* her husband must be having sex with every pretty young thing. If she were in his position, she would. *Projection.* Because of the way they are raised, women are especially vulnerable to transferring their own unacceptable desires onto their mates.

From the day she is born, the little girl is rewarded for remaining close, tied to mother. The infant is confused about the boundaries between mother and self; where she leaves off, where mother begins.

Symbiosis starts with mother's kisses and ends by becoming its own reward. When she lay against mother's breast, there was no burning issue of proving herself a different gender. One day those breasts would be hers, that smell, that texture of skin. The closer she stayed, the greater the reinforcement. Why move away?

Painful as it was for the young boy to establish his gender as different and opposite from mother's, the process powers his separation from her. He gets kisses for being "a little man," independent. Away from women, he feels powerful, strong. At the heart of Carol's symbiosis is a terrible question: What will happen to me if he should leave?

The woman who meshes with her mate, who doesn't even like to watch TV alone, would rather live with unsatisfactory sex than tell him what she would like. Having to put it into words would break the symbiotic union. Her partner is inside her head. He is supposed to know what she wants. By the same token, she is inside his head and knows what *he* wants. When a woman like Carol finds matchbooks from the Bide-A-Wee Motel in her husband's jacket pocket, it can mean only one thing. Never mind that the Bide-A-Wee was the only motel open on his last grueling sales trip and that he slept alone. When we are "as one," the beloved wants what we want. Symbiosis intensifies projection.

If Carol's husband is indeed involved with one of these women who frequent her imagination, she has reason to fear abandonment. She is totally dependent on him, not just for the roof over her head but for the inner security she has found all her life in attachments to one person or another. He is also the source of her self-esteem: "I am envious of his position in life, which I realize I share only by being his wife."

Like most of us, Carol probably has greater resources for emotional survival than she is aware of. But she has never used them, neither tested nor practiced them in a life where she didn't feel safely contained within his image.

"Women are traditionally raised to think of themselves as a success or failure in terms of their relationships," says psychotherapist Leah Schaefer. "When a woman is jealous and fears another woman is breaking up her marriage, part of the jealousy is her sense of failure."

Carol raised children, managed her household, performed countless highly responsible roles. But the satisfactions of self-reliance were never taken in. To acknowledge her separateness would dissolve the symbiosis. It would be like saying to her husband, "I am big enough to survive without you." Only by remaining small and dependent can she maintain what she thinks is her lifeline: attachment. Can you name a more fertile breeding ground for jealousy?

In the young girl's life, the advent of sex is attended by a special problem: Can she win men's love without losing her mother's? "Female-dominated childhood tends to make jealousy more complex for women than for men . . . ," says Dorothy Dinnerstein. "Under prevailing conditions the little girl, if she is to develop the early orientation to gender that will later allow her to feel heterosexual passion, must overcome an initial handicap. What is required of her is a central shift of erotic allegiance: It is to this shift that Freud and his students point, more unanimously than to the shaky theory of penis envy, as a basis for their working assumption that woman's sexual disadvantage is inevitable. . . . The girl's original love, they remind us, was, like the boy's, a woman. Upon this prototypic erotic image, the image of man must be superimposed. . . .

"In the girl's case, this jealous concern about one's place with the parents is typically more deeply two-edged. The father's animal allure is likely to be more powerful for her than it is for the boy. . . . At the same time, the mother is for the girl, as for the boy, the parent around whom bodily based tender passion was first organized. This means that for her, love of this kind is more evenly directed toward both parents than it is for the boy, and rivalry with the mother for the father's love is more evenly balanced against rivalry with the father for the mother's. The growing insight that this balance is scheduled to tip mainly in the father's direction is on some level wounding. *To realize that one is a female, destined to compete with females for the erotic resources of males, is to discover that one is doomed to renounce one's first love* [emphasis added]."[8]

Dinnerstein's point that many women never quite "renounce" that first love—mother—explains much of women's jealousy. Female psychology often contains a stronger need for mother/women's approval than for the passion of heterosexual love. This inhibits the inevitable competition for the male. Since the rival stands in some significant relationship to the unconscious memory of the all-powerful oedipal mother, the daughter enters battle encumbered by ambivalence dating back to the cradle. With all her most primitive passions having been met or thwarted by women, the betrayed woman is unable either to face her rage at the man or to openly compete for him. What is lacking in the woman's jealous experience is the strength/determination/courage that derives from early heterosexuality. Without it, sexual deprivation, loss of the erotic mate, is not the goad it is to men.

Men do many disservices to women. They do not deny them sex. Women suppress their own sexuality and choose not to compete opposite other women for its expression. Once again, as Bruno Bettelheim says, fairy tales illustrate "the workings of our psyche: what our psychological problems are, and how these can best be mastered."[9]

"In 'Cupid and Psyche,'" he writes, "the oracle and the sisters tell Psyche that Eros is a terrible dragon; in 'East of the Sun and West of the Moon' it is her mother who tells the girl that the bear is likely to be a troll —with the clear implication that she had better look and find out. The witch who suggests tying a string around the husband's leg in 'The Enchanted Pig' is an older female. Thus, the fairy tale subtly suggests that it is older women who give young girls the idea that males are beasts; that girls' sexual anxieties are the result not of their own experience, but of what others have told them. The stories also imply that if girls listen and believe this, then their marital happiness will be in jeopardy. The enchantment of the animal husband is usually the work of some older female: Aphrodite, who actually wanted Psyche to be ravaged by an abominable beast; a stepmother who cast a spell on the white bear; a witch who enchanted the pig. This fact repeats the motif: *it is older women who make males appear as beasts in the eyes of young girls* [emphasis added]."[10]

Bettelheim continues: "Since our mothers—or nurses—were our earliest educators, it is likely that they first tabooed sex in some fashion; hence it is a female who turns the future groom into an animal. At least in one story of the animal bride we are told that it is the child's naughtiness which causes the change into an animal, and that it is the mother who does it."[11]

In switching her focus from women to men, mother to father, the little girl learns that the dilemma goes beyond merely changing love objects. If she were to turn from mother's small, safe and known world to enter the larger, freer—even if a bit frightening—world of male values, a question of treachery would enter. She would be extending her horizon beyond that of other women. Men's view of life as an ever-expanding universe stands opposite women's conviction that there is only so much. If one woman gets more, there is less for every other. The male world is based on open competition. Women's world denies competition. Should the girl decide to permit herself life on a man's scale, the wrath of other women would be overwhelming. It is a rare woman for whom the approval of other women is not the base line for action.

"There is no evident biological component in such personality traits as assertiveness and competitiveness," concludes a recent study on sex differences. Male or female, what determines how competitive we are is heavily influenced by training. The conspicuous inhibition against competition and aggression found in women does not come from the genes but from society.

"When a rival enters, why do so many women shoot right past competition into hopeless certainty that they have already lost?" I ask Dr. Michels.

"What you are saying is that women *are* competitive, but they are inhibited from showing it," he replies. "Women have been socialized to lose angrily rather than risk public defeat and humiliation in trying to win."

When young girls first get out of the house, away from mother's watchful eye, the friendships they form significantly repeat what they individually had with mother: symbiosis and defense against competition. There is no female equivalent of the boy gang, no spirit of camaraderie in which sexuality is explored, separation and independence encouraged. Nor is the brightest and the best taken as model. Sameness and uniformity are the rule. The prettiest girl—born with extra power no one can control—must especially watch her step. She can have nothing more because she already has so much. Very early, beautiful women learn not to flaunt their beauty. It arouses too much envy.

The relationships young girls set up with one another in these latency years are tight and exclusive. The hours apart are unbearable; witness their time on the telephone. The twosome cannot tolerate an outsider. Adolescence will need broader reinforcement, wider groupings, but right now three little girls cannot play together. Inevitably, it arouses a jealous situation. One is always being left out. It is a forecast of what she will later fear in a triangle with a man. Infusing their best friend with the same life-and-death power that mother had over them, girls never really get a rest from envy.

Though the boy gang has no interest in girls, boys are always on the girl's horizon. Meanwhile, she waits, practicing with other girls the tight union she will later try to establish with a man. "You will be my best friend and I will be your best friend and you must promise never to like anyone more than me." This is an early version of The Rules, which every little girl learns. Boys' rules, learned through games, are different. They teach open competition. Girls' rules do just the opposite: They deny competition. Women do not find out through repeated experiences that while they may lose today, they can still win tomorrow. That is why the world ends—or seems to—when they lose a man.

When boys enter—adolescence—the young woman gracefully and unhesitatingly switches her symbiotic allegiance. But things must proceed by the book, The Rules. When you do what and how often and with whom, while not written down, is indelibly inscribed in each girl's mind. To break The Rules might win the man, but would turn every woman's hand against her. The Rules make sure that no one girl gets more than her share. Virginity used to be the Number One Rule. The form is different today, the content is the same. Says one fifteen-year-old, "If you sleep with more than one guy at a time, you're labeled a Sex Queen. No one talks to you." If life is going to be limited, it must be limited for everyone.

With so many rules, sexuality becomes fraught with anxiety. Best to give oneself over to the man, give him the responsibility. Best to lie in his arms and be Swept Away—two words that carry so much significance for women that they are used in sex-education manuals with almost no further explanation. The words describe the epidemic need adolescent girls feel *not* to use contraception.

"I was a virgin when I married," wrote Carol. "I left it to him to set our sexual pace and I never dreamed of another man. I left responsibility for my life to him. It may have been a foolish decision, but in those days it was thought to be a womanly gift, something that made him feel more manly. I didn't want to 'wear the pants' in the family."

These lines are at the heart of Carol's despair, her fear and certainty she is losing her husband to younger women. She cites no evidence of infidelity. She just "knows." Projection.

"Are you jealous?"

"I used to be. I danced it away." She is an attractive twenty-five-year-old woman, married to a film star.

"Danced it away?"

"It was ruining my life. I realized it wasn't him I didn't trust. It was me.

I was still looking for Prince Charming, the next guy around the next corner. I hadn't yet made my husband Number One. Once I decided what my priorities were, once I realized I didn't want any other man—only him—I stopped worrying if he was sleeping with his leading lady."

Once the film star's wife consciously decided that *she* didn't want any other man, she stopped projecting her own forbidden desires onto her husband.

Projection is not exclusive to women. There are a lot of jealous men who try to lock up their wives, accusing them of flirting with every man who approaches. But his suspicion that she is going to be unfaithful doesn't stem from sexual repression.

Most men are more separate than women, therefore more conscious of their sexuality and their sexual fantasies. A successful projection lays the evil desire on the other and keeps the projector pure, unconscious of errant wishes. Men get no points for being "innocent." We raise men to be proud of their sexuality. Which is not to say it is always easy for a man to commit adultery. Matters of conscience enter for him as strongly as for a woman. But he is not ashamed of his sexual desires. Sitting beside his wife and watching TV, he'll say, "Oh boy, I'd like to make it with that one!" His wife may mime displeasure and jab him in the ribs, but on the whole, she expects her man to be sexually alert. One difference between the sexes is that she would never allow herself to make a similar comment about a male TV star. As sexually active as many women are today, most still *do not own their sexuality.* Not taking the sexual initiative allows them to maintain the idea of themselves as Nice Girls. Nice Girls hide their sexual feelings. They project them onto the man. He is a beast; she is Snow White. She is jealous.

There is a composite couple who repeatedly crops up in the practice of marriage counselors and therapists. Like Carol, the wife is convinced her husband is having an affair with his secretary, the blonde at the party last night, her best friend. He doesn't know what his wife is talking about. "Maybe he isn't totally faithful," one therapist said to me. "Maybe he is. The reality is that basically he is a quiet, unassuming guy. She is the outrageously flirtatious one. The fantasies in the air are born in *her* mind. She invents them, won't face them, then angrily turns around and accuses him, saying they are really his."

An old male joke refers to the wife as "the ball and chain." But the other end of the chain is around *her* leg. She is locked up too. The notion of sex with the handsome stranger may be exciting but it threatens something felt to be even more important: union with him, replica of the lifeline she once had to mother. The classic feminine solution is to suppress fantasies of sexual adventure as, long ago, sexuality itself was suppressed. Like rage, desire just doesn't go away. The end result of successful projection is that since she is innocent, she is therefore free to accuse him of wanting to break the symbiotic tie. If she can make him guilty enough, he won't. That it was her own wandering eye that first threatened the union is denied.

If I knew Carol, I would say to her (as I do to myself): The next time you are jealous because you see your husband talking animatedly to another woman, stop and think. Are you certain he is setting up an assignation because you "know" him—or because you refuse to know yourself? Is your anxiety/anger/jealousy caused by your desire to wander, or his? The only evidence so far is that he is talking to someone—about what, we don't know. What we do know is what you are feeling. *What are you feeling, Carol?* Is it a desire to make love with the attractive new man who's escorted your best friend to the party?

I have spelled out these notions of projection in elaborate detail because marriage counselors tell me that is what they must do. "The jealous woman doesn't know—doesn't want to know—that she is the one who wants to have sex. Therefore, you must repeat and repeat and explain the mechanism of projection to her. Pushed hard enough, she may admit it."

"Biologically, and in terms of intensity, a woman can have as much sexual desire as a man," says Dr. John Money. "Social forces and the way women are raised make women put their sexual feelings away someplace and live in a kind of sexual twilight or blindness, even today. But that's a cultural fact. Not biology."

A respectable argument can be made on either side of the question of whether you can love more than one person at a time. There is less need to debate whether you can feel sexual attraction for more than one person at a time. While most of us choose monogamy, it is a matter of values and not nature. My own feeling is that to ignore the existence of random, sexual impulses does not so much ensure monogamy as it does projection.

In societies where sex is taboo, it goes underground, becomes obsessive. Guilt intensifies the glamour of the forbidden. The Victorian Age in England has also been called the Age of Pornography. It is no accident that the institution of the duenna and the harem developed in the extraordinarily sexually repressive societies of southern Europe and Araby. It was inconceivable that if a young man and a young woman were left alone for five minutes, they would not leap into bed. Therefore, the older generation (society), envious of their opportunity, and projecting their own desires, went to great lengths to keep young people chaperoned.

Cultural anthropology teaches that different people in different ages and places have invented untold variety of structures to organize sexuality. How often Robertiello has reminded me that men's desire for polygamy is not necessarily a reaction formation to the too-close attachment to any one woman. "It is often derided as 'men's fear of intimacy,' " says Robertiello. "That may be true for some men. For others, polygamy is a valid choice. They are doing what they want to do, not merely reacting against women. To say that all men who are polygamous are neurotic is reductionistic."

"Agreed," I reply. "But if we are to grant men polygamy as a choice valid as any other, must we not give women the option of polyandry on the same nonjudgmental terms?"

Powerful cultural norms still value monogamy and low threshold of desire in women more than explicit sexuality. Women are just beginning to integrate their sexuality into their whole lives. But in terms of reinforcing sex-role behavior, sex is still more a male experience than female. By which I mean, when a man has sex, regardless of how satisfying the orgasm, he has once more validated his manliness.

"How are your orgasms?" someone asks Woody Allen.

"They're always right on the money."

In terms of self-esteem and masculinity, men are much less discriminating about sex. Even if it is sex with a whore, just the fact of "doing it" is psychologically satisfying. As for a woman, I think the sex act outside a love relationship can make her feel many things, many of them good. But I don't think she feels more womanly through the pure sex experience itself. Not enough time has gone by.

A number of major sex surveys have been published since I began this book. All agree that more women are having more sex than ever before, and beginning at an earlier age. In the forties, Kinsey reported that only 3 percent of women had given up their virginity by the age of sixteen.[12] In 1982, a survey done by the very conservative *Ladies' Home Journal* found that 70 percent of respondents had become sexually active before age twenty.[13] The surveys also agree that women are having more extramarital affairs than ever.

Do the new figures on more and earlier sex for women add up to more happiness? If they do, why don't more women candidly go after what the Constitution guarantees them—the pursuit of happiness? Why don't more women take the sexual initiative?

Questions about significant change are impossible to answer easily because change occurs on three different levels and at three different rates.

The first level is change of *attitude*. This includes what we think and what we say. We read something in a book, see something in a film, sit next to an articulate person at dinner. The new information seems cogent. The next morning the new opinion is ours. Attitude changes quickly.

But would we act on our new attitudes? What we do—*behavior*—is the second level of change. Last night the articulate person at dinner persuaded us that multiple sex was perfectly OK. To say it is one thing. To do it is something else. Our behavior changes more slowly than our attitude.

The third and most significant level of change is the one that ironically, we disregard most often, and that subsequently gets us into the most trouble. *It is how we feel deep down in our gut.* We are persuaded that multiple sex is acceptable. We may even translate our attitude into behavior. Why then, when we wake up the next morning, do we feel profoundly guilty that we have done something wrong? *We acted on our new attitudes before they had become integrated into our deepest value system.* The feeling of what is right, what is wrong, comes to us from our parents. They got it from their parents. That changes very slowly and is beyond superficial intellectual decision.

Here is a story of a woman who acted on her new attitudes while her deepest feelings were still rooted in early training.

"I have fallen in love with a man ten years younger than I," she says. Beautiful and successful, she is thirty-eight. "He'd worked in my company for about a year. I seduced him. It was wonderful. I swept him off his feet."

She is terribly unhappy today, but we smile, then laugh out loud at the wicked joy in her words. The memory of her glorious seduction is short-lived. She is anxious, hollow-eyed; "jealous" is the word she uses to describe her feelings about her beautiful affair. Lack of control over her life led her to a therapist, who brought us together.

"Professionally, economically, intellectually, this man and I are worlds apart," she continues. "It's never been my pattern, younger men. The men in my life had always been older and more successful than I. But something happened once my own career took off. If I drew a trajectory of the people attracted to me, in relation to my professional success, there is a very close correlation: The more successful I get, the younger the men who are attracted to me."

"But he didn't make the first move," I say.

"No, no, no. It was me. I was so high on my life, my good fortune that day . . . I just walked across the room and put my arms around him. I'd had fantasies of him. His body is just . . . beautiful, no other word for it. And he's serious about his work; I loved that about him too. His earnestness. And I knew he wanted me. But he's so shy, he'd never . . .

"I thought he'd faint when I kissed him. His knees buckled, literally. We were on location. It was a work site. There were other people around, out of sight but within earshot. I think it was the most thrilling thing I've ever done, my first seduction. I've never felt so sure of myself, so . . .

womanly. Yes, I know it's men's work, taking the initiative, but that day, I don't know how to explain it . . . everything worked. It *was* the right thing to do.

"Was it a power trip? Yes, in that I'm sure it was my success that allowed me to do it. But I was being me. Waiting for boys, waiting for men, I'd hated that. All my life it seemed that the wrong men had approached me; the ones I wanted didn't pick up on my signals, or they didn't want me. I suppose it occurred to me that day that I didn't have to wait anymore.

"In the beginning, the gap between us worked for him too. I could feel his pleasure that he had won me, his pride that I'd chosen him. I couldn't wait to get to work, to see him, be around him. We were both on fire. Stolen lunches, stolen trips. I held nothing back from him. Being the older, wiser one, I thought if I showed him my emotion, my love, in a way that men had never directly shown me theirs, I could make him happy. I guess men don't want what women want.

"I tried so hard not to overwhelm him. I tried to use the age difference, what wisdom I have to cushion everything for us. When he said it made him feel like a gigolo for me to pay, I told him it was all expense account. It was. Do you know what fun it is to open a world to a man, to fly him first-class across the country, hotel suites, limos, the kinds of restaurants he'd never seen? I'm used to those things. But with him, it all became thrilling. It was exhilarating, sexually, to be the one who gave him so much.

"True, we didn't have a whole lot to talk about. He doesn't read much; Tolstoy's my favorite author. But I wasn't looking for an intellectual peer. Men have always seen me as smart. I wanted to be loved for being lovely, giving, warm. . . . I wanted to really give to someone. We were sexual peers. We went places together no other lovers have taken me. For the first time in my life, my fantasies during sex were about the man I was with. I would connect that man in my head with the man who was inside me, and get so high, so high.

"I guess I was in way over my head. The cool woman of the world who'd convinced him that life was too short to pass up our mutual attraction—the woman he'd fallen in love with—vanished. Suddenly I needed him in this desperate sort of way. It all just flip-flopped. One day I felt so in charge, so happy for being able to give him so much. One day he couldn't keep his hands off me; the next day I couldn't make contact with him. He began withdrawing, holding back emotionally. I know he still loved me. I've never doubted that, but we lost ourselves, each of us. The great seductress became this baby who—well, I don't know how to explain it other than to say I wanted *him* to take care of *me!*

"In the end, I've never been so hungry for a man, for a crumb, a word, a touch. The hungrier I got, the more he withdrew. He took advantage. He even withdrew sexually, not totally but enough. He spoiled it.

"The last time I saw him, that last night, in the middle of making love, I did something I'd never done before. I asked him if he'd been with someone else during the days he'd avoided me. 'Yes,' he answered. He was on top of me. I threw him off me; I screamed at him; I wept. I lay beside him all that night, wanting to kill him, but to crawl inside him too and be safe. It was a terrible, terrible, jealous scene.

" 'I thought you were different,' he said. He said it so sadly. He thought he'd found 'a real woman.' It had to end. I'd lost all self-respect.

"Near the end, he said something I'll never forget: 'I don't know who I am anymore.' "

While this story differs in many ways from the traditional version of older man/younger woman, there is a powerful parallel. When the gap between two people is too big, when one person has all the power, the dependent partner finds it increasingly difficult to handle his envy. In a story like this, where the roles are reversed, when it is the man who is in the dependent position, it dramatically illustrates the heart of Klein's theory. This young man's lover had the power to give him the world, but she also had the power to take it away. This is traditionally the male role. When the young man says, "I don't know who I am anymore," the heart clutches sympathetically at his loss of identity. The woman wanted to give him everything, but despite her good intentions, she took away the little he had.

If it were a younger woman and an older man, we would be less able to understand her anxiety. Hasn't the powerful man given her a beautiful house, clothes, money, everything she's been raised to expect? How ungrateful of her to feel resentment. On her first married morning, a bride does not wake and cry with terror, "I don't know who I am anymore!" What she consciously feels is relief and fulfillment. "Now I know who I am."

It is instructive that this man's first reaction to powerlessness is the same as that of many a wife. He begins to hold himself back, to withhold sex. He doesn't stop loving her, but he is in a rage, too. As Klein teaches us, envy of her power makes him bite the hand that feeds him. He spoils a good thing.

His next reaction to loss of identity is to have sex with another woman, to reestablish his independence. He didn't think she would be thrilled if she found out, but he didn't expect such enormity of jealous rage. She had everything, he must have thought: power, money, position. Women nearer his age, women who were dependent, had always tried to possess him.

How could he know that a gloriously self-sufficient, powerful woman would also find herself irrationally in need of being taken care of when she fell in love? "I thought you were different," he said.

The woman began the affair on an omnipotent high, wanting to give herself and the man a ride free of all the petty jealousies she'd felt in a more traditional relationship. Somewhere along the line, it all "flip-flopped." Lying in the arms of the man she loved, and whose salary she paid, she felt the words irresistibly forming on her lips: "Take care of me."

Crazy as it sounds, the young man had become her symbiotic connection. She invested him with all her self-esteem, wanting to see him as the powerful one in the relationship. She felt alive only around him and feared being left. In an effort to rearouse his ardor, she even resorted to petty maneuvers to make him jealous. Miserable as she was at his withdrawal, she did not seek the balm of alternative sex—as he did. How was he to know she had projected an unspoken contract onto him to which he had never agreed? "I will be faithful to you and you will be faithful to me." When he broke the contract, she felt betrayed. She did all the things the traditional "little woman" does. Why not? In the end she was younger, less powerful than he. Abandoned and jealous, she was a child.

The mechanism of jealous projection extends beyond the purely sexual. It is not just sex that woman has been taught to suppress; not merely man's erotic possibilities that she envies. It is the whole range of human experience from which women have been excluded—emotions, liberties, movement, powers of speech, ease, choice, spontaneity. Since these freedoms were inhibited at the same time she was taught to suppress sexuality —adolescence—is it not logical that they are forever after combined and confused with sex?

When a woman's mind suddenly projects a jealous fantasy because her husband is late getting home, it is not necessarily naked sex she is imagining. Just as likely, it is a picture of him walking into a bar, striking up conversation with a pretty woman on the commuter train. Initiative, mobility, conversation, these are avenues to sex. Avenues closed to her. "My mother made me feel that my tongue would turn black if I spoke to a boy before he spoke to me," a woman says.

Oh, to have men's ease! Men's options! How the wife envies him. How sure she is that from entering the bar, opening that conversation, his union with the other woman will lead to intimacy. How often she herself has sat and waited for a man, anticipating, hoping he would do with her exactly what her unfaithful husband must be doing now. She can see the whole scenario: the walk across the room, the half-humorous opening remarks. . . . She imagines and resents the simple ease men have in the world more clearly and poignantly than she imagines the sexual act itself.

And now that the wife has accused the husband and they've had a jealous argument, just look how he slams out the door! Where is he going? He is free to go anywhere, enter any public place, meet anyone. Mixed with fear/anger that he will find someone else—fueling her jealousy—is envy: to be able to come and go as one pleases! *Mobility.*

It doesn't matter that in reality the poor guy may be miserable and alone. Women overestimate men's ease at picking up women. Never mind. She knows he has ways of replacing her. Even a whore is a sexual alternative. If he sleeps with her often enough, he will fall in love with her. The wife would. If she had men's options. God damn them!

Once it was the little girl, not the little boy, who knew all the answers, raised her hand in school, and was delighted to speak them out loud. Clinical tests show that female infants learn language faster. It is also known that little girls learn to read earlier and have larger preschool vocabularies.

The awesome sexual energy of adolescence should power mental, physical, intellectual maturation. Now is when the girl should try once more for the separation and individuation she slept through in mother's arms. Instead, for most women, adolescence is the time they learn to retreat, to hold back and infantilize themselves.

The spontaneous gesture, the act of daring, the brilliant thought that is the first spark of creation, they are all of a piece with the exhilaration of sexuality. Or should be. When the adolescent girl learns to leave initiative and responsibility to the man, the conduit between brain and tongue soon becomes rusty. Just as swinging a tennis racket requires practiced muscular control, so does speaking; and the more firmly the basis for this motion is laid in the central nervous system, the faster and more easily we get the words out. "Think before you speak," the girl is told. It is not long before she believes she cannot speak for herself, just as she cannot take care of herself.

We don't listen to women's voices. As linguist Robin Lakoff notes, "women's language" is tentative, less specific, more polite than men's. Rather than risk offending, most women would rather not be heard at all. What comes out has to be agreeable to the greatest number of people and therefore of the lowest common denominator of interest.

"There is also evidence suggesting that women tend to utter declarative statements in the 'question intonation,' " says Dr. Sally McConnell-Ginet. "For example, if they are asked 'What is that you're reading?,' women are more likely to respond with a question ('A newspaper?') rather than a declaration ('A newspaper.')"[14]

Vocabulary and tone of voice work to keep women in their place, submissive and subordinate to men. Women perpetuate these patterns and men recognize them. The smiles and giggles that punctuate women's speech are both apology and devaluation of whatever the woman is saying. In another study, says Professor Candace West, 75 percent of conversations initiated by women are interrupted by men. In three other studies, it was found that in conversations initiated by either men or women, when interruptions occurred, they were by men an extraordinary 96 percent of the time.[15] Women do not interrupt.

Theologian/philosopher Mary Daly makes a scholarly connection between speech and power. "In the Middle Ages, *glamour* and *grammar* were associated in the popular mind," she says. "If you look in the dictionary, you find that *glamour* is in fact really a corruption of the word *grammar*. Originally they were the same word. *Glamour* meant a witch's power to cast a spell; often the power to make the male member disappear. Women in those times were burned for exercising and practicing *glamour*.

"The reason *glamour* and *grammar* were so associated is that in those times people thought occult practices involved learning; to practice *glamour*, you had to know *grammar*.

"However, in our time, *glamour* has deteriorated into shallow, absolutely artificial meaning, just as *grammar* has deteriorated into merely a tidy set of rules. The original, magical, deep meaning of these words—with all their elemental overtones—has, under patriarchy, deteriorated. The history of language is filled with words whose meanings have changed in this depraved manner."

"If men wanted to keep women in their place," I say, "by depriving them of their 'magic,' their *grammar/glamour*, surely women have aided and abetted the cutting off of one another's tongues?"

"Oh, I think the problem of envy is rock bottom. Starting with male envy in a society of scarcity, envy is what makes women do each other in."

Built into women's fear of abandonment—a part of jealousy—is this learned, "ladylike" inhibition of an inalienable right: freedom of speech.

In a lecture at Sarah Lawrence College last weekend, Margaret Mahler said that after the first three years of life, the adolescent years are the most critical phase of character development.[16] Ah, yes, I thought, adolescence. A second chance.

Or a reversal. It threw me a terrible curve.

I was eleven and had just got things under control. I had learned to conquer the fear I had never dared to name: being abandoned. I was the most popular girl in town, president of my class, member of student government, captain of every team, a straight A student, and brave. God, was I brave.

Breathtaking in its immediacy, adolescence offered me the intimacy I'd always wanted, but only on terms that reversed the world I'd made. Overnight, all the courage and talent I'd practiced as a little girl became useless —in fact, a handicap—when it came to winning boys. I died for boys, but I was not merely less successful than my friends at winning men's love— that was indisputable. I seemed to have a need for these mysterious, wonderful people, these men, more desperate than that of my friends. I have never gotten over it, adolescence.

Like many others I have interviewed, I didn't blossom into a woman from the brave little girl I had been. I abandoned her along with all that was most admirable in me. I wasn't good at being a Girl-Girl, an ideal formed at puberty, which had beauty at its core. Terrified of being left out, of not measuring up in femininity, I tried even harder at secondary characteristics. I became adept at checking spontaneity in midflight; the excited gesture, the exuberant step was reined in. Taller than everyone in my class, I tried to make myself small. I learned to dance with my knees bent. To be absolutely sure no clever thought slipped out, I emptied my head. I had been a very articulate little girl. I bit my tongue so well, I literally had to learn in later years to speak fluently again.

I know public speaking is a nightmare for many people. *But I had once been good at it.* I can vividly remember the feeling of panic, trembling, the wet palms that soaked my notes the first time I lectured ten years ago. Nothing, not even economic security, has increased my self-confidence more than finding my voice again. Today, I look forward to speaking. It is exciting to know I will be able to finish any paragraph I start. And if my writing has improved in ten years, nothing has contributed more than the relearned ease of putting thought into speech.

"I haven't been everywhere, but it's on my list,"[17] says a Susan Sontag character. Marilynne Robinson writes of her heroine, "Every story she told had to do with a train or a bus station."[18] Mobility is what the new woman is about. Behind the traditional woman's fear of being alone, of going anywhere without a man, was her learned inability to speak for herself.

Did I envy those beautiful southern girls, opposite whom I felt so gangly in my height, so "masculine" in my competitive, assertive secret self? Oh, yes, I surely did, all the more so for having once been their leader. But I was never aware of envy. I defended against it by making the most beautiful girls my best friends, by idealizing them and, I suppose like analyst Erika Freeman, hoping that through my association with them, some of their assets would rub off on me.

I dreamed at night of the boy I desired, for whom I waited, for whom I wished on every star. If allowed, nothing would have kept me from winning him, from trying, competing. But only waiting was allowed. I lay under my white eyelet canopy and wished myself small and helpless to the sound of recorded music. The allure of men, the promise that union with a man held out, was that by being a Nice Girl, obeying The Rules, I would be rewarded with someone powerful enough to meet all my needs. Having abandoned self-sufficiency, those needs were enormous.

No man can love a woman enough to make up for that kind of sacrifice. Nor is that the meaning of love. It is unfair to ask it either of love or of a man. But women do. Not only does he have his own power, she feels. She has invested her own in him too.

Here is the boy, intimidated by the girl's beauty, feeling she has all the power. Do adolescent boys have any notion of their idealized image in the girl's mind? Or of how much of herself she is willing to surrender or remake to be the kind of woman he wants? Men are puzzled when women read betrayal in actions they feel insignificant. "I was just talking to her." What baffles the man is that the jealous woman responds as if he had actually been sexually unfaithful. He doesn't understand that in her mind, attention paid to another woman threatens "the something special" she feels is exclusively hers. She doesn't want to tie up just his sex; she wants him to be as immobilized, as focused on her, as she is on him.

For some women, the sexual act in itself does not necessarily threaten "the something special." She may not like her husband's infidelity, but it does not end her world. Perhaps there were so many fears attached to sex when she was growing up, so much anxiety over competition with mother, that when adolescence came along she hovered at the edge, but never went through. Sex was never important in her life. It is not important in the life she shares with her husband. She is what an analyst friend calls a Latency Girl.

She grew up; her menstrual cycle began. She had boyfriends, married and had children. She has a nice, healthy, attractive Girl Scout quality about her. But the idea of herself as a sexually alive person opposite a man —that never took. Laura, whose story follows, is a good example of the Latency Girl.

"I watched my mother put up with my father's hypocrisy for years," says Laura. She is fifty-one. "He liked to boast that he put women on a pedestal. He held my mother up to us as a paragon of virtue. She never looked at another man. She gave in to him on everything. Everyone knew he had other women. The humiliation and anger she must have swallowed! I'd hear her cry at night.

"Of course she was jealous. She loved him in some crazy way. She never thought of divorce. She was miserable with him, but would have been more miserable without him. It's not as if she didn't have a choice. A friend of his, a friend of the family's, was in love with her. Was for years. I'm sure of it. But my mother never acknowledged it. I think it would have terrified her. I've always believed she was afraid my father would abandon her if she even looked at another man. That was entirely in her own mind. I doubt he would have noticed. I swore I'd never end up like her. But here I am.

"I met my husband when I was in college. It was like magic. I couldn't believe how wonderful he thought I was. We married after graduation. I worked until he got through graduate school and then we started our family. It was all planned, all part of the beautiful life I had always dreamed of. It *was* wonderful. His work went very well. Both children went to college and now have their own families.

"Some years ago my husband fired his secretary. Out of spite, she called me. She said he'd been having an affair. Yes, I was hurt, jealous. But I knew who the woman was. A strumpet. Not a woman he could take seriously. He would never leave me for her. Women are attracted to my husband. I learned to live with that. I never wanted to rock the boat.

"Recently I found out he was involved with a woman who's a vice-president at our bank. I talked to my best friend. 'Ignore it,' she said, 'just as you always have. John loves you. Nothing has changed except you know something you didn't know before.'

"But I have changed. I cannot contain my anger. I had played by the rules. I was a good girl. My daughter always said she couldn't understand why I gave up my dreams of going to law school. 'Because I wouldn't have married her if she hadn't,' my husband used to say with a smile. He meant it. I took a kind of smug satisfaction in hearing him say it! So self-sacrificing. Such a good little woman—how could he not be grateful and love me for it? I should have saved something for myself . . . but the fifties were all about togetherness and I bought it. I wanted to be the little woman behind the big man. I was proud that my husband depended on me, that my opinion meant so much to him professionally. He talked everything over with me, but while the decisions and ideas were often mine, in public he got the credit. We both lived off his life.

"I never minded his idle flirtations. I didn't begrudge him his whores. Sex for its own sake wasn't what was important between us. But a bank vice-president . . . ! I realize now deep down inside, I envied all the glory he got. This new woman who'd used her brains to push herself ahead, she made me realize the absurdity of my position. I can see myself in her eyes, a joke! I always knew I was smarter than he, but I'd bought the package. . . . I would have made a great lawyer!

"The only difference between me and my mother is that today the betrayed wife climbs down off the pedestal and gets a divorce. John did not want the marriage to end. I do. It isn't his body I imagine him giving her. The betrayal is that it was the man I helped to make and form. Do they discuss me when they have their filthy sex? He's giving *me* away, that's how I feel when I think of him with her. When I moved out, John was aghast. My lawyer says he wants to give me the house, some kind of guilt settlement. The only way I would ever enter that house again would be to kill him. I was thinking that when I read about Jean Harris killing that doctor. I'll tell you something. Men had better watch out. Jean Harris just broke the ice."

Laura's husband said to her he'd only started having affairs because she was no longer interested in sex. That was true, she tells me. She hadn't planned to give it up, but the desire went. Maybe it never was there. Oh, there was a passion at first, but sex . . . if she were to be honest, she would have to admit that just being held had always been the nicest part of sex. She's never masturbated. Couldn't imagine it. She doesn't miss sex.

Dr. Carol Cassell is president of the American Association of Sex Educators, Counselors and Therapists. "The Latency Girl," says Dr. Cassell after reading Laura's interview, "didn't disappear with the sexual revolution. If women really wanted to recognize themselves as sexual, the rate of unwanted pregnancies would not be so high. By being unprepared for sex —not using contraceptives—women hide from their responsibility. Yes, women are having more sex than ever, but they are still coyly leaving initiative to the man. It doesn't matter how intelligent you are or how successful, if you keep yourself a little girl in your intimate life . . ."

"You're left wide open to jealousy."

"Right," she says. "Studies show that what inhibits women is fear of men's disapproval if they show themselves as too sexual."

"Some women even have intercourse knowing they are at the peak of fertility in their cycle."

"They'd rather take a risk than stop and say, 'I have to use birth control.' That would diminish their feeling of being swept away by passion. The National Association of Broadcasters did a survey on ads on TV for contraceptives. A surprising number of women who were most at risk— age eighteen to thirty-four—were overwhelmingly opposed. Close to sixty percent against."[19]

"On a recent *Donahue* show," I say, "there was a young woman who'd not been allowed to speak at the graduation ceremonies because she had become pregnant. A woman in the audience got up and said, 'I have to ask, you were an honor student, didn't you know something about birth control?' And she said, 'Yes, but I just couldn't use it.' "

"The nice middle-class girl who lives in the suburbs," says Dr. Cassell, "they're the ones astonishing everyone in the field. They are going right through the top of the charts, a terrific high rate of pregnancy. Their reasons for not using contraceptives are right out of the fifties."

"If you see birth control as a statement that you are sexual," I say, "and still have the feeling that Nice Girls Don't, how can you use contraceptives?"

"As long as women were on the pill, the whole thing could be kept sort of vague. Today a lot of young women use other forms of contraceptive, not so easily kept secret. They may have the diaphragm right in the bedside drawer, but they don't get up and use it. The troubling statistics show that most abortions are done on women over twenty. They are young adults. How can they be so irresponsible about getting pregnant?"

"One man told me he stopped bringing up birth control. When he did, the woman thought he wasn't 'serious' about her. 'But, in fact,' he told me, 'it was only because I was serious that I was concerned.' "

"Men get messages from women," says Dr. Cassell, "but they also have their own ideas. They haven't changed much either. I just spent a week working with medical students in Indiana. It's amazing how many men would say, 'I know intellectually the woman I'm with is not a virgin, but I simply block out the fact that she's had more than one, two, three—tops —sexual partners.' Remember, these are medical students in their thirties."

I tell Dr. Cassell about studies done by psychologists and sociologists in the United States and Canada. They found that taking responsibility "helped people cope by giving them the opportunity to change their behavior . . . in a way that would help them avoid becoming a victim in the future."[20]

"If you take the sexual initiative," says Dr. Cassell, "you risk rejection. But you keep the options. Knowing you have options reduces your vulnerability to jealousy. But the most reliable surveys I've seen say that men are still almost invariably the ones who initiate sex."

"Why do women so doggedly refuse to even pick up the phone?"

"Every woman I ask mentions rejection," says Dr. Cassell. "Women are not prepared for rejection. It's so personal. It's not like being turned down in a business deal. You yourself have been found not good enough."

When a woman phones a man and gets turned down, she feels the same pain a man feels. But there is a special feminine pain added. She takes his no not just as rejection but as punishment. She has gone against The Rules. She is sitting in her three-window office, dressed for success, but has just been reduced to a naughty little girl.

"All the magazines say it's perfectly okay to telephone the man, but I just couldn't do it," says Liz. She is thirty-eight, recently separated, and is head of her own employment agency. "I had to feel that he wanted me, that I had been chosen by him. So I had to wait. Wait for him to phone. If I pursued him, it would not work out. The funny part of it is how accessible people are by phone. I did have his telephone number. But there's that invisible line that women just don't cross.

"I'd been married at eighteen. My husband and I decided we needed time on our own. I wanted to be independent. I wanted to be free to experience the sexual revolution, the smorgasbord everyone said was out there. I didn't want to get tied down. But right away, I meet a man, we have an affair, and there I am, waiting for him to call. I didn't know any other way to act."

As Liz speaks, I note how her voice changes. Intellectual one moment —what she knows. Emotional the next—how she feels.

"Women have a special way of waiting by the phone," she says. "Not casual. It's very intense. You are totally trying to make yourself available so that there are no barriers to this romance. It was the intensity of the waiting that bothered me. How it really interfered with other things, not being able to go out with friends, afraid to even go to the supermarket for milk. I had to be there in case he called. It's just bizarre. Men—he may want to hear from you but if your line is busy, he'll hang up and go out and play softball. Whereas you just sit there and die. During that waiting, it wasn't like I had a lot of loving fantasies about how great this guy was. It was this high-keyed kind of tension, anxiety. 'Is that him? Is he going to call?' "

"You were out of control," I say.

". . . and humiliated! I have a sixteen-year-old daughter who moons around the house. I'm always telling her, 'Don't just sit there, call him!' And here I was, acting just like her. And the anger, at him, at me! The jealous fantasies of 'I wonder who he's with?' I'd replay the awful fantasy, fleshing out the image of him with another woman from bits and pieces of what he'd said and done. . . ."

"You don't think younger women today are better?"

"I see it not only with my daughter, but in the young women I work with. There's something primitive in the way we operate. He has to want you, conquer you. You have to be there. You have to be chosen by him. *He has to call.*"

Liz's words touch a chord; something said several years ago by anthropologist Lionel Tiger. It never really went away, his declarative, emphatic explanation that certain jealous reactions are healthy, "built-in." Dr. Tiger and I may not totally agree, but I find his emphasis on the positive and biological aspects of jealousy a valuable counterweight to the almost universal belief that jealousy is weak, demeaning, wrong.

I telephone and tell him of Liz's lament that she must be crazy to sit at home, jealously waiting for a call from a man with whom she is having an affair—instead of going out and perhaps meeting a new one.

"It's not crazy," says Dr. Tiger. "Even though she may not plan to have children with this man, or even be able to have children, the emotions that are involved when a female edits a possible cadre of male companions are exactly the same as those of a woman choosing a father for her unborn children. Exactly the same."

"You're saying it's biological."

"Of course, of course."

"We're talking about jealousy. . . ."

"Well?" he says.

"Well?"

"Why should a woman care that someone takes a penis and puts it into a vagina other than her own?" says Tiger. "Big deal. Except it matters. And matters deeply. The reason it matters is because it is essential to the whole management of the reproductive system. In any species."

"You aren't saying there is value in the double standard?"

"The double standard is basic. Whether we like it or approve of it or not. Females have more at stake, and in virtually all cultures they are more careful about choosing partners than are males. Males are, by and large, promiscuous. By and large, females are not. And the reason is that if the female gets impregnated, she has to make a major investment in time. She needs, or at least is entitled to, a male to rely upon. Therefore, she has to choose very carefully."

"What does this have to do with a woman who just wanted to have a sexual affair and suddenly finds herself jealously waiting by the telephone?"

"When you talk about jealousy, and the difference between love and sex, it's like the difference between up and down, gravity . . . the motion with respect to known forces. They are both part of the same thing. The relationship between sexuality and what we call love is that love is another word for durable and generalized sexuality, or vice versa."

"If you're saying there is no difference between love and sex, I don't agree."

"In the biological sense you cannot make that distinction and it is idle to try. The effort to distinguish between love and sexuality is precisely what causes the well-meaning but irremediable pathology of people who feel that they should be nobler than the husband or wife who is jealous when the partner has 'merely' had a love affair, because, after all, 'It's just sex; it isn't love.' "

"The TV program *20/20* did a segment on jealousy recently. 'How can it be controlled?' Barbara Walters asked. As if jealousy was something to be stamped out. Why do people denigrate the emotion?"

"Because people have no understanding of human biology. They don't understand that the emotions are powerful, vital and highly significant forces and that they reveal real problems in today's existence which, in natural and evolutionary terms, we've coped with for millions of years. Jealousy is one of these emotions."

"Don't you think the increased interest in jealousy has to do with women's new mobility, sexuality . . . ?"

"It's a new game. An entirely new game. Since females have at last got to control contraception when they want to, it's all up for grabs. There's never been a society in history where one sex could control reproduction."

"If jealousy were a purely destructive emotion, and had no good qualities attached to it, would it have evolved out of the species?"

"Of course. The reason jealousy is so powerful and persistent is because it's been an irreducible feature of any sexual selection. Any pair that mated successfully had to believe their hectic endeavor was worthwhile. What I'm suggesting is that sexual selection has always been a tricky issue and trickier for women than for men because of the investment they have to make of time, personal resources and everything else. Looked at harshly but also with sympathy, the reality is that women who are not jealous may simply end up having less control over the goods, services, affection and sharing that males could provide."

"And you? Have you been jealous?"

"Yes. And I think it was a healthy jealousy. Close contact with another person was a threat to the integrity of my connection with a particular woman. It's healthy to try to fight that. If it's an important relationship, it's important to protect it. It's ludicrous to assume that the person who says, 'Well, I don't care. I can rise above it,' is displaying magisterial nobility. In our culture, many people think that any experience, however miserable, should be turned into something unique and psychologically rewarding or improving. Nonsense. What a notion—that it is lofty-minded to live calmly with the fact that the person you love is also in love with another person! That's original sin, as far as I'm concerned."

It has taken me how many thousands of pages, written and rewritten, to come to an emotional grasp of something taken in only intellectually at the beginning of this research: It is not jealousy that is destructive. It is envy that gives jealousy a dirty name. Envy that comes disguised as jealousy, a misnomer that elevates the nasty emotion so that we confuse it with and excuse it as love.

There are no experts on jealousy. But if we do not understand that appropriate jealousy is a protective emotion that alerts us to defend what we cherish, how can we keep envy from destroying what we love? We cannot prove or disprove anything Lionel Tiger says. But I find reassuring and profound parallels between his anthropological approach to the value of jealousy and Hanna Segal's words:

"In a way, jealousy is almost invariably an accompaniment of love. It is a positive element in that it makes you reassess whether you really love the other person. Also, it makes you aware that you don't own the other. Inappropriate jealousy—possessiveness, destructiveness, excessive envy—that is a different matter. If people could declare themselves free of jealousy, what would it mean? It would mean that they really don't value the other person, that nobody else is better than they—arrogance—or that nobody would want the love object, which is devaluation. A certain modicum of jealousy, a wish for a more exclusive relationship, is, I think, a part of love. It is inevitable and a lot of harm is done by denying jealousy."

Women think men have all the power; men think women have all the power. The confusion of sex-role reversal in contemporary society has been the stuff of several recent movies. Speaking of her role as a man in *Victor/Victoria*, Julie Andrews says, "I discovered that even though we've come a long way, men have it made in terms of their freedom."[21] On the male side, a thirty-eight-year-old man I interview says, "After seeing *Tootsie*, I wanted to go home and put on one of my wife's terrific sexy dresses. And lots of great fur. And really high heels, so that I was a knockout. Then I'd go out and pick up four construction workers. Then go to the hospital and have a baby. Then I would breast-feed the baby. Then I'd go to the Copa in a strapless drop-dead sequined evening gown and sing a torch song."

"What about the baby?" I ask.

"Oh, I'd hold the baby in one arm while I sang."

When he tells the story, we laugh. But it is only half a joke.

This man loves pretty women. He is married to one and I am sure one of the reasons he won her is his humor. He is not as beautiful as the women he adores. He must have suffered a lot of rejection. Women's power.

Power that women themselves often don't feel, so preoccupied are they with their view of men's power. Two years ago this man's wife had a baby. He loves his son. His face collapses when the baby preferentially reaches for the mother. On Sunday mornings, "When the baby lies between my wife and me," he tells me sadly, "my son kicks me."

How this man loves beautiful women. How he envies them. In Robertiello's immortal words, "All a beautiful woman has to do is *be!*"

Tell that to a beautiful woman.

> *Only God, my dear,*
> *Could love you for yourself alone*
> *And not your yellow hair.*[22]

How to write about jealousy and give appropriate emphasis to women's youth and beauty. The amount of envy it breeds. Between the man and the woman. Between women.

The power of women's beauty is so enormous, it must be denied or devalued. In the verse above, the woman's beauty is made to seem alien and opposite to her. Almost her enemy.

"You don't know you're beautiful until someone tells you, and no one told me. Least of all my mother." It is difficult to believe the speaker is approaching sixty. Her figure is perfect, her face almost unlined. Her name is Marion.

"My mother didn't know how to be a mother. She and my father were divorced when I was two. From photographs I see now that I was a very pretty little girl. I was a platinum blonde. My father must have been crazy about his first child. I think I was a threat to my mother for my father's affection. I never thought I was pretty though. . . .

"My mother was always telling me how ugly my feet were. She said my hands were big and made for work. My nose was ugly, my singing voice was terrible. She told me that her breasts . . . her doctor said he'd never seen such beautiful breasts. Now I have a manicure and a pedicure every week. I had my nose fixed. I found out my feet were very small, much smaller than hers."

"She was envious of you."

"As a kid, I always thought there was something wrong with me. What was wrong was our relationship. It was shocking to finally realize she viewed me as a rival and a threat. When she married again, we were left with housekeepers so she could travel with her new husband. I never missed her. I felt guilty about that, about not being able to cry when she went away.

"I married when I was in my teens and had three children, one after another. That's drudgery. I began reading a great deal. I went back to school. Came out of that sleepwalking stage and began working. I got divorced. I found out that I was pretty.

"I always hated being in a bathing suit because my mother told me that my legs were long and gangly. The first thing I did when my husband and I split was to buy a bathing suit and go to the beach. I found out that I was sensational. I'd had no idea of that. I was twenty-seven. It was like beginning another life. I became a model. I remember this pair of green Jax pants I bought. I wore them on my first assignment. I knew from people's reactions that I was really something."

"Coming into your beauty is heady stuff," I say.

"I discovered I had to be very careful. I could not be friendly with men. It led to things I could not control. Just a smile and the man felt it was an invitation. My second husband was my agent. He was the one who put me into modeling. I told myself I was in love with him and that he would be a good father to my children. We were married eight years. The money I made paid for my husband's office."

"Before we began the interview, you told me that your daughter fell in love with your second husband."

"She was the youngest child of my first marriage. She fell in love with him as little girls fall in love with their fathers. He started her off in modeling the way he started me. To this day, he is her agent. When she became a child model, he wanted me to retire. I was at the peak of my career. I didn't exactly understand why he wanted me to quit. I learned quickly. If they know you have a daughter as old as Alice, they won't hire you. When she became a super-model, it ended my career . . . before I was ready."

"Had you saved any money?"

"I never saw any of the money I made. I was working very hard, I was very successful, and there were no savings. I'm a person who saves. He was a person who spends. The divorce was his idea. He asked me for a divorce five times during our marriage. He wanted to make me beg. He wanted to keep the power over me. I was frightened of being alone again."

"Your second husband promoted jealousy between you and your daughter."

"Yes. When Alice was thirteen, she had a thirty-eight bust and my husband would buy her bikinis. She was beautiful. But she was embarrassed. And flattered. She didn't know how to handle it. He did things that made her feel guilty; excited and guilty. Because she hated me. I wasn't the kind of mother that other kids had. I'm sure she was jealous of the way I looked. She always reproached me for not looking like her stepmother. 'That's the way a mother is supposed to look.'

"One time there was a big movie screening. I didn't want to go. So he took Alice. At the party afterward, she danced with him. She was probably fifteen. She tells me now that she was feeling so many different things

. . . elated to be there, terrible about being there. He did play us off, one against the other."

"So she envied your beauty. And you? Did you envy her?"

"I think I may well have. But I did everything I could not to have the same relationship with my daughter that my mother had with me. My mother did so many things that I hated. My mother was competitive with me; my daughter was competitive with me. I felt like the person in the middle. Yes, I did feel competition with Alice. . . . Those bikinis my husband bought her, they were bothersome to me. Because my mother—you know, that doctor who said she had the most beautiful breasts he'd ever seen? And here I was with a daughter with a thirty-eight bust at age thirteen."

"You didn't discover beauty until you were almost thirty," I say. "So just as you were coming into your own, here's this daughter who professionally undermines you. You'd be inhuman not to feel resentment."

"Alice's first marriage was a complete rebellion against me. It was all because of anger, hostility, to get away from me. My daughter . . . she got the job; she got the man. . . ."

"You mean she got your second husband to act as her agent?"

"Yes. She got the job; she got the man; she got the agent. I took her to lunch not long ago. I said, 'I have something to say to you. I want you to look at it upside down, inside out, backward, digest it, roll it around, live with it. Now this is what I want to say to you: You never took anything away from me. You never took anything away from me.' I wanted her to know that."

"But she did take it away from you."

"No, she didn't. She didn't take anything away from me."

"I mean she did get the job; she did get the man; she did get the agent."

"Whether it's true or not, I did not want her to feel that I felt that way. I don't know if I ever got through to her. Maybe she understands it now because her daughter is going through the same thing with her gorgeous husband."

"You mean your daughter's daughter is now in love with her stepfather?"

"Yes. I think Alice feels less guilty now. I often think we'd both be better off if we'd been plainer. I've come to see now that there is a detrimental side to beauty. Sometimes when I'm getting dressed, I'll undo what I've just put on because it's too much. I'll go back and put on a scarf or a skirt that doesn't work. To make it off. I loved having the figure I had, I loved it. But it made women cry. I've had women cry. One time there was this bathing suit, fantastic, black, one-piece, my God. We went to visit some people on the beach. I had the children with me. When we left, there was a woman at the door. She said, 'Tell me those aren't your children.' And I said, 'This is my second marriage.' She started crying. She said, 'I knew it.' "

"What do you mean?"

"The jealousy. This woman cried with relief that these were not my children, because I couldn't look the way I look and have children that old."

"But they were your children."

"Of course."

"You lied to her."

"I've done that many times. I had to or they'd hate me."

"So you are aware of the envy and jealousy you arouse in others?"

"In other women. It's an awful thing. Just awful. The other night we were playing a game with friends. It's about what you want, and what you'd be willing to pay for it. The game makes you stop and think. I said I wanted aggression. I think of aggression differently than most people. I see it as something benign. It gives you a motor to deal with the world. I said I wanted to be able to stand up for myself and I wanted to be able to go and get. I wanted power. Power. The others asked what I was willing to give up to pay for aggression. They decided I should give beauty for it. I said, 'Fine. I'd be happy to give beauty for it because beauty has been worthless to me.' "

"Were they surprised?"

"Yes. They said, 'Would you be willing to have a hunchback?' I thought that price was too much. 'No, no,' I said, 'I will be just plain. A plain woman would be fine. I'll take less aggression.' My perception had been that plain women did every bit as well as I did. I was really an old person before I got rid of my act. That was being despondent and pouting and all that sort of thing to get my own way. It didn't always work. As a child I had a really hot temper. But I found that only gave me trouble. In fact, when I was a young woman, married with a couple of kids, I got us evicted because of my temper. It ended my birthday parties. I've learned to suppress my anger, my rage."

The male defense is to put the beautiful woman on a pedestal, out of reach, desexualized, adored for her purity and constancy. If she comes down from the pedestal, men's envy of her unleashed power says she is a whore. The male's resentment of women's beauty is reinforced by the envy of other women. The beauty knows that if she were able to break free of the Madonna/Whore split, and capitalize on her looks, other women would destroy her. *Or so she thinks.* She assuages her sisters' resentment by self-devaluation. She complains about her crooked nose. What crooked nose? you ask, seeing only perfection. Never mind. Even when the nose is surgically changed, the beautiful woman quickly finds other defects. She diets.

Diet organizations acknowledge that 95 percent of their clients are women.[23] I find it significant that at the time in history in which women are taking powerful positions in men's world, they are also striving to reduce their size. In an article titled "How Women's Diets Reflect Fear of Power," the author concludes, "The male-dominated culture calls for slender women, unconsciously seeking to limit the symbolic physical expression of their power. And women themselves accept this tyranny . . . because of their own ambivalence about their bodies. . . . Our culture has another kind of response to the awesome girth and power of woman that we experienced in our infancy. We have strong, ambivalent feelings about the relationship between a woman's power and her size, and they are reflected in our dislike for large, fleshy women. . . ."[24]

How Kleinian that sounds—"women's power . . . large, fleshy women." And no one fears her power more than the woman herself. Men don't talk women into dieting. Women try to keep themselves small. Not out of fear of men, but out of fear of who/how they may become, if they get too big.

Men compete with the phantom giant penis. Women compete with the more beautiful, younger women. And they don't compete. The denial of competition between women, laid down by The Rules of adolescence, which declare that no one woman shall have more than another, tells the beautiful woman that she already has too much power. A beautiful woman tells a joke. Another woman turns to her and says, "Hey, you aren't supposed to be funny. You're the pretty one."

I've committed the same stupidity myself. Sitting with a group of women discussing sports, I heard a ravishing woman describe how good she'd been at baseball.

"You mean you were athletic as a girl?" I blurted out.

Her beautiful green eyes filled with pain. "Why do you ask? Because I'm so fat?"

I was caught aback. Another woman kindly filled in. "Because you're so pretty," she said, understanding what I meant. A foolish way of thinking, left over from my girlhood. Being plain, I had to work on other talents.

The night-cream conglomerates put doubt into the hearts of women with even flawless skin. Envy—hyped by the cosmetics industry—makes each woman devalue her own looks and overestimate that of others. From this low point of self-esteem, it feels impossible to compete. "What a gorgeous woman! No wonder Charlie prefers her to me." The other woman may be merely attractive, but the jealous wife has judged herself out of the running: upper arms flabby, hair mousy and thin. She abdicates all claim to attractiveness in the service of protecting herself against envy of her rival.

In *Femininity*, Susan Brownmiller writes:

"How one looks is the chief physical weapon in female-against-female competition. Appearance, not accomplishment, is the feminine demonstration of desirability and worth. In striving to approach a physical ideal, by corsetry in the old days or by a cottage-cheese-and-celery diet that begins tomorrow, one arms oneself to fight the competitive wars. Feminine armor is never metal or muscle but, paradoxically, an exaggeration of physical vulnerability that is reassuring (unthreatening) to men. Because she is forced to concentrate on the minutiae of her bodily parts, a woman is never free of self-consciousness. She is never quite satisfied, and never secure, for desperate, unending absorption in the drive for a perfect appearance—call it feminine vanity—is the ultimate restriction on freedom of mind."[25]

Though she doesn't have to prove her womanliness as a man must labor at manliness, a woman knows her value in the marketplace lessens with age. Not every man wants a beautiful woman, but all respect her power. When a little boy is reminded, "Beauty is only skin deep; don't judge a book by its cover," he learns a powerful message: Women's beauty is important. "But that's changed," you say. To which I respond with a quote from a recent survey cited in one of the leading women's magazines:

In a class of fifth-grade girls, 75 percent honestly ranked themselves the least attractive girl in the class. And if you think we grow body-wise with age, try the results of this study on for size: Almost 70 percent of the women studied described themselves as overweight when in fact only 39 percent were.[26]

Like you, I know women whose inner beauty lights up every room they enter. But men still do the choosing and a woman's desirability in the marketplace has *something* to do with her face and youth.

Men marry down. Women marry up.

"I noticed that when the story of Mary E. Cunningham's rise and fall at the Bendix Corporation broke," writes Anne Taylor Flemming, "it was women, other successful women, who were often quicker than men to ascribe that rise to her blond beauty and to her inferred romance with Bendix chairman William M. Agee. I heard these women, at parties, in restaurants, well-accoutered in their gabardine suits and gold chains, hint, in well-bred innuendoes, that Miss Cunningham had used her sexuality to get ahead. She was too young, they said wistfully, too lovely, they said enviously, not to have. Her resignation from Bendix they took as confirmation of their suspicions."[27]

When women collectively decided to change their lives twenty years ago, beauty was the first thing to go. If anything of importance was to be accomplished, women couldn't afford to have sister pitted against sister. It made sense. The battle of envy and jealousy over beauty gave way to more important wars. Spending time on your looks was taken to show a lack of seriousness. Gloria Steinem hid her beautiful legs in jeans. You could hardly have women challenge men for an equal share of power while preoccupied with competing for the most successful man. Beauty was hooted down to make room in women's lives for new forms of power.

I sometimes think women abandon nothing, merely take on more. To the role of major housekeeper and child rearer, women have now added breadwinner, while returning in recent years to the task of beauty maintenance more ferociously than ever. For instance, a few years ago two magazines appeared on the newstand. One *(Mademoiselle)* contained a national survey on young women ages seventeen to thirty. The results showed a startling idealism, an optimism out of touch with reality. Over half the respondents expected to make it to "the top of my field," and to earn more than $25,000 a year—a salary then made by only 2 percent of working women.[28] Fully three quarters expected to find egalitarian husbands who would share fifty-fifty in housework and child rearing.[29] Eighty percent declared confidence their lives would work out as they had planned.[30]

Meanwhile, on the cover of *Life* magazine, fifty-year-old Elizabeth Taylor smiled at us with a face so cosmetically lifted and lighted, one was thrown thirty years back in time. Whatever other women had been doing —working, raising families, aging in the process—Ms. Taylor and the moguls of Time, Inc., reminded us that little had changed regarding the real power of women.

A twenty-seven-year-old industrial designer arrives in a huff for an interview with me. She is irate that rude men have been blowing kisses at her on the street. She is wearing a blouse so transparent her nipples show. Her skirt is so tight it tucks in under her ass. She saw her provocative image in the mirror before she left the house. And she did not see it. She unbuttons the top button of her blouse. She buttons it back up. Half of her wants to put her beauty on display; half of her wants to keep it hidden. The beautiful, powerful woman doesn't just frighten men and other women. She frightens herself too.

"There's a built-in reflex to take the elitist woman down a peg or two," writes film critic Molly Haskell. "That reflex, sadly, is stronger today than it was in the '30s and '40s, probably because there are more of us who want to 'do it all' or 'have it all,' and more areas in which to feel anxious and inadequate. We can swoon over a male paragon, while his female equivalent has rough going. A man can 'have it all'—a Harvard education, looks, glamour, wealth, well-shaped thighs—and can be a professional dynamo, and no one will in the least resent him, but bring on a female Warren Beatty and you'll have the audience hissing. The solution is the one devised by Hollywood years ago: Neutralize her, domesticate her, by removing one or more of her options. Demand a sacrifice. Splatter egg on her face."[31]

It is not just society that keeps women from full realization; women themselves feel they must choose between love and work, marriage and a career. It is not merely because of time, practicality and economics. The inhibition against the accretion of too many powers comes from within. Both man and woman retain unconscious fear of the All Powerful Woman. Both split the mother into good and bad, keeping the loving mother intact, while projecting their destructive impulses onto the bad, powerful monster of the nursery, the evil witch.

Men are not afraid of accruing too much power. Becoming big takes them even farther away from mother; identifies them more fully with father. Being the same sex as mother, women unconsciously fear that if they get too powerful, they will *become* the destructive mother-woman of their nursery fantasy.

Does this explanation of female self-diminishment sound overly psycho-analytical? I think it adds a new element of understanding to the enigma of women's fear of success. In contrast to the overly optimistic *Mademoiselle* survey on combining career and marriage, here are figures that reflect reality: In a 1982 survey by a management recruiting company, of 300 executive women—average age forty-six—only 40.7 percent of the women are married as against more than 94 percent of executive men polled three years earlier in a similar survey. (In the earlier survey, women could not be included since only eight replied.) Even more dramatic, 27.6 percent of the women polled were in the never-married category, compared with fewer than 1 percent of the men in the earlier survey.[32]

In the seventies, says Dr. Cassell, the largest group of divorcees were women who'd been married in the 1950s. Their marriages had lasted twenty, twenty-five years or more. The biggest divorced group in the 1980s is women in their late twenties. "Now marriages break up before seven years." In five, seven or ten years, when the optimistic woman in the *Mademoiselle* survey loses her husband, will her own success ameliorate her rage/envy at *him*—for making more money that she does? At *her*—for being younger than she is?

As the anxiety of ambition takes its toll on women's faces, youth and beauty will be ever more time-related. A man's face is a map of his life. If he's powerful enough, a woman can read something lovable into each crag and cranny. Every morning a woman investigates her mirror for the damage done in the night.

Too much beauty in a woman can frighten a man. If he lost her to a more powerful rival, he would lose face too. He chooses a safer partner. But should his fortunes and self-esteem rise, he feels entitled to the beautiful woman. Threat of loss abated, gap closed between beauty and power, he drops his plain partner for someone commensurate with his new status. Fitzgerald's Gatsby returns to spread his wealth across the lawns at the doorstep of the beautiful Daisy Buchanan. A match that was out of sync ten years before when Gatsby was penniless is now charged with appropriate sexual desire. We all understand. Understand why Gatsby worked so hard, and why Daisy succumbs. Power is drawn to power.

In a less literary vein, the eighty-year-old face of America's most beloved baby doctor, Benjamin Spock, appears in the tabloids. His new wife is in the picture too. She is more than forty years younger than he. Less than ten years ago, I remember reading an interview with the rejected wife who had helped him write his famous books. What rage, what betrayal in that woman's face. Do we think less of the man? It is the way of the world. The young beautiful woman is the prize our culture awards to power.

In every woman's life the clock ticks, taking away her one irreplaceable asset, leaving her open to the most ignominious form of jealousy because it denigrates everything else that she is. Intelligence, bravery and creativity cannot be expected to count opposite younger flesh.

> When I was young and miserable
>   and pretty
> And poor, I'd wish
> What all girls wish: to have a
>   husband,
> A house and children. Now that I'm
>   old, my wish
> Is womanish;
> That the boy putting groceries in
>   my car

> *See me. It bewilders me that he*
> *doesn't see me.*
>
> "Next Day"
> RANDALL JARRELL[33]

A man acquires power as he ages; the woman on his arm never grows old. Where did this idea originate, that women must lose as they age? With men? With women themselves? To be so entrenched, it requires the assent of both.

When all possibilities of physical beauty are focused on one sex, the other must feed upon the first. It is unhealthy. It is what women have always objected to . . . men's stares, men's pawing, as if they were hungry. They are. And hunger makes them angry that these people, these women, can withhold themselves if they choose. One of the displacements that works most painfully against both sexes is that the woman must satisfy the man's inner hunger to be admired not for his wallet and achievements but for himself.

This desire to be looked at and applauded is stronger in some of us than in others, but it is human and universal. In our wacky distribution of what is allowed each sex, the pleasure of being adored for oneself, of seeking the eye of others for personal gratification, has traditionally been women's.

When did Robertiello stop going to see the naked ladies?

When I first met him ten years ago, he told me he often went to the burlesque houses on the West Side. I was stunned. I thought it contemptible, and told him so.

"One of the reasons I like to see ladies exhibiting themselves," he said to me, "is that they are doing what I can't. In other words, I'm getting off vicariously on the strippers' exhibitionism and narcissism."

Wearing a woman on your arm isn't the same as being admired for yourself, no matter how beautiful the woman. There is a residue of dissatisfaction, sometimes anger, which often turns up in men's sexual fantasies. The man turns his own exhibitionism around and takes pleasure in thinking of the woman exhibiting herself to other men. She doesn't merely strut and preen in pretty clothes. In the scenario he invents, she bares her genitals in public, exposing herself to other men. An exaggerated reversal of what he wants for himself.

It occurred to me several months ago—was it during the writing of the Self-Esteem chapter?—that Robertiello hasn't mentioned going to burlesque in years, literally. There is something else that has been happening without either of us having commented upon it: He's become a much snappier dresser. Gone are the shiny, baggy pants, the wornout and shapeless sweaters. His wife used to cut his hair. It looked it. Now the shaggy beard and mane of graying curls have a certain expensive symmetry.

"The more I've been able to be directly narcissistic and exhibitionistic myself," he said, "the less I needed to go to burlesque."

"What changed a life pattern?"

"A lot of it had to do with my reading. Kohut's books gave me an understanding of narcissism I hadn't had before. My defense of being self-effacing . . . it was like I suddenly had permission to get attention for myself."

"No wonder you dedicated one of your books to Kohut."

"You were a big influence too."

"You identified with me?"

"Oh, yeah. You were a role model. I mean, look at you. You are someone who is exhibitionistic/narcissistic. You dress to be looked at; your writing is revealing. Our talks are so personal. We tell each other everything. By my being connected to you, and your doing all that . . . you made it all right for me to do it too, you know?"

"That's when you started buying clothes that fit?"

"If I was going to those fancy restaurants with you, I had to look as nice as you . . . or try to. Before I knew you, I never went to those places."

For a period of years, during the writing of *My Mother/My Self*, Robertiello and I used to have a weekly Wednesday lunch. When I found out how much he loved good food, and that he'd never been to most of New York's great restaurants, I suggested we meet at Lutèce, Le Cirque, The Four Seasons—a different superb restaurant each week.

I remember one afternoon at La Grenouille. Finishing a bottle of La Tâche 1964, a few tears fell into his glass. I thought it was the subject we were discussing . . . abandonment, separation, death, the usual luncheon fare. "Oh, no," he said, "I'm crying because it's so wonderful. I wouldn't be here if it weren't for you."

I was moved. Especially since he was paying.

"I always needed someone to make me spend money on myself," he reflected more recently. "You fulfilled that role. You always pushed me to be more expansive."

"I was pushing you to buy the more expensive La Tâche," I laughed.

"But I would never have been there without you. I guess that's also when I stopped going to burlesque. I'd look at you in your fancy clothes and go out and get some for myself."

"Thus allowing yourself exhibitionism, instead of having the naked ladies do it for you."

"But you never understood something about burlesque. You went *'yuck'* because you thought it was disgusting and male chauvinistic. . . ."

"I thought it was dirty old men masturbating under their raincoats. . . ."

"Maybe some of them do but women never understand the power of their beauty over men."

"And that men envy them for being able to show off and parade, for getting all the goodies just for being pretty . . ."

"Women just don't get it."

"No, they don't," I sighed.

"Most men don't feel attractive," says Dustin Hoffman, about his role as a woman in *Tootsie.* "There's this tremendous repressed narcissism, because we want to be more attractive, so we get a good-looking girl next to us. . . ." In portraying a woman, the actor was shattered to find he could not make himself into an attractive one. Then came rage at how he was treated by men. Devastated that his homeliness as a woman made him invisible to men, Hoffman nonetheless had to realize he himself had committed the same sin.

"I could feel that number printed on me," says Hoffman, "that I was a 4, or maybe a 6. And I would get very hostile. I wanted to get even with them [men]. But I also realized I wouldn't ask myself out."[34]

Feminists fight the double standard of aging by encouraging women to tell their ages honestly. Do we ask a man how much money he has? "I don't talk about my age," says French Film actress Anouk Aimée. I don't think anyone should ask or say the age of a woman. I find it very unfeminine and I find it very rude. Who cares?"[35]

Who cares? Clearly Anouk Aimée. She is realistic. So long as a woman's youth is her currency, should we ask her to reveal her assets? When there is economic equality between the sexes, when women's power is no longer time-related, only then perhaps will the double standard of aging change. I think it will take more. I think it requires a change in how we raise our children, so that the monster/mother isn't always a woman.

When I ask men if they can picture the big screen filled with the face of a sixty-five-year-old Jane Fonda being caressed by a man's lips, they cannot focus. I try Dan Stern, that superbly sympathetic and rational man.

"If you'd asked me five years ago," he said, "I would have answered differently. Lately I have been attracted, sexually, to some older women. Women in their sixties, one even seventy. Could I imagine myself in bed, caressing them?" He closes his eyes. "I'm trying to see if I can get past that, if I could conquer a feeling . . ."

"Aha! You have to get past something . . . !"

"True. I don't know what it is."

My editor reminds me that many men continue to desire their wives for thirty, forty years. She warns me that I am generalizing and that absolutes ring false. But I know this aversion, which even Stern cannot name, is there. It goes beyond the merely erotic. Old female flesh is disturbing, frightening, even disgusting.

I telephone Robertiello. Luckily a patient is late.

"Those photos of Picasso at age eighty-five, standing on the beach," I say, "wrinkled as a prune, but we know he has a young wife waiting in his bed. No one is put off. In fact, we smile. But if it were an old female Picasso . . ."

The idea catches Robertiello. He hasn't thought about it either. "It's so irrational," he muses, "a break in human symmetry. I don't know, but I'd guess it has to do with mother stuff. It's so primitive."

"You mean Klein?"

"Yeah. That whole business of the child wanting to tear the mother's flesh apart . . ."

"Let me read you something Brigitte Bardot said about old age: 'It is horrible, you rot, you fall to pieces, you stink. . . . I'm 48 and not so pretty. I wouldn't inflict this sight on anyone anymore.' "[36]

"Just listen to the words she uses—'you rot, you stink'—it's so close to that idea of a wish we all had . . . the earliest envy. Mother's body. Old age reveals her split-off half, the monster we always hated."

"But we created her," I say. "When I think of the soft, saggy under arm older women get . . ."

"Oh, that really fits in with Kleinian theory!" says Robertiello excitedly. "Because it isn't even sex-linked. Men and women both are afraid of our impulses to destroy mother."

"It is time that destroys, not us. The breasts become wrinkled . . ."

"Look at what you just said, Nancy. Why did you pick breasts to become old and destroyed instead of eyes, the nose . . . ? I think the parts you chose to mention were no accident . . . the sagging arm is like a breast. That was obviously unconscious. It means something that you picked those two particular areas as the most unattractive. I've got to hang up. My patient's here."

"Hold on, one last thing," I say quickly. "Why are women always the monsters? The Eumenides, the Furies, the Harpies, Medusa? Why is there no male counterpart to the figure of the witch?"

"We don't associate the horror of withered old flesh with men because it's women who raise us. It's against them we feel all that infant rage. The Furies are our own envious fury at mother, projected back at us."

"But it wouldn't be that way," I say, angry at the unfairness of it all, "if men too raised children. . . ."

The phone is dead. He's hung up.

I sit on the edge of the bed, holding the buzzing instrument, as if to keep my connection to him while I write a note for our next talk: Does this throw an entirely new light on why men go for younger women? The usual reason given is that biology and evolution put a premium on female fertility. Men can reproduce at almost any age, but women cannot. This is obviously true, but maybe as important is this: The younger the woman, the more reassurance the man has that she is not secretly the powerful Kleinian witch mother he has unconsciously feared and struggled to get away from all his life.

I understand men who tell me they are terrified of the rage of a jealous woman. The monster they fear is the monster of the horror film, the creature who tears the flesh out of the man's belly. It is projection, his fury at the all-powerful mother whom he wanted to destroy for withholding.

But it is also reality. "Hell hath no fury like a woman scorned." It used to be that jealous women contained their rage and walked into the sea, took an overdose of sleeping pills or put their heads in a gas oven. Destruction takes a less passive form in women today. Jean Harris, the eminent and very proper headmistress of the Madeira School for girls, picked up a gun and shot her unfaithful lover. A landmark case.

By 1980, Jean Harris's love affair with Dr. Herman Tarnower, the famous Scarsdale Diet Doctor, had lasted fourteen years. She was fifty-seven. For a long time, Harris had known Tarnower was seeing other women. She hadn't liked it, but had accommodated rather than lose the man who had become her entire world. When it became clear that his increasing focus on the much younger Lynn Tryforos was going to push Harris out of his life, she drove from Virginia to Scarsdale, New York, and shot Tarnower in his bed. The timing was prophetic; at least to me. The shooting was almost simultaneous with the beginning of my research. When Harris claimed that she was not jealous, I remember thinking, "The woman must be crazy."

I read an early book on the Harris trial and found it wanting. I had hoped to interview Harris myself. But then came Shana Alexander's book. Her research was so complete, her access to Harris so prolonged, intimate and empathic, I doubted I could learn more on my own. If I choose to draw on Alexander for these speculations, it is because her intelligence helps clarify a killing that tells us so much about envy and jealousy today. As Shana Alexander said when she first saw Harris, "She reminds me of me."[37] She reminds me of a lot of women. She reminds me of me.

When Jean Harris fell in love with Herman Tarnower, it was as never before in her life. Love allowed the dependent needy child in Harris to emerge. With total enthusiasm, she surrendered her self-sufficient and domineering self to intimacy. Tarnower became not only a mirror of herself as a woman but her symbiotic connection, her entire repository of identity and self-esteem. One of Harris's psychiatrists referred to her loss of Tarnower as an "amputation."

Jean Harris was forty-three, divorced and working full time when she met Tarnower. She had raised and supported her children on her own. At twenty-three, she had married a man far less aggressive, less ambitious than she. Thus she remained as her temperament had always dictated: in charge. One of Tarnower's major attractions was that he took charge. She loved it that he made all the decisions. He made her feel pretty, feminine and taken care of. He breathed life into what sounds like an otherwise desperately lonely existence:

"From the time I was a young woman," Harris says, "the only prayer I ever prayed was, Just give me the strength to get through this day, one day at a time."[38]

Jean Harris had lived by the Nice Girl Rules all her life. When she became Tarnower's lover, she broke those rules, continuing the affair even when she knew there would be no marriage, even when she knew there were other women. By her own rules, she was a tainted woman. But she had reason to stay. She had lived by the white-glove script and got nothing back. Tarnower accepted her as an equal and as a woman.

Like so many women today, Jean Harris was caught between her mother's submissive generation and a world in which she was a chief executive, acting "like a man." Tarnower healed the split. Ideally, falling in love is a mutual affair, "taking care of" one another. In the beginning, that is how it was. Then Tarnower withdrew.

But not totally. He kept her dangling, always waiting, never sure of when she could see him again. He became the parent, allowing her to see him when she was a good girl, literally banishing her from his presence when she didn't behave. It was a replay of the Kleinian life-and-death situation where one person has all the power, either to give or withhold himself. Harris constantly lived in terror of being abandoned.

As a protection against her destructive rage, Harris marshaled Klein's defenses: She idealized Tarnower into a god and devalued herself. When she allowed herself to remain Tarnower's lover with no promise of marriage, she surrendered conscience to him. It was the beginning of her deterioration. She transferred the burden of her own demands on herself —that she be a person of the highest moral integrity—onto him. He became her ego ideal, her narcissistic extension. He had to be above everyone, high enough to meet the standard of her cruel superego, which demanded superhuman perfection. Now that she was so low, he had to be perfect enough for the two of them.

Remaining Tarnower's lover meant, to a woman of Jean Harris's ethical background, a total compromise of her integrity. "Integrity" was a word Harris used often during the trial. She repeatedly demeaned her rival as low and said Tryforos's usurpation of her place was an attack on her integrity. These were taken to be snobbish remarks. They hurt her defense. It was unfortunate. The correct interpretation of what Harris meant by integrity was self-esteem. Being replaced in Tarnower's heart by a woman whom she could not respect lowered Tarnower and thus diminished Harris's own self-esteem.

Harris had a symbiotic contract with Tarnower which existed only in her head; having abandoned to him the part of herself on which she placed greatest value—her integrity as a moral person, a quality she'd drummed into the female student bodies of every school she'd headed— he must be ideal. If he was less, then she was less. She hated the Scarsdale Diet book. If he was the kind of person who wrote pop best sellers, then she too, by extension, was cheap and commercial. If he was not Bayard, the perfect knight, *sans peur et sans reproche*, she was just a whore.

To preserve the man she loved, to preserve herself, Harris split off the bad doctor who wrote faddish diet books, and who slept with inferior people like his nurse, Tryforos. What remained was the other half, the idealized god who meant life itself. As if in a textbook example of the results of splitting, all was revealed in a famous letter. When read at the trial, Harris's closest friends could not believe she had written it. The letter accused her rival of being a slut and a whore, and sounded as if it had been written by a whore. All the vile and ugly parts of Tarnower, which Harris could not afford to see in him, she smeared on herself and her rival. The Kleinian monster inside, which she had refused to project onto him, erupted in that letter.

Using almost Kleinian imagery herself, Shana Alexander writes: "The Letter was the work of a lady driven mad by her own demons. Buried resentments pour forth from its pages like the tiny devils with pitchforks that gush from the mouth of victims of demonic possession in Medieval paintings."[39]

One of the rules Harris imposed on her defense lawyers was that not one bad word be said about Tarnower. She wanted the trial to vindicate not her but her romance, her lover. If she were to be acquitted by proving he was a rotten bastard who deserved what he got, if he were morally flawed, the sacrifice of her integrity to him would be a dirty joke. She crippled her own defense.

The prosecution called the case "jealousy pure and simple . . . discarded mistress, having lost her man to a younger woman."[40] Harris repeatedly denied that she was jealous. She wanted to be honest; believed in honesty and justice so totally, she never doubted vindication if she told the truth. When a woman as intelligent as Harris maintains with such consistency that she is not jealous, we ought to listen carefully.

Certainly she was in a jealous situation. It was clear Tarnower was leaving her for good, abandoning her for a younger woman. *But she didn't kill the other woman.* Various forms of envy were flying around within the triangle. She certainly envied the other woman's youth and beauty. We know that Harris devalued her own looks to an almost pathological degree. At her trial she was still attractive enough to have been nicknamed "Miss Pretty" by one of the guards. But her self-image was such that she had decided against plastic surgery five years earlier for fear that it would make her look "even uglier [than I already am]."[41]

A constant thorn to Harris was that Lynn Tryforos represented a way of being a woman that Harris could never imitate. Harris hated it that Tryforos defined femininity by acting like a servant to Tarnower. "I wish I had been born a doormat, or a man,"[42] says Harris. Being a doormat meant to Harris all the passive, self-sacrificing behavior that traditional women performed to cajole men. She half bought this definition of womanliness but could not find it in herself to act that way. To be fair, Tarnower never asked her to. But in the end, he rejected her in favor of a woman who did act like his servant.

"I was a person and no one ever knew."[43] What did Harris mean by that? her attorney asked. Weeping, Harris replied, "I don't know. . . . I think it had something to do with being a woman who had worked for a long time, and had done the things a man does to support a family, but (sob) still a woman. I always felt that when I was in Westchester I was a woman in a pretty dress [going] to a dinner party with Dr. Tarnower. . . . In Washington I was a woman in a pretty dress and the headmistress. But I wasn't sure who I was . . . and it didn't seem to matter. . . . I was a person sitting in an empty chair. . . ."[44]

Harris's ultimate rage wasn't directed at Tryforos; if she wasn't in the doctor's bed, another woman would be. I think this is why she said she wasn't jealous. Something in her knew that her real emotion—though she didn't name it—was directed at Tarnower. It was envy. He could have saved her life, but chose not to.

One line of Harris's defense was that she intended to kill herself when she brought the gun to Tarnower's house. She was in a frenzy of drug deprivation. For days she had been out of the pills Tarnower had been prescribing for her for years. She was exhausted, depressed by the worst professional crises of her life; she wanted to talk to him one last time.

I believe she did intend to kill herself. Or part of her did. When she got to his bedroom, was the doctor concerned for her, compassionate? Tarnower greeted her arrival with irritation. Once more he turned away from her. She killed the person her unconscious meant to kill.

"I agree with that," says Robertiello. "But, Nancy, be careful that you don't make this sound like a pathological surrendering of herself. Tarnower didn't ask her to surrender herself. She did it very happily. Maybe she did lose part of her identity. But on the whole her love affair with Tarnower was a joyful experience. Even after he died, she said that he was the most important thing that ever happened to her." Robertiello loved Shana Alexander's book.

"I don't think Tarnower comes out as such a villain," he continues, "except in the cruel, insensitive way he handled leaving Jean. And the way he plied her with drugs, making her dependent on him in that way. In a lot of ways I identify with him. What I like about him is what she liked about him. He needed a lot of narcissistic reflection and acclaim. He was a social climber and needed women around. But whatever his needs, he was the kind of guy who found a way to get them gratified."

"So he was selfish."

"Selfish isn't a dirty word. You don't impose a moralistic system on a person in terms of evaluating him. If you take the morals out of it, he wasn't such a bad guy. *She* never thought he was a bad guy."

"Friends of mine in Scarsdale liked him."

"You and I would probably like him in terms of his having a presence, being direct, for real, not being a wimp or an unconscious sneaky manipulator. His manipulations were up front."

"He really did represent and give her a part of herself that had been wiped out."

"But not just in a sexual, male/female way," says Robertiello. "He didn't have all that inhibiting Anglo-Saxon bullshit that she was brought up on and which crippled her. She never accused him of misusing her. He never put her down or diminished her personhood, or her 'masculine' parts. He didn't destroy them in terms of using her as a cunt. He shared a lot of very important, intellectual and spiritual experiences with her. He didn't just respond to the baby in her, he responded to all of her, to the baby, to the woman, to the man, if you will. A total response. At a certain point, somebody else came along who interested him more. That's life."

"Everything you read about Tarnower depicts him as a bastard," I say. "Both books were written by women. It's interesting that you like him.
. . ."

"He was a good father to Harris for a long time. He really was the good daddy she needed but never had."

"Harris's mother represented all the subservient stuff that she hated."

"She must have needed her father very badly as a girl, both as a source of love and as a model for action and getting things done. But he rejected her viciously. He didn't just deny her closeness that would have allowed her to introject him as a model. He also withheld from her any acknowledgment of her womanliness."

"That is a special gift a father can give his daughter better than anyone."

"If you are a little girl with a lot of 'masculine' sex-role characteristics, so powerful they refuse to be tamped down into a conventional picture of what a woman is, then more than ever you need a good father. One who says, 'You're a beautiful young woman and I'm really tickled with you.' Harris got that from Tarnower. He responded to her as a beautiful woman but also as a very capable person."

"So many young girls today grow up in single-parent families without daddies. Who's going to give them confirmation they can be aggressive and competitive and still be desirable women?"

"I don't think for a moment Harris doubted she was a woman," says Robertiello. "But she didn't think she was feminine, maternal, nurturing, womanly. Performing like a man for so much of her life set up tremendous envies for Harris."

"The envy of the new woman for the traditional woman," I say.

"And the other way around too," he says. "The traditional ones are envious of the independent ones. It increases all these problems between women."

"Oh, 'The War Between the Women,' " I say. "That's the title of something I've brought to read you." I get up from the floor and stick my head practically under the lampshade. "Christ, Richard, this is only a forty-watt bulb. Why do you keep this place so dark? You afraid someone will see . . . ?"

"Read."

"This is from a study by sociologist Kristin Luker. Her point is that women activists on either side of the abortion issue are fighting a vicious war over far more than abortion itself. 'Their feelings on abortion,' Dr. Luker said, 'are embedded in a larger world view, so for them to question their beliefs about abortion would be to challenge an interrelated set of values about the roles of motherhood, the sexes, of morality, of religion and of human rights.' And listen to this: Luker goes on to say, 'The prolife people spent as much as 40 hours a week on the issue,' but she couldn't find a pro-choice activist 'who put in more than five hours.' . . ."[45]

"That's because," says Robertiello, "for the pro-life women, their whole identity is in question. It's a consuming passion."

"Here's Luker's profile of each camp. 'The typical antiabortion activist is a 44-year-old [woman] who was married at age 17 and has three or more children. Her father graduated from high school only, although there is a better than even chance that she went to college. She does not work outside the home. . . . Her husband is a small-business man or lower-income white-collar employee, and the family income is less than $30,000 a year. She attends church at least once a week, and is most likely a Catholic.

" 'Her counterpart on the prochoice side is also married and 44. She was married at 22 or older and has one or two children. Her father is a college graduate, and she is likely to be one too. She is employed and is married to a professional man. Their combined income is $50,000 or more. She rarely attends church.' "[46]

"The pro-life woman," says Robertiello, "really feels the new woman denigrates everything her entire life stands for. All her repression and sacrifice . . ."

"On the other side, women who work outside the home feel that pro-choice is integral to their whole lives. The battle isn't being fought overtly in terms of envy—you don't hear that word—but it's certainly there."

"Don't forget," says Robertiello, "the pro-choice women have a lot of envy too. They must envy the traditional woman who is taken care of, who doesn't have to fight to preserve her position, who doesn't have to compete in a man's world. . . ."

"She may have chosen to give up the traditional role, but she hasn't got the sureness of womanliness, had she stayed home like her mother. . . ."

"On the other hand, the pro-lifers envy the working woman being the heroine of the day, getting all the attention in the media."

"So the abortion issue is like the shooting of the Grand Duke at Sarajevo. It's part of a much bigger war. What women have at stake is *who is the real woman?*"

"This is very much what we were talking about with Harris," says Robertiello. "Tarnower solved the conflict for her by applauding both her professionalism and her womanliness."

"But then he stopped loving her."

"It was unlikely she'd ever replace him. First of all, there aren't a lot of guys around like that. Second, she didn't have the wherewithal to get another one."

"I was interviewing a woman recently who veers between older men and much younger ones," I say. "She is thirty-six and has a good job. Right now she's with a man much younger than she. She refuses to let him see any of his women friends. Her previous affairs had been with men twenty and thirty years older. She had never been jealous because, in her eyes, she had the power. She was the pretty young thing. What makes her jealous today is that her new lover is the pretty young thing."

"Sounds like the daddy figures affirm the little girl in her," says Robertiello, "and the young guys affirm those strong 'masculine' qualities that made her so successful in business. This woman can't find both in one person. Tarnower was rare in that he gave Harris both. That's why losing him was such a stunning blow."

"You really did identify with Tarnower," I say, standing up. "It's seven o'clock; I'd better get home."

As if he hadn't heard me, Robertiello goes on. I plug the tape recorder back in. "The book did a lot for me personally," Robertiello muses. "Enhanced my own feeling about myself. In some ways Tarnower is like a carbon of me. I've also taken my women all over the world on trips. I've reinforced their feelings about themselves as women. But I also respected their so-called masculine ambitions. Almost all the women I've been with have grown professionally. They've gone to graduate school, increased their practice, developed in their profession. I gave them the stuff they didn't get from their fathers. Even when I broke up with a woman, I never felt like I was a bastard who had victimized her. I did feel affirmed by that book."

"Affirmed? Tarnower got killed!"

"I almost got killed several times."

"That's because you promise women you'll be there forever and they foolishly believe it. They could risk stepping outside the dependent role and becoming successful on their own. But then, like Tarnower, you abandon them."

"I've never understood the enraged reactions from women when I left them. Like, how can you be so furious with me after all I've done for you?"

A perplexing moment. Am I to understand Robertiello really didn't know why women were so furious when he left them? He has described himself as so terrified of their anger, he literally cowered in a corner. "I've always been more afraid of women than of men," he has told me many times.

He knows his pattern. First he figures out exactly what the woman needs, then offers himself as the perfect answer to her prayers, all the while promising never to leave. In the end, because he does not get anything back out of the one-way relationship, he takes his departure. "Richard." I say, "you're an analyst. Aren't you being deliberately and self protectively naive?"

"I really didn't feel losing me was all that big a deal."

I look at him, taken aback for a moment. He isn't joking. Nor is this false humility. He is a mixture of self-inflation backed by self-devaluation —like most of us.

"I met a lover I had not seen for ten years." He is still talking. "She said that after I left her she'd been depressed for a year. I was astonished. Hell, I didn't even know she'd cared, so to speak. I knew she loved me, but I didn't think I was that important. Tarnower made me realize how rare it is for a man to be able to respond to both the ambitious, 'masculine' side of a woman and to the feminine too. The book explains it. I gave them everything they'd ever wanted and then pulled it away."

"That's why you like the book," I say. "You found a brother in Tarnower."

"Even if Harris killed him, she didn't want to denigrate him in any way. She said Tarnower was emotionally the most important person in her life. That said she knew Tarnower had given her a lot and confirmed that I had given my women a lot too. I had never realized how important I had been to these women. Now that I do, I can understand why they always wanted to destroy me when I left."

"You broke your promise, Richard."

"When I make the promise that I never will leave, I'm not conning them. I have total belief that I never will leave."

"That's why you're terrified of a woman enraged," I say. "You told me that you could kill when someone breaks a promise, even if it's only a promise to meet you at seven and they don't come until eight. You're afraid she's going to feel the same way you do. You think these women are going to kill you. . . ."

"They want to. . . ."

"They haven't yet. . . ."

"Not literally, but figuratively. The things some of them have done have been vicious, incredible."

"What makes them so threatening is that you endow them with so much power. . . ."

"I project my own rage onto them. They become the giant killer mother of the nursery. What makes me so envious is that I know I cannot make it without a woman."

"You have two support systems. The first is this office, your patients who see you as God. This place is your kidney machine. The second is your woman who adores you. If you get home and Susan is merely talking to her sister on the phone . . ."

"Not merely. *Especially* if she's talking to her sister."

"You're jealous."

He laughs nervously.

"Which you call sibling rivalry. You'd better watch out. Harris is the tip of the wedge. Women are buying guns."

"You mean literally?"

CHAPTER NINE

Betrayal: An Afternoon with Medea

*I*t is a beautiful Sunday afternoon in April. Everything in me resists going into the dark theater. The critics say Zoe Caldwell's performance as the betrayed Medea is a once-in-a-lifetime event. I am writing a book on jealousy and here is one of the world's great classics on the subject, revived as if on cue. I have postponed buying tickets for months. I say it is because I am bored with the theater. The truth is I don't want to see the fleshed-out emotions about which I have been writing for so long. Only notice in this morning's paper that the play will close in three days gets me to the matinee.

Usually in the theater I daydream. From the moment the curtain rises on the enraged Medea, abandoned by Jason, I am riveted. What is burning this woman? Jealousy? Envy? Betrayal? Euripides adds an important clue I myself had not yet attached to jealousy.

> Medea: Jealous for the sake of Jason?
>   I am far past wanting Jason.

"She wants herself back, not him," says Zoe Caldwell to me.

It is three weeks after the performance. We are sitting in my office, tape recorder on the coffee table between us.

"She'd given herself totally to Jason," Zoe continues. "That's what you must not do. You lose your identity. Medea had given away family, country, everything for him. Then he betrayed her. Oh, no, she did not want him back. She was not a deserted suburban housewife. She was a barbarian princess. She wanted to get herself back."

I ask Zoe what she thought Medea meant when she tells Jason she is ashamed of having loved him.

"She had been his equal in every way. And he brought her down. She was humiliated to find that she had married a hero and he had turned into a politician. In one of the versions, she says to her sons, 'Your father has stolen your life away,' meaning Jason has betrayed his pride in their marriage."

"What infuriates her is that by becoming a wheeling, dealing politician, he was no longer a man she could respect."

"The two of them were capable of anything."

"They were the golden couple."

"Absolutely. He was the man she needed in order to feel herself feminine. She needed him to be up there, the hero. If he suddenly brings himself down here"—Zoe's memorable gesture includes my ceiling and floor—"then all her femininity goes. He has betrayed her to the feminine core."

"The Greeks considered her a barbarian. They were so rational that they even suspected love. One of the townswomen says, 'Too much love burns down the roof.'

" 'A little love is a joy in the house. A little fire is a defense against the cold. But a great love burns the beams of the roof. . . .' "

"It is much safer to settle for a little love. . . ."

"Big, big love is very difficult to keep."

"In her rage at being betrayed," I say, "Medea kills everyone—the rival princess, the King, even her own sons. But she doesn't kill Jason. . . ."

"To kill Jason would not get her back what she wants. Only when Jason is brought down and is totally without power, only when she can see him reduced, impotent, his future destroyed by the death of his sons, can she get her own self back."

"At one point Jason says to her, 'Your jealousy has ruined everything.' "

"Jealousy is too weak. When you are jealous you want to kill the blond girl. Medea does kill her but jealousy is not what consumes her. More important than the blond princess is Medea's humiliation at having been belittled. He diminished her, dirtied everything. 'Must I look into my sons' eyes and see Jason forever?' she says. Even her sons' eyes remind her of her humiliation. She is not whining some little complaint about Jason copulating at the palace. What she says is, 'Must I see this thing that has made me dirty, made me less, made him less, the children less, everything less?' "

"But she does feel something about her rival. . . ."

"Of course she does. Medea is older. And she is dark of skin. Medea kills her but the girl is a pawn. The rivalry is just one element within a bigger, darker picture. It enrages Medea that Jason would accuse her of mere jealousy."

"Then it is vengeance. . . ."

"Vengeance is also too weak. Medea wants destruction. To go beyond human limits. By destroying everything, pulling the world down, she regains her power."

Zoe has told me that after the performance people would often come backstage and say, "Oh, God, I feel so much better and healthier."

"Catharsis?" I say.

"The Greek theater was not just for entertainment. That's where we've gone terribly awry. For them, yes, it was a kind of purging. Aristotle's famous theory. The drama was to make you well. . . ."

"By identifying with the characters we get beyond our individual self, beyond the secret suspicion that only we are so awful. . . ."

"Yes," says Zoe. "The Greeks would go to the open-air theater, sit in the sun with all their friends and the other citizens around them. They would see human beings go to the limits of everything. Mothers killing children, marrying sons. All this very strong stuff done right out there in sunlight while they are having wine and a nice picnic. If you watch people on stage doing extraordinary things, much wilder than anything you would consider doing; if you have seen the consequences and experienced some person going through all that, going beyond the limits like Medea, it's almost as though you have done it yourself. The actor has done it for you. You have lived through it and come out the other side. Of course you feel better."

"When you think about it, Medea has a contemporary feeling . . . a woman coming to terms with power. Medea didn't feel that Jason raised her from lower status to his own loftier one. She didn't find a bigger identity through him."

"She didn't even want to be a Greek . . . who considered themselves so wonderful they thought everyone outside Greece was a barbarian. To Medea being Asian was to be superior. It was an old knowledge. An old religion. She never felt inferior to the Greeks. And Euripides . . . You know, women of Euripides's time loathed this play. They loathed the fact that he gave a barbarian woman such terrific wit and intelligence superior to the Greeks. They loathed the fact that he showed a woman who was not subservient to the King, but capable of outwitting and indeed killing the King. They hated it that Medea was not subservient to her husband, didn't just keep a nice house and make the children her world. They hated Medea for being the kind of woman who was capable of moving and destroying. I think she is an extraordinary heroine, a great and glorious woman."

"Up to the last minute, you believe she may not kill the children. But the emotions working on her are too powerful. Her envy of Jason's power . . ."

"Envy? I never felt that! In fact, I despised him. Just the physical presence of him, that he would do something that was so beneath the marriage we had made!" Impassioned in her denial of envy of Jason, Zoe speaks in the first person. She becomes Medea. "No, no," she says, "I never felt envy!"

"By envy, I mean envy of his power," I say. "Not envy of him. Envy of the power he had over you, over your life. Power to debase and ruin and destroy your happiness when he could have kept you the golden couple . . ."

The light is coming up in her eyes.

"Ahhhhh . . . envy of the power he had over me . . ."

"I'm speaking of primitive envy. The infant's envy of the breast, the mother's power to give life or take it away. Take it up a few levels to a traditional couple where the man has all the power. The woman is, consciously or not, enraged at him. She loves him but if the power gap in the relationship is too big, she envies him. Yes, he gives her a beautiful house and clothes, everything. But that means he also has the power to take it away. The choice is his. She loves him; she hates him. She envies his power. Until Medea comes to Greece, she and Jason are equals. Suddenly he has all the power."

"Oh, yes. That's right. And she'd given him everything. Given up everything. Not just her country and family. Her powers too. She kills people right, left and center for him."

"What a fall. For the first time in her life she is powerless. She was a princess . . . her fall was from such a height. Now she is dependent on him."

"It is so destructive, dependency. It doesn't breed like love. It's rotten for desire. Yes, oh, yes, dependency. You envy the other person the power he has over your life. Oh, my God, you just said something that explains so much. Oh, oh, *Envy!*"

"He could make her wretched, or he could save her. She had killed her own brother for him. . . ."

"They were deep, deep in blood," says Zoe. "I mean, they went through the world laughing, but they were deep, both of them, deep in blood. So suddenly this barbarian princess, she is dependent on him, this proud woman. She is enraged. She is jealous. Yes, most of all she is envious. And when you have these feelings of powerlessness, you wish to get power over the other person or at least stop his power over you. And these little boys, her sons, are there all the time reminding her that everything is wrong, wrong, wrong. Their vulnerability is the thing that would make you want to hurt or hit or kill them. I didn't understand child abuse until I had children. I never abused my children but I did come to understand it."

Zoe tells a story about when she was breast-feeding her first son, Sam. It happened on a day when she was very busy, had too much to do. She was tired and had no milk when Sam wanted it. "I was on my own that day. All that the baby wanted was milk. That's all. And I couldn't give it to him. My feeling of impotence, of not being able to give the baby—the baby that I'd wanted so much—was so extreme . . . and the baby was screaming and screaming and screaming. Nothing I did, nothing I did, a bottle . . . no, that was no good. He wanted my milk and I didn't have it. I felt so impotent . . . it was the first time I really and truly understood child abuse."

A startling picture of envy seen from the mother's point of view. The baby filled with envious hatred because the withholding breast will not give him what he wants. The mother's retaliatory response to that rage— the baby is not giving her what she wants.

"Having known envy and jealousy early in life," I say, "I think most people try to keep themselves closed off from those feelings. How many of us marry our great passion? Women are learning what men have always known: It's hard to lead a passionate life, where your life is always on the line, and hold a job too."

"Until I met my husband, I always had to pretend with men. I mean, I loved some stunning, extraordinary fellows . . ."

"I bet you did." Did I mention this woman's beauty? She is a powerhouse.

"I always had to pretend that I was a little less," Zoe says. "A little less something, a little less bright, a little less talented, a little less powerful. And I thought, 'Do I have to go through my whole life feeling I've got to be a little less?' "

"Women don't understand why men are angry today, why they won't 'commit' themselves. Women have ruined men's defenses. Men are exposed to their envy of women. You're not going to commit yourself to someone you envy."

"When I married Robert, I felt it had to be mateship, like my mum and dad. It was going to be for life and I better feel I can be myself . . .

'I'm me,' not *'I'm not quite me.'* Not being me, making myself less, had always ruined relationships with men. With Robert I suddenly realized that I was with a fellow with whom I could be strong as I wanted to be. He's always okay. I could be as clever as I wanted to be and he was always still intact. In fact, he always took me a bit further."

"That was Medea and Jason. She was too much woman, too powerful for most men. How many men would have taken her on? Jason asked extraordinary things of her and she did them. How he must have envied her courage. After the golden fleece adventure, when he wanted to settle down and play politics with the boys at the palace, he wanted a littler, 'white limbed' girl. He wanted to defend himself against all that female power. He betrayed Medea."

"I don't get jealous of Robert," Zoe is saying, still on her own track. "Because I don't feel dependent on him."

"You do not feel easily replaceable in his life?"

"That's exactly the phrase. I feel it would be his bad luck. I also feel it would be mine. I don't think he's easily replaceable. I can't imagine a marriage after Robert."

We talk about a recent Broadway production of *Othello*. Zoe had been brought in to "doctor" the production.

"It must have been a heady year," I say. "Not only playing Medea but directing *Othello* as well."

"Othello has absolutely nothing to gain by killing Desdemona. Everything to lose. He kills her because of the assault on his manhood. Male pride. Iago and Othello and myself, the actors, we talked a lot about this. The real jealousy is Iago's jealousy of the power that Othello has. But it isn't jealousy, it's *envy*, right? Envy between Othello and Iago. In the beginning, Iago has so little power, Othello has so much. Very gradually, what happens is that the feminine part of Iago slips in little things, little ideas, suspicions. They make no impression on Othello at first. Eventually Iago gets all the power. He is the one who just sits back. It is Othello now who is moved to ask, Please tell me more, don't tell me, tell me, no more, no."

"Planting suspicion of Desdemona was Iago's way of equalizing their power."

"The way of making himself the most powerful man on that stage, in that play, in the world. Because he then also has power over Cassio, who is well-born, a Florentine. Iago was Milanese, had no money, no background, an outsider. So he went into the army. He envies Cassio, envies his past and his high position. If you don't feel this envy from the beginning of the play, you never can understand why Iago makes so much trouble."

"You directed Desdemona to treat Iago like a servant. . . ."

"Which makes for resentment, envy, rage. Out of which you can make a lot of mischief. You can do true evil. Envy makes you want to bring somebody down, down, down where the iguanas play."

"With Cassio, Iago envies his higher position. With Othello it's envy . . ."

"Iago's rage is a blue-collar worker's absolute fury at a potent, extraordinary black man in great power."

As Zoe is leaving, we pause at the door. "I find it very interesting," she says, "the idea of power. The idea that what rankles in envy is the power someone has over you. I'd never thought of it in that light."

But she played Medea in that light. I had to do no more than mention the idea of envy for Zoe Caldwell to understand perfectly. It is Klein who has given her and me a new frame of reference in which to put what we already knew: that we hate the people who have the power to put us in hell when they could raise us to heaven.

Technically, of course, betrayal is not jealousy. Therefore I did not have a chapter on betrayal in my outline for this book. I include it now because the people I interview remind me how we overlap jealousy and betrayal.

"If he danced too long, too close, too much with another woman, I'd be jealous," a woman tells me. "But if he made love to her, then I'd feel betrayed."

One might say that jealousy is *before* the fact; betrayal, after.

Defining *betrayal, The Oxford English Dictionary* makes no reference to either envy or jealousy. Nor are any of the citations concerned with betrayal in the romantic/sexual sense. The same is true of *Webster's* and *American Heritage.*

Betrayal and jealousy are different, but they can coexist. Within the jealous situation, along with jealousy of the rival and envies flying in all directions, there can also be an additional and terrible sense of betrayal. It is not always there. When it is, an extra engine of destruction is added. From *The Oxford English Dictionary:*

betrayal
1. A treacherous giving up to an enemy.
2. A violation of trust or confidence, an abandonment of something committed to one's charge.

"An abandonment of something committed to one's charge . . ." Like my heart, my love, my self. Isn't that what love is? A promise, a contract. If we surrender, lay down our defenses, commit ourselves to the beloved's care, he will not betray us. If, as in the case of Medea, he does, our vengeance will have all the infantile destructiveness of the dependent Kleinian child. Betrayed, most of us do not kill, but the wish is there. *A promise has been broken.*

Perhaps one of the reasons so many marriages fail is that each party has a different conception of the central contract. "Most of the things we do," says psychoanalyst Erika Freeman, "we do because that's the bargain we make with the world. I won't steal from you if you won't steal from me. Even though women grow up knowing that men aren't necessarily monogamous, they still believe in magic. They really believe that if they are good little girls, the world will be all right. Women whose fathers left home unconsciously expect to be betrayed by their own mates. If they aren't, they believe it's because of that magical bargain: *They* were monogamous, and so their husband was."

So many of the bargains we make are silently made within ourselves. She: "I will be a virgin until I marry. It will be my dowry. He will be grateful and never leave me." He: "I will give up all my dreams of adventure and work steady and hard and pay the mortgage. She will be grateful and never leave me."

Does he understand the weight of her sacrifice, the terms of her contract? Does she understand his? When she learns of his infidelity, the marriage is ruined in her eyes. To him it was just a one-night stand. To her it was an act of betrayal. When he accuses her of jealousy, she will be semantically correct when she denies it.

Women do not have a monopoly on feelings of betrayal. Especially nowadays. I know a woman whose adulterous affair was discovered by her husband. He was emptying a wastebasket and found a letter. They were both virgins when they met and married. She was attracted to him because he was so much like her father: strict, straight as an arrow, "an absolutist." She also says his character was the reason she began the affair. She wanted "romance," a man to acknowledge her beauty and sexuality as her husband/father never did.

When her husband discovered the infidelity, he felt his manhood put in question. He felt betrayed. He had always been totally faithful. This man, who had loved his wife with all his heart for fifteen years, decided overnight that the marriage was over. She pleaded, telling him the affair was just that. For him the contract had been broken. Like Medea, he said, "I am not jealous. I do not want her back."

She was more lively, more attractive, perhaps more important, more professionally successful than he. If he was envious, the contract had always kept it in check. What he wanted now was revenge. He threw her out of the house, even though they had built and paid for it together. He went into the basement and began pressing weights, setting his newly competitive eye on the wife of the man she had slept with. In her words, "he spewed his sperm" over the entire community.

The adulterous wife totally bought his condemnation. Overnight, the adventuress became the Scarlet Woman. Friends noticed that her voice had become that of a little girl. She had broken a contract with him, but also with herself/mother/society. Not enough time has gone by for most women to posit their sexuality without feeling it is a breach of contract, a betrayal of the Madonna idealization of womanhood.

I tell Hanna Segal this story. "The husband didn't want her back," I say. "In understanding jealousy, how important is that?"

"I never thought about it before," she says, "but it seems to me that in nonpathological jealousy, the main aim would be to get the love object back. That says that your love is still there. You either want the person back or, if the situation is hopeless, you resolve to let the person go."

"So when this man—like Medea—says that he's not jealous, that he doesn't want her back . . ."

"It means, 'I don't love her/him anymore.' So what I'm dominated by is not love or jealousy but revenge. Betrayal is different from jealousy. You see, if I loved a man who was already in love with another woman, I would hate her, not him. But if the man promised me love, and betrayed me behind my back, then the reaction is to the betrayal."

"Did Melanie Klein write about betrayal?"

"I don't think she did, but I am sure it is important. For instance, if children are very involved with narcissistic mothers who always make them feel 'You're my one and only,' that is taken as a promise. When that promise is broken—*which it must be* because 'You're my one and only' is a lie—then the child feels betrayed."

We seem to be getting close to a definition of the ability to love, which has eluded me throughout this book, as it has in my life. "The idea of loving someone," I say, "wanting them back, wanting revenge, being hurt, wanting to hurt . . . it's all so contradictory."

"The way I would see it," Mrs. Segal says, "has to do with the relative strength of love versus destructiveness. And I would relate destructiveness to envy."

"So the stronger your love . . ."

"The less you would be preoccupied with envy, destruction and revenge. With love, the fear of hurting the object would be on your mind."

"So, if you truly love," I say, knowing my own record, "you would want what is best for your beloved. Even when you were jealous, you wouldn't whip right into revenge. . . ."

"If the person you love wants someone else, you would either want to get them back or you would let them go and mourn their loss. You would want what is best for them."

I sigh. "Do you have a definition of love?"

"No," she smiles.

"Are you jealous?"

"It's not jealousy," he says defiantly, though that is what his friends are whispering behind his back. Everyone in town knows of what he calls his "fucking around." In his best-selling autobiography of his career as a philosopher, it is given an entire chapter. Now his wife has trapped him in his own game.

"If it's not jealousy," I say, "what would you call it?"

"It has to do with money. *My* money. I'll be damned if I'll give her another cent."

"In your first marriage you wrote that your wife fucked around. You didn't care. What's different this time?"

"In that marriage, she did, I did, that was the deal on which the marriage was based. But in this one, I married for respectability. She was to stay home and be the mother of my child. What I did on the side was my business."

"That's the double standard."

"Of course it is. But she had no right to object. She knew the terms going in and she accepted them. Now she's forty years old and wants to play around. Well, she can't fuck around and have my money too."

The conversation ends. He is right. He is not jealous. Love was never the issue. He has been cheated in a business deal. She broke the contract. Betrayal.

When we lie in the beloved's arms, we suspend mistrust. That is why love feels so good and why so many distrust this kind of surrender. If the beloved should betray us we would feel reduced to a powerless child.

The child does surrender to the mother, to the breast; I have heard it called the oral triad. Being held, sucking at the breast, falling to sleep. "I have often had that kind of surrender at the breast, as an adult," Robertiello recently said. "There is a feeling of complete peace and security. I suppose women get it when they are held in a man's arms. I'm sure you can get it without the literal breast. It's like relaxing all your defenses, letting down all your protections against bad things happening, letting Mama take over the whole thing."

What is puzzling about my friend is that knowing the degree of surrender he wants with a woman—and offers them too—how can he be surprised at their rage when he betrays them?

Man, born of woman, has a special memory of betrayal. Long before the oedipal years bring the boy face to face with sexual betrayal, there is union with mother which in the child's eyes is an unbreakable contract.

A man tells me a story:

"You're a good little girl," his mother says to his little sister.

"And I'm a good little boy," he says, certain of the reply.

"No," she says. "You're not."

The answer is so stunning he remembers it to this day. He was four, his sister two. It was in fact one of his earliest memories, the first being his sister's birth. Why do the words ring as clearly in his ears today as they did more than forty years ago?

"It was the first unexpected, and in my mind false, thing my mother ever said." The broken contract.

He had a brother and a sister, eleven and fourteen years older than he. A late arrival, he was his mother's little boy, her darling. When his sister was born, he could not understand how the bargain between mother and son, the promise she would love him forever, could be over. Hadn't *forever* and *exclusively* been intertwined in the little boy's mind?

Today I ask the grown man if the shocking reverberation of his mother's label of him as "bad" opposite the hated but "good" sister stayed with him because it explained why she had brought this interloper home, thus perfidiously breaking their first and most important contract.

"I never expected women to be fair," he says, "until I met my wife. Nor have I ever given much weight to other people's opinion of me."

The fine print in the mother's contract says she has to be only a good mother. In the child's, it says she swears to be perfect. For the boy there is an additional clause. In the long ago, now forgotten, mythical male memory, the all-powerful mother could have solved the dilemma of attachment and separation. Didn't she kiss away his tears at night? She not only controlled his life, but heaven and earth too. If she did not show him how to be a man and have her too, it was because she chose not to. Almost the first lesson a boy learns is that women betray you.

"I resented my mother . . . ," writes Sheila MacLeod, for not protecting her against her father's belief in corporal punishment. "It seemed to me that she should have taken my part, should somehow have defended me from my father. . . . I could hear him say to her, 'She's not even trying. I despair of her!' My mother would answer inaudibly . . . whether immediately or eventually, she would acquiesce, and I resented her acquiescence, not only because of its consequences for myself, but because I didn't understand why she, an adult, would not, or could not, stand up to him."[1]

Sheila MacLeod is writing about her history as an anorexic, trying to understand why starvation came to be a form of power in a world where she had no other. She quotes Erik Erikson, who sums up not only Mac-Leod's childhood but I think everyone else's too: "The polarity adult-child is the first in the inventory of existential oppositions (male-female being the second) which makes man exploitable and induces him to exploit. The child's inborn proclivity for feeling powerless, deserted, ashamed and guilty in relation to those on whom he depends is systematically utilised for his training, often to the point of exploitation."[2]

Notice that Erikson puts the adult-child relation before the male-female in order of time and power. No matter how early Dan Stern and the Baby Watchers are now coming to believe that infants can discern between male and female parents, there is no doubt they can tell the difference between bigness and littleness even before that. Erikson is talking about an era so archaic in everyone's history that gender differences are not yet important. He is talking about the reign of the Kleinian mother.

In MacLeod's unconscious, not only was her mother an adult, she was also the Kleinian mediator of life and death. For so powerful a figure not to stand up for her was the sheerest betrayal.

"It seems so obvious," I say to Robertiello, "that so long as a child's infinite needs are met by only one person, all kinds of spoken and implicit promises must be broken. How much strength, patience and goodness can one person have?"

"We always get back to this," he says. "Shared parenting."

I sigh. For him and me, it is an ideal. In practice, far too late. "Still, some of us never give up," I say. He knows what I am talking about.

"We keep hoping we'll find someone who will meet those early unrequited needs," he says. "When we get older, we say, Well, I didn't get it then, but I'll find somebody. And then we fall in love."

Robertiello wants desperately to drink at the sweet waters of surrender in a woman's arms. To do so, he must first defend himself against any possibility the woman might betray him, again, as mother did. Before he can surrender, he must strip her of all power. Before he can allow himself to become dependent on her, she must be totally dependent on him.

Here he is speaking of an infant's surrender: "When the infant lies at the mother's breast, he feels powerless but in a good way. When you relax at the breast, you give up your power, like Medea did. She said, 'This guy is so great that I can leave everything to him, put myself in his hands. He'll always admire, love, and take care of me.' That's a great feeling. The infant feels, 'I am going to put aside all my hatred, all of my thanatotic death wishes and I'm going to totally relax and see her as a completely good mother forever.' "

Robertiello continues: "It's ridiculous to say an infant cannot feel this. All you have to do is look at an infant's face and see these emotions. And you know that you feel it when you're in the same place. So the infant is in Nirvana but the next time he cries because he wants Mama to feed him, Mama is making some chicken soup and she literally doesn't hear him or she does hear him, but she's got the hot soup pot in her hand— whatever. So she takes five minutes before she gets there with the breast. He goes bananas."

"Just like you hate to be kept waiting in a restaurant. You go into a deep funk."

"That's true. I hate my food to be delayed."

"The infant feels, Mom, you broke the contract. . . ."

"The kid assumes," Robertiello says, "that Mama is always going to be there, like she was when he was at her breast. To put the baby's accusation into words, 'You didn't make me wait then . . .' "

"So why are you making me wait now?"

"He wants to tear her breasts off."

"Klein's envy . . ."

"But the sense of betrayal is there very strongly too."

"What eases the sense of betrayal," I say, "is that most infants in time learn that mother is doing her best. If he is not too constitutionally envious, the child begins to surrender his demand that she be perfect and settles for the good enough breast, the good enough mother. He has her inside him so strongly that even when she's not there—or not there fast enough—he knows she soon will be."

"The next time mother doesn't respond to his first cry, he doesn't guiltlessly go into thanatotic wishes. He feels guilty for wanting to destroy her. And he makes some kind of reparation like gently touching her face or whatever. Then he feels gratitude for the good mother instead of envy."

"Do you ever feel grateful for what the women in your life have given you?"

"I have a lot of trouble taking in good things. Gratitude is an emotion I haven't felt much."

"I think there's a connection between inability to feel gratitude and the way you set up women for betrayal. . . ."

"It's hard for me to acknowledge that somebody is giving anything to me. . . . That's where I get into spoiling. If I acknowledge that someone is really generous to me, giving me something I need, that puts me in a position where I need *them*. I'm dependent on them, on their continued giving. That makes me vulnerable to Kleinian envy. So what I do to prevent that is to spoil it. I say, 'Why should I be grateful to her? She isn't giving me anything, or what she's giving me is shit.' "

"Give me an example with Susan."

"I minimize what she does for me because I don't want to acknowledge how important she is to me. Maybe I don't want to know myself how much I would be devastated if I lost her. What happens is that I feel she is giving the good stuff to her sister. What she's giving to me is bullshit."

"Doesn't Susan resent this?"

"And how! The next step is that Susan feels her gifts aren't being acknowledged. She decides, 'I'm not going to give this son of a bitch anything.' "

"And then you say, Aha! I was right. She really . . ."

"Really isn't giving me anything. It has a snowball effect. A male patient of mine never let any woman be important to him. He's fifty years old and very active sexually. As soon as he fell in love with a woman he devalued her."

"To protect himself from how much power she had over him."

"Men defend against these feelings much more than women. By cutting off, by not letting themselves be really close to a woman. Men refuse to be grateful to women; they devalue what the woman gives, devalue her whole role."

"To admit gratitude would set up an intimacy, a dependency. . . . And to see yourself as dependent not only opens you to envy, it is also unmasculine."

"Now we're talking about one of the major differences between the sexes. Why, quote, Women are emotional and men are withdrawn."

"The man says, Who needs you? I can get along without you very well. And the woman says, I need you but I hate you because I need you."

"Maybe when we get through the Envy Battle between the sexes, a relationship will have evolved in which men will not be enraged that women have a monopoly on emotion and women will not be enraged that men have a monopoly on money and power."

"Richard, why can't you practice what you preach?"

"When we set up housekeeping together," Robertiello says, talking about a woman with whom he lived for several years, "she felt I was totally committed to her and that there was no way we would ever break up. I did promise her that. At the time I meant it. So she felt she could trust me to be with her forever. She broke with her father and brother, who didn't like me. I became her guru, her god, everything."

"Then one day you tell her it's all been very nice but you want to move on. . . ."

"She was totally bereft. She had given up everything she ever had. When I left, she had nothing."

"She didn't know you had another woman?"

"It wasn't jealousy. Even if she had known, the other woman wouldn't have mattered. When it was clear I wasn't coming back, she says, like Medea, 'You betrayed me. You promised to be here forever, so I totally gave myself over to you.' And she had. She totally surrendered herself."

"So you had all the power."

"What added the poison to her feeling of betrayal was that she had *given* me the power."

"The humiliation she must have felt," I say. "It is as if twenty or thirty years of maturity, sophistication, layers of defense, have been stripped away . . ."

"Exactly, exactly . . ."

". . . you have laid yourself bare to this person . . ."

"Like a baby. Like a sweet, innocent, naive baby . . ."

If he understands it so well, why does he ask it of women, to surrender everything to him?

Something in his crooning tone of voice when he just said "like a sweet, innocent, naive baby" confirms why he is not answering my question. He is the baby. He is putting women in the helpless position he once was in: when in his own words, he was dependent on his mother and she "betrayed" him, dropping him for his sister and then for his brother.

CHAPTER TEN

Memoirs of a Jealous Woman Part Three: Siblings and Revenge

*H*ow do you end? It's over. Trust is dead. But love's transactions are still in motion: Need, dependency, the expectations of first love, they mock us with a ghostly life of their own.

In the beginning, long ago, we realized our prince/princess was flawed. The blemish became what we loved most. Ah, the healing properties of love. Behind acceptance of the beloved's imperfection was a certain self-congratulation. Only we could love so much. As long as love was in progress, we refused to strike a bargain with anger; we lived with it anyway. Anger—hidden, under the bed, in a box, buried.

Love doesn't end in a day. And then it does. The tombstones roll away and all the buried demons rise. Rage is supreme.

Good-bye is never a handshake.

I had known for months that Jack and I were over. There was Guadeloupe. But what I did with the French soldier was an exploration, a venture outside the monogamy I thought I couldn't live without. A walk in space, lifeline still tied to Jack.

I could return to him. I did. I loved him. I hated him.

For four, maybe five months, we stayed together. Hot, passionate months. But terrible. Summer arrived. In four days we boiled to an end.

I remember the first of those days. Sometimes memory is a smell. Mine is a touch, the feel of sheer silk moving across bare skin as I stepped from the steam of a July night into the cool darkness of a little Eastside bar called The Renaissance. Jack seldom went above Twenty-first Street. But his friend Bill was writing a column on the place. The pale little bit of silk hung, weightless, from my nipples and became what the night was all about. Whether or not it was true, I felt all eyes were on me.

The dress was new. I had nothing on underneath. When I'd met Jack, I had the full Lady's Wardrobe of Underwear. He talked me out of everything. I walked around in a state of semiarousal in those days, always conscious of what I didn't have on. The price we exhibitionists pay for excitement is imminent humiliation.

I took Jack's seat at the bar. He and Bill stood on either side, smiling at me. The dress provoked me to tell a story I'd heard at lunch that day from an old friend, a staid Wall Street type. The broker and his wife had recently been to a party. A woman had removed all her clothes, and then proceeded to undress as many men as were willing. "Jane and I left, of course," my friend had said, still in shock. But others had joined in the fun.

Bill laughed. Jack did not. Too late, I saw my mistake.

I'd thought a story of sexual abandon would excite Jack. But it was someone else's abandon, not his. Further evidence that he wasn't moving fast enough. To me the story was one of excess. To him it was a reminder of where he should have been yesterday.

I had come very far very fast. The naked green dress was something I slipped on over a Nice Girl. That was its thrill. I would take it off later. That was its safety. I was both people. Jack wanted to abandon the past. I did not. Summer heat. It was getting to him. He was hungry for the sexual riches "out there."

When I finished my story, he took his drink to the end of the bar and sat alone. I had created my own rival. If the woman in the story had walked in the door that minute, I didn't have a doubt in the world which of us he'd choose. Short of removing my dress and topping her performance, there was nothing I could do.

I handled anxiety in my usual way. I smiled more brightly. Bill was off on a soliloquy against marriage. People laughed and bought each other drinks. I could understand why Jack admired Bill. His cynicism about the lives our parents had chosen matched the times. "A fool and his money are soon in a ranch house." But unlike the rest of us who came to the party in costumes of the sixties, Bill came as himself.

"I always think people should get married as soon as possible," Bill was saying. "That way, when they get divorced they're not too old."

"You're just looking for a good argument," I said.

He smiled and bought me a stinger.

In bed that night, just before he came, Jack said, "You're thinking about Bill, aren't you? Wishing he were here."

It wasn't an accusation. There was no hurt in his voice. More like hope. He wanted someone else in bed with us. The missing link, the next logical step in our adventure.

"Get off me!" I screamed. "Get out of here!"

It was more rage than the moment deserved. But the anger had been there a long time, as long as my knowledge that I wasn't enough. I wanted no one in our bed. Not even in my fantasies were there other men. Jack was still so mysterious and frightening, he was the other man.

He put on his clothes and went home.

The next day Jack and I went to Fire Island for the weekend, as planned. But a new chapter had begun. We would be on the beach and he would leave. Hours later he would reappear on the deck of whatever house the party had settled on. I would wake in the night and he would be gone. The houses we played in that summer were in the vanguard of mid-sixties experimentation. There were enough booze, grass, hallucinatory drugs and available sexual partners to sate the greediest. Jack had tried it all, had tried it first. He was looking for something more. Or had he found it?

It is one thing to feel the center of attention in a beautiful naked green dress; daring, grown-up, in control. Something altogether different, sitting on the deck of a summer house, conspicuous before strangers. The public humiliation of being abandoned. I moved from party to party with people who were more Jack's friends than mine.

"Where's Jack?"

"Oh, he'll turn up in a minute or two," I would smile.

"Where is your mother?" Teachers buzzed around me, at the end of my first day at school. I stood inside the white picket fence as car after car, mother after mother, picked up other little girls. Finally, after everyone had gone, she arrived.

So would Jack. Meanwhile no one must see the pain. Why was that so important? In that crowd, no one would have cared if I'd had a hysterical collapse. That summer, four people had already been carted away by helicopter ambulance for overindulgence. But I cared.

"Everyone always said you were the happiest little girl they'd ever seen," my mother persists to this day. That is true. People did say that.

I held my drink—smiling—and prayed for Jack's return. There was nothing he had done for which I would not forgive him, if he would just come sit beside me. At one A.M. on Fire Island there is nowhere to run. Of course it had nothing to do with geography. I was losing an obscure competition I hadn't entered. One I would lose at my peril, I knew not why.

At Saturday night's "early" party, Bill came to sit beside me. Drunk and happy, he let me know without words that he knew I was not; and he was sorry. The woman he was with soon removed him, steered him to another side of the room, to another house. She knew before Bill and I—as future losers in love do—that I was the enemy.

I did not yet see Bill. It was too soon. All emotion focused on Jack, all energy used for control. At some point in the night, Jack walked up over a sand dune, bounded up onto the deck and sat beside me. No questions were asked. Just before Sunday's dawn, we went back to the house where we were staying. We made love. He didn't stay. "I've got to walk around," he said with that crazy desperation. He was off into the night. For all I know, walk is all he did; walk is all he'd ever done.

Who was the rival? Free-floating jealousy can be the most painful. Fixed on an individual, fear and rage can be contained. But unfocused separation anxieties are like a "sickness unto death." The enemy is everywhere. I thought the enemy was Jack. It was in me.

The person I wanted to be existed only in his eyes. Had I lost myself totally in him it might have been simpler. We would have continued our unique exchange of sexual permissions. Except Jack's were the only fantasies left to explore. Mine had gone as far as I wanted.

I had always known what was right and wrong for me. I had to. Left too much on my own as an adolescent, missing the rules concerned parents had laid down for my friends, I'd made up my own. Boys offered everything I'd always wanted. To be held promised heaven. Or hell, if I wasn't careful. The rules I made were stricter than anyone else's. My rebellion with Jack was against nothing more than my own overly rigid conscience. I had followed his wildness because I trusted the part of him that, like me, was anchored in the past. Thanks to me—to my permission—it was that part of himself that he was ready to jettison.

He should have left me. He was the teacher. But we were still lovers. And so, while the ship was sinking around me, I lay in bed and secretly put together another ship to save myself. A ship within a ship, built on survival and rage.

Sunday's return to the city brought not one harsh word from me. He had expected recriminations. He was grateful and showed it. Monday I called him from my office and offered to buy lunch. We had enchiladas and Carta Blanca at our favorite Mexican restaurant. After which we shared a joint in the garden of the Museum of Modern Art. I took the afternoon off. The best sex in months. At seven, I said I was leaving. He sat up in bed and watched me dress.

He never said, "Where are you going?"

He said, "You are beautiful inside and out."

He yelled it as I walked out the brownstone door. He was standing at the top of the stairs, naked. I knew he was hoping a neighbor would walk out and see him.

The taxi ride was a cool forty blocks uptown. I had showered but could still smell him on my skin, and taste his sweet breath. Another man's scent on me would excite Jack. What would it do for the man I was going to meet? His name was Parker.

Parker was very handsome and very rich. I had picked him because of the experience these qualities had brought him. He had already tried everything Jack wanted, and he wanted me. When I'd telephoned that morning, he'd been pleased to hear my voice. We'd met about a year ago, just after I'd become involved with Jack. We'd had a few dinners. When I said, No, there was someone else, he had smiled. "Ah, the faithful type." He said it nicely. He could afford to. He was not a mean man. And life had taught him that most things he really wanted he got, if he was generous. He'd been generous with me.

When the taxi turned into the graceful drive of River House, I felt an emotional shift in gears. Vases of fresh flowers filled the lobby. The formal politeness of the gray-haired retainer who ran the elevator promised everything would be all right. I hadn't been among these people, in this country, for months. Before I could ring, Parker's man opened the door. I could hear voices on the terrace. As I walked out to join them, I began to sense how much I had changed. There had been more consolidation than I had thought. Neither part of Jack's world nor of this any longer, I was somewhere between. Like Parker. By birth and any other set of credentials, he belonged here. By choice, he was an outsider too.

"How did you get away?" he'd asked over dinner our first night.

We'd been talking about families.

"I always knew I didn't want what everyone I grew up with wanted," I'd said. "I felt different."

We were glad we'd had conventional pasts. "Having the old rules makes the new ones more meaningful," Parker had said.

"The ones you make up."

It was easy to be with him again.

The other people were as I remembered them. Perfectly dressed. Parker was the only one among them who held a wild card that attracted me. A lack of complacency. Had I not been involved with Jack when we met, I would not have rejected him. Ironically, tonight's infidelity would happen only because my own fidelity had been found wanting. I was still trying to become Jack's fantasy woman.

As the others rose to leave, Parker looked at me. I remained seated. He saw them to the door. The rest of the evening was so easy, I couldn't help wondering if he knew. What I'd come for, why I needed him. If he did know I was using him, he had enough confidence to believe he could turn any advantage his way.

I had little heart for what I was doing. Had his hands and mouth not been so expert and patient, I doubt he could have entered my dry body. His own was tan and hard from daily sessions at the Racquet Club. In the dark I might have loved that perfect body were it not for his penis. So different from Jack's, so wrong. I'd forgotten the abruptness of that moment, the feel of a new lover's penis. So much invested in an organ, this tender relationship with a part of a man's body. Is it like that for men? Does the inside of a new woman, the walls and muscles of her vagina, feel alien at first? Is there a shock that first time, sadness at something past and lost even in the happy prospect of love to come?

"You're like me," Parker was saying. "You never lose yourself." He was lying beside me.

"You have a wonderful mouth."

But he could never be my teacher. Though his lovers had been men and women and he'd done everything Jack feared would be used up before he got to it, he lacked Jack's puritan seriousness. I lay in Parker's arms. Following Jack's directives, I did not feel guilty. I felt nothing.

"There, there," Parker was saying, running his hand gently down my back. I was crying.

In the morning, he lent me dark glasses.

"Will I see you tonight?" he asked.

"No."

"Ever?"

"You are too famously fickle for a jealous woman like me."

"You are too faithful."

Jack telephoned the apartment while I was changing. By the eager love in his voice I knew he'd tried to reach me earlier. He asked me to lunch. My confusion melted before his artistry with jealousy, the exuberant delight he took in my presence. My own less enthusiastic handling of the emotion the previous night had obviously worked. Things would be better now. He would see I was not so easily replaceable.

New York can be as small as any town. Walking back to the office, we ran into Parker leaving La Caravelle. Jack immediately knew it was Parker I had been with. The knowledge seemed to excite him. Once again I felt that infusion of added love from him. He couldn't wait, he said, for the night ahead. It was spent in an artist's loft, where the hostess ended lying on her bed, knees raised, while a man, naked except for dark socks and shoes, licked hungrily away at her. I saw only the tail end, so to speak, when someone sitting next to me in the main room nudged and pointed. The bedroom door was open. Three people stood at the foot of the bed watching and waiting their turn. One was Jack.

I wasn't surprised the next day when Jack's call didn't include getting together that night. I didn't ask where he was going; I still needed to be part of his life. And because I knew he would love me more for anything I did that would allow me to accept him, I called Parker and said yes to dinner.

The night ended back at River House with Parker and an old friend of his, an attractive man who brought humor. When Parker led the three of us to bed, I didn't resist. If I was following Parker's lead, the other man was clearly following mine. It was a first for him too. Did he think Parker and I went in for threesomes regularly? It didn't matter. I had my own reasons and whatever his were for making love to me while Parker watched, I was surprised at how easy it all went. It had to do with not caring too much. With not loving anyone there at all. We were all nice people.

I left before dawn, knowing with a sinking heart that while I could never have done this with Jack, I was now prepared to accept it if he did it. I could only hope he would never tell me; never force me to know.

He did.

The next night in the middle of the party, he took two people, a man and a woman, into the bedroom. They stayed locked in there, it seemed, for hours. Why didn't I immediately leave? More of that old unfinished business, I suppose; the need not to let people see I'd been humiliated, destroyed. But I had been. I was absolutely burning with a false hope that the bedroom door would magically open and the betrayal be seen never to have happened.

We didn't meet for a week. When he did call, I said I'd come to the Mexican restaurant. Over the obligatory Carta Blanca, I controlled the urge to reach across the table and kill him. Instead, I took him back to my apartment and fucked him as never before. Jack, the great man of words, could not speak. I still loved him.

I saw Jack at least once a day or night, whenever I wanted him, the whole of the next week. When I didn't see him, I saw Parker. I never bothered to make the bed when Jack was coming, and if he noticed the stained sheets or empty champagne bottles around the usually immaculate apartment, it only seemed to excite him more.

On the seventh night, I did him one better and took him and two other men to my place and had them all. After that, his eyes told me I never had to worry again: He was mine. He would never find a woman like me. One who united his past and his future. One who accepted all of him.

The next morning I flew to London with Parker. I was gone a long time. As long as it took.

When I came home I married Bill.

What is the connection between jealousy and revenge?

When we are jealous, not all of us want to hurt back. When my husband sees me in intimate conversation with another man, he may feel something, a momentary threat, even pain. Essentially he sees whatever I do as something I am doing for myself, not as an act against him. That is how he is. I think that is how he's always been, the way he grew up and learned to think about himself. He knows he is not easily replaced.

In a reverse situation, when I feel threatened, I punish. On the way home in the car, I may not speak to him. I turn away in bed. That is how I am. Because of what I had with my mother? In part.

Bill and I had different beginnings, different histories of love and loss. Our needs to control, the capacity for trust, are not at all alike. His mother was a warm maternal person. And though his father never liked him—"He was always in a rage"—he had two brothers, ten and twelve years older. "They were my heroes," he says. "I thought they were perfect. I could never understand why they were always quarreling between themselves."

When Bill was two years old, a sister was born. His father smiled. He was never angry with his little girl. After three sons, the powerful, loving mother now had a daughter, someone in her image. Bill had been her baby. His place had been usurped. "I always knew there was something special between them," he says. He says it now without rancor or resentment. For two reasons.

First, the bad sister was punished. "Want to see a movie?" he said to her one day when they were little. He was hiding half a lemon inside his fist. He told her to press her eye against the peephole. "I shot the acid in her eye" is how he's always told the story. I've heard it several times. I never understood the drama in his voice until now. To little Bill, it *was* acid. He was blinding her. Eventually he did find a way to eliminate her. For taking his place, stealing his mother, he expelled her from his family. He rarely sees her. Never speaks of her. She doesn't exist.

His brothers do. On a very large scale. That is the second reason rivalry with his sister hasn't dominated his life. "My brothers were my fathers," he says. "They saved my life." He has said it often. Whenever he sees them, he repeats this enormous gratitude, how much he owes them. I have noticed that they don't like hearing it. They change the subject.

Once a brother even got angry. "You're the one Pop hated. He hated you more than any of us," the brother said. It was such a cruel and unnecessary thing to say. Bill's brothers resented their own goodness to him. Of course. Who had been "the good father" to them? No one.

Families.

We are reluctant to accept that whom we sleep beside, and how soundly, is determined by what we had with mother in the first year of life. It is easier to come to terms with oedipal jealousy—our ability to compete against rivals, based on a more grown-up time of life. But something still is missing. There is more to my intimacies with men, fears of rejection, than can be explained by analysis of my relations to my mother and a missing father. Where did I learn this need to hurt back, my pre-emptive pattern of striking first against the unfairness of jealousy?

How does my sister fit into all this?

The question becomes passage into a discussion I've spent a life avoiding. In this I am not alone. Freud himself left his siblings out of his memoirs. To read his life, it is as if they didn't exist. He eliminated them. Revenge. For what? For having been born.

I too would have left my sister out. What has she to do with my adult torments over men? But this book has taken on a life of its own. That is what a writer wants, and doesn't want. To stop controlling. To give the book its head. To be led by the unconscious. To this:

From the beginning, we were a triangle. A mother and two daughters. "When I brought you home, I put you in Anna's arms," my mother says. Anna was my nurse. My sister hadn't had a nurse. She was the first-born. She had my mother and father.

I have always known there was something special between my mother and sister. I used to think it went no further than what I saw—criticism, heated reaction, intense and tearful emotional exchange. I told myself I was well out of it. Why then this lifelong sense of being left out? I now know that "the something special" my mother and sister shared was my father. A time when my mother was a happy woman. When she had a husband and my sister had a father. I never knew those years. I never knew him. By the time I came along the magical, mythical epoch was over. My sister was part of the great mystery no one was allowed to talk about. I was shut out by time itself.

"I think that sibling rivalry is much more important to everybody, male and female, than sexual rivalry," said Robertiello years ago, almost at the beginning of our talks. To me the idea seemed misleading. I decided he was hiding again, putting up deceptive screens, calling jealousy anything but what it really was.

There was the story about when he was twelve. His mother had brought a distant cousin into the house to live with them. The girl was fourteen. "I was so jealous of the attention my mother gave her that I stepped out onto a fifth floor window ledge. I threatened to jump if my mother didn't promise to send her home. Clearly this was sibling stuff. A replay of me and my sister and also my brother. My sibling rivalry is enormous."

Robertiello's earliest memory: He is two years old and is suddenly sent away from home without explanation, to unknown relatives in the country. He is under the dining-room table, crying and miserable. When he returns home, they tell him he has a brand-new baby sister. This is the first he knows of her. She has taken his place in his parents' room. He is put in with his grandparents. "My sister literally stole my bed!"

Bruno Bettelheim: "When the story [of Goldilocks] is told from the perspective of Baby Bear, Goldilocks is the intruder who suddenly comes from nowhere, as did the next younger sibling, and usurps—or tries to usurp—a place in a family, which, to Baby Bear, was complete without her. This nasty intruder takes away his food, ruins his chair, even tries to drive him out of his bed—and, by extension, to take away his place in his parents' love. Then it is understandable that it is not the parents' but Baby Bear's voice that 'was so sharp, and so shrill, that it awakened her at once. Up she started . . . and ran to the window.' It is Baby Bear—the child—who wants to get rid of the newcomer, wants her to go back where she came from, never to see 'anything more of her.' Thus the story gives imaginative body to the fears and wishes a child has about an imagined or real new arrival in the family."[1]

Robertiello's infinitely tangled and painful beginnings—plus relentless intellectual curiosity—led him to twelve different analysts over a period of thirty years. It was only with the thirteenth analyst, who went with him to his sister's grave, that the sibling question arose. "I went to the cemetery expecting to feel terrible remorse. What came out beside my sister's grave was a torrent of rage." Not at his mother. Not at his father. But at the sister whom he'd loved and hated and lost.

"Among individually and family-oriented psychotherapists," write psychologists Stephen Bank and Michael Kahn, "the experience of being a sibling is rarely described. Psychoanalytic literature and commentary is, surprisingly, almost devoid of reference to Freud's viewpoint about the relationships among brothers and sisters. The American Psychoanalytic Association's Committee on Indexing produced a cross-referenced subject index on Freud's work which does not mention 'brothers,' 'sisters' or 'siblings.' While therapists may occasionally discuss sibling relationships with their patients, the sibling experience is rarely a major focus of treatment

. . . neo-Freudian theory takes almost no account of the sibling relationship as a major force in the life of an individual."[2]

"What was [Freud's] own experience as a sibling?" write Bank and Kahn. "And how could this experience have influenced his way of seeing his patients? Finally, did Freud's sibling experience influence the way in which he characteristically handled relationships with peers, equals, and rivals?"[3]

The answers are important for the light they cast on Freud's theories, the lacunae that exist in the psychoanalytic process, wherein discussion of siblings is rarely emphasized. To this day, Bank and Kahn have received not one letter in response to what I consider to be their extremely provocative article in *The Psychoanalytic Review.*

Sigmund Freud was the firstborn. His mother adored him, her "golden Sigi." When Freud was about ten months old, a brother, Julius, was born. Freud resented Julius. When Julius died at the age of nine months, Freud was left with a "lifelong tendency toward self-reproach." There was another important "sibling" relationship with his nephew John, who was, by odd family marryings, a year older, and who dominated and tyrannized the younger Sigmund. Freud writes, "Until the end of my third year we had been inseparable; we had loved each other and fought each other and, as I have already hinted, this childish relationship has determined all my later feelings . . . with persons my own age."[4]

Says Freud's famous biographer Ernest Jones: "The problem of the family relationships came to a head with the birth of the first sister, Anna, when he was just two and a half years old. How and why had this usurper appeared, with whom [Freud] would have once again to share his mother's warm and previously exclusive love?"[5]

There is a significant parallel between the relationship of young Freud to his sister Anna and Freud's later analysis of his first child patient, Little Hans. In both cases the arrival of a younger baby sister, and rival, is not given full weight.

The case of Little Hans ("The Analysis of a Phobia in a Five-Year-Old Boy") is a classic exposition of the oedipal triangle. Few people think of it in the sibling context. Which is the precise point made by Bank and Kahn: Though Freud discusses the trauma for Little Hans when his sister is born, the sibling triangle is seen as subordinate; used only as a lens for analyzing the more determinative oedipal struggle. Doesn't the case of Little Hans become even more interesting if we recognize that two *equally* important triangles exist, one on top of the other: sibling and oedipal?

Little Hans is three and a half when his sister is born. For the first few days after Hanna's arrival, the boy was, in Freud's own words, "naturally put very much in the background." He is "suddenly" taken ill with a sore throat and "in his fever" declares he doesn't want a little sister. When visitors praise the baby, Hans sneers. Hanna isn't beautiful. She doesn't even have teeth. He develops a great need for mother's attention. He hopes mother will drop Hanna into the bath water and let her drown. He later declares he wishes the baby were dead. A year after the little girl is born, Hans develops a phobia about going outdoors. He is afraid a horse might bite him. Hans also shows a great anxiety about his penis; he constantly wants to be reassured that everyone—father, mother, animals, even a steam engine—has a "widdler."

An obvious seat of this anxiety is mother's warning that if he touches himself she will have a doctor cut it off. Freud diagnoses the boy's anxiety at leaving the house as disguised oedipal fear. The horse will bite and castrate him. And sure enough, in a visit to Freud, Hans makes a simple association between his father and a horse (one with a big penis) that recently frightened him. The classic oedipal explanation is presented to the boy in suitable language and he agrees, yes, he would like to push daddy out of mother's bed and marry her himself.

Father: And then you'd be alone with Mommy. A good boy doesn't wish that sort of thing, though.
Hans: But he may think it.[6]

Freud himself remarks that "the most important influence upon the course of Hans's psychosexual development was the birth of a baby sister." Having thus given primacy to the sibling relationship, Freud proceeds along strictly oedipal lines as if he'd been merely paying lip service to the sibling triangle. I am left wondering why he did not take his own statement more seriously. Would it have meant forsaking, or at least changing the emphasis of, all he had thought and written up to that time?

The oedipal triangle worked through, however, Freud declares the case closed. A complete developmental theory, one that would mesh oedipal and sibling triangles, has been tantalizingly signaled and then abandoned. Neither Freud himself, nor Harry Stack Sullivan, nor Frieda Fromm-Reichmann nor any of the other famous psychodynamically oriented therapists employed sibling theory. To Freud, say Bank and Kahn, "the sibling relationship has no separate life of its own."[7]

Questions remain. Was there a connection between Hans's castration anxiety and the birth of a sibling who, shockingly, did not have a penis? In fact, Hans's anxiety to believe everyone must have a "widdler" is so strong, he convinces himself he can see that even little Hanna has one.

How are we to understand Freud's glossing over of Hans's defensive misperception of reality? Why is the overlapping of sibling and oedipal triangles not expounded upon? "Some six months later," Freud writes, "[Hans] had gotten over his jealousy and his brotherly affection for the baby was only equalled by his sense of superiority over her."[8] Freud himself teaches that the more primitive the emotion, the more enduring the effect. The possibility for ambivalence—that Hans might feel both love and hate—is not opened up.

As a boy, Freud lived in splendid isolation from his brother and sisters, the only one to have his own room. He was the genius of the family and insisted on being treated as such. He dominated everyone, leaving them out of his life to the point where he would usually eat alone, ignoring their existence by reading a book. He was so rivalrous with his fiancée's close attachment to her brother that Freud threatened to call off the engagement. When Freud's sister Anna married that same charming brother-in-law, Freud did not attend the wedding.

Freud's intolerance of rivals continued in his conduct as autocratic head of the psychoanalytic movement. Ferenczi, Jung, Adler, Abraham, were given the role of siblings; each other's rivals, never Freud's. Anyone who disagreed with Freud was expelled. It has been suggested that Melanie Klein's placement of the oedipal triangle in the first year of life was her effort not to be cast out of the Freudian family. In books by and about Freud's adherents, we are repeatedly struck by how personal supposedly intellectual differences became. Disagreement with Freud was somehow shameful, ungrateful, betrayal; a symptom of neurosis in itself. Members of the inner circle would even stop speaking to the offender.

Freud was the master. He still is. But I think Bank and Kahn's point is well taken. Freud's personal history did influence his theories. Not only did he subordinate the sibling issue, but when he did discuss it, he saw it through his own lens: He darkened it.

"A small child does not necessarily love his brothers and sisters: often he obviously does not," wrote Freud. "He hates them as his competitors, and it is a familiar fact that this attitude often persists for long years, till maturity is reached or even later, without interruption."[9]

Brotherly love is denigrated. Commenting on *Totem and Taboo*, Bank and Kahn note that to Freud, "siblings . . . get along only because they are working out oedipal guilt. Brotherly love has no separate life of its own; it could not have occurred without being derived from a collectively shared oedipal conflict."[10] Historically, Freud's phrase *sibling rivalry* has in itself given unhappy bias to subsequent discussion.

Bank and Kahn see five principal themes—all negative—in most of Freud's references to siblings. These are:

1. One dominates, the other is dominated.

2. They have a harmful influence upon each other's development.

3. They compete with one another in a hurtful way. One comes out the loser of the battle for parental resources and love. For both to win is impossible.

4. Eroticism between siblings is normal, yet this erotic bond may be perverse rather than helpful.

5. Siblings feel frequent and continuing underlying rage at one another.[11]

But is rage all we feel?

I have found few therapists able to speak with clinical authority about the wider issues of sibling relationships. Analysts are men and women, subject to fear and repression like the rest of us. They go through years of analysis as part of their training. They come out of the process with backgrounds comparable in learned technique. Each remains the unique product of his personal past.

Some will do their best work with patients who suffer from problems they have faced themselves. Others may be helpful in everything but the one painful area of their lives they have not been able to work through. I have often thought we should choose a therapist as carefully as we do a mate.

Bank and Kahn are pioneers. *The Sibling Bond,* their recent book, to me heralds a new field of science. They push past the single-mindedness of rivalry to explore the full spectrum of emotion between brothers and sisters.

"There is no normative language to define a sibling relationship, to say what it ought to be," Bank tells me. "I think that helps explain the complexity of what goes on between siblings; why we have avoided analyzing it. There is a commandment that you should honor your father and mother. Fifty states in the union have laws against parents abusing children. There are codes and traditions that govern how a parent and child should treat one another. There is nothing like that for siblings. You, Nancy, were probably freer writing about you and your mother than you will be writing about you and your sister."

I smiled at his words last summer, unconvinced. How did he know what I'd gone through in my efforts to see myself in my mother? Bank's words have proven prophetic. After a half dozen false starts on this chapter, my

lower back has once more gone into spasm. My doctor worriedly pre-
scribes a CAT scan.

I am half carried crosstown to a clinic where I am gently rocked in a
giant iron X-ray machine. From another room, a woman's voice orders me
to breathe, not to breathe. While some part of me hopes that the doctor
will prescribe indefinite bed rest and *absolutely no typing*, I think about
the first book I tried to write, a highly autobiographical novel of a woman's search for identity through sexual attachment to one man after another. The mistaken thesis not only flawed the novel; my body recognized
it as a distortion in me. Shoulder inflamed, back in spasm, I ended by
having to stand at a tall bureau to write, my right arm rigidly strapped
across my chest, while I typed with the left.

"Enough," I said, when the orthopedist suggested surgery.

Instead, Bill and I boarded a freighter for Italy. My body was miraculously restored after three weeks in the Roman sun. The book was abandoned as many first novels should be.

There is no sailing away from this book.

"With almost four years invested in jealousy," I say to my friend as we
leave the clinic and she helps me into a taxi, "you would think I was ready
for siblings. Why is my body betraying me? A last-ditch effort on the part
of my unconscious . . ."

". . . maybe warning you to leave this stuff out." And then, as if to
console me, her confession: "When I was four," she says, "they told me
when my mother went to the hospital that she would bring me back a
beautiful doll. Instead, she brought back this *baby!*" Her voice sounds
angry as a four-year-old's.

"What did you feel?"

"One day when I was five, I crawled into her crib, lifted my dress and
peed on her sheets. She was supposed to be toilet trained."

We laugh. "I've never told that story before," she says, blushing. I love
her for telling me. How very human she seems at that moment.

There has of course always been a kind of low-key interest in siblings.
Popular and professional periodicals regularly deal with optimum times to
have a second child, significance of sex and IQ of each child, the structural
meaning of being oldest, middle, youngest or only. Beginning with Adler
in 1928, special emphasis has long been given by such well-known clinicians as Levy and Winnicott to the influence of rivalry on personality.
More recently, Victor Cicirelli, professor of development and aging psychology at Purdue University, has been studying the birth order and spac-
ing of siblings. The amount of interest, the pace of research has intensified. The 1984 Biennial International Conference on Infant Studies,

attended by professionals in psychopathology, biology, behavioral pediatrics, cognition, linguistics and sociology, featured over a dozen papers on sibling issues.

However, the subject is so new that one of the questions asked most often is still unresolved.

Dan Stern: "Everybody says you should wait a few years between children. I'm not sure that's necessarily true. I've seen kids who are as little as fourteen months apart manage to get around the usual sibling rivalries. Until you have a categorical and symbolic sense of self, which doesn't happen until around age two, you're not at the point of development where the birth of a younger sib gets woven into your envy and jealousy system. Of course, both children continue to grow and develop—so the interaction a year or two later will be very different. That is to say, getting born in itself is not the only thing a younger sib can 'do' to elicit envy or jealousy. Accordingly, the age difference at birth may not be so crucial."

On the other hand, here is Hanna Segal: "I never try to influence my own children with my theories . . . but the one thing I tell them is 'Be sure the first child is at least two and a half before you have another.' "

One of the most interesting findings by psychologist Victor Cicirelli is that if siblings have a good relationship early on, it tends to continue throughout life. If siblings have a poor relationship, it may become dormant later. But if a crisis occurs in which they have to help elderly parents, or if there is a disputed will, ancient rivalries resurface. In his work with elderly siblings, Cicirelli's research confirms that "there is a tendency to continue the early relationship throughout life."

Memory is fickle, protectively selective. Who wants to remember the arrival of a sibling, especially if one was very young and the world was turned upside down? By the time someone is old enough to be interviewed, whatever happened in the preverbal years has been largely forgotten. The new researchers begin with the earliest days.

"What is so moving and upsetting for tiny children when they are displaced by the arrival of a new baby is that they have no words to express what they are feeling," says Judy Dunn. "I think that explains why we have ignored the significance of these early years for so long."

Judy Dunn is British, a developmental psychologist. What makes her research on siblings unique is that she observed the whole family in their home, beginning during the mother's pregnancy with the second child. To date, there is no other longitudinal study like it. Her paper was titled "Siblings and Mothers: Developing Relationships Within the Family." She is in town to deliver a follow-up paper at the Biennial International Conference on Infant Studies. She has been generous enough to come to my apartment where I have now lain in bed for eight days, unable to move. As we speak, the tape recorder is on the blanket between us.

"The child's misery is so unfocused," she says. "It is as if they don't know what they are so miserable about. In the middle of a nice game with mother, they burst into tears. Why they are so unhappy is that their life has been destroyed. Even more confusing is that at the same time, many of them adore the baby. Children love babies. It's so unsettling, so painful . . . to feel and yet not to have the faculties to understand your grief."

"Unfocused misery." Sometimes when Judy Dunn is talking about two-year-olds, my mind goes to a man and woman. Instead of mother and child in the nursery, there is a couple having dinner in a little French restaurant. Something is said or not said. Suddenly, things aren't as they were. We feel threatened. What can we say or do with our "unfocused misery"? We light a cigarette and sip our wine; we feel confusedly little. We are regressed.

"After my brother was born, I used to pack my suitcase regularly and walk out the door," says a twenty-seven-year-old woman. "Of course, I always came back. I was four. When my family laughs about it today I say, 'But I wanted you to stop me. That's why I was always leaving.'"

Today when this woman is jealous of her lover, she walks out. She gets as far as the laundry room in the apartment building. She sits on top of the dryer and weeps. She waits.

"You never come after me anymore," she accuses on her return.

"You were angry," he says, "and told me to leave you alone."

"You weren't supposed to believe that," she says despairingly.

Walking out is still her jealous revenge. It's humiliating but it's what she does. What is bewildering to her is that she still does it even though she knows he has learned not to come after her.

When we are little and our parents don't pick up on our "unfocused misery," we punish them. We hurt back as they have hurt us. The enormity of our revenge (in our eyes) is in direct proportion to the pain they caused by loving this interloper, this "other" child. Why don't they respond to our manipulations? Eventually, fear tells us how much we still need them. We crawl out from under the neighbor's bush where we are hiding and take our little suitcase home.

"During our research," says Judy Dunn, "one of the most helpful things was that although the first child was only one and a half to three years old when the second was born, they talked to us a lot. One minute they'd be saying they liked their little sister. The next minute they'd say, 'It was nicer before the baby was born.' There is tremendous warmth and affection between some siblings. Between others, very little. Between most, there is both. Even in families where the first child is most hostile to the baby, if anyone ever said, even with a laugh or teasingly, 'I'm going to take him away,' the first child would leap to the baby's protection. That is why I feel the whole notion of describing what a child feels about the arrival of a brother or sister as jealousy is misleading. I think ambivalence, more than any other word, describes what goes on between siblings. It is a deeply ambivalent business.

"If I were writing a book about jealousy, and siblings," adds Dunn, "I'd want to stress this. To say what a lot of support and solidarity there can be, as well as the horror of displacement."

Psychologists like Dunn, Bank and Kahn take us beyond Freud's limited conception of sibling rivalry. They propose a reassessment of the formation of identity to include not only the parent/child relationship, but the developmental role played by brothers and sisters. This may sound like ordinary common sense. Given the overwhelming weight Freud and his followers assigned parents in our development, it is a radically new path. Perhaps the partners we look for in adult life have as much to do with what we had—or didn't have—with our siblings, as with our parents. Vulnerability to the loss of those partners, our jealousy, may be more determined by loss of parental love to a sibling than by oedipal loss. "Siblings," say Bank and Kahn, "may at times be *more influential* in each other's development than the parents."[12]

"Are you jealous?"

He stops work and looks at me with a flash of anger. He is refinishing an antique refectory table in our dining room. He is thirty years old.

His partner laughs. "Ask Larry about his younger brother."

"I consider myself an only child," Larry says before I can get out a single word. A response I have often heard.

"Who expelled the brother from your family?" I ask. "You or your parents?"

Bang with the hammer. "Me!"

"What's the age difference?"

"Two. He was born premature, kind of sickly. My parents treated him like Dresden china. 'Don't you even touch him!' they told me. He used to get away with murder. Medically speaking, he was fine after the first year. But they still protected him, specially from me. He used to provoke the hell out of me, always punching, pushing me when they weren't looking. I'd feel this anger start up and then I'd cool it. It got so I couldn't express anger at anyone. There was a group at school that used to beat me up. They knew I was an easy target. One day they kicked the hell out of me. I went to my father. 'Stop crying,' he said. 'Be a man!' That did it.

"A week later, the same guys jumped on me on our own front lawn. I grabbed this one guy. I had him by the ears and I was beating his head against the pavement. I just kept pounding him into the pavement and yelling, 'I'll kill you, you motherfucker!' I can still hear my mother calling from the house, 'Now, Larry, don't you use language like that.' I have a really bad temper. I was all-state fullback. I try to curb my anger because I know what I'm capable of. That's why I got into this work. Working with my hands on beautiful things, it's soothing."

So is the woman he chooses to live with. She is gentle, loving, totally monogamous. "What would I do if she weren't?" says Larry. "I'd kill her." He says it with his arm around her, pressing her to his side, love all over his face. He is the one who wanders. He is flagrantly indiscreet. More important than the joy of stolen sex is the satisfaction of putting the woman he loves in a jealous triangle. He was once the pained, passive victim. Now she is. An illustration of one of the truest psychological maxims I know: In adult life, we often actively re-create traumas we once passively suffered. This time, we put ourselves in the victor's role. Revenge.

"Don't touch the baby," his parents had said. "The baby" had made his life miserable. He could have killed the baby for getting all their attention, for secretly taunting him, knowing Larry could not retaliate. The unexpressed rage grew and grew until it was so enormous, he dared not let anyone see it. Until he was fourteen. Then he almost killed another boy. Recently, Larry's landlord threatened on false grounds not to renew his lease. When the police came, Larry had him by the ears and was beating the guy's head against the pavement.

"Why do you think there's been so little work done connecting siblings to later relationships as adults?" I ask Dan Stern. He and Judy Dunn are old colleagues. It was he who introduced me to her, calling her research, "the best in the field."

"I don't know," says Stern. "When you think how awfully important it is, it's hard to understand why people just haven't paid attention. It's been very important in my life."

"The sibling thing?"

"If I didn't understand how my sister fits in, I would never get all the ramifications of my oedipal development. In fact, sibling relations can account for much of what we have traditionally understood to be oedipal conflict. What happened with your sib is always very high on the list. Sometimes the highest."

It's uncanny. After years of neglect and avoidance, a psychologist in England, several others in this country—all suddenly digging around the same sore, sensitive area at the same time. They were unknown to one another until recently. It is as if something in the cosmic ethos starts us looking for clues, answers, when the world can no longer afford the absence of understanding.

The family lies about us like broken pieces of an old-fashioned jigsaw puzzle. Nothing fits the way it used to. Parents no longer are the useful blueprints they have always been. Bewildered children grow up in a time when change occurs at the rate of geometric progression. We can no longer afford to drift into sex, marriage, parenthood. We need the missing pieces—an honest look, a clear picture of our relationship to our brothers and sisters.

There used to be rules most of us lived by: Sex outside of marriage was bad, marriages were till death do us part, and children grew up to respect and become like their parents. Even when the rules were disobeyed, they offered the advantage of firm and known ground from which to push away. What our parents said was what they meant. No longer. If present trends continue, a child born in 1983 has a 40 percent chance of experiencing parental divorce and a 20 percent chance of experiencing a second one.[13] With three out of four divorced men and women marrying again within five years, experts say that by 1990, more people will be part of a second marriage than of a first.[14]

In such tumultuously changing times a sibling may be a child's greatest constant. Siblings have long supported each other's efforts to separate and learn independence from parents. In an era of one-parent families, they will look to one another more than ever.

Bruno Bettelheim: Hansel and Gretel emerge from their adventure with the wicked witch "as more mature children, ready to rely on their own intelligence and initiative to solve life's problems. As dependent children they had been a burden to their parents; on their return . . . they bring home the treasures [of] . . . new-won independence in thought and action, a new self-reliance which is the opposite of the passive dependence which characterized them when they were deserted in the woods."

Stories like Hansel and Gretel, Bettelheim goes on, "direct the child toward transcending his immature dependence on his parents and reaching the next higher stage of development: cherishing also the support of age mates. Cooperating with [age mates and sibs] in meeting life's tasks will eventually have to replace the child's single-minded reliance on his parents only."[15]

"One of the things that make the sibling relationship unique," says Bank, "is the capacity for identification. You have lived with the same parents, shared the same experiences. You can put yourself inside your brother's or sister's skin. You know them better than anyone else does. And they you. There is nobody else in the world, whether you like it or not, who has known the same parents in pretty much the same way. The outside world may see your family as that nice Mr. and Mrs. Jones. The truth is your father is a gambler. Your mother's not a loving person. Only you, your brother and sister know this, and each other."

By confirming each other's perceptions, serving as a reality check, siblings give each other additional help in separation and individuation. An extremely helpful function of the sibling bond, one that is rarely discussed. "It's very hard to know who your parents are all alone," says Dan Stern. "You can figure it out by yourself, but it takes longer and it's harder. Children see the world differently than adults. They are very good at reading what people are about. Kids have their own perspective. It's amazing to watch the whole communication system, the private language that brothers and sisters set up. It's very important."

"Because it allows them to continue this business of staying separate from their parents?"

"It's very reassuring if someone you trust names reality out loud. 'Don't you realize Dad is a drunk?' You didn't really know that. All you knew was that Dad came home and became goofy and fought with your mother. You thought, Well, that's just the way it is."

"Not knowing the truth, always trying to figure out the mystery, keeps you tied," I say. "Something's wrong and you think it's your fault."

"Then your brother or sister, who's just a few years older, says, 'Dad had a mental problem long before you were born.' All of a sudden it falls into place. Nobody else but a sibling could have said that and have it work the same way."

"Do kids have to get along to help one another separate?"

"They don't even have to like each other."

Stern tells a story about a woman from a cold and ungiving family. By all the usual developmental rules, she should have ended badly. Ironically, what saved her was her determination to be as different as possible from her sister. This became one of the foundations for her separation.

"Her older sister," says Stern, "while beautiful, was both passive and frightened. The younger sister used her as an image of everything she *did not* want to be. This constituted a source of strength. The younger sister worked hard and excelled in this and that. She was popular. She schooled herself to be as ambitious as her sister was timid.

"What she did was individuate herself, not so much from the mother as from the sister. What is not usually recognized is that in separation, people often use siblings just the way they use parents. Of course, it's easier for sibs to do this if they are different sexes. In this case, what helped was that the sisters were born at different times in the parents' emotional life together. The sisters sprang from different archeological eras in the family history.

"While it could be said that the younger sister was disadvantaged because she was born when the mother and father were not getting along, she turned even that to her advantage. She made the lines of difference work for her. Okay, she said, I'm going to run my life by a different set of rules, to different tunes. And if you, mother, father and sister, shared some special time before I came along, well, I'm going to be part of something that *you* don't know about. I'm going to make myself so different, *you* are going to be left out. And," concludes Stern, "she did. She used her sister as a negative model to separate and finally outshine them all."

"That helps explain something you see every day," I say. "Brothers and sisters turning out as different as possible from each other."

The most convenient repository for revenge is a sibling. You know their secrets; you know what makes them angry; you know what makes them sad. "You know about their lusts," says Stephen Bank. "You know where they hide their erotic books; you know their bra size; you know they don't like the bathroom door open when they're going. There is a unique system of checks and balances in the sibling relationship. If your brother humiliates you in front of someone, you can make his life miserable."

Envy and rage begin with mother. "When sibling jealousy is extreme," says Hanna Segal, "the usual case is that the child has a fantasy of totally possessing mother. The birth of a new sibling is such a dethronement. The absolute hatred which cannot be directed toward the mother is switched to the sibling." When a sibling touches off hatred, our feelings are not tempered by dependency. We do not rely on our sibling for life. Unshielded and naked fantasies of revenge become temptingly realizable.

Kill thy father or mother? It is a sin. The laws are not so rigid regarding brothers and sisters.

"There are no holds barred between siblings," says Dunn. "It's such a naked relationship. Every irritation is acted out; every provocation is responded to. The kind of things you try and repress with your parents—and even more so with your own children—you don't hide from your siblings. Out it all comes."

A child's revenge on mother is literally kid stuff. We want to punish her, but what can we do? We bite the breast, says Klein, but that is merely spoiling a good thing for ourselves. When the sexual jealousies of the oedipal years arouse terrible desires for revenge, we dare not carry these fantasies into reality. Father is too big. To actualize our feelings for revenge, we need people our own size . . . or smaller.

"Isn't the baby beautiful," the three-year-old boy says to his grandmother. She is holding the new little sister.

"Yes, she is," grandmother agrees.

"See how sweet she sleeps," says the boy

"Like a cherub."

"Let's hurt her."

At three, we haven't learned to edit our thoughts. Misery and love, out it all comes. Unlike the reservoirs of rage at mother that must be buried, anger at our siblings is constantly on tap. We learn to hide our wars from mother. What goes on between us can be kept secret. Mother thinks we get along fine, merely that we argue too much. She doesn't know the secret punishments and reprisals, the emotional bartering and blackmail that goes on behind closed doors.

"Sibs are marvelous for learning about revenge," says Stern. "They are good for learning all the realities of the legal and penal system. They work that way much more than parents do. Sibs are the ones who say to you, 'If you don't do that by Tuesday, I'll make you sorry.' And they do. Sibs are the ones who say, 'Okay, you can use my bike, but it'll cost you a dollar an hour.' What they often give you is a much better indoctrination into daily reality than your parents."

"Supposedly parents give us the adult reality of sane people."

"Sibs treat each other in that irrational way the world really works. I've never known a pair of sibs who didn't go through long periods of extraordinary revenge antics."

"Robertiello says that only children have a harder time with jealousy because they never learned to share. But Judy Dunn referred me to a psychologist at the University of Texas. Toni Falbo did special research on only-child families. She says that 'onlies' learn from grandparents, parents, other family members and friends what people with siblings learn. That it all averages out. She does not think onlies are more prone to jealousy than people who have siblings. Each theory sounds plausible, but they contradict one another."

"It's all so new. We'll have to wait for consensus to form. My own feeling is that onlies grow up with the notion that life should be fair. They believe in fairness. Which is an extraordinary thing to believe in. If you've been through normal sibling experience, you just know that life isn't fair at all."

"You learn from sibs that you can quarrel and make up. If you grow up thinking any harsh word is The End, it seems to me you're left wide open to jealousy."

"But some sibs never fight. That's their bargain. It's too dangerous. If they fought, it would all come out. That they don't like each other, and if they had met on the street, they'd never be friends."

"A lot of couples do the same thing. They don't dare fight."

"For the same reason."

My dentist is filling a cavity. Every six months we meet anew. Every six months he asks me how the book is going. Whatever chapter I may be on, he has an appropriate story to contribute. Today, as I stare speechless into his eyes, he tells me about the time his son put baby brother's tricycle in the driveway—with baby brother on it—so that Dad couldn't miss running him over as he backed out. My eyes roll knowingly. He drills on, smiling for us both at the human condition. The pretty hygienist, standing behind him, tells her own sibling horror story. When she was six months old, her mother took her from the crib for father's morning kiss. Her left leg kept crumbling under her. It was broken. The hygienist's three-year-old brother had not been able to resist the little leg poking through the crib slats. He bent it back upon itself, the wrong way. Justice.

"But my sons are great friends now," says the dentist. "My brother is my best friend," choruses the hygienist.

When we are very little, rivalry between brother and sister is expected. That's how kids are. It is further expected that when we grow up, early intensities of desire to maim and kill will be forgotten. Sometimes they are worked through. Very often, early patterns of relating live on unconsciously. We may become friends. We may not. If we consistently choose love partners who do not wish us well, it does not occur to us that an early sibling enmity might be in the process of reenactment. Good Freudians all, if we look to the past for answers, we think first and only of our parents.

"I remember photographs of them all taken before I was born," a man tells me. "My brother and sister, my mother and father. Summer days on Puget Sound. Right after the war. They seemed so young and innocent. My parents looked really happy then. I remember those pictures and thinking, They look so happy. I didn't like those pictures."

His name is Jeff. Thirty-eight years old, tall, handsome, a very likable man. The look in his eyes is beguiling. Someone put it succinctly: "He looks like he wants to be hugged."

"When my father came home from work," Jeff tells me, "he'd say, 'Where are my loved ones?' And we'd all line up like ducks for kisses. And hugs."

"You were the middle child of five. . . ."

"I always wanted to be the first one so I'd get the best hug and kiss. But I always had to wait. I felt my father gave the first two kids great hugs and kisses and the last two great hugs and kisses. . . ."

I ask how his older brother and sister reacted to his arrival in the family.

"I always felt I was not welcome. They used to tell me that I was not their real brother, that I was adopted. I believed it for years. It troubled me. I kept going to my parents and asking, 'Are you sure I'm yours? Or did they mix me up at the hospital.' I'd ask them to show me my baby bracelet. My brother and sister had baby bracelets. My mother couldn't find mine. Maybe she'd lost it. That confirmed every suspicion my brother and sister had planted in my head. 'See, you're adopted,' they'd say.

"I was told I was an ugly baby. My mother says, 'You looked like a little Japanese. I'd look into that crib and think, Oh, my God, the first two were so pretty. Now I've got an ugly one.' I heard that, over and over, that I was really an unattractive baby. My mother says I grew into my looks by the time I was ten. But even today it's hard for me to believe."

"Was your mother pretty?"

"A beauty. Both my parents have movie-star looks. She knows she's good-looking. So is my younger sister. She looks just like my mother, who calls her 'My *même chose.*' I think my mother's favorite children were my younger sister and my older brother. My father's favorites were my older sister and my younger brother. There was always this feeling: I wasn't enough."

I tell him it's hard to believe that he could feel so left out, an orphan of his own childhood. It isn't just his looks that draw you in and make you want to like him. He emanates sympathy, an empathy right down to the bone. I ask him where he thinks he got his lovable qualities.

"Both my grandmothers were fabulous to me. Of all their grandchildren, they loved me the most. My father has a capacity for a gentle kind of love for everybody. He got it from his mother. My mother doesn't have it at all. Whenever my parents would have one of their jealous fights, my mother would attack my father's mother. She was very competitive with her.

"My way to get approval and love was to do all the chores. My brother would never do his share. I would cover up for him. I would wash the windows, his and mine. I'd go to my grandparents' house and do the windows there too. I wanted someone to say, 'You're a good boy; I love you.' "

He is still that way. He takes care of his friends. He's the one you call at three in the morning if you've lost your key and are locked out. He "washes everyone's windows." He is loved in return. Though he doesn't believe it. To this day he is still sure others are preferred over him. I ask him how this feeling of being forever the one left out affected his adolescence.

"My first girl was the prettiest in school. When she rejected me, I never let that happen again. After her, I never got in a situation where I wasn't in control."

"You picked people who didn't have the kind of power she did."

"They were less beautiful, less popular, less something. Or else they needed someone to push them around. It's an ugly thing to say. After that first one, I used to treat women badly."

In school, he was always class president, captain of the baseball team. "It was very easy for me to have pals."

"Do you think that all the presidencies and captaincies, all the buddies, had anything to do with need for approval? Like the extra chores you did, the extra windows . . . ?"

"It's shocking you said that. Because I think that's totally true. I constantly felt I didn't get the same attention. So I really worked for it."

"So you learned to compete by being nice?"

"My mother came from a really competitive family. She had a twin brother and a younger brother. Her father encouraged the three of them to compete for his love. Whoever was the best at sports, they got to ride in the car with him. But you were the favorite for only that day."

"Your mother's father stirred up competition, and she had a twin. She got a double dose."

"Her mother was a simple, sweet woman who didn't like to go to all the business and social functions my grandfather had to attend. So, from an early age, about eleven, he began to take my mother. She was very attractive and flashy. My mother acted as her father's hostess. Which set up another dose of competition. Between my mother and her mother."

"How do you feel about competing?"

"As a boy, I loved to compete. That was not my choosing at first. It was my mother's. She had us all swimming competitively, beginning when we were very young. Each race we were in, all five of us, I remember whenever I would come up to take a breath, my mother would be screaming, running along the pool after us, telling us where the competitors were. It was like she was in the pool, in the race herself."

"So the competition between you and your brothers and sisters was intense."

"I was convinced my older brother hated me from the moment my mother brought me home from the hospital. He's competitive still. We had a talk and he said, 'I always wished I was like you.' It was like a bolt out of the blue. It explained so much of the horrible things he used to do to me."

"When you all competed against each other, did your mother give you a feeling—like her father had given her—that the one who won also won her love?"

"That's right. That's right! You never could win enough races."

"What's it like when you get together today?"

"We've got over all the old rivalries. We're all good friends. Whenever we get together, we remember how much we hated our parents' fighting. All of us had the same fear. That we'd turn out like our parents, fighting and tearing at whoever we loved or who loved us. Whenever they went out, all the kids knew they'd come home fighting. I knew my parents had this really hot sexual thing going for each other. Somehow it didn't work for them. It made them all the more jealous. They'd do this thing where my father would flirt with the most attractive woman in the room. My mother would flirt with the most attractive man. I think flirtation is a form of competition. After a while they couldn't make up in the bedroom for the damaging things they had said and done to each other. I was sixteen when they got divorced. The funny thing is, only my brothers and sisters remember their fights. For some reason I don't get, I blanked it all out."

When Jeff was nineteen, he had his first homosexual affair. He lives very happily today with a man who has been his business partner and lover for twelve years. They are known as The Best Couple.

"Given your history," I say, "weren't you nervous starting up with Philip? Someone who is so flirtatious?"

"That's just what I fell in love with, that flirtatious business. I just fell in love with him."

"Does the flirting ever cause trouble?"

"Our first two years, we didn't trust each other. We'd both been hurt in previous relationships. We had to work very hard to stay together. You're right about the flirtatiousness. I loved it but at the same time, if he pulled that with someone else, I'd just get crazy. We fought all the time. I would punch out anybody who responded to him, literally just go over and punch him in the face."

"You never punched Philip?"

Jeff looks horrified. "Oh, no, no! That doesn't mean I wasn't on to him. Since he was afraid he was going to be left again, his flirtations were a way of controlling the situation. By making me jealous, he would be making me leave. That way, it would be his choice, not mine."

"A variation on an old theme. 'I'll force you to leave me before you decide to do it yourself.' "

"Finally, I had to say to him, 'Look, you'd better face it. You can make me jealous all you want; I'm not going anywhere.' So that settled that. He can still make me jealous, but I know it doesn't mean he's going to crawl in the sack with somebody. He's only flirting to elicit a response from me. He does it if I'm not giving him enough attention. Which reminds me of something I wanted to say earlier. When people come on to Philip, I'm jealous and mad because he's my lover and they're trying to take him away. But part of me is also mad they are not coming on with me."

"That's envy."

"I thought envy had to do with material goods. . . . But you're right; I envy something he has that I don't have. He's so sure everyone will love him. And they do."

"Are you careful not to arouse jealousy in him?"

"I used to do it because I didn't feel attractive. Arousing jealousy showed I was loved. I realize now it is dirty pool. I feel more secure about myself these days. I don't need to do that so much. When I meet people, it takes a long time to feel I can reach out and touch them. When the barrier is broken, I can't touch them enough. Philip understands that is because I didn't get those hugs when I was a kid. He knows it's not sexual. It's just warmth I want, friendliness. Every once in a while, I'll overdo it. All Philip has to say is, 'You're being very friendly today.' It's a signal. I'm making him uncomfortable."

"You felt you were the runt of the litter," I say, "the unfavored sibling. It would be natural for you to suspect anyone you're attached to would prefer someone else. Competition would lead to a loss. What makes jealousy painful is this certainty you're going to lose."

"We had a rule from the start. Monogamy. If Philip was monogamous, there'd be no contest; I couldn't lose. I always feel that if anyone leaves, it will be him. What I have with Philip is the best I've ever known. But in a way, it's like every time I've been in love . . . a kind of panicky, trembly thing starts up inside of me."

We agree that jealousy isn't always destructive. Sometimes it's a signal, a warning—Look out for the primary relationship. "The gay world is so openly sexual," I say, "if you two can pick up on one another's signals that way, you're ahead of most couples."

"If I see Philip's worried eye on me, first I wonder if it's rational. If he's right, I cut it off right then and there. Even if he's wrong, I'll probably stop because it's torturing him and he's letting me know it."

"If you were to walk in on Philip with someone else . . ."

"Oh, I'd kill him." The reply is matter-of-fact.

"You would kill him."

"I would kill him. I would kill him. He and I set up rules. If either one wanted to change the rules, we'd talk about it first. That would give each of us a choice. But if I found him in bed with someone else, it would be that old business again of feeling that I'm not enough."

"You keep coming back to those words. . . ."

"It's my real problem. Those words sum up my insecurity. I guess it comes from when I was a kid, my father always holding my older sister, my mother preferring the others. . . ."

Just before he leaves, he says the most amazing thing. "Are you sure it is jealousy we've been talking about?"

I ask him to define jealousy.

"I think I confuse it with betrayal."

"The broken promise."

"We've been talking so much about my brothers and sisters. Isn't jealousy strictly involved with someone you love? The first jealousy I ever saw was between my mother and father. I guess that remains my model. And maybe I'm jealous myself because I didn't get enough love from them. But I don't think that what went on between me and my brothers and sisters was important enough to be called jealousy. . . ."

Dr. Stephen Bank: "If eight- and twelve-year-olds could write books on psychology, eighty percent of them would be written about siblings. By the time you're old enough to articulate what you feel about your brothers and sisters, you are seventeen and off to college. You never really worked out how you felt about that other person at the appropriate time. So the emotions and conflicts get 'frozen.' You develop other options, other loyalties. What you had with your siblings no longer seems so significant and yet the capacity to torture in a very intimate, almost unspoken way is still there."

"You make it sound like a marriage," I say.

"In terms of torture, the relationship which is a close second is marriage." He tells me a story of how early sibling revenge gets played out later in marriage.

"A man had a younger brother who always publicly upstaged him. What do you know—he marries a woman who constantly does the same thing. By this time, he has become exquisitely sensitive to the tiniest signs of being upstaged, though he has absolutely no idea where this comes from. He wreaks the revenge on his wife he couldn't on his brother. He humiliates her. He is sexually neglectful. He upstages her by flirting with other women. There is a sort of mafioso message operative at all times, which is 'I'll kill you. I'll kill you softly, but I'll kill you, and nobody will know that I am killing you.' Spouses really know how to torture one another."

"But you have to be careful in marriage," I say. "A spouse can walk out on you. Sibling ties go on forever no matter what you do."

"That's not quite true. The possibilities for revenge with a sibling are endless."

In addition to teaching and practicing therapy, Dr. Bank writes a column in a paper I remember from my own school days. *My Weekly Reader* is for fifth- and sixth-graders. He receives hundreds of letters a year. "How you express your revenge, or do not, depends on how emotionally and psychologically dependent you are on one another. There are so many ways you can be attached. How much freedom do you really have to get away from the sibling? What if your brother is making a fool of you in front of your friends? If he takes what is yours? Your options for revenge, for controlling his behavior, for fighting back, are relative. How mature are you? Are you smart enough to outthink an older brother? Even more important, how much do you need that brother? I mean socially, with your homework, as a buffer with your parents? Siblings can provide many services for one another. They are willing to take enormous amounts of abuse because they know there is a payoff down the road. I think you can see this with spouses too."

By 1990, it is estimated, the majority of "mothers will hold jobs outside the home, including more than half those with children under six. One of four children under ten will be living in a single-parent household and most of their parents will be working, or would be, if they could afford child care."[16] These economic realities, perhaps more than anything else, have brought the sibling issue to the fore. Older siblings have become attachment figures, surrogate mothers and fathers, little caretakers of their littler brothers and sisters. Sometimes the roles are assumed lovingly, sometimes with tremendous resentment. Once again, ambivalence would seem to be the word.

"Freud's pessimistic viewpoint about siblings," write Bank and Kahn, "was articulated within the parent-oriented culture in the Germany of Freud's time. Western culture at the turn of the century focused . . . upon the parents as primary providers of emotional resources. In Freud's day there was little interest in the power of peer groups. Freud lived as do we in a culture that emphasized hierarchy and one-upsmanship while deemphasizing collateral relationships among equals. The power differential between parents and children seemed much more interesting to Freud and his followers than did the warmth and connectedness of the sibling group. . . .

"Freud's clinical milieu did not predispose him towards the study of siblings. Freud treated patients from intact families: he did not, generally, study one-parent families. The nature of one's clinic population defines the boundaries of one's theory. Freud's families, as disturbed as they were, had not experienced the kinds of disruptions that force children into closeness with each other. The typical family structure of Freud's patients involved two parents and two children. The mutual support functions siblings often play in large one-parent families in which the family's division of labor must be shared by all were not likely to be visible in the upper-middle class Viennese families who sought help from Freud. . . . That his ideas about siblings have received such great acceptance attests in part to the continued (and perhaps questionable) agreement that parents rather than siblings exclusively determine psychological development."[17]

Bank and Kahn's point is well illustrated by a story of three siblings. By the time Joan was born, the family pattern was set. For six years there had been only two children. Bobby, the eldest, had long adjusted to sharing mother's attention with sister Liz, who was two years his junior. Markedly different in temperament, Liz was happy to be Bobby's slave. "Hold my feet," he'd order her while he watched TV.

From the moment she was born, Joan was in rivalry with Bobby, an attention-getter just like him. They even look alike. When I interviewed Bobby, his first words were "Joan's always competing with me!"

Joan's first words were "Did he tell you about Bobby Boy Football?"

He had. It was a childhood game he played with Liz. She would try to get from one corner of his bedroom to the other without being tackled. "It was a very physical game," he said laughing, "as close as we got to doctor games." But Joan was never allowed to play Bobby Boy Football.

Today Joan lives with a married man. She has been with him for years. He promises to get a divorce. He never does. Standard oedipal explanation would be that Joan is trying to win the unobtainable married man just as she tried to win father from mother. The truth is that Joan's father was hardly ever around when she was growing up. *The most glamorous man in the house was Bobby.* The operative triangle from which she was most painfully left out was Bobby Boy Football.

Bobby's complaint that Joan always competes with him is nearsighted. She doesn't so much compete *with* him as *for* him.

In a study on children who had been orphaned in the war and brought up together in a nursery, Freud's daughter Anna noted a wide range of emotional exchanges between the children—love, hate, jealousy, rivalry, competition, but also protectiveness, pity, generosity, empathy and understanding.[18] "But Anna Freud specifically said that none of this would have happened in a normal family," says Judy Dunn, "because according to this thinking, what matters in a normal family is what happens between mother and child. Siblings are only important in that they compete for their parents' love.

"What we found in our research made nonsense of this," Dunn continues. "In no way would you say there was just rivalry or jealousy between these two small children. There was a wide span of emotion that clinicians up till now didn't think a one- or two-year-old was capable of feeling. In one family you'd have children bashing each other over the heads and in a different family you'd have these sweet one- and two-year-olds, who ac cording to the textbooks aren't able to understand that people have feelings and intentions. That is absurd. These two-year-olds understand enough about upset—their own and their siblings—to comfort and to control.

"Like everyone else, I had been studying the mother/child dyad as something separate from the other relationships in the family, leaving out what went on between the two siblings. It occurred to me it was absurd to leave these blinkers on. That an awful lot of what is going on in the family has to do not with what happens between mother and child but with what is going on between the two siblings, with what went on between the older child and the mother prior to the younger child's birth, and between each child and the father. How did the arrival of this baby, this tremendous upheaval in the family, affect each of these relationships? And as the baby grew, how did the relationship develop between the two sibs?"

What Dunn found in relation to jealousy was an "extraordinary degree of consistency." The first child's reaction to the arrival of the new baby was a very good predictor of how they would get on during the year that followed. If they got on well or badly when the older child was two and a half, Dunn found in a follow-up visit made when that child was four that while the content of what the children were doing together might be different, the degree of affection or hostility remained the same. A colleague, Robin Stillwell, has just completed additional research on Dunn's families. She found the consistency held. There was a parallel between the way siblings got on with each other when they were little, and how they got on in friendships outside the home four years later.

"Nobody's looked at it," Dunn says. "Empathy, friendship, the various emotions that go into one child's caring about another—it was assumed none of this pertains to little children. That's nonsense."

"This 'extraordinary consistency' you mentioned—does it mean our pattern with siblings may be predictive of adult jealousy?"

She sighs. "That's where you're lucky. As a writer, you can speculate. I am cautious by profession. I can only tell you this: There has been research employing large samples. It shows strong correlation between unhappy sibling relationships in three- and four-year-olds and behavior five years later that could be called antisocial. But the crucial things this early relationship tells us about adult relationships . . . it's just been ignored."

Dunn describes an emotional negotiation, the kind of practical, even sophisticated, empathy that two-year-olds aren't supposed to be capable of. When the new baby cried, the two-year-old would bring a cookie to console her. In various other ways, however, the firstborn showed he was hostile. The mother told Dunn the older child did it only to keep *her* from paying attention to the infant. She boiled it all down to simple rivalry. Dunn saw something much more complex.

"What fascinated me," she says, "was not only that the two-year-old understood what was going on between mother and infant, but how effective he was at doing something about the triangle. He knew what the baby's state was. He knew what would comfort the baby. And he had figured out how he could prevent his mother from paying attention to the baby."

The two-year-old was, in Dunn's words, "capable of both comfort and control."

"It reminds me of how some women act in a jealous situation," I say. "Being less powerful, we become expert manipulators, keeping track of everyone's emotional state. A woman will recognize another woman is her man's type before he does. 'You look like you could use a nice cold drink, Harry. Let's go downstairs to the bar.' In the name of solicitude, she has steered him away from a rival."

Since most of our talks have been about children and mother, I ask Dunn how father fits into her research. "Most fathers are child lovers, rather than baby lovers," she says. "Many don't become really interested until the child is around age three or four. At that point, the child, too, often becomes much more intensely involved, so it's reciprocal. Both mothers and fathers report this is when the *expressed* affection for the father becomes most intense.

"In many families, the moment father does something with the younger child, the older is jealous and looks miserable. My conversations with mothers at this age are like hearing the same tape again and again: 'My husband doesn't see how upsetting it is to the older one when he plays with the baby.' "

"If father were involved from Day One," I ask, "wouldn't it lessen children's jealousies?"

"Absolutely. In families where father had a close relation to the first child before the baby was born, where the feelings were intense and warm, fewer things went wrong when the baby arrived. A good relationship with the father means conflict in the family is far less acute."

"Father is a new prize. They've been through it all a thousand times with mother."

"And he's just not tuned in to the child's world, the child's feelings. Overt jealousy is seen far more clearly in relation to the father than to the mother."

Men are far less able than women to remember or talk about the emotional content of their early sibling relationships, say Bank and Kahn. It is a point of male pride to be cut off from emotions. One can understand that fathers, unfortunately, are not empathic. It is easy to understand that fathers may not see the pain in their children's eyes, but when Dunn says that empathy in children is a new idea to professionals, I grow confused.

Could it be denied that tiny children who weep when a doll is hurt, when a puppy whimpers, are showing empathy? In the very silence parents maintain, children sense anxiety in the house. They put themselves in their parents' place. They join in the parents' silence.

A child's ability to feel and identify with what is going on in someone else is at the heart of a story told by Dr. Berry Brazelton. A doctor noticed that a two-year-old boy who had come with his mother to the doctor's office grunted every time he leaned over. There was no physical reason. The doctor asked the boy's mother if she was pregnant. She said no, but two days later phoned to say she was indeed pregnant. How did the doctor know? "I told her I'd been groping for a reason why the boy would be grunting as he bent over, until I noticed that she did too. This was a completely unconscious response to her new, unrecognized pregnancy. The boy had picked up on and identified the changes in her even before she had recognized them herself."

There is a connection I am trying to make between the capacity for empathy in children and how its moderating effects on sibling rivalry might temper later jealousy. "It just goes against experience and common sense to deny that tiny children are empathic," I say to Dan Stern. "Why has the idea hung in so long?"

"Because kids don't talk."

"It's that simple."

"That's the biggest simple. There's also historical precedent," he adds. "The concept of childhood itself is new, a luxury product of the Industrial Revolution. When so many children died young, parents could not afford to become attached. Before modern medicine, people didn't want to know how much small kids could feel and suffer because of the high infant-mortality rate."

"So the adult desire for control enters," I say.

"Babies terrify people, except their mothers. There is something really scary about babies. Adults need to keep some distance. We don't want to believe anything big or important can be happening inside that little head."

"But people in the caring professions must have known better. . . ."

"Yes, but they didn't have hard evidence. Now we do. New work suggests that true empathy may start as early as thirteen, fourteen months. Martin Hoffman, a psychologist at the University of Michigan, is an expert on empathy in kids. He has a nice example about a twelve-month-old boy. When this baby was upset, he pulled his ear and sucked his thumb.

One day he saw his father was visibly upset. The little boy went to sit in his father's lap. What he did was suck his own thumb and pull his father's ear."

Psychologist Carolyn Zahn-Waxler has also done special research in the area of empathy. "I don't think children are allowed much practice in exhibiting empathy," she says. "If a parent feels depressed, it's upsetting to know how much your sadness can affect a small, vulnerable child. 'Run out and play', mothers say. 'Everything is all right.' The child may know it is not. It is the very mark of his empathy that he does not let his mother know that her sadness makes him feel sad.

"Also, there are competing demands on mother's time," Zahn-Waxler continues. "If a child wants to help when a younger child begins to cry, it is quicker for a busy mother to handle the problem herself. Another reason parents don't reward empathic conduct is if they keep the child's compassion to a minimum, they feel their child won't be taken advantage of in later life."

Can we afford to ignore children's capacity for empathy even as we assign them the role of surrogate parent in our crumbling families? Women's role has changed. Men are making complementary changes. As adults decide to transform their lives, to work outside the home, to divorce, to remarry, or to live together, the child's role changes too. Men and women may choose to live alone. They can take care of themselves. A child has no such choice. Without a father, with a mother who is often absent, one child will seek to find in another what he cannot get from a parent. In Judy Dunn's study, over one third of the younger siblings turned to the elder for comfort when upset.[19]

"After mother," says Dr. Michels, "father is a second chance." The statement resonates with hope. Sadly enough, we've come to the point today where for many a child, it is the sibling who is the second chance.

"In a world as frustrated and discontinuous as ours, a child experiences inconsistency all the time," says Michael Kahn. "Rather than an initial closeness with mother, which is gradually outgrown as the child gets a firm sense of self internalized, what we are getting today are people with disturbances stemming from this choppy quality of their early lives. It has to do with the loss of an ongoing environment, loss of an intimate family setting due to our crazy rate of divorce, separation and disappointments in love. What kids experience now is an uneven rate of development. They are focused to be older than their years. The sibling somehow gets inserted as a proxy attachment figure, someone from whom a younger child can experience some sort of steadiness and contact, object constancy rather than object loss."

Couples plan their children today. "They are not going to have five, they are going to have two," says Kahn. "Time and dual careers dictate that they have them closer together. The sibling relationship gets intensified." Brothers and sisters will define one another's identity more than ever.

The idea that adult jealousies grow not only out of parent/child relationships but out of those of siblings too is persuasive. How much more complex it all becomes when sibling and parent come in the same package.

"When the older sibling is delegated to the role of mother's helper," Kahn continues, "sometimes he takes on the job out of his or her own needs, the older seeking nurturance from the younger. You often see this. They love to cuddle or carry that younger sib around. They love to get that primitive feeling and body contact, the holding, cuddling they missed out on and still need. It looks like a very pretty picture, but when that happens, our research shows, both children experience an ambivalence.

"The younger child is attached, trying to get nurturing from a four-year-old who is struggling for his or her own needs. Even as the older child cuddles the younger, he is angry, disappointed and jealous. Warmth and love are in the air, but he's giving it, not getting it. Both children, unable to articulate the rage that might more appropriately be directed toward the parent, now begin to direct it toward each other."

The kind of nurturance one can get from a sibling is second-rate. While it may save a child's life, it cannot compare to the expressive, differentiated and intelligent caretaking we get from a fully developed adult who loves us. "Therefore," says Stephen Bank, "the supply of love that you receive from a brother or sister is always insufficient."

"You never quite believe in what you are given," I say.

"You would always feel you hadn't gotten quite enough. That leaves you prone to jealousy."

In his therapeutic practice, Dr. Bank makes a point of trying to relate sibling patterns to adult identity. He is willing to go further in this connection than any professional I've interviewed. I think his approach is prophetic. "If you had a powerful attachment to a brother or a sister and it was marked or scarred in a repetitive or compulsive way," he says to me, "your sibling can have an even greater effect on your adult pattern of intimacy than the role your parents played."

Bank tells me the story of a woman who grew up in an upper-middle-class family, "very stuffy." The father was alcoholic, the mother nonmaternal. "As a child," says Banks, "she turned to the next available person to get what she couldn't from her mother. This was an older sister who was five when she was born. The older cuddled and treated the younger like a baby doll. After all, the sister had the same impoverished beginning, the same withholding mother. She was very needy herself. She gave the younger one the nurturance she herself had missed out on. But having grown up in this cold background, the older sister resented what she was giving away.

"There began a history of baby sister seeking out older sister for warmth. The older sister would give it, but also expressed her resentment by doing some absolutely vicious things. She would take the little girl into strange neighborhoods and abandon her there. That was at ages three and eight.

"Go up one more developmental level, ages ten and fifteen. The younger sister is molested by a father in a household where she is baby-sitting. The older sister calls her a whore. Some years later, at the younger sister's wedding, the older sister flies across the country to attend. First, she gets her sister drunk the night before her wedding. Though she had promised to come help her get dressed the next morning, she doesn't turn up. Finally, at the wedding itself, she appears in this provocative sexy dress, absolutely upstaging the bride. In her late twenties, the younger sister lands in the hospital with a life-threatening illness. What she gets from the older is a one-line note: 'Hope this finds you feeling better.'

"Believe it or not, all her life the younger felt that her sister was the most wonderful person in the world. She required intensive therapy to help her get the blinders off. Therapy helped the angry sibling to define just who she was really mad at."

"Doesn't Klein enter here?" I say. "A defense against envy of the powerful figure is idealization."

"Very definitely. Instead of hating the figure she could not afford to lose, she idealized her—'the most wonderful sister on earth.' Traditional analysts have been dealing with these mechanisms on a parent/child basis. If in your life, your brother or sister was a dominant figure, you have to see them as they truly are. In therapy, the murderous rage at her sister finally came out."

I ask Bank if he knew what kind of husband the younger sister chose.

"The attachment was very similar to what she'd had with her sister. The basic template inside her head predisposed her to pick somebody who would be a little fulfilling but essentially frustrating. Who would treat her kind of good but mostly bad. When the sisters were nine and four, the mother gave a piece of string to the older. She tied it to the younger."

"You mean like a leash?"

"What the string did was give the older sister the total control the mother had resigned. The girl could only go a certain distance. The sister would give a little tug and she'd come bounding back. This became a metaphor for every intimate relationship. There was no tangible string, but she had a sense that she was always on the other person's tether. She anticipated having to look for how far she could go with each man. She was always afraid, looking over her shoulder, lest she go too far and be pulled viciously back. There was no sense of autonomy."

"No sense of self . . ."

"The door open to jealousy."

"Freudian analysis would say she picked a cold man and tried to make him into the loving mother she never had," I say.

"Don't put it all on mother," Bank replies. "The most powerful attachment was this sister who filled the vacuum left by the mother. The woman found someone who would treat her as coldly as mother or as ambivalently as her sister. The sister was more available than mother. She was also a more interesting model of how one could be."

"Did ideas of revenge enter?" I ask.

"Not only did they enter, but they were very useful to her. After she became aware of her rage, and she had identified the older sister's pattern of pretended love, she retaliated. She refused to attend her sister's daughter's graduation in which the daughter was class valedictorian. That may not sound like a big deal, but it was the first step in getting even."

"Paying the sister back."

"And that made her feel terrific. It did not make her feel like a grown-up, it did not make her feel like a whole person—but it was a first attempt to use power, the power of the payback. I don't recommend revenge, but I have found that sometimes it is an important step that people need in gathering up their dignity. First and foremost, revenge is a function of justice. It helps overcome feelings of inadequacy and inferiority."

"For some people, the desire for revenge is simultaneous with the first whiff of jealousy. . . ."

"It's the humiliation," says Bank. "Many people have low thresholds for humiliation. If your sibling wants to hurt you, you can believe that no one will know how to do it better. It will be done and be done in a way that is exquisite. It's the experience of having your pants taken off in public, your cherished ideals, your fondest picture of yourself degraded in front of others, or in front of yourself. No human being can handle the experience of humiliation—male or female. Being castrated, neutered, laughed at, really hurt and assailed makes people come to certain life decisions. 'Never again will I ever let this happen to me.' "

During the various drafts of this chapter, I've had to return to bed; back spasms. Ideas come swimming up. I've been thinking of when I was young, when I was eleven. Something Stern said during our last interview about adolescence . . .

"It does its own magical work," he'd said. "It adds something that was never there before. It reorganizes old experiences in sexual terms."

When I was eleven, I fell in love with my best friend's brother. Having nothing better to do one hot night, he'd kissed me. How to describe that kiss? My first. More than that. I'd never been held by a man, never been caressed. I moved into my friend's house. To be near him, to be available instantly should he desire to repeat what had happened. My mother was used to my extended overnights in homes where there was a complete family: daddy, mother, children. One day she telephoned and mentioned to my friend's mother that my sister was sitting home alone. To my horror, my sister was invited to join us in the country.

That afternoon while Molly and I swung from the trees in our Girl Scout shorts, my sister was parked down the road, half hidden by Spanish moss. In the same car where I'd been kissed. In the same arms that had held me. The only arms, the only man, who'd ever loved me. She'd taken him away.

It was dark when they reappeared. She was wearing his jacket. They were holding hands. While the hushpuppies boiled in the cauldron of fat and the grown-ups stood around the big wooden table laughing and swilling down sweet oysters picked fresh that day from the Johns Island oyster beds, again and again I swallowed my confusion and pain. There was nowhere to run, nothing to do, no one to whom I could explain my anger. No place to hide my humiliation.

My sister was a sweet child. She meant me no malice, not in that eleventh year, not ever. The anger between us was one-sided. When I was little and she tried to hold me, I'd push her away. When we played games, I had to win. I'd cheat. Losing meant little to her. If I didn't win, I'd start a fight. I was the younger, but I was the meaner. I'd beat her up. I was the competitive one, the winner. Until adolescence. When she bloomed into an utterly beautiful creature. It was a competition I could not win.

Of course I've left my sister out. Left her out of my life as far back as I can remember, pretending she had nothing to do with me, with who I became and what I refuse ever to let happen again.

I had lost my father to her. I lost my first love to her. Twenty years later, it was what I felt when Jack took those two people into the bedroom and closed the door. I'd lost to my sister again.

Dunn: "The sibling is the longest relationship in one's life. It goes on until you die and no other relationship does."

Bank: "Those transactions we had with our brothers and sisters remain unconscious because whatever you're transacting with a sister or brother who is only a year or two age difference from you, it's all preverbal. It's all without language, without cognition. Whatever you went through with your parents, you might not have had words, but they did. When you're talking about children, you're talking about symbolic, nonverbal, gut-level, primitive interactions with no language to accompany it. Therefore, you get these preverbal hooks lodged in your gut; the way your sister smelled, the way she bit you."

Unable to sit at the typewriter, I have taken to writing on an enormous blackboard propped up beside my bed. I want to make a diagram of how emotions feed from birth into adult jealousy. But their overlapped, embedded quality defies any linear diagram I can trace with chalk. Only in my mind's eye can I make sense out of the list, twisting and turning the emotions one upon the other into a giant DNA-like braid. Sometimes I stack triangles one on top of the other, the oedipal on top of the sibling. It all begins so early. The possibilities for richness and complexity in a family increase geometrically when you go from one child to two. Even more when there are three. The chances for love increase. So do the chances for loss.

I can see where my preoccupation with the notion of empathy has been leading. It is at the heart of the vital lesson in Dunn's work: There is a fount of emotion that can be tapped to meliorate rivalry. If a child's capacity for compassionate understanding is encouraged early enough, he learns significant alternatives to mindless and automatic fighting and competition. Empathy can moderate jealousy.

"Dunn's work is wonderful," says Stephen Bank. "She was the first to blueprint with hard data the age at which empathy and caring start." Though Bank and Kahn's work was published about the same time as Dunn's, envy doesn't occur to Bank. It is as if he profits from what he teaches: He doesn't see her as a rival but as an ally. Dunn's findings parallel his own. He feels reinforced and grateful.

"The implication in her work is that at two and a half years a sibling can be taught that he can make discriminations. Not only about his own feelings, but about those of someone else. In Dunn's study, when mothers took time to communicate that the new baby was not an alien and hostile intruder, but a helpless little human being with feelings and fears just like his own, the older child could understand these ideas and act on them.

"Another determining factor was how mother treated the older child when the baby was present, the amount she included the elder as a significant, helpful, thoughtful caretaker. So he never felt left out. You can hear his eagerness in conversations Dunn recorded in the home. He speaks of the newcomer in warm terms. When Dunn returned months later, lo and behold, a spirit of charity prevailed. One of life's great truths had been learned: It is better to give than to receive. No child believes that unless he's lived through it himself.

"However, when parents were too burdened with their own personal problems, when they didn't take time to prepare the older child—if they simply discounted his feelings and ability to understand—Dunn found that sibling rivalry was much more intense. The rivalry became imprinted. What is important in her work is the implication of where revenge, anger and jealousy start."

Rivalry is natural. The intention is not to try to eliminate it but to teach a child a message that is best taken in early in life: That brothers and sisters need not deal with each other solely in terms of power: What are you taking away from me? What can I grab back from you?

The notion that we can feel love and hate at the same time is intimacy's first law. It is best learned in childhood with our first peers, our brothers and sisters. If we do not take in love's ambivalence then, it is almost impossible to come to terms with it later. When we feel Kleinian fury at the power of the beloved, we do not recognize it as the other face of love. We do not feel guilty for hating someone who loves us.

"And at that point," I say to Robertiello, "envy becomes destructive, right?"

He is glum. His voice is hardly resonant at the best of times. Today he is almost inaudible, his words cut off and distant. Then I remember. He and Susan are leaving in two days for the Caribbean. Never mind that I'm the one who is being left. When separation is in the air, no one suffers more than he. He's mumbling something about a patient's dream of destroying his newborn child.

"What?" I say.

"This guy's in his late twenties," he speaks up. "His new wife just had a baby. He had a dream about a woman who had a lot of baby fat, 'a kind of baby woman' he called her in free association. She had breasts on the front but also breasts on her buttocks. All four of the breasts were burned, scarred; terribly burned. The symbols in the dream are barely disguised. His new child is a baby daughter. The dream was a combination of destroying the baby and his wife—the woman who had baby fat on her. It wasn't just a dream of rivalry with his baby, but also a putdown of his wife by sticking breasts on her buttocks."

"It sounds so Kleinian," I say. "He's afraid the breast will be taken from him and given to the baby. He destroys the breast. But it's also a sibling rivalry dream. . . ."

"He had a lot of rivalry with his siblings. When he was little, he felt they got all the good stuff from his parents."

"It's so crazy," I say. "In the dream, he treats his own child as a sibling."

"Men with pregnant wives have these dreams about destroying the baby all the time. It scares the hell out of them. It's so standard. The baby is almost always perceived on some level as a sibling rival."

"Because she is carrying the child, a woman isn't going to see the unborn baby that way."

"She may very well later. When she sees the child involved with the father. My wife saw our daughter as a rival. She thought I loved the little girl more than I loved her. Which, in fact, I did."

"I once told a friend one of the reasons I hadn't become a mother was I didn't want to share Bill with another child. '*Another* child?' she said."

"Catching you up on your Freudian slip," he laughs. "That shows you'd be rivalrous with your own child. I think more women are than is commonly recognized. When a mother overpossesses a child, she isn't criticized. She's a 'good mother.' What she may be doing is locking the child away from the father. Keeping the child her possession eliminates the child as a rival."

"When a woman gives birth, the husband sees her as more maternal than wifely. He's competing with the child for the mother."

"A man might be jealous of his son for taking mama away, yes. But men can be rivalrous whether the child is a daughter or a son. For instance, the guy whose dream I told you, he had a little daughter. Instead of seeing her as a love object for himself, he immediately saw her as a rival who was going to take away his wife-mother."

"What about when your son was born?"

"My wife was crazy about him. Having a son was a thrill to me, my masculinity confirmed. He was a chip off the old block. At the same time, I was consciously furious at my wife's attention to him. I was ready to kill them both." He pauses. "Which is exactly what I feel when I go home and Susan is on the phone to her sister. I'm furious. I want her to hang up and pay attention to me."

"Jealousy does have a special meaning to you. You're not necessarily jealous of someone your woman sleeps with. You *are* jealous of people who invade your special territory. You could lose Susan to her sister."

"And that's so central to what jealousy is all about. You are jealous of people who are a threat to the 'special something' between you. Susan's sister happens to be like my sister. I mean, she's beautiful, vivacious, charming. And, like my sister, she's dying."

"You once said your father was the same way. If he came upon your mother talking on the phone to her sister, he became insanely jealous. He made her hang up."

"Susan's sister really cares about her in a way I don't think I'm capable of. She can get into Susan's head in a way that invades my special territory. I've promised Susan that I would always be there for her, and while I mean it at the time, I know the sister means it for always. I think the reason I can't allow myself to love Susan as intensely as I'd like has something to do with my sister."

"You're afraid Susan will leave you."

"She'll die and leave me."

"Like your sister. It's always women you're jealous of, never men."

"That's not true. It's the sibling I'm jealous of, either sex. The genuine feeling people have for others in their family. For instance, I didn't give a damn when my second wife came on with my best friends. But once she said something flirty to my brother. I was depressed for three days. I could hardly get out of bed."

"Sartre once said that he didn't much care if the woman with whom he was having an affair was also seeing someone else. The essential was that he should come first. Why does that have the same ring to me as what you just said about you and your brother?"

"You are associating to the idea of siblings being rivals for mother's attention. What Sartre might be saying is that he is resigned to the fact that the woman-mother might have other sons. What he demands is that she love him most. I wanted that myself, but I never got it."

"How old were you when your brother was born?"

"Nine and a half. I remember seeing my mother nurse him. That's when I pretended to run away from home. I hid in the closet and listened to them all going crazy with worry. How I loved it. They really did care. I wanted revenge for being displaced in my mother's affections."

"What did you mean when you said not allowing yourself to love Susan has something to do with your sister?"

"Thirteen years ago when my analyst took me to my sister's grave, all that came out was rage and anger. Trying to figure out why I can't really love Susan got me beyond that, put me in touch for the first time with my real love for my sister. Not just the rage, but the loving bond between us. My sister aced me out of the family. She did a bad thing to me. At the same time, she was the only loving person in my entire childhood. To maintain a relationship, you have to deal realistically with dichotomy and ambivalence. My number is just the opposite. I idealize the woman."

"That protects you from knowing how envious you are of the power she has over you, how much you need her. There's no dichotomy or ambivalence in any of your affairs or marriages. But no woman's perfect. When she lets you down, you go straight from seeing her as a perfect goddess to seeing her as useless. You never get into your envy of women. You never feel guilty for being envious and angry at people who love you. When you're through, you just dump her and get a new one. You can't live without a woman."

"I need someone to affirm me, not just sexually but in my total existence. If your siblings were preferred to you—as mine were, God knows—your self-esteem is likely to be tenuous. You have a tremendous need all your life long for someone to make up for that, to see you as perfect. A positive reflector. I think a reason for jealousy is fear of loss of the other person as that reflector.

"Susan is my positive reflector. She makes me feel I'm the most wonderful person on earth. In my mind, she does that only because of what I give her. But I know what I give is for selfish reasons. The love and approval she gets from her family are given generously, without ulterior motives. So whenever she talks to them, I'm angry and terrified she's going to realize my love is narrow and mean—ungenuine—compared to theirs."

"Don't be so hard on yourself," I say. "From everything you've told me, it's not all manipulation. The dialogue you set up with a woman resembles the dyad of mother and child. She's getting a very intense relation."

"Without it I feel emptiness."

"But you're angry with every woman because she might abandon you as your mother did, or die on you as your sister did. What kind of prospects have you for a great relationship?"

"The answer is none at all! I've never made it with anyone in a really good way, that lasted. That's obvious."

"Maybe one reason is women are interchangeable for you."

"Absolutely."

"It's not the specific woman, it's the role she plays. . . ."

"Absolutely."

"You don't really . . ."

"I don't really love them."

A naked statement. I am embarrassed. He is not. He goes on. "I can put on a great show of loving someone. Pseudo-intimacy, pseudo-sexuality, pseudo-adoration, worship, idealization . . . I can give women these things better than any man. That's why I'm not jealous of other men. When it comes to genuine feelings of loyalty, closeness—the way families feel—I'd be crazy if I ranked myself high in any of those. I can't give loyalty, deep-down caring. But Susan's sister could. She gives her the real McCoy."

"Have you ever envied other men for being able to love?"

"I think other men are as incapable of real love as I am. I don't think men really love women. Understand? But relatives love women; thei mothers, their sisters, their brothers do. And I'm not so sure a woman can love a man. Not nowadays. There's too much conflict and anger, too much mistrust and vying for position. Too much envy."

"Sometimes I think you idealize women so you can yank it all away. Revenge."

"I need their love. But I do need the revenge too. I want to get back at women for what my mother did to me. First she dropped me for my sister and then for my brother. He's her favorite to this day. I'm still jealous of the attention he gets from her. I don't love her and she doesn't love me. There isn't even a pretense on either side. But between her and my brother there is love both ways."

"Consciously you need women's love. Behind that, you want to do them in."

"To do to them what Mama did to me. First when my sister was born, then with my brother. Make them feel like they're in heaven, in the Garden of Eden, and then suddenly plunge them into hell."

"What are you saying, Richard?" I exclaim. "Your mother never gave you any love! That's the one thing you've always told me."

"She didn't? Of course she didn't. I know that."

I realize how pat this sounds. But sometimes that is just how things happen. With nothing more than a shake of his head, he proceeds to reinterpret his life.

"Since my mother never gave me love, she can't be the one who yanks it away. It was my sister who loved me. My pattern of getting love from women and then inflicting revenge on them isn't based on my mother . . ."

". . . but on your sister!"

"She's the only one who ever gave me love. Offered all the good stuff and then died. That set the pattern. My revenge is to fulfill every one of a woman's wishes and then yank it all away."

"You never realized that your sister was more important than your mother?"

"I was acting it out rather than analyzing it. I told you, I never focused on my sister either in my life or in my analysis until late. Why should I examine it? I wasn't consciously frustrated. I was getting a helluva lot of gratification acting out my revenge fantasies against my sister. Seducing women and then abandoning them was turning the tables on what my sister did to me."

"By acting out repressed emotions, you kept the original stuff buried. . . ."

"And thus maintained the repression. Simple classic Freudian stuff and I missed it. I never questioned what it meant: that I had to beat out every woman. Tennis, Botticelli, gin rummy, in every competitive game, I beat the hell out of them. Some of them sensed I was getting off on it and didn't like it. They knew I wasn't just playing Parcheesi. I just laughed at them. I didn't want to change."

"You were winning."

"That business of attaching women to me and then abandoning them reversed what happened between me and my sister."

"I remember when you left your wife. All the life went out of you. You don't leave. You die on people."

"What my sister did to me."

Silence.

I start the conversation again a few keys down the emotional scale. "How competitive are you with Susan?"

"The competition is intense. More sibling than maternal. Which confirms what we've been saying. I was never competitive with my mother. I certainly was with my sister. And I am with Susan. The problem is she's one of the best tennis players I know. That gets us into very heavy stuff."

"What'll you do if she beats you?"

"I'm really apprehensive. We'll be staying at a beach and tennis club. When she's playing her best, she can beat me. I don't like that. It's not something I look forward to. It's like my balls or my life or whatever is on the line. I've avoided all that several times by just volleying with her rather than playing for points."

"You've got a huge edge on her professionally. . . ."

"I have to have the edge in *every* way. Because with my siblings, I never thought I could win. I never thought I had anything that could make Mama love me more than them. I want to love her so badly."

Who is he talking about? His mother? Then I realize.

"I'm afraid," he says, "that Susan will value me less than her sister. I could lose out to her sister. I could lose out to her mother because . . ."

I sit forward to hear what he says.

". . . because they really care about her. I'm not a very loving person."

CHAPTER ELEVEN

Gratitude and Love

"*D*id you beat him in tennis?" I ask Susan.

She and I are sitting in the apartment she shares with Robertiello. Hanna Segal is in town from London. In an hour and a half (two psycho-analytic sessions), the three of us are going to hear her lecture. Susan and I have met before, but never without him. She is tan and pretty from their vacation in the Caribbean. He knows we are talking about him.

"We just rallied." She pauses, looks across the room as if for explana-tion. There is none. "We didn't play for points."

"You played tennis every day and no one won or lost?"

"We're both so competitive," she says. "I get so anxious playing against Dick, I'm a wreck."

"You want to beat him?"

"I do and I don't. I'm a better player so I should. I often beat people who can beat him."

"But you don't beat him."

"It isn't just psychological. His game is hard to counter. I do better against someone who plays more aggressively."

"He's always telling me he's a killer on the court. . . ."

"He plays defensively. He doesn't take chances that can lose the point. I play more aggressively—and I make more mistakes."

"Tennis is so important to him," I say. "He tells me it's where he works off his oedipal rages."

"I have played him and won, but more often he wins. Even when we just rally, we're both secretly counting points. . . . It's ridiculous."

"Why do you think you lose?"

"What goes through my mind is, Am I losing because I'm afraid of being rejected if I win? Am I losing because . . . Who's going to be destroyed? Him? Me? The relationship . . . ?"

We talk about her work. She is studying at an analytic institute and has a private practice. She was just beginning when they met. Do I understand how much she owes him? Her tone is urgent. Yes, I understand very well. Then, knowing what I want to hear, she switches the subject to her sister. Beginning at the beginning:

"I'm thirty-eight," she says. "I grew up in Arlington, Virginia. Both my parents are alive and still married. I had a sister who recently died. She was sixteen months younger than me. When I heard my voice just then on your machine, it sounded so much like hers that it was eerie."

"You were close?"

"Very. And looked alike and talked alike."

"Affectionate?"

"Yes. Very. But also competitive. Most of the envy and jealousy in my life are connected to my sister."

I know Susan has studied Klein. I'd once borrowed her copy of *Envy and Gratitude*. Handing it to me, Robertiello had warned against losing it. The pages were heavily annotated in the margins.

"Was the rivalry open?" I ask.

"On both parts. She may have been more competitive. I was certainly more envious. She was vivacious, prettier. In adolescence she was more popular, had more dates. At *my* senior prom she arrived with the handsomest guy in school. I didn't have any date at all until the last minute. Earlier on though, I think I envied her relationship with our mother. She and my mother were birds of a feather."

"You felt something special between them that left you out?"

"Always. She was my mother's daughter, and later she followed my mother's pattern. That is, she grew up, married, had children. . . ."

"You chose a career."

"In temperament I was more like my father. He was not as outgoing as my mother and sister. He was more introspective, reflective."

"You were your daddy's girl."

"He loved me but it didn't carry the same weight as the relationship my sister had with my mother. I envied those qualities that gave her that special *in.*"

"Did you feel guilty when your sister became ill?"

"And how. I would dream about when we were kids almost every night. There were also terrible dreams about her dying. My mother in a big black limousine driving to the cemetery, and me . . . standing on the curb . . . I'm not allowed to be with her. Dreams that go back to murderous feelings I had when we were little, when she was born. . . . As for her, her one goal was to beat me in tennis."

"Tennis is an emotional subject with you."

"It was very big in our family. We were all very competitive, playing in country-club and state tournaments. Sports were more important than scholastic achievement or culture or anything else."

"Didn't you say your father was intellectual?"

"Yes, but tennis was very important to my mother."

"Why didn't you latch onto your father, make him your ally?"

"He wasn't around enough. Like most fathers. He played Saturday golf."

"According to Klein, the person you'd be envious of wouldn't be your sister. It would be your mother."

"Yes, but I couldn't afford to show envy of her. I needed her too much."

"She had all the power a mother has. In your case, she also had the power to pick you over your sister. . . ."

"And she didn't!"

"It's less threatening to deny envy of the mother and to displace those murderous feelings onto a sister."

Susan nods. "I'm in a similar position with Dick. I'm dependent on him. Not only emotionally, but for all the help he gives me in my career. I see him as more powerful, with more professional status, more money, experience and prestige."

It used to be that women wanted their men to be more powerful. The woman lived through the man and assimilated his status. Envy got buried behind the facade of the little woman and the big man. Susan wants Robertiello to be wiser, more powerful than she. It is the model she grew up with. She also wants to be as successful as he; the model on the cover of today's women's magazines. So far it's a standoff. On the tennis court she cannot allow herself either to win or to lose.

"When we first met," says Susan, "I thought Richard was perfect. I still admire him professionally more than anyone. He is more in touch with the unconscious than any other teacher or supervisor I've had. I have learned more from him in the last three years than in any other period in my life. I love him; I admire him. I envy him too."

When Richard and Susan met and fell in love, they idealized one another, as do we all. One of the sources of magic in the "in love" stage is that there is no envy. We are as one and therefore the power of the beloved is ours. Romantic love cannot last. Time reveals our prince/princess to be imperfect. The primitive expectations aroused by first love remain unsatisfied. The beloved is withholding what he could give us, if he chose to. Resentment and envy destroy the mutual idealization.

Susan's admiration was less ambivalent before she loved Richard. Before, as she says, she became emotionally dependent on him. It gave him so much power over her life. How can she not envy him?

"Someone like Richard . . . four marriages, lots of women," I say. "He has to win in tennis. He has to win in love. Can you live with his streetcar philosophy, that if you lose one woman another will be along in five minutes?"

"In the beginning, I asked him a million questions about his previous women. It was important for me to outdo them, to feel better than they were. I wanted to know what he liked about them, why they broke up. I was in competition with the entire female pantheon from his past. I've even been jealous of you."

"I can understand that."

"You and Dick work together so well. You have an intellectual rapport, a kind of easy companionship that makes me jealous. Or am I talking about envy?"

"A jealous situation, with all kinds of envious components flying around inside . . . envy of me, envy of him."

"Also, you've known him longer . . . so what you have with him may be more substantial. I ask myself, Are you more intelligent? Are your conversations with Dick on a deeper level? Maybe there is jealousy, but I think the envy is more powerful."

I read Susan something I had brought to show Robertiello. It's from the new Doris Lessing book:

> Envy. Jealousy and envy, I've always used them interchangeably. A funny thing: once a child would have been taught all this, the seven deadly sins, but in our charming times a middle-aged woman has to look up envy in a dictionary. Well, Phyllis is not jealous, and I don't believe she ever was. It was not the closeness and friendship of Joyce and me she wanted, but the position of power. Phyllis is envious.[1]

"The more I write about jealousy, the more I come to believe envy is the heart of it. Envy feeds jealousy and makes it all the more bitter. . . ."

"And all the more irrational! You are very important to Richard. I should be glad that he has such a good friend as you. He doesn't make friends easily. At the same time, how can I not resent you?"

How smoothly Susan's speech moves from love to resentment and back again. Would that life followed suit . . . that arguments and rages didn't end everything. Or feel as if they might. "Why do you think every time we argue it's The End?" says Bill. It is true. The first angry sentence is not yet completed and mentally I've begun to pack my bag. I'll be the first out the door. We are bound to hate the ones we love. Who could hurt us more? The trick is to be able to express the hate and then return to love; for the memory of past happiness to be so deeply embedded that regaining and restoring it is worth any pain.

"What happened when Richard met your sister?"

"I was convinced he would like her more than me. That he would find her more attractive. This was before she got sick. I felt if she had been the least flirtatious, he would leave me and go off with her. It was the most jealous I have ever been."

Susan's mother had preferred the sister. Why wouldn't Richard? How ironic that Richard and Susan both suffer from sibling rivalry. Successful, attractive men can take Susan to dinner. It gives Richard no qualms at all. The only rival he fears is someone within Susan's family. Consciously or not, knowing the intensity of the bond with his sister, he does not believe his love could win against Susan's feeling for her sister. The only time he was jealous was when Susan's sister's illness took her away from his side.

"Do you feel you need Richard more than he needs you?"

"It feels to me like I am more dependent on him than he is on me. With men in the past, I used to call it fear of abandonment, jealousy. But with this dependency on Richard comes a lot of envy. I could 'kill' him, thinking that he could leave me tomorrow and replace me, and that it would be harder for me to replace him."

Susan has just described herself in terms better suited to an infant. "I am dependent on him and he's not dependent on me." These are her feelings. The facts are different. "Richard has vulnerabilities," she once told me. "Being in an intimate relationship with him for three years, I can see he doesn't have the inner resources, the certainty of self, that I think I have." She also knows she is ". . . the sum total of his emotional life. . . . When he is with me, I feel I am his sole source of love." A powerful position but one Susan's self-devaluation cannot take in.

The need to protect herself from destructive envy of Richard is stronger than her need to believe in the real power she has in the relationship. She puts herself in the position of a child. In love with a man, she acts as she once did in the arms of a woman.

Envy is getting in the way of love. We get past envy and develop the capacity for love in the first year of life. Can the process be learned in Susan's thirty-eighth year, in Robertiello's sixtieth?

"There are things I have in mind to say," says Susan, in a formal voice that says she is speaking for the record. "May I? Dick is very generous in our relationship, very giving in material ways. But I'm not sure he is giving from a sense of fullness within himself. The first trip he took me on, to Italy, every place we went was like a gift in which he showed me something that was beautiful, and very special to him. The pleasure is just being with him, but I don't think he realizes that."

"He doesn't feel he is enough."

"All he really has to do is to be who he is." Susan sighs. "He has given me a lot. Sometimes though, when he gives and gives, I find myself slipping into a certain way of thinking: 'Don't think all this generosity is making me happy, because I'm really more anxious than ever before in my life!' "

"The more he gives, the more terrible it would be if he took it away. . . ." The more he gives, the more it emphasizes her dependence on him.

"Am I biting the hand that feeds me?" Susan asks almost rhetorically. "I may be ungrateful out of envy, that he can give so much. Materially, there's little I can do for him in return. I can go to the Xerox machine for him or get stamps from the post office. But I can't give, at least not in the same way."

In her eyes, the relationship is unequal. The inequality allows Richard to sleep at night. In the end it makes him angry. He feels unnurtured by these women he has turned into dependent children. Robertiello wants to be able to love Susan. To do so, he will have to let go some of his ascendency and control. In choosing Susan, he has made a good first step; she is an ambitious, competitive woman. He is also taking a risk.

"You want what he has," I say. "What if you succeed?"

"That is what frightens me. I took him to a party recently. The one person there he established a rapport with . . . of every woman at the party, she was the most vulnerable, the least competitive."

"Were you jealous?"

"I don't want to have to compete with someone in vulnerability. Do I have to keep myself small to keep his love? He encourages me, pushes me to succeed, to be independent. But at the same time . . . it's as though he's attracted only to women he can't possibly envy. We started out really well. There seemed to be more of a balance. In the last year we've had some pretty bad fights and have come close to breaking up. Sometimes I feel he wants a completely independent, autonomous, 'grown-up' woman —who is completely dependent on him."

When we meet and fall in love we are in balance. Then, as Susan says, reality enters. At least once a day, Robertiello used to say to her, "Promise you'll never leave me." It was the talisman of her power. He doesn't say it anymore. His power continues. She misses hers.

"He fears being left just as much as I do," Susan says. "But he deals with separation anxiety in a different way. He leaves first. I think he does it so that he can't be left."

When I asked Richard what he loved most in Susan, his answer was unhesitating. "Her warmth," he said. He would love to be as open and unguarded with friends and relatives as she is. He cannot be. He envies her warmth. Jealously he guards it for himself.

It is one of the sad ironies of human nature that Susan does not think her warmth is enough. She compares herself to her sister and mother, and finds herself wanting. Susan's mother looked at the younger daughter and saw mirrored there the qualities she liked most in herself. She did not see them in Susan. As a tiny child, the pain of being excluded from the union of sister and mother damaged Susan's self-esteem.

"You're just like your father," the mother would say. Susan knew it wasn't meant as a compliment. She is her father's daughter. She shares his love of literature, inherited his temperament. She remembers walks alone with him in the woods as among the most precious hours of childhood. But the walks happened only in the summer when the family was on vacation. More important, her father was not at the center of emotional power in the family. Mother was. How could father's reassurance sustain her? How could being told she was like him build self-esteem? He was peripheral. The time she had with him was hardly enough to make her feel their relationship was as important as what she perceived her sister had with her mother.

"Would it have made a difference if your father had played a larger role in your life from the beginning?" I ask.

"All the difference in the world. When I felt left out by my mother and sister, I would have had someone on my side."

"What did you miss getting from him?"

"I knew he approved of me as an intelligent person. But I had a kind of androgynous feeling when I was growing up. What I wanted from him more than anything was affirmation of me as an attractive female. I wanted him to see me as pretty, womanly. I wanted it desperately."

If in her earliest years Susan had felt her father to have as much power as her mother, she would have suffered less destructive envy; envy of mother-woman's power. This was hardened to a murderous edge by sibling rivalry with a prettier sister. In Susan's oedipal years, and again in adolescence, her father had a second chance to give his daughter what she needed. His smiling eye could have integrated her tenuous hold on sexuality with the "masculine" intellect that was so like his.

Like many women, Susan fears independence jeopardizes her chances of keeping a man's love. Her jealousy is grounded in an equation that dependence equals femininity and that other women are more vulnerable than she. Of course she is attracted to Robertiello. He does the work her father left undone. He cheers for her success. He loves her as a woman and tells her that independence carries reward in the male eye. But does he mean it?

"Do you want to marry?" I ask.

"We almost married a year and a half ago. I was against it. Now I would like to. I'm not sure Dick would. Given his track record . . . maybe we'd be better off staying as we are."

"What are you two going to do?" I ask. "Keep volleying, never play for points?"

"When we play it's like two gladiators in the ring. I don't know how he feels; certainly he is determined to win. As for me, I get so anxious I want to throw up."

"Do you feel that way with other people?"

"With other people it passes. It's like stage fright. I can use it to play better, but with Dick . . ."

"To win is to lose."

"What I want is to be able to choose. I could accept losing to him if it was my deliberate choice to be a 'wimp,' to lose on purpose; or I could accept losing if it turned out he was a better player. But what I have now is this unconscious fear, this inhibition against I don't know what."

"Tennis is a metaphor of all the things going on between you. The game is still on. How do you think it's going to end?"

"It might be that he'll give up trying. He's sixty years old. He's had a lot of women, marriages, long-term relationships. If we broke up, if *he* initiated a breakup, it might be that he just threw in the towel."

"What would you do if you found he was seeing another woman?"

"I would be hurt. I would be angry. I would cry. Then I would leave him."

"You want children?" I ask.

"When I was in my twenties, very much. But a few years ago, I became less sure. I'm very involved in the work I do."

Susan is on her feet, gathering purse and papers. She has a patient to see. The arrangement we've made is that in forty-five minutes we will meet again in Richard's office. Then the three of us will take a cab down to New York University, where Hanna Segal is going to lecture. Meanwhile I will wait here in their apartment.

"I'm not sure now that I ever did want kids," she says, "or I probably would have had them by now. I do know my not having children when we met was one of the things Richard found desirable. If we had a child . . . it might destroy the relationship."

"He'd be jealous of his own child."

"He needs it all," she says and leaves me alone with my thoughts. She could beat him in tennis and she does not. The decision, the indecision, make her physically ill. She is fighting her own competitive nature. Three years ago when she met Richard, she stopped wanting a child. She has decided to turn from what mother taught was women's greatest source of power to forge a relationship and career her mother would never understand. Richard will be her child and she will be his. I can't help wondering, Is she giving up too much? Who is wise enough to say?

There are many reasons men and women want children. Often it is to repair and restore the love felt to be lost when the initial romantic idyll fades. In the patriarchal world, the powerful role of motherhood balanced the score between the sexes, cooling the woman's envy of male dominance, giving meaning to the male role of providing ever more material status. But justification of the parents' lives is not the role of a child. Too often the child became the woman's possession. With only one emotionally operative parent, one source of love, the child had only one outlet for reaction and rage. Susan's father had an insubstantial presence in her life. Par for the course.

Study after study shows the average father spends seconds, not even minutes, a day with his baby. In terms of what matters most to a child— the constancy of *being there*—mother is all. How can any child express resentment of dependence on this one all-powerful person? Susan could not.

Envy of women/mother's power became so destructive, frightening, it had to be denied. Women were devalued. Women themselves, born of women, bought the devaluation. It protected them against their envy of the patriarchal male. More important, against the envy of other women.

Once mothers instructed their daughters always to let the man win. I'm sure many still do. It ensured the dependent position, supposedly making the woman more desirable, the man less likely to abandon the helpless creature. Many women today feel it morally wrong to lose—anything— when you could win. Men's philosophy.

From a bad arrangement of manipulation, deception and defense against envy, we have gone to open war. The new battle between the sexes: envy of one another's power. Envy that intends—consciously or not —to demean, devalue and destroy that which is quintessentially other, male or female. Our attacks on one another are seemingly as free of guilt as our destructive pollution of the world. There is little gratitude.

There can be none, says Klein, without conscious awareness of guilt at wanting to damage and spoil someone or something that has been good to us. "One of the deepest sources of guilt," she says, "is always linked with envy of the feeding breast, and with the feeling of having spoilt its goodness by envious attacks."[2] The infant cannot move out of his envious position, his resentment that mother has all the power, until a sense of guilt enters.

This is one of Klein's great insights, so unexpected and ironic that people refuse to recognize its power. How can guilt be put in the service of love?

If envy is built into human nature, so is the capacity to deal with it. If the infant has a memory of good enough mothering, if he has received sufficient gratification at mother's breast, gratitude will follow. The infant will fight his own impulse to destroy the loving relationship. He will feel guilty at hating someone who has given him so much pleasure.

Writing this I remember how Hanna Segal pointed out to me that *gratification* and *gratitude* have the same etymological root. Is it so surprising then that those of us who did not get enough early gratification are unable to feel grateful for whatever we do get, and are guilty that we cannot love?

When the infant who has had good enough mothering feels envy, he wants to restore the good breast his hatred has attacked; wants it enough to accept the self-accusation, the pain, that accompanies guilt. Rather than give free rein to destruction, he wants to regain the blissful communion he once knew with mother. In the many ways a tiny baby knows how to return love, to feed the mother from the same supply she has given him and which he has internalized, he makes the reparative act, which continues to restore the good breast whenever destructive feelings of envy arise.

The battle of love versus hate, life versus death, is inevitable and continues throughout life. As Klein says, "In an adult, dependence on a loved person revives the helplessness of the infant and is felt to be humiliating."[3] One of the ambivalences of love is to know the other holds our fate in his hands. No matter how happy he makes us, there is an undercurrent of fear, resentment. What if he should leave us? This leads to the desire to get our own back. We are angry at feeling so weak and dependent. Consciously or not, we close our hearts and lash out at the beloved.

Translating Klein broadly, the outcome depends on the quality of the relationship to date. If it has been loving enough, if we have been given love in abundance, more than we feel we deserve, memory of the beloved's generosity will give us pause. We will feel guilty for wanting to spoil the source of so much pleasure. How can I hate someone who has shown me so much love? The memory of former happiness shines so strongly we want to overcome present difficulties. Only when our guilt is faced, only when we open ourselves to realization that the nastiness and meanness is within us do we then cast about for ways to restore the love we once had.

We make reparations. We say we are sorry. Partly for the bad words of the moment, but much, much more to restore the universe of well-being the beloved once made of our life. Having acknowledged guilt and atoned for our anger, our heart opens again. We no longer have to rationalize that our behavior is the other's fault.

"Admitting that you hate the beloved object out of envy," says Hanna Segal, "is to admit that this person does have admirable qualities. Or else why would you envy him? So accepting your envy, feeling the guilt at wanting to hurt someone you admire, reestablishes trust in the love object." Trust in the good qualities we admired to which our envy blinded us.

"But when Klein speaks of gratitude," I say, "doesn't she mean something more than simply saying, 'Thank you,' or 'I'm sorry'?"

"Being grateful to your lover or husband when he is good to you is one thing and is obvious," says Hanna Segal. "Klein means something much deeper. She means the full gratitude one feels for the totality of experience, all the happiness you owe to the person." Only when we own up to our destructiveness can we accept the good in the other. What is required for love's expression is gratitude's victory over envy.

On the other hand, if the relationship has not been loving enough; if it was built on possessiveness, narcissism, sexual exploitation, dependency or fear; if the breast/lover has not given us enough gratification, the desire to restore the relationship will obviously not be as strong. In the hot red light of anger, the flaws we didn't want to see are revealed. "He wasn't jealous because he loved me so much but because he wanted to protect his ego." Whatever is wrong, "it's his fault, the withholding bastard." We don't feel guilty when we hit back; we feel vindicated.

It's been said that the sexes today don't so much love as mutually exploit each other. How can there be gratitude? When the relationship is no longer useful, it ends. It wasn't love; it was a bargain.

It used to be that women were the ones who made reparation. In terms of economic and political power, they were—and still are—the weaker sex. If someone didn't quickly make a conciliatory gesture, the relationship would end and the woman would die. Or so she thought. Looked at more positively, women were the caretakers, the peacemakers; so proficient at holding the world together, it has been postulated that women's reparative talents are in the genes. In sum, women had no right to their anger. Their rage was their peril. It was neither nice nor feminine.

As women come to share more of men's world, there is less inclination to be seen as weak, the one who makes the reparative gesture. Admirable as are the goals of the women's movement, the engine at the heart is partly fueled by envy of male dominance. Justified envy, but envy nevertheless. Relationships between men and women today are left without a built-in conciliator. "Don't get mad, get even." Rather than restoring the love we have damaged, we keep score.

And the score is dumbfounding: "Of the estimated 85.4 million households in the United States as of March [1984] . . . nearly 20 million consisted of a single person." One quarter of the population lives alone.[4]

Fifteen, twenty years ago, when women decided to change, *they changed.* Men could not stop them because men had not been their jailers. In matters of conscience, it is women who are society's permission givers. If it were not so, women would enjoy their bodies and men would not feel like dirty little boys for enjoying theirs.

If women wanted men to share the power of raising children, men would. It is natural for a man to love his child. What is unnatural is that so many fathers abandon their children. The failure to make child-custody payments has reached epidemic proportions. It is as unnatural as a woman having a child without a man, using him as a convenience merely to furnish her with sperm. Both are vengeful, destructive acts of envy. Men's and women's angry desire to ruin and spoil one another for withholding the love each feels is his or her due. Angry, envious men and women carrying on a war in which no one loses more than the child.

Perhaps the dyad of mother and child was never sufficient to counteract envy. The social lie was that the love of one parent was enough to raise a grateful child. With the passing of an ordered, structured society, old defenses are breaking down. There has never been so much envy. If the entire framework of a child's future happiness, of ability to sustain and repair relationships, is based on memory of the earliest gratification in life, why not maximize the chances?

The more constancy in love a child is given, the greater the amount, the more gratitude a child feels backward and forward. Backward to the parents who gave it to him in full measure, forward to the people who will allow him to express his abundance in return.

The question is monumental and yet so simple it answers itself: How can we not conclude that the love of two parents—shared parenting from the moment of conception—is the single most important goal we have before us? I know of no greater confirmation of Klein's and Freud's belief in the death wish than the fact that society is running as fast as possible in the opposite direction.

In the forty-five minutes that are left before I walk to Robertiello's office, let me tell you a love story. It is different from Richard's and Susan's in that it involves a man's love for his wife and son.

The man's name is Don. We met about a year ago. His wife, Angela, was then four months pregnant. Don and Angela had been trying to conceive for two years. Now that the dream was coming true, Don was astonished by his ambivalence.

"In the early days of Angela's pregnancy," he said, "it suddenly hit me in the gut. I remembered my mother's pregnancy with my brother. I was four. No one had prepared me. I have no memory of her stomach getting bigger. Just awareness one day that I had to do jobs and chores because she no longer could. I felt all kinds of unwelcome responsibilities being laid on my shoulders. And I felt terrible resentment."

The same feelings came back when Angela became pregnant. Along with elation and solicitude, there was jealousy, a sense of being unimportant and left out. Don wanted a child. He loved Angela. Resentment gnawed at his love. Guilt was his dirty secret. How could a grown man have such destructive thoughts about his own unborn child? I asked Don to keep a journal of what he was feeling.

This is what he wrote: "When my brother was born, I refused on principle to go to the hospital and see him. I was four years old. My aunt knew I wanted a toy cash register very much. She said she would buy me one if I went to the hospital. I wasn't going to be bribed. No way was I going to see this intruder. Who asked him to come into the world?"

Don has no memory of his mother either holding or breast-feeding the new baby. "A block," he said. "Total denial." What he remembers is rage at his baby brother. Lukewarm as he'd always felt his mother's interest in him to be, he'd lost even that. "But my brother, he was indulged: He got away with things my parents would not tolerate in me."

The younger boy didn't do his share of household chores. He was loud and boisterous. Don watched him manipulate his way out of work, a free ride that Don had always been denied. Don redoubled his efforts to be important around the house. He became more serious than ever. "It left me with a tremendous sense of unfairness at having to be the more responsible child in the family."

Don thought that when Angela became pregnant, what he had with her would be enlarged. Instead, once again something was being taken from him.

By an association that is easy to follow, after Don tells me this, he speaks of his mother. He finds it difficult to remember moments of closeness with her. He writes in his journal: "I never felt my mother could sit down and be unanxious enough just to be with me and listen. My father could, even though he felt a lot of demands and pressures from his business. I identified very closely with him." Don's father became the center of his life.

By age five Don was reading *Time* magazine so they could have conversations. At six, he graduated to *The Wall Street Journal.* As "the intruder" learned to speak, Don worked even harder at being a student worthy of his learned father. He wanted them to have something so special together the interloper would be excluded. Don felt his father had high expectations of him. He was to be an adult, grown-up, mature. Don was eight.

The indulged younger brother struck up his own kind of relationship with his father. Don watched the two of them play ball, tell each other jokes and laugh together. His brother was his father's playmate. Don had never seen this lighter, easier side of his father. He wanted to be the playmate.

Don decided his father wasn't doing a good enough disciplinary job with the boy. "So I sort of stepped in." Don became the overly strict authoritarian he felt his brother needed. He outdid his father. As far back as he can remember, Don was his brother's keeper. A job he hated.

When he grew up, Don had a pattern of picking cold women and trying to warm them up. To make them love him. It was a replay of what he'd had with his mother, and more, an ongoing act of infantile omnipotence. Don had always perceived his sibling to be preferred by his parents; he was sure women would prefer other men to him. He was constantly open to jealousy until he met Angela. "Angela reminds me of my grandmother. She has the same giving, accepting, loving qualities. The best thing I ever did was marry Angela."

Before Angela became pregnant Don had found an intimacy with her he'd never experienced, the coveted sense of playfulness he'd always wanted, an escape from burdensome seriousness. He welcomed Angela's paycheck. What a pleasure that all the responsibility was not his! He was her playmate.

He wrote in his journal: "With Angela, I feel a second chance of getting some of the nice maternal warmth and love. As her pregnancy progresses, why do I feel I might lose this? It requires a conscious effort not to withdraw from her. I know it is some form of childish retaliation for leaving me out. My worst feeling is one of negation when friends and relatives focus on Angela. I am left with a desolate feeling that I am only here to make sure she is okay. I exist only as the sergeant at arms. Doesn't anyone think I might need support?"

Twenty years ago, perhaps even ten, an expectant father would have been ashamed to make this lament. It wasn't manly. But twenty years ago, even ten, it wasn't manly to allow your wife to work, to recognize that her paycheck was as important as yours. This is not to say that men did not feel the same jealous loss of which Don writes. They just shut up about it.

Don enrolled in a YMCA class for expectant fathers. He learned it was not uncommon for a man to have destructive dreams about his unborn child. Don's were sometimes conscious fantasies, coming to mind at the end of a long day's work, when he felt most drained. He would hope that the baby wouldn't make it. "It's just a fantasy," he tried to console himself. And in the next fantasy, he did indeed see himself holding and loving his child.

He wrote the bad fantasies down because he didn't want to forget them. He feared that if they got buried deep inside there would be distance between himself and his child, competition, rivalry. He would have to mask it with even more of the cold authoritarianism he hated. He promised himself he would do better than his father, be physically close to his child from the minute the baby was born. He saw his child as a source of love.

These are the things Don felt, the ambivalences buried in his heart. What the world saw was a supportive husband, a man who could not do enough for his pregnant wife. He told Angela he wished he could carry the baby with her. But he also feared that when the baby arrived all that would be left for him would be responsibility.

Don wrote in his journal: "I don't want to be the boss."

Angela had a high-risk pregnancy. Two previous miscarriages led her doctor to prescribe no sexual activity. Don wrote in his journal: "It is selfish but I feel deprived. We are always running to the obstetrician-gynecologist, buying maternity clothes, looking for furniture for the baby. Angela is always tired. I am working late hours. By the time I get home, she is conked out. Why is the father so unimportant?

"Am I being irrational? If I don't express what I'm feeling, if only to myself, I'll become long-suffering and withdraw from Angela and the baby. *I refuse to let that happen.* Writing these things down helps.

"We are taking Lamaze now. It helps deal with the stresses. I'll walk in all uptight after running around to stores—I hate shopping!—then I have this terrific satisfaction. Lamaze gives me the feeling I'm sharing the pregnancy with Angela. What a pleasure to see the ripples when the baby kicks! To hear the heart beating! Just when I feel there are too many burdens, that everything has been taken away from me, I get something in return when Angela includes me. I know it is a strain for her to give me this, she is so preoccupied with her pregnancy. I love her when she does it."

Angela and Don had a son who is now three months old. "As each month passes," says Don, "I get more connected with him."

"And the ambivalence?" I ask.

"It waxes and wanes. I can be jealous of the attention she gives him but when we care for him together, it makes all the difference. I'm not just talking about a mechanical division of time, so many hours given to me to take care of the baby. When I feel Angela is looking over my shoulder, when her whole posture expresses she is just waiting for me to do something wrong, it makes me feel not that I am a co-parent but that the baby is hers and I am her assistant. I don't want to feel that I am merely the guy who brings home the paycheck."

Don's last sentence marks a milestone. Men of his father's generation, more than anything else, wanted to be the ones who brought home the paycheck. "I would never allow my wife to work." Children were women's responsibility. Any inner twinge of jealousy was covered by the satisfactory knowledge that he was economic support for them both.

Don takes off one full day a week to spend with his son, and tends to him on weekends too. He feeds and bathes the baby every night. He writes in his journal: "I believe there is a natural possessiveness Angela has for the baby. She is a wonderful mother. But when she criticizes me for the way I feed or change him, I want to say, 'You take the kid and you take care of the kid twenty-four hours a day, seven days a week, and don't bother me.' When she holds onto him, when she locks me out, I want to say to her, 'Okay, but I'm going to find my satisfaction somewhere else. I'm gonna lock you out.' "

My editor fills the margin with big red letters: "Poor Angela, now she's got *two* babies to worry about!"

Her comment does not surprise me. If Don sounds petulant it is because I have asked him to say exactly what he is feeling, without the usual male censorship. If Angela's side of the story is missing, that is intentional. We know a great deal about how women feel in men's world. We know very little of the reverse.

I asked Don to keep a journal because I wanted to capture the almost embarrassing reality of what it feels like to a man, entering the sacred mother/child dyad, resisting the urge to run from babyish feelings to higher, safer, "masculine" ground.

However, my editor is a mother. She has tried to read the manuscript not only professionally but also as "Everywoman." Because I know her feelings will indeed be mirrored in other mothers, I consult my favorite Baby Watcher, Dan Stern.

"I hear reactions like Don's all the time," he says. "Your editor's comment is right, but so what? A part of Don is a baby too and that baby part is not going to be well taken care of during the first months of his son's life. That's what he's bitching about and why shouldn't he? Even before men got involved in child rearing, they felt jealous, left out. Typical reactions were to find another woman or to lock themselves into their work and hobbies."

Says psychologist Penelope Leach, "We have put our males in a no-win situation. We must move to accept the idea that two parents and one or two children are an easier equation than one parent and one or two children. I resent on behalf of males that they are screamed at to do what they are not permitted to do."[5]

The way Don locks Angela out is to work even harder. He has proposed a new division for his company. Preparing projections of profit and loss demands as much time as he is willing to give. Don had every intention of being fully involved in his son's life. He and Angela had discussed with pleasure and in great detail their mutual belief in shared parenting. The discussions had not prepared him for what he calls Angela's "possessiveness" of their child.

Angela means to include Don, but she "forgets." When he pins the diaper, she repins it. When she is at the office, she telephones home to check up. Sometimes he does forget to do something, but the baby is not in peril. All this criticism emphasizes what he already fears: that a woman has a natural affinity for the child, which a man can never learn. That he has no organic place in the family and will always be an outsider, the provider; the "sergeant at arms." This undermines Don's resolve to be the nuturing parent of his fond dreams.

How can he not envy the ease with which he sees Angela tend the baby? He forgets that before their son was born, Angela too had nightmares of dropping the infant. Watching her breast-feed their son, how can he not be envious of her, jealous of the child? How unimportant his own body seems beside hers. Small wonder men have tried to remake the world in the symbol of their phallus. It is an effort to gain mastery over memory of dependence on the breast.

How tempting to return to the model of fatherhood he knows best. Don's father didn't hold, bathe or nurture him. He was an intellectual friend. He was not the role model Don needs today. Well-intentioned fathers like Don find that when it comes to actual, intimate involvement with their children, their own life has not furnished appropriate emotional resources. After years of cutting off any soft or "womanly" emotion, there is anger at the realization of being so poorly equipped. This is exactly the moment when the man needs the wife's encouragement most: "You're wonderful with the baby. You're holding him just right."

My editor takes to the margin once more with her angry red ink: "Who's telling *her* she's wonderful with the baby? There's something off-key in the Don/Angela story!"

"I understand why your editor thinks it's unfair," says Dan Stern. "But when you talk about fairness, it must be recognized that no matter what Don does, Angela is getting something he isn't. You've got to remember that the mother is the one who 'has' the baby in a very profound sense. She has fulfilled her major biological role according to the species. He has not. There is almost no way the scale is not going to be heavily tilted on her side in point of view of benefits.

"The father doesn't get this enormous sense of accomplishment that most women do after the baby is born. He doesn't have this very sustaining thing going for him. Breast-feeding for instance is a very sexual thing for many women—especially during that period when they can't have sex with the husband. It's a highly charged piece of business that she is conducting with this relative stranger. Meanwhile, he's sitting on the outside, having to do more, getting less. One might say, 'The poor woman, she's waking up every four hours!' But at the same time, she has something to show for it that is wonderful. Both as an internal feeling as well as an external product. The father doesn't.

"Each couple works out a certain amount of chronic, sustaining behavior that they perform for each other. The woman's capacity to provide that for the man is greatly compromised when the baby comes. It would be unrealistic to think otherwise. It would be equally unrealistic to expect him not to be disturbed. For men like Don, it is like a repetition of when younger siblings were born."

"Modern couples," I say, "set up this expectation that there is going to be relative equality. Are you saying that's unrealistic?"

"When Angela breast-feeds," says Stern, "it means she is the only one who can really do it. There is no more potent connector than breast-feeding. While Don is prepared to do his share, pay his dues, the fact is that he *is* 'the sergeant-at-arms' in the first months."

"A lot of men tell me," I say, "that it feels a little bit like their wife has taken a lover because her real emotional involvement is much more with the kid than with them."

"That's life," says Stern, philosophically. "That is the way you react when your partner is taken away from you in both a psychological and physical way."

Mothering has been women's only role, only occupation, the prime definition of womanliness for so long that even those who don't care for their children will demand to be seen as if they do. Irrational as it may seem, they resent any good mothering offered by fathers, nurses, aunts and housekeepers. Fear that someone is doing their job better becomes more important than concern for the child. The good nurse, the good house-keeper are fired. The aunt is asked not to interfere. Father is told he is doing it wrong.

Many women say they would be deliriously happy to have a husband who would take an equal share in raising children. The subtext to this statement is that if she tells him he is as good at child rearing as she, it feels to her as if she is giving away her birthright. The unconscious meaning is that she does not so much want an equal but, as Don says, "an assistant."

The role of raising and civilizing children is usually not seen in terms of power. It is more often described in terms of sacrifice and responsibility. To admit that motherhood is the most powerful role of all would shake what is left of the patriarchal world. Is it so surprising then that men wish to keep whatever dominance they have, and are reluctant to give women equal pay for equal work? History does not furnish many examples of the gracious abdication of a ruling class.

"How do you make women aware of their unconscious need to keep mothering exclusively theirs," I ask pediatrician Berry Brazelton, "even as they ask their husbands for help?"

"Just by saying it in print," says Dr. Brazelton, "you'll help make them conscious of it. The question you want them to ask themselves is, 'Do you want to maintain your Number One position at the cost of making your husband feel left out?' You are going to need him later. The baby is going to need him even more."

Ask any man who had the most power over him. Ask when he felt most dependent. The odds are high he will not name his mother. He defends himself from this memory today as he did when he first escaped from women's domination. He devalues women's power, obliterating any traces of "femaleness" he might find in himself.

The usual male defenses against envy of women are anachronistic. How to idealize a woman who competes with you in the marketplace? How to devalue her when she beats you out? When men today lose their wives to their children, lose the children to their wives, there is no "all-male" club to which to retreat for identification and reinforcement. Just to mention the male locker room is to evoke a derisory smile. Men have been made to move over for women in a world they once owned. To restore the balance, men must take their rightful place in the home.

Since 1974, Swedish law has permitted mothers and fathers of newborn infants to stay home for a combined total of nine months. It is a paid leave of absence and the nine months can be shared. For instance, a father can take a leave for six months and the woman three. By the years 1981–1982, fewer than 10 percent of eligible fathers took advantage of this law. Most men who did stayed home only a short time. The average was one month.[6] If Don is representative, if more and more men are finding that the joys of work have been overrated, why isn't the option of paternity leave more enthusiastically taken up?

Pediatrician Berry Brazelton: "Men instinctively think of their children as a source of love, but a prohibition has been built into human males. If you look at animal behavior, young male monkeys will pick up a small baby and cuddle and croon to it unless they are prohibited. In our society men feel they are not allowed to do that. It is not men's work. We are in the process of changing that. We've got to. We will be in deep trouble if men are not included, not just to back up their wives but to flesh out their children." And to flesh out their own lives.

When Don is jealous of his three-month-old son, he remembers how he lost out to his younger brother's playfulness. Don writes in his journal: "Sometimes I have fantasies of being totally irresponsible. I have allowed bills to amount unpaid for two or three months!" For a man whose boyhood dream was a toy cash register, this is serious dereliction.

Are absent fathers who allow child-custody payments to go unmet so different from Don? Envy and jealousy, resentment at being locked away from their children are added to the new despair at no longer being sole support of the family; in these men, taken to the extreme step. Calling them inhuman tempts us to dangerous oversimplification: Women are good; men are bad. Can we be surprised if men act the antisocial role they have been assigned?

"A man used to take pride in providing for the mother and child," says Dan Stern. "Now he can't do that. He really can't." Brazelton tells me of an impoverished African society in which men who lost their traditional roles became drunks and ran away from their families. "They were lost to society." Closer to home, the nineteen-year-old son of friends quietly hanged himself one night three months ago. He left a note absolving his parents. It was not their fault. "I cannot," he wrote, "compete as a man in this world."

Like many families today, Don and Angela need two paychecks. Now that the baby has arrived, they need the money she earns more than ever. Don is acutely aware of economic reality, but has developed ambivalence about his wife's working. She always did have economic importance in their family; now she has the baby too.

When she recently told him of important new work she'd been assigned, with an increase in pay, he found he could not praise her. His immediate reaction was to work still harder, stay longer at the office, even if it meant he would see his son less.

Don writes in his journal: "I am being spiteful, hurting only myself. No one told me to work harder, but I do. And I resent it. I love Angela. I am angry at Angela. I got mad at her the other day for spending so much money. *My* money! I never thought I would think of it that way. I miss how we used to be. I don't want to undo the baby. I love the baby. Yesterday I bought Angela a new dress and told her I was sorry. She laughed and said, 'Sorry for what? You're wonderful. I love you.' Then I fed the baby and bathed him and held him for a long time. All the bad feelings went away."

Angela is surprised at Don's apology when he offers the new dress. She can see nothing he has done to hurt her. It is only within himself, and in his journal, that the wishes exist to strike at her and "undo" the baby. Klein makes no bones about it: In the unconscious the wish is to do murder. At the same time, Don remembers the warmth, love and acceptance Angela has brought into his life. His guilt leads him to want to protect Angela from his own destructiveness.

"The urge to make reparation," says Klein, "and the need to help the envied [person] are . . . very important means of counteracting envy. Ultimately this involves counteracting destructive impulses by mobilizing feelings of love."[7] We hate those we have injured. We love those we have benefited. We think someone will love us more when we give them a present. This is true, but in Klein's thinking, superficial. The deepest feelings of love mobilized when Don makes a reparative gift *are in him.*

Everyone who reads Klein has his or her interpretation. In our talks, how often I heard Hanna Segal preface a point with "I think what Mrs. Klein meant here was . . ." What I like most about Klein is that she makes acceptable the ugly ambivalence that must accompany love. She shows how conscious awareness of envious, destructive feelings can repair love.

This is exactly the work Don is doing. Using his journal, he faces emotions that untold generations of fathers were not allowed to express. So ingrained is our prejudice that men be strong and silent that Don's admission of jealousy often sounds like whining. Having picked and applauded him for his honesty, I've then found myself having to resist the temptation to edit out his "weakness." *Jealousy is not weakness.*

Dr. Brazelton: "Even with the most cooperative wife, a father's jealousy of his child cannot be totally avoided. Jealousy has to be seen in a new way. It is not necessarily unhealthy. It can be a positive force leading men to reevaluate their role. If they don't identify with the baby and the wife's maternal role, they miss a crucial opportunity to change their own lives, just as the wife is changing hers. In my life, I was motivated by longing to be as important to my children as was my wife. I turned this longing into my career."

It is envy that has given jealousy a bad name. Saying we are jealous when indeed we are envious allows us to hide our nasty murderous emotions behind the grandeur of the word. Within the jealous triangle Don is envious of what the baby has, those qualities that take the focus of Angela's love from him. It does not matter that these are the same lovable qualities that Don himself adores in his son. Love and envy coexist. It is Don's work to separate them. That is what his reparative act—the gift to Angela—was meant to do.

What makes envy so galling to acknowledge is that it affirms the other person to be our superior and we hate him for it. How much less painful for Don to erect men's traditional defenses, to idealize Angela into a Madonna, so perfect she is safely elevated out of his world. His anger cannot reach her. But her love cannot reach him. To Don's credit, he hasn't done this. He never may. Nevertheless, the ambivalence is there.

"If we could acknowledge more of [our] aggression," Hanna Segal says, "we would have a greater chance of coping with it because in the vicious cycle of paranoia, if we can't accept our own aggression and say it is we who are bad, then it augments our aggression and makes it guilt free." If I am all good and nice but there is hate in the air, it must be you who is angry and is persecuting me. Anything I do back to hurt you is your fault.

Women angrily say they cannot find men who will make a loving commitment. Men say the commitment women ask for today gives the woman all the power. In 1984, twice as many men live alone as did in 1970.[8] Leaving women out can be a conscious choice. It may also be a form of retaliation. When Don felt that his wife had the major power, his reaction was to withdraw, to bury himself in work. A share in the responsibility for avoiding that dead-end solution, in which both husband and wife lose, must rest with Angela.

Dr. Brazelton: "When a woman becomes pregnant, it is natural for her to withdraw into herself. But she should make a conscious effort to let her husband participate in the immense change heralded by pregnancy. She is about to enter a new role. Men are beginning to want part of that role for themselves. Later on, the wife is going to need him and will be angry if he is not there. The more she includes him now, the more she is laying up money in heaven. If she helps him avoid jealousy of the child, he will be eager to become her ally."

Quite so. What deters men is that it is far more difficult for them to move into women's world than it is for women to move into men's. Going out and earning money is a mature, independent act for a woman, a step into the future. To a man, women's world is the one he ran away from in boyhood. It represents retreat, regression and loss. Women may not like men's hostility in the marketplace, but they are encouraged to persist. For a man to force himself upon the idealized pair, mother and child, is almost unthinkable.

Men fear women. And they fear the place where they were once small and impotent, the nursery. A mother with a child, even if it is *his*, can scare a man away. Conversely, she is the best one to bring him in. Women encouraged other women to crash through the Men Only barriers. Few men are praised or admired by other men if they take on what is called women's work. Because there is no monetary value attached to parenting, because it arouses men's great anxiety about gender identity, men look down on it.

Before the Industrial Revolution, the question of who made the more important contribution to the welfare of the family would have seemed pointless. It was only when monetary value could be assigned to work performed—with the money usually being earned outside the home—that the male role came to be seen as preeminent in the family. *Even though he was the one more absent.*

In recent, more affluent times, the locus of value has shifted again. A man is not measured so much by the quality of life he provides his family. The question is, Does he bring home more bacon than the neighbor? The goal of earning more had value, was even commendable, as long as it served a function: providing greater security and well-being for the family. When earning money became an end in itself, a step up in competition with the neighbor; when accumulating money came to be seen as a means of allaying envy, the economic process turned destructive.

When women measured their value solely as the money-earning man's extension, how could they not be envious? The most vital business of the human race, begetting and rearing children, was assigned monetary-value-zero. Families were admired not for how well they raised their children, but for the number of cars in the garage. Symbol had replaced reality Beginning in the 1960s, the envious need to enrich and embellish the self turned unloved children against their affluent families and against the greed-oriented society.

The hippies' slogan was No Ownership. They stood for love. Since they knew nothing of love except their need for it, eventually they fell back on the model they knew best: their parents' lives. The children's revolution of love failed.

"The flower children said, 'Let's make love, not war,'" says Hanna Segal. "They wanted to do away with aggression and live in Lotus Land. The danger of the pacifist position is the denial of aggression. We have to recognize aggression. We have to recognize there are things to be fought for."

"I thought it interesting," I say, "that they equated possessiveness of one another with possessiveness of things and wanted to get rid of both."

"By throwing out possessiveness of one another," she says, "they threw out love and attachment. I was there when it was in decline. They idealized love. In truth, their movement was tremendously destructive and cruel. The notion of giving up possessiveness must also have been a defense against tremendous greed. Because when things didn't work out, they turned to greed."

A study in 1981 found that the most money-oriented people were between the ages of eighteen and twenty-five.[9]

While Klein's theory essentially deals with the first year of life, I feel she also explains much of our loveless and destructive world. In greed for ever more power, lovers and leaders alike destroy what once fed them. In public and private life, "nonnegotiable demands" escalate. And the reparative act is almost unknown. Guilt is painful, humiliating. How much easier to say the other is wrong, is the persecutor; to shore up these defenses with ever shriller accusations and faultfinding.

There are no good men! A woman who had a child through artificial insemination says she did it "because I didn't want anyone to come to me in a year or five years and say, 'I have rights where this child is concerned.'" If her daughter ever asked who her father was, "I would tell her the truth. I would say, 'There wasn't anyone Mommy loved enough to make a baby.'" There are no good women! "They want to steal your job during the day and cut your balls off at night." There are no good people. End the relationship. Slam out the door. Stockpile lovers, fame, wealth, power, *stuff.* All in the unending quest to make others envy you as you envy them. "Never apologize, never explain." Meanwhile, devalue all that has been so painfully acquired because it wasn't what was wanted in the first place.

"I think women who have children on their own," says Dr. Berry Brazelton, "they often don't dare trust themselves to have a heterosexual or equal relationship. They have to be in control in a sort of total way." The drive to control birth is assertion of women's greatest power. The envious male analogue—the ultimate one—is determination to control death.

Psychoanalyst Robert J. Lifton: "Scenarios of nuclear war . . . are, for the most part, projected by men. . . . And there are indeed male elements in our entire nuclear arms race, particularly the embrace and worship of weapons. This is a form of what I call 'disembodied male play,' play without persons, without bodies. . . . I think men are much more prone to that form of disembodied play than are women. . . ."

"Women, because of their capacity to create life, have always had a special symbolic relationship to nature. Woman is, in fact, perceived *as nature*, and many cultures have their own equivalent for our 'mother earth' or 'mother nature.' *Destruction of nature is, in our imagery, closely tied to destruction of women and the sources of human life* [emphasis added]."[10]

Let me repeat that Klein does not extend her theory on envy and gratitude to politics. I must admit that the parallel had not occurred to me until recently. But now it makes a kind of terrifying common sense.

Says Klein: "Greed is an impetuous and insatiable craving, exceeding what the subject needs and what the object is able and willing to give. At the unconscious level, greed aims primarily at . . . devouring the breast: that is to say, its aim is destructive introjection. . . ."[11]

How many times did I argue with Robertiello that greed was worse than envy. "It's the worst sin of all against another person."

"Reread Klein," he said, handing me the book.

Even when I found the relevant passage, my intuitive feelings were so strong that the words remained just that. Words on a page. It's taken all these years for me to accept the profundity of what she has to say: Envy is even more poisonous than greed in that it seeks to destroy the very source of life. Like greed, "envy not only seeks to rob . . . but also to put badness, primarily bad excrements and bad parts of the self, into the mother, and first of all into her breast, in order to spoil and destroy her."[12]

The envious blame their frustration on the selfishness of everyone else and so seek to poison and punish the happiness of all others. As the infant puts "bad excrement" into the mother's breast from which it feeds, the envious make shit of everything, polluting the air we breathe, the water we drink, the earth that supports us. The top one percent in America do not feel they have enough.[13]

"My friend Robertiello and I keep arguing about the difference between envy and greed," I tell Hanna Segal.

"If you are greedy," she says, puffing on her little cigar, "you want your object to be bountiful, good, providing you with as much as it can. You take and take and take and suddenly realize the object is exhausted. But you didn't set out to destroy."

"And if you are envious . . . ?"

"You set out to take everything possible so that no one has more than you . . . so that the object is spoiled and has nothing left to give anyone else." Seeing my confusion, she tries again.

"Let's talk of the life and death instincts. The life instinct is 'I want to take everything good that there is.' In situations of anxiety, the life instinct can lead to greed and become destructive but it didn't start that way."

"Then a greedy world would lead us to planting more—more crops, more fish, always wanting more food. . . ."

"But we don't. We destroy the mother earth instead, because we are envious that others will get more than we. Add to that the paranoia that we are the object of envy of others . . . in the end, it leads to destroying all life."

"That is how you link envy and the death instinct?"

"You destroy the earth, the breast that feeds you. Also, the living infant part of you. It's not only the object but your own feelings and attachment that must be destroyed. This really is choosing death instead of life."

The envious do not love. They possess. Of course they are jealous. "When you love somebody," says Hanna Segal, "you want something pretty exclusive with them. But when love exceeds a certain limit it becomes damaging. It begins to infringe upon the other's life, upon their minds and their possibilities. Love has become possession. When you possess the other person, it has more to do with envy and greed and with your own narcissism than with love." To my mind, one of the most important quotations in this book.

That the beloved has a life of his own, that everything he does for himself is not an act of withholding, is an idea that is incomprehensible to the envious. The envious person wants more, everything; to possess the beloved's mind and heart. When we own him we control him. We cannot be envious of anyone we control. We guard our beloved jealously, not because of love, nor even because we wish him well, but because loss of our possession would reveal the hollowness within; our emptiness to ourselves.

Where does my certainty come from that the destructive components of envy, which feed possessiveness and jealousy, would be mitigated if there were two parents from day one? Is it based on my own absent father?

If, when life began, there were a triad instead of a dyad, we would have two sources of love. Security would be enhanced if two people watched over us. When we cried in the night, when we needed to be held, there would be inner knowledge that if one parent didn't come, the other might. Even when our needs were not instantly met, one sex would not be singled out as the frustrating one. "Mother blaming" would lose its focus. With two outlets for our rage, envy of mother's power—envy and hatred of women—would be diminished.

Like love, our rage would be spread around. Having the love of one parent at our back, we would not fear our anger at the other. It is fear of anger that makes us project it outward. We would not decide mother is the one who hates and is persecuting us. One of the most difficult lessons in life would be learned at a time when we could take it in most easily: Hate is part of the love relationship. Feeling it doesn't mean the relationship is destroyed.

With two parents physically and emotionally internalized, fear of abandonment would be eased. Going from one pair of arms to another, not as a treat when daddy comes home but as a matter of course and routine, symbiotic attachment would move with less anxiety into healthy separation. We would not be fixated on one person to the exclusion of the world. Two sources of love would free us from growing up with the terrible feeling that the one beloved is irreplaceable. From the beginning of life, when mother got angry, when she wasn't present, didn't father's arms bring balm and peace? In later years there would be less infantile dependency, less jealousy based on the life-and-death fear that if a lover is lost, there will never be another.

If we had two working parents—two people working at parenting—we would have two models to idealize and introject. Both a man and a woman to imitate and from whom to borrow those qualities that build self-esteem. If mother weren't brave and independent, father would be. If father lacked patience, mother did not. If our self-image was built from both male and female components, we would deal better with a world in which men's and women's lives, roles and work overlap.

Gender identity would not be so easily threatened. From the beginning, what men and women did was sustain our life, and each felt equally important. When self-esteem is high, we lose our mortal fear of jealousy. Should jealousy arise, we know we are not easily replaceable. We do not surrender upon the entrance of a rival. We fight the good fight.

If women encouraged men to take their rightful and equal place in the rearing of children, fathers would enter their children's lives long before the oedipal years, avoiding the dreadful anxieties that are thus forever after attached to sexuality. On a pre-oedipal, presexual level, we would have intimately known father all along, giving the relationship roots that run back to birth itself. Because father, no less than mother, taught us the rules of life, men would get the respect from children they want; a respect based on fact, not on fear.

An unhappy female pattern is to use sex to win a man and then try to wring from him the kind of presexual satisfactions once found in symbiosis with mother. If a girl's father were as familiar to her as her mother, she would have felt the pull of independence; known that the more mature joys of sexuality are headier than the comforts of closeness to mother. Not confusing claustrophobic clutching with passion, she would not demand her lover see her as the be-all and end-all of life. And she would grant him the same freedom, the same room to breathe.

If a man had held and bathed and toilet-trained his daughter, she would not despise her genitals as a dirty secret that women share. A self-inflicted trap that leaves every woman open to the jealous certainty that other women are cleaner, more desirable than she. An involved father would not allow the natural competition between women in the family to remain hidden, guilty and embittered.

When a daughter grew up, she would not see herself as the automatic loser—the one eternally left out in any jealous competition. Since there had been a triangle from birth, sexual rivalry would not come as a shattering surprise.

What if a boy were nurtured and cared for by his father as well as his mother? He would not see women as holding the monopoly on love; emotion would be men's business too. Being less merged with a woman, the boy wouldn't have to compulsively assert maleness by denouncing and sneering at all things female. When the oedipal years came, wanting mother would not mean father would seek revenge. Nor would he so easily project castration fantasies onto the older man. Haven't they been friends for four or five years? When the boy grew up—male identification and certainty of gender beginning from the day of birth—he would not feel a woman must be jealously guarded as a possession, a male status symbol. Losing her would be exactly that: loss of love, not the loss of his balls.

"When the father is absent," says Hanna Segal, "the infant feels in possession of the mother. He is so guilty of his envious desires to destroy her because of her power over him that he is incapable of making reparation. When the father is present, the child feels he cannot possess mother. He cannot destroy her and spoil everything with his envious rage because father is seen as mother's protector."

The father also protects the child. He doesn't allow the mother to possess and overcontrol. The triad opens up the love relationship. It is no longer a tight, interdependent world of two. The child raised by both parents would not have a pattern of intimacy based on owning, controlling and limiting. "Any normal person is jealous," says Hanna Segal, "but not every person goes out of control. . . . The more secure you feel in your internal object in which is based your self-esteem, the *less* you need *desperately* to possess and control. Simply put, if jealousy is fear of an intrusive third person, a child raised in a nurturitive triangle would feel less jealous.

"The absence of fathers," Hanna Segal continues, "is one of the things that has gone fatally wrong in our civilization. It creates a vicious circle. If a child does not have a father, he cannot identify with an image of the father protecting the mother. He cannot identify with a caring couple. It is very important for the child that a father should be there, not just for him, but there for the mother."

The picture of father taking care of mother is love seen at its ideal best. It soothes the child to know father stands guard between his unconscious rage and mother. It expands the self-centered notion that love is exemplified by how mother takes care of him. An infant is too greedy to learn generosity based just on how his own needs were met. Love never means more than "What's in it for me?" Father gives the child a new picture to introject, of altruistic concern for another person. One of the saddest facts of our time is that altruism is suspect; everyone expects his neighbor to act only from selfish reasons. The most ordinary act of human decency—coming to the aid of a defenseless person—is so extraordinary it rates a medal and a phone call from the President.

If gratification received in the first year of life begins the Kleinian process that ends in gratitude and love, two parents optimize a child's chances. Unless a child gets this gratification, he will not learn love; he will learn possession and control. "It is the memory of gratification," says Hanna Segal, "which helps him become aware of his guilt. The impulse is to overcome destructive envy, make reparation and restore the loving relationship. This means giving up his possessiveness because restoring an object means restoring its independence."

I am not saying that shared parenting would end jealousy. That is impossible. The goal is to reduce the murderous poisons of jealousy, its irrational force. We have no better guide for this than Klein. It is the envy hidden with jealousy, she says, that gives it the power to wreck human life. If envy is to be mitigated it is best done in the first year of life. If it is to be done then, two parents can do it better than one.

The fathers we see pushing the baby carriages through the park are the heroes of the day. And yet, and yet . . . why do we think of them as somehow insubstantial; failed; almost figures in a cartoon? "I have strug-

gled to shed my out-of-date personality and grow into new-man mode.
. . ." writes Russell Baker in an amusing essay. "There has been bad
feeling about my attempt to share in the child rearing . . . our youngest
child is 30 and married. . . . I won't even mention the diaper problem."[14] Along with a million other readers, I chuckle at Russell Baker—a
man's man even if he does sit at a typewriter.

Less amusing is a study on corporations and two-career families. Eighty-
three percent of the corporate respondents believed more men feel the
need to share parenting responsibilities, but only 9 percent of the corporations offered paternity leave.[15] There is something resentful in us—yes,
even envious—that doesn't want our children to have it better than we
did. It leaves an enormous gap between what we think and what we do.

"I think it's the last change in gender role that will occur," says Dr.
Michels. "It is the one thing that is closest to out-and-out biology.
Women have very different attitudes about a child they carried in their
bodies for nine months than men do. It would be strange if it were
otherwise. It would be strange if two people had the same intensity of
interest in an infant if one carried it in her body while the other had only a
psychological belief that he had something to do with its development."

"You're not saying that only a mother can do a good job raising a
child?"

"I'm not talking good or bad. I'm talking powerful or weak. The average expectant mother has to have more powerful ties than the average
expectant father."

"Then sexism is not the issue here."

"Gender-related roles in child rearing are more than social construc-
tions. They are more than the residue of outmoded sexist traditions."

"As women gain more power outside the home, will they surrender to
the father some of the power they have over the children?"

"These things will change," says Dr. Michels. "But based on the biology of the woman carrying the child and the intimacy of breast-feeding,
they are going to be the last gender specific roles to change . . ."

"If they ever do change," I finish his sentence.

I had this conversation with Dr. Michels four years ago. As my work
took its head, galloping me toward the inevitable conclusion that shared
parenting would lessen envy and jealousy, Dr. Michels's words have never
left my mind. They are a warning against easy optimism. Things will
change, he says. They may not change enough. Will they change in time?

I will ask Robertiello what he thinks. I close the door to the apartment
he and Susan share and walk up Madison Avenue toward his office, turning left into the familiar street. Ring three times, up one flight of stairs,
open the door. What is this? The door to the waiting room is closed,

behind it muffled voices. Robertiello's own door is tightly shut, so who is in the waiting room?

I take a chair in what used to be the kitchen, now neatly fixed up as a new, if minuscule, waiting room. In exactly three minutes the mystery will solve itself. Robertiello is the master of punctuality. Why am I vaguely resentful? So many tears over mothers and daughters and fathers and siblings have been shed here, so many hours, so many years. The place has the associations of home. Robertiello has moved the furniture without consulting me!

Exactly on time, his door opens. His patient leaves and he stands in the doorway looking at me. He has put on a suit and tie for Hanna Segal.

"Who hung curtains in the kitchen?" I ask. "Who's in the waiting room?"

"Susan's in there with a patient," he says. He looks shy. "She's going to get her own office soon."

I follow him into his office. I am surprised. This apartment, these rooms have always been his refuge, a place away from his women. The waiting room is where he used to have his assignations. There is a story of a wife walking in on him, an anecdotal picture of the naked Robertiello scampering for life into his office and cowering behind the desk. He was sure she was going to kill him. In her place he would.

"Giving Susan the other room," I say, "that's very generous. Turning over a new leaf?"

"I hope so. I want Susan to have her own successful practice. I'd like someone to stay with me not because I've brainwashed her but because she chose to."

"You want Susan to stay."

"I don't want her to go."

"And the old streetcar philosophy?"

"Oh, that was just a defense."

Just like that? My mouth opens. Nothing comes out. Does he want me to believe he's abandoned the structure that has so long defended him against jealousy?

"If I really believed it," he says, "I wouldn't have had to say it so often, right?"

This is where we began. A lifetime of insistence that women were like streetcars. If one left, another would be along in five minutes. Is this where we end? At some recent time, at a moment never described to me, did he come to the realization that his defenses were costing him too much? Has he begun to face his jealousy? He has practically admitted that Susan could not be easily replaced.

For most people, changing the emotionally protective pattern of a lifetime would mean hesitation, ambivalence, anxiety. Not him. Remaking himself is what he does.

"What changed your mind?" I ask.

"Experiences with patients, some things said in group therapy. It all sort of came together."

I wait to hear my name, a word of thanks: "And our talks, Nancy. They helped too." He doesn't say it.

How many times over the years has he sat up in his chair and said to me, "I never realized this before . . ." The insight was his but wasn't I the goad? Hadn't he told Susan that no one pushes him the way I do?

"What about our talks?" I say.

"That too." He says nothing more.

If I want gratitude, I will have to bluntly ask for it. It isn't necessary. I know him too well. Lewis and Clark have reached the headwaters of the Jealousy River. We won't be meeting again. If I feel abandonment in the room, I know he does too.

Susan's door opens. Her patient leaves. When she walks in, I get up from where I am sitting next to Robertiello. He stands too. A moment of awkwardness. I realize this is the first time in over ten years that he and I have not been alone in this room.

On our way out, I see that the old waiting room has been redecorated. New curtains, plants, a pair of handsome chairs.

"What happened to the old daybed that was in there?" The one on which he used to have his assignations.

"The Salvation Army wouldn't take it."

Headed downtown in a taxi, Richard and Susan discuss whose turn it is to pay the cleaning woman. I am still thinking about what he said. If Susan makes it professionally, she will be able to leave him. She is almost twenty-five years younger than he, mobility in itself. Can he live with all that? He has given her the waiting room.

Robertiello is impressed by how many people have turned out to hear Hanna Segal's lecture. "I've never seen such a big crowd," he says.

In England, the Kleinians are called the B Group. The title of A Group belongs to the more orthodox Freudians. Eminent psychoanalysts and professors of psychiatry are hauling in extra folding chairs, standing in the aisles to hear Klein's greatest living disciple. These are the people who will decide if Melanie Klein is going to get an A in America.

The lecture is clinical. Descriptions of case histories; difficult dream interpretations. I am preoccupied with triangles, deeply aware of Hanna Segal, Robertiello and me in the same room. Me and my two teachers. Susan and me flanking Robertiello in the audience, another triangle. I am grateful to him, hopeful for her. I wish I didn't doubt his plucky resolution.

"Come on, I want to introduce you," I say when the lecture is over. Hanna Segal is still at the lectern. The three of us approach.

"This is my friend Dr. Robertiello," I say to Hanna Segal. "The man of whom I spoke to you in London. He's the one who told me to read *Envy and Gratitude.*"

She asks how my own book is going. "I'm up to gratitude," I say. "Why was it easier writing about envy than love?" We laugh and I ask if at the end of Kleinian analysis patients were grateful.

She pauses, smiles. "Sometimes," she says.

For a few minutes she and Robertiello discuss dreams. We leave and walk through Washington Square Park. Susan shines in his presence. Robertiello in love. We pass the corner of Thirteenth Street where Jack once lived. I am thinking of something Berry Brazelton said, that a child who grows up in a house without a father never stops being hungry for a man. If I had been less hungry, I would not have had to possess Jack. I would not have been so jealous. If I had been less hungry for a man . . . there wouldn't be this slapping sound as we walk, my foot slack as it hits the pavement. The nerves in my leg still unhealed from all the anxious, cramped sitting at the typewriter. Which is what it has all been about. All the books, all the writing, all the years. To find out why nothing satisfied the hunger, no man, ever.

"The best thing for being sad," Merlin advised the fatherless young Arthur, "is to learn something. That is the only thing that never fails. You may grow old and trembling . . . you may miss your only love, you may see the world about you devastated by evil lunatics, or know your honour trampled in the sewers of baser minds. There is only one thing for it then —to learn. Learn why the world wags and what wags it. That is the only thing which the mind can never exhaust, never alienate, never be tortured by, never fear or distrust, and never dream of regretting. Learning is the thing. . . ."[16]

Robertiello is saying something. "You see, Nancy, you're no longer a little girl. You can talk to Hanna Segal and hold your own. You don't have to go to the authorities for answers. You're an authority yourself."

Is he telling me he can no longer be my father? He never was.

He is leaving me before I can leave him.

Notes

Chapter One

1. Sigmund Freud, "Certain Neurotic Mechanisms in Jealousy, Paranoia and Homosexuality," *Collected Papers*, p. 232.
2. Leslie H. Farber, *Lying, Despair, Jealousy, Envy, Sex, Suicide, Drugs, and the Good Life*, pp. 182–183.
3. Linda Wolfe, *The Cosmo Report* (New York: Arbor House, 1981), p. 240.
4. "The *Playboy* Readers' Sex Survey, Part One" (January 1983), p. 4 of reprint.
5. "Psychosemantics" is from *Soul Murder: Persecution in the Family*, Morton Schatzman (New York: New American Library, 1973).
6. Lily B. Campbell, *Shakespeare's Tragic Heroes*, p. 148.
7. Ibid.
8. Joel Greenberg, "Relationships: Analyzing the Pangs of Jealousy," *The New York Times*, July 27, 1981.
9. Gordon Clanton, "Frontiers of Jealousy Research: Introduction to the Special Issue on Jealousy," *Alternative Lifestyles*, Vol. 4, No. 3, August 1981, p. 266.

Chapter Two

1. Ernest Becker, *The Denial of Death* (New York: The Free Press, 1973), p. 55.
2. Harris Dienstfrey, "Early Sorrow and Mass Hysteria," *Psychology Today*, February 1983, p. 74.
3. Sylvia Brody, "Psychoanalytic Theories of Infant Development," *The Psychoanalytic Quarterly*, Vol. 51, No. 4, 1982, p. 580.
4. Donald W. Winnicott, *Playing and Reality* (London: Tavistock Publications, 1971), p. 10.

5. "Hearts and Minds: What Do College Men and Women Really Mean to Each Other?" *Glamour,* August 1981, p. 231.

6. Bruno Bettelheim, *Freud and Man's Soul,* pp. 15–16.

7. Melanie Klein, *Envy and Gratitude,* p. 194.

8. Ibid., p. 198.

Chapter Three

1. George M. Foster, "The Anatomy of Envy: A Study in Symbolic Behavior," *Current Anthropology,* Vol. 13, No. 2, April 1972, p. 173.

2. George Foster, "Cultural Responses to Expressions of Envy in Tzintzuntzan," *Southwestern Journal of Anthropology,* Vol. 21, No. 1, Spring 1965, p. 26.

3. Helmut Schoeck, *Envy: A Theory of Social Behavior,* p. 10.

4. Ibid., p. 16.

5. Melanie Klein, *Envy and Gratitude,* p. 181.

6. Sheila MacLeod, *The Art of Starvation: A Story of Anorexia and Survival* (New York: Schocken Books, 1982), p. 72.

7. James Grotstein, "Book Reviews," *The Psychoanalytic Quarterly,* Vol. 51, No. 1, 1982, p. 149.

8. Hanna Segal, *Klein,* p. 36.

9. Ibid., pp. 41–42.

10. James Grotstein, "Book Reviews," *The Psychoanalytic Quarterly,* Vol. 51, No. 1, 1982, p. 150.

11. Ibid., p. 152.

12. Melanie Klein, *Envy and Gratitude,* pp. 179–180.

13. Jerome Neu, "Jealous Thoughts," in *Explaining Emotions,* ed. Amelie Oksenberg Rorty, p. 438.

14. Melanie Klein, *Envy and Gratitude,* p. 181.

15. James Grotstein, "Book Reviews," *The Psychoanalytic Quarterly,* Vol. 51, No. 1, 1982, p. 149.

16. Judith Rossner, *August* (Boston: Houghton Mifflin Company, 1983), p. 26.

17. George M. Foster, "The Anatomy of Envy: A Study in Symbolic Behavior," *Current Anthropology,* Vol. 13, No. 2, April 1972, p. 184.

18. Peter Shaffer, *Amadeus,* act I, sc. 12.

19. Melanie Klein, *Envy and Gratitude,* p. 182.

20. Jerome Neu, "Jealous Thoughts," in *Explaining Emotions,* ed. Amelie Oksenberg Rorty, pp. 440–441.

21. Leslie H. Farber, *Lying, Despair, Jealousy, Envy, Sex, Suicide, Drugs and the Good Life,* p. 43.

22. Mary Cantwell, "Fellini on Men, Women, Love, Life, Art and His New Movie," *The New York Times,* April 5, 1981.

23. Heinz Kohut quoted in "Oedipus vs. Narcissus," by Susan Quinn, *The New York Times Magazine*, November 9, 1980, p. 126.
24. Melanie Klein, *Envy and Gratitude*, p. 176.
25. Leslie H. Farber, *Lying, Despair, Jealousy, Envy, Sex, Suicide, Drugs and the Good Life*, p. 44.
26. Melanie Klein, *Envy and Gratitude*, p. 196.
27. Ibid., p. 201.
28. James Grotstein, "Book Reviews," *The Psychoanalytic Quarterly*, Vol. 52, No. 2, 1983, p. 295.
29. Melanie Klein, *Envy and Gratitude*, pp. 187–188.
30. Jane E. Brody, "Guilt: Or Why It's Good to Feel So Bad," *The New York Times*, November 29, 1983.
31. Philip Blumstein and Pepper Schwartz, *American Couples: Money, Work, Sex*, p. 312.
32. Sydney Harris, "Enough Hardly Ever Is," *The Miami Herald*, February 8, 1982.
33. Melanie Klein, *Envy and Gratitude*, p. 181.
34. Henry Fairlie, *The Seven Deadly Sins Today*, p. 67.
35. Herman Melville, *Billy Budd*, in *Great Short Works of Herman Melville* (New York: Harper & Row, 1969), p. 459.
36. William Shakespeare, *Hamlet*, act III, sc. 1.
37. John Fowles, *The Magus* (Boston: Little, Brown and Co., 1977), pp. 54–55.
38. Nora Johnson, *You Can Go Home Again* (New York: Doubleday, 1982), p. 268.

Chapter Four

1. Jerome Neu, "Jealous Thoughts," in *Explaining Emotions*, ed. Amelie Oksenberg Rorty, p. 452.
2. Leslie Farber, *Lying, Despair, Jealousy, Envy, Sex, Suicide, Drugs and the Good Life*, p. 41.
3. Willard Gaylin, *Feelings*, p. 103.
4. Maya Pines, "New Focus on Narcissism Offers Analysts Insight into Grandiosity and Emptiness," *The New York Times*, March 16, 1982.
5. Judith Rossner, *August* (Boston: Houghton Mifflin Company, 1983), p. 376.

Chapter Five

1. Barbara Lazear Ascher, "The New Jealousies," *Vogue*, September 1983, p. 216.
2. Sigmund Freud, "Certain Neurotic Mechanisms in Jealousy, Paranoia and Homosexuality," *Collected Papers*, p. 232.

3. Ibid., p. 233.
4. Ibid., p. 234.
5. "The *Playboy* Readers' Sex Survey, Part One" (January 1983), p. 4 of reprint.

Chapter Six

1. Helmut Schoeck, *Envy: A Theory of Social Behavior*, p. 98.
2. Quote from Anatole Broyard's book review of *Margaret Mead: A Life* by Jane Howard, *The New York Times*, August 23, 1984.
3. Carol Gilligan, *In a Different Voice*, pp. 9–10.
4. Ibid., p. 42.
5. Marcel Proust, quoted in Cyril Connolly, *Previous Convictions* (New York: Harper & Row, 1963), p. 208.
6. Rhoda Koenig in a review of *Clare Boothe Luce* by Wilfrid Sheed that appeared in *New York*, March 1, 1982, p. 70.
7. Wilfrid Sheed, *Clare Boothe Luce*, p. 15.
8. Ibid., p. 9.
9. Ibid., p. 135.
10. Ibid., p. 163.
11. Ibid., p. 129.
12. Jennifer Allen, "Hers," *The New York Times*, June 10, 1982.
13. Bryce Nelson, "Aggression: Still a Stronger Trait for Males," *The New York Times*, June 20, 1983.
14. Anne Taylor Flemming, "Women and the Spoils of Success," *The New York Times Magazine*, August 2, 1981.
15. Robert Nozick, *Anarchy, State and Utopia*, p. 240.
16. Arthur and Cynthia Koestler, *Stranger on the Square* (New York: Random House, 1984), p. 72.

Chapter Seven

1. Sigmund Freud, "Tendency to Debasement in Love," *Standard Edition* (Vol. 11), p. 183.
2. Leonard Michaels, *The Men's Club* (New York: Farrar, Straus & Giroux, 1981), p. 62.
3. Melanie Klein, *Envy and Gratitude*, p. 223.
4. Peter Gay, *The Bourgeois Experience*, p. 144.
5. George Leonard, *The End of Sex* (Los Angeles: J. P. Tarcher, 1983), p. 104.
6. Peter Gay, *The Bourgeois Experience*, p. 154.
7. Karl Marx and Friedrich Engels, *The Communist Manifesto* (Northbrook, Ill.: AHM Publishing Corporation/Crofts Classics, 1955), p. 28.

8. Phyllis Rose, *Parallel Lives: Five Victorian Marriages* (New York: Alfred A. Knopf, 1983), p. 8.
9. Catherine Clifford and Carin Rubenstein, "The American Woman's Pursuit of Love," *Self*, October 1984, p. 82.
10. Isaac Asimov, "Male Humor," *The New York Times Magazine*, June 5, 1983.
11. George Dullea, "Widowers and Their Grieving," *The New York Times*, September 12, 1983.
12. Dorothy Dinnerstein, *The Mermaid and the Minotaur*, pp. 48–50.
13. Clara Thompson, "Penis Envy in Women," *Psychiatry*, Vol. 6, 1943.
14. Leslie Farber, *Lying, Despair, Jealousy, Envy, Sex, Suicide, Drugs and the Good Life*, p. 45.
15. Michael Castleman, *Sexual Solutions* (New York: Simon & Schuster, 1980), p. 31.
16. "Hearts and Minds: What Do College Men and Women Really Mean to Each Other?" *Glamour*, August 1981, p. 328.
17. "The *Playboy* Readers' Sex Survey, Part One" (January 1983), p. 3 of reprint.
18. Joyce Johnson, *Minor Characters* (Boston: Houghton Mifflin Company, 1983), p. 79.
19. William F. Buckley, Jr., "The Clubhouse," *The New York Times Magazine*, August 28, 1983.
20. Paul Theroux, "The Male Myth," *The New York Times Magazine*, November 27, 1983.
21. Phil Gailey, "A Nonsports Fan," *The New York Times Magazine*, December 18, 1983.
22. Ruth Benedict, *Patterns of Culture*, p. 26.
23. "Wedding Bells (Are Breaking Up That Old Gang of Mine)" by Sammy Fain, Irving Kahal, and Willie Raskin.
24. Walter Goodman, "The Luck of the Draw," *The New York Times Magazine*, August 7, 1983.
25. Barbara Ehrenreich, *The Hearts of Men*, p. 38.
26. Ibid., p. 51.
27. Andrew Hacker, "Money and American Families," *The Miami Herald*, February 19, 1984.
28. *Statistical Abstract of the United States*, 1985 ed.
29. Patricia O'Brien, "Times Are Tough All Over—Even for the 'Rich,'" *The Miami Herald*, March 21, 1982.
30. Samuel G. Freedman, "Rabe and the War at Home," *The New York Times*, June 28, 1984.
31. Helen Dudar, "As Rabe Sees Hollywood," *The New York Times*, June 17, 1984.
32. Ellen Goodman, "When Kramer Jilts Mrs. Kramer," *The Miami Herald*, April 30, 1983.

33. "Hearts and Minds: What Do College Men and Women Really Mean to Each Other?," *Glamour*, August 1981, p. 328.
34. Leila Tov-Ruach, "Jealousy, Attention, and Loss," in *Explaining Emotions*, ed. Amelie Oksenberg Rorty, p. 472.
35. Marcel Proust, *Remembrance of Things Past*, p. 415.
36. Sigmund Freud, "Certain Neurotic Mechanisms in Jealousy, Paranoia and Homosexuality, *Collected Papers*, p. 232.
37. Ibid., p. 233.
38. Allan Compton, "Current Status of Drive Theory," *The Psychoanalytic Quarterly*, Vol. 52, No. 3 (1983), p. 393.
39. Mark J. Sedler, "Freud's Concept of Working Through," *The Psychoanalytic Quarterly*, Vol. 52, No. 1 (1983), p. 97.
40. Lewis Yablonsky, *Fathers and Sons* (New York: Simon & Schuster, 1982), p. 49.

Chapter Eight

1. George and Ira Gershwin, "Someone to Watch Over Me."
2. Ibid.
3. "More People Waiting to Marry," *The New York Times*, August 27, 1984.
4. Trish Hall, "Many Women Decide They Want Their Careers Rather Than Children," *The Wall Street Journal*, October 10, 1984.
5. Bruno Bettelheim, *The Uses of Enchantment*, p. 297.
6. Dorothy Parker, "A Telephone Call," *The Portable Dorothy Parker* (New York: Viking Press, 1973), p. 119.
7. Carol Cassell, *Swept Away*, p. 67.
8. Dorothy Dinnerstein, *The Mermaid and the Minotaur*, pp. 43–45.
9. Bruno Bettelheim, *The Uses of Enchantment*, p. 275.
10. Ibid., p. 297.
11. Ibid., p. 283.
12. "The *Playboy* Readers' Sex Survey, Part One" (January 1983), p. 3 of reprint.
13. Ellen Frank and Sondra Forsyth Enos, "The Lovelife of the American Wife," *Ladies' Home Journal*, February 1983, p. 119.
14. Glenn Collins, "Men's and Women's Speech: How They Differ," *The New York Times*, November 17, 1980.
15. Ibid.
16. Daniel Goleman, "Analyst Focuses on Life's Early Years," *The New York Times*, March 13, 1984.
17. Susan Sontag, "Unguided Tour," *A Susan Sontag Reader* (New York: Vintage Books, 1983), p. 381.
18. Marilynne Robinson, *Housekeeping* (New York: Bantam Books, 1984), p. 68.

19. Carol Cassell, *Swept Away*, p. 142.
20. Jane E. Brody, "A Broader View of Victims' Psychology," *The New York Times*, January 17, 1984.
21. Mary Cantwell, "The Sexual Masquerade Is Conveying a New Kind of Message," *The New York Times*, January 16, 1983.
22. William Butler Yeats, "For Anne Gregory."
23. Kim Chernin, "How Women's Diets Reflect Fear of Power," *The New York Times Magazine*, October 11, 1981, p. 38.
24. Ibid., p. 44.
25. Susan Brownmiller, *Femininity*, pp. 50–51.
26. Margaret Wolf, "Body Confidence," *Self*, May 1982, p. 64.
27. Anne Taylor Flemming, "Women and the Spoils of Success," *The New York Times Magazine*, August 2, 1981.
28. Carol Tavris, "The Love/Work Questionnaire—Who Will You Be Tomorrow?" *Mademoiselle*, March 1982, p. 140.
29. Ibid., p. 235.
30. Ibid., p. 236.
31. Molly Haskell, "Women in the Movies Grow Up," *Psychology Today*, January 1983, pp. 18–20.
32. Elizabeth M. Fowler, "Women as Senior Executives," *The New York Times*, November 10, 1982.
33. Randall Jarrell, "Next Day," *The Lost World* (New York: Macmillan, 1965).
34. Leslie Bennetts, "Tootsie Taught Dustin Hoffman About the Sexes," *The New York Times*, December 21, 1982.
35. Anouk Aimée, "They Told *W*," *W*, March 25, 1983, p. 4.
36. Brigitte Bardot, "People, Etc.," *The Miami Herald Tropic*, March 20, 1983.
37. Shana Alexander, *Very Much a Lady: The Untold Story of Jean Harris and Dr. Herman Tarnower*, p. xiiv.
38. Ibid., p. 263.
39. Ibid., p. 283.
40. Ibid., p. 218.
41. Ibid., p. 118.
42. Ibid., p. 96.
43. Ibid., p. 255.
44. Ibid., p. 256.
45. Nadine Brozan, "Profiling Activists for and Against Abortion," *The New York Times*, July 21, 1984.
46. Ibid.

Chapter Nine

1. Sheila MacLeod, *The Art of Starvation: A Story of Anorexia and Survival* (New York: Schocken Books, 1982), p. 31.
2. Ibid.

Chapter Ten

1. Bruno Bettelheim, *The Uses of Enchantment*, p. 223.
2. Stephen Bank and Michael D. Kahn, "Freudian Siblings," *The Psychoanalytic Quarterly*, Vol. 67, No. 4 (Winter 1980), p. 493.
3. Ibid., p. 494.
4. Ibid., p. 498.
5. Ibid., p. 500.
6. Ibid., p. 496.
7. Ibid., p. 497.
8. Ibid., p. 496.
9. Sigmund Freud, quoted in Stephen P. Bank and Michael D. Kahn, *The Sibling Bond*, p. 197.
10. Stephen Bank and Michael D. Kahn, "Freudian Siblings," p. 497.
11. Ibid., p. 494.
12. Ibid., p. 493.
13. Sandra Blakeslee, "Major Study Assesses the Children of Divorce," *The New York Times*, April 10, 1984.
14. Andree Brooks, "For Stepfamilies, Sharing and Easing the Tensions," *The New York Times*, January 10, 1983.
15. Bruno Bettelheim, *The Uses of Enchantment*, pp. 164–166.
16. "Who'll Mind America's Children?" *The New York Times*, March 29, 1984.
17. Stephen Bank and Michael D. Kahn, "Freudian Siblings," pp. 502–503.
18. Anna Freud, *The Writings of Anna Freud, Vol. III*, "Infants Without Families: Reports on the Hampstead Nurseries, 1939–1945," written in collaboration with Dorothy Burlingham, pp. 560–561.
19. Judy Dunn, "Sibling Relationships in Early Childhood," *Child Development*, Vol. 54, No. 4 (1983), p. 795.

Chapter Eleven

1. Doris Lessing, *The Diaries of Jane Somers: The Diary of a Good Neighbour* and *If the Old Could . . .* (New York: Vintage Books, 1984), p. 140.
2. Melanie Klein, *Envy and Gratitude*, p. 195.
3. Ibid., p. 223.

4. Matthew L. Wald, "The American Dream Is Changing: A New Outlook Takes Shape in Shared Housing," special real-estate supplement to *The New York Times*, October 28, 1984, p. 29.

5. Eden Ross Lipson, "A New Child-Centered Guide for Nurturing Parents," *The New York Times*, June 2, 1984.

6. Kathleen Teltsch, "Swedish Feminists See a New Sense of Apathy," *The New York Times*, July 9, 1982.

7. Melanie Klein, *Envy and Gratitude*, p. 220.

8. Barbara Ehrenreich, "A Feminist's View of the New Man," *The New York Times Magazine*, May 20, 1984, p. 39.

9. Carin Rubenstein, "Money and Self-Esteem, Relationships, Secrecy, Envy, Satisfaction," *Psychology Today*, May 1981, p. 40.

10. Robert Jay Lifton, "While There's Life, Can We Still Hope?" *Vogue*, October 1984, p. 227, p. 216.

11. Melanie Klein, *Envy and Gratitude*, p. 181.

12. Ibid.

13. Patricia O'Brien, "Times Are Tough All Over—Even for the 'Rich,'" *The Miami Herald*, March 21, 1982.

14. Russell Baker, "Male Mystique," *The New York Times Magazine*, July 8, 1984.

15. John Naisbitt, *Megatrends* (New York: Warner Books, 1982), p. 234.

16. T. H. White, *The Once and Future King* (New York: G. P. Putnam's Sons, 1958), pp. 171–172.

Bibliography

Alexander, Shana. *Very Much a Lady: The Untold Story of Jean Harris and Dr. Herman Tarnower.* Boston: Little, Brown, 1983.

Bank, Stephen, and Kahn, Michael D. "Freudian Siblings." *The Psychoanalytic Review,* Vol. 67, No. 4, Winter 1980, 493–504.

Bank, Stephen P., and Kahn, Michael D. *The Sibling Bond.* New York: Basic Books, 1982.

Beecher, Marguerite and Willard. *The Mark of Cain: An Anatomy of Jealousy.* New York: Harper & Row, 1971.

Benedict, Ruth. *Patterns of Culture.* Boston: Houghton Mifflin, 1959

Bettelheim, Bruno. *Freud and Man's Soul.* New York: Alfred A. Knopf, 1983.

Bettelheim, Bruno. *The Uses of Enchantment: The Meaning and Importance of Fairy Tales.* New York: Alfred A. Knopf, 1976.

Blumstein, Philip, and Schwartz, Pepper. *American Couples: Money, Work, Sex.* New York: William Morrow, 1983.

Brody, Sylvia. "Psychoanalytic Theories of Infant Development and Its Disturbances: A Critical Evaluation." *The Psychoanalytic Quarterly,* Vol. 51, No. 4, 1982, 580.

Brownmiller, Susan. *Femininity.* New York: Linden Press/Simon & Schuster, 1984.

Cambell, Lily B. *Shakespeare's Tragic Heroes: Slaves of Passion.* Magnolia, Mass.: Peter Smith, 1960.

Cassell, Carol. *Swept Away: Why Women Fear Their Own Sexuality.* New York: Simon & Schuster, 1984.

Chernin, Kim. "How Women's Diets Reflect Fear of Power." *The New York Times Magazine,* October 11, 1981.

Clanton, Gordon. "Frontiers of Jealousy Research: Introduction to the Special Issue on Jealousy." *Alternative Lifestyles: Changing Patterns in Marriage, Family and Intimacy,* Vol. 4, No. 3, August 1981, 259–273.

Clanton, Gordon, ed. "Special Issue on Jealousy." *Alternative Lifestyles:*

Changing Patterns in Marriage, Family and Intimacy, Vol. 4, No. 3, August 1981.

Clanton, Gordon, and Smith, Lynn G. *Jealousy*. Englewood Cliffs, N.J.: Prentice Hall, 1977.

Clifford, Catherine, and Rubenstein, Carin. "The American Woman's Pursuit of Love," *Self*, October 1984.

Dinnerstein, Dorothy. *The Mermaid and the Minotaur: Sexual Arrangements and Human Malaise.* New York: Harper Colophon, 1976.

Dunn, Judy. "Sibling Relationships in Early Childhood." *Child Development*, Vol. 54, No. 4 (1983), 787–811.

Ehrenreich, Barbara. "A Feminist's View of the New Man." *The New York Times Magazine*, May 20, 1984.

Ehrenreich, Barbara. *The Hearts of Men: American Dreams and the Flight from Commitment.* Garden City, N.Y.: Anchor Press/Doubleday, 1983.

Euripides. *Medea and Other Plays*. Translated by Philip Vellacott. New York: Penguin, 1963.

Fairlie, Henry. *The Seven Deadly Sins Today*. Washington: New Republic Books, 1978.

Farber, Leslie. *Lying, Despair, Jealousy, Envy, Sex, Suicide, Drugs, and the Good Life.* New York: Harper Colophon, 1978.

Foster, George M. "The Anatomy of Envy: A Study in Symbolic Behavior." *Current Anthropology*, Vol. 13, No. 2, April 1972, 165–202.

Foster, George M. "Cultural Responses to Expressions of Envy in Tzintzuntzan." *Southwestern Journal of Anthropology*, Vol. 21, No. 1, Spring 1965, 24–35.

Freud, Anna, in collaboration with Burlingham, Dorothy. "Infants Without Families: Reports on the Hampstead Nurseries, 1939–1945." *The Writings of Anna Freud, Vol. III.* New York: International Universities Press, 1973.

Freud, Sigmund. *Civilization and Its Discontents.* Translated by James Strachey. New York: Norton, 1962.

Freud, Sigmund. *The Psychopathology of Everyday Life.* New York: New American Library, 1964.

Freud, Sigmund. "Certain Neurotic Mechanisms in Jealousy, Paranoia and Homosexuality." *Collected Papers of Sigmund Freud, Vol. 2.* Edited by Ernest Jones. New York: Basic Books, 1959.

Freud, Sigmund. "Tendency to Debasement in Love." *The Standard Edition of the Complete Psychological Works of Sigmund Freud, Vol. 11.* Edited by James Strachey. London: Hogarth Press and The Institute of Psychoanalysis, 1955, 177–190.

Friday, Nancy. *Men in Love*. New York: Delacorte, 1980.

Friday, Nancy. *My Mother/My Self.* New York: Delacorte, 1977.

Gay, Peter. *The Bourgeois Experience: Victoria to Freud*, Vol. 1: *Education of the Senses.* New York: Oxford University Press, 1984.

Gaylin, Willard. *Feelings.* New York: Ballantine, 1979.

Gaylin, Willard. *The Killing of Bonnie Garland: A Question of Justice.* New York: Simon & Schuster, 1982.

Gilligan, Carol. *In a Different Voice: Psychological Theory and Women's Development.* Cambridge, Mass.: Harvard University Press, 1982.

"Hearts and Minds: What Do College Men and Women Really Mean to Each Other?" *Glamour,* August 1981.

Klein, Melanie. *Envy and Gratitude and Other Works 1946–1963.* New York: Delacorte, 1977.

Kohut, Heinz. *The Analysis of Self: A Systematic Approach to the Psychoanalytic Treatment of Narcissistic Personality Disorders.* New York: International Universities Press, 1971.

Kohut, Heinz. *The Restoration of the Self.* New York: International Universities Press, 1977.

Lasch, Christopher. *The Culture of Narcissism: American Life in an Age of Diminishing Expectations.* New York: Norton, 1979.

Lifton, Robert Jay. "While There's Life, Can We Still Hope?" *Vogue,* October 1984.

Neu, Jerome. "Jealous Thoughts," in *Explaining Emotions,* edited by Amelie Oksenberg Rorty. Berkeley: University of California Press, 1980.

Nozick, Robert. *Anarchy, State and Utopia.* New York: Basic Books, 1974.

Peterson, James R., in collaboration with Kretchmer, Arthur; Nellis, Barbara; Lever, Janet; and Hertz, Rosanna. "The *Playboy* Readers' Sex Survey: Part One." *Playboy,* January 1983.

Pines, Maya. "New Focus on Narcissism Offers Analysts Insight into Grandiosity and Emptiness." *The New York Times,* March 16, 1982.

Proust, Marcel. *Remembrance of Things Past.* Translated by C. Scott Moncrieff and Terence Kilmartin. New York: Random House, 1982.

Robertiello, Richard. *A Man in the Making: Grandfathers, Fathers, Sons.* New York: Richard Marek, 1979.

Robertiello, Richard. *Your Own True Love: The New Positive View of Narcissism.* New York: Richard Marek, 1978.

Rorty, Amelie Oksenberg. *Explaining Emotions.* Berkeley: University of California Press, 1980.

Scheler, Max. *Ressentiment.* New York: Free Press, 1961.

Schoeck, Helmut. *Envy: A Theory of Social Behavior.* Translated by Michael Glenny and Betty Ross. New York: Irvington, 1966.

Schoenfeld, Eugene. *Jealousy: Taming the Green-Eyed Monster.* New York: Holt, Rinehart & Winston, 1979.

Segal, Hanna. *Introduction to the Work of Melanie Klein.* New York: Basic Books, 1973.

Segal, Hanna. *Klein.* London: Fontana, 1979.

Segal, Hanna. *The Work of Hanna Segal: A Kleinian Approach to Clinical Practice.* New York: Jason Aronson, 1981.

Shaffer, Peter. *Amadeus.* New York: Harper Colophon, 1981.

Shakespeare, William. *Othello.* Edited by Kenneth Muir. New York: Penguin, 1981.

Sheed, Wilfrid. *Clare Boothe Luce.* New York: E. P. Dutton, 1982.

Tavris, Carol. "The Love/Work Questionnaire—Who Will You Be Tomorrow?" *Mademoiselle,* March 1982.

Thompson, Clara. "Penis Envy in Women." *Psychiatry,* Vol. VI, 1943.

Tov-Ruach, Leila. "Jealousy, Attention and Loss," in *Explaining Emotions,* edited by Amelie Oksenberg Rorty. Berkeley: University of California Press, 1980.

White, Gregory L. "Inducing Jealousy: A Power Perspective." *Personality and Social Psychology Bulletin,* Vol. 6, No. 2, June 1980, 222–227.

White, Gregory L. "Relative Involvement, Inadequacy, and Jealousy: A Test of a Causal Model." *Alternative Lifestyles: Changing Patterns in Marriage, Family and Intimacy,* Vol. 4, No. 3, August 1981, 291–309.

Nancy Friday invites readers to contribute to her ongoing research on jealousy and envy, with particular emphasis on how sibling relationships contribute to the development of these emotions. Please be as specific as possible, stating age, family background, personal anecdotal history, and any other biographical information you feel pertinent.

Send to:

Nancy Friday
P.O. Box 634
Key West, Florida 33040

ANONYMITY GUARANTEED